MEMOIRS

DAVID ROCKEFELLER

MEMOIRS

RANDOM HOUSE / NEW YORK

Library of Congress Cataloging-in-Publication Data
Rockefeller, David.
Memoirs / David Rockefeller.
p.   cm.
Includes index.
ISBN 0-679-40588-7
1. Rockefeller, David. 2. Bankers—United States—Biography. 3. Chase Manhattan Bank.
4. Banks and banking—United States—History.   I. Title.
HG2463.R6 A3   2002   332.1'092—dc21
[B]   2002024800

Printed in the United States of America on acid-free paper
Random House website address: www.atrandom.com
2 4 6 8 9 7 5 3

Book design by J. K. Lambert

To the memory of my mother,

ABBY ALDRICH ROCKEFELLER,

and my wife,

PEGGY McGRATH ROCKEFELLER

CONTENTS

MEMOIRS

GRANDFATHER

There is a picture of all the men in the family waiting at the Tarrytown station for the train carrying Grandfather's casket from his winter home in Ormond Beach, Florida. He died quietly in his bed on May 23, 1937, at the age of ninety-seven. While the official cause of death was sclerotic myocarditis, it would be simpler to say he died of old age. I had known him as "Grandfather," not the "robber baron" or great philanthropist of the history books. He had been a constant presence in my childhood: benign, indulgent, revered by my father, John D. Rockefeller, Jr., and by the family as a whole.

Looking at that picture today, I find it remarkable how well it captured our relationships with one another, where we were in life, and, perhaps, where we would all be going.

John, characteristically, stands on the periphery. Thirty-one years old, he is the oldest son, inheritor of the dynastic name. After he graduated from Princeton, Father put him on the boards of many family institutions, among them the Rockefeller Foundation, the Rockefeller Institute for Medical Research, and Colonial Williamsburg, grooming him to be the family leader, but he is shy and uncertain of his abilities.

Nelson, also characteristically, has managed to situate himself at the exact center of the picture and stares authoritatively at the camera. At twenty-nine he will soon become president of Rockefeller Center.

Laurance, twenty-seven, the philosopher and businessman, gazes into the middle distance. He was emerging as a leading investor in the aviation industry and, with Eddie Rickenbacker, the World War I Flying Ace, would soon buy a large stake in Eastern Airlines.

Winthrop is the handsomest. Somehow Mother's Aldrich features— which one might describe as having a lot of "character"—combined with the Rockefeller genes to produce almost movie-star good looks. Win is the most troubled of us and never quite fitted in. Now twenty-five, he is working as a "roughneck" in the Texas oil fields.

I am the youngest, twenty-one years old, and look very wet behind the ears. I have just completed my first year of graduate work in economics at Harvard and will leave that summer to continue my studies at the London School of Economics.

Father, beginning to show his sixty-three years, presides over us all, completely forthright, a friendly, kind face. Perhaps a little distant.

==

We brought Grandfather back to the mansion that he and Father had built twenty-five years earlier on the family estate at Pocantico Hills. Called Kykuit, the Dutch word for "lookout," its hilltop site commands a magnificent view of the Hudson River. The next day, with only immediate family and a few close friends present, we held a service for him. I remember it was a beautiful spring day, the French doors open to the terrace, and the Hudson River a glistening blue below us. His favorite organist, Dr. Archer Gibson, played the large pipe organ in the main hall, on which we used to pretend to perform when we were children. Harry Emerson Fosdick, senior minister of Riverside Church, which was built by Father, gave the eulogy.

After the service, as everyone milled about, Mr. Yordi, Grandfather's valet, gestured to me. Yordi, a dapper Swiss fellow, had been Grandfather's valet and constant companion for thirty years. I knew him well, but he had always been reserved in my presence. I went over to him, and he pulled me aside, into a deserted hallway. "You know, Mr. David," he began (from as early as I can remember, the staff always addressed us in that way, "Mr. Rockefeller" being too confusing with so many of us having that name, and first names would have been too familiar), "of all you brothers, your grandfather always thought you were the most like him." I must have looked very surprised. It was the last thing I expected him to say. "Yes," he said, "you were very much his favorite." I thanked him somewhat awkwardly, but he just waved his hand and said, "No, no, I just thought you should know." I didn't really know what to make of it. I thought it would have been Nelson, but I couldn't pretend I wasn't pleased.

"THE STANDARD"

Grandfather had started at $5 a week as a clerk in a dry goods store in Cleveland, Ohio, and went on to found and run the Standard Oil Company, which for all practical purposes *was* the oil industry in the United States until the Supreme Court ordered the trust dissolved in 1911 after a long period of acrimonious litigation. Many of the companies that emerged from the breakup still exist: ExxonMobil, Chevron, Amoco, and about thirty others as well.

Standard Oil made Grandfather rich, possibly "the richest man in America." He was also, for much of his life, one of the most hated. The tabloid press attacked Standard's business practices and accused it of crimes—including murder—in its relentless efforts to eliminate all competition and perfect its monopoly of the oil industry. Grandfather was the target of Progressives, Populists, Socialists, and others discontented with the new American capitalist order. Robert La Follette, the powerful governor of Wisconsin, called him the "greatest criminal of his age." Teddy Roosevelt used him as a whipping boy in his effort to bring the industrial monopolies to heel. Ida Tarbell, who through her writings probably did more than anyone to establish the image of Grandfather as a greedy and rapacious "robber baron," wrote: "There is little doubt that Mr. Rockefeller's chief reason for playing golf is that he may live longer to make more money."

Today most historians would agree that the picture painted of Standard in those contemporary accounts was highly partisan and often inaccurate. Grandfather and his partners were tough competitors, but they were guilty of no more than the common business practices of their day. It was a different world then. Few of the laws that regulate business competition today were in place. Standard was operating on the frontiers of the economy; it was new, unexplored territory, in some cases literally like the Wild West. Muckrakers idealized the first years of the petroleum industry as some kind of entrepreneurial Eden. It was, in fact, exceedingly cutthroat. Prices gyrated wildly, with huge swings in production and alternating gluts and droughts of oil. Refiners and producers were bankrupted and driven out of business overnight. Grandfather was no romantic; he thought the situation was speculative, shortsighted, and wasteful, and he set about to correct it in a tough-minded fashion.

The accusations that Standard cheated widows of their inheritance, bombed rival refineries, and drove competitors into ruin by any means available—all gleefully repeated by Tarbell and others—were absolute fiction. The real story is that Standard was considerably more honorable in its dealings than many of its competitors. During the process of consolidation, Standard offered not only an honest, but often a generous price for competing refineries—so generous, in fact, that competitors often reentered the business simply for the opportunity to be bought out again. Grandfather's partners complained bitterly about this persistent pattern of "blackmail," but he continued to buy in order to complete his plan.

Standard was a monopoly. At its height it controlled 90 percent of the domestic oil industry and was trying hard to buy up the last 10 percent. Grandfather, however, never saw anything wrong with dominating the market, not only for the owners and workers in the industry, but for consumers and the country as a whole. This runs so contrary to textbook assumptions that many people find it hard to credit his sincerity on the matter. But as Standard's market share increased, the cost of petroleum products to the consumer—principally kerosene during Standard's first decades—dropped dramatically. Kerosene became universally available, and Standard's product was cheaper and better. The company invested in new technologies to improve the range and quality of its products and to develop new uses for by-products that earlier had simply been poured onto the ground or dumped into the nearest river. Gasoline is the most obvious example of a waste product that eventually found a prime use in the internal combustion engine and became the most valued petroleum product.

It was Grandfather's policy to lower prices, believing that the less expensive the product, the more of it people would buy; and the larger the market, the more economies of scale Standard would be able to employ. Without having studied economics, he understood the meaning of "elastic demand." He always believed that it was good practice to "do a larger volume of business at a smaller profit per unit." Many economists talk of business as "responding to market demand"; but that isn't how Grandfather operated. He also *created* demand by setting up new channels of distribution at home and abroad. For instance, as a marketing device, Standard often gave away lanterns to ensure that consumers would buy kerosene to burn—much as Gillette gives away razors so that the customer will continue to purchase razor blades. Grandfather drove his associates to buy refineries, to develop new oil fields, and to increase production long before demand existed. Standard acted most aggressively during economic downturns when others retreated, because Grandfather had a long-term vision of the industry and how it should be operated.

A number of factors distinguished Standard from its rivals: a willingness to invest in new technologies, a constant concern for the cost of production, and great attention to the marketing of its products. Grandfather successfully integrated within one cohesive organization the diverse elements of the industry from production at the wellhead to the final delivery to the customer. Standard was the first modern, fully integrated economic enterprise. That was Grandfather's greatest achievement: building the petroleum industry and, in the process, creating the modern corporation. It was an organizational triumph that transformed the business world.

The American public welcomed the Supreme Court's dissolution of the Standard Oil Trust in 1911 with great acclaim. However, it should be remembered that the ultimate result of Grandfather's consolidation of the oil business was a cheaper, better, and more reliable supply of petroleum that helped the United States make the transition from a decentralized, agrarian nation to a highly centralized industrial democracy.

EQUANIMITY IN THE FACE OF THE STORM

M y father, who later had his own troubles with the press, used to describe with a kind of envy Grandfather's equanimity in the face of the storms raging against him. When Grandfather read the Tarbell book, he remarked to everyone's consternation that he "rather enjoyed it." In my view it was Grandfather's deep religious faith that gave him his placid self-assurance in the face of personal attacks, and supreme confidence that enabled him to consolidate the American oil industry. He was a devout Christian who lived by the strict tenets of his Baptist faith. His faith "explained" the world around him, guided him on his way through it, and provided him with a liberating structure. The most important of these principles was that faith without good works was meaningless. That central belief led Grandfather to first accept the "doctrine of stewardship" for his great fortune and then to broaden it by creating the great philanthropies later in life.

Grandfather was raised in modest circumstances in central New York State. William Rockefeller, his father, was something of an absentee parent and had a shady past, but his mother, Eliza Davison Rockefeller, who actually raised Grandfather and his siblings, was an extraordinarily devout and principled woman.

In our secular age it is difficult for us to understand a life that was so governed by religious faith. For many, too, a life lived according to the strictures of the Baptist faith—no drinking, smoking, or dancing—seems a painfully dour existence. But Grandfather wore the commandments of his religion, all the things that would seem to us such burdens, with ease and even joy. He was the least dour man I have ever known; he was constantly smiling, joking, and telling shaggy dog stories. Often at dinner he would start to sing softly one of his favorite hymns. He wasn't singing *to* anyone; it was as if a feeling of peace and contentment were welling out of him.

As a boy I would occasionally walk up the hill to Kykuit from my parents' home, Abeyton Lodge, a distance of about a quarter mile, for breakfast or lunch with Grandfather. For breakfast Grandfather invariably ate oatmeal, but with butter and salt rather than cream and sugar. He ate very slowly, chewing every bite very thoroughly, because he thought this an important aid to digestion. He said one should even chew milk, which he did!

Grandfather rarely took his meals alone. Friends and associates, many from the old days in Cleveland, often stayed with him, frequently for extended periods. Meals were long and leisurely, and the conversation informal and congenial. Business was never discussed; instead, Grandfather would joke with his cousin and longtime housekeeper, Mrs. Evans, a rather stout and kindly woman who would return his good-natured jibes in kind. On a few occasions I dined with him at Kykuit as well. After the meal we all moved to a sitting room where, as his guests talked, Grandfather would doze quietly in his easy chair. He always retired for the night at a very early hour.

At other times Grandfather enjoyed playing a card game called Numerica. The cards were square with only one number on each, and the game was designed to test and improve mathematical reasoning. Grandfather always served as the dealer—and the winner of each round always received a dime and the losers a nickel.

On one occasion when I was a bit older and Grandfather was in his nineties, he accepted my invitation to a chicken dinner at the Playhouse, which I prepared. Both he and Mrs. Evans came and pronounced the meal "quite delicious!"

I also visited Grandfather at his homes in Florida and Lakewood, New Jersey. Grandfather loved golf and built private courses at Pocantico and Lakewood. When I was a teenager and just learning the game, we would play a few holes together. By then Grandfather played for the exercise and rarely completed a full round.

In June 1936, as Grandfather's health began to fail, I paid him a short visit in Ormond Beach. He was pleased, as always, to see me, but he was noticeably feeble and tired. He spent most of his time sleeping or sitting quietly in his room. We spoke briefly about matters of little consequence, but he seemed content just to have me in the room with him. He allowed me to take several photographs of him sitting in his chair. It was the last time I saw him alive.

===

Grandfather was a deeply religious man, but he never judged or condemned others who did not share his beliefs. As a teetotaler his entire life, Grandfather was a rarity at Standard, where most of his closest associates were anything but pious men. John Archbold, a onetime rival who became a close friend, was a very heavy drinker, and Grandfather made it a lifetime project to reform him. Grandfather formed intense friendships with his business partners, including Archbold, Henry Flagler, and his brother, William, who were with him from the earliest days at Standard. On the rare occasions when I heard him mention his business career, he spoke of the fun they had, despite the hard work and long hours, as confederates in a grand new enterprise.

Grandfather was modest by nature, and while he lived a life possible only for those of great wealth, he was comparatively frugal. At a time when the Carnegies, Fricks, Harrimans, and Vanderbilts were building grand mansions along Fifth Avenue, Grandfather bought a home on a side street whose previous tenant, Arabella Worsham, was the mistress of Collis P. Huntington. It was a very large brownstone, and Grandfather bought several lots beside it into which the family would later expand, but it says something about him that he never bothered to redecorate it. Miss Worsham's red plush wallpaper and heavy, ornate Victorian furniture remained there as long as Grandfather lived.

His one indulgence seems to have been trotting horses. He kept a number of matched pairs, and he enjoyed driving them at Pocantico and in Central Park, where he would occasionally become involved in races with his brother and close friends.

Grandfather was totally lacking in vanity. He gave little thought to surface appearances. As a young man he had been good-looking, but in the 1890s he contracted a painful viral infection, generalized alopecia, which affected his nervous system. As a result of the disease he lost all his hair. In one photograph from this time he is wearing a black skullcap, which made him look a bit like the Merchant of Venice. Later he wore wigs.

Some people, notably Ida Tarbell, thought his physical appearance repugnant; others disagreed. Initially, John Singer Sargent was reluctant to paint Grandfather's portrait. However, after lengthy conversations during the sittings, they became friends. In the end, Sargent told Father he wanted to paint a second portrait because he had become intrigued with his subject and said that Grandfather reminded him of a medieval saint.

"THE ART OF GIVING"

The truth is that Grandfather found managing his fortune, which had reached almost a billion dollars by 1910, to be a problem. His annual income from Standard Oil and other investments was enormous, and given Grandfather's meticulous nature, it had to be spent or invested properly. Since he was uninterested in acquiring French châteaus or Scottish castles and was appalled at the idea of buying art, yachts, or suits of medieval armor—all activities engaged in by his more extravagant contemporaries—Grandfather worked out a characteristic solution: He invested a good portion of his income in coal mines, railroads, insurance companies, banks, and manufacturing enterprises of various kinds, most famously the iron ore business, and eventually controlled much of the rich Mesabi Range in Minnesota.

But increasingly, after Grandfather retired from Standard in 1897, he occupied himself with a different form of investing: philanthropy, which he referred to as the "art of giving." In doing this he would have as profound an effect as he had with Standard Oil.

From the time he was a young man just starting in business, Grandfather recorded every item of income and expense, including charitable donations of as little as a penny, in a series of ledgers, beginning with the famous "Ledger A," which are preserved in the Rockefeller Archive Center in Pocantico Hills. Keeping records became a family tradition. Father followed Grandfather's example and tried to have my generation do the same with varying degrees of success. And I tried it with my own children with even less success than Father.

In doing this Grandfather was following the religious injunction to tithe, or give a tenth part of his income to the Church and other good causes. As his earnings grew, his charitable donations kept pace, usually reaching the tithe to which he had committed himself. By the mid-1880s, Grandfather found it difficult to handle charitable contributions by himself. It was, in fact, one of the chief causes of stress for him in those years. He felt obliged not only to give but to give *wisely*, which is a lot more difficult. "It is easy to do harm in giving money," he wrote. By then his annual income exceeded a million dollars, and disposing of just 10 percent of it was a full-time occupation. His eventual solution was to employ the Reverend Frederick T. Gates, a Baptist minister, to develop a more thoughtful and systematic way to assess the individuals and organizations who requested funds. Fortunately, Gates was a man with a broad education and considerable wisdom. Over the next several decades they planned the distribution of more than half of the fortune; most of the rest ultimately went to Father, who dedicated his life to carrying on and expanding their work.

Some have said that Grandfather and Father, along with Andrew Carnegie, invented modern philanthropy. That may be true, but it may also claim too much. What the two of them did was emphasize the need to move charitable activities away from treating the symptoms of social problems toward understanding and then eliminating the underlying causes. This led them both to embrace a scientific approach and to support the work of experts in many fields.

Grandfather's first major philanthropic project was the creation of the University of Chicago in the 1890s. It was only after the turn of the century, however, that Grandfather put his business cares behind him and devoted himself primarily to philanthropy. One of the first initiatives he undertook was the Rockefeller Institute for Medical Research, founded in 1901.

Grandfather's vision, developed in close collaboration with Gates, my father, and the first director of the institute, Dr. Simon Flexner, was to establish a research facility modeled on the Pasteur and Koch institutes in Europe. In creating the institute Grandfather followed the same principles he had first tested at Standard Oil: He hired good men and gave them scope. While he had been intimately involved in the inception and planning, once the institute was up and running, he made it a point not to interfere with its management. He felt it appropriate to hand over the reins to the educators and scientists who were specialists in their field. Father became president of the board of trustees to ensure that the policy of independent scientific research was strictly maintained.

The General Education Board, Grandfather's next major initiative, grew out of his desire to create a public education system in the South that would benefit blacks as well as whites. Grandfather provided the GEB with almost $130 million in endowment and operating funds over its thirty-year existence. The GEB worked closely with local and state governments to achieve its goals. It is one of the first and most successful examples of public-private cooperation that our family has always promoted.

The Rockefeller Foundation, founded in 1913, was the first philanthropic organization with a specifically global vision and the culmination of

Grandfather's efforts to create a structure capable of wisely managing his assets for benevolent purposes. Grandfather provided more endowment for the foundation—approximately $182 million, more than $2 billion in present dollars, over a period of ten years—than for any other institution. The foundation fought against hookworm, yellow fever, malaria, tuberculosis, and other infectious diseases. In later years it became a leader in developing hybrid varieties of corn, wheat, and rice that served as the basis for the Green Revolution, which has done so much to transform societies around the world.

"PUBLIC RELATIONS"

The charge has often been made that Grandfather's charitable giving was no more than a public relations ploy to burnish his image after a lifetime of rapacious profit-making. If that had really been his motivation, would he have needed to spend half a billion dollars to achieve that end?

Public relations pioneer Ivy Lee is often credited with developing the plan that included everything from the creation of the great foundations to having Grandfather give away shiny dimes, which would replace his image as a ruthless robber baron with that of a genial, kindly, and benevolent old man. Most of this is quite preposterous. Grandfather handed out dimes as a means of establishing an easy rapport with people whom he met casually on the golf course, at church, or walking down the street. It helped break the ice with them, and put them at ease, and it usually worked.

In fact, Grandfather had so little interest in the public relations benefits of his philanthropy that he wouldn't allow his name to be used for the University of Chicago or the General Education Board, and it was only with great reluctance that he agreed to use his name for the Rockefeller Institute. It is hard to imagine that Grandfather, who refused to allow Standard Oil to refute the libels being spread by the muckrakers, would instead devote the larger part of his fortune to manipulating the public's view of him. One would have to believe, which I do not, that he experienced a crisis of conscience that compelled him to throw off his "ill-gotten gains."

Grandfather never breathed a sigh of remorse to my Father, his grandchildren, or anyone else about his business career. He believed Standard Oil benefited society, and he felt comfortable with his role in creating it.

What, then, explains Grandfather's philanthropy? In my view it flowed from his religious training and the experiences of his own life. Ida Tarbell and her intellectual descendants have chosen to picture Grandfather as the essence of greed and the epitome of selfish individualism. Grandfather was a strong individualist, but he defined the term differently. He rejected the idea of individualism as selfishness and self-aggrandizement. Instead, he defined individualism as the freedom to achieve and the obligation to return something of value to the community that had nurtured and sustained him. I believe this was both the source and object of his philanthropy.

As for Father, far from being ashamed of Grandfather, he was immensely proud of him and his many achievements. If Father had conflicted feelings—and he did—they were that he didn't measure up. For much of his life my father, one of the greatest philanthropists in history, thought of himself as simply following in the footsteps of a greater man.

CHAPTER 2

MOTHER AND FATHER

When my parents married on October 9, 1901, the press headlined it as the union of the two most powerful families in America: the son and heir of John D. Rockefeller and the daughter of Nelson Aldrich, Republican majority leader in the U.S. Senate and, according to some, "the General Manager of the Nation."

Father had been taken with my mother from their first meeting, but he agonized over whether to propose to her for an almost fatal length of time. It is indicative of Father's earnestness that when he finally asked the Senator for his daughter's hand, he launched into a lengthy explanation of his financial prospects, apparently anxious to demonstrate that he was a sound match. The Senator, somewhat amused, stopped him in mid-sentence and said, "Mr. Rockefeller, I am only interested in what will make my daughter happy."

That Father did make Mother happy, and she him, I have no doubt. They were exceedingly close—perhaps too close, as I will explain in a moment—and I believe they loved each other very much. Mother brought to Father and to the marriage a sense of joy and fun that he desperately needed.

Mother grew up in a large family of eight siblings, five boys and three girls, in Providence, Rhode Island. Mother was third in age, the second oldest daughter, and was particularly close to her father. Her father played a key role in setting high tariffs and creating a more flexible currency and a more stable banking system through the formation of the Federal Reserve System. Mother recalled him and his Senate colleagues debating legislation while playing poker and enjoying a few drinks at his

Washington home. Grandmother Aldrich had been an invalid for many years, so for a decade or so prior to her marriage, Mother often served as hostess for her father. She was thrust into the center of the Washington scene and was not only comfortable but supremely adept at handling the demands of "society."

Grandfather Aldrich loved travel and greatly appreciated art. Mother and her siblings often accompanied him to Paris, Rome, and London, where he attended official conferences. At an early age she came to know Paris and its art world, and became comfortable with the new forms and ideas emerging at that time.

INFLUENTIAL STANDARDS, EMOTIONAL FRAGILITY

The family Mother married into couldn't have been more different from hers. Her siblings, especially her older sister, Lucy, kidded her about the "straitlaced" Rockefellers, and in the beginning worried if she would be able to adapt.

For most of Father's childhood his mother, Laura Spelman Rockefeller, was the dominant figure in his life. She had the principal responsibility for his upbringing and education, and was a strict disciplinarian. Her parents were deeply religious and had been active in both the antislavery and temperance movements. Her portraits and photographs reveal a formidable individual not easily given to mirth.

Grandmother Rockefeller provided Father with most of his religious training, his strong sense of moral rectitude, and the first intimations that he would bear a heavy responsibility for the stewardship of the family's immense fortune. Grandmother Rockefeller joined the Woman's Christian Temperance Union soon after its founding, firmly convinced that "demon rum" lay at the heart of all the social problems of the time: poverty, vice, and crime. As a young boy Father attended temperance meetings regularly and, when he was ten, signed a pledge to abstain from "tobacco, profanity, and the drinking of any intoxicating beverages." Until he entered college, Father's life was centered on his family and the Baptist Church. Father's college years at Brown University provided him with the first opportunity to break free from his mother's influence, but it was a difficult task and he never quite succeeded. He did, however, explore new ideas that gradually broadened his understanding of the world around him and formed a number of friendships that lasted his entire life. Most important, at least from my perspective, he met my mother and began the courtship that would end in their marriage more than eight years later.

Even with the leavening of a college education, a secure family life, and a large circle of friends, Father approached life with a considerable amount of insecurity. His marriage, despite his initial doubts and hesitation, was a godsend. Mother's high spirits, gregariousness, and sociability helped him deal with his shyness and introspection, and helped compensate for what he felt keenly were his deficiencies. In Mother he found someone who could understand, care for, and protect his emotional fragility. He wanted her to be with him always—if not immediately by his side, then immediately available. He wanted to retreat with her into their own private circle of two. From one point of view it was romantic, and I believe their relations with each other were extremely intense and loving. From another point of view the bond they shared was exclusive of all else, including the children. And therein lay the source of much tension for Mother.

We grew up realizing that if we were to have any of Mother's attention, we would have to compete with Father for it. We knew how much she cared for us and enjoyed spending time with us, and it was apparent to us that the conflict between his needs and ours caused her much anguish. It was a never-ending struggle for her and the cause of great stress; and it was something she was never able to resolve. Father expected Mother to be there for him when he needed her, and his needs in this regard were practically insatiable.

A BEAUTIFUL WOMAN

Despite that tension—which strongly underlies my memories of childhood—whenever I think of Mother even today, it is with a sense of great love and happiness. I suppose by contemporary standards she would not be considered a beautiful woman. Nelson and I inherited her Aldrich features, most prominently the Aldrich nose. However, I thought of my mother as beautiful, as did many of her friends and acquaintances, because those features were animated by such liveliness and infused with such warmth. It was a beauty that was hard to capture in a photograph or a painting, and, in fact, few visual images do her justice. Strangely, the best likeness of her is a drawing done after her death by Fred W. Wright, who took it from a very good photograph of her holding Nelson's eldest son, Rodman, when he was a small boy. Somehow it captures her expression better than any formal portraits.

Along with the Aldrich physiognomy I inherited from Mother a good deal of the Aldrich temperament. Her calm disposition was in distinct contrast to the more tense, driven quality of Father and some of my siblings. I always felt a special rapport with her. Mother loved small children, and no doubt being the youngest gave me an advantage. My brothers often accused me of receiving special treatment, though both of our parents made a conscious effort never to show any favoritism. But Mother and I had an easy relationship. We enjoyed many of the same things. One of my strongest memories is her love of art and how she subtly and patiently conveyed it to me. Beautiful objects came alive in her hands, as if her appreciation provided them with a special aura of beauty. The longer she looked at a painting, the more she would find in it, as if by some magic she had opened new depths, new dimensions not accessible to ordinary people.

There was little of the "collector" in Mother; having a complete set of something was of much less interest to her than enjoying the quality of each object. By her side I absorbed some of her taste and intuition, which in her was unfailing. I learned more from her about art than from all the art historians and curators who have informed me about the technical aspects of art history and art appreciation over the years.

While "officially" Mother and Father agreed on all vital questions of our upbringing and spoke to the children with one voice, they were poles apart in temperament. It wasn't lost on us children that Mother didn't attend our morning prayer meetings, preferring to stay comfortably in bed, reading the paper or answering correspondence. Or, that she brought into the house daring new art forms—often along with the artists who produced them— that upset Father. Or, that her face lit up whenever she had a chance to be with us or play with us alone. She loved adventures and the unexpected. Being spontaneous came naturally to her, and she derived the greatest pleasure from doing things on the spur of the moment.

DUTY, MORALITY, PROPRIETY

Father was the opposite. He wanted life to follow an orderly pattern. He liked to know what he was going to do and in what order, with whom and how. Whether in the city or on vacation, the day would be planned out in advance, and deviations from the plan were not greeted with pleasure. I remember his saying, when someone proposed a new activity, "But we *planned* something else." For him that was reason enough not to do it.

When we moved to Maine for the summer, Father's trunks would be brought out three days before we left; some were the old-fashioned steamer trunks which had a lid that opened from the top. Others were known as "innovation trunks"; they opened out and had room on one side to hang suits, and drawers on the other for linen. He would fill half a dozen or more trunks and bags for the two or three months he would be away. To begin with, he and his valet, William Johnson, would start selecting and laying out what to take—overcoats, sweaters, suits, riding clothes, and so forth. Then William would do the actual packing.

Dress was decidedly more formal in those days; in the winter Father wore a black tie to dinner every night, and Mother a long dress, even when the family dined alone. Still, the quantity of clothes they carried everywhere was astounding. Father never ventured out even in the summer without a coat in case the weather turned cold, and he always wore a hat outdoors. A photograph of Father and me taken one summer during my college years on a motor trip through the Southwest shows us seated on a wool lap robe under a lone pine tree in the middle of the Arizona desert. Father is wearing a suit and tie, felt hat on his head, and the ever-present coat lying nearby.

I have no doubt Father loved his children, all of us, very much, but his own rigid upbringing undoubtedly contributed to his inflexibility as a parent. He was formal, not cold, but rarely demonstrably affectionate. Nevertheless, he was *physically* more present during my childhood than many fathers, and perhaps more than I was with my children. He worked hard, but mostly in his office at home where he did not wish to be disturbed. He was with us in Pocantico on weekends and spent summer vacations with us in Maine, but on the emotional level he was distant.

There were exceptions. When we took walks, rode horseback, or traveled together, he would sometimes talk candidly about his own boyhood and listen to my concerns with real interest and tenderness. Those were important moments in my life.

However, the procedure Father preferred whenever we had something important to deal with, especially an issue with significant emotional content, was an exchange of letters. This happened more frequently when we went off to college and when my parents were on extended trips, but it was the preferred mode of communication even when we were all living under the same roof. Father dictated his letters to his secretary, who typed and mailed them—with one copy for the files!

Although Father's love for us was heartfelt and sincere, his sense of parental duty prodded him into frequent soliloquies on duty, morality, and proper behavior. My brother Laurance to this day remembers with some distress the letter he received from Father after he was voted "most likely to succeed" by his class at Princeton. Father reminded him that he would have to spend the rest of his life truly earning the good opinion his classmates had of him. Such a response was fairly typical of Father.

But underneath Father's formal, correct exterior was a tender, warm side that came out if one of us was in trouble. This revealed an aspect of his personality that was very precious to me. It helps explain Mother and Father's close relationship over nearly five decades. I knew I could count on his love and support when I really needed him even if he might disapprove of something I had done.

Father was a complicated person. Grandfather was a self-made man who created a great fortune starting with nothing, an accomplishment Father would have no opportunity to emulate. Even after he had built a solid record of achievement, he was plagued with feelings of inadequacy. He once described his brief involvement in the business world as one of many vice presidents at Standard Oil as "a race with my own conscience," and in a sense Father was racing all his life to be worthy of his name and inheritance.

In his early thirties Father suffered a "nervous collapse"—we would now call it depression. It was then that he began to withdraw from active involvement with Standard Oil. In order to recover his health, Father took Mother and my sister, Abby, then only a year old, on a month's vacation to the south of France. Their stay there lengthened into six months, and even when they came back, Father retreated to his home and rarely went out. It was almost a year before he felt able to return to the office, and then only part-time.

Perhaps it is understandable that he never told me directly of this episode, although once or twice he hinted that as a young man he had some emotional problems. The first time I became aware that he had gone through some difficult times was a few years after I graduated from college when a close friend of mine was experiencing a similar bout of depression. Father spent hours with him, and my friend said that when Father spoke about his own experience, tears rolled down his face. It was only then that I understood how serious his depression had been.

Once Father overcame his depression, he resigned from Standard and devoted himself exclusively to philanthropy and the management of Grandfather's personal affairs. As a result, during the decade of the teens, Grandfather began to transfer some stocks and other properties to him, but it was still in relatively small quantities. In 1915, the year I was born, when Father was forty-one years old, he owned outright only about $250,000 of Standard Oil stock.

What was Grandfather waiting for? I am not sure he ever intended to leave a great fortune to his children. His original plans for Father's inheritance were probably the same as for his daughters: He would leave Father enough to be comfortable, to be "rich" by most measures, but by several orders of magnitude less than it turned out to be. Grandfather truly believed it when he said, in the context of philanthropy, that "there is no easier way to do harm than by giving money," and he felt it applied most particularly to his own children. Frederick Gates wrote Grandfather a memo about how Grandfather's fortune was "piling up" into "an avalanche" that would "bury him and his children." Grandfather was probably a bit stunned at the size of his fortune as it continued to appreciate long after he had retired from Standard Oil. He saw his son, who was struggling to deal with his own emotional problems and to find his place in the world, already weighed down with more responsibility than he could bear, and he probably concluded that dumping an immense fortune on him wasn't going to help matters. Thus, until 1915, Grandfather probably planned to give the bulk of his fortune to philanthropy either before his death or through his will. What changed his mind was Ludlow.

LUDLOW

The "Ludlow Massacre," as it has come to be referred to in history books, was one of the most famous or infamous events in American labor history. It was also one of the seminal events in my family's history as well.

Ludlow, a coal mining town in southern Colorado, was where Colorado Fuel & Iron (CF&I), a company in which Grandfather owned nearly 40 percent of the shares, operated a number of mines and other facilities. Grandfather, already well into retirement, still maintained large holdings in many companies, but he looked upon them as a passive investment in securities and did not pay close attention to their management on a daily basis. Father sat on the board of CF&I, but corporate meetings were held in New York, and he never visited the company's operations in Colorado.

In September 1913 more than nine thousand miners represented by the United Mine Workers struck all the coal operators in the southern Colorado fields, including CF&I, over a number of grievances, including wages, hours, safety conditions, and, most important, union recognition. Months of sporadic violence between the strikers and guards employed by the companies forced the governor of Colorado to call out the National Guard. The situation worsened through the winter, and on April 20, 1914, open warfare erupted. During the course of a pitched battle between the strikers and the guardsmen, eleven women and children suffocated to death in a small crawl space under their burning tent; scores of others on both sides were killed and wounded in the days following this event, eventually forcing President Woodrow Wilson to dispatch federal troops to enforce an uneasy truce.

It was a terrible tragedy, and because the name Rockefeller evoked such powerful emotions, Grandfather and Father were dragged into the middle of the conflict. There were even demonstrations outside our West 54th Street home denouncing the Rockefellers for the "crimes" of Ludlow.

Father appeared before several congressional committees investigating conditions in Colorado, both before and after the Ludlow tragedy. At first he took a hard-line position against the strikers, undoubtedly influenced by Gates, who considered the strikers little better than anarchists. After Ludlow, Father began to question the soundness of Gates's position. He removed the despised head of CF&I and hired Ivy Lee, who suggested that Father retain a labor expert to help him resolve the issues. Lee was much more than an image maker. He convinced Father that he would have to address the underlying causes of the miners' discontent.

Father then hired William Lyon Mackenzie King, who would later become prime minister of Canada. Mr. King became Father's closest friend, and at his recommendation, Father implemented an "industrial representation plan" at CF&I that became a milestone in labor relations. Father traveled to Colorado with King and spent several days meeting with the miners and even dancing with their wives at a square dance.

Father's objective was to improve labor relations in the United States by addressing the grievances of labor and persuading businessmen to recognize their broader responsibilities to their workers. For that reason his involvement with labor issues did not end with Ludlow but remained a central interest for the rest of his life. In the early 1920s he established a company, Industrial Relations Counselors, to advise corporations on labor relations. It was well received, and a number of large American corporations, including several in the Standard Oil group, used its services.

=

Ludlow was a rite of passage for Father. Although not a businessman by talent or inclination, he had demonstrated his skill and courage. What must have impressed Grandfather most was Father's determination and strength of character under very trying circumstances. Moreover, he had displayed these qualities during a time of intense personal tragedy; in March 1915 his beloved mother, Laura, died after a long illness, and his father-in-law, Senator Aldrich, died of a massive cerebral hemorrhage a month later. These events took place only a short time before my birth on June 12, 1915. It was a period of trauma for both my parents.

=

Ludlow and its aftermath seem to have convinced Grandfather that his son was fully qualified to bear the burden of managing his great fortune. Beginning in 1917, Grandfather began to transfer his remaining assets to Father—about one-half billion dollars at the time, which was equivalent to about $10 billion today. Father promptly set about restructuring his life to deal with the responsibilities that great wealth had brought him. Essentially, his goals would be the same as those expressed by the motto of the Rockefeller Foundation: improving the "well-being of mankind throughout the world." This meant continuing his active involvement with the institutions started by Grandfather: the Rockefeller Institute for Medical Research, the General Education Board, and the Rockefeller Foundation, where he already had significant leadership responsibilities. But it also gave him the opportunity to initiate projects of his own—projects that would range over practically every field of human activity from religion to science, the environment, politics, and culture.

CHAPTER 3

CHILDHOOD

I was born in my parents' home at 10 West 54th Street on June 12, 1915. Their home wasn't a château with turrets, crenelated walls, and expansive ballrooms of the sort built by the Vanderbilts and others along Fifth Avenue, but it wasn't exactly simple, either. At the time it was the largest private residence in New York City and had nine floors and an enclosed play area on the roof. Below it there was a squash court, a gymnasium, and a private infirmary, where I was born and where family members would go if sick with a contagious disease such as the measles or mumps. On the second floor was a music room with a pipe organ and a large piano; it was here that my parents hosted recitals by such noted artists as Ignacy Jan Paderewski and Lucretia Bori.

SURROUNDED BY ART

The house was filled with art from many parts of the world, the style and period of which reflected my parents' very different tastes and personalities. Mother's taste was eclectic and ranged from the art of the ancient world to contemporary work from Europe and the United States. Her interest in contemporary American artists emerged during the 1920s. Under the guidance of Edith Halpert, owner of the Downtown Gallery, Mother acquired works by Sheeler, Hopper, Demuth, Burchfield, and Arthur Davies. It was during this time that Mother came to know Lillie Bliss and Mary Quinn

Sullivan, who shared her excitement about modern art. The three of them were concerned that talented artists had little prospect of being shown by a museum until they were dead—if then. They decided to establish a museum of modern art where the works of contemporary artists would be shown. It was through their initiative that the Museum of Modern Art (MoMA) came into being in late 1929.

Although Father provided Mother with ample funds for her personal needs, she did not have independent resources to buy expensive works of art; oil paintings by Monet, Manet, Degas, Matisse, and others were beyond her means. Instead, she acquired prints and drawings by several of these artists, eventually forming a remarkable collection, much of which she later donated to MoMA.

Father disliked modern art. He considered it "unlifelike," ugly, and disturbing, and discouraged Mother from hanging contemporary art in those areas of the house that he frequented. Though respectful of his views, she remained undaunted in her growing interest. In 1930, Mother retained Donald Deskey, the designer who later supervised the decoration of Radio City Music Hall, to transform what had been the children's playroom on the seventh floor of Number 10 into an art gallery.

Father's more traditional tastes prevailed in other parts of the house, although Mother's influence and good taste was very much in evidence there as well. Indeed, Mother fully shared Father's appreciation of ancient and classical art, as well as the art of the Renaissance and post-Renaissance periods. Mother loved beauty wherever she found it, but Father's taste was restricted to the more conventional and realistic art forms.

Shortly after building Number 10, my parents ran out of space for some of the large and important pieces they had acquired, so they bought the house next door. Connecting doors were cut through the walls from Number 10 on three floors. It was here that Father displayed some of his favorite works, including ten eighteenth-century Gobelin tapestries, *The Months of Lucas*, woven originally for Louis XIV, and the early-fifteenth-century set of French Gothic tapestries, the famous *Hunt of the Unicorn*.

I was fond of the Unicorn Tapestries and often took visitors through the room where they were hung, explaining to them, panel by panel, the story of the hunted unicorn. One of the visitors was Governor Al Smith of New York, who, as a guest at my sister's wedding, listened patiently to my monologue and later sent me a photograph of himself signed "To my pal, Dave, from Al Smith," as a thanks. In the late 1930s, Father gave both sets of tapestries to the Metropolitan Museum of Art, and the Unicorn Tapestries continue to be the central feature in the Metropolitan's Cloisters Museum in Fort Tryon Park near the northern tip of Manhattan Island.

Father's pride and joy was his comprehensive collection of Chinese porcelains from the Ming and K'ang-hsi dynasties. He had acquired a significant portion of J. P. Morgan's enormous collection in 1913 and maintained his intense interest in these beautiful objects for the rest of his life. Many of the K'ang-hsi pieces were huge beakers, taller than I was as a boy. They stood on specially made stands and were conspicuously displayed in several rooms on the second floor at Number 10. They looked very imposing—and overwhelming. He also bought many smaller pieces, including figures of mythical animals and human figures that were delicately painted and beautifully wrought. To this day I have a picture of him in my mind, examining the porcelains he was thinking of buying with a magnifying glass to ensure they had not been broken and restored.

Mother also loved Asian art, but she preferred the ceramics and sculpture of the earlier Chinese and Korean dynasties, as well as Buddhist art from other parts of Asia. She had what we called "the Buddha room" in Number 12, filled with many statues of the Buddha and the goddess Kuan-Yin, where the lights were kept dim and the air heavily scented with burning incense.

Mother had another partner in her collecting, her oldest sister, Lucy. Aunt Lucy had been almost completely deaf since childhood, and one had to stand very close to her and shout into her ear to be understood. Despite this handicap she was an intrepid traveler, and during the 1920s and 1930s she wandered the world visiting many out-of-the-way places at a time when travel was much more precarious, particularly for unmarried women. In 1923, while traveling on the Shanghai Express between Peking and Shanghai, Aunt Lucy's train was attacked by bandits. Several people on the train were killed, and she was kidnapped. She was taken on the back of a donkey into the mountains, where the plan was to hold her for ransom. When the bandits learned that government troops were in hot pursuit, they abruptly abandoned her. Aunt Lucy made her way in the middle of the night to a walled village. She was refused entry and spent the night in a doghouse outside the gate before being admitted in the morning. She was rescued later that day.

Aunt Lucy bought art everywhere she went—often in remote spots and at modest prices. Not infrequently she bought things for Mother and would ship them back in large crates to our home in New York. Fortunately, Aunt Lucy had excellent taste. She developed a keen interest in Japanese bird and flower prints and Noh dance costumes, highly prized in Japan and quite rare, from the Edo Period (1600–1868), acquiring a rather large number of both over a period of forty years. In addition, she accumulated a superb collection of antique European and English porcelains, including a complete set of the eighteenth-century Meissen *Monkey Band,* modeled by Johann Kändler. Before her death in 1955 she left most of these collections to the Rhode Island School of Design, to which my mother also gave her important collection of eighteenth- and nineteenth-century Japanese prints by the great artists Hokusai, Hiroshige, and Utamara.

SCHOOL DAYS

During the week our daily routine never varied. We were roused early for a quick breakfast, preceded by morning prayers in Father's study. Father required us to learn selected verses from the Bible, which he called upon us to recite. Each of us then took turns reading a psalm or another passage from the Bible. We ended with a prayer. Father, strict but gentle, would explain to us the meaning of what we were reading. Making jokes or cutting up was sternly discouraged. Prayers lasted ten or fifteen minutes; neither Mother nor my sister, Babs, attended.

Except for John, we all attended the Lincoln School at 123rd Street and Morningside Drive near Harlem. Father considered it important for boys to get exercise, so every morning we strapped on our roller skates in the front hallway and headed uptown on Fifth Avenue along the border of Central Park. When we were younger, Winthrop and I got only as far as 72nd Street, whereas Nelson and Laurance often went to 96th Street. Following along behind us in a Nash sedan to pick us up when our energies flagged was one of the three Irish Concannon brothers, who had originally worked as coachmen and who all learned, with varying degrees of success, to drive a car. They had difficulty adjusting to sitting behind a wheel and were happiest driving one of our electric cars, which were popular before the advent of Henry Ford's Model T, because, like a hansom cab, the driver perched on top like a coachman.

Lincoln was not a typical private school like Browning or St. Bernard's for boys or Chapin or Brearly for girls, where the children of most wealthy families studied. Tuition was quite low to make it accessible on a competitive basis to children from all backgrounds. Lincoln was coeducational, and the student body was representative of the City's diverse population. In my class there were a few children from the families of wealthy businessmen and bankers, but most of my classmates were from middle-class academic or artistic families. One of them, Tessim Zorach, was the son of the well-known sculptor William Zorach, whose wife, Marguerite, painted and wove tapestries. A few were the children of very recent émigrés to this country; one was even a White Russian émigré. My classmates were quite intelligent and, like me, were more interested in activities other than sports.

It was Lincoln's experimental curriculum and method of instruction that distinguished it from all other New York schools of the time. Father was an ardent and generous supporter of John Dewey's educational methods and school reform efforts. Father and the other founders of Lincoln believed that modern schools had to be more than places where facts and formulas were memorized and recited verbatim; schools had to become the place where individuals learned how to think and solve problems on their own. Teacher's College of Columbia University operated Lincoln, with considerable financial assistance in the early years from the General Education Board, as an experimental school designed to put Dewey's philosophy into practice.

Lincoln stressed freedom for children to learn and to play an active role in their own education. In most subjects we did not have detailed reading assignments from a textbook but were instructed to go to the library and find information for ourselves. Essentially, we were taught how to learn rather than being forced to simply repeat facts that had been drilled into our heads. But there were some drawbacks. In my case, I had trouble with reading and spelling, which my teachers, drawing upon "progressive" educational theory, did not consider significant. They believed I was simply a slow reader and that I would develop at my own pace. In reality I have dyslexia, which was never diagnosed, and I never received remedial attention. As a result my reading ability, as well as my proficiency in spelling, improved only marginally as I grew older. All my siblings, except Babs and John, had dyslexia to a degree.

On the other hand I had some very good teachers at Lincoln. I attribute my lifelong interest in history to Elmina Lucke, my sixth grade teacher, who made the past come vividly alive. While Lincoln may have left me in some ways unprepared, I was able to enter Harvard at age seventeen and complete my academic requirements there with moderate success.

POCANTICO

During the winter the family spent the weekend at the estate in Pocantico Hills in Westchester County, just north of where the Tappan Zee Bridge now crosses the Hudson River. We drove up in a Crane Simplex sedan with a roof high enough for a person of average height to stand upright inside. It had folding side seats and could comfortably accommodate seven people including the chauffeur. For children it seemed like an endless journey—there were no modern highways, and the trip from Manhattan took about one and one-half hours—and I remember distinctly the smell of the plush fabric on the seats that always made me feel a little carsick.

Grandfather started buying property in Pocantico in the early 1890s close to his brother William's estate on the Hudson River. Southwestern Westchester County was still very rural then and had large areas of woodlands, lakes, fields, and streams—all teeming with wildlife. Eventually the family accumulated about 3,400 acres that surrounded and included almost all of the little village of Pocantico Hills, where most of the residents worked for the family and lived in houses owned by Grandfather.

The wooden house my grandparents occupied burned down in 1901. Rather than rebuild, they simply moved down the hill to a smaller place, known as the Kent House, where they were perfectly content. After a great deal of prodding by Father they finally built a larger and more substantial house on the top of the hill near where the original structure had stood. Grandfather occupied Kykuit from 1912 until his death in 1937, and then Mother and Father moved into it.

My parents' first home in "the Park," Abeyton Lodge, was a large, rambling wooden structure down the hill from Kykuit. Abeyton's cheerful interior was filled with oak paneling and floors, which gave it a warm and comfortable feeling. A wide golden oak staircase ascended from the entrance hall to the second floor, and a huge oak table almost filled the front hall. It was on that table that I recall seeing the front page of the *New York Herald-Tribune* the day the stock market crashed in 1929. There were fireplaces in many rooms, including several of the bedrooms. The one in the living room was always lit in cool weather and contributed to its friendly and inviting atmosphere. Bookcases with glass doors lined an entire wall and held sets of books by well-known authors, Charles Dickens and Robert Louis Stevenson among them, as well as bound copies of *Country Life* and *St. Nicholas* magazines, both relics of Victorian America. The only painting in the house of any distinction was a large George Inness landscape.

There was a long hallway between the living room and dining room where the heads of big-game animals lined the walls. I have no idea where they came from, because Father certainly never went on an African safari, but this wasn't too long after Teddy Roosevelt's time, and mounted animal trophies were much in vogue. There was also a stuffed Emperor penguin standing in the front hallway. Admiral Richard Byrd had presented it to Father in gratitude for the financial support Father provided for his expeditions to the polar regions. Admiral Byrd visited us frequently in those days, and on his first expedition to Antarctica he telegraphed me from Little

America saying he was naming a relay camp after me. That was an exciting thing for a thirteen-year-old boy. Byrd discovered mountain ranges near the Ross Sea, and he named one of them the Rockefeller Range, a name it still bears to this day. Another famous visitor was Charles Lindbergh, who spent a weekend with us soon after his solo flight across the Atlantic in 1927.

A spur of the New York Central, the Putnam Division, ran right through Grandfather's property, and there was a small station just outside the entrance gate. I recall hearing the whistle and the chugging of the steam engine as I lay in bed at night. Outside my bedroom window stood a big maple tree that turned bright red in the autumn. When the leaves fell, I could see up the sloping lawn past the sheep grazing on the golf course—a Scottish shepherd herded a flock of sheep around the property to keep the grass down—and all the way up the hill to Kykuit.

I had developed an avid interest in nature study, particularly collecting beetles, as a result of a class in natural history I attended, along with Henry Ford II, one summer in Maine. On warm spring nights I would hang up a linen sheet against the stucco wall on the porch off my bedroom and put a light in front of it. Beetles and other insects would swarm toward the light in large numbers, and in a short period of time the sheet would be covered with crawling life. On a single evening I could easily collect thirty or more species of beetles. It is a sad fact that the same result could not be produced today, clearly due to the extensive use of insecticides. As a child the strident sounds of the katydids, cicadas, and other members of the insect orchestra would keep me awake at night. Now, late in the summer, we sometimes hear a few katydids sawing away, but very few. Sadly, Rachel Carson's *The Silent Spring* was all too accurate about the impact that pesticides would have throughout the world.

There were two electricians who lived on the estate, named, appropriately, Mr. Bell and Mr. Buzzwell. Mr. Buzzwell's daughter, Louise, was exactly my age, and this fact convinced me when I was five that the two of us were destined to be married. When the snows fell, the endless sloping lawns around Kykuit were ideal for sledding, and Louise and I often raced down the hills together. Except for Louise and a few other children of estate employees, there wasn't much companionship. I would sometimes bring friends out for the weekend, but more often I spent my days alone.

The estate was nevertheless a child's paradise. When I was in my early teens, Father built a huge playhouse just up the hill from Abeyton Lodge with a gymnasium, indoor pool, bowling alley, squash court, and the kitchen where I had prepared Grandfather's chicken dinner. A decade later Father added an indoor tennis court lit by a vast glass dome, with a sitting area for observers and fireplaces to keep them warm in the winter. There were an infinite number of places to play, but I remember usually having to play alone or with a tutor who came out for the weekend.

SUMMERS IN SEAL HARBOR

Summers were always spent in Maine at the Eyrie in Seal Harbor on the southeast shore of Mount Desert Island, not far from Bar Harbor. We would celebrate Grandfather's birthday on July 8 in Pocantico and head north the next day. The movement of the household was a complicated logistical task and required weeks of preparation. Large trunks and suitcases were dragged out of storage and packed with everything we might need during the nearly three-month stay. On the day of our departure, workers loaded them on trucks along with ice chests containing pasteurized Walker-Gordon milk for the children on the train. Everything was delivered to Pennsylvania Station and loaded on the train. Abeyton Lodge was filled with a wonderful bustle and sense of anticipation as we hurried about collecting all of those things that we *had* to have with us: books, games, and athletic equipment.

In the mid-afternoon of what was invariably a hot and humid summer day, we would leave Pocantico for the drive to New York City. The family and household staff filled an entire Pullman sleeping car. In addition to Mother, Father, and the six children, there were nurses, tutors, personal secretaries, Father's valet, waitresses, kitchen maids, parlor maids, and chambermaids—each a distinct vocation—to take care of some one hundred rooms in the Eyrie, which had been enlarged considerably by my parents after they bought it in 1908. In addition to the Pullman sleeping car, Father had a horse car hooked onto the train to accommodate the horses and carriages he always brought for the summer. A groom would sleep there so that no accidents occurred during the sixteen-hour train ride.

The Bar Harbor Express originated in Washington and stopped in Baltimore, Philadelphia, and New York to add sleeping cars. We boarded at about five in the afternoon for the overnight trip through New England. The following morning, as if by magic, we would be passing by the sparkling blue waters along the rugged coast of Maine.

We would climb down excitedly from the car when it arrived at the Mount Desert Ferry at the head of Frenchman's Bay, breathing in the balsam-scented Maine air and pointing to Cadillac Mountain looming in the distance. Father supervised the unloading of trunks, luggage, horses, and people. Each of us boys helped carry parcels down the dock to the Norumbega, a side-wheeler, which would carry us to the island.

With everything safely stowed aboard, the Norumbega would pull slowly away from the pier for the four-hour voyage to Seal Harbor. The ferry stopped first in Bar Harbor, where many of our fellow passengers would disembark, along with their many steamer trunks and other possessions. Then the Norumbega would steam round the headland, toward Seal Harbor, and finally, in mid-afternoon, we would dock. After a journey of almost twenty-four hours we had finally arrived, with the whole summer stretching deliciously before us.

In contrast it now takes barely two hours to reach Ringing Point, my Seal Harbor home, by plane from Westchester. While it is a good deal faster, I am nostalgic for the sights and sounds of the train and ferry, and the sweet anticipation of an endless summer in Maine.

One of my earliest memories is from Seal Harbor. There was a report that a dead whale had washed ashore on a nearby island. Father arranged for a boat to take family members over to view the carcass. Barely three, I was considered too young to accompany them. I remember standing on the dock weeping bitterly as the others left and complaining to my governess that "in my whole life I had never seen a whale" and would probably never see one ever again.

=

By 1900, Bar Harbor had become one of New England's most fashionable summer resorts, on a par with Newport, Rhode Island. The rugged coastline along Frenchman's Bay flanking Bar Harbor was covered with immense gabled mansions of the rich, and the harbor was filled with large pretentious yachts. Seal Harbor, although only nine miles away, remained much quieter and more conservative. My parents thought Bar Harbor too flashy and ostentatious, and spent little time there. Families such as the Atwater Kents of radio fame, the Dorrances of Campbell Soup, and the Potter Palmers from Chicago gave elaborate parties, with bands playing on yachts anchored just off their property and dancing all through the night. Speedboats carried guests back and forth, and champagne flowed for all ages.

My parents disapproved of such opulent displays, especially because of the liquor that was in abundant supply even during Prohibition. Many rumors circulated about the high society of Bar Harbor; it was even whispered that Mr. Kent kept a mistress! Of course, I was too young for most of this and heard about it primarily from my brothers.

Father spent much of his time during the summers riding horses and driving carriages along the fifty-five miles of carriage roads he had built on land he owned as well as within Acadia National Park. They were marvels of engineering and meticulous planning, and provided spectacular views of the ocean, mountains, lakes, and forests.

Father didn't like sailing and rarely ventured out on the water. He preferred outdoor activities on the ground: horseback riding, carriage driving, and long walks through the woods. This was a great disappointment to Mother who had been raised on Narragansett Bay among a family of sailors. Eventually Father bought a beautiful thirty-six-foot racing sloop, an "R" boat named the *Jack Tar,* undoubtedly as a concession to my older brothers. Being the youngest, I didn't get much sailing time on it, although when I was seventeen, a friend and I sailed one hundred miles east to Saint Andrews in New Brunswick across the treacherous waters of Passamaquoddy Bay. *Jack Tar* had no engine, so Captain Oscar Bulger, who worked for the family for many years, followed along in his lobster boat in case two very inexperienced sailors got into real trouble.

I have always loved Maine, but I now realize that I felt a certain sense of isolation during my summers there. There was a large household of servants, tutors, and governesses, but because everything was available at the Eyrie, I never took tennis lessons at the club or went to a sailing class at the Northeast Harbor Yacht Club with other children. I never became part of a group as most children did whose parents summered at Seal Harbor. At the time I am not sure I realized what I was missing. I liked the series of French tutors whom Father had selected to be our companions, and they did their best to keep me entertained, but they were hardly substitutes for the companionship of children my own age.

=

I do fondly remember my nurses—governesses, really—who took me under their protective wings. My first was Atta Albertson—for some reason I called her "Babe"—who was with me until I was ten years old. She had served as a nurse with the U.S. Army in the Philippines during World War I, and I remember hearing about the delectable qualities of mangoes for the first time from her. Many years later on my first trip to Asia I tried them, and they have become my favorite fruit. After Babe came Florence Scales, whom I called "Puss"; one of the kindest, sweetest ladies imaginable, she would read to me as I worked on my beetle collection.

My sister's companion, Regina DeParmant, a Russian aristocrat whose family had fled the Revolution, was beautiful with dark hair and eyes; she spoke exquisite French but could barely get by in English. She was very kind and would often play a board game with me called Peggaty, at which I was very good, or thought I was, because she would usually let me win.

SIX DIFFERENT PERSONALITIES

My siblings viewed me as being far too young to be worth playing with. The eldest, my sister Abby, whom we called Babs, was twelve years older than me. When I was a young child, she was already a debutante, out every night until early morning; once or twice I remember her getting home as I was strapping on my roller skates and heading off for school. John, two and a half years younger than Babs, was next in line and already in long pants—literally; we all wore knickerbockers and long socks until well into our teens—so I also considered him almost part of the adult world. Nelson and Laurance were also quite a bit older, seven and five years, respectively, and Win, the closest to me in age, was my senior by three years.

It's interesting how very different siblings can be despite the similarities of their upbringing and genetic inheritance. The two oldest, Babs and John, bore the brunt of Father's own severe upbringing and personal rigidity.

=

From my earliest memory Babs had already entered her rebellious phase, which in one way or another lasted most of her life. Father clearly wanted his first child to be a devout Christian woman and to do things he felt a well-brought-up lady should do. He truly adored Babs, but in his eagerness to have her become a paragon of modesty and charity, he badgered her constantly with lectures on good behavior and the obligations of wealth. Babs would have none of it. If Father wanted her to do something, she would refuse or do the opposite. For instance, Father strongly disapproved of alcohol and tobacco, and offered each of us $2,500 if we didn't smoke before the age of twenty-one, and another $2,500 if we made it all the way to twenty-five. This was not an insignificant sum, either, considering the size of the allowances we received. I don't think Babs even tried. She smoked as ostentatiously as possible in front of our parents.

Babs was most adamant in her refusal to give money to charity. Grandfather and Father expected all of us to follow their example and encouraged us to contribute 10 percent of our allowances to church and other charitable causes. In the beginning these were very small amounts—only a few dollars a month—but Father saw this practice as an essential part of our moral and civic education. Babs refused to give a cent, as a way of show-ing her independence. She suffered for it financially because Father was less generous to her than he was to his five sons.

The rebellion was not a happy one on either side. Father was distressed by her behavior and hurt by her animosity toward him. For Babs, life just be-came more and more difficult. One episode when she was in her early twen-ties had a lasting impact on her life. She was ticketed for speeding in her Stutz convertible and was terrified at what Father might say when he found out about it. Her fiancé, Dave Milton, was an attorney and tried to get the ticket "fixed" through a judge he knew. The press picked this up, and the story appeared on the front page of the tabloids for several days. My parents were upset, but my sister even more so. In the end, seeing her real distress, Father was understanding of her plight and did not react as she had feared. But from that day forward she was terrified of public notoriety. She retreated into herself and ceased being the gay, fun-loving party-goer she had been.

Babs was intelligent, capable, and beautiful, but after that event life never seemed to work for her. She loved to travel, but the most trivial inconve-niences or delays overwhelmed her; she was upset if the bathwater wasn't the right temperature or if meals weren't served precisely on time or if she had not brought just the right clothes for the weather or a dinner party. As a result she could think of nothing else and viewed all her trips as failures. It was as if her rebellion had been turned inward, where the struggle would continue, forever unresolved.

When I was ten and Babs twenty-two, she married Dave Milton. His fam-ily had been friends of our family both in Seal Harbor and in Pocantico. At first she saw marriage as a way to escape from Father, and while she at-tended major family events and kept in touch with Mother, she lived a very separate life.

=

John, of course, had *the name*. He was John D. Rockefeller 3rd, the eldest son and the heir apparent. Of all the children, John was the most like Father in personality; he was hardworking and conscientious, and had a strong sense of duty. But Father's standards were so high and exacting that John could never hope to win any final or complete approval from him. Every achieve-ment or success was taken for granted—that's how a Rockefeller *should* be-have, after all—and, furthermore, one should be careful not to get a swelled head about it and think you're superior. Since perfection was the norm, all John could do was fail. Though probably not articulated in words, Father's response always made him feel he should be able to do better.

It's not surprising that John had a "nervous disposition." He was extremely shy and awkward in social situations, so self-conscious that he would agonize for days over things he had said or thoughts he was thinking. He was, like Father, something of a hypochondriac, always concerned about his health and plagued throughout his childhood by a series of allergies and illnesses, though none of them was serious. Perhaps because he was so much like Father, John was destined to have, apart from Babs, the greatest conflict with him, but that would not come out in the open for a number of years.

John and Abby took opposite approaches in dealing with Father. Abby rebelled and tried to be in every way as different as possible; John, especially in his youth, tried to please Father, to be everything he could ask for, to be as good, dutiful, and giving as Father wanted him to be. In some ways it was just as futile. While at Princeton, John asked Father if he could bring a car down for use during prom week. Father acceded to his wish but expressed deep disapproval. Characteristically, Father elevated what was a simple and almost classic request from a son to his father—to use the family car—into an opportunity to teach a moral lesson. He said that in his own college days he had not had a horse because he did not want to be different from the other boys, and he stressed the valuable "democratic" role John would play by "getting along without a car when others were having them." John wrote back that he felt there was a limit to the sacrifice Rockefellers ought to feel it their duty to make to promote the democratic spirit. It was as close to sarcasm as John ever allowed himself to get, and in fact he ended the letter with an apology.

==

It can't have been easy for John, either, to have Nelson always nipping at his heels. Nelson was the first in my generation to test successfully the limits of Father's precepts on the proper way to raise children.

The contrast between John and Nelson was dramatic. Where John was painfully shy and self-conscious, Nelson was sociable and outgoing and loved to be the center of attention. The duties and obligations that weighed John down seemed to roll off Nelson easily. It was as if Nelson had looked at Babs and John and decided he wasn't going to make either of their mistakes in his relations with Father—there would be no futile rebellion and no slavish subordination to the Rockefeller image. If he broke the rules, as Babs did, it wouldn't be done ostentatiously to anger Father but to have fun, get away with it, or secure some important result. If, like John, he was setting out to please Father, it was to achieve a clear and calculated objective—to get what he wanted—and he often succeeded.

Nelson was named for Mother's father, Senator Nelson Aldrich. But even though Nelson admired both grandfathers, he thought it significant that he had been born on Grandfather Rockefeller's birthday. He let one infer from this coincidence that he was the true *Rockefeller* standard-bearer. Yet his own career more closely paralleled that of Grandfather Aldrich, the career politician. In any case, Nelson was politically astute, even wily, within the family. He was a natural leader and radiated self-confidence. The burdens of duty, as defined by Father, did not weigh him down, and he seemed to relish being a member of a prominent family. He was also the mischievous one in the family; he surreptitiously shot rubber bands at the rest of us during our morning prayers and was not the slightest bit concerned when Father reprimanded him.

I idolized Nelson. In a household full of duties and constraints, Nelson knew how to have fun and acted as if the constraints were only minor obstacles that could be easily avoided. Most of the time he miraculously escaped serious discipline, and even the punishments that were meted out to him never really seemed to stick, because Mother enjoyed his liveliness and independence and, perhaps, in the secret and subtle ways that mothers can, encouraged his jaunty misbehavior. On the rare occasions when he took notice of my existence and asked me to join one of his adventures, my life was immediately transformed into something larger, better, and more exciting.

==

Laurance—the unusual spelling is because he was named after our grandmother Laura—was the philosopher and the creative one. Quiet like John and a bit detached, he was less shy and more venturesome. When he was at Princeton and roomed with a rather fast crowd, he told me that he believed in trying anything once. He was quick and witty, but not an especially good student. His natural charm and whimsical manner made him very attractive to girls, to whom he warmly responded. As a young man, however, he searched endlessly for the right road to follow in life. Later on he became a highly successful venture capitalist as well as a conservationist. His interest in unconventional ideas never diminished.

Nelson and Laurance formed an inseparable team, and they remained uniquely close within the family throughout their adult lives. Nelson, as the more aggressive and outgoing of the two, was invariably the ringleader in their exploits, but Laurance, in his more quiet and engaging way, would keep his end up. Zane Grey's western novels were their favorites, and they emulated characters from these stories in their behavior. As a result Nelson took to calling Laurance "Bill," because that sounded more Wild West than Laurance, and he continued calling him that until the day he died.

Even as a young boy Laurance showed evidence of his later financial acumen. He and Nelson bought several pairs of rabbits from the Rockefeller Institute, bred them at Pocantico, and then sold back the offspring for a handsome profit. A few years later the two of them, with some help from John, built a log cabin as their secret hiding place in the woods near Mother's garden in Maine. It was built with logs from trees they chopped down and dragged to the site with a pony. It was quite skillfully done, though I only saw the cabin as an adult because they had strictly forbidden Win and me from going anywhere near it, and I was sufficiently intimidated by their warning that I never attempted to find it until years later.

=

Winthrop faced an unusually difficult situation within the family. Nelson and Laurance were a club to which he wasn't invited. I, three years his junior, was a club he didn't want to join. He was teased unmercifully by them and gave me full measure of the grief they inflicted on him. Win did not have a particularly happy childhood. He was, as was I, somewhat overweight and awkward, and received a great deal of ridicule from Nelson and Laurance, who gave him the nickname Pudgy. Once Nelson coaxed Win onto a seesaw, and when he was high in the air, jumped off, sending poor Win crashing to the ground. Win picked up a pitchfork and chased Nelson, fully intending, I'm sure, to skewer him if Father hadn't intervened.

Later in life, after Win had been governor of Arkansas for two terms and was suffering from chronic alcoholism, Nelson made some gestures of support, but Win saw them as halfhearted and very belated. Win was deeply embittered about the condescending treatment he felt he had always received from Nelson.

As the youngest I received the special attention of my Mother, but there were fewer compensations for Win. Win had exceptional natural qualities of leadership, which he demonstrated during his distinguished military service in the war and later during his political career in Arkansas. But he was never comfortable with his social and intellectual peers. He spent much of his time with fair-weather friends, who looked up to him because of his money and position. He hated school and was actually somewhat relieved when he was expelled from Yale during his junior year. Win was restless, iconoclastic, and full of energy. I think he desperately craved Father's approval, but his academic failures and undisciplined comportment with friends of whom my parents did not approve meant that Father rarely granted him the acceptance and approval he sought.

=

As children we recognized that we belonged to an unusual, even exceptional family, but the effect was different on each of us. For some it was a burden, for others an opportunity. Mother and Father cared for each of us deeply, wanted the best for us, and tried to show us, each in his or her own way, the kind of life they thought would be most fulfilling. Mother was a remarkable woman whose elegant style and gracious behavior affected everyone, especially her children, in a positive way. Father was a more austere and certainly a more awesome figure. However, much of what I learned about myself and my family's traditions came as a result of his efforts to expose me to the special travails associated with the Rockefeller name and the realities of the world I would inevitably inherit. His accomplishments were an inspiration to me.

CHAPTER 4

TRAVELS

Father, busy as chairman of the Rockefeller Foundation and the Rockefeller Institute, as well as many other activities, was a somewhat remote figure to me and my siblings. Virtually the only opportunity we had to see his less formal side was on the many memorable trips we took with him during our childhood years. These early trips, as much as my formal education, helped develop the interests I would pursue and the man I would become.

The trips—four of which I will allude to here—were not typical family vacations. We traveled from the down-at-the-heels town of Williamsburg in Virginia to the towering Grand Tetons in Wyoming and from the resplendent palace of the Sun King at Versailles to the banks of the upper Nile in Nubia. They were extraordinary adventures, which gave me an insight into the values that motivated Father to make philanthropic gifts, not always as part of a grand design but spontaneously, because there were opportunities to do things that needed to be done. These trips also planted the seeds of my own later passion for travel and international affairs.

LIFE SAVERS AND HERSHEY BARS

Father understood that children become restless, especially on long automobile trips, and invariably brought along Life Savers, Hershey bars, and other goodies, which he doled out at appropriate moments along the way. He also used the trips as a means of teaching us how to travel. He showed us that by packing a bag neatly we could fit in more clothes than if we simply threw them in a jumble. He taught us to fold suit jackets so that they would not be rumpled when we took them out of the bag. He assigned each of us jobs, such as seeing that the luggage was distributed to the proper rooms when we arrived at a hotel and tipping the baggage carriers, the doormen, and others who helped us along the way. The older children handled paying the hotel bills.

RESTORING THE PAST: THE SPRING OF 1926

In the spring of 1926, Mother and Father took Nelson, Laurance, Winthrop, and me on a trip to Philadelphia and then on to Virginia to visit Revolutionary War and Civil War sites. Father also had agreed to speak at Hampton Institute, the famous Black college in Hampton, Virginia, that had received a great deal of financial support from the family. We spent a day on the campus speaking to students and attending a church service.

The next morning we climbed into the car for the trip to Richmond, where Father was to meet with Governor Harry F. Byrd to discuss conservation work in the Shenandoah Valley. Father had decided earlier that he wanted to stop in Williamsburg, home of the College of William and Mary, to see the work that was being done to renovate the national memorial hall of Phi Beta Kappa, the first chapter of which was located on the college campus. Father had been elected to this national honorary fraternity when he was an undergraduate at Brown and had agreed to lead the fund-raising campaign for the building. Our guide for this brief portion of the trip was to be the Reverend Dr. W.A.R. Goodwin, rector of Bruton Parish Church and a part-time development officer for the college.

Dr. Goodwin met us on the road into town early in the morning of a glorious spring day, with the dogwood and azalea in full bloom. He showed us the memorial hall and then led us around the sleepy village that had been the capital of Virginia before the American Revolution. But after the Revolution, when the capital moved to Richmond, the town entered a long period of slow decline. Many of its splendid public buildings, including the Governor's Palace and the House of Burgesses, had literally fallen into ruins. Dr. Goodwin was an eloquent tour director and a very good salesman. When we visited a handsome but dilapidated brick building known as the George Wythe House, he extolled its fine architecture but pointed out with sadness its state of disrepair. Father picked up on the observation and later agreed to provide the funds needed to restore the house.

That was the modest beginning of Father's most significant project in historic restoration, a project that gave him as much pleasure as anything he did in the field of philanthropy during his lifetime. Over a period of more than thirty years he spent some $60 million in acquiring and restoring the central portion of the town to its authentic colonial condition. Today Williamsburg is a pilgrimage site for millions of Americans and a place to which presidents of the United States have proudly taken visiting heads of state to catch a glimpse of an earlier America and its customs and traditions.*

EXPLORING THE WILD WEST: THE SUMMER OF 1926

The first extended trip I took with my parents was to the American West in the summer of 1926. We traveled in a private Pullman railway car, the Boston, which was usually reserved for the chairman of the New York Central Rail Road. We left the car on sidings at various points along the way and visited national parks and other sites of interest by automobile. In addition to Mother, Father, Laurance, Winthrop, and me, our group included a French tutor, who wrote long letters every day to his fiancée in France which he claimed were purely philosophical, and a young doctor from the Rockefeller Institute Hospital. We completed a ten-thousand-mile circuit of the country in a period of two months.

Father was a committed conservationist and used his western trips (he traveled there almost every year) to learn about the national park system and meet park superintendents. Two men in particular impressed him: Horace Albright of Yellowstone and Jesse Nusbaum of Mesa Verde in southwestern Colorado. We saw both of these men on the 1926 trip, and the meetings had important consequences.

==

We stopped first in Cleveland, Ohio, where we visited Grandmother Rockefeller's grave. Father stood there quietly for a few minutes as the rest of us watched him from a distance. Then we toured the old Rockefeller home on Euclid Avenue where Father was born and had spent his boyhood. He told us stories about his boyhood days and how different things were before

---

*Dr. Goodwin and I hit it off immediately. Father wanted his involvement with the project to remain secret for as long as possible, and so Dr. Goodwin and he used the code name "David's Father" in their correspondence to throw the press off the scent.

electricity and the automobile. We also visited Forest Hill, where Grandfather had a summer home for many years. Father was then developing it into a middle-class suburb, really a planned community similar to the ones in Radburn, New Jersey, and Sunnyside, New York, in which Father also had an interest. The "Rockefeller Homes" were an innovative departure and had attracted a great deal of national attention, although the project never proved to be a financial success.

Just as important to Father was a visit to the coal fields of southern Colorado, scene of the Ludlow Massacre. We spent a day in Pueblo touring Colorado Fuel & Iron's large steel mills and meeting representatives of the company union. Father greeted a number of the men by name, and they seemed pleased to see him. I remember being a bit startled by the experience but impressed with my father's forthright manner and the easy way that he dealt with the men and their families. It was an important lesson for a young boy to learn.

We began our real vacation, at least from my point of view, when we reached Albuquerque. The Southwest was incredibly mysterious and interesting to me, and filled with all sorts of exotic characters: Indians, cowboys, ranchers, and artists. We visited a number of the famous pueblos along the Rio Grande, and at San Ildefonso we met the celebrated potter Maria Martinez and watched her make her black-glazed pots, which would later become so famous and valuable. I celebrated my eleventh birthday in Taos, and that evening our group perched on a roof to watch the traditional fire dance ceremony at Taos Pueblo.

Mother was impressed by the artistic merit of Indian artifacts, as she often was by the simple beauty of good handicrafts. She and Father purchased Navajo rugs and silver jewelry, Pueblo pottery, baskets, beaded saddlebags, and other objects wherever they could find them. Mother was also quite taken by the paintings of Indians and other western subjects done by American artists who had established an art colony a few years before in Taos. She and Father were particularly drawn to the very realistic work of Eanger Irving Couse and Joseph Henry Sharp and bought a number of their paintings.*

Father became more aware of the need to preserve Indian art and to protect ancient archaeological sites as a result of this trip. We spent several days

---

*Mother and Father decorated a rest house near the Eyrie Garden in Seal Harbor with many of these works of art. The house and its contents remain to this day just as my parents arranged them. This is the only place left that shows Mother's interest in furnishings coupled with Father's passion for Southwest Indian artifacts.

at Mesa Verde with Jesse Nusbaum, who took us through the Anasazi cliff dwellings there. Nusbaum also spoke to Father about the depredations of "pot hunters" and others who invaded old sites and totally ruined the historical record for the sake of unearthing a few pieces of pottery. Largely as a result of this trip Father supported the creation of the Laboratory of Anthropology in Santa Fe, an institution that continues to exist to this day as part of the School of American Research.

=

After Mesa Verde we visited the Hopi villages in the Painted Desert and the south rim of the Grand Canyon before moving on to California. After a few days in Los Angeles, where I got my first glimpse of the Pacific, we boarded the Boston for the ride through the Sierras to Yosemite National Park. We spent almost a week at Yosemite and saw El Capitan, Bridal Veil Falls, and Glacier Point. Father spoke here also, as was his custom, with the national park people, who brought to his attention the need for funds to improve public access within the park and to acquire additional acreage to protect the giant redwoods, *Sequoia gigantea*, from the woodman's axe.

After a short stopover in San Francisco we headed south for Santa Barbara, where I experienced my first earthquake, and then back north again for a few days on the Monterey peninsula. We then headed for the great groves of coastal redwoods, *Sequoia sempervirens*, north of San Francisco. The year before, Father had made an anonymous pledge of $1 million to the Save-the-Redwoods League to enable this group to purchase one of the last remaining virgin stands of these trees in the area around Dyerville Flats. Even now, more than seventy years later, I can recall the incredible beauty of those redwoods standing like tall sentinels in the groves near Eureka.

=

Our party finally reached Yellowstone on July 13. We had been on the road for more than a month and had grown a bit weary of constant traveling. Yellowstone quickly revived our spirits.

Horace Albright presided over Yellowstone, the crown jewel of the National Park System. He took us to see Old Faithful and a number of other sites in the park, many of which could only be reached on horseback in those days. Albright urged Father to visit Jackson Hole, just south of Yellowstone, and we drove with Albright to see for the first time the Grand Teton Mountains, probably the most magnificent peaks in the Rocky Mountains, which only recently had been set aside as a national park. As

Albright pointed out, however, the drive through Jackson Hole, from which one had the best view of the Tetons, was marred by ugly signs and tumble-down roadside stands.

Both Father and Mother quickly saw Albright's point, and Father would later acquire anonymously the sagebrush-covered floodplain of the Snake River at the foot of the mountains in order to extend the park and preserve its beauty. Over a period of several years he bought more than thirty thousand acres and then offered it to the federal government if they would include it and a number of other parcels controlled by the Forest Service and the Bureau of Land Management within the park. It was nearly twenty years, however, before the Roosevelt administration would finally accept the gift.

A collateral benefit from Father's purchase of the Snake River land was his acquisition of the JY Ranch, a beautiful dude ranch on the eastern end of Phelps Lake, nestled at the foot of the Tetons. We had lunch there in 1926, and it became a favorite place for our family members to visit in subsequent years.

We started the homeward trek in late July and made one final stop in Chicago to see Aunt Edith Rockefeller McCormick, one of my father's sisters, at her palatial home on North Michigan Avenue. Aunt Edith was quite flamboyant and had recently divorced her husband of many years, Harold Fowler McCormick, the son of the founder of International Harvester, Cyrus McCormick. Aunt Edith was a devoted patron of the Chicago Opera and had also spent a great deal of time being analyzed by Carl Jung. She obviously relished her position as one of the grandes dames of Chicago society; she entertained us at a formal luncheon complete with liveried footmen in tights behind every chair.

FRANCE AND THE RESTORATIONS: THE SUMMER OF 1927

Although my parents felt their children should first get to know their own country, they believed it was just as important for us to learn about European cultures and civilization. So in 1927 they took Winthrop and me to France. Four years earlier Father had offered to place a million dollars at the disposal of the French government to repair sections of the Rheims Cathedral damaged by German artillery, and to restore the portions of Fontainebleau palace and the Palace of Versailles, where the leaking lead roof threatened the integrity of the limestone walls and made the famous Hall of Mirrors, where the treaty ending World War I had been signed, too dangerous to be used.

France was still reeling from the enormous human loss and physical destruction of the Great War, and neither the French government nor wealthy citizens of France were in a position to assume responsibility to protect or restore these monuments of incomparable architectural beauty and historic significance.

Once the French government had accepted Father's offer, he retained his old friend and the Beaux Arts–trained architect Welles Bosworth to supervise the restorations. Over the course of the next decade he provided more than $2 million for these projects.

We had a chance to inspect the work that had been completed to that point during our 1927 trip. We spent a week at Versailles in the lovely old-fashioned Trianon Palace Hotel so that Father could spend time with Bosworth and the French architects going over the details of the work under way. The conservator of Versailles gave Winthrop and me a special pass to ride our bicycles in the park and to climb over the vast lead roofs of the palace.

Winthrop and I were particularly intrigued by the restoration of Marie Antoinette's "Le Hameau," an exact replica of an eighteenth-century farm village filled with miniature houses, barns, and a dairy. Marie Antoinette had been a devotee of the writings of Jean-Jacques Rousseau, the great romantic philosopher, and seems to have heeded his advice about returning to nature, at least on occasion. She constructed a bucolic fantasy where she could escape from the stress of court life and palace intrigue with a few of her friends. There she dressed as a shepherdess and tended a flock of sheep. Not wanting to be too removed from the conveniences of court life, however, the Queen also built a small opera house, seating less than one hundred people, where she would go to be entertained by great musicians and singers. The story is also told that the Queen objected to the smell of the sheep and would send word of her arrival so that they could be perfumed.

During the remainder of the trip we traveled in two huge Spanish-built Hispano Suissa limousines with uniformed chauffeurs through the château country of the Loire Valley and then on to Mont-Saint-Michel and the wonderful coasts of Brittany and Normandy, which Mother particularly loved because of its associations with the great masters of the Impressionist school.

=

I returned to France in 1936 with my parents to participate in the ceremony rededicating Rheims Cathedral. Jean Zay, the minister of culture in Leon

Blum's Popular Front government, gave a banquet in Father's honor at the Palace of Versailles to express the French government's appreciation for Father's assistance, and named a street for him there as well. A few days later President Albert LeBrun decorated Father with the Grand Croix of the Legion d'Honneur, France's highest decoration, in front of a large and distinguished gathering at the Elysée Palace.

Sixty-four years later the French government generously awarded me the same decoration at the Palace of the Legion of Honor in Paris. It was a particularly meaningful occasion because the only other living American to hold that rank is President Ronald Reagan.

THREE MONTHS AMONG THE PYRAMIDS: THE WINTER OF 1929

Father was enthralled by the discoveries of archaeologists who had uncovered so much about the emergence of the great civilizations of antiquity. As a young man he had taken a special interest in the work of the University of Chicago's Oriental Institute, headed by the distinguished Egyptologist Dr. James Henry Breasted. For a number of years Father supported Breasted's work in Luxor and at the Temple of Medinet Habu across the Nile just below the Valley of the Kings.

In late 1928, Dr. Breasted invited Mother and Father to visit his "dig" in Egypt and to review the work of the institute. Neither of my parents had ever been to that part of the world, and after some discussion they readily agreed to go. I was in the ninth grade at the time and quickly made it obvious to my parents that I wanted to go with them. I had read about the discovery of King Tutankhamen's tomb only a few years earlier, and a trip to Egypt seemed to me the most exciting of adventures. Father was concerned about my missing so much school because of the length of the trip, which would last for more than three months, but I finally persuaded him to let me go on the grounds that I would learn so much from the experience. He agreed on condition that a tutor went along to keep me up to date on schoolwork. This was the best deal I could get, so I eagerly agreed.

We sailed from New York on the S.S. *Augustus* in early January 1929. At the last moment Mary Todhunter Clark, known as Tod, who was a close friend of Nelson's from summers in Seal Harbor, came along as well.

In Cairo we spent a week at the elegant old-world Semiramis Hotel, where a colorfully dressed dragoman served as our interpreter and guide. We visited the Sphinx, and I rode a camel out to Giza, where I climbed the

Great Pyramid. We saw whirling dervishes dance in the Arab Quarter one evening and visited mosques and the ancient Arab university of el Azhar. Best of all for me were the bazaars, where I spent as many hours as I could, fascinated by the women dressed in black robes whose faces were always veiled, and by the exotic wares sold by hundreds of small shopkeepers from their tiny stalls facing onto narrow streets of the souk. The pungent smells of the spice market, the sounds of hammering on copper pots and bowls that were being fashioned, and the colorful displays of rugs and textiles caught my fancy, and I quickly learned to bargain for everything, offering but a fraction of the listed price for anything I was interested in. There were swarms of flies everywhere, clinging to freshly dressed meat hanging from hooks in the butchers' stalls, and hordes of beggars, many of them children with trachoma who had fluid running from their milky white eyes.

From Cairo we headed up the Nile on a large *dahabiyah* (a passenger boat) to see Dr. Breasted's excavations at Luxor. I still remember the picturesque *feluccas* sailing on the Nile, the farmers patiently raising buckets of water from the river with *shadoofs* (a counterbalanced sweep) to irrigate their fields, which for centuries has fed millions of people in defiance of the desert. There were many other important ancient sites on the way, and each evening after we tied up along the riverbank, Dr. Breasted gave a slide lecture on the monuments we would see the following day.

After Luxor and Karnak we continued on to the Second Cataract at Wadi Halfa, the first town in the Sudan. On the way we passed the beautiful Temple of Philae, now submerged under Lake Nasser following the construction of the High Dam at Aswan in the 1960s. We also saw the magnificent Temple of Ramses II at Abu Simbel with its four colossal statues of a pharaoh carved into the face of the cliff. Half a century later I visited Abu Simbel again after the entire temple, including the great statues, had been cut free and lifted hydraulically to the top of the cliffs, to protect it from the rising waters of the Nile behind the Aswan Dam. Reinstalled in this new setting in front of an artificial cliff, it looked as imposing as when I had first seen it in 1929.

I continued to pursue my interest in beetle collecting and even managed to find a sacred scarab, a beetle that lays its eggs in a ball of dung and then buries it in the sand. The ancient Egyptians worshiped the sacred scarab, believing it to be an intermediary between the living and the underworld of the dead. Tod playfully teased me about my hobby, so I bought an inexpensive wedding ring and gave it to her in the presence of my parents and others, claiming that I represented Nelson in asking for her hand in marriage. Everyone except Tod thought this was quite amusing, since we all knew she had high hopes for just such an event. Indeed, soon after we returned from the trip, Nelson did propose, and they were married the following year.

We also visited the Cairo Museum of Antiquities and found it in appalling condition with mud-encrusted sarcophagi and beautiful ornaments resting on bare shelves, poor lighting, and inadequate identification. In 1925, at Dr. Breasted's urging, Father had offered $10 million to rebuild the museum in order to provide a better setting for the world's greatest collection of antiquities. Inexplicably, the Egyptian government refused, and Father always suspected it was the result of pressure from the British government, which was not anxious to see an intrusion of American influence even in cultural affairs.

We drove on to Palestine through the Nile delta and along the coast. We toured the holy places in Jerusalem and traveled down to Jericho, where I took a swim in the salty Dead Sea, a thousand feet below sea level. We then proceeded north to Beirut through the Jordan Valley and along the Sea of Galilee. The associations of this area with the Bible and the ministry of Jesus Christ made this a deeply meaningful part of the trip for Father and, I confess, for me as well.

Although Father's proposal to build a new museum in Cairo foundered on the rocks of international politics, he was much more successful with a similar idea in Jerusalem. Wandering the Via Dolorosa, visiting Bethlehem, the Garden of Gethsemane, the Dome of the Rock, and the Wailing Wall on the site of the Second Temple convinced Father that something needed to be done to preserve the antiquities of the Holy Land after centuries of neglect by the Ottoman Turks. Again, with Dr. Breasted's encouragement, Father offered to build a museum of archaeology to house these antiquities and provide the facilities for scholars to study them. This time the British government, which controlled the Palestinian Mandatory State, agreed with the proposal wholeheartedly. The Palestine Archaeological Museum, often referred to today as the Rockefeller Museum, still exists in east Jerusalem and houses, among many other marvelous things, the Dead Sea Scrolls.

===

Looking back I realize the debt I owe to my parents for my education. While the Lincoln School did a creditable job in providing me with a formal education, my parents did more. They brought to our home some of the most interesting people of the time. On our many trips and excursions they opened our eyes to nature, to people, and to history in a way that expanded our interests and stimulated our curiosity. They made us feel the excitement of the opportunities open to us and recognize the role the family was playing in so many areas. These experiences gave us an education that transcended formal learning.

CHAPTER 5

ROCKEFELLER CENTER

During my childhood and teenage years Father was involved in a number of major projects in and around New York City. He seemed to have a hand in everything, from the creation of public parks and the preservation of the natural landscape and the building of museums and churches to the provision of adequate and affordable housing for the City's burgeoning population. Many of Father's initiatives—the Palisades Interstate Park, the Cloisters and Fort Tryon Park, and Riverside Church—have become part of the City's incredible physical landscape. Ironically, however, Father will be most remembered for a project he never intended to undertake and that inadvertently led him to become a major real estate developer.

A NEW OPERA HOUSE

Father's most important project was, of course, Rockefeller Center. It was his most visible endeavor and has had a lasting impact on urban design in New York and around the world. The project began quite modestly, but it turned out to be an enormous venture that exposed him to serious financial risks without bringing him any financial return. Yet, paradoxically, Rockefeller Center is, with the possible exception of Standard Oil, the business venture with which my family is most closely linked. I will return to the story of Rockefeller Center again, but this is the place to introduce it—at the beginning.

Mother commissioned Stefan Hirsch, a promising young artist, to paint the view from my fifth-floor bedroom window at 10 West 54th Street in 1930. Hirsch's cityscape, *Midtown Range,* is dominated by the glowing white towers of the Chrysler and Empire State Buildings rising majestically in the distance and punctuated by the graceful spires of Saint Patrick's Cathedral in the middle ground. The foreground, the neighborhood just to our south, much of it owned by Columbia University, is flat, featureless, and undistinguished.

The reality was even grittier. As commercial activity surged northward through Manhattan during the first decades of the twentieth century, older residential areas were overwhelmed and transformed. Columbia's property, bounded by Fifth and Sixth Avenues between 48th and 51st Streets, was composed mostly of four-story residential brownstones, many of which were being converted to small retail businesses or subdivided into small apartments. With the advent of Prohibition in the mid-1920s, nightclubs and speakeasies selling bootleg liquor also appeared, and there were rumors that a number of brothels had opened as well. The neighborhood, once the exclusive preserve of the Vanderbilts and Astors, had become seedy and down-at-the-heels. Father owned substantial property just to the north and was concerned about the deterioration of property values.

By the mid-1920s the neighborhood had become a prime candidate for redevelopment. Columbia University received little income from the properties, and with most of the leases expiring between 1928 and 1931, the trustees decided to look for a builder who could develop the entire parcel. An attractive potential tenant, the Metropolitan Opera Company, also appeared on the scene.

At the time, the Metropolitan Opera House was located in the heart of the Garment District, at 39th Street and Broadway, a part of town not much different then from what it is today. Built in the early 1880s, the house also had become inadequate for the needs of the company—especially its crowded backstage areas and poor sight lines. For some time the Met directors had been searching for a site on which to build a new opera house. Thus, in early 1926, when Otto Kahn, the Met's chairman, learned that Columbia wanted to improve its midtown property, he decided to explore its potential for the opera.

At that point, in early 1928, Father came into the picture. He was impressed by Columbia University's aspirations and the opera's plans to build a new opera house as the centerpiece of a carefully planned commercial and residential development on the Columbia property. This would be just the thing, he felt, to upgrade the area and safeguard his own properties.

After months of consultation with real estate experts, architects, and businessmen, followed by detailed negotiations with the university and the opera, Father signed a Definitive Agreement and Lease with Columbia on October 1, 1928, agreeing to rent the twelve acres of Columbia's land for an initial period of twenty-four years at an average rent of $3.6 million a year. The agreement with Columbia gave Father the option to purchase the central block for $2.5 million, but only if the construction of an opera house was firmly committed. If the opera house plans failed to materialize, the land would revert to Columbia, which would then be free to incorporate this block in the broader lease. Although Father assigned the lease to a holding company, the Metropolitan Square Corporation, he remained "liable as a principal and not as a surety on all of the covenants and promises contained in the Agreement." This was a fateful clause in that it made Father personally responsible for all financial obligations related to the development, whether or not it reached fruition.

All participants agreed that the project would be called Metropolitan Square because of the opera's role as the "anchor tenant." The first site plan placed the opera house on the western portion of the central block between 49th and 50th Streets—where 30 Rockefeller Plaza now stands. Father proposed, and the leaders of the Met and Columbia agreed, that the eastern portion of this block, fronting on Fifth Avenue, would be developed as a small park with an open plaza to give the opera house the proper setting, after which the park would be donated to the City. This first plan envisioned apartment buildings, department stores, and hotels on the two blocks adjacent to the opera house, which would be subleased to developers who would be responsible for financing and constructing their own buildings.

When Father signed the lease in 1928, everyone believed the plan would go forward as originally envisioned: The opera would sell its old house, and Father, having bought the land from Columbia, would transfer the title to the Met, which would reimburse him for the cost of the land and his expenses. The Met would then finance the construction of its new facility, and Father would be off the hook financially for the central block of the site.

In short, Father saw his role in the project as that of a facilitator. He considered it neither a real estate investment nor a charitable gift. He had no thought of making money from the deal, but he didn't expect to lose anything, either. He knew there would be carrying costs between the time the lease went into effect in 1928 and when the area was fully developed, but depending on the subleases negotiated, he expected to come out even. Things did not work out that way.

GOING IT ALONE

A year after Father signed the lease with Columbia, the stock market crash changed the situation totally. The first domino to fall was the Metropolitan Opera. The Met board found it impossible to sell its old house and went to Father with a take-it-or-leave-it proposition: Unless he donated the land to them outright and helped finance the construction of the new opera house as well, they would withdraw from the project. Father was outraged and promptly rejected their proposal.

Losing the opera was bad enough, but with the deepening economic depression, the individuals and businesses that had earlier expressed interest in building on the other blocks also began to back out, even Standard Oil of New Jersey. For Father it was the worst of all worst-case scenarios. Columbia refused to renegotiate the lease or even to modify it significantly. Father was stuck with leasing the property on the original terms—with no tenant. For the university, of course, the deal was a bonanza that would turn out to be its principle source of income for the next fifty years. Columbia had Father over a barrel and was very content to keep him there.

The situation Father faced in the first months of 1930 must have been frightening. If he did nothing to improve the property, he stood to lose about $5 million a year (counting rent, real estate taxes, and other expenses), which over the twenty-four years of the lease would amount to approximately $120 million. Developing the land without the firm promise of tenants, however, posed even greater risks. The construction cost for a project of this kind was enormous, and given the state of the economy, there was no assurance that tenants could be found once the buildings were completed.

In later years Father would be praised for his courage in going forward with the project. He once said to a friend: "Often a man gets in a position where he wants to run, but there is no place to run to. So he goes ahead with the only course open to him, and people call that courage." That may be so, but it still took a lot of courage for Father to face the risks and uncertainties that confronted him. All of a sudden he found himself thrust back into the world of business where he felt no special interest or aptitude, and once again was faced with the prospect that he might not be able to live up to the role he had been assigned, that he wouldn't be able to fulfill his obligations.

But as Father had demonstrated at Ludlow when he found himself with his back against a wall, he accepted the challenge and moved forward unflinchingly to do what had to be done.

Father consulted with the several distinguished architects and builders who had worked with him in developing the original project, and an alternative proposal was quickly devised. The new plan—the second iteration of what would now be called Rockefeller Center—in contrast to the original envisioned an entirely commercial development.*

To finance the project Father negotiated a $65 million line of credit from the Metropolitan Life Insurance Company, the largest such arrangement any insurance company had made up to that time. Father was furious at the 4.5 percent interest rate and told everyone that Fred Ecker, the chairman of Met Life, had forced him to pay an exorbitant premium. But it was the best deal he could get, and the high rate was in itself an indication of the riskiness of the project. Met Life also insisted that Father give his personal guarantee on the loan, making him the ultimate guarantor of both the lease and the loan.

The Met Life loan took care of cash flow problems, but it did not relieve Father of his own financial obligations to the project. For more than five years in the 1930s during the main period of construction, Father spent between $10 and $13 million a year on the Center, which he financed from his personal income and through the sale of oil stock, sometimes at very depressed prices. Father's expenditures on construction, taxes, lease payments, and other aspects of the project from 1929 to 1939 totaled $125 million, or the equivalent today of more than $1.5 billion. It might surprise people to learn that although he lived until 1960, Father received no income from this massive investment and recouped less than half of the capital he had invested.

But Father's cost in building Rockefeller Center cannot be measured only in dollars. As with everything he did, he applied himself singlemindedly to the task, agonizing over minor details and meticulously supervising the work of the architects and builders. Constant worry took its toll. He was plagued by migraines and would often come home from the office in such a state of nervous exhaustion that he would have to lie down on his couch, not to be disturbed for an hour or more in the evening before dinner. He often used the service of a Swedish masseur who seemed to bring some

---

*Among the architects was the young Wallace K. Harrison, and the principal builder, the man who really built Rockefeller Center, was John R. Todd, grandfather of Christine Todd Whitman, the former governor of New Jersey.

relief. He suffered recurrent bouts of bronchitis and other ailments, which the stress he endured probably exacerbated. I recall that he was physically tired during much of this time, and he and Mother spent several weeks each winter either in Taormina, Sicily, or Tucson, Arizona, trying to get some rest and relaxation from the ordeal.

Nevertheless, he persevered and in the process provided thousands of jobs for New Yorkers during the worst part of the Depression. Union leaders were vocal in their appreciation of Father, and years later my friends in the building trades—men such as Harry Albright and Peter Brennan—still spoke with deep gratitude of Father's courage and generosity.

RESCUING THE PROJECT

For the project to be viable economically, Father needed tenants. The turning point, undoubtedly the salvation of the project, came in the summer of 1930 when David Sarnoff, chairman of the Radio Corporation of America (RCA), and Owen D. Young, chairman of General Electric, which held a controlling interest in RCA and also owned Radio-Keith-Orpheum (RKO), a major producer of motion pictures and a chain of movie theaters across the country, agreed to lease one million square feet of office and studio space in the project's major building at $2.75 a square foot and to pay an annual rent of $1.5 million for four theaters that would be built on the property. With this major tenant in place, architectural planning could move ahead for most of the site. Just as important, by linking a real estate project with radio and motion pictures, two of that era's most dramatic new technologies and growth industries, an excitement and cachet was created that would not have been possible with the Metropolitan Opera. When the deal was announced, David Sarnoff spoke enthusiastically of a "Radio City" rising on the site, a name that caught on almost immediately.*

Securing NBC as the principal tenant of the main building was critical, but the other sites remained open. Congress agreed to special legislation that provided duty-free status for goods imported by firms taking space in the Center, and a number of foreign firms took long-term leases in some of

---

*In a project filled with ironies, this was a rather intriguing one. Father disapproved of mass popular entertainment. A few years earlier there had been a bit of a family crisis over whether or not to buy a radio. Father was adamantly opposed but eventually agreed to buy one on the conditions that the instrument would be played quietly and would not be placed in the main sitting room of the 54th Street house.

the smaller buildings. This allowed construction to proceed on the British Empire Building and La Maison Française, the two low-rise buildings on Fifth Avenue between 49th and 50th Streets. The press immediately christened the garden in between them the Channel Gardens, à la the English Channel.

The Center had an enormous amount of space to fill, and this produced an intense competition for tenants with other landlords in the midtown area and even further afield. The Chrysler Building and the Empire State Building, both completed in the early 1930s, were especially strong competitors because of their proximity, superb architecture, and modern conveniences. The Empire State Building even had mooring posts for blimps!

As Rockefeller Center neared completion, Father persuaded Standard Oil of New Jersey, in which he was still the largest individual shareholder, to lease all of the final building that would be built on the original site. Other companies and institutions with which Father had a close identification also took leases. For example, Chase National Bank agreed to open a branch, on condition that it would have exclusive banking rights throughout the Center for a number of years. The Rockefeller Foundation, the Spelman Fund, and Industrial Relations Counselors—Father was chairman of each—also rented small amounts of space in the Center.

=

Despite its difficult beginnings, Rockefeller Center became a universally acclaimed real estate property. The clean, bold thrust of its modernist lines and the Art Deco motif, plus its underground shopping malls, open plazas, and rooftop gardens, gave it a simple beauty, elegance, and imaginative quality that silenced even its harshest critics.

More than an architectural success, Rockefeller Center became a city planning paradigm known for maintaining the highest standards of security and cleanliness while promoting its creative design and aesthetic appeal. In many ways it is better known and more respected as a model of urban design today than it was in the decade after it was built.

HELD HOSTAGE BY A LEASE

While Rockefeller Center was a success aesthetically and architecturally, its financial viability remained uncertain for many years. The biggest problem, at least once the Depression eased and a measure of normality returned to the nation's economic life, was the Columbia lease.

Stated simply, while Father, and later my brothers and I, owned the buildings, the university owned the land. The lease provided Columbia with an unusual amount of control over a broad range of routine business activities—for example, the types of businesses that could locate in the Center and the amount of rent that could be charged. Most important, the lease prohibited Father from selling any or all of the buildings, offering outside investors a participation in the ownership, or assigning the lease itself to any other individual or corporation without Columbia's prior agreement. Father tried to get the lease restrictions modified, but the university routinely refused his requests. Essentially, the lease held Father hostage and the next generation of the family as well. The original lease ran for twenty-four years, until 1952, with three option periods of twenty-one years each, potentially a full term of slightly less than one hundred years. However, the specific terms of the lease as well as its dollar amount were renegotiable each time it was up for renewal.

The greatest financial burden to the family was the obligation to pay the rent regardless of tenant income. The greatest financial threat to the family was Father's personal guarantee of the lease, an obligation that passed on to my brothers and me when we bought the equity shares of the Center after World War II. In addition there were several onerous covenants. One required Father to maintain an escrow fund equal to three years of lease payments that had to be invested in U.S. Treasury Bonds, which carried a very low interest rate. Another restricted the payment of dividends until all the original debt on the Center had been paid off, an event that did not occur until 1970.

What all this meant was that during Rockefeller Center's first five decades the family received virtually no return on the investment despite the fact that my father had poured his heart and soul—and a good portion of his fortune—into the project.

A CONTROVERSIAL MURAL

An interesting subplot to Rockefeller Center's early history concerns the mural commissioned for the entrance lobby of the RCA Building. As part of the plan to make the Center aesthetically pleasing, a number of artists received commissions to decorate the buildings and the open spaces. Paul Manship's golden *Prometheus*, which still gazes silently over the sunken plaza, was one of these works and has become a hallmark of the Center. Father was less fortunate with another selection.

In the late 1920s my mother had come to admire the work of Diego Rivera, an extremely talented Mexican painter and muralist who had studied in Paris before and during World War I and became part of Matisse's artistic circle. Like many artists of his generation, Rivera was left-wing in his political orientation and was even a member of the Mexican Communist Party for a time.

Alfred Barr, the young director of the Museum of Modern Art, brought Rivera to Mother's attention. Barr and Rivera had lived for a short time in the same rooming house in Moscow in 1928, and Barr was impressed by the Mexican's talent and personality. When Barr proposed that MoMA give Rivera a one-man show in 1931, both Mother and Nelson were enthusiastic. Mother commissioned a painting from him and also bought a number of the watercolors he had done in Moscow in 1927. With this money Rivera was able to visit New York for the first time.

Mother and Nelson came to know Rivera well, and he was a frequent visitor in my parents' home, where I met him on several occasions. He was a very imposing and charismatic figure, quite tall and weighing three hundred pounds. He spoke very little English but perfect French in addition to Spanish. On one or two occasions he brought his wife, Frida Kahlo, with him. Frida was a fascinating and exotic young woman whose artistic talents were comparable to her husband's. Today her works command prices in the New York auction market that are even higher than those paid for Diego's.

The MoMA show in December 1931 firmly established Rivera's reputation in the United States. And when the time came to commission a mural for the front lobby of the RCA Building, which was just being completed, Mother and Nelson argued strongly in favor of giving it to Rivera. He submitted a sketch for consideration, and after much discussion among the architects and managing agents about Rivera's reliability, it was approved. On the basis of this sketch a contract was drawn and signed by all parties, and Rivera agreed to a payment of $21,500 for a project that he estimated would take about three months to complete.

Rivera arrived in New York in early 1933 to start work on the fresco after a very difficult experience at the Detroit Institute of Art, where his just-completed murals were attacked as anti-Christian and anti-American by many, including Father Charles Coughlin, the famous "radio priest."

It would appear that Rivera decided to use the Rockefeller Center mural to make a strong political statement. *Mankind at the Crossroads*, as Rivera titled the work, was filled with contrasting images drawn from the Marxist canon: class conflict, oppression, and war as the theme on the "capitalist" side of the fresco; peace, cooperation, and human solidarity on the "communist" side. The solution to these conflicts, at least in Rivera's view, would come from the application of science and technology for the benefit of all. He filled the fresco with microscopes, telescopes, movie screens, and gigantic gears and levers to underline his point. When the mural was almost finished, he added a prominent and quite unmistakable portrait of Lenin joining hands with workers from around the world. This idyllic and somewhat fanciful grouping was balanced by a deftly done scene on the "capitalist" side of well-dressed men and women dancing, playing cards, and drinking martinis, all positioned under a microscope examining a slide filled with viruses of "social" diseases. The backdrop for this was a scene of policemen beating workers while Catholic priests and Protestant ministers looked on approvingly.

It was quite brilliantly executed but not appropriate for the lobby of the RCA Building. Nelson tried to persuade Rivera to eliminate, at the very least, the portrait of Lenin. But the artist refused to change anything, saying that rather than mutilate his great work he would have the whole mural destroyed! Nelson pointed out that he had not been commissioned to paint communist propaganda and that, based on the original, much less provocative sketch, there was no reason to accept the work as finally executed. In the end, when no compromise could be reached, Rivera was paid in full and dismissed. An attempt was made to remove and preserve the fresco, but it proved impossible, and this work of art had to be destroyed.

In the late 1930s, Rivera reproduced the mural, with more than a few embellishments, including a portrait of Father drinking a martini with a group of "painted ladies." This mural is prominently located on the central staircase of the Palacio de Belles Artes in Mexico City. In the immediate aftermath of the destruction of Rivera's mural, there were expressions of outrage from the arts community in New York, Mexico, and elsewhere. They accused the family of committing a sacrilege against art and of violating Rivera's freedom of expression. In the view of artists and liberal thinkers more generally, the fact that the artist was guilty of deceit, meanness, and publicly insulting a family that had befriended him and helped promote his career seemed not to matter.*

---

*Perhaps Senator Daniel Patrick Moynihan had the last word on this controversy. He noted at a dinner in Washington soon after the breakup of the Soviet Union that it was a shame the mural had been destroyed because the almost complete eradication of monuments to Communist leaders throughout the Soviet Union and the old Eastern Bloc might have left it the only remaining image of Lenin anywhere in the world!

BICYCLING THROUGH BRITAIN

While I was aware of Father's worries about Rockefeller Center, as a teenager I had other interests and concerns. I graduated from the Lincoln School in June 1932, and as a graduation present I set off on a bicycle trip in the British Isles with a school friend, Winston Garth, and a French theological student and tutor, Oswald Gockler. The trip was inspired by tales Father had recounted to me of a similar trip he had taken in England when he was about the same age.

We sailed tourist class on a Cunard liner to Southampton and then went by train to London. We had no sooner arrived at our hotel than the telephone rang and a very English voice announced that she was the Marchioness of Crewe, that she and her husband, the Marquis, had just returned from New York where they had taken part with my parents in the dedication of the British Empire Building in Rockefeller Center. My parents had told them of our proposed bicycle trip, and she was calling to say that on that very evening the Duke of York—who later became King George VI—was giving a dinner dance at Saint James's Palace and that I was invited to attend with her. The event was in honor of his brother, the Prince of Wales—who would, of course, succeed to the throne within a few years as King Edward VIII and then abdicate—and other members of the Royal Family. Dinner would be at 8:30, white tie and tails. I should pick her up at 8:00.

I was stunned and nervously replied that I had no evening clothes with me and could not possibly attend, to which the Marchioness replied with authority that this was a royal invitation I could not refuse. I mumbled something to the effect that I would see what I could do and hung up, looking petrified at my friend Win who had not been invited.

Fortunately, my aunt Lucy was in town, so I called her in desperation. She said it was a great opportunity and that I should go. I should call the concierge about renting evening clothes and get the hotel to order a Daimler with a liveried chauffeur in which to fetch Lady Crewe. My day was ruined, but I followed instructions and arrived on time to pick up the Marchioness, only to find when I appeared at Crewe House, her grand mansion in Mayfair, that I was to ride with her in her Rolls-Royce. My Daimler could follow.

Saint James's Palace is a sixteenth-century stone structure at the end of St. James's Street, facing out on Green Park and Pall Mall. For centuries it has served as the residence of senior members of the Royal Family. On our arrival we were greeted by Coldstream Guards standing rigidly erect with their red jackets and high beaver shakos, an imposing beginning for the evening.

We entered the palace and proceeded down long corridors paneled in dark wood. Kings and queens from the Stuart and Hanoverian dynasties peered down at us from the walls as we walked slowly toward the great drawing room to be presented together.

I was received with great courtesy by the Duke and Duchess of York, who made a real effort to make me feel comfortable. But small talk with a seventeen-year-old American boy did not come easily for them, and the conversation was difficult for me. Lady Crewe introduced me to the other "royals" present that night and to a bewildering variety of dukes, earls, and countesses. The only other American present was Lady Nancy Astor, the wife of Lord Waldorf Astor and herself a viscountess. Lady Astor, the first woman ever elected to the House of Commons, was a formidable intellectual who presided over the somewhat notorious Cliveden Set, which would later be accused of pro-German sympathies. She, too, did her best to put me at ease, but after a few embarrassing pauses, Lady Crewe whisked me off to meet her brother, Lord Roseberry, whose father had been prime minister in the 1890s.

Before I left—alone in my rented Daimler—Lord Roseberry invited my two friends and me to spend a night with him in his castle in the north of England. Our visit gave me my first exposure to the formalities of an English country estate with its hierarchy of servants headed by an all-powerful Jeeves-like butler who unpacked our saddlebags filled with dirty clothes as if we were British royalty.

The bicycle trip was a great adventure and quite unlike my brief and unexpected introduction to the Royal Family. We covered a considerable part of Britain, from Cornwall in the southwest to the Highlands of northern Scotland, stopping mostly in small inns along the way. We interspersed a few days of bicycle riding with train rides to the next area we wanted to visit. In those days this was easy to do since trains were run very informally. One bought a ticket for a seat and another for the bicycle. When the train pulled into the station, one simply put the bicycle in the baggage car and found a seat in a passenger car. There was no red tape, and no one ever thought of the possibility of the bicycle's being stolen.

We had no letters of introduction and relied on our guidebooks for modestly priced places to stay. In Scotland, however, we visited our Lincoln School classmate Donald Barrow, whose father managed Skibo Castle, Andrew Carnegie's estate near the northern tip of Scotland. Our hostess was Mrs. Carnegie, a friend of my parents and the widow of the great industrialist and philanthropist who had been a friend of my grandfather's.

Altogether we bicycled some six hundred miles and covered a good deal more ground by train. It was a wonderful learning experience—far away from Rockefeller Center and Father's troubles—and left me with a lasting affection for the United Kingdom and fit and ready for my freshman year at Harvard.

CHAPTER 6

HARVARD

Mother strongly influenced my choice of colleges. Father had deliberately avoided stating a preference to any of his sons, believing the choice should be ours alone and refusing to influence our decisions in any way. The result was that, somewhat to his disappointment, none of us attended his alma mater, Brown. Mother, on the other hand, wanted one of us to go to Harvard. Her favorite brother, Winthrop Aldrich, was a Harvard man, and she hoped one of us would follow in his footsteps. My brothers had attended other colleges, so I was her last hope, and although she put no overt pressure on me, her quiet persuasion influenced me greatly.

Although I entered college at seventeen, this was not due to academic brilliance. I entered first grade at Lincoln when I was five—a year earlier than most—because all my brothers were in school and I didn't like being left alone at home. Lincoln's strong focus on individual development allowed me to keep up with my class, and I graduated at the age of sixteen. What Lincoln had not taught me was disciplined work habits, and it had done a poor job of teaching me reading, spelling, and grammar, although my dyslexia certainly played a role in that also. This made my first year at Harvard a bit of a grind, but I did manage to attain a B average by diligently applying myself to my studies. Academically, the year was not a serious problem for me.

SOCIALLY AWKWARD

It was socially that I felt like a misfit. I was not only a year younger than most of my classmates, but I had grown up in a protected environment and was unsophisticated and ill at ease with my contemporaries. My brothers had largely ignored me, so most of my social interaction had been with adults. In fact, I was far more comfortable talking with public figures or famous artists than I was with people of my own age.

I entered Harvard with eleven hundred other men, of whom only two had been classmates at Lincoln, and neither was a close friend. I lived in a single room on the fourth floor of Thayer Hall, the oldest freshman dormitory in Harvard Yard, and took my meals in the Union, located across Plimpton Street from the Widener Library. Wandering around the yard, in classes, and at meals in the Union, I came into contact with many boys from elite prep schools, such as Groton, Saint Mark's, and Saint Paul's. They all seemed to be my antithesis: good-looking, athletic, self-confident, and smartly dressed in Harris tweed jackets and gray flannel trousers. I admired them from afar. They represented the epitome of college fashion and sophistication, but I had little to say to them, and they showed no great interest in talking with me, either. Instead my closest relations were with other residents of Thayer Hall, including Walter Taylor, my class's sole African American. Walter also seemed out of his element and a bit lost, so we had much in common. Sadly, for reasons I never learned, Walter did not return to Harvard after that first year.

I realize now that had I gone to boarding school, as so many sons of wealthy parents did, I would have been part of the very group I secretly envied but with which I felt so ill at ease, and my life at Harvard would have been more immediately pleasurable and certainly very different from what it was. Upon reflection almost seventy years later, however, I do not believe the rest of my life would have been as interesting or constructive as it has been. Having to deal with my early insecurities at Harvard and to struggle for academic achievement and social acceptance made me a more open-minded and tolerant person.

THE ALDRICH FAMILY

While my freshman year had lonely moments, two circumstances laid the groundwork for my becoming more fully and happily engaged in college life.

The first was that several of Mother's family lived in the Boston area. Mother's youngest sister, Elsie Aldrich Campbell, lived with her family in Brookline, only a few miles from Cambridge. She invited me to meals and encouraged me to bring my college friends. She always made us feel welcome. A good many years later Benjy Franklin, one of my roommates and a frequent visitor to the Campbells', married Aunt Elsie's daughter, Helena.

I also made numerous trips to Providence to visit Aunt Lucy Aldrich at her home, 110 Benevolent Street, where she, Mother, and their siblings were born and raised. Outspoken in her opinions and mercurial in her feelings, Aunt Lucy was full of life and great fun to be with.

BENJY AND DICK

The key moment in my freshman year was meeting George S. Franklin, Jr. (for obvious reasons known as Benjy) and Richard Watson Gilder.

Benjy was the son of a prominent lawyer in New York City and two years older than I. He had a brilliant mind and was an excellent student. He was serious-minded and a strong competitor in anything he did—a good tennis player and excellent racing sailor. He won the summer championship in the Atlantic Class of sailboats at the Cold Spring Harbor Yacht Club on Long Island for nine years in a row.

Dick Gilder was more lighthearted but no less brilliant. He was the grandson and namesake of the founder of *The Century Magazine* as well as a grandson of the great artist and founder of Tiffany & Company, Lewis Comfort Tiffany. Dick was a fine athlete and played on Harvard's varsity squash team. He was also quite handsome, and girls found him almost irresistible. Dick loved to argue and to take strong positions, usually contrary to the conventional wisdom, on political or economic subjects.

As prep school graduates, Benjy and Dick had many friends at Harvard. They included me in their circle, thereby dispelling my sense of isolation. We lived together in Eliot House for our three final years at Harvard in close proximity to several other friends. In fact, by our senior year our suite of rooms—consisting of four bedrooms and two living rooms—was called the "goldfish bowl." I am not sure exactly what people meant by this, but it may have been because all of us were from prominent families and had a certain level of recognition around campus.

Oliver Straus of the R. H. Macy family was also a suitemate until he left college his junior year. Walter Rosen, Jr., took his place. Walter was the son of the head of a prominent New York private bank, Ladenberg, Thalmann.

His mother played the theremin, a black box containing an electrically charged field. It was played by passing one's hand through it in mystifying, languorous motions; this changed the electrical field and produced ethereal sounds somewhat like the music in science-fiction movies. We all thought this very amusing, although for a time she had a serious coterie of musical admirers.

In senior year we connected a third suite occupied by two other friends: Ernst Teves, the son of a German industrialist, and Paul Geier, whose family had founded the Cincinnati Milling Machine Company.

I went out for soccer as a freshman but disliked it immediately since I had no experience or talent for competitive sports. I switched to squash racquets in the winter and golf in the fall and spring. I had a short stint as assistant business manager for the Harvard *Daily Crimson*, but otherwise I remained unconnected with most organized school activities. My social life revolved around debutante parties in Boston and visiting the homes of my relations and classmates who lived in the area. Junior year I was asked to join the Signet Society, a lunch club that I greatly enjoyed because many interesting faculty members lunched with undergraduates on a regular basis; this included Harvard Law professor Felix Frankfurter, who soon after was appointed to the Supreme Court.

CHALLENGING COURSEWORK

My father expected me, as he did all his sons, to take courses that were challenging and meaningful and that would be helpful later in life. Father had an excellent academic record at Brown and was elected to Phi Beta Kappa, and although he never said so, I am sure he hoped each of his sons would do at least as well as he had done. As it turned out, Nelson did the best of all, despite a dyslexic condition far worse than mine, and *was* elected to Phi Beta Kappa at Dartmouth.

All freshmen were required to take at least two yearlong introductory courses. The most memorable of these courses was History 1, Modern European History, taught by the flamboyant Master of Eliot House, Professor Roger Merriman. It was an enormously popular and interesting course that covered the political and economic development of Europe from the Middle Ages to the outbreak of World War I. Merriman was a forceful lecturer who made history come alive.

My long-term interest in beetles and other insect life enabled me to take a graduate-level course in entomology during the second semester of my freshman year. Professor William Marton Wheeler, the great authority on the social life of ants, taught the course, and I got an A–, my only A during four years of college!

My interest in entomology led to another outside activity my first year at Harvard. Through the Philips Brooks House, an organization sponsored by Harvard to encourage volunteer student activities, I taught a class once a week in nature studies to a group of young teenagers at Lincoln House, a settlement house in south Boston. Every spring I took members of the class out to the country to hunt for insects and learn about trees and wildflowers. One of the boys, Fred Solana, the son of a Spanish stonemason, showed much more interest and aptitude than the others. As a result I asked him to help with my beetle collection, which I had brought to Harvard. For the next three years I employed Fred to catalogue and care for the specimens. I also helped modestly with his expenses at Boston College. After the war Fred joined the Chase National Bank where he had a fine career, but he never lost his interest in beetles. For twenty-five years he came to Hudson Pines every Saturday to work on the collection. My children loved to sit with him in the basement while he worked and became very attached to him.

A SUMMER IN HITLER'S GERMANY

Satisfying Harvard's language requirement caused me some real difficulties. I had not studied classical languages at Lincoln—Dewey's philosophy viewed Greek and Latin as irrelevant to the modern world—and so I was required under Harvard's rules for graduation to demonstrate proficiency in two modern languages. My French was good enough so that I was able to handle an advanced course in French literature my sophomore year where the lectures were given in French by a well-known scholar, Professor André Maurice.

German was a different matter. I found it difficult to keep up with the introductory course and dropped it at the end of the first term. My alternative was to pass a reading examination, and to prepare for it I decided to spend the summer of 1933 in Munich studying German.

I lived in a *pension* run by Hans Defregger and his wife, and took German lessons every day with Frau Berman, a remarkably talented teacher. Her intensive "immersion" program worked well, and while I could not have translated Goethe by the end of the summer, I did pass the reading exam when I returned to Harvard that fall!

The Defreggers were well known in the Bavarian art world. My host's father, Franz von Defregger, was a respected nineteenth-century Romantic artist whose paintings were well represented in the Neuespinakotec in Munich. Frau

Defregger took a great interest in her guests and took us on weekend trips by car to nearby parts of Bavaria and sometimes even farther afield. She was well versed in German art and history, and we visited many historic sites, including the wildly exuberant rococo churches in southern Bavaria, such as the Wal Fahrt Kirche auf dem Wies. During the course of our tours she introduced me to the magnificent paintings of Albrecht Dürer and Lucas Cranach and the exceptional wood carvings of Tilman Riemenschneider. Frau Defregger explained the architectural mysteries of the Nymphenburg Palace and the development of beautiful medieval towns such as Rothenburg and Nuremberg. I came to appreciate the relaxed fun-loving ways of the Bavarians and acquired a feel for German history and the incredible culture that had produced those marvelous works of art. In the evening we would often visit Munich's renowned Hofbrau Haus, an immense beer hall, where we would drink giant steins of beer and sing along with the rest of the huge crowd.

At the same time I saw the new Germany that Hitler was bringing into being, a glimpse that left me uneasy and uncomfortable. The Defreggers introduced me to one of Hitler's close friends, Ernst (Putzi) Hanfstaengl, who handled press relations during the Führer's rise to power in the 1920s and 1930s. Putzi, a tall, bushy-haired man with an easygoing artistic temperament, was part American and had graduated from Harvard. The deferential way in which he was treated suggested the apprehensions that people felt even then about anyone with a close connection to the iron-willed new leader of Germany. Later he broke with Hitler and fled to the United States.

Already, only a few months after Hitler had taken power, people were speaking in hushed terms about the Gestapo, and there were reports of "concentration camps" where political opponents of the new regime had been sent. The first laws purging the German civil service of Jews and those of Jewish descent had already been implemented. I found it personally offensive that the worst kinds of anti-Semitic language were openly tolerated, not least because I was working closely with Frau Berman who was Jewish. I was indignant as well that quite a few people seemed to accept without serious question the Nazi claims that Jews were responsible for all of Germany's economic problems and that they deserved to be punished.

THREE MEMORABLE PROFESSORS

That fall in Cambridge I had to select a more specialized area of study, and I chose English history and literature. I also opted to pursue a "degree with honors," which entitled me to have a tutor, in effect a faculty advisor, whose role was to help with course selection and to recommend outside reading that would broaden my base of knowledge in a field of concentration. It was customary for an honors student to meet with his tutor two or three times a month to discuss academic progress and even issues of a more personal nature.

My first tutor was F. O. Matthiessen, a highly intellectual professor of English literature. Unfortunately, he and I had little in common. I felt as uncomfortable with him as he did with me. I simply was not ready to take advantage of his subtle and sophisticated mind; therefore, for my last two years I switched to Professor John Potter, a historian and later Master of Eliot House, who was more accessible.

I was also fortunate to study under three men who opened my mind to creative thought and powerful new ideas. The titles of their courses now sound narrow and pedantic, but the way in which they taught them opened up a new world that I had previously only dimly perceived.

Professor Charles McIlwain taught British constitutional history from the time of the Magna Carta to the sixteenth century. A distinguished lawyer, McIlwain traced the political evolution of England from its feudal origins to the emergence of a centralized state in which the rule of law was an increasingly important element. McIlwain used legal and historical documents, beginning with the great charter itself, to illustrate his points, but he breathed life into those dusty documents and made us see them in their historical and human context. I began to understand the reasons that democracy and the rule of law are so important in any society, as well as why it has been so difficult to achieve them.

The same year I took Professor John Livingston Lowes's course on the poetry of Samuel Taylor Coleridge and William Wordsworth. The most exciting part of the course was the analysis of Coleridge's two greatest poems, "The Rime of the Ancient Mariner" and "Kubla Khan." We used Lowes's book, *The Road to Xanadu*, which painstakingly identified the influences on Coleridge as he wrote those two masterpieces. Lowes had read not only everything Coleridge had ever written but everything he had ever read as well, and he identified all the personal and literary influences that inspired this great Romantic poet when he wrote his epic poems. I also learned that good writing—writing that conveys ideas lucidly and elegantly—is the result of a combination of factors that may begin with inspiration but also includes personal experience, formal learning, exhaustive research, and a great deal of hard work.

Abbott Payson Usher's economic history of England from 1750 to 1860 was a revelation of a different kind. Usher was a dull lecturer but a meticulous scholar who uncovered the hidden processes of economic change. He showed how successive inventions and innovations in plowing, fertilizing, and the use of improved seeds had revolutionized agricultural production in England. Over the same period, the introduction of the one-cylinder steam engine, coupled with the many inventions relating to the manufacture of iron, textiles, and other industrial products, had changed the lives of the ordinary man and woman in England. The facts were not new, but Usher explained their interrelationships in a manner that was a model of clarity. He made history come alive and seem real to me. Years later, as I wrestled with the difficult problems of economic development and social change in Latin America and other parts of the world, I would often recall Professor Usher's analysis of the complex process by which history unfolds.

As I discovered a number of times in the course of my education, an inspiring teacher can stimulate thinking in a manner that has little to do with the subject matter in question. I will always be grateful to Professors McIlwain, Lowes, and Usher for teaching me how to reason.

SUMMER INTERLUDES AT HOME AND ABROAD

The summer following my sophomore year, Paul Geier and I took part in an entomological expedition in the Grand Canyon organized by the American Museum of Natural History. The expedition was led by Dr. Frank E. Lutz, curator of entomology at the museum, with whom as a boy I had spent two summers at the Station for the Study of Insects near Tuxedo Park, New York. The purpose of the 1934 expedition was to study the variation of insect species at different altitudes between the bottom of the Grand Canyon and the top of the nearby San Francisco peaks. It was an ecological study, a term little used at that time, which demonstrated that insect species at the bottom of the canyon were common to Mexico, whereas species at the summit of the peaks a few miles away, but ten thousand feet higher, were indigenous to Alaska. In short, altitude, with corresponding temperature changes, may be as important as latitude in determining the distribution of insect species. That summer I understood more clearly than ever before nature's underlying order.

At the end of the summer, to my pleasant surprise, Father joined me for a week. This had not been planned, and I have never fully understood why he decided to endure the two-day train trip to meet me; it was so uncharacteristic of him to do anything impulsively. We spent a week visiting the Hopi villages in the Painted Desert, Monument Valley in northern Arizona, and the great Anasazi ruins in Canyon de Chelly.

Although I was nineteen years old, it was really the first time that Father and I had been alone for any length of time. We were both relaxed, and he talked openly about himself and his childhood. It was one of the best times we ever had together.

=

In the spring of 1935, Dick Gilder and I decided to spend the summer touring Europe by car. We were motivated in part by two art courses we had taken and a desire to see firsthand some of the masterpieces of European art we had studied. In fact, we managed to visit some thirty museums in six countries. At the same time, however, we became absorbed by the ominous political situation in Germany, which left us deeply concerned about the future.

We sailed tourist class on the S.S. *Olympic* and took with us in the hold the Model A Ford touring car that Father had given me for use while I was at college. We drove across the Low Countries and stopped in Paris for a few days before driving on to Germany, where we spent two weeks.

The country had visibly become the Third Reich. As we made our way through Germany, we saw posters in public squares with slogans denouncing the Jews as Germany's "ruination." Half the population seemed to be in uniforms of one kind or another. One evening when Dick and I were in a tavern on the outskirts of the Black Forest, a group of soldiers came in, sat at a nearby table, and entered into conversation with us. They were curious about the United States and very talkative; by the end of the evening they had told us their life stories. They could not have been friendlier—until a couple who had been hiking in the Black Forest entered the tavern. A pall fell over the room. We only began to understand what was going on when the soldiers conspicuously turned their backs on the new arrivals and began talking in a loud voice about the Jews and the menace they represented to Germany. When the couple left, a soldier turned and with a raised right arm said, "Heil Hitler"—the obligatory salutation in Germany. The woman very politely said that she didn't use the official salute but wished them a good night anyway. They then walked out the door. We felt very uncomfortable and left soon thereafter.

=

Dick and I would often listen to the radio at night, and I would translate the broadcasts of Hitler's impassioned diatribes as best I could. Even without being able to understand every word, we sensed Hitler's powerful hold on the German people, which we also saw in the growing regimentation of daily life. Just hearing the cadence and drama of Hitler's oratory left Dick enraged and terrified, and by the end of a speech he would have tears of anger in his eyes. Dick later said that it was those bloodcurdling broadcasts that had convinced him we would eventually have to fight the Nazis. Anybody with that kind of hypnotic power to move and mold people was dangerous, he said.

MEETING PADEREWSKI AND FREUD

From the Black Forest we drove into Switzerland where we crossed the Rhine and continued on to Geneva. On the way we stopped in Morges to call on Ignacy Jan Paderewski, one of the world's great musical figures who had also been prime minister of Poland for a brief period right after World War I. I had met him when he gave a concert at my parents' home in New York the year before and had been charmed by his personality as well as his playing. He was an impressive man with a shock of long gray hair. He greeted us with great warmth and enthusiasm and took us on a tour of his property. From there we visited the library Father had built for the League of Nations a few years before.

Soon afterward my sister-in-law Tod joined us for a portion of the trip. Tod and Nelson were living in England that summer while Nelson worked at the London branch of the Chase National Bank. Before leaving New York, Dick and I had invited her to join us for a week but had little hope she would be able to make it. We were pleasantly surprised when she actually agreed to come. She met us in Lucerne, and from there we drove through the Swiss and Austrian Alps. My Model A had no trunk, and there was barely room for Tod and our bags, but we managed well and had a congenial time. This happy adventure thoroughly scandalized Aunt Lucy, who thought it terribly inappropriate for a married woman to travel unchaperoned with two young men. In fact, it was all quite innocent. Tod and I had developed a good relationship on our Egyptian trip six years earlier, and she and Nelson had served on several occasions as chaperons at the house parties I gave at Abeyton Lodge during college vacations. Tod was like an older sister to me, and I think she was very pleased to get off on a spree with two college boys.

After our tour of the Alps we drove through Austria to Vienna, where we visited Sigmund Freud. The visit was arranged by Dick's aunt, who had been analyzed by Freud and had stayed on with the family as a companion and coauthor with Anna Freud of many books on child psychology. Freud by that time was quite old and was suffering from cancer of the jaw, but despite his evident discomfort, he was very friendly to us. He seemed less interested in discussing Freudian psychology—about which we knew next to nothing anyway—than in talking about his extraordinary collection of Egyptian, Greek, and Roman artifacts, which crowded his study and living areas. He was intrigued that I had been to Egypt and questioned me closely about what I had seen and learned. I found out later that Freud had become almost obsessed with the idea of phylogeny, specifically the historical evolution of the ego, and thought about little else. We also spent some time with Anna Freud discussing the more familiar aspects of psychology. She must have been persuasive because I informed my parents that "certainly the Freudian doctrine has been much twisted by half-baked critics, as what we heard from her was most sane."

THE ROCKEFELLER INHERITANCE

The fall of 1934 proved to be a crucial time for me and for the future of my family. In December 1934, Father decided to set up a series of irrevocable trusts for Mother and each of his six children with an initial value of approximately $60 million. The 1934 Trusts, as they are referred to within the family, allowed Father to pass on at least a portion of the family's wealth without estate taxes through three generations. Today these trusts hold the majority of the family's wealth. Without them, much of the Rockefeller fortune would have gone either to the government in taxes or to charity.

=

As strange as it may seem, I never took for granted that I would inherit great wealth. Naturally, I knew Father was very wealthy, but I also knew the Depression was taking its toll on his fortune as well as everyone else's. I well recall receiving a letter from Father during my freshman year in which he stated that the way things were going, I was very likely going to have to "work for a living." While admittedly this is what most people expect to do, it was more surprising coming from one of the wealthiest men in the country.

I knew Father was balancing many competing and even contradictory demands from among his extensive philanthropic commitments and financial obligations for Rockefeller Center and the necessity to make provisions for his family. Father understood that we needed a certain amount of economic independence, which he would have to provide. But he believed all of us were too young and too inexperienced to handle large amounts of money without expert supervision and guidance. *His* father, after all, hadn't begun passing on any sizable sums to him until he was in his forties, and as I have noted earlier, it may not have been Grandfather's initial intention to leave him a major part of his fortune at all. My guess is that Father would have preferred to wait some years before he decided how to distribute *his* fortune.

Ironically, it was Franklin D. Roosevelt's tax policies targeted at the wealthy that persuaded Father to act when he did. Steep increases in both gift and estate tax rates in 1934 convinced Father that he had no alternative if he wanted to provide us with independent means. However, his real concerns about our maturity and inexperience led him to establish trusts with very strict limits on access to income and invasion of principal by any of the beneficiaries.

Father's original intention was to give each of his children a small but gradually increasing income until we reached the age of thirty. The trusts were set up to accomplish that objective. Until we reached thirty the income from the trusts in excess of what was paid out to us, rather than being reinvested, was distributed to a number of named charitable institutions, among them the Rockefeller Institute and the Riverside Church.

In 1935, the first full year the trust was in operation, I received only $2,400, a tiny percentage of a much larger income. This income was to cover all my living and college expenses, apart from tuition, then $400 a year, which Father continued to pay during the remainder of my college years. On occasion I did find myself a bit short of cash and had to ask Father for an advance. He usually viewed my requests as an opportunity to impart wisdom and guidance. In one letter he wrote me in 1935, he noted disapprovingly that

> you have spent far more during the period than your anticipated income—which as you say is, of course, poor financing and is a mistake. . . . That I am somewhat disappointed at you again being in financial difficulties, you have of course imagined. When you were getting $1,500 a year you had no difficulty. As increases have been made, the difficulties have seemed to grow greater. The old saying that one is apt to lose one's head with growing prosperity is a very true one. I hope from now on your financial plans will be such as to give no further occasion to believe this is true in your case. The $400 will be sent today to your bank account.

At the time the 1934 Trusts were created, Father informed Laurance, Winthrop, and me that our trusts would contain assets of significantly less value than the ones he had established for Mother and our older siblings. Father wrote me a letter to explain his reasons. It gives a good sense of his feelings about the dangerous mixture of youth and money: "When I first talked with you about this matter, I had in mind to establish trusts for you three younger boys in the same amounts as for the older children. On further thought, I have come to the conclusion that to do so would be unfair to you . . . first, because it might result in your being put in a position where you would find yourself bewildered and unprepared because suddenly saddled with heavy and relatively new obligations . . . Secondly, it would . . . seriously curtail the opportunity for current guidance and advice during formative years which it is a father's duty to provide."

However, when Congress increased the gift and estate tax rates in 1935, Father had to change his strategy. He reluctantly concluded that it was now or never if he was to increase the value of the trusts for his three youngest children, so he added additional assets to ours and thereby equalized the value of all the trusts at about $16 million. It was not until several years later that I was told the value of my trust.

In mid-June 1935, Father wrote to me shortly before Dick and I left on our trip to Europe:

I should have preferred not to take this step now but circumstances seem to have forced me to do so. The knowledge of how to manage and handle property wisely is best acquired through gradually increasing experience. That thought has been uppermost in my mind in all the gifts I have made for your benefit. . . . I am putting great trust in you. I know, however, that you will never give me a cause to regret it.

Affectionately, Father.

CHOOSING A CAREER

My senior year was occupied with writing my senior thesis on Fabian socialism, "Destitution Through Fabian Eyes." The essay pointed to the fact that the traditional European approach to poverty was based on the Christian precept of atoning for one's sins by giving alms to the poor. The focus was more on the benefits in the afterlife to the donor than on the notion that individuals had a social obligation to provide assistance to people in need. Fabian Socialists, under the leadership of Beatrice and Sidney Webb, took the opposite view. They saw the provision of a minimum standard of living for everyone as a basic right of all citizens and an inherent responsibility of government.

The concepts advanced by the Webbs and other Fabians established the foundation for the work of Sir William Beveridge, then the director of the London School of Economics, where I would soon go to study. Sir William, later Lord Beveridge, became one of the principal architects of the welfare state, which began to gain acceptance in Britain in the mid-1930s.

With my undergraduate years coming to an end, I had no clear idea of what I wanted to make of my life or even what I wanted to do immediately after graduation. I was inclined toward pursuing something in the international field, and I leaned toward something independent of the Family Office since three of my brothers were already there. Postgraduate studies in business or economics had some appeal, but even that was not a clear objective. I felt the need to get advice from someone I respected and whose own life had been successful.

Over the years I had come to admire William Lyon Mackenzie King, who had become a close friend of Father's through their work together in the aftermath of the Ludlow strike. Mr. King later assumed leadership of the Liberal Party in Canada and became prime minister in 1935. He often stayed with my parents when he was in New York and sometimes visited Seal Harbor as well. He was always warm and friendly to me, and I felt comfortable talking with him. The Mackenzie King I knew did not correspond at all with the steely, remote, and offbeat reputation I later learned he had in Canada.

After consulting Father, I wrote Mr. King asking if I could visit him in Ottawa to seek his advice. Mr. King quickly responded by inviting me to spend a weekend with him in the spring of 1936. During our long hours of conversation on my options and interests, it became clear that a career in either government or international banking made the most sense for me. In either case, Mr. King felt I would be well served by taking a Ph.D. in economics, a course that he himself had pursued many years earlier. Not only would this be good training in a field of knowledge useful to both government and banking, but it would also give me credibility with people who otherwise might feel that any job I had was principally because of my family's influence.

Mr. King's arguments were convincing, and I decided to remain at Harvard for one year of graduate work in order to begin my study of economics under Joseph A. Schumpeter, the famous Austrian economist. After that year my plan was to attend the London School of Economics and then finish my studies at the University of Chicago so that I could acquire as broad a background as possible. By spending time at three universities I would have a chance to work with many of the world's greatest economists.

CHAPTER 7

LEARNING FROM
THE GREAT ECONOMISTS

In mid-September 1936, Dick Gilder and I attended the Republican Convention in Cleveland and watched the nomination of Governor Alfred Landon of Kansas as the forlorn hope to run against the immensely popular President Franklin D. Roosevelt. My family had supported the Republican Party since the 1850s—Grandfather told me that he had voted for Abraham Lincoln in 1860—and I considered myself a Republican as well. The party regulars were pessimistic about their chances and deeply divided between the progressives, who opposed the New Deal but saw a necessary role for government in the economic life of the country, and the conservatives, who were convinced that the United States was undergoing a Bolshevik revolution and wanted to return to the laissez-faire world of the nineteenth century.

With the convention over, Dick and I returned to Cambridge and reoccupied our old suite of rooms in Eliot House. Dick entered Harvard Business School, and I, with some trepidation, began the demanding course of graduate study in economics.

SCHUMPETER AND KEYNES

I soon knew I had made the right decision. I began graduate work just as John Maynard Keynes's controversial ideas on state intervention to stimulate economic activity provoked an explosive debate within the profession and more broadly.

I was most influenced that year by Joseph A. Schumpeter. In fact, one of the intellectual high points of my graduate work was his basic course in economic theory. Schumpeter was already considered one of the world's premier economists. He had been active in politics in Austria and had served briefly as minister of finance in 1919. He had also run a private bank in Vienna for a time in the 1920s. He arrived at Harvard in 1932 and was in his mid-fifties when I met him in the fall of 1936.

Schumpeter was most interested in the entrepreneur's role in the process of economic development, and by the mid-1930s he had emerged as one of the principal champions of the neoclassical economic tradition. But he was not a simple defender of the old order. He agreed with Keynes that something had to be done to deal with the unprecedented levels of unemployment of the Depression and the political and social instability it had produced. However, he rejected the central element of Keynes's theory that without government intervention the capitalist economy is vulnerable to prolonged periods of massive unemployment and reduced levels of economic activity.

Schumpeter feared that Keynesianism would permanently substitute government control for the normal and healthy operations of the marketplace. He was quite alarmed at the impact these "unorthodox" ideas were already having on the fiscal, tax, and monetary policies of a number of Western countries, including the United States.

Fit, trim, and aristocratic in bearing, Schumpeter had driven horses competitively when he was younger. He was also a great admirer of the female sex and was rumored to have had many elegant amours. He once said in class that he had three goals in life: to become the greatest economist, the greatest lover, and the greatest horseman of his generation, but felt he had not yet fulfilled his ambitions—at least in respect to horses! Unlike most Harvard professors he dressed stylishly in well-tailored suits, with a silk handkerchief jutting out of his jacket pocket. Arriving in class with an air of being in a great hurry, he would throw his overcoat on a chair, whip his handkerchief from his pocket, flip it out toward the room, then fold it and carefully mop his brow and the top of his balding head before saying, in his heavy German accent, "Ladies and gentlemen, let us begin."

Paul Samuelson, who has since become a renowned economist in his own right, was also in Schumpeter's class that term. Paul already had a master's degree in economics and was a superb mathematician as well. Since economics was already becoming reliant on mathematical analysis, Schumpeter would often call on him to go to the blackboard and write out complex economic formulas, which I usually didn't understand. I had entered the graduate program with little knowledge of calculus, which had already become critical to economic analysis. Although I had written my senior thesis on a subject bordering on economics, I had taken only two rudimentary economics courses as an undergraduate and had a lot of catching up to do.

Paul's formidable knowledge of economics made me all the more self-conscious about my own modest background. However, at the end of the first term I remember going to the bulletin board outside the classroom to check our posted grades. To my great surprise and delight I got an A–, a much better grade than I had expected. I was standing there feeling thrilled with myself when Paul arrived. He had received a solid A. He also looked quite pleased until he saw my grade, listed just above his. His face fell immediately. Clearly his grade lost significance if a novice like me could get an A–.

HABERLER AND MASON

Professor Gottfried von Haberler's course on international trade also influenced me greatly. A charming man with courteous European manners, Professor von Haberler had just arrived on campus that fall with a reputation as a staunch defender of free trade. His ideas were ignored in the 1930s when nations around the world gave in to the siren song of protectionism, but they would have a great impact after World War II when international trade expanded and world economic growth surged dramatically.

Professor Edward S. Mason's equally interesting course covered the nascent area of international economic development. Mason emphasized the technical inputs needed to stimulate broader economic growth in what we would later call the "underdeveloped world." His pioneering work would make him one of the leading proponents of foreign economic assistance in the years after World War II, a subject that would engage me deeply as I became involved with Latin America and Africa later in my career.

The courses with Schumpeter, Haberler, and Mason provided me with a superb introduction to the study of economics and a solid grounding in economic theory as it was evolving during that critical period. I also discovered that I enjoyed the subject and maybe even had a flair for it.

THE LONDON SCHOOL OF ECONOMICS

Since my first year of graduate study had gone well, I decided to go on to the London School of Economics and Political Science, commonly known as the LSE. Fortunately, I found a genial companion to share the adventure. In the course of my graduate year at Harvard I became acquainted with Bill Waters, a fellow resident of Eliot House whose father ran a manufacturing company in Minneapolis. I discovered that Bill also planned to spend the following year at LSE. We struck up a friendship and decided to room together in London.

The night before we sailed from New York in late September 1937, several friends gave us a farewell dinner at Giovanni's Restaurant. Our hosts included Benjy Franklin, Dick Gilder, and also Margaret (Peggy) McGrath, the young lady whose company I had long enjoyed but still just considered a good friend. Bill sat next to Peggy at dinner and was greatly taken by her. After we settled into our stateroom on the S.S. *Britannic,* he said, "What are you waiting for? Why don't you marry Peggy?" I was more than a bit taken aback, but somehow the suggestion struck a responsive chord. I wrote to Peggy once I arrived in London and to my delight had a prompt response. From this modest start was born a relationship that meant everything to me for the next six decades.

My father's connections with the LSE (both the Laura Spelman Rockefeller Memorial and the Rockefeller Foundation had provided sizable grants over the years) helped solve the problem of housing in London. Father knew Sir William Beveridge, the director of the LSE, who was retiring to become master of University College, Oxford. Sir William, to whom I had written at Father's suggestion, offered to lease us his flat in Elm Court in the Middle Temple, one of the famous Inns of Court nestled just within the ancient walls of the City of London between Blackfriars Bridge and Fleet Street.

This was a rare opportunity for us, to live in the heart of London only ten minutes' walk from the LSE and in one of the few Elizabethan buildings that had survived the Great Fire of London in 1666. The flat was quite small, but there were two bedrooms, a dining room, living room, and kitchen. Best of all, Sir William left us his laundress, Leily, who agreed to cook for us and take care of our rooms. In fact, she did everything for us *except* wash our clothes! Leily was an absolute gem, and her presence allowed Bill and me to entertain guests and live very comfortably.

Unfortunately, my close connection with Sir William made life more difficult for me in some ways. As I wrote to my parents, Sir William "definitely belongs to a regime that is past and which is none too well liked by the great majority of the staff. . . . Most of the trouble seems to rise out of petty jealousies and school politics. The fact nevertheless remains that I am looked upon a bit skeptically by virtue of being such a good friend."

It was not the last time that I would encounter suspicion because of the privileged or controversial company I kept.

HAROLD LASKI: PIED PIPER OF THE LEFT

In those days the LSE was widely considered a hotbed of socialism and rad-icalism. Founded by the Webbs in the 1890s to help achieve their Fabian Socialist goal of a just society based on a more equal distribution of wealth, its walls had always given shelter to men and women who tested the limits of orthodoxy. During the 1920s and 1930s its reputation owed much to Harold Laski, a very popular political science professor who enthralled well-filled classrooms with his eloquent Marxist rhetoric.

Laski dominated the teaching of government and sociology at the LSE for three decades and was by far the most flamboyant and controversial figure at the school. In person, Laski was a small, sharp-faced man with a power-ful and aggressive intellect; in his lectures he spoke in full paragraphs, the final word or phrase of which drew his thoughts together with a sudden and startling clarity. Although Laski was enormously popular with the student body, I found the intellectual content of his lectures superficial and often de-vious and misleading. They seemed more propaganda than pedagogy; he was indeed a pied piper.

I had one personal experience with Laski that revealed something of his true character. Before I went to London, William E. Hocking, a professor of religion at Harvard, gave me a letter of introduction to Laski. The two had met when Laski taught at Harvard from 1916 to 1920. During the infa-mous Boston Police Strike of 1919, Laski sided with the striking police and denounced the authorities, including Governor Calvin Coolidge. Laski be-came persona non grata at Harvard; people refused to speak to him when they passed him on the street. Hocking befriended Laski and took him into his home during the most difficult period. Though Hocking had no sympa-thy for Laski's political opinions, he apparently thought they had become friends.

When I presented Hocking's letter to Laski, he scanned it briefly, threw it aside, looked up with a bored expression on his face, and said, "I have no more use for Hocking." I was appalled! I wrote Father a letter in which I didn't mention the incident—I think in a curious way I found it almost em-barrassing—but I did observe that Laski's radicalism appeared to come more from "envy of those who are more successful than pity for those who are less well off."

Laski, who saw the state as "the fundamental instrument of society," was particularly influential with students from India, who flocked to his classes and seemed bewitched by his rhetoric. In the judgment of many, Laski had a greater influence on India's and Pakistan's economic and political policy when those British colonies achieved independence after World War II than any other individual. India's dominant Congress Party, for instance, was largely controlled by people who had learned socialism at his feet, and his ideology exerted a powerful influence for many years.

HAYEK AND ROBBINS

The economists at LSE were much more conservative than the rest of the faculty. In fact, its economists comprised the major center of opposition in England to Keynes and his Cambridge School of interventionist economics.

My tutor that year was Friedrich von Hayek, the noted Austrian economist who in 1974 would receive the Nobel Prize for the work he had done in the 1920s and 1930s on money, the business cycle, and capital theory. Like Schumpeter, Hayek placed his trust in the market, believing that over time, even with its many imperfections, it provided the most reliable means to distribute resources efficiently and to ensure sound economic growth. Hayek also believed that government should play a critical role as the rule maker and umpire and guarantor of a just and equitable social order, rather than the owner of economic resources or the arbiter of markets.

Hayek was in his late thirties when I first met him. Indisputably brilliant, he lacked Schumpeter's spark and charisma. He was a dull lecturer, very Germanic and methodical. His writings were ponderous and almost impossible to read—or at least stay awake while reading. Nevertheless, I found myself largely in agreement with his basic economic philosophy. Personally, he was a kindly man whom I respected greatly. On more than one occasion I remember his taking from his wallet a crumpled, dog-eared paper on which he had written a list of the remaining "liberal economists." He would look at it sadly and sigh. He was convinced that the list was shrinking rapidly as the older believers in the free market died off and most of the newer economists followed the new Keynesian fashions. I feel sure that Hayek, who died in 1992 at the age of ninety-three, felt greatly reassured by the resurgence in support for the market among the majority of economists and many political leaders in the 1980s. Unfortunately, I never had a chance to discuss this with him or to find out if he had made up a new and longer list!

My favorite teacher at the LSE was Lionel Robbins, later to become Baron Robbins of Clare Market, who took over as head of the economics depart-

ment the year I arrived. At that stage of his career Robbins was a firm advocate of the market and dedicated opponent of government intervention. But
he was much less dogmatic and more eclectic than most of the other neoclassical economists I met during this time. He stressed logic and sound reasoning over the new fashion of econometrics. He would often say that one
should make a distinction between what *actually* happens in the real economy and what we might *wish* to happen.

Robbins clashed with both Laski and Keynes during the 1930s over a
number of key political and economic issues. Robbins and Keynes first tan-
gled in 1931 while serving on a government advisory committee examining
the problem of unemployment. Keynes pushed his demand-side ideas—
public works, tax cuts, and deficit spending—which Robbins successfully
opposed. Later, though, Robbins joined the ranks of those favoring an increased role for the state in the management of economic life, calling his
earlier disagreement with Keynes "the greatest mistake of my professional
career."

Robbins wrote and spoke English with great elegance and style. After the
war his interest in the arts began to take precedence over economics, and he
became chairman of the National Gallery and a director of the Royal Opera.
Lionel was one of the most broad-gauged and cultivated men I have ever
known, and I valued his friendship until his death in 1984.

SOCIALIZING WITH THE KENNEDYS

Bill and I had a varied and pleasant year. We met a number of interesting
people and learned a great deal about the country and its people. Bill
was a delightful companion, and we spent weekends bicycling in the countryside, playing golf, or visiting new friends at their country homes. On a few
occasions we went to Oxford or Cambridge to see Harvard friends who were
also studying in England. On one trip to Cambridge we saw John Kenneth
Galbraith and his wife, Kitty. I had known Ken at Harvard when he was a
young instructor in agricultural economics. Ken was a great admirer of
Lord Keynes and had gone to Cambridge specifically to study under the
great man. Although we had sharply divergent views on economics and politics, that never prevented us from maintaining a cordial personal relationship through the years.

On one occasion Randolph Churchill, Winston Churchill's son, then
writing for *The Evening Standard*, came to interview the "Rockefeller" who
had come to study in England, and the next day his column revealed that I

was in the country to find myself an English bride. The story was reprinted throughout the British Empire. Within a few weeks I was inundated with marriage proposals, many accompanied by photographs, from scores of prospective brides from as far away as Nigeria.

Halfway through the year Joseph P. Kennedy arrived with his wife and a number of his children to take up his post as ambassador to the Court of Saint James. Within a relatively short time Kennedy would become very unpopular in Britain, first for his allegedly pro-Nazi sympathies and then for opposing U.S. aid to Britain and France after the outbreak of war. But in early 1938 that was all in the future, and he was liked and respected by the British political and financial establishment.

The Ambassador quickly became a fixture on the London social scene, photographed often in nightclubs and at gala parties in Kensington. He and Mrs. Kennedy also entertained lavishly at the American embassy. They gave an extravagant dance to introduce their daughter Kathleen to British society, to which I was invited. It was there that I first met John F. Kennedy, who had come over from Harvard especially for the party. Although we were contemporaries at Harvard, we had never met before. Jack was an attractive, sociable young man, slight in build with an unruly shock of dark red hair. He seemed eager to get my impressions of the political situation in Great Britain.

Kathleen was pretty, vivacious, and a great success in London. She later married the Marquis of Hartington, but that year she was uncommitted, and I enjoyed her company on a number of occasions. (Tragically, Kathleen and her husband were killed in a plane crash shortly after the war.)

PEDRO BELTRÁN: FUTURE PERUVIAN PRIME MINISTER

I made a number of enduring friends during that year in London, but the most impressive was Pedro Gerado Beltrán, a man almost twenty years my senior. Pedro came from a prominent Peruvian landholding family and was the owner and publisher of the influential Lima newspaper *La Prensa*. He had taken a degree in economics from the LSE twenty years earlier and had served as head of the Peruvian central bank by the time I met him. Pedro was in England to take care of family business interests, but he was an intellectual at heart and spent several days a week at the LSE sitting in on economics courses that interested him. A charming, urbane bachelor, he introduced me to some quite beautiful women I probably would not have met otherwise.

Pedro was such an impressive man that I gave him a letter of introduction to my brother Nelson, who had started to develop a keen interest in Latin America. This proved to be serendipitous a few years later when President Roosevelt appointed Nelson Coordinator of the Office of Inter-American Affairs and Pedro became Peruvian ambassador to the United States.

REVISITING THE THIRD REICH

During the Christmas 1937 recess, Bill and I traveled to Germany. I remember particularly the "wool" clothing made out of wood pulp; the real wool, I suppose, had been commandeered by the military.

In Munich we witnessed the massive funeral procession for General Erich Ludendorff, the virtual leader of the German army during World War I and Hitler's compatriot in the Beer Hall Putsch of 1923. The largest crowd I had ever seen jammed the Ludwigstrasse, Munich's main boulevard. Fully armed SS troops, standing rigidly at attention, lined both sides of the street. As Bill and I pushed up to the front, the funeral cortege began to pass with Hitler at the head of columns of goose-stepping soldiers. I snapped his picture with my Leica camera as he swaggered past acknowledging the stiff-armed Nazi salutes and the thunderous cries of "Sieg Heil." I had never seen anything like the frenzied adulation of that crowd or experienced such an overpowering sense of discomfort at what that adulation represented.

After this chilling encounter I spent the rest of the holidays in Frankfurt with a close Harvard friend, Ernst Teves, and his father, a prominent German industrialist. We attended a number of parties, including an elaborate costume ball where the Frankfurt socialites seemed almost frantically bent on having a good time. From my conversations I learned that many people believed Hitler's aggressive demands for the return of German territory would lead inevitably to war, although no one wanted to protest. It also appeared to me that the growing regimentation of daily life, the menacing Nazi ideology, and the flagrant persecution of Jews and others had produced a strong undercurrent of fear and anxiety. People seemed to be afraid of saying or doing the wrong thing. "Heil Hitler!" was the mandatory greeting for everyone. Swastikas were everywhere, and people deferred obsequiously to Nazi party officials whenever they encountered them. The gaiety of the parties I attended seemed forced and hollow. I returned to England feeling depressed about the future.

THE DALMATIAN COAST AND GREECE

During our Easter holiday in 1938, Bill and I joined three Harvard friends for a trip down the Adriatic. We took all of the passenger accommodations on an Italian freighter sailing from Venice. The cabins were small but clean and comfortable, and the food surprisingly good, considering that the entire five-day voyage cost each of us five pounds (then $25), everything included! We stayed for a few hours each in Trieste, Zara, Split, and Dubrovnik in Yugoslavia and Durazzo in Albania, and ended the trip in Bari, Italy.

We flew from Bari to Athens where we rented a car and drove through the Peloponnesus to Sparta and Mount Parnassus and then back along the Gulf of Corinth to Delphi. While having a drink at the bar of the Grand Bretagne Hotel in Athens, I ran into Professor Kirsopp Lake, who was famous for his popular course on the Bible at Harvard. He asked me to go with him, his wife, and stepdaughter, Silvia Neu, to Salonika by overnight boat. From there he and I would take a smaller boat to the peninsula of Mount Athos, where he would be looking for manuscripts in the libraries of orthodox monasteries. The invitation was too tempting to turn down.

Silvia Neu turned out to be a very agreeable companion on the boat trip, and the three days on Mount Athos were unforgettable. We stayed each night at a different monastery as the guests of the monks, many of whom Professor Lake knew from earlier trips. The monasteries, built during the Middle Ages, are perched on the slopes of Mount Athos, with the incredibly blue Aegean spread out below. At night the stillness was broken by the hauntingly beautiful chanting of the monks, and the air was thick with incense. To my disappointment, because I found Silvia quite appealing, the monasteries were exclusively male; females—human, animal, or otherwise—were strictly forbidden. As an entomologist, however, I was amused to discover a number of copulating beetles.

I had expected to spend several days in Rome with Ambassador William Phillips and his attractive daughter, Beatrice, but that part of the trip had to be cut short because of my trip with Professor Lake. My plane from Salonika to Rome stopped unexpectedly in Tirana, Albania, where I found there were no hotel rooms available. By good chance I ran into an entomologist working for the Rockefeller Foundation on a malaria eradication program, and he offered to share his small house with me for the night. It had been a memorable vacation.

THE UNIVERSITY OF CHICAGO

After a year in London I was eager to return to the United States to complete my graduate work at the University of Chicago, which boasted one of the premier economics faculties in the world, including such luminaries as Frank Knight, Jacob Viner, George Stigler, Henry Schultz, and Paul Douglas. I had heard Knight lecture at the LSE and found his more philosophical approach to economics quite compelling. Lionel Robbins knew Knight well and urged me to study with him. The fact that Grandfather had helped found the university played a distinctly secondary role in my choice.

=====

The Chicago "school of economics" has gained a great deal of fame and not a little notoriety over the past fifty years for its unwavering advocacy of the market and strong support for monetarism. These ideas are intimately associated with Milton Friedman, whose views have now come to symbolize a Chicago School that is strongly doctrinaire in its insistence that government should not interfere at all with the market and the natural pricing mechanism. Friedman also argues that business should concentrate exclusively on optimizing profits and should not be sidetracked by involvement in outside activities that are "socially responsible."

While Friedman later became an associate of Professors Knight and Viner on the economics faculty, I have no doubt they would have resisted being categorized as members of the Chicago School in the narrow present-day meaning of the term. They both favored the "invisible hand of the market" over government intervention as the best means to sustain economic growth, but I believe they would have objected to Friedman's cavalier dismissal of corporate social responsibility.

KNIGHT, VINER, AND LANGE

When I arrived in Chicago in the fall of 1938, I was able to persuade Professors Knight and Viner to become members of my thesis committee. Oskar Lange, a refugee scholar from Poland, also agreed to serve on the committee. I already had a general idea for a dissertation topic—Professor Hayek had suggested the idea of economic waste to me in

London—but I sought the help of these distinguished economists to help me formulate a more specific proposal.

Frank Knight occupies a revered position among the world's economists. His best-known book, *Risk, Uncertainty and Profit*, is unusual in its insistence that ethical considerations had to be incorporated in the process of economic analysis. His probing questions in books and lectures, testing the moral validity of economic dogma, produced many heated debates.

Knight doubted the claims of New Deal planners that an increase in the coercive powers of government automatically leads to an increase in people's well-being and happiness. At the same time Knight criticized those who talked only of the efficiencies of capitalism without recognizing the moral issues involved and the obvious failures of the existing system to address important social problems.

Jacob Viner was best known for his theoretical work on international trade. Like Haberler at Harvard, Viner advocated unobstructed trade as a means of generating economic growth. As a teacher Viner was known for his tough and demanding manner in the classroom. Logical and incisive himself, he was intolerant of students who did not meet his standards. He was famous for throwing them out of class if they failed two or three times in a row to come up with the correct response. He'd simply say, "You're not up to this class. Good-bye," and that would be it. With me, however, he was always friendly and willing to be helpful when I consulted him on my thesis. Perhaps it was fortunate for me that I was simply his advisee, not in one of his regular graduate seminars.

Oskar Lange was less renowned as an economist than either Knight or Viner, but he added a different and important perspective to my thesis. Lange was a Socialist and a leading exponent of market socialism. His book *The Economic Theory of Socialism* purported to demonstrate that "market socialism" was not a contradiction in terms and could be much more efficient than laissez-faire capitalism. Clearly, this notion has never been demonstrated in real life, but Lange carried off his argument with elegance.

Lange was one of a large group of émigré scholars who came to the United States with the assistance of the Rockefeller Foundation during the 1930s, fleeing political and religious persecution in Europe. Chicago hired Lange because of his capability in mathematical statistics and knowledge of Keynesian economics, and he became an American citizen in 1942.

After the war Lange resumed his Polish citizenship and became ambassador to the United Nations. He later filled a number of posts in the Polish government, which by then was increasingly dominated by Communists. Lange was a kind, gentle, and eminently likable man, not a demagogue like

Laski. I believe he returned to Poland more out of a sense of patriotic duty than because he was a committed Marxist. I saw Lange several times at the U.N. after the war, and it was clear he was a torn and unhappy man.

LIFE ALONG THE MIDWAY

The university contained a fascinating mixture of individuals, many with strong personalities and convictions, beginning with the head of the university. Robert Maynard Hutchins dominated the university and consistently outraged the city's business establishment. Known as the "boy wonder," Hutchins had resigned his position as dean of the Yale Law School to accept the presidency of Chicago at the age of twenty-nine. He quickly threw the campus into turmoil by abolishing football and restructuring the undergraduate degree program. Hutchins favored a broad-gauged liberal arts education for undergraduates focused on the "Great Books" program developed by his friend, the Thomist philosopher Mortimer Adler.

Hutchins's reforms alienated many of the faculty, who were also put off by his arrogance and dictatorial ways. Hutchins also fought an ongoing series of battles with Chicago businessmen and politicians, of whom he was contemptuous, viewing them as limited in their vision and parochial in their interests. Mrs. Hutchins was of little help. An artist with severe psychological problems, she refused to support her husband in any way. She also raised eyebrows and started tongues wagging by sending out as a Christmas card in 1938 her drawing of their nude daughter.

=

Despite my family's role in creating the university and sustaining it during its early years, Hutchins never invited me to a function at his home during the year I lived there. However, I suspect Hutchins may have encouraged his vice president, William B. Benton, one of the founding partners of the advertising firm of Benton & Bowles, to spend some time with me. Benton introduced me to a number of interesting people, including Beardsley Ruml, the enormous cigar-smoking Hungarian who had been a close advisor to my father during the years that he ran the Laura Spelman Rockefeller Memorial, the foundation that helped underwrite the development of the social sciences in many American universities. Ruml, like my father, had been a strong supporter of government reform efforts, not just by eliminating corruption and graft but by strengthening the civil service and improving the management of municipal and state governments.

Ruml put me in touch with the Public Administration Clearing House in Chicago, which had received substantial funds from the Spelman Fund (yet another family philanthropic foundation). It was through that organization that I began to understand the important role government at all levels should play and considered government service as a possible career path.

Benton also arranged for me to see Philip La Follette, the governor of Wisconsin, to discuss whether I should enter politics. La Follette's advice was that I could never get elected to public office with my name—unless I bought a farm in the Midwest and established a new life and image. That ended my thoughts of a political career. I could not imagine being so hypocritical as to pretend to be something I was not. It would be a subterfuge that people would quickly see through.

=

At the social functions I attended during that year in Chicago, I often felt uncomfortable because many of the other guests were slavish followers of the isolationist line trumpeted daily by Colonel Robert R. McCormick's *Chicago Tribune* and were outspoken "America Firsters," actively hostile to any involvement with the rest of the world. A famous America First rally was held during the summer of 1939 at Soldiers Field, and I recall the roar of approval from the crowd as it cheered the speech of my childhood hero, Charles Lindbergh, who had become the standard-bearer of the isolationist cause.

My year in Chicago was productive intellectually, but I longed to return to a more congenial environment. Since I had completed my required year of residency and passed my general qualifying exams (not an easy task with fifteen economists peppering me for three hours with searching and very technical questions), I decided to write my dissertation back in New York at Kykuit.

I had another and much more important reason to do this: Peggy McGrath. I had been courting her much more seriously since my return from London and wanted to be closer to her, hoping our relationship would continue to grow.

=

I owe a great intellectual debt to the remarkable economists with whom I studied. My mentors were truth seekers who believed that economics could shed light on an important aspect of human behavior and thereby help improve society. They were all political moderates who were willing to listen to reason regardless of where they found it. I like to think I have followed their example. I am a pragmatist who recognizes the need for sound fiscal and monetary policies to achieve optimum economic growth. I recognize, however, that otherwise sound policies that ignore real human needs are not acceptable and that safety nets have an essential place in our society. However, my greatest concern is that the pendulum has swung too far in the direction of unaffordable safety nets with too little attention given to sound policies that will stimulate economic growth.

CHAPTER 8

A DISSERTATION,
A WIFE, AND A JOB

My return to New York coincided almost exactly with the outbreak of World War II. In the end, the Anglo-French policy of appeasement had failed to mollify Hitler or to deflect him from his goal of creating a Greater Reich and making Germany paramount once again in Europe. I read the newspaper accounts and listened to the radio reports with mounting dread as the irresistible blitzkrieg overwhelmed Poland. It was a new kind of warfare, and I wondered what the future held in store for me and my many friends in Germany, France, and Great Britain.

My primary task that fall was completing my dissertation. I chose to live in Pocantico rather than in my parents' home on Park Avenue to avoid the wonderful distractions with which New York City abounds. Living at Kykuit worked out well for me on several accounts, not least of which was my proximity to Peggy McGrath. My parents came out for weekends, but otherwise I was alone. I made the sitting room next to what had been Grandfather's bedroom into my study. During meals I played rolls of music on the pipe organ, which worked just like a player piano. I especially liked the arias from *Madame Butterfly* and *Tristan und Isolde*. Whenever I needed a break from the rigors of intellectual inquiry or the "terror of the blank page," I could play golf, ride horseback, go for a swim in the Playhouse, or walk in the woods overlooking the Hudson. Actually, it was a pleasant existence.

I began work on my dissertation with some trepidation since I had never been involved in a project that required such concentrated research, thinking, and writing. Moreover, I was totally on my own with no professors to turn to for guidance. I was painfully aware that I had to produce a document demonstrating original thinking on a subject of economic significance.

"REFLECTING" ON IDLENESS AND WASTE

My subject, "Unused Resources and Economic Waste," dealt with one aspect of a much wider issue: whether to rely principally on market forces or governmental intervention to correct the extraordinary levels of unemployment and the underutilization of industrial capacity that had characterized the era of the Great Depression. Hayek and the neoclassical economists placed their faith in market forces, while Keynes and many others argued that only government intervention, including deficit financing or "pump priming," along with fundamental economic restructuring could return the United States and other advanced economies to full employment and prosperity.

The narrower aspect of the contentious debate that I examined was industrial plant utilization, a question that had received little attention from economists until the 1930s. By then large industrial firms—automobile plants, steel mills, and the like—employing thousands of workers dominated the American economic landscape. As a result of the Depression many of these plants were idle or operating at only a fraction of their capacity. To many this situation was wasteful in the sense that factories were not being used while enormous numbers of people were without jobs and in great personal distress. Many argued that pumping government funds into the economy through the construction of public works or direct relief payments to the unemployed would raise the level of national income and stimulate activity in the private sector, which in turn would utilize idle capacity and increase employment. The specific issue I addressed was whether idle plant capacity was wasteful in the sense that many economists were asserting.

Both Hoover and Roosevelt had inadvertently pumped money into the economy through annual budgetary deficits. Even though conditions slowly improved over the course of the 1930s, there remained a large and seemingly permanent body of unemployed in the country, and a significant percentage of the industrial plants remained idle. Economists sought the cause for this situation and offered a wide array of remedies. I felt that many of the studies had failed to define their terms accurately, and their conclusions might be used to justify inappropriate and unwise fiscal and regulatory policies.

For instance, The Brookings Institution published a series of analytical studies in the mid-1930s that supported the case for permanent government intervention. One volume argued that "underconsumption is a permanent malady, inherent in the present form of industrial organization," and that the failure to fully employ all resources was not only wasteful but an inevitable part of our economic system. The solution proposed was a permanent program of public works, the easing of restrictions on lending and credit, and a greater role for government in the planning of economic production.

More telling, I thought, was the explanation for the failure to achieve the ideal of full and continuous use of plants—the "stupidity and lack of foresight of entrepreneurs." Thus, if businessmen could not be trusted to plan intelligently, others had to assume the role.

Statements like this led me to delve into the economic and moral meaning of waste and under what circumstances unused plants are in fact wasteful. I found that at the heart of these arguments was an unsound and fallacious premise that considered idleness and waste synonymous. In fact, they are not. For instance, it would be wasteful to *reopen* a factory if changes in taste and technology rather than insufficient demand had forced its closing. More important, most of these studies assumed that the primary reason for unused capacity or idle resources—and therefore of high unemployment and low income in both good times and bad—was the selfish decision of entrepreneurs and corporate managers to keep production low in order to obtain high prices and large profits.

I found this argument preposterous. There are many reasons that a businessman decides *not* to use a portion of his available capacity: difficulty in purchasing materials, seasonal fluctuations, high taxes, excessive regulation, or even a failure to correctly read the market itself. If a factory is closed because of changed technology or consumer taste, it might be more wasteful to keep it running than to scrap it and build a new factory.

I concluded that the failure to use an economic resource per se is not evidence of waste. In practical policy terms this means that citing the existence of idle factories as justification for interventionist government policies can lead to inappropriate actions and counterproductive results. On the other hand I also made it clear that in an extreme circumstance, such as an economic recession that severely reduced aggregate demand, pump priming was not only defensible but necessary.

At the time my thinking about how and why businessmen made decisions had been molded to a large extent by the economists I had studied with, but in rereading my thesis today, it is clear that I was strongly influenced not only by Schumpeter, Hayek, and Knight, but also by my grandfather.

In discussing the behavior of businessmen like him, I pointed out that those who believe the entrepreneur is motivated solely by the desire to "maximize profit" are mistaken. Clearly, the desire to make money is one important motivation, but there are others, often just as important. As I wrote in my dissertation: "Entrepreneurship offers at once an opportunity to satisfy man's creative, his power-seeking, and his gambling instincts. . . . It would be misleadingly simple to ignore the fact that interest in the process of achievement is itself a goal to many who regard profit as a more-or-less worthwhile by-product."

In other words, part of the joy of business is achieving what one has set out to do, accomplishing goals that are important, and building something that has permanence and value beyond oneself. In addition to the profit motive and personal fulfillment, I argued that businessmen make decisions based on their assessment of their impact not only on their balance sheets and income statements but also on the needs of their workers and the broader community.

Grandfather would have agreed with these propositions. The profit motive provides the discipline for achievement, but individual goals are formed by the larger society and only have meaning and value if they embrace and mirror the needs and objectives of the broader society. I have tried to put these principles into action during my own business career.

I devoted about six months of nearly full-time effort to the project and finished the dissertation in April 1940. I can still remember placing the finished manuscript in envelopes and mailing them off to Professors Knight, Viner, and Lange. I was anxious, as every author is, about my readers' reactions, but I was convinced that I had done a good and thorough job. My committee agreed, and four months later I received my doctorate.

PEGGY

That fall and winter were not devoted solely to intellectual hard labor. Courting Peggy McGrath provided me with a very pleasant diversion and eventually with the most important relationship of my life.

Peggy and I had known each other for years, but we had started to see one another more frequently and seriously only after I returned from London. Her father, Sims McGrath, was a partner with Cadwallader, Wickersham and Taft, a prominent Wall Street law firm. Her mother, Neva van Zandt Smith, was the daughter of a former president of the Pennsylvania Railroad. The McGraths had suffered financial losses during the Depression but lived comfortably in an attractive, white colonial-style house on "The Narrows" Road in Mount Kisco, exactly twenty-two minutes' drive from Kykuit. That route became well worn during the winter of 1939–40.

Peggy preferred the quieter life in Westchester County. She adored her horse, Soldier, whom she cared for herself and trained to jump and foxhunt. She had many friends in and around Mount Kisco and enjoyed dropping in on them unexpectedly during her rides, often staying for dinner. Peggy was full of fun and adventure, and was always the first to join in with something new and unconventional.

Even as a child she enjoyed playing practical jokes. Old friends who attended the Rippowam School in Mount Kisco with her recalled the time that she and one or two others, including her sister, Eileen, placed a wedge of Limburger cheese behind a radiator on a wintry Friday afternoon before leaving for home. School officials had to cancel classes on Monday as they worked desperately to air out the building.

Later, Peggy spent one year at the Shipley School, a rather stuffy girls finishing school outside of Philadelphia. She was known as Batty McGrath and delighted in skirting the regulations, especially the ones meant to keep the girls in their rooms in the evening. She had learned through careful observation the location of every creaky board in the building, a skill that allowed her to move about silently to visit her friends.

I witnessed a number of Peggy's practical jokes myself. One time she planted a device on the engine of Benjy Franklin's beloved new car. When Benjy pressed the starter button, there was a loud bang and a huge cloud of smoke. Benjy jumped from the car with a look of horror on his face and searched frantically under the hood until he noticed the rest of us laughing hysterically.

Peggy inherited her father's strong sense of integrity and scrupulously adhered to a high moral standard. She inherited her mother's excellent taste in many things, particularly the ability to select and wear attractive and flattering clothes, a talent made easier by her having an exceedingly good figure.

===

While Peggy preferred life in the country to the social whirl of the city, she loved parties. In fact, we first met at a debutante party on Long Island in the early 1930s and often saw each other at dances and other parties during my college years. Both of us enjoyed waltzing, and this interest led to many enjoyable evenings together. The St. Regis Roof and the Rainbow Room were our favorite spots, and one evening we won a polka contest at the Rainbow Room.

From the time I first met Peggy, I knew there was something different and compelling about her. I was not yet in love with her, but I found myself seeking her out more than other girls at parties. She had style, she was fun to talk with, and she was a great dancer. So when I returned to New York in the fall of 1939, my feelings changed significantly. I wanted to be with her as much as possible and found myself calling her on the phone several times a day. She often visited me at Kykuit. We listened to the player organ together or picnicked at some beautiful spot on the family property, where we would go on horseback. We took long walks together through the woods, talking for hours on end. A strong friendship turned into something much more passionate.

By early spring I was thinking seriously about asking Peggy to marry me, but it was not until June that I actually got the courage. Peggy gave me the answer—twenty-four long hours later.

When I told my mother—I had never mentioned the possibility to her before—she said dryly but with amusement, "Well, David, I'm not entirely surprised because I read the telephone bills, and there have been a great many calls to Mount Kisco."

In order to buy an engagement ring I drew out all my savings, about $4,000, which comprised my available resources at the time. Asking Peggy to marry me was the best decision I ever made. We spent fifty-five wonderful years together. There were rocky moments along the way, but our love deepened with each passing year.

THE LITTLE FLOWER

With my dissertation completed and my doctoral degree in hand, it was time to consider a career. I had no clear idea of what I wanted to do, but I knew that I had no interest in joining the Family Office where John, Nelson, and Laurance were already working.

While I was in Chicago, Bill Benton and Beardsley Ruml told me about Anna Rosenberg, a labor and public relations advisor who had good contacts with important political leaders, including President Roosevelt, Governor Herbert Lehman of New York, and Mayor Fiorello La Guardia. Benton contacted Anna and told her of my interest in government service. After we met, Anna suggested that I take occasional days off from my dissertation to learn about different aspects of New York City's government. She arranged visits to several City agencies, including a municipal lodging house and soup kitchen. On another occasion I spent the day sitting with a children's court judge while he disposed of juvenile delinquency cases.

These experiences piqued my interest in public service, and when Anna suggested I might enjoy working with Mayor La Guardia, I quickly agreed. Anna made the necessary arrangements, and on May 1, 1940, I reported to City Hall to begin working as a secretary to the mayor for "a dollar a year."

I was assigned a large office separated from the Mayor's more resplendent chambers by a smaller room occupied by his two stenographers. My responsibilities took me in and out of La Guardia's office a dozen times a day, and I sat in on many conferences and staff meetings, which often were both contentious and loud. I also drafted replies to the dozens of letters that came in every day. I dictated responses to a stenographer and sent them in to the Mayor for his signature. La Guardia seemed satisfied with my efforts, and more often than not he signed my suggested letters without making any changes.

La Guardia, known as the Little Flower, had an explosive temper, though he could turn it on and off at will. He often turned it on. While sitting in my office answering correspondence or talking to a merchant in Brooklyn who was complaining about the lamppost in front of his store being too tall, I would suddenly hear him throw something down on the desk and yell to a trembling subordinate something like "You stupid SOB. How am I supposed to run a city with this kind of incompetence?" The rant would continue for several minutes, and a short while later I would see whoever had been the brunt of his rage slinking from the office.

The commissioners who ran the departments of the City's government were not spared this treatment, either. One of them, William Fellowes Morgan, Jr., the commissioner of markets, came from an old New York family and had accepted La Guardia's job offer out of a sense of civic duty. However, whenever La Guardia received a complaint about Fellowes's department, he would summon him into his office and berate him with the same foul language that he used with everyone. Poor Fellowes would just sit there cowering, practically shivering in a mixture of shame, anger, and fright.

La Guardia was cruel to his secretaries as well. These women worked incredibly long hours and were completely devoted to him. But late in the afternoon, if the Mayor discovered a typo in a letter or some such thing, he would bawl them out unmercifully until they were reduced to tears.

His negatives aside, La Guardia was an extremely impressive man and an extraordinary politician. He was certainly the best mayor New York City has seen in my lifetime—at least until Rudy Giuliani came along. One has to recognize that if La Guardia was impatient and hot-tempered, he had a lot to be impatient about: He was cleaning up a city whose government had become synonymous with corruption. A few years earlier the infamous James J. (Jimmy) Walker had allowed graft to reach new heights of flamboyance and artistry. Most City employees assumed they would be promoted only by paying off the proper person. Robbery, extortion, murder, and prostitution flourished while judges were paid to look the other way.

La Guardia cleaned up New York through the force of his personality and the strength of his character. When he yelled at people, it was because of some festering corruption, inefficiency, or sloppiness. He drove himself hard and expected the same from the people around him. He didn't hesitate to call people in the middle of the night to demand that something be ready for him by a certain time the next day.

He was also a showman: His huge seven-passenger Chrysler limousine was equipped with flashing lights, siren, and a police radio to keep him informed about major accidents and fires around the City. When he heard about a fire, he would change course and race off to the scene, put on his fireman's hat, and start giving orders. He was so colorful that the firemen didn't mind, and the people of New York—and the newspapers—loved it. La Guardia could be heroic, too; he once helped rescue a firefighter pinned under a burning beam. He took an intensely personal interest in every aspect of the City—even on occasion flagging down speeding motorists and lecturing them on safe driving.

The Chrysler was a movable office. Not uncommonly he would grab me as he left City Hall so that I could ride with him to edit his correspondence or to discuss a project of interest to him. We would spend the trip engrossed in business, and then he would jump out as we arrived at the next event on his schedule and with no preparation—sometimes I doubt he knew where he was going till he got there—deliver a speech perfectly tailored to his audience. And he was *sincere*, but not with the false sincerity that is the stock in trade of so many politicians. La Guardia was a believer, and it showed.

I remember accompanying the Mayor to the opening of a new Sanitation Department facility somewhere in Brooklyn built with money provided by the federal government. The audience was the student body of a local grade school. I know for a fact that he had no idea he was going to be talking to children that day. But he launched into a description of, first, the value of the Works Progress Administration and its role in providing jobs during the Depression, and then of the Sanitation Department and its critical importance to the working of the City. From there he moved smoothly into a celebration of democracy, of which the Sanitation Department was clearly a vital element, and then of America itself. The children were spellbound. I'm sure all the sanitation workers felt like heroes. By the end of the speech I had tears in my eyes. It had all been impromptu, but it came from La Guardia's heart and was enormously effective.

=

The one commissioner who held his own with La Guardia was Robert Moses. Moses was a power in his own right. He had been a legislative aide to Al Smith when Smith was in the New York State Assembly and worked closely with him after Smith became governor in the 1920s. Moses was an intense man, the driving force behind the creation of New York's impressive system of state parks, and a large part of its transportation system as well. Indeed, Moses remained a power in the City and the State for more than fifty years. During that time he held a variety of posts, but regardless of the titles, Moses was always a doer and a builder. There were few things related to the City's infrastructure that did not go through one or another agency controlled by him. I would have firsthand experience with this after the war when I worked with him to redevelop both Morningside Heights and lower Manhattan.

Moses was a Yale graduate, and unlike many politicians he was personally incorruptible. He was a dedicated public servant who demonstrated what well designed and well-managed government programs could accomplish, but he could often be ruthless and autocratic in reaching his goals.

Moses was a match for La Guardia in every way, in intellect as well as in sheer strength of character. He would casually say hello to me as he entered the Mayor's office in a calm and gentlemanly manner. A few moments later I would hear the two of them start a shouting match that reverberated to the ends of the halls. But these arguments had a different outcome when Moses was involved; La Guardia respected him, and though he would get angry, he treated Moses as an equal and wouldn't try to humiliate him the way he did others.

=

During my year and a half with the Mayor, my biggest project was renting commercial space at La Guardia Airport, which had opened in 1939. The airport was the Mayor's pride and joy, and he wanted it to be economically self-sustaining. The main terminal had been designed without the inclusion of rentable commercial space, an omission that made the Mayor's goal difficult to achieve. William A. Delano, the architect, and I found areas where stores and display cases could be placed, and then I went out and leased the spaces. I turned out to be a pretty good salesman. Cartier took a small area at the head of a curved stairway for a jewelry counter, and I sold other space to a flower shop, a bank, a haberdashery, a brokerage office, and a beauty salon.

Airplanes were still a novelty in 1940, and thousands of people visited the airport daily just to watch them land and take off. We installed an observation deck on an enclosed balcony overlooking the runways and charged a modest admission fee. The "Skywalk" was an immediate success and generated almost $100,000 a year in revenue.

In late May 1940, a month after I began work, I was alone in the car with the Mayor and told him of my plans to marry. Assuming that Peggy accepted, I told the Mayor we would be married in the early fall and that I would like time off for a honeymoon. The Mayor expressed enthusiasm and wished me success. A few weeks later I told him that Peggy had accepted my proposal, and he took us out to dinner at the Tavern on the Green in Central Park and then to an open-air concert at City College's Guggenheim Stadium to celebrate. He also agreed to give me time off for my honeymoon!

Peggy and I married on September 7, 1940, in a charming little Episcopal church, Saint Matthew's, in Bedford, New York. My brother John served as best man, and my other brothers and college roommates were ushers. The McGraths held the reception at their home, and there were more than two hundred guests, including Henry Ford, his son Edsel, and a number of older friends of both families.

We honeymooned at the JY Ranch in the Grand Tetons, one of the most beautiful places in the world. We took a five-day pack trip through Yellowstone National Forest, where we each shot a bull elk. (In later years both of us lost our interest in hunting, but our love for wilderness pack trips continued unabated.) But mostly Peggy and I spent time with each other, enjoying the first experience of marriage and making plans for our future. It was a time that I still treasure in my heart. All too soon we had to return to New York.

"PREPAREDNESS"

While I continued to work for La Guardia after my marriage, by the late summer of 1941, American entry into either the European war or a hostile confrontation with Japan became more and more of a possibility.

Defense spending increased dramatically in mid-1940 after the fall of France, both to increase our own "preparedness" and to supply the British (and later the Russians) with armaments and other supplies.

Government contracts for every imaginable item—from tanks to chocolate bars—stimulated the conversion of old factories to new uses and the construction of many new ones all across the country. The speed with which all of this was done spawned a number of unanticipated problems: inadequate medical facilities, nonexistent housing for war workers, strains on the local water and food supplies, and overwhelmed school districts. To cope with these and many other problems, the Roosevelt administration set up the Office of Defense, Health and Welfare Services (ODHWS), another of the hundreds of "alphabet agencies" that existed at the time. Regional offices were established across the United States, and Roosevelt asked Anna Rosenberg to head the New York region.

Anna was a frequent visitor to City Hall, and one day she stopped in my office to say that perhaps the time had come for me to become involved with the "preparedness" effort and work with her as assistant regional director of ODHWS. The timing seemed good to me. I had enjoyed working for La Guardia and had learned a great deal about City government, but a year and a half seemed long enough. The job Anna offered me was salaried, and I felt it would give me the administrative experience that I never had with La Guardia.

Anna assigned me responsibility for a large area of upstate New York. The companies opening factories there faced a number of problems, but employee housing was the most acute. At the tail end of the Depression, people were still willing to move long distances to find a good job, and the housing in many of the small cities and towns along the Saint Lawrence River and Canadian border—Watertown, Massena, and Ogdensburg—was inadequate to meet this large influx. I spent most of my time trying to mediate among impatient businessmen, harassed local officials, and the federal bureaucrats who controlled the funds needed to build the housing. I learned to negotiate and to cope with the unexpected on a daily basis.

Less than three months after I took the job, the Japanese bombed Pearl Harbor. A new and very different chapter of my life was about to begin.

CHAPTER 9

THE WAR

It was a wintry afternoon in New York, and Peggy, Dick Gilder, and I were in a cab on Fifth Avenue headed to the Frick Museum. The cabby had his radio on when the announcer interrupted to tell of the attack on Pearl Harbor. We were all in shock. The three of us went on to the Frick and walked through the rooms in silence. Dick especially liked the Vermeers, and we looked at them together. Their beauty calmed us for the moment.

The next day Dick quit his job at Tiffany's and enlisted in the Air Force. His action didn't surprise me. Dick had believed war with Hitler was inevitable since our trip to Germany six years before. His views were not popular; most of the people I knew, including many of my family and most of Dick's, were opposed to the United States entering the European war. That was natural enough given the horrors of World War I, and it was a much more widely held sentiment than we acknowledge today. The year before, Dick and I had been asked to join the Council on Foreign Relations, and I remember Dick arguing strongly for intervention on the side of the British. Many of our elders at the council vehemently disagreed.

Shortly after college Dick had married his childhood sweetheart, Ann Alsop, and they had two small children, George and Comfort. Dick was devoted to his family, but duty to his country and to the principles he believed in had to come first. After Germany invaded Poland, he started flying lessons so that he would be prepared when war came. He rose at five in the morning, drove to Floyd Bennett Field on Long Island, and flew for an hour or so before reporting for work at Tiffany's at nine.

In early 1942, before he left for flight training, Dick and I had lunch at the Harvard Club. Neither of us had any experience with war, but we had heard the reports from Europe and knew the life expectancy of combat pilots was not great. Dick said he thought it unlikely that he would return from the war. I remember his words: "David, I have a wonderful wife and two beautiful children. I hope I can count on you and Peggy to look after them if anything does happen to me." For the first time I fully understood the depth of his convictions and realized that I might soon be losing my best friend forever. In a subdued and shaken voice I assured him: "Of course we will, Dick. You can count on us."

Although I admired Dick for his strong beliefs and his decisiveness in acting on them, I was ambivalent about enlisting immediately myself. Peggy was not having an easy time adjusting to being a Rockefeller and had just given birth to our first child, David, Jr. I also felt more than a few misgivings about how I would handle military service. I persuaded myself that my war-related job would exempt me from active military service. Certainly Anna Rosenberg could pull a few strings if I asked. I was classified III-A because of my dependents, which meant I would not be drafted for some time, so I felt there was no need for an immediate decision.

AN UNSETTLING CONVERSATION

Until, that is, I had an unsettling conversation with Mother in her sitting room at 740 Park Avenue. My parents lived near us, and I stopped by a few times a week to say hello. One evening she brought up the war. Mother had long been a pacifist and, before Pearl Harbor, firmly believed the United States should remain neutral. Starting in the late 1930s, however, Mother became convinced that Hitler and his allies posed a profound threat to the United States and, indeed, to the deepest values of Western civilization. Her doctor told me later that with each domino that fell before the Nazi war machine—Austria, Czechoslovakia, Poland, and France—Mother experienced severe psychosomatic reactions, becoming extremely anxious and physically ill.

No doubt one of the things Mother had long dreaded was the conversation she was having with me. She was gentle but firm in expressing her view that the United States had to fight to safeguard our way of life and that men who were eligible ought to do their part by enlisting. They should not wait to be drafted. It was their "duty." I remember her saying the word softly but emphatically. I was taken aback, not because it appeared she had changed her mind about the war but because she was telling me it was time to go off to fight and possibly die in the process. It was upsetting for me, and obviously it wasn't easy for Mother, either. I knew Mother was right and that I had been indulging in wishful thinking. I discussed it with Peggy, who agreed. In mid-March 1942 I enlisted in the Army as a private even though Father could have used his influence to get me a commission.

BASIC TRAINING

I began basic training at Fort Jay on Governor's Island on May 1, 1942. Governor's Island lies off the southern tip of Manhattan. I slept in the barracks, which also housed the grooms for the officers' horses. Each room in the barracks accommodated several score of enlisted men who slept in double-decker cots. I slept above one of the grooms. As the weather got hotter, the "aroma" of my bunkmate's clothes, reeking of horse perspiration mingled with his own, grew stronger. He was an amiable fellow with very little education, but we got on well—save for the scent—and I valued his knowledge of horses and his many small kindnesses to me.

Basic training consisted of endless hours of close-order drill, calisthenics, learning how to care for and fieldstrip our weapons, and, of course, the inevitable KP duty. At first the Army was something of a shock. It was at once threatening because it was all so new and, at the same time, boring and arduous. I had entered the Army with serious misgivings about my ability to cope with its rigors physically or to adapt socially. I had never been a good athlete, and I was not good at most competitive sports. Thus, having occasional bits of time to play baseball was more nerve-racking to me than close-order drill. At the outset I wondered how I would fare mixing with people from very different backgrounds, tastes, and skills.

As it turned out, basic training went surprisingly well. Submitting to military discipline and getting on with my fellow trainees was much less of a problem than I had anticipated. I had a strong sense of duty, of doing what I was told (perhaps not so surprising, given my upbringing), and following orders was the primary attribute demanded of an enlisted man.

I recall at one point that a few of us were assigned to paint the kitchen in the officers' mess hall. I followed instructions faithfully, painting quite a bit more steadily than some of the others who had a more lackadaisical attitude toward Army orders and work. It certainly wasn't my intention, but this impressed the officer in charge of the detail and also the other enlisted men. They were amazed that a Rockefeller was willing to do manual labor. I soon realized that I wasn't as inept as I had feared; that I could get along and even become friends with people with whom I had few things in common.

=

Of all the brothers, only Win and I enlisted. Win joined the infantry, went through officer candidate school at Fort Benning, and saw combat in the Pacific. He was seriously wounded when his troopship took a direct hit by a kamikaze off Okinawa in 1945. My eldest brother, John, first took a job with the Red Cross in Washington and then was commissioned in the Navy as a lieutenant in 1943. He worked for a special interagency group in Washington, the State-War-Navy Coordinating Committee, that planned for postwar governments in Japan and Europe. Nelson, as Coordinator of Inter-American Affairs, was, of course, exempt from military service. Laurance, however, had not yet decided what he would do, and that was the occasion of a somewhat cruel but nevertheless funny practical joke that Peggy and I played on him.

After the first few weeks of basic training I was able to spend weekends at home with my family. Laurance and his wife, Mary, lived in an apartment in the same building at 115 East 67th Street. One Saturday they invited us for dinner. Peggy took some of Father's office stationery and wrote Laurance a letter, signing it "Father." The letter mentioned an admiral who had pulled a few strings and arranged for Laurance to be inducted immediately into the submarine service. It was all set; Laurance would sign up and enter training the following week. The letter closed with heartfelt expressions of pride and warm good wishes to his brave son in what Father knew would be a "challenging service for his country."

Peggy had the letter delivered that morning, so Laurance would be sure to see it before dinner. When we arrived, Laurance looked quite ashen. He showed us "Father's letter," and we played along for a short while but didn't have the heart to keep it up. Laurance was so relieved when we told him the truth that he forgot to be angry with us.

Later, Laurance, who had learned a great deal about the aviation industry through his early business investments, was commissioned a lieutenant in the Navy and worked on the design and production of aircraft.

PAINFUL LOSSES

I got my corporal's stripes shortly after finishing basic training and was assigned to the Counter-Intelligence Corps on Governor's Island. In August I was sent to Washington to join a counterintelligence task force training for assignment in the Middle East. We met in the basement of an obscure government building for two weeks and heard rumors that we would be sent to Cairo in the near future. While I was awaiting orders, however, Colonel Townsend Heard of the American Intelligence Command asked for my transfer to his unit, which was about to be moved to Miami. I confess this came as a welcome surprise. Somehow I could not see myself as an "undercover agent" in the bars of Cairo. The transfer was arranged, and early that fall I reported for duty in Miami Beach, where Peggy and young David joined me. We rented a small house on La Gorce Island, and I bicycled to work each day. My duties were not very impressive or important—serving as a messenger and standing guard duty.

During this time Dick Gilder was stationed at an air base in northern Florida. When he learned that his wing was soon going overseas, Dick wrangled a twenty-four-hour pass that allowed him to visit us before his departure. I was on guard duty when he arrived—making sure the colonel's horses, stabled on the Firestone estate, were not hit by falling coconuts!

Dick came out to be with me for part of the night. We talked of nothing special, but everything seemed important at the time, and I cared very much that he had made the effort to see me. He reminded me of the promise I had made to him in New York, and I told him that he could depend on us. When I was relieved, we went back to the house to spend a few hours with Peggy. Early the next morning we took Dick to the station. As the train pulled out, Peggy and I turned to each other, both knowing somehow that we would never see him again.

We spoke to Dick one last time when he called from his home in Tyringham, Massachusetts, just before he left for England. His wing refueled in Gander, Newfoundland, and then took off for the North Atlantic crossing. Dick's plane and two others in his flight were lost without a trace. Ann learned later that the planes had been held in Gander because of indications that the engines had been tampered with. One would have to suspect sabotage as the cause of their disappearance. The war had barely begun, and already I had lost my best friend and Ann was a widow with two small children.

Before the war ended, two other close friends would die. Walter Rosen, whose mother played the theremin, tried to enlist in the Army Air Corps but was rejected because of his eyesight. He then joined the Royal Canadian Air Force and was killed during the Battle of Britain. Bill Waters, my roommate from the LSE who only a few years earlier had stood with me watching Hitler march through the streets of Munich, died when his plane crashed outside of Kano, Nigeria. He and his crew were part of the vast armada that flew across the South Atlantic and Africa, and finally over the "hump" of the Himalayas to Chungking, to supply the Nationalist forces of Chiang Kai-shek.

OFFICER CANDIDATE SCHOOL

After a few months in Florida I asked Colonel Heard's permission to apply for officer candidate school. He told me the competition was quite strong and that the best chance for getting a prompt acceptance was to apply to the Engineer OCS School at Fort Delvoir, Virginia, which had a reputation as the system's toughest. My application was accepted, and I began the demanding three-month course in January 1943.

OCS was much more rigorous than basic training, both intellectually and physically. At the end of the course we had to complete a twenty-mile march carrying an M-1 rifle and a field pack weighing eighty pounds. That night we pitched, and then immediately dismantled, pup tents in the deep snow and straggled back to camp at 5 A.M., only to be awakened two hours later for calisthenics. I was pleased to discover that I could handle the tough and disciplined side of the military as well as excel in the classroom.

I was commissioned a second lieutenant in the Engineer Corps in March 1943 and received orders to report to the Military Intelligence Training Center at Camp Ritchie, Maryland, after a two-week leave. Peggy was already well along in her second pregnancy, so I was grateful for a short break that enabled me to be with her in New York. As the fates would have it, Peggy went to the hospital to give birth to Abby only a few hours after I left for Camp Ritchie. I got the news on my arrival and was granted a three-day pass to return to New York to see her and my newly arrived daughter.

The two-month course at Ritchie trained officers for intelligence work with combat infantry units. The focus of our training was the battlefield; we studied the order of battle and combat tactics of both Allied and enemy forces, learned map-reading skills and reconnaissance procedures, and mastered techniques for the interrogation of prisoners of war. Each of us chosen for the course had been selected because we had special talents, such as language skills and familiarity with foreign cultures, that would be useful in the European Theater of Operations, our group's ultimate destination.

I met a number of interesting men at Camp Ritchie who would intersect with my life later on: Philip Johnson, then a junior architect who had already been involved with the Museum of Modern Art; John Kluge, who was born in Germany and later would found Metromedia; John Oakes, who later edited the *New York Times* editorial page; and Fred Henderson, part Apache Indian and a regular Army officer who made a career with the CIA after the war. His son, Brian, joined Chase in the 1960s before going on to a senior position at Merrill Lynch.

After completing the course I was appointed an instructor in the French section of the school and remained for an additional three months to teach French army organization, giving the lectures in French. This assignment provided me with a good background for the task that I would face for the final years of the war in North Africa and France.

DUTY IN ALGIERS

In late August 1943 my pleasant interlude in the Appalachians ended. On a lovely summer morning I opened sealed orders that assigned me to the Joint Intelligence Collection Agency (JICA) of the War Department and directed me to report immediately to Washington.

I spent the next month at the Pentagon, where I learned that I would be assigned to JICA's detachment at General Eisenhower's Allied Force Headquarters (AFHQ) in Algiers. My fluency in French, knowledge of the prewar European political situation, and time as an instructor at Camp Ritchie seemed to qualify me as a French "expert"—or so the War Department believed.

I left Washington on September 23, 1943, with about one hundred other servicemen crammed onboard a noisy, drafty DC-4. We crossed the North Atlantic to Prestwick, Scotland, seated side by side along the fuselage in "bucket" seats, a hard metal bench with shallow indentations on which you planted your buttocks. The thirteen-hour flight was an exhausting experience.

I had spent two days in Prestwick waiting for transport to North Africa before I ran into William Franklin Knox, the Secretary of the Navy, whom I had met when I was a student in Chicago. He offered to take me on his plane—which had much more comfortable seats—as far as Rabat, Morocco, where I was able to pick up a ride on a military plane to Algiers.

Because I was entering a combat zone, the Army issued me a .45-caliber pistol, two magazine clips, twenty rounds of ammunition, a first-aid kit, a compass, and a pair of suspenders (which I promptly lost). I was also given little information booklets with helpful advice on how to behave in North Africa: "Never smoke or spit in front of a mosque." "Don't kill snakes or birds. Some Arabs believe the souls of departed chieftains reside in them."

"When you see grown men walking hand in hand, ignore it. They are not 'queer.' " One book admonished the reader that staring at Muslim women or touching their veils could start a riot!

None of this prepared me for the beauty of wartime Algiers. The city stretched for miles in a crescent along the aquamarine Bay of Algiers. The modern French city, built close to the harbor, had wide boulevards, handsome government buildings, and private villas interspersed among parks filled with date palms and flowering plants. Nearby was the older Arab city with its winding streets, whitewashed buildings, and slender minarets, crowned by the Casbah, the ancient Moorish citadel. The Sahel Hills framed the city, and in the distance loomed the coastal mountains. Allied shipping crowded the harbor, and the streets were filled with military men from around the world: Americans, British, Australians, Indians, South Africans, as well as Arabs and Berbers and, of course, the French.

By the time I arrived in Algiers, the real war had moved on. Rommel's Afrika Korps had been driven from its last bastion in Tunisia, and Eisenhower had captured Sicily in a lightning campaign. In early September, Allied forces crossed the Straits of Messina and started the long and bloody campaign up the Italian peninsula. The beauty of Algiers masked the intrigue that simmered just below the surface. The intense battle within the French Committee on National Liberation (CNL) for control of the Vichy French civil and military authority in North Africa absorbed everyone's interest. And central to that struggle was the question of whether General Henri Giraud or General Charles de Gaulle would control the CNL.

Giraud was one of the leaders of France's brief and ineffectual struggle against the Germans in 1940. Captured and interned, Giraud escaped from the fortress of Koenigstein in Austria and made his way to unoccupied France. Untainted by collaboration with the Germans and deeply respected by the French officer corps, Giraud seemed the ideal candidate to replace Admiral Jean-François Darlan as chief of state in North Africa. Following Darlan's assassination in December 1942, Giraud, with the full backing of President Roosevelt and his senior advisors, became the commander of French military forces. It appeared to be only a matter of time before he took control of the political structure as well.

Charles de Gaulle, who would become one of the great figures of the postwar period, was still an obscure military man with a small following and few financial resources in 1943. After the French defeat in 1940, de Gaulle organized the Free French from the remnants of the army that had made it across the Channel after Dunkirk, and proclaimed the French Government in Exile. Although most of the French officer corps detested de Gaulle, Churchill respected his fighting spirit and pressed Roosevelt at the January 1943 Casablanca Conference to include de Gaulle's Free French in whatever political structure was established in North Africa. The outcome was that the two rivals were forced together in a "shotgun wedding" and told to work out their differences.

INITIATING AN INTELLIGENCE NETWORK

By the time I arrived in Algiers, the Giraud–de Gaulle marriage was on the rocks. The two had spent ten months maneuvering deviously and incessantly against each other. While de Gaulle had clearly gained the upper hand in the political struggle, it was by no means certain that he would prevail. Their continuing conflict demanded solid intelligence both because of its implications for the war effort and the impact it would have on postwar France.

The Joint Intelligence Collection Agency North Africa (JICANA) was composed of about ten officers and thirty enlisted men drawn from all of the U.S. intelligence services. We operated from an office on le boulevard du Telemly, and the officers shared quarters in a private villa across the street. Our primary job was to "collect" intelligence produced by the military intelligence services operating in North Africa and to pass this material along to Washington and London. JICANA functioned as a clearinghouse and a postal service. This was not a particularly arduous task and left the officers with a great deal of leisure time, which was devoted to sampling the quite palatable local vintages and scrounging black market restaurants for rationed delicacies not available to the general public.

I found the work disappointing. I had been led to believe that I would be involved in a much more active intelligence-gathering operation that would utilize my specialized training. Colonel Byron Switzer, my commanding officer, felt differently. An engineer with little intelligence background, the colonel believed JICANA had no mandate to originate its own intelligence reports. Shortly after my arrival I wrote my parents that "no one seems to know what I am supposed to do."

After a few weeks of collating reports prepared by other agencies and growing increasingly frustrated, I asked Colonel Switzer if I could try my hand at reporting on political activities and economic conditions in the region. After some hesitation he agreed to my request, and I set about creating my own intelligence "network" from scratch.

Frankly, this was an almost impossible task for someone in my position. I was only a second lieutenant and was competing with the more established intelligence services—including Colonel William Donovan's Office of Strategic Services. However, I did have a few advantages. I spoke French and understood the political and economic situation better than most. In addition, I had letters of introduction to a number of influential people, two of whom proved to be of immense help.

Henri Chevalier, Standard Oil of New Jersey's general manager in North Africa, had lived in Algiers for many years and had wide contacts within the business community across North Africa. Henri introduced me to a number of *colons* (Algerians of French descent) and to others who had left France after the German occupation. Among the latter was Alfred Pose, the powerful head of the Banque National pour le Commercial l'Industrie's branch system in North Africa, who introduced me to influential Arab businessmen and political leaders.

Prime Minister Mackenzie King, my father's old friend, wrote on my behalf to General George Vanier, the senior Canadian representative in North Africa. The friendship I developed with General Vanier brought me into contact with a number of people in the Allied diplomatic community and with members of the CNL, whom it would have been difficult for me to meet otherwise. Vanier's military attaché, Colonel Maurice Forget, invited me to join a ten-day trip through Morocco with a group of military attachés. That trip provided me with a number of new contacts and a broader understanding of the precarious French position in North Africa.

I also began to meet senior people in Allied diplomatic circles and in the CNL, among them Ambassador Robert Murphy, a staunch Giraud supporter who had prepared the way for the Allied landings in North Africa. I also met several of Murphy's famous vice consuls, such as Ridgway Knight, who would later join me at Chase. It was in Algiers that I first became friends with William Paley, the founder of CBS, who ran the psychological warfare program in the theater, and C. D. Jackson, one of Paley's deputies and later publisher of *Fortune* magazine.

Within a few months I developed a large and well-placed network of informants, which enabled me to report thoughtfully on the evolving political situation in North Africa. Colonel Switzer saw the merit of my work and gave me a free hand, even to the point of allowing me to make forays—about ten thousand miles of it in a jeep—throughout Algeria, Morocco, and Tunisia, as well as a two-week trip to Cairo and Istanbul to deepen my contacts with French intelligence officials. Presumably, the reaction from Washington was favorable since I was not told to stop.

GIRAUD VERSUS DE GAULLE: AN INSIDE VIEW

The most valuable contacts I developed were within the CNL command itself. Two men in particular enabled me to obtain an inside view of the rivalry between Giraud and de Gaulle. A friend of Mother's introduced me to de Gaulle's aide-de-camp, Etienne Burin des Rosier. Like most of de Gaulle's entourage, Etienne kept a chilly distance from most Americans, but he was friendly to me and occasionally provided me with useful information.

Even more responsive was Léon de Rosen, Giraud's aide-de-camp. A refugee from the Russian revolution, Léon had worked his way up from a menial job to become director of the Fiat assembly plant in Provence. He joined the French Foreign Legion in 1939 and became one of Giraud's aides in late 1942. Léon and I became good friends, and he was quite willing to provide me with information on the struggle between de Gaulle and Giraud, because, no doubt, he felt it would be communicated to sympathetic ears in Washington.

Even Léon recognized that Giraud's political ineptness and connections to conservative political circles made winning the political struggle with de Gaulle a difficult proposition. De Gaulle, on the other hand, was astute and ruthless, and step by step he outmaneuvered his older rival. As the year progressed, Giraud became increasingly isolated, and as I drove down the boulevard de la République, the main street of Algiers, I saw more and more flags displaying the blue and white cross of Lorraine, de Gaulle's liberation emblem, flying next to the tricolor.

By April 1944 the struggle was over. De Gaulle forced Giraud from the CNL and sent him in exile to the town of Mostaganem, near Oran. A few weeks later and shortly after Giraud survived an assassination attempt, Léon invited me to visit them for a long weekend. I talked with the general for several hours, and he told me in detail about his escape from prison, his months hiding out in the south of France, and his negotiations with the Allies in the weeks leading up to the North African invasion. Giraud was a proud man with all the soldierly qualities, and he had accepted his defeat with dignity and sadness. He gave me fascinating insights into the political situation, which had important consequences for the postwar period, which I passed on to Washington.

==

Much of my reporting focused on the anticolonial movement that was gaining strength among the Arabs and Berbers throughout the Maghreb. This was of considerable significance since the U.S. government was on record as favoring the independence of colonial areas in Asia and Africa after the war. In one report I said: "German propaganda in North Africa among Arabs no longer effective. Arabs supporting the Allies. No fundamental hostility between Jews and Moslems in Algeria. . . . Arabs' principal antagonism is toward the Colons. . . . Communism said to be spreading rapidly. . . . Ultimate objective of Moslems in North Africa said to be political and economic equality with other national groups."

It was clear to me that even though Algeria had been incorporated within "metropolitan France," the Arabs and Berbers resented French control. The beginnings of the Arab revolt that would culminate in Algerian independence in 1960 could already be seen during World War II. However, it would take a savage colonial war and the near collapse of the French Republic itself before that occurred.

=

Although my duties in North Africa were not hazardous, there were moments of extreme danger. The closest I came to death was on a routine flight from Morocco to Oran, and it wasn't from enemy fire. I was on a DC-3, sitting, by chance, with Adlai Stevenson, who was on a mission as an assistant to Secretary of the Navy Knox. We encountered severe turbulence, but the real problem was cloud cover, which made it impossible to get visual bearings to land in Oran. The plane was not equipped with radar, and the pilot circled for a long time hoping for a break in the clouds. Looking over the pilot's shoulder I saw the gas gauge needle pointing ominously to empty. The pilot was visibly nervous, Adlai had turned green, and I probably looked the same. As a last resort the pilot took the plane down through the clouds to get his bearings, hoping we didn't hit a mountain in the coastal range. We descended for what seemed like an eternity before breaking through the clouds above the landing strip at an altitude of about one hundred feet. The pilot landed safely, bringing a terrifying flight to a prosaic conclusion.

TO HOME AND BACK

In July 1944, Colonel Switzer arranged for me to act as a courier to escort our intelligence pouch to Washington. On my arrival I was given a fifteen-day leave to visit Peggy and the children. There were now three; Neva, the youngest, had been born in June, and I saw her for the first time. It was a welcome respite and one that few GI's ever had. It also gave me an opportunity to reassure Peggy that I cared for her and missed her, and tell her how important she was in my life. She had cause to wonder since my letters, though frequent, arrived after delays of several weeks. The problem was the "V" mail system; one wrote letters on a single sheet of paper, which were censored, microfilmed to reduce their size for shipping to the United States, then blown back up to normal size, and finally mailed. This cumbersome process caused Peggy much stress and anxiety. My stay was painfully short; we hardly had time to get reacquainted before I had to leave.

SOUTHWEST FRANCE

I returned to Algiers just before the Allied invasion of southern France in August 1944. The city had become a backwater, and there was little for me to do. I desperately wanted a transfer and finally received new orders in early October transferring me on a temporary basis to "T" Force, a frontline intelligence unit attached to General Alexander Patch's Seventh Army, which had moved north along the Rhone River to join forces with General George Patton's Third Army near Lyon. I joined the unit near Dôle in eastern France. The front was only a few miles away, and there was a constant movement of men and supplies toward the Rhine and the steady rumble of artillery.

"T" Force was the brainchild of Colonel James Pumpelly, who had been the deputy commander of JICA in Algiers when I first arrived. The unit's mission was to travel with frontline combat troops and seize critical scientific and technological information before the enemy could destroy it. However, the colonel had a different job in mind for me. He had been impressed by my work in Algiers and asked for my transfer to handle a special assignment. Eisenhower's headquarters, Pumpelly told me, had little reliable intelligence about the immense area west of the Rhone and south of the Loire rivers, which had been bypassed in the rapid pursuit of the German armies toward the Rhine. There were reports of German SS units operating in this area, and other accounts that the French Communist resistance controlled vast portions of the countryside and would launch an insurrection when the time was right. Along the border with Spain, units of the Spanish Republican Army were known to be still active. As resistance groups evened old scores by purging collaborators with drumhead courts-martial and summary executions, there was a danger that the situation might degenerate into civil war.

Colonel Pumpelly ordered me to assess the political situation, the state of the economy, and the degree to which foreign forces or indigenous radical groups posed a threat to Allied forces or the authority of the new French government in extreme southwestern France. Although Pumpelly gave me a general idea of my mission, he left it to me to make my own way.

MEETING PICASSO

Since the successful completion of this mission would require assistance from the newly established French Provisional Government, I went to Paris to request help from some of my old friends from Algiers who had moved to France with de Gaulle. I spent a few days visiting government offices and the Deuxième Bureau of the Army and was given several "To Whom It May Concern" letters that would prove of great value.

One morning I ran into Henri Laugier, the former rector of the University of Algiers who had been a member of the CNL in Algiers. He invited me to lunch with him at the home of his mistress, Madame Cuttoli, an art dealer in Paris with whom my mother had dealt before the war. Her husband, an elderly, semi-senile former senator from the Department of Constantine in Algeria, was confined to a wheelchair in his upstairs bedroom. Much to my delight the fourth member of our luncheon party was Pablo Picasso, who, Laugier informed me, had also been a lover of Madame Cuttoli before the war.

Picasso, though not yet the preeminent artist he would become, was already a well-known personality. He was subdued and did not talk much about his wartime experiences, which he had spent quietly in the south of France. Upon his return to Paris in the autumn of 1944, he had immediately joined the Communist Party. Nonetheless, he was warm and friendly to me, and was pleased Mother had been an early collector of his drawings and prints, which she had acquired through Madame Cuttoli in New York before the war.

It was a memorable if somewhat disconcerting meal. The aged senator remained upstairs while his wife, Picasso, Laugier, and I enjoyed a sumptuous meal. Neither Madame Cuttoli nor her amorous friends were the least embarrassed by their past or present relationships, even when we all visited her husband in his bedroom.

CUT OFF FROM THE WORLD

I returned to Luneville in early November 1944 to make final preparations for the trip. Colonel Pumpelly assigned me a jeep and a young Navy yeoman driver, Buddy Clark, who doubled as a stenographer. We towed a small open trailer filled with five-gallon cans of gasoline and large quantities of C rations since both fuel and food were in short supply in the area. Buddy and I were completely on our own during the entire six-week period. I don't recall any other time in my life when I was so completely cut off from the rest of the world for so long.

The area we had been assigned was the ancient lands of the Languedoc, the Midi, and Gascony. It was a glorious trip through some of the most beautiful country in Europe. The last of the harvest was being brought in, and the distant peaks of the Pyrenees were white with the first snows of winter as we drove from Perpignan to Toulouse. Only a few hundred miles away millions of men were locked in savage combat.

We visited the regional capitals of Nîmes, Montpellier, Perpignan, Toulouse, Pau, and Bordeaux, where I met the new commissioners of the Republic appointed by de Gaulle. I was well received and had no difficulty getting them to talk about the political and economic situation in their areas. I also spoke with many people I met along the way who represented a variety of backgrounds and points of view. In many of the places we visited, we were the first Americans anyone had seen since 1940. It was a fascinating and, at some points, a nerve-racking mission.

Returning to Luneville in mid-December, I dictated reports on each *departement*, which were sent to AFHQ and Washington. I had found nothing to substantiate the reports of subversive elements roaming the countryside, but there was great political and economic uncertainty, as well as anxiety about the progress of the war. With winter fast approaching and food and fuel supplies low, I suggested the situation could deteriorate quickly if supplies were not sent in from the outside.*

INTELLIGENCE GATHERING IN PARIS

Although I had hoped to remain in France after completing my mission, the Army had other plans. I was sent back to Algiers and spent a desolate Christmas there waiting for a new assignment. Finally, in February 1945, just after I was promoted to captain, I received orders to report to Paris as an assistant military attaché.

A few weeks later General Ralph Smith was appointed military attaché. General Smith had served in France during World War I, married a French woman, and spoke the language well. He had fought in the Pacific and com-

---

*More than four decades later I discovered my reports had been preserved, and I was able to get copies of them from the National Archives in Washington.

manded the assault on Makin Island in 1943. General Smith brought with him as an aide Captain Warren T. (Lindy) Lindquist, who had won the Silver Star for bravery at Makin. Lindy and I became friends and also got along well with General Smith, who asked us to share his quarters on the boulevard Saint-Germain. Once again my responsibilities as an AMA were not clearly defined. General Smith was a combat officer with little intelligence experience. When I told him what I had done in North Africa and southwestern France, he suggested that I set up a similar political and economic intelligence unit, reporting directly to him. He assigned Lindy to work with me, along with two lieutenants, one of whom, Richard Dana, had been a friend of mine in New York and would, like Lindy, work for me after the war.

I built the intelligence operation around my contacts with members of de Gaulle's government. Rather quickly we were reporting on the Provisional Government and its internal conflicts. We kept a particularly close watch on the competing French intelligence services—the Army's Deuxième Bureau, the Gaullist Secret Service, and the remnants of Giraud's intelligence apparatus. We learned that Jacques Soustelle, head of the Gaullist operation, had been ousted after a "heated cabinet discussion." André DeWavrin, who used the *nom de guerre* Colonel Passy, replaced him. The Colonel was believed to have been a member of the Cagoulards, the rightist group that had almost toppled Léon Blum's Popular Front government in a 1937 coup attempt. I had written a report on Passy the year before, saying, "There are few people in Algiers more generally feared, disliked, or distrusted. . . . He has openly expressed the desire to get control of the police of France so that he can eliminate the elements he considers undesirable."

Somewhat naively I sent out a questionnaire to U.S. military commands asking for all material on French intelligence. Not surprisingly, Colonel Passy learned about my inquiries. Although everyone did it, it wasn't *comme il faut* to be caught spying on one's allies. Within days Colonel Passy summoned me to his office. He seemed in a good mood and ushered me to a seat with a friendly wave of his hand. We chatted amiably, then he said, "Captain Rockefeller, we have come to understand that there is information you would like to have about our services." He looked at me and raised his eyebrows as if to say, "Isn't that so?" I nodded. I could tell he was clearly enjoying my agony. "But my dear captain," he continued, "really, all this is readily available to you if you will just ask us for it. Please tell me what you would like, and we will be glad to provide the information." I thanked him for his offer and left as quickly as possible.

Fortunately, not all our efforts were quite that inept. We prepared a steady stream of reports on the critical economic situation and the increasingly unstable political scene. De Gaulle was running into serious trouble by the late spring of 1945. His arrogance, inflexibility, and single-mindedness, qualities that had been so essential to his political triumph over Giraud in Algiers, created serious problems as the French went about the task of forming a permanent government and drafting a new constitution. Within a year he would fall from power.

While we developed most of our information through our own network of informants, a good part of it came as a result of the dinners that we hosted for high-ranking French officials at General Smith's residence. A well-stocked wine cellar and a fine table proved to be a wonderful inducement to revealing conversation.

THE AFTERMATH OF WAR

On May 4 the Germans surrendered and Paris celebrated VE day. It was a beautiful spring day that turned into an evening of wild celebration. The embassy closed, and we all went out into the streets for a party that lasted all night. That night and for a brief time afterward one had the unique experience of having Parisians be friendly to you precisely *because* you were an American!

Paris, physically untouched by the war, was the most beautiful I had ever seen it. The scarcities caused by the war actually burnished the city's many charms. Gasoline was strictly rationed, so the streets were virtually empty of cars. I walked across the Seine to the embassy every morning and saw only an occasional automobile. Instead, the streets were filled with women on bicycles riding home from the markets with long loaves of bread under their arms, sitting carefully on their long skirts that would catch the wind and billow out behind them as they rode.

I was eager to return home but had not yet earned enough "points" to be demobilized. In the interim, General Smith sent me on several interesting missions. One, only ten days after the surrender, took me to Frankfurt and Munich. Allied bombing had almost destroyed both cities, and it was shocking to see the extent of the devastation. I saw my old Harvard friend Ernst Teves in Frankfurt for the first time since 1938. Ernst had volunteered to work for the U.S. Occupation as soon as the war ended. Our meeting was difficult, and Ernst's account of his war years was distressing for a friend to hear. He had never become a Nazi, but the compromises he had made in order to keep his family's business operating eroded his principles and coarsened his values.

In Munich I returned to the Kaulbachstrasse, where I had lived with the Defregger family in 1933. The street was covered with rubble, and most of the houses had been destroyed. Somehow the Defreggers' house had escaped serious damage, and the family greeted me at the door. They were amazed and overjoyed to see me, and crowded around, shaking my hand and asking questions. I was glad to see them and relieved that they had survived the war, but it gave me a strange feeling to see them again after so many years. The war and its terrible passions now stood between us: the deaths of Dick Gilder, Walter Rosen, and Bill Waters; the destruction I had seen across France and Germany; the wasted years away from my family. The Defreggers had not started the war—indeed, they had suffered from it— but the horrible tragedy had begun in that city, and I had watched its "evil genius" walk through Munich's streets only a few years before.

The next day I visited Dachau, the infamous concentration camp nestled incongruously amid the gentle hills north of Munich. The camp's inmates had been evacuated, but one could still see the barracks in which they had been housed and the grotesque crematoria where their emaciated bodies had been burned. Scraps of striped cloth still hung in the rusting barbed wire beneath the guard towers. It gave me an understanding I had not had before of the horrors of the Nazi regime, the full extent of which we would only discover with the passage of time.

COMING HOME

In August, Uncle Winthrop came through Paris, and we talked about my plans for the future. He said that a career at the Chase National Bank, of which he was chairman, was the logical path for me to follow. I didn't give him a firm answer but said I would think seriously about it.

Orders recalling me to Washington came through in early October. I wrote Peggy that I had no way of knowing the day of my departure, nor would I be able to notify her when I did find out. Peggy was so impatient that she went to Washington to stay with Nelson at his home on Foxhall Road. Each day for a week she drove to the airport and anxiously scanned the crowds of arriving servicemen. Each day she returned home disappointed. When I finally squeezed aboard a plane, it landed in New York. I called her immediately, but it was another day before I could join her in Washington.

Peggy and I were overjoyed to be together again, and it is difficult to find the words to describe my emotions when I saw my three children, David, Abby, and Neva, although to them I was a stranger. It was some time before they accepted the fact that I was their father and not just a competitor for their mother's time and attention.

The war years had taken a toll. While I had been traveling and getting to know interesting people, Peggy had a different experience. She had endured the restrictions of rationing and the constant fear that I would not return. It was a lonely and difficult time for her. What I had not known was that Peggy was in the midst of a perplexing struggle with her mother, who treated her as if she were still a child, telling her how to dress, how to furnish our home, and how to bring up the children. Peggy resented this but felt powerless to resist it and never told me about it until years later. She was under enormous psychological pressure, which contributed to her recurring periods of depression.

Peggy battled depression for more than two decades. The key moment came when she broke free from her mother and sought psychological counseling. In the end she overcame her problems, and the last twenty years of her life were her happiest.

=

Men of my generation often refer to their military service as good or bad. I had a good war. I had been confused and apprehensive at first but soon learned to adapt and then how to use my newly acquired skills effectively for the benefit of my country. I look back at the war years as an invaluable training ground and testing place for much that I would do later in my life. Among other things, I discovered the value of building contacts with well-placed individuals as a means of achieving concrete objectives. This would be the beginning of a networking process that I would follow throughout my life.

CHAPTER 10

EMBARKING ON
A CAREER AT CHASE

Soon after returning home I accepted my uncle Winthrop Aldrich's offer to join the Chase. It was not an easy decision because I still had a strong interest in working for government or in the not-for-profit sector. I discussed my alternatives with a number of people, including Anna Rosenberg, who thought the Chase would be useful training for a year or two but that I "would not find it challenging enough to stay with as a career." Anna was wrong. Indeed, for the next thirty-five years I devoted myself to the fascinating and personally rewarding life of a commercial banker. During those years I had a number of opportunities to serve as a cabinet officer or in ambassadorial posts. I did not accept any of those attractive offers, but I have no regrets since my career at Chase provided me with a strong challenge and different, though equally satisfying, ways to participate in civic and government affairs.

THE CHASE NATIONAL BANK

The bank I joined in April 1946 was an impressive organization with a distinguished history. The Chase National Bank had been formed in the 1870s, grown through a series of mergers early in the twentieth century, and emerged from the war years as the country's largest commercial bank. At the end of 1945, Chase had total assets of $6.1 billion, deposits of $5.7 billion, and seven thousand employees, many of them, like me, recently discharged from the armed forces. Chase took special pride in being the biggest and best "wholesale" bank in the country, handling the credit needs of major U.S. corporations, serving as a "bankers' bank" for thousands of domestic and foreign correspondents, and financing a substantial portion of the nation's foreign trade. On the other hand, Chase had little interest in the "retail" side of banking or in expanding its international operations, two areas that I would take special interest in and would push aggressively for the following thirty years.

ROCKEFELLER "FAMILY" BANK

Chase has often been called the Rockefeller "family bank," suggesting that we owned or at least controlled the bank. Neither has ever been the case, although my family has had a number of strong ties with Chase over many years. Early in the century Grandfather acquired shares in a number of New York banks, including the Equitable Trust Company, one of Chase's predecessors. In 1921 he gave his stock interest in the Equitable, amounting to about 10 percent of its outstanding shares, to Father, making him the bank's largest shareholder.

However, no one in my family had any direct role in the management of the bank until late 1929, and even then it was the result of an unusual series of events. Equitable's law firm, Murray & Prentice, had handled corporate and trust work for my family over the years. My uncle Winthrop Aldrich, Mother's youngest brother, joined this firm in 1918 and rose rapidly to become a senior partner, handling the Equitable Trust, among other clients.

In the wake of the 1929 stock market crash, Father and other stockholders became concerned about the Equitable's stability. A short time later, when the president of the Equitable died suddenly, Father suggested that Winthrop step in on a temporary basis. Winthrop accepted the position reluctantly, insisting that he would take it only for a year.

After Winthrop became president, he sought a banking partner to provide domestic strength and support. He found that partner in Chase, one of the strongest domestic banks in the country. In early 1930 he negotiated the merger with Chase, creating what was at the time the largest bank in the world. Father strongly backed the merger and was allowed two representatives on the new bank's board, out of a total of twenty-five. Although his stock ownership was reduced by the merger to about 4 percent, Father remained the largest shareholder in the combined bank. After the merger,

Albert Wiggin, the prominent and very successful chairman of Chase, became the chairman of the combined bank, and Winthrop assumed the presidency.*

WINTHROP ALDRICH

Winthrop Aldrich was a handsome man with pale blue eyes and the rather distinctive Aldrich nose that I also inherited. He was enormously charming and very prominent in the social life of New York, but became more than a bit pompous as his prestige and position increased.

From what he later told me, Uncle Winthrop had every intention of returning to his law firm shortly after the merger. But the situation changed dramatically in late 1933 when Albert Wiggin admitted at congressional hearings that he had lent large amounts of the bank's money to himself and his associates on favorable terms and that they had made $10 million selling Chase stock short during the 1929 crash! With strong pressure from Father, who was appalled by the revelations, Wiggin and two other senior officials resigned in disgrace. The Chase board decided that Winthrop, long a staunch advocate of ethical business practices and of banking reform, was the most qualified person to lead the bank through the crisis and persuaded him to remain as chairman.

Winthrop insisted that such misbehavior had been made easier because commercial banks were allowed to own investment banking subsidiaries, which facilitated the self-dealing practiced by Wiggin and others. He testified before Congress in 1933, strongly supporting the two major structural reforms enacted that year: the Glass-Steagall Act, which separated commercial from investment banking, and the Securities Act, which created the Securities and Exchange Commission and compelled corporations to register their stock and make regular and substantial financial disclosures.

---

*The National City Bank (now Citigroup) was really more of a Rockefeller bank than Chase. William Rockefeller, Grandfather's brother, owned a substantial percent of National City's stock and was closely associated with James Stillman, the bank's president between 1891 and 1909. Two of William's sons married two of James Stillman's daughters; their clan became known as the Stillman Rockefellers, and their family maintained a close relationship with City Bank over the years. In the 1960s, Stillman Rockefeller, William's grandson, was chairman of First National City Bank when I became president of the Chase. However, by this time Stillman and his family owned less than 1 percent of City Bank's stock, and my family about 1 percent of Chase's. While Stillman and I had cordial personal relations, we were not close friends and were unabashedly ardent competitors.

Wall Street and the American banking community respected Winthrop, and the Chase prospered during the twenty years of his stewardship. Winthrop, however, had not been trained as a banker and rarely became involved in the day-to-day operations of the bank. He preferred the role of business statesman and emerged as a prominent spokesman for the American banking industry. The downside of Winthrop's detachment at Chase meant that a cadre of senior officers with more limited views about banking dominated operations and hindered the development of an effective management structure and organization.

THE CHASE CULTURE

It did not take me long to discover that Chase had both enormous strengths and some significant weaknesses. As I saw it, the most serious of the latter were our inadequacies in the field of management and our limited international presence. Although the bank was powerful and influential, in many ways it was still the creature of a much simpler era. We had no budget, no comprehensive business plan, no formal organizational chart—in short we had few of the tools considered essential for the effective management of a large and complicated financial enterprise. I remember going in to see Winthrop and arguing that, given the problems that Chase faced—slow growth and an alarming decline in deposits—a budget was essential because it would help us plan for the future and deploy our assets and personnel more intelligently. Winthrop's response was that the bank had never had a budget, and there was no reason to adopt one now.

The narrow attitudes and predispositions of the Chase officer corps was another problem. Only a few had college degrees. The majority had risen through the ranks, starting as tellers or cashiers. As a group, with some notable exceptions, they lacked a breadth of vision or an awareness of political and economic factors that might affect the bank or their profession. Most Chase officers subscribed to the idea that the "science" of banking—finance, accounting, and arbitrage—could be taught, but the "art" of banking, its real essence, could only be learned through a lengthy apprenticeship that had its origins, as far as I knew, in the time of the Medici. This system had been highly successful in its time; rigorous standards of accounting and credit analysis had always been demanded of our loan officers. However, Chase officers tended to dismiss the newer management disciplines—human resources, planning, marketing, and public relations—as unworthy of the time and attention of credit officers. In the minds of the old guard, who would dominate the bank well into the 1960s, the model officer was a man who made good, profitable loans; everything else was left to those of lesser talent.

$3,500-A-YEAR SUBWAY "STRAPHANGER"

During my first twelve years at Chase, until I became a vice chairman in 1957, I rode to work on the Lexington Avenue subway. Like many of my fellow commuters I became expert at folding the newspaper lengthwise, reading standing up, one arm grasping the strap, while clutching my brief-case between my legs.

In an atmosphere where neither higher education nor management skills were considered important, having a Ph.D. in economics was not something I advertised. It would have seemed effete. However, I did suggest to Winthrop Aldrich that having a Ph.D. in economics meant, at the very least, that I should not be required to take the bank's excellent credit training program, and, unfortunately, he agreed. I was thirty years old and anxious to get going with my career; my head was full of bigger visions than analyzing balance sheets and income statements. It was a decision I regret and certainly paid for later on when I was trying to change the bank's culture. It meant I never spoke the same language as those I was trying to convince. It only increased the conviction of many that I was never a *real* banker anyway.

Graduates of the new credit courses started as clerks and became officers after a year or so—if they performed well. I began as an assistant manager, the lowest officer rank, in the Foreign Department at an annual salary of $3,500. I was assigned to one of twenty or thirty wooden desks in a room that ran the length of the tenth floor of 18 Pine Street. Each desk had two chairs, one on each side, for customers and/or a secretary from the pool. It was here that I spent my first three years at Chase.

Jerome (Packy) Weis, the department's personnel director, guided me through a rotation of the thirty-three geographical and functional units in the Foreign Department. This was my first exposure to the bank's inner workings, and I emerged from it somewhat mystified. I wanted to make sure I understood each unit's role, so I made notes after completing each one. Although I had never had formal training in organization management, I could not understand the wisdom of a structure where thirty-three units reported directly to one person. I proposed as an alternative the clustering of units so that only six or seven managers would report directly to Charles

Cain, the department head. Charlie's reaction was polite (I fear my name caused him to be more so than he might have been otherwise), but no changes were made in the department's structure.

EUROPE: LITTLE MARKETING IMAGINATION

The Foreign Department's main function was maintaining relations with our global network of more than one thousand correspondent banks, all closely linked to our principal business of financing international trade in a number of commodities, such as coffee, sugar, and metals. Chase required these correspondent banks to maintain substantial "compensating balances" with us. These were enormously profitable interest-free deposits that constituted the bulk of our deposit base. Domestic credit officers viewed them as the only valuable aspect of our international business. We did no underwriting of business transactions or financing of mergers and acquisitions.

Although Chase had only a modest network of nine branches scattered across Europe, the Caribbean, and the Far East, Winthrop saw real opportunities for Chase overseas. Indeed, it was one of the things that he had talked to me about during our meeting in Paris in 1945. His enthusiasm for international business was one of the principal reasons I decided to join Chase.

My first assignment in the Foreign Department was the development of "new business" from the affiliates of American corporations for our branches in London and Paris. Although I was still quite innocent of the intricacies of banking, sales was something that I understood. My time with Mayor La Guardia had taught me a few things, and I found that I enjoyed meeting people, talking business with them, and closing the deal.

I worked on the project for about six months with an experienced younger banker named James Watts. We developed a rather impressive list of more than five hundred firms and identified ways to approach them. I then set off for Europe by steamer in July 1947 to put our plan into operation. (In those days you went by boat because air travel had not yet been perfected.) I could have saved the cost of the voyage.

Much of London had been destroyed by the wartime bombing. The British government still found it necessary to ration food and fuel, factories and offices remained closed, and whole neighborhoods had been obliterated by the blitz and "V" bombs. The face of London had changed markedly, but the Chase London branch remained mired in the past. While the country cried out for credit to rebuild, Chase did not pursue corporate lending for fear of offending its British bank clients. Instead, it continued to provide financial market information as a courtesy to visiting executives of American corporations, to engage in routine foreign exchange, and to provide traveler's letters of credit. We continued to serve our customers tea and crumpets while cashing their checks, but our major American competitors actively exploited the new business opportunities, including making loans to the subsidiaries of our principal domestic customers.

The Scotsman who ran the bank's operations viewed my "new business" efforts to get major American companies to open accounts with "his" branch with great skepticism. While I had some modest success in attracting business, the branch manager found my methods unseemly; I drove a rented car to make calls on prospective customers in their offices. In his view, clients always called on a banker in his office if they had business to discuss.

The situation in Paris was worse. Chase had little contact with either U.S. subsidiaries or French corporations. In essence, we were no more than a post office for our American clients. They used our offices at 41, rue Cambon, across the street from the Ritz Bar, as a convenient mailing address. We changed money for them and handled their traveler's letters of credit. The manager, an American who had headed the branch for twenty-five years, never learned to speak French; anyone who needed to see him had to speak English!

With only two European branches, managed by bankers with little imagination and no marketing savvy, Chase's operations clearly required a more aggressive strategy.

LATIN AMERICA: UNTAPPED MARKETS

By the end of 1947 I had become frustrated with the difficulties of trying to coax clients to bank with our London and Paris branches, and asked to be transferred to the Latin American section of the Foreign Department.

Latin America had become a more important area for Chase, just as my own interest in its business, culture, and art had grown. During a second honeymoon right after returning from the war, Peggy and I had traveled through much of Mexico and became fascinated by that country's impressive pre-Conquest culture, turbulent colonial period, and vibrant contemporary spirit.

Nelson's visionary plans to assist Latin America's economic development had also stirred my imagination. After resigning from the State Department in August 1945, Nelson set up two organizations—the not-for-profit American International Association for Economic and Social Development (AIA) and the for-profit International Basic Economy Corporation (IBEC)—to provide technical assistance and financial capital for the economic development and diversification of Venezuela and Brazil.

I was so taken by his plans that I asked my Trust Committee for an invasion of principal so that I could invest a million dollars in IBEC. For many years IBEC was one of my largest personal investments.

=

In 1948, accompanied by Peggy, I made my first business trip to my new territory. We toured the Chase branches in Puerto Rico, Cuba, and Panama, as well as the bank's trade finance operations in Venezuela and Mexico. I discovered that Chase's position and prospects varied a great deal from country to country. We dominated the market in both Panama and the Canal Zone; in Cuba we were major financiers of the sugar crop but did little else; in Puerto Rico our position was insignificant. I returned from this initial tour convinced that Chase could greatly increase the scope of its business. I reported my reactions in a memorandum to Winthrop Aldrich in March 1948. In referring to the Caribbean branches, I wrote:

> My general impression of all three branches is that they have been run in accordance with conservative commercial banking policy, but there has been little overall thinking or philosophy as to what their role should be in the communities where they are situated. . . . It is my impression that there may be ways, if we were to look for them, in which Chase could be constructive positively in helping these countries formulate and carry out programs to raise their standard of living through improved agriculture, more efficient distribution and increased industrialization.

Reading these words more than a half-century after I wrote them, I am amazed at my temerity in criticizing the operations of the bank to its chairman. But there was no doubt about the need to change the way we did business. I noted in the same memo:

> Unquestionably the trend towards nationalism and all that it connotes is on the increase in Latin America. The day has passed when our Latin neighbors will tolerate American institutions on their soil unless those institutions are willing to take an interest in the local economy. I believe it is to our own interest, therefore, as well as others, that Chase

should rethink its policies with respect to Latin America in general and our southern branches in particular.

Much to my surprise, my superiors allowed me to experiment with the variety of services we offered and to expand our Latin American operations.

CATTLE AS COLLATERAL IN PANAMA

P anama seemed an excellent place to begin the process of change. Chase had operated in Panama and the Canal Zone for twenty-five years and held 50 percent of all the bank deposits in the combined areas. We financed shipping tolls through the canal, the export of the sugar and banana crops, and the business of local merchants in Panama City and Colon. However, our deposits far exceeded our loans, and the Panama manager and I agreed that Chase should use a larger share of our local deposits to promote economic growth in Panama.

To begin with, we opened a branch in the isolated western province of Chiriqui in a small town called, coincidentally, David, to provide loans to cattle ranchers. With little access to credit, these ranchers found it impossible to develop their operations, so we initiated the practice of securing our loans with their animals as collateral. I went to David in 1951 for the opening of the branch and took a hand in branding some of our collateral cows with the Chase logo!

By making credit available we enabled the ranchers to expand their businesses, generating some large revenues for the bank and earning Chase a reputation as a foreign bank committed to the well-being of the Panamanian people. As nationalistic passions over the ownership and operation of the canal grew stronger, Chase's willingness to assist in the development of the local economy became important in maintaining our favorable position.

SUGARCANE AND REVOLUTION IN CUBA

C uba, the "Pearl of the Antilles," presented equally alluring opportunities but some very significant dangers in terms of political stability. Since the Spanish-American War, the United States had developed a dominant position in the Cuban economy, which had become heavily dependent on the production of sugarcane and its export to the U.S. market.

While Chase was the lead American bank in financing the sugar crop, sugar exports represented only about 20 percent of the island's commercial business. We had little or no role in the other sectors of the economy—tobacco, mining, or tourism. I believed that Chase should become more broadly based and needed to do it quickly. I came up with a novel proposal, at least for that time. I suggested that we buy into a local Cuban bank with an existing branch system. With head office approval I entered into conversations with the president of the Trust Company of Cuba, the largest and best run of the Cuban banks. Largely for reasons of Cuban national pride, nothing came of our proposal, so as an alternative we opened two more branches in Havana.

It was just as well that we didn't succeed in buying a bank. On January 1, 1959, Fidel Castro overthrew the authoritarian Batista government. Although *The New York Times* described Castro as a "democratic and anti-Communist reformer," things didn't quite work out that way.

Within months Castro had established the first Marxist, pro-Soviet government in the Western Hemisphere. In 1960 he seized $2 billion worth of U.S. property, including all of Chase's branches. Fortunately for us he overlooked the fact that we had an outstanding loan of $10 million to the Cuban government secured by $17 million in U.S. government bonds. In response to the seizure of our branches we sold the collateral and quickly made good our losses. Reportedly, when Castro learned what had happened, he had the president of the central bank summarily executed for his negligence.

"OPERATION BOOTSTRAP" IN PUERTO RICO

In my 1948 memo I described Chase's position in Puerto Rico as "lamentable." Winthrop Aldrich had personally authorized the creation of the branch in 1934, but almost nothing had been done in the intervening years to develop its potential.

Ironically, nationalism—a threat to the bank's operations in most other parts of the world—in this case provided us with a unique opportunity. In 1948, Governor Luis Muñoz Marín, who had led the effort to secure "commonwealth" status for the island, began to implement "Operation Bootstrap," his plan to develop and diversify the island's resources. I viewed this as a ready-made opportunity for Chase to expand its business.

I got to know Muñoz Marín and his able secretary of economic development, Tedoro Moscoso, quite well. Since credit was the key to their development efforts, we introduced a program of lending to private purchasers of government-owned enterprises. For instance, we lent the Ferre brothers a million dollars to acquire a steel plant.

Chase eventually became one of the island's leading "offshore" banks, and after being rebuffed in our effort to acquire Banco Popular, we increased the number of Chase branches on the island and built a handsome building designed by Skidmore Owings and Merrill in Hato Rey as our headquarters.

===

By the end of 1949 the changes we had introduced in the "southern" branches had begun to show strong results. Our traditional correspondent business grew steadily, but so did our new business. In contrast with my experience in Europe, the staff in our Caribbean branches seemed eager to embrace new ideas. One such idea was to hire and promote citizens of the countries in which we operated, which sent an important message to the local community about our intention to be a constructive partner. Hiring qualified local personnel was a policy that Chase would begin to pursue as we expanded aggressively around the world in later decades.

By the early 1950s our branch system in the Caribbean had emerged as the most dynamic part of our overseas operations. I was eager to use our Caribbean strategy—branching, buying into local banks, and expanding into new lending activities—as a model for expansion into other parts of the world, most immediately into the big countries of South America.

EXPANDING IN SOUTH AMERICA

Two years after joining the Latin American section and helping to improve our Caribbean results, I was promoted to vice president and took over responsibility for all our activities in Latin America. As quickly as I could, I embarked on an extensive six-week trip to the major countries of South America to assess the potential that might exist for business expansion.

In those days there was no jet service, so we endured long hours on four-engine turboprop Constellations cruising slowly over the endless Amazonian rain forest and picking our way carefully through the treacherous peaks of the Andean cordillera.

The 1950 trip was in many ways a watershed event in my life. I saw that banking could be a truly creative enterprise—creative in the sense that my old professor Joseph Schumpeter defined the term—and that Latin America was a place where economic development might take hold with spectacular results. Before that trip I had kept Anna Rosenberg's admonition firmly in mind; afterward I found myself fully committed to a career at the Chase.

My traveling companion and guide on that trip, Otto Kreuzer, was an old Chase hand who had spent a good part of his professional life in Latin America. Otto chain-smoked cheap cigars. He lit his first one while he was reading the paper in bed in the morning and continued puffing on them all day long and well into the evening. The smoke was so noxious that I would hang out the window of our car for fresh air as we traveled between meetings. My coughing and hacking and obvious discomfort made no impression on him. Otto simply lit up another cigar.

But Otto knew our operations intimately, and he gave me a thorough introduction to every aspect of our business. In those days each of the South American countries depended on the export of a few major commodities for the preponderance of their foreign exchange earnings. Peru exported cotton, sugar, and copper; Chile, copper and nitrates; Argentina, vast amounts of wheat and beef; Venezuela, petroleum products; Brazil and Colombia, coffee, billions of beans every year.

Chase financed a good portion of this trade by extending short-term letters of credit, usually no longer than three months' duration, to the exporters, who were also clients of our local correspondent banks. While the business was profitable, when demand for these commodities fell and prices dropped, as they did on a regular basis, the bank lost business and revenue. Also, as these economies expanded and relied less heavily on commodities, the bank's income became vulnerable. We needed to expand our product offerings.

Loans to governments emerged as one of a number of new opportunities. Over the years Chase had maintained good relations with the central banks in the countries where we operated, and I thought we could build on those relationships. I recall one instance when I agreed on the spot to the Brazilian finance minister's request for a $30 million short-term loan against the country's coffee crop.

In a more important departure from prior bank practice, I persuaded Chase to participate, along with the U.S. Treasury and the International Monetary Fund, in a $30 million loan to Peru at the request of my old friend Pedro Beltrán, then the president of the Peruvian central bank, to stabilize its currency in the foreign exchange markets. The Peruvians provided no collateral for the loan, but they agreed to adopt a program of fiscal reform laid out by the IMF. This was the first time that a private bank in the United States had cooperated with the IMF in such an arrangement.

While loans to governments could be risky if they were not carefully crafted and well secured, I was convinced that they could provide us with profitable business and open doors to a broader range of private business lending as well. It was no secret that senior officers on the domestic side of the bank viscerally distrusted lending to foreign governments, especially in the lesser developed world. They felt the return was too small and the risk too great. My disagreement with George Champion, then the head of the United States department and a rising power in the bank, on this issue was the beginning of a schism that would widen considerably over time.

AN ATTEMPT TO DEVELOP CAPITAL MARKETS

I learned after only a brief acquaintance with Latin America that economic growth was lagging due to the lack of medium- and long-term credit for equity financing. While there were a few *financieras* that channeled private funds into new enterprises, merchant or investment banks, such as those found in profusion in Europe and the United States, simply did not exist. Except in the field of government bonds, capital markets capable of underwriting security issues were completely absent.

North American and European commercial banks compounded the problem because they rarely extended credit for more than three months, and then only for trade-related activities. It was an area of real frustration for Latin American entrepreneurs who wanted to expand and diversify their businesses but lacked the capital resources to do so. Here was a glittering opportunity for Chase, but we had to find our way around a legal obstacle before we could proceed.

The Glass-Steagall Act of 1933 prohibited U.S. commercial banks from participating in domestic investment banking. They could do so overseas through the provisions of the Edge Act of 1919. Chase had an Edge Act corporation, but we had used it solely as a real estate holding company for our branches in Paris and the Far East. We amended the charter to permit investment banking and created a new subsidiary called Interamericana de Financiamiento e Investimentos, S.A. as a joint venture with IBEC to underwrite and distribute securities within Brazil. I recruited fourteen of our Brazilian correspondent banks to join us as shareholders, and we launched the new company in early 1952.

Interamericana made money during its first two years of operation, but then hit a stagnant period when the Brazilian economy fell into recession. We never recovered our momentum. Pressure built within the home office to cut our losses, and despite my pleas to correct the problems and wait for better days, I lost the fight. In 1956, Chase sold its share of Interamericana to IBEC.

In retrospect I have no doubt that the concept underlying Interamericana was sound, and our Brazilian partners were among the strongest banks in the country. Unfortunately, few at Chase had any interest in or sympathy for the idea. We needed first-rate investment bankers to run it and enough time to prove the idea could work. Even though several bright junior officers were assigned to the project, we never found an experienced senior investment banker to head the operation.

Ironically, after Chase gave up on Interamericana, IBEC converted it into a mutual fund, Fundo Crescinco, the first of its kind in Latin America. Most of our Brazilian partners rolled over their investment into the new company, which proved to be enormously profitable and still exists today. Many of our original Brazilian partners also created their own investment banks, a further indication of the validity of our original concept. Sadly, Chase had fumbled a major opportunity.

THE STRUGGLES WITHIN CHASE

My efforts to get Interamericana launched were among my last activities in the Foreign Department. In September 1952 I was promoted to senior vice president and assigned responsibility for the bank's New York City branches and customer relations.

During my six years in the Foreign Department I saw that radical changes in management structure and style needed to be adopted to enable Chase to be a more aggressive and profitable financial services institution. As I rose through the hierarchy, from assistant manager to vice president, I was able to implement some changes, but as a relatively young officer in a department of secondary importance, I did not have the clout needed to make a broader impact in any of the areas that I thought were fundamentally important. Furthermore, among old-line officers in both the domestic and international areas, I sensed some resistance to the changes I proposed and concern about the role I was playing in the bank.

My introduction to international banking had been eventful, replete with a number of successes and some failures. But it would take a full decade more before my concerns about international expansion and a more sophisticated professional management and organizational structure began to be accepted.

CHAPTER 11

LAUNCHING A
PARALLEL CAREER

I had other responsibilities beyond Chase that claimed my attention after the war. The most important of these were my wife and children, and the affairs of the Rockefeller family, particularly in the areas of international relations, urban affairs, culture, and education. Over time, each of these areas would become of intense importance to me, consuming an expanding portion of time and creating what can only be called a "parallel career."

ESTABLISHING A HOME LIFE

My first and most important challenge was to reconnect with my wife and children. I made a start by establishing a permanent home in New York where they would feel secure after my wanderings and the uncertainties of the war years.

During the war Peggy had found an apartment on Fifth Avenue, and they were living there upon my return. Peggy, our fourth child and third daughter, was born there in October 1947. She was the first of three children who came to be known as Series B. Richard ("Dick," as we always called him, named for my dear friend Dick Gilder) and Eileen followed at two-year intervals. Even with three children it became clear that we would have to move.

Peggy found a house on East 65th Street that fit our needs perfectly. It had enough rooms to accommodate our growing family and a friendly atmosphere, almost like a country house; it featured a large living room with eighteenth-century English pine paneling and a small, cozy garden at the rear. We bought it in mid-1948, and it would be our New York City home for the rest of the century.

On weekends we took the children to Pocantico Hills, first to the Stevens House inside the walls of the estate, but within a short time we took them to our own home. My sister Babs, recently divorced, decided to leave the beautiful redbrick Georgian House just outside the Pocantico Estate, designed for her in 1938 by Mott Schmitt, and move to Oyster Bay, Long Island. Knowing that we wanted a larger country home, Mother persuaded Babs to sell us the house. Hudson Pines, as we named it, was located across a public road from the family estate. It included forty acres of land, a caretaker's house, a stable, flower and vegetable gardens, and some barns—just what we were looking for in a country place.

Peggy and I also established a base on the coast of Maine for our summer home. My childhood summers had been spent in the Eyrie on Mount Desert Island, and it was there that I learned to sail and developed a deep interest in nature. I wanted my children to have the same exposure. Peggy had been there with me to visit my parents several times before the war, and she shared my love of the mountains and coastal islands. We were delighted when my parents offered us the use of Westward Cottage, a simple white New England frame house close to the ocean. When Father realized we were happy there, he generously gave us the house.

MAKING ENDS MEET

The only real drawback to acquiring three homes in one year was that we needed a considerable amount of furniture for three rather large houses. This presented a serious financial challenge since I had no capital of my own and was dependent on the income from the trust that Father had established for me in 1934, which in 1946 amounted to slightly more than $1 million before taxes.

The operative phrase was "before taxes." During the war the tax rate on incomes of more than a million dollars increased to nearly 90 percent—in my case exactly $758,000 in 1946—after first deducting charitable contributions of $153,000. As a result I was left with less than $150,000 in discretionary income. So even with a gross income of a million dollars, what I was left with in terms of spendable funds was clearly modest.

Both Peggy and I had been brought up to be economical in our expenditures, but we both wanted the things we owned to be of good quality. By good fortune, soon after the war we met Cecil Turner, an English dealer who had started the Antique Dealers Fair in London's Dorchester Hotel. Cecil understood our budgetary limitations but was impressed with our insistence on furnishings of good quality. He took us under his wing and taught us to recognize quality and to spot fakes. Over the years he helped us buy many fine pieces of eighteenth-century English furniture at prices we could afford.

Our zest for antiques extended also to porcelain, silver, and glass, a taste that had been encouraged by my mother and Aunt Lucy, both ardent connoisseurs and collectors. Perhaps it was just as well, at least for the sake of our pocketbook, that it was not until we had completed the furnishing of our homes that we became interested in French Impressionist and Post-Impressionist paintings.

Thanks to Peggy's considerable talents, good taste, and thrift, we managed to furnish our homes without ever using an interior decorator. Peggy obtained a decorator's license, enabling her to buy furnishings at a 30 percent discount. Peggy's first chance to develop her skills as a decorator had occurred right after our marriage when Father told her that he would pay for the furnishing and decoration of the Stevens House if she would be responsible for doing it. Within a short time she had shopped around to find attractive furniture, rugs, and draperies at wholesale prices. To Father's amazement and admiration Peggy had bought everything needed for $5,000! Over the years Peggy made our homes cozy and inviting. As our financial resources increased, I like to feel they had style and elegance as well.

ORGANIZING AS BROTHERS

In early 1946, when all five brothers returned to New York to pick up the threads of our lives, Father was still the overlord of the Family Office, the acknowledged moral leader of the many Rockefeller philanthropies, and master of the substantial family fortune. It soon became apparent that the brothers needed to present a united front in dealing with Father if the process of generational transition was to move forward more swiftly and in harmony with our vision for the future.

Nelson had taken the initiative before the war in organizing our generation. He suggested we meet on a regular basis to talk about our careers as well as to explore how we might work together on issues of common interest. At the outset we met every two months or so, often at the Playhouse in Pocantico but sometimes at one of our homes.

The brothers' meetings served a practical purpose both in managing family affairs more efficiently and in giving us a chance to keep in touch with one another on a more personal level. The five of us had widely diverging and, in some ways, conflicting interests, but largely because of these regular get-togethers we maintained a basic respect and affection for one another, something that has not always been the case with other wealthy families.

We asked Abby to join us, but she wasn't interested. We also asked Father to sit in with us, but he also declined. He seemed uncomfortable, almost threatened, by the prospect of facing all of his sons at the same time, perhaps out of concern that we might confront him with unanimous decisions with which he disagreed. Mother would have enjoyed the experience, but I think she felt awkward joining us when Father had declined our invitation. So she, too, declined, leaving us to meet by ourselves.

My brothers unanimously elected me secretary of the group, responsible for keeping minutes, since I was the youngest and "the only Ph.D." I retained that position during the thirty-eight years that we held the meetings. In later years our divergent careers and busy schedules made regular meetings impossible, but there was never a year when we didn't meet at least twice.

We began meeting in 1940 and initially did little more than bring one another up to date on our individual activities and plans. We soon decided, however, that philanthropy was an area in which closer cooperation could be beneficial. Each of us received annual requests from a number of charitable organizations, and each tended to respond differently depending on our inclinations and financial resources. We decided it would be more efficient and effective to pool our gifts to organizations such as the United Jewish Appeal, Catholic Charities, the Federation of Protestant Welfare Agencies, the United Hospital Fund, the Red Cross, and the United Negro College Fund. The result was the incorporation of the Rockefeller Brothers Fund (RBF) in late 1940. For the first twelve years of its existence the RBF had no endowment. Instead, each of us made annual contributions proportional to our income. Arthur Packard, Father's senior philanthropic advisor, served as director and helped us determine the allocation of funds.

A decade later our individual annual contributions to the RBF had grown to the point that we were able to support organizations which individual brothers had initiated or in which one of us had a special interest. Nelson, for example, had created the American International Association (AIA) to provide rural credit and advice to farmers in Brazil and other South American countries, similar to the U.S. government's agricultural extension programs. RBF became a substantial funder of this effort. John was deeply concerned about the dangers of escalating world population growth long before most people recognized the urgency of this critical issue. The RBF provided crucial support to John's Population Council during the early years of its work. Over time, the fund provided us with the opportunity to work together and to forge a philanthropic philosophy that reflected our generation's values and objectives.

BUYING ROCKEFELLER CENTER FROM FATHER

N o subject loomed larger in our meetings after the war than the future of Rockefeller Center. During the first eighteen years of its operation, the property had not generated enough revenue to fully cover interest and taxes, let alone amortize the debt owed to the Metropolitan Life Insurance Company and to Father. After construction was completed in the mid-1930s, Father had covered the Center's operating deficit for almost a decade. Through the end of 1944, Father had invested a total of $120 million: $55 million in common stock and another $65 million in interest-free notes. As a result the common stock, all of which Father owned, was worth very little.

Nevertheless, Nelson, who had served as president of the Center for a few years prior to the war, saw great long-term potential in the property. He was convinced that once the debt was paid off, it would be an increasingly valuable asset. He encouraged the brothers to take advantage of the "great opportunity" he saw by asking Father to sell us the Center's common stock. With our concurrence Nelson pressed Father on the matter, and while Father saw merit in his arguments, he explained that he was not a totally free agent. Before he could sell his stock, he had to obtain the permission of both Columbia University, which was the landlord, and Metropolitan Life, the principal debt holder. Met Life readily agreed, but the university gave its consent only after the terms of the lease were modified to incorporate iron-clad guarantees that the lease payments would be made and that the common stock could not be sold to anyone outside the family. An additional provision stipulated that no dividends could be paid so long as any of the original debt remained outstanding. My brothers and I agreed to these stiff conditions because we believed the long-term financial future of the Center was bright. However, some of these restrictive lease covenants would continue to limit the Center's flexibility and marketability as long as Columbia remained the landlord.

In 1948, after ironing out these complexities, Father sold us his Rockefeller Center stock for its appraised value of $2,200,000. The five of us acquired ownership of the Center with its eleven fully occupied buildings in a prime location for $440,000 apiece. Taking ownership of the company, however, meant assuming its debt of $80 million: $20 million still owed to Met Life and $60 million to Father. In 1950 we repaid the final portion of the Met Life loan, and the following year we made a payment of $2 million on the debt to Father.

How to deal with the remaining debt generated a good deal of intra-family tension before it was finally resolved. Father was seventy-eight in 1952, and his health, never robust, had begun to decline. His lawyers became increasingly concerned about the impact that holding the Center's notes would have on his estate. Shortly after we purchased the common stock, Nelson proposed that Father forgive the indebtedness so we could free up the funds needed to modernize and possibly expand the Center. Father countered by pointing out that this would oblige him to pay $26 million in gift taxes, so he declined. Since canceling the debt was not feasible, we proposed that Father give the notes to the RBF, which badly needed an endowment. In fact, Nelson felt so strongly about this that he threatened to resign as chairman of the Center if Father did not agree with our proposal. Father eventually yielded and gave the notes to the RBF. In so doing he effectively ended his financial involvement with Rockefeller Center, leaving its management entirely in our hands.

Father's contribution of $57.7 million to the RBF had great significance for my generation. As the Center paid down the debt over the next seventeen years, the RBF gradually built up an endowment enabling it to support new initiatives that had not been possible previously. The Rockefeller Brothers Fund emerged as my generation's most significant joint philanthropic endeavor, and it was the principal vehicle for our support of groups in fields such as population, conservation, economic development, urban affairs, and basic scientific research.

Rockefeller Center would become an increasingly valuable investment not only for my brothers and me but also for our heirs. For Father, however, the venture had been almost a total financial loss. All told he invested $55 million in common stock and $65 million in personal notes. (This does not take into account the "opportunity cost" of financing these obligations by selling securities, primarily oil stocks, at rock-bottom prices during the Depression.) On a total investment of $120 million he received $2.2 million for the common stock and was repaid only $7.5 million on the notes. Few people realize that despite the long-term benefits produced for his descendants, Father sustained a direct loss of more than $110 million as a result of his courageous decision to proceed with the building of Rockefeller Center during the Depression.

BUYING THE POCANTICO ESTATE

Another important topic of discussion at the brothers' meetings was the future of the 3,300-acre Pocantico estate. By the late 1940s the tax consequences of property transfers had become quite costly, and steps had to be taken to deal with Father's potential estate problems.

Nelson, without informing any of his brothers, approached Father about selling the Pocantico property to us. Father was somewhat reluctant to do this because he had been responsible for the design and construction of Kykuit when he was a young man and had supervised the development of the property into one of the most beautiful estates in the country. Understandably, he was not keen on giving up control of a property that had meant so much to him for the better part of his life. However, Nelson then implied that if he refused to sell, none of us would be interested in remaining on the estate. That was stretching the truth by quite a bit, but Father, faced with what he thought was an ultimatum from his sons, agreed to the immediate sale.

In January 1951, Father formed the Hills Realty Company and folded the entire estate into it, taking back stock valued at $700,000 in return. The following year he sold all the Hills stock to the five of us, retaining a life interest for himself—a reasonable compromise from my point of view. Each brother paid just over $152,000 for a one-fifth undivided ownership in the full estate.

RESTRUCTURING FAMILY HOLDINGS

High personal and corporate income tax rates forced my brothers and me to find sensible ways to restructure our major holdings in order to generate more income and increase their capital value. Rockefeller Center was our largest single asset, so our primary objective was to eliminate its divided ownership whereby Columbia owned the land and my brothers and I the buildings. A few months after our purchase of the common stock we asked William Zeckendorf, the principal in the Webb & Knapp real estate firm, to examine our options. Bill suggested that we create a new corporation to purchase both the land and the buildings, which would amortize the debt over a period of twenty-five years. When we approached Columbia with this proposal they turned it down cold.

Bill then suggested restructuring the Center's finances to take advantage of the favorable tax treatment of real estate income. His point was that real estate corporations—companies that earned more than 50 percent of their income from rent and related sources—paid taxes at the 7 percent level, whereas all other corporations were subject to a 50 percent tax on their net earnings. The Center's earnings had grown steadily since we had bought it, almost doubling to $1.9 million in 1952. Bill emphasized that we could almost match that amount with income from securities and still qualify for the lowest corporate tax rate.

But there was a major problem. The Columbia lease did much more than establish the annual ground rent; it literally governed all aspects of the Center's financial structure and prohibited us from making logical and sensible changes in the corporation's financial structure. For instance, we had to maintain $14 million in U.S. government bonds in an escrow account at all times to guarantee payment of the rent, and the Center's working capital fund had to be kept at a level of $30 million, of which no more than 25 percent could be invested in stocks. This meant that more than 90 percent of the Center's investment portfolio *had* to be invested in low-yield government bonds, returning less than 2 percent interest a year.

If the Center was ever to generate the higher returns it needed to finance capital improvements and pay down debt, we had to persuade Columbia to modify these anachronistic and punitive provisions in the lease.

Columbia's lawyers and accountants saw our point—that an expanding and more profitable Rockefeller Center would be as valuable to the university as it was to our family. They agreed to remove the restrictions on both the escrow account and the working capital fund, but only in return for a substantial increase in rent. We began the new investment program in early 1953, just before a period of enormous appreciation in stock values. Our strategy and timing proved to be excellent.

===

Hills Realty posed an entirely different challenge. The company's only income came from securities we had added to its portfolio to cover the cost of maintaining the Pocantico estate. We could only benefit from the 7 percent corporate tax rate if we added income-producing real estate assets. In order to achieve this result, we borrowed money through Hills to acquire an interest in the Carlyle Hotel in Manhattan, which we later swapped for a much larger stake in the Moorestown Shopping Center and an industrial park in Edison, New Jersey. Eventually we also added the ground lease for the Parke-Bernet auction gallery on the Upper East Side. The income from these properties generated significant revenue, which was offset against the returns from Hills's stock market securities. This ingenious use of the tax code allowed us to mitigate the high levels of personal and corporate taxes we paid on other sources of income during this period.

A TRADITION OF PHILANTHROPY

The Rockefeller philanthropic tradition was simple and unadorned. It required that we be generous with our financial resources and involve ourselves actively in the affairs of our community and the nation. This was the doctrine of stewardship that Father himself had learned as a young man and had carefully taught us. We had been greatly blessed as a family, and it was our obligation to give something back to our society.

Although Father hoped each of us would become involved with one or more of the organizations with close family connections, we were also free to pursue our own interests. I was drawn to the work of educational and cultural institutions, especially the University of Chicago, the Rockefeller Institute for Medical Research, and the Museum of Modern Art. My travels during the 1930s and my experience during the war had sharpened my awareness of international affairs, which I would develop through active involvement with the Council on Foreign Relations, the Carnegie Endowment for International Peace, and International House of New York. Finally, working with Mayor La Guardia had kindled a deep interest in the complexity of urban life that would now be expressed through service on the Westchester County Planning Commission and a lead role in creating Morningside Heights, Inc., one of the first private efforts in the United States to deal with the problem of urban decline and renewal.

REINVENTING THE ROCKEFELLER UNIVERSITY

My first exposure to the management of an educational institution came on the board of the Rockefeller Institute for Medical Research. Father had been the driving force in the creation and expansion of the institute that Grandfather had created in 1901, and in the late 1940s he still served as the president of its seven-member board of trustees. Father took great pride in the pioneering work of the institute's scientists in the fields of biology, pathology, and physiology and in the practical impact their research had on the treatment of infectious diseases such as yellow fever, syphilis, and pneumonia.

Father supported the institute's fundamental mission, the pursuit of scientific knowledge, even more strongly. He understood that basic research in the biological sciences had to come first and that direct applications would follow inevitably. The seminal work of Peyton Rous in uncovering the viral origins of cancer; the efforts of Albert Claude, Keith Porter, and George Palade in mapping cell structure and function; and the discovery by Oswald Avery, Colin MacLeod, and Maclyn McCarty that DNA carries genetic information were the real measure of the Rockefeller Institute. These advances had transformed the nature of scientific inquiry and medical practice, and fulfilled the mission that Grandfather and Father had in mind when they established it in 1901.

Despite its rich history, the institute stood at a crossroads in the late 1940s. There were tough questions about its leadership, scientific mission, and funding. Father planned to retire in 1950, and the director, Dr. Herbert Gasser, a Nobel Prize–winning neurobiologist, would follow him a few years later. Father assumed that my brother John, who had long served as a trustee, would succeed him in the top board leadership position. But in early 1946, John decided to resign from the board to concentrate on the Williamsburg Restoration and the Rockefeller Foundation. It then became clear that I would have to carry on the tradition of family responsibility for this vital research organization.

When I succeeded Father in 1950, the first thing we needed to do was determine how and, even more basically, whether the institute should survive. There were a few on the board who actually favored closing down the institute since its original mission had been largely achieved. For me that was not an option. But we needed to determine what specific role the institute should play within the field of biomedicine.

Funding was also an important issue. Grandfather had endowed the institute, and Father had added money and land for expansion. The portfolio had been well managed and appreciated over the years to about $100 million in 1950. In order to preserve its complete independence, however, the institute had never accepted funds from government or even other private sources because Father thought this would lessen the independence of the researchers in carrying on the work they thought important. As a result, by the mid-1930s, expenses had overtaken income, forcing staff reductions and negatively affecting the scope of research. Without a policy change permitting us to seek new sources of revenue, the institute risked becoming a distinctly second-rank organization.

We needed a comprehensive evaluation of the institute, and at my instigation the trustees asked Dr. Detlev Bronk, president of Johns Hopkins

University and the chairman of the National Academy of Sciences, who was also a member of the institute's board of scientific directors, to chair a committee to provide it. Bronk, a physiologist and biophysicist with a sterling reputation, believed in the critical role of independent scientific inquiry and admired the institute's pioneering work. But he and the other members of the committee, including me, agreed that changes were needed if the institute was to survive in a more competitive and challenging environment.

The Bronk committee spent a year reviewing the institute's scientific work and its financial and physical resources. We consulted with scores of leading scientists and educators from around the world. Our review concluded that the time for a completely freestanding research institute had passed and that we needed to supplement our basic research with a strong educational component and increase our contacts with the outside world.

For fifty years the institute had been operated as a community of like-minded scholars. The head of each autonomous laboratory was free to pursue his scientific inquiries in his own way, subject only to the canons of his discipline and the review of his peers. That system, which the great physicist Niels Bohr referred to as the "Republic of Science," had worked well in the past, and none of us, particularly Det Bronk, wanted to infringe upon scientific freedom. However, that freedom had to be balanced to a degree with the need for stronger centralized direction, greater collaboration, and an awareness of financial reality.

Bronk was the prime mover on the committee. As our study moved forward, there was a growing feeling that he would be the best successor to Dr. Gasser. In the end, with the board's enthusiastic support, I persuaded Bronk to leave his post at Hopkins to become the new director of the Rockefeller Institute with a mandate to introduce the reforms that had been proposed.

Bronk's assumption of the directorship in 1953 became, in effect, the "second founding" of the institute. His principal task was to transform a research institute into a biomedical graduate university. He started on the transition process almost immediately. In late 1953 the trustees voted to incorporate under the laws of the State of New York as a graduate university empowered to grant both Ph.D. and M.D. degrees. At the same time we merged the board of scientific advisors with the board of trustees. This group appointed Bronk president, and I became the chairman. We received our new charter in 1954 but did not formally change the name to The Rockefeller University until 1965, more out of sentimental attachment than anything else.

Bronk also moved quickly to broaden the range of disciplines represented on campus by inviting mathematicians, experimental and theoretical physicists, psychologists, and even a small number of philosophers to join the faculty. The independent laboratory system was maintained, but academic ranks were introduced and the former title "member of the institute" was exchanged, often reluctantly, for the more pedestrian "professor."

We admitted the first group of ten graduate students in 1955. In keeping with the institute's long tradition, they worked closely in the laboratory of a senior scientist, learning firsthand the essentials of the discipline. Throughout his tenure Bronk insisted on personally interviewing all candidates for admission and insisted on the highest standards of excellence.

All of these changes required additional funding, and Bronk proved to be quite adept at finding new sources of revenue. He had played a seminal role during both the Truman and Eisenhower administrations in creating the National Institutes of Health and the National Science Foundation. Both agencies emerged as significant funders of scientific research in the United States, and a significant portion of their annual budgets flowed into the university beginning in the late 1950s.

During this time Bronk and I worked closely to expand the university's physical plant. We added a nine-story laboratory building, a residence hall for graduate students and postdoctoral fellows, an auditorium, and a beautiful international-style residence for the president, designed by my friend Wallace K. Harrison.

My tenure as chairman, which ended in 1975, embraced a dramatic period of scientific progress in the field of biology—the genetic revolution—unleashed by the discovery that genes were composed of DNA. This discovery, as medical historian Lewis Thomas has written, "opened the way into the biological revolution which continues to transform our view of nature."

Today, its mission refined, its governance restructured, and its finances reinvigorated, The Rockefeller University continues to play a pivotal role in harnessing science and technology to search for answers to life's most perplexing health-related questions. Our reinvention of the institute in the early 1950s was the essential first step in this process and one in which I am quite proud to have played a part.

ALGER HISS AND THE CARNEGIE ENDOWMENT

I was still an assistant manager in Chase's Foreign Department when I received a visit one morning in early spring 1947 from the new president of the Carnegie Endowment for International Peace. Alger Hiss was a tall, lanky man with a handsome chiseled face. He had an agreeable manner, was gracious and charming, and I liked him immediately. After the usual pleasantries Hiss told me I had been elected to the board of the Carnegie Endowment, and he hoped I would agree to serve.

The endowment was established by Andrew Carnegie in 1910 to pursue his interest in the prevention of war and the creation of an effective system of international law. Nicholas Murray Butler, president of Columbia University and a Nobel Peace Prize laureate, had led the endowment for twenty years and made it one of America's most respected foundations. Butler had just retired, and Hiss had been chosen as his successor.

Hiss had had an impressive career for such a young man. A graduate of Harvard Law, he had studied under Felix Frankfurter and then clerked at the Supreme Court for Oliver Wendell Holmes. During the New Deal he served in both the Department of Agriculture and the Justice Department before shifting over to the State Department. He remained at State until the end of World War II and traveled with the American delegation to the Yalta Conference—a fact that would cause considerable consternation when he was later accused of being a Soviet spy.

I was flattered to be asked to join the endowment's prestigious board, which included such luminaries as General Dwight D. Eisenhower and Thomas J. Watson, the founder of IBM. John Foster Dulles, the eminent international lawyer, was chairman, and it was to him that I attributed my selection because I had known him and his family since my college years. Foster had a reputation for being cold, austere, and puritanical, but the man I knew had a good sense of humor and could be a wonderful companion. His daughter Lillias had been part of a small group of friends during my college days and one of Peggy's closest friends. In fact, when I was courting Peggy in the late 1930s, she always stayed with the Dulleses at their New York town house.

When I mentioned Hiss's offer to Nelson, he told me in confidence that a high-level FBI official had warned him there was reliable information indicating that Hiss was a Soviet agent. I reported this to Foster, who said he didn't believe it. Given Dulles's prestige, experience, and reputation as a strong anticommunist, I accepted his judgment and joined the endowment's board in May 1947. A year later the spy charges against Alger Hiss would become front-page news.

At the time, the board members of the endowment were preoccupied with the mundane issues of program and physical location. In fact, the board meetings were devoted to contentious debates about moving our headquarters from New York to Washington and whether we should rent or build. We finally agreed to remain in New York—*where* in New York was the issue.

I turned to Bill Zeckendorf, and he offered us one of the building sites he had acquired on the west side of First Avenue, across from where the new U.N. building would be erected. Although the area was still filled with abandoned slaughterhouses and decaying commercial buildings, Bill felt the U.N. and other related projects would permanently transform the area. He recommended that we buy the parcel before land values skyrocketed and then put up our own building.

Several of the more conservative board members thought the plan far too risky and criticized spending the endowment's limited funds on a construction project in an unproven location. The endowment's longtime treasurer opposed the project and resigned from the board, predicting it would bankrupt us. However, a strong majority of the board backed the proposal, especially after I was able to persuade Winthrop Aldrich to open a Chase branch on the ground floor. Once the building was completed, we rented much of the building to not-for-profits and easily handled the mortgage payments. As Bill Zeckendorf predicted, the area around the U.N. quickly became one of New York's prime neighborhoods and continues to be so to this day.

AN EVENING WITH ALGER

The allegations against Hiss first surfaced publicly in August 1948. In testimony before the House Un-American Activities Committee, Whittaker Chambers, a former editor of *Time* magazine as well as an admitted former Communist, identified Hiss as a member of his party cell during the mid-1930s and a participant in a Soviet spy ring. When Chambers repeated these accusations outside the halls of Congress, Hiss sued him for libel and set the stage for a courtroom drama that preoccupied the country for years. A few months after Chambers's accusations, the Carnegie board assembled for the most awkward dinner I have ever attended. When Alger arrived, the atmosphere grew tense, and when we sat down to eat, the chairs on either side of him were not filled. Embarrassed by what was happening, I sat on his right, and Harvey Bundy took the chair on his left. William Marshall Bullitt, an outspoken, choleric lawyer from Louisville, Kentucky, sat on my right. Bullitt was elderly and very deaf, and provided a running commentary during dinner in a loud voice as to why Hiss was a traitor and should immediately be fired from the endowment. I leaned forward, trying vainly to shield Alger from the verbal barrage, but Bullitt's insistent voice penetrated every corner of the room.

After dinner Alger excused himself so that the board could discuss its agenda for the following day, including the matter of his continuing employment. We were polled one by one, and the vote was unanimously in favor of firing Hiss immediately, until it was my turn to vote. I disagreed, saying that while the accusations were heinous, they were still only accusations. Until Hiss was found guilty, it was incumbent upon us to treat him as an innocent man. I suggested that it would be appropriate to ask him to take a leave of absence, since he couldn't function effectively at the endowment under the circumstances. Tom Watson and others supported my position, and in the end the board compromised by offering Alger a paid leave of absence, which he accepted.

The Hiss-Chambers case dragged on into 1949, when Hiss was convicted not of espionage, but of perjury in denying before Congress that he knew Whittaker Chambers. Hiss denied until the day of his death in 1996 that he was a Soviet spy, and his supporters continue to maintain his innocence. Once the evidence was all in, it appeared to me that he was a Soviet agent.

On the other hand it was also evident that opportunistic politicians were using the Hiss case to attack the New Deal and to oppose a stronger international role for the United States by claiming that Communists had infiltrated the federal government as part of a massive "international conspiracy." The emotions stirred up by the Hiss case marked the emergence of a dangerous tendency in our political life. Since then, both the left and the right have routinely demonized individuals and carelessly attacked our governmental institutions in an effort to impose their own rigid and intemperate ideological views on the rest of us. In time I would emerge as a favorite target of both extremes.

RECRUITING A PERSONAL STAFF

It was not long before I realized I needed help in dealing with my many outside involvements. For a few years after the war the Family Office, financed almost completely by Father, handled these relationships. In addition to legal, accounting, and investment services, a staff of twenty people managed a vast array of civic and not-for-profit involvements for me and my siblings. Arthur Packard, Father's philanthropic advisor, and his young assistant, Dana Creel, helped with my not-for-profit activities, but they were not an adequate substitute for a personal staff.

In 1947 I hired Eleanor Wilkerson as my personal secretary. She was an expert stenographer and skillful in arranging social functions and dealing with all manner of complex situations. Eleanor was a pillar of strength for the next three decades and worked closely with Edna Bruderle, my bank secretary, to keep my schedule under control. These two remarkable women were well organized and efficient, and handled people with sensitivity and tact.

In 1951 I decided to add a personal assistant to manage my growing philanthropic interests. After a brief search I turned to a colleague from my Army days in Paris, Warren Lindquist. After the war Lindy had worked at the Chase for five years before taking a job as an assistant to R. Peter Grace, chairman of W. R. Grace and Company.

Lindy helped me with Rockefeller University, the Carnegie Endowment, International House, and a host of other involvements. He took charge of my correspondence and scheduling, and strategized with me on my role in various organizations. Lindy later played a central role in guiding my substantial personal real estate investments. As Lindy became more fully occupied with real estate matters and the scale of my personal involvements and responsibilities increased, I hired additional staff. Richard Dana and DeVaux Smith were longtime friends, and I had also served with them during the war in Europe. John (Jack) Blum, a young Milbank, Tweed lawyer assigned to the Family Office, assisted Lindy in his work.

I gave my associates considerable independence, although we consulted on a regular basis. All of them and their successors—Richard E. Salomon, John B. Davies, Jr., Alice Victor, Patricia Smalley, Christopher Kennan, Peter J. Johnson, and Marnie S. Pillsbury—handled their responsibilities with great tenacity and intelligence. They extended my reach and influence dramatically. Without them I could never have balanced my work at Chase with my "parallel career."

CHAPTER 12

BUILDING THE CHASE
MANHATTAN BANK

On January 19, 1953, John J. McCloy succeeded Winthrop Aldrich as chairman of the Chase National Bank. In many ways Jack was an unusual choice to head one of the country's largest commercial banks. Like Winthrop, Jack had been trained as a lawyer, not a banker. He had been a partner at Cravath, Henderson and de Gersdorff, Wall Street's most powerful firm, for more than a decade before World War II and had worked closely with a number of investment banks and large corporations. Right after the war he became a name partner in another of the Street's prestigious firms, Milbank, Tweed, Hope, Hadley & McCloy, which numbered among its clients both the Chase National Bank and my family. However, during his many years as a practicing lawyer Jack had no direct experience with the highly specialized world of commercial banking.

Obviously, in making their choice the Chase board had looked beyond Jack's limited banking background to his distinguished public service career. He had entered government service in 1940 as a special assistant to Secretary of War Henry L. Stimson and became an assistant secretary the following year. He served in that capacity for the remainder of the war and emerged as a key member of President Roosevelt's circle of advisors.

In late February 1947, Jack assumed the presidency of the World Bank, a post he held for more than two years, until his appointment as the U.S. High Commissioner for Occupied Germany. Working closely with Chancellor Konrad Adenauer, Jack presided over the creation of the West German state, its rearming, and its inclusion in the Western Alliance. His tenure proved to be a great success, and he returned to the United States in July 1952 a well-known and deeply respected figure.

Although Jack had never made a loan or analyzed a balance sheet, he had enormous prestige and was a great natural leader—qualities that suggested he would understand how to manage a large organization like the Chase. His appointment as chairman gave encouragement to those of us who had been working toward an expanded international program for the bank.

A CURIOUS RELATIONSHIP

Given the similarity in our interests, I was disappointed that Jack and I never developed a close personal relationship. That may have been the result of the great differences in our early lives and a peculiar episode in Jack's that seems to have scarred him for life.

Jack was born, as he often recalled, on "the wrong side of the tracks" in Philadelphia. His father died when he was quite young, and it was only by dint of hard work and exceptional ability that he made his way through Amherst College and Harvard Law School, and on to a distinguished career.

Despite his own great achievements, Jack seemed wary, perhaps even resentful, of what I appeared to represent in financial and social terms. Frequently at gatherings I attended, Jack related the story of his first contact with my family. He had worked his way through college and law school in part by tutoring during the summer and had traveled to Maine in the summer of 1912, three years before I was born, hoping to get a job on Mount Desert Island. One of the families he decided to contact was mine. Jack always imparted the story at great length—walking the quarter mile from the main road up to the Eyrie, knocking on the massive door, and explaining to the butler why he was there, only to be turned away with the explanation that a tutor had already been hired for the Rockefeller children that summer. And that ended the story. I confess that I never understood the significance he attributed to it. Making an unannounced call didn't seem to be the best way to go about securing a summer job, and Father, in fact, always arranged for tutors and other summer companions months before we moved to Seal Harbor.

Jack must have told the story in my presence a hundred times, the last time in 1985 when I succeeded him as chairman of the Council on Foreign Relations. The story always made me feel uncomfortable.

Jack's inability to resist retelling this anecdote demonstrated ambivalence toward me and my family, maybe even latent hostility. His feeling was probably deepened by a comment Nelson was said to have made to him at the time he became chairman of Chase. Nelson reportedly told him the "family had used its influence" to make him chairman and that one of his jobs was to ensure that "David would succeed him when he retired." It seems quite possible that Nelson made the comment or one quite similar to it. He could be quite high-handed and no doubt thought he was doing me a favor. But if Nelson did make a statement of this kind, it certainly was not the result of a family decision or a request from me. It would have been highly inappropriate for anyone in the family to make such a demand. Unfortunately, *if* the story was true, it may have permanently altered Jack's attitude toward me.

In any event, Jack's ambivalence may have been a factor in his refusal to play a more decisive role with the directors of the bank in selecting his successor in 1959. His indecisiveness, whatever its cause, would have profound consequences for me personally and for the bank. Quite possibly Jack could never look at me without remembering the long, dusty walk up the hill in Seal Harbor and the big wooden door being closed quietly but firmly in his face.

MODERNIZING BANK MANAGEMENT

The longer I worked at Chase, the more uncomfortable I became with its antiquated management structure. While our basic lending business was well handled, there were severe shortcomings in most other areas: decentralized management with many autonomous fiefdoms, inadequate personnel administration, and no budget and/or business plan. Any management consultant would have been appalled, but we refused to let any of them in the door.

In the summer of 1952, just before I took over as head of the New York City District, Kenneth C. Bell, a vice president with similar views, and I began to assemble information on this issue. Although assessing the bank's organization had nothing to do with our jobs—or anyone else, as far as we could tell—we wanted to see whether we could suggest a more efficient and rational structure. Our research turned up some startling and even alarming facts. For example, the directors of the nine geographical "districts," which handled corporate business around the country as well as all the heads of our twenty-nine domestic branches, reported directly to the president of the bank. Few apparently ever received instructions or oversight from him. They operated as they pleased. On paper, Chase had a highly centralized structure; in reality, clear-cut responsibility and accountability did not exist.

Taking these astounding facts into account, my colleague and I designed a simplified structure that reorganized the bank along functional lines. We kept our conclusions private, preferring to wait for a favorable moment to bring our organizational proposals forward.

COLLISION COURSE

I had been moving up quite rapidly in the bank, as had George Champion. George was eleven years my senior and had graduated from Dartmouth in 1926 where he had been an all-star football player. He joined the Equitable Trust Company right after college and came to Chase through the merger. Over the course of the 1930s and 1940s, George had become one of the bank's most outstanding lending officers. Corporate customers and bankers across the country respected his skills and business acumen, and were glad to do business with him. He was an ardent golfer and enjoyed a hearty good time at the nineteenth hole as well! George was named head of the Commercial Banking Department, the bank's most important unit, in 1949.

It became increasingly apparent to many that George and I were on a collision course, both seeing ourselves headed for the chairmanship of the bank.

The moment of truth for our reorganization plan came in September 1952 when President Percy Ebbott called me into his office to tell me that he was promoting me to senior vice president. He talked in vague terms about my responsibilities, which would be related to the branch system in New York. Percy's description was so obscure and nebulous that I frankly had no idea what I was expected to do or how I would relate to the other parts of the bank. I thought the time was right to bring up the reorganization plan that we had been working on for the past few months.

The next morning I brought in our organizational chart and laid it all out for Percy. We proposed to combine all the bank's corporate business under George Champion in a new "United States" Department. A department called Special Industries would be created and would include the Public Utilities group and the Petroleum and Aviation departments. I would take charge of a third new one, the Metropolitan Department, with responsibility for all the retail branches in the city as well as relations with our many large corporate customers headquartered there. Certain key staff functions, such as public relations and economic research, would be included in my new domain. I told Percy that both activities deserved more emphasis than they had previously been given.

Our suggested reorganization plan also called for the retention of three existing departments: Trust, Bond, and my old area, Foreign. A senior vice president would head each of the six major departments, and they and they alone would report directly to the president. Most important, each of these senior officers would be given well-defined responsibility for a specific area of the bank's operation.

Percy seemed quite pleased with our ideas and particularly intrigued by the "novel concept" of an organizational chart. He took the proposal to Winthrop, who gave it his endorsement. As I had anticipated, George Champion was enthusiastic about the new arrangement since it gave him responsibility for the area of the bank he considered most important. It also gave me authority over an aspect of the bank's business that I believed would be increasingly important in the coming years. The board authorized the reorganization, and it went into effect on the first day of January 1953, just as Jack McCloy took over. Chase now had—at least on paper—a modern and potentially more effective corporate structure.

MERGER MANIA

When he retired from Chase, Winthrop Aldrich told Jack McCloy that there were three things he had failed to accomplish during his nineteen years as chairman: first, finding a merger partner to expand the bank's branch system and strengthen the retail side of its operations; second, building a new headquarters to house the bank's widely dispersed workforce in lower Manhattan; and third, making Chase a truly international bank. Jack took these words to heart and began immediately to seek a merger partner.

By the early 1950s all the major New York banks, as well as those in Chicago and California, began to search for new sources of lendable funds to meet the increasing credit requirements of their corporate customers. Some commercial banks, such as the Bank of Manhattan, had followed a retail strategy designed to broaden and strengthen their deposit base. Their deposit base had grown appreciably, while the great wholesale banks, such as Chase, City Bank, and Guaranty Trust, had seen their corporate deposits decline. Chase had about $6 billion in deposits at the end of 1943, but only $4 billion by the end of 1954. In contrast, the Bank of Manhattan's deposits had increased—by almost $300 million—over the same period, and so had the number of small depositors. It became apparent that the acquisition of retail-generated deposits would have to play a role in the activities of even the largest commercial "wholesale" banks.

Thus, in the mid-1950s there was a veritable mating ritual of mergers—almost all of them linking larger commercial banks having substantial corporate business with smaller retail banks, which had large and growing consumer business. All of these mergers were driven by the need for wholesale commercial banks to acquire branches so that they could gain access to new deposits.

"JONAH SWALLOWS THE WHALE"

The Bank of the Manhattan Company, chartered by the New York State Legislature in 1799, was the second oldest bank in the state. Aaron Burr had been one of its original incorporators. The Manhattan Company had been chartered as a water company to provide freshwater to New York City, but Burr and his associates shrewdly slipped a phrase into the charter that allowed the company to use its excess capital "in the purchase of public or other stocks, or in any money transactions or operations not inconsistent with the laws and constitutions of the State of New York." Thus, the *Bank* of the Manhattan Company came into existence.

Burr's subterfuge outraged Alexander Hamilton and his associates, who up until then enjoyed a banking monopoly through their Bank of New York. This undoubtedly played a role in the bad blood between Burr and Hamilton, which led to their famous duel on the heights of Weehawken in 1804, in which Burr killed the former Secretary of the Treasury. (Chase still owns and displays the dueling pistols used by the two.) The Bank of Manhattan prospered over the years and continued to function under its original 1799 charter. By the early 1950s its most important asset had become its network of fifty-eight retail branches in New York City, double that of Chase. Measured by total assets of $1.7 billion, however, the Bank of Manhattan was only one-quarter Chase's size.

Winthrop Aldrich had tried to combine the two banks in 1951 and the merger had actually been announced in the press, but the attempt proved unsuccessful, due primarily to a powerful personality clash between Winthrop and the Bank of Manhattan's chairman, J. Stewart Baker.

Jack McCloy was a more artful negotiator, and he skillfully overcame Baker's personal reluctance and a number of nettlesome legal obstacles by agreeing to merge the much larger Chase into the state-chartered Bank of Manhattan. This strategy flattered Baker's ego and achieved Chase's objective to expand its retail banking. And so, on March 31, 1955, the smaller Bank of the Manhattan Company technically absorbed the much larger

Chase National Bank, leading one newspaper to run the headline "Jonah Swallows the Whale."

The merger created a financial powerhouse with deposits of $7 billion, capital of $550 million, and total assets of almost $8 billion. Most important, from the point of view of Chase, the number of domestic branches swelled to eighty-seven, the third largest in New York City. In addition, the new Chase Manhattan Bank moved past First National City Bank in terms of total assets—making us the second largest bank in the world, behind only the Bank of America.

SEEKING OUTSIDE GUIDANCE

Prior to opening for business on that April morning in 1955, McCloy and Baker had agreed to an interim corporate structure and division of senior level responsibilities. Jack McCloy had handled Baker's vanity adroitly by giving him the jobs of president and chairman of the executive committee, while retaining the chairmanship for himself. In a master stroke at the time, but one that would create problems only a few years later, McCloy also agreed to alter the bylaws so that both he as chairman and Baker as president were named co–chief executive officers.

Just below the top level, a new title of executive vice president was created. I was named executive vice president for planning and development with responsibility for all staff functions, and George assumed the same rank and retained control of the commercial banking group.

The complicated task of integrating the personnel and operations of these two large institutions, each with a strong personality and a distinct culture, could not be accomplished easily, but it was essential to do it in a manner that would both heighten morale and maintain momentum.

The merger presented us with a unique opportunity to develop a more responsive and effective corporate culture. Some of us felt strongly that the best course would be to hire one of the established management consulting firms to design a more integrated and effective organizational structure. But others in the bank were opposed, bridling at the idea of bringing in an outside consulting firm to do work that we could better perform ourselves. Once again we were locked in a stalemate between the "old guard" and the "modernizers." Happily, we found a compromise.

My friend Peter Grace had faced a similar situation with many of his old-line executives in restructuring W. R. Grace and Company. Peter had found a workable alternative by hiring Gerald Bower, an independent consultant who had worked for General Electric for many years. Bower did not bring a large team of experts with him; instead, he asked senior management to assign eight or ten capable officers to work with him in studying the company. Bower found that this procedure assisted the process of analysis greatly and made it less threatening to company management. Although George Champion and most other senior lending officers remained dubious, Jack McCloy was convinced, and we hired Bower to do the study in May 1955, only a month after the merger.

Bower submitted his final report later that year. Basically, it refined the organizational changes that my associate and I had suggested in 1952 by describing more clearly the operational areas of the bank and definitively establishing lines of authority and responsibility. Bower also strongly recommended that we either establish or strengthen a number of specialized departments—corporate planning, personnel, marketing, and public relations—and recruit trained professionals to manage them. During my entire time at the bank these critical staff functions had been relegated to individuals whose only qualifications were that they had not shown a special aptitude for making loans. I thought this had been a grave error, so now as the executive in charge I was determined to give those staff functions proper recognition and authority.

Despite resistance from George Champion and the "barons" in the United States Department who resented the loss of their autonomy, the organizational changes that Bower suggested were implemented by the end of 1956. By streamlining the structure and strengthening the management process, this represented a significant turning point in Chase's history.

CONSOLIDATING IN LOWER MANHATTAN

In early January 1955, shortly after the merger was announced, Jack gave me another important assignment: figuring out what to do about a new Chase headquarters. It had been clear for some time that we needed to consolidate our widely dispersed activities. Chase had absorbed more than fifty smaller banks over the years, and as a result had operations in nine separate locations scattered throughout the financial district, including our increasingly crowded headquarters at 18 Pine Street. Our looming merger with the Bank of Manhattan made our space needs even more acute.

The issue was not *whether* we should move—all were agreed to that—but *where* we should move to. The financial community in lower Manhattan was unhappy with the crowded streets, poor public services, and antiquated buildings, and many had already taken steps to leave the area. Midtown

Manhattan was the preferred destination for most. The City had grown enormously in the postwar years, but almost all that growth had taken place above 34th Street, with dozens of corporations relocating there each year. Meanwhile, not one new building had been built in the financial district since the beginning of the Great Depression. Lower Manhattan was stagnating, many of its famous financial institutions were planning to follow their corporate clients uptown, and there was general talk of "grass growing again on Wall Street."

No one wanted to be the last to leave. We all owned substantial amounts of property, which would have plummeted in value if the financial community began to move northward en masse. First National City had already announced that it would move many of it operations to a new building on Park Avenue that was scheduled for completion in 1959, though the bank's chairman had assured Jack McCloy that he had no plans to relocate their headquarters. But Chase was perceived as the bellwether; everyone seemed to be waiting for our decision.

My personal view was that it was vital to keep the financial district intact in the Wall Street area and that Chase had to take the lead in the process. This was partly sentiment. The area was rich in history; it included the original Dutch settlement of New Amsterdam; it was where George Washington had taken his oath of office and Congress had convened for the first time. The New York Stock Exchange had begun its operations there in 1817. Grandfather's Standard Oil headquarters had been located at 26 Broadway for many years. But sentiment should never be the basis for a business decision involving many thousands of people and hundreds of millions of dollars. I also felt there were compelling practical reasons for Chase to remain in lower Manhattan. The concentration of the financial industry in such a small area along with the New York Federal Reserve and the major stock and commodity exchanges created enormous efficiencies. Together we formed an integral and increasingly critical part of the world's financial nervous system. These strengths would be jeopardized if any more of the major institutions left. And there were signs that some were seriously considering that option. Even the board of the New York Stock Exchange had indicated that it would move to New Jersey if a threatened stock transfer tax were imposed. If the major banks left lower Manhattan, the Stock Exchange would have added incentive to depart, and that, I felt, would have precipitated a general business diaspora, which would have been an economic and financial disaster for New York.

I persuaded Jack McCloy to hire a qualified outside firm to assess the business climate and potential downtown. This comprehensive review confirmed that the area was in the midst of a profound economic transition.

The major shipping firms, long a mainstay of lower Manhattan, were moving to other cities, and other businesses were leaving for midtown Manhattan and New Jersey. Most financial institutions—banks, brokerage houses, and insurance companies—were feeling nervous and giving indications that they might follow their customers to other parts of the City or even out of state. Our consultants concurred with me that Chase should remain downtown but urged that we do so "in a sufficiently definitive and dramatic way that people would recognize it as a decisive move on our part."

AN OPPORTUNITY WE COULDN'T REFUSE

The clinching factor in the decision to remain downtown turned out to be an opportunity we simply couldn't refuse. I had been working with Bill Zeckendorf, the flamboyant, larger-than-life real estate mogul who a decade earlier had sold my father the land on which the United Nations built its headquarters. Bill was an enormous man in all senses—three hundred pounds of energy and ideas—who operated from a round penthouse office in a building he owned on Madison Avenue in midtown. Bill and I had been exploring ways in which Chase could dispose of its scattered properties and find a single location for our new headquarters. Bill had already proposed a number of solutions, but none seemed workable. I became discouraged about the prospects of remaining downtown.

Then at seven o'clock one morning in late February 1955, Bill telephoned me at my home on 65th Street with urgent news. I was just finishing breakfast and about to grab the paper to head off for the subway. He said he would pick me up in his limousine so we could talk on the way to the bank.

Bill, who was familiar with every major real estate deal in New York, had just learned that the Guaranty Trust Company was about to sell a building it owned that occupied the block between the Federal Reserve Bank of New York and Chase's main building on Pine Street. As soon as I settled in the back of his seven-passenger limousine, Bill sketched out his imaginative game plan. The first step would be for Chase to acquire the Guaranty Trust building. Then we would begin to acquire all the other buildings on the block east of our headquarters on Pine and at the same time sell our many properties dispersed throughout the Wall Street area. If everything went according to plan, we would then ask the City to give us permission to close Cedar Street between our two blocks so that we would have a large parcel—

especially by Wall Street standards—on which to build a new headquarters. Bill pointed out that this was the last opportunity to assemble a space in lower Manhattan that would fit our needs. But we had to move quickly because he had learned the Guaranty Trust was closing the deal that very day. I was astonished by the audacity of his proposal, but he convinced me that we should do it. The question was whether we could persuade Jack and the Chase directors to move swiftly on the matter.

We arrived at Chase and rushed up to Jack's office on the fourth floor. Jack was impressed by Bill's presentation and immediately called the president of Guaranty Trust, who confirmed that the deal would be completed within a few hours. Jack was able to persuade him to delay the sale for twenty-four hours to give Chase a chance to make a counteroffer. Within a few hours Jack contacted Director Frederic W. Ecker, head of the Chase Real Estate Committee. Ecker, experienced in real estate matters, immediately saw the importance and desirability of the proposal and agreed that we should pursue it. The other members of the Real Estate Committee concurred with Ecker's view, and the $4.4 million purchase was closed within a day of Bill Zeckendorf's urgent call to me. Chase would remain downtown.

A DRAMATIC NEW BUILDING

Once Chase had acquired the land, we turned our attention to the kind of image we wanted to project and the kind of building that would be sufficiently striking to make the statement we needed to encourage others to remain in lower Manhattan.

I called Wallace K. Harrison for advice. He was the architect who had first come to prominence for his work on Rockefeller Center and later became a principal architect for both the United Nations and Lincoln Center. Wally had become a friend over the years, and in retrospect I'm a bit embarrassed because Wally could well have assumed that *he* was the best architect for the job. In any case, he graciously accepted my explanation that since we were such good friends, I wanted to select someone else to avoid the appearance of favoritism. Wally unhesitatingly recommended the firm of Skidmore, Owings & Merrill.

The Skidmore firm had come to prominence in the late 1940s with its innovative international-style designs. The most influential of these in New York was Lever House at Park Avenue and 53rd Street, which embraced the pure functional style that Mies van der Rohe and Le Corbusier had pioneered two decades earlier in Europe to take advantage of new construction materials such as aluminum and sheet glass and new technologies such as air-conditioning.

Another recent Skidmore building—a small branch bank for Manufacturers Trust on Fifth Avenue at 43rd Street—had attracted my attention. Completed in 1954, this small architectural gem created a sensation because it was such a departure from traditional bank buildings in both form and feeling; it was a simple glass box with an aluminum skeleton. The door to the giant vault—usually the sacred and secret core of the bank, hidden away in the bowels of the building—was visible from the street! But it was the light, almost ethereal quality of the building that caught everyone's attention.

I contacted my friend Nathaniel (Nat) Owings, one of the founding partners of the firm, whom I had met while a student at the University of Chicago. I told him that we wanted to create a "statement building" to reflect the fact that Chase was a progressive institution, willing to blaze new trails in architecture that would symbolize dramatic changes in management style and culture. Nat and I spent many hours with Bill Zeckendorf discussing the two very different alternatives available to us: The first was to construct two separate conventional buildings on our two blocks. The second, the one Bill Zeckendorf had envisioned from the beginning, was to combine the two parcels by closing the section of Cedar Street between them and erecting one building—not another massive, hulking office building but a shimmering skyscraper set on a large open plaza. It would introduce a revolutionary new city planning concept to lower Manhattan.

The financial district at that time was a solid mass of buildings jammed along the narrow streets close to Trinity Church: Wall, Cedar, Pine, Nassau, and William. For more than a century this had been the most valuable real estate in the world, and when new structures were erected, the owners used every square inch permitted by the building code. The canyons of Wall Street may have been picturesque, but they also created a crowded, dark, and almost claustrophobic feeling at street level. The wind-tunnel effect could be ferocious as well, and hordes of dignified lawyers, bankers, and stockbrokers pursuing their escaping homburgs and derbies was a common sight on a blustery day.

Zoning laws now mandated that a new building had to fit within an "envelope" determined by its size and location on the block. This meant an office building had to be stepped back as it rose in height to let in more light and air into the streets below. The higher you went, the less usable space there would be. The result was inefficient and architecturally unappealing buildings. To encourage more open space, skyscrapers of any height were permitted as long as they occupied no more than 25 percent of a lot. No one on Wall Street had been bold enough to commission this type of building. They felt it wasted valuable land and cut down on the amount of usable building space.

Bill, Nat, and I were not convinced by these arguments. Nat assigned Gordon Bunshaft, the architect responsible for both Lever House and the Manufacturer's branch, to the project. After studying a variety of possibilities, Gordon proposed a sixty-story rectangular tower with no setbacks on a large plaza. To maximize flexibility and efficiency, the building's structural columns were placed outside the skin and inside around the elevator shafts. This provided each floor with a more uniform and unobstructed working space than traditional buildings provided. Gordon also intended to use modular construction, which allowed the installation of the electrical wiring and plumbing, heating, and air-conditioning ducts in a regular pattern in the floors and ceilings. This innovation, which has become the industry standard, would afford versatility in office layouts and make renovations quick and inexpensive.

Another ingenious aspect of Gordon's design cleverly blunted potential criticism that too much valuable space would be lost by building on such a small portion of the land. The foundation for the building would be dug eighty-five feet below the surface to bedrock, allowing for an additional five floors—each with three times the work space of the tower floors—underneath the plaza. The main banking floor would be located underground and lit by natural light from an open-air sunken pool. Floors below that would contain a garage, auditorium, cafeteria, the gigantic bank vault, and storage space.

Gordon's design was the first head office of an American bank in the contemporary style and the first building in lower Manhattan surrounded by a large open plaza. This building would make the definitive statement that I thought essential.

Jack McCloy became an ardent supporter of the one-building approach. Fred Ecker, although in his eighties, also embraced Skidmore's unconventional design. With those two powerful backers, we had little trouble, despite the grumblings of a few in the old guard, in getting the Bunshaft international-style design approved by the board of directors.

Now we needed the City to agree to close part of Cedar Street so we could build on the two-block parcel. The key to getting the plan approved was to have the support of Robert Moses, whom I had known since my days with La Guardia and more recently at the Morningside Heights project. I went to see Moses, who, among many other official positions, was the chairman of the City Planning Commission. Much to my relief, Bob proved to be an easy sale. He believed that a dramatic gesture was needed to save Wall Street, and he liked the concept of opening up more space and letting a little more light into the gloomy downtown streets. Once we had his okay, other needed approvals came easily. In exchange for the City's yielding the land under Cedar Street, we agreed to widen all the sidewalks around the new One Chase Manhattan Plaza.

Soon after construction began, we turned our attention to interior decoration. Gordon noted that the new building would be cold and unappealing without special decoration. Neoclassical buildings, he pointed out, were embellished by columns, pediments, and ornamental sculpture, but none of these decorative elements could be incorporated into our building. He felt that Chase should consider buying contemporary works of art to enhance the public spaces inside the building.

I liked the idea and discussed it with Alfred Barr, the chief curator at the Museum of Modern Art, who fully agreed. Jack McCloy was also open-minded about the proposal, and we formed a small committee that included leading art experts, Gordon, Jack, and myself, to select quality pieces of modern art for the building. We set aside $500,000, which in those days was enough to acquire a representative selection of modern paintings. From this relatively modest beginning the world's first significant corporate art collection has grown to one worth almost $100 million.

=

Construction began in late 1956, but we immediately ran into an unanticipated problem: water. In digging the foundation, the engineers discovered an underground stream about fifty feet below the surface. To deal with this problem and the tidal flow of the East River, which affected the water table under the building, we had to erect a cofferdam the size of the property, a costly modification since it had to be installed before we could begin excavation. The foundation itself was almost 100 feet deep, and eventually more than 225,000 cubic yards of earth and rock were removed. As a consequence, work was delayed and construction costs escalated dramatically. A number of citywide strikes slowed the work even more, and drove up expenditures as well. The preliminary estimate for the building alone was $55 million; in the end the full cost, including land and furnishings, was $145 million. Twenty-five years later, however, the market value of the building was almost three times that amount.

I was more than a bit apprehensive about the immediate critical reaction to our novel bank headquarters. I need not have worried. "One Chase" received rave reviews in publications that ran the gamut from *Forbes*, which praised the "fresh and hopeful cast it has given the old financial district," to *Architectural Forum*, which called it "the boldest and quite possibly one of the soundest investments made on Wall Street."

It is now widely acknowledged that Chase's decision to remain downtown was pivotal in quelling the threatened exodus of other banks and financial institutions, and was a key first step in the renaissance of Wall Street.

The late 1950s was the beginning of an eventful period for me and for Chase. We began the process of transforming an antiquated management structure and entrenched corporate culture into something more rational and capable of dealing with the contemporary world. We recommitted to lower Manhattan and in the process influenced others to remain there as well. And we built a dramatic edifice to serve as our headquarters—a building that exemplified the "new" Chase Manhattan Bank.

Despite the bank's progress during this period, not everyone at Chase supported or appreciated the changes I had sponsored. One executive in particular stood largely in opposition to the vision I held for the bank and the direction I thought it should follow. My conflict with this man would develop into a major struggle for power within the bank in the years immediately ahead.

CONFLICT

In December 1956 we put in place the final pieces of the plan that fully merged Chase and the Bank of Manhattan. I was promoted from executive vice president to vice chairman of the board, and George Champion became president and chief operating officer. We became the clear front-runners in the race to succeed Jack McCloy when he retired in early 1960. The stage was set for a competitive struggle between us that would last fifteen years.

STRUGGLE FOR THE "SOUL" OF THE BANK

George Champion was one of the best-known and deeply respected bankers in the United States. His election in 1958 to the presidency of the Association of Reserve City Bankers was testimony to this fact. George knew all our major corporate clients, and they valued his advice and friendship. He was sound, smart, professional, and level-headed. No other man so thoroughly personified the conservative banking culture of the Chase, a culture that I felt needed to change.

Being a credit officer and a "damned good one" was all he cared about, and as far as he was concerned, it was all the bank should care about, too. He had worked hard to make Chase the country's foremost wholesale domestic bank, catering primarily to large U.S. corporations. Filling their credit needs had always been Chase's primary function; it was the principal source of our revenue and profits, and anything else, for George, was largely a diversion and a waste of resources. Over time, I came to understand that he had a visceral distrust of international expansion. He once told a group of credit trainees that "we would lose our soul" if the bank went international.

I saw Chase's challenges in a different light. My training and experience was not on the lending side. Rather, I had spent fourteen years in the bank's Foreign and Metropolitan Departments. I understood the bank's people and culture, and appreciated its great strengths and enormous potential as well as its glaring organizational and management weaknesses. I saw Chase's future in terms of increased services to a worldwide clientele.

Almost from my first days at the bank George and I sparred over goals and vision. Our debates were heightened by our very different personal styles. George was hale and hearty and occasionally loud. I was much more reserved, and my manner of communicating more subtle. But our conflicts were fueled by more than contrasting personalities. Part of it was that George saw me as his principal competitor in the bank's hierarchy. More important, he and I fundamentally disagreed on how the bank should be organized and where it should be headed. George seemed wedded to the past, content with Chase's role as the preeminent domestic bank. I saw the need for dramatic change and sought to lead the bank in new directions both internally and around the world. As our careers progressed, these basic philosophical differences sharpened, and our personal conflict intensified.

"TROJAN HORSE"

As president and chief operating officer George was in a dominant position, but he could not thwart all my ideas during the late 1950s since, as vice chairman, I reported directly to Jack McCloy and the board. During those years I devoted most of my time to building our new headquarters in lower Manhattan, integrating the personnel and programs of the post-merger bank, and trying to introduce a more effective management structure. These tasks did not provide me with any direct involvement with the lending areas of the bank, which remained George's territory.

However, I used my staff as a kind of "Trojan horse" to initiate quietly a number of important changes. Although my group concentrated on operations, marketing, management development, employee relations, advertising, and public relations—all essential elements of a modern corporation—the department also included an upgraded economic re-search group and a newly minted organizational planning unit. Both of these operations, once they were up and running, became significant in an-alyzing the medium- and long-term banking environment in which we op-erated and in suggesting measures to capitalize on it. Inevitably, or so it seems in retrospect, this moved Chase in the direction I thought it should be moving. And as long as I restricted my activities to the bank's staff functions and did not intrude directly on its fundamental business, George left me to my own devices, which I suspect he viewed as relatively harmless.

END-RUNNING THE INTERNATIONAL DEPARTMENT

There was one line department for which I had responsibility after the re-organization. It was called, rather vaguely, Special Investments, and through it I was able to expand the bank's activities to several foreign coun-tries and to broaden the scope of our financial services in cooperation with, but independently of, the International Department.

I had to proceed in this way because while Jack McCloy sympathized with my view of international diversification, he never took any concrete actions to force the bank onto this new path. In some respects he had no other choice. Throughout his tenure Jack relied on George and his team of domestic lend-ing officers to provide stable growth and acceptable earnings. As late as 1960, Chase had a total loan portfolio of just under $5 billion but only about 5 per-cent in loans outside the United States. So while Jack hedged his bets by allow-ing me to follow through on a number of projects, he never engaged in the difficult task of confronting the bank's domestically based culture.

In 1955, at the time of the Bank of Manhattan merger, we operated only seventeen foreign branches, nine of them clustered in the Caribbean—four of which I had sponsored myself. Our modest presence overseas stood in stark contrast to City Bank and the Bank of America, both aggressively ex-tending their already extensive overseas networks in Europe, South America, and the Far East. In terms of foreign branch networks we were far behind our two major U.S. competitors, and the gap was widening.

The Foreign Department, strongly supported by George Champion from his position as head of the United States Department, resisted expanding the range of products we offered beyond short-term trade finance and the tradi-tional areas of correspondent banking. It pursued this course more out of fear than calculation. Our foreign correspondent banks supplied a substan-tial portion of our low-cost demand deposits, the principal base for Chase's domestic lending. In the late 1950s the demand for bank credit increased substantially, but our deposits failed to grow at a comparable rate, raising the possibility that we would have to curtail our lending as we approached the limits established by the Federal Reserve. Under these circumstances George did not want to take any steps that might jeopardize relationships with our foreign correspondents who maintained large deposits with us.

I considered this view shortsighted. Those deposits were very important, but we had to move beyond correspondent banking by opening more overseas branches, acquiring foreign affiliates, and providing a broader range of products, including ones that might require longer-term lending and even direct investments. I was convinced that in doing this we would not jeopardize our correspondent balances since I believed our correspondents needed us more than we needed them. Initially my arguments were not accepted, but I pressed ahead to develop our international activities through a number of vehicles.

COMPETING WITH EX-IM

President Dwight D. Eisenhower had entered office in 1953 proclaiming his intention to rely more on the U.S. private sector to finance foreign trade. This seemed to offer Chase the opportunity to enter the field of medium-term trade finance an area that private commercial banks had neglected to that point, leaving the field almost totally to the government-financed Export-Import Bank.

At my prodding we enlisted the cooperation of other U.S. commercial banks to create a facility that provided one-to-five-year medium-term credit for the financing of "big ticket" export items, such as steam shovels, electric turbines, earthmoving equipment, and railroad locomotives. We called on correspondent banks in the Northeast and Midwest, and eventually persuaded the National Bank of Detroit, the Mellon Bank in Pittsburgh, and the First National Bank of Boston to join with us and Chemical Bank of New York in launching a new trade finance corporation. We also called on many of our corporate customers, such as Caterpillar, International Harvester, John Deere, General Electric, and Westinghouse, to inform them of our plans. Finally, we spent a great deal of time in Washington with Ex-Im officials, who under their charter were required to "assist" private lenders in the promotion of American exports. However, we had learned from our customers that they were far from satisfied with Ex-Im's performance. They complained of maddening delays, endless red tape, and relatively high-cost financing.

All of this encouraged us to incorporate a joint venture, which we called the American Overseas Finance Corporation (AOFC), in June 1955. Each partner purchased equal shares of the $10 million issue of common stock. Jack McCloy, a strong proponent of the idea, served as the chairman, and I became a director.

AOFC quickly demonstrated that our assumptions had been correct. It financed a number of trade deals and established lines of credit for several American manufacturers. By the end of 1956, AOFC held total assets of $11 million and had commitments to purchase more than $22 million in commercial paper; a modest beginning, perhaps, but the earliest private sector effort to respond to American exporters' critical need for medium-term financing.

Ex-Im officials viewed our entry into the field with alarm. They reacted by lowering interest rates to our potential customers in order to keep their business. Discussions—including a stormy one between McCloy and Secretary of the Treasury George Humphrey—failed to resolve the issue, and our partners became concerned about the competitive rivalry that was emerging between AOFC and Ex-Im. The other directors of the AOFC decided to sell the business rather than risk the displeasure of the regulators in Washington. We sold the company in May 1957 to IBEC for what we had invested in it.

I was quite disappointed by this outcome, but although AOFC fell short of my ambitious expectations, I was pleased that Chase had emerged as an innovator in an important area of trade finance and, more important, had demonstrated to George Champion and his disciples that we could extend our international reach and at the same time strengthen our relationships both with correspondent banks and our large U.S. corporate customers.

INVESTING IN THE DEVELOPING WORLD

Shortly after the incorporation of AOFC, the Special Investments group explored another dimension of the international market by creating a subsidiary to invest in the developing world. We felt Chase should play an active role in the economic development process, and by doing so we could get in on the ground floor in Asian and African countries that had just thrown off the shackles of European colonialism as well as in nations still struggling to modernize their economies, as in Latin America.

During my trips abroad I had noted the weakness of capital markets and the inability of local businessmen and entrepreneurs to borrow in order to finance growth. Interamericana had been an early and perhaps poorly conceived effort to address this problem in Brazil, yet the need for long-term infusions of capital still persisted there and in most developing nations. One approach was to invest directly in local companies, especially in those key sectors—such as mining, commercial agriculture, and manufacturing—that could generate jobs and produce consumer goods for the local market. Creating industrial development banks in countries with good economic profiles was another method that might enable us to leverage our funds with those of local investors to stimulate productive diversified investment.

We had to be creative in accomplishing these goals since U.S. government regulations prohibited commercial banks from directly entering the investment banking field either alone or in combination with others, even outside the country. As a result, we restructured our existing Edge Act corporation (see Chapter 10) into a so-called nonbanking company, which allowed it to make direct investments outside the United States.

From the very start we avoided the two problems that had complicated our previous efforts in Brazil and with AOFC. We chose partners with a strong commitment, and we found competent leadership to run the bank. We hired an experienced investment banker to run the operation, and in August 1957 established the Chase International Investment Corporation (CIIC). I became CIIC's chairman, and we invited several experienced outsiders to join our board of directors.

As a matter of policy we invested only in new projects and always with a "know-how" partner who understood the business and the local economy. CIIC quickly became active around the world. Among other initiatives it invested in a profitable textile mill in Lagos, Nigeria, the first major private industrial project with an American interest in that country. We also established a development bank in Iran, in partnership with Lazard Frères and a local Iranian group. The Industrial and Mining Development Bank of Iran was the first development bank organized by private investors and served as the model for others that we established later in the Ivory Coast and Panama. Both the Iranian and Nigerian projects were profitable, although each had to endure the uncertainties of politics in the developing world. The Iranian bank became a nationally important institution before it was seized by Islamic revolutionaries during the hostage crisis of the late 1970s.

CIIC then took a major stake in the Esperance Land and Development Corporation in western Australia, which held title to 1.4 million acres on the shores of the Great Australian Bight. The Esperance project turned what had been an arid and virtually barren wasteland into a prosperous agricultural region.*

In its early years CIIC produced good results on most of its investments and spectacular profits from at least one—an equity position in an oil refinery in Puerto Rico that returned several million dollars in a period of two years. As CIIC succeeded, the arguments against expanding the bank's international activities were much harder to make from within the bank. CIIC gave us a chance to establish a presence in parts of the world where Chase had little exposure. Slowly but surely we began to create an image as an American bank with a concern for the well-being of the countries where we did business. In several cases CIIC also opened the door to opportunities for broader Chase activities in later years. The foundation that we laid in those areas in the 1950s was consistent with my vision for the international expansion of the Chase.

But my ability to push this expansion aggressively was contingent upon my being given a position of greater authority in the bank, and my future role in the fall of 1959 was by no means clear. My fate rested in the hands of the twenty-three men who formed the board of directors of the Chase Manhattan Bank and would collectively select Jack McCloy's successor.

SHOWDOWN FOR THE TOP JOB

Jack McCloy had been scheduled to retire in March 1960, but the board was divided on the choice of his successor and asked him to stay through the end of the year while they sorted things out. From the board's perspective George was the logical choice as CEO. He was fifty-six, eleven years my senior, and had been with the bank since the late 1920s. I, on the other hand, was relatively young, and many on the board did not consider me a "real banker." My principal responsibilities had been in management and marketing. I had never been a line credit officer, although, unlike either Winthrop Aldrich and Jack McCloy who became chief executives with very little knowledge of the inner workings of banking, I had spent fourteen years immersed in the operations of Chase and had encouraged a number of innovative changes. A large majority of the board recognized that policy changes of the kind I had been pushing were necessary and inevitable. They

---

*Peggy and I were intrigued by the plans to improve soil fertility by adding trace mineral elements and fertilizer. We bought a sixteen-thousand-acre lot in partnership with Benno Schmidt and operated it as a sheep ranch.

seemed to appreciate my creativity, but apparently they wanted a chairman with a solid record in credit and lending, areas where George obviously excelled.

I have little doubt that a majority of the board would have jumped at the chance of appointing George as chairman and chief executive officer *if* I was willing to stay on in a subordinate position. Frankly, I was not. I had worked with George for fourteen years—the last four in a roughly equal position—and I was convinced that if he had sole responsibility, he would lead the bank in a direction that would prevent Chase from becoming a serious force in international banking. I made it clear to board members who sounded me out, particularly J. Richardson (Dick) Dilworth and Jack McCloy, that I would leave the bank if the board chose to give George full and unchecked authority.

My response created a difficult dilemma. The directors were not prepared to make me chairman and chief executive. Had they done so, George would have resigned, a risk no one was prepared to run. Faced with a showdown between George and me, the board blinked. They suggested a face-saving compromise: George would become chairman, and I would be president, but we would be considered "co–chief executive officers." Although George would have full control of the day-to-day operations of the bank, we would share responsibility for policy decisions.

But I wanted more than the appearance of equal authority. I feared the board's proposal would not provide me with the clout necessary to stand up to George on critical issues. I dug in my heels and insisted that I be named chairman of the executive committee as well as president and that the agreement be in writing and signed by the two of us. Without these conditions I believed that George would unilaterally redefine the terms of the mandate and that I would find myself powerless to do anything about it. The final agreement was negotiated through intermediaries—George and I never met face-to-face to discuss it—but in the end we both signed. The dual CEO arrangement was the only viable alternative; both of us had reservations, but we hoped it could be made to work. The announcement of our joint appointment in October 1960 included the following language: "Each will be concerned with and responsible for all aspects of the Bank, but each will supply special leadership in certain areas of his total responsibility. Mr. Champion will give particular attention to the operational and lending policies of the Bank, to the investment funds in its portfolio and to its fiduciary responsibilities. Mr. Rockefeller will give particular attention to forward planning with emphasis on manpower, facilities and markets, to activities abroad and to domestic expansion."

Our joint appointment was a prescription for conflict and indecision. Co–chief executive arrangements rarely work because they represent an uncomfortable compromise. Institutions do best when they have strong and *unified* leadership. George and I were never able to provide that leadership since we disagreed so profoundly about the direction in which the bank should move. His reluctance to commit to the aggressive program of international expansion that I proposed led to delays and missed opportunities. We lost ground to our archcompetitor, City Bank, which continued to expand aggressively and consolidate its position around the world. The real competition should have been with City Bank and the other American international banks, not between George and me.

Concealed within the boilerplate of the press release was the inescapable reality that George and I had each been given veto power over the actions of the other. George was always a consummate professional, but in his heart he never accepted the agreement we had both signed. I suspect that he never fully forgave me for challenging his right to become chairman and sole chief executive officer of the bank.*

"BUMPING" UP AGAINST TASTE

An incident from our first days in joint command highlighted our basic incompatibility and typified the manner in which we would deal with most issues. Not surprisingly, it concerned the bank's art program and the choices we were making to furnish and embellish the modern design of our new head office.

In contrast to the modern decor of most of One Chase Manhattan Plaza, George decorated his office with antiques. For his desk he used an attractive eighteenth-century English curved hunt table, and his walls were hung with rather conventional paintings. A large Remington bronze sculpture of a bucking bronco took pride of place in the center of his office. With these decorative elements in place, George believed that his banking friends from around the country would be reassured that he had not been corrupted by the "wild and modern" ideas I had introduced to the bank in the new building.

---

*Peter Drucker, the esteemed management consultant, was retained to help make this arrangement work, but even Peter could not bring it off. He refers to this assignment as his greatest failure.

Some of the art selected by the Art Committee, of which I was a member, simply exhausted George's patience. One of the first pieces of sculpture acquired was by Jason Seley, a composition of automobile bumpers welded together, forming a kind of bas relief that measured about seven feet long and seven feet high. It was hung against a red mosaic tile wall on the concourse level of One Chase Plaza and to my mind was well suited to the location.

The mistake we made was putting it up during lunch hour. A crowd of Chase employees gathered around to watch the installation. When they realized that this piece of art was "just a bunch of bumpers," there was a stir of protest. Someone called George to tell him what was going on, and he got extremely exercised. He sent down instructions to take the bumpers down immediately. I decided not to press the matter for the time being.

As part of our purchase agreement the piece was to go on a year's traveling exhibition before we could have it, so I decided to buy it personally and figure out what to do with it when it returned. A year later I discussed it again with the Art Committee, all of whom still felt it was an excellent piece and very appropriate for the location. We waited for a weekend when no one was around to hang it in its original location. There it was on Monday morning when everybody came to work. Nobody said a thing; the bank bought it back from me, and it has remained in place ever since. During the entire time George and I never discussed the controversial artwork.

A HOUSE DIVIDED

The "bumpers" episode revealed a great deal about how George and I dealt with each other, most often by indirection and usually through intermediaries. As much as possible we avoided outright confrontation.

On those occasions when George countermanded a decision of mine that I felt was too important to let go by, I would take it to him personally and try to find a solution. If the disagreement was strong enough, we could end up pretty close to the borderline of incivility. George would be abrupt and condescending, explaining to me that I "obviously didn't understand" the fundamentals of banking. I couldn't deny his superior competence as a credit officer, but there were often other issues where I felt my competence and judgment were at least equal to his. When I would remind him that we had coequal authority, he would remind me that the agreement gave him discretion in day-to-day matters of loan decisions and treasury policy. I would counter by saying that the issue had long-range policy implications and was therefore within my jurisdiction as well. Sometimes this circular process would continue without result for weeks. In most cases we worked out a compromise, but on a few rare occasions I told him that I would take the matter to the board. Rather than have that happen, George would usually capitulate.

To be fair, George and I agreed on many issues, most notably the domestic expansion of the bank, which became possible as national and state regulatory restrictions began to ease in the early 1960s. Although we avoided open confrontation, our differences were widely recognized among officers in the bank, with the result that those with an idea they wanted to promote would go to whichever of us they thought would be most sympathetic, an informal procedure that quickly became known as "weathervaning." In a very real sense we became a "house divided," caught up in our own struggles with no consensus on how to move forward or even on which way "forward" was.

Most of our disagreements concerned the manner and degree to which we would internationalize the bank, but here rapid changes in the global economy clearly supported my views.

CONFRONTING A NEW GLOBAL ENVIRONMENT

Jack McCloy turned over a very healthy company to George Champion and me on January 1, 1961. During his eight years as chairman the bank's assets had almost doubled, to more than $9 billion; deposits had increased to just over $8 billion; loans and mortgages had risen to nearly $5 billion; and our net operating earnings had tripled, to almost $75 million. Chase was the leading commercial bank in New York City and trailed only the Bank of America nationally. However, I saw two major vulnerabilities in our otherwise favorable position.

First was our deposit base, which had not kept pace with the explosive growth in credit demand despite the addition of the Bank of Manhattan's large retail deposits and the creation of many new branches within New York City, to which outdated federal regulations confined us. It was only in mid-1960 that New York State's banking regulations were eased to permit New York City commercial banks to branch into the adjacent Westchester and Nassau County suburbs.

The second problem was the low level of our foreign lending. While Chase retained its position as the top-ranked U.S. bank in foreign correspondent banking, we were not a "leading international bank" either in terms of our physical presence or as a supplier of credits. I considered the old guard's commitment to maintaining the primacy of domestic lending tantamount to acquiescing in our becoming a second-tier institution, which might, over time, threaten our survival as an independent bank.

Because I argued for a bold strategy of foreign expansion that George viscerally opposed, our joint tenure at the bank would be an extended and often unpleasant struggle for primacy.

CHAPTER 14

DIFFICULT TRANSITIONS

Mother died early in the morning of April 5, 1948. She died in her bed at 740 Park Avenue in New York City with Father by her side. She had complained of some discomfort earlier, and as she described her symptoms to the doctor who had been called to her bedside, she lay her head back on the pillow and was gone. The doctor attributed her death to a "tired heart."

Nelson called me with the news, reaching me at the bank just after I arrived for work. I can hardly express the grief I felt at her death. Peggy and I had spent the two previous days with her at Kykuit, a peaceful weekend filled with quiet talks. Though we could see she was tired and frail, there had been no dramatic symptoms or warning of what happened so suddenly. Mother loved children, and I will forever remember a final picture of her holding our tiny daughter Peggy in her arms, her loving smile reflected in the little one's face. As we drove back to the city Sunday night, Peggy and I agreed that the weekend had been very special; everyone had felt particularly close to Mother, more so than usual. But for the second time we had a premonition, as with Dick Gilder several years earlier—an intense, sad feeling that this might well be the last time we would see Mother alive.

We had all drawn from the infinite well of Mother's love, and it had sustained us more than we knew. Her passing left a void in all our lives, but no one felt the loss as deeply or desperately as Father. He and Mother had been inseparable throughout their forty-seven years of marriage, and like vines whose braided branches grow together, their lives had become one.

A PROFOUND LOSS

While Mother's death took its heaviest toll on Father, it had a profound effect on me as well. No one else had had a comparable influence on my beliefs, my tastes, and my capacity to enjoy the world around me. My love for her was very great. She was pure of heart and put her family and her deeply held convictions ahead of all else.

At the same time she was fun to be with. She loved the beauties of nature: flowers, the song of the wood thrush in the forest, and the crashing of waves on the beach in Maine. She also loved people. Her standards were high, however, and she was intolerant of those she felt were shallow, lacking in moral principles, or pretentious. She was gentle and the essence of a lady, but unyielding and insistent on issues that she considered important.

Mother read a great deal: history, novels, biography, and sometimes detective stories. She believed that the more one knew about the world, the greater the chance one had to achieve something important. She taught me the enjoyment of learning and living life to the fullest, of savoring the excitement of meeting new and interesting people, of tasting new food and seeing new places, and of exploring the unknown.

Mother was also fond of adventure. When someone came up with a daring idea, she was always prepared to explore it—provided, of course, that Father was not around to discourage her from it! Of the six children I believe Nelson and I were the two who most shared her love of people and adventure. But Mother scrupulously avoided playing favorites among her children; she was devoted to all of us.

THE MATISSE WINDOW

I do not recall who first suggested commissioning a window in the Union Church at Pocantico, the little church just outside the gates of Pocantico, as a lasting memorial to Mother, but the idea was quickly and unanimously accepted by all the brothers and Babs. Nelson, then president of the Museum of Modern Art, was designated to work with Alfred Barr in finding the right artist.

Alfred suggested Henri Matisse; Mother had known him quite well and owned a number of his paintings and drawings. Matisse was in his eighties, however, and it was uncertain whether he would be able to undertake the work. While we felt a rose window over the altar would be the most suitable location, thick wooden mullions broke up the circular space and placed severe limitations on any artist's creativity. But Matisse had begun to focus almost exclusively on intricate abstract compositions of pure color, which could be adapted to the window's configuration. In addition, Matisse had just completed a magnificent set of stained-glass windows for the Dominican Chapel of the Rosary in Vence in the south of France, which demonstrated his great competence in this difficult medium. Happily, Matisse agreed to our request.

It turned out to be his last work of art—the maquette was in his bedroom when he died. The rose window was a beautiful, simple, and appropriate masterpiece. We dedicated it on Mother's Day 1956, and it reminds me of Mother every time I attend church in Pocantico. The sunlight streaming through it creates a wonderful radiance and feeling of joy.

REMARRIAGE AND WITHDRAWAL

After Mother's death, Father was sad and lonely, and we worried about him. I thought a change of scene might help him deal with his grief, so in May, just a month after Mother died, I proposed that he and I set off on a quiet drive together. He eagerly agreed and suggested that we take the Blue Ridge Parkway from Washington to Asheville, North Carolina. It was the height of springtime, and the hills were gloriously beautiful, with the rhododendrons and mountain laurel in full bloom. We had a cozy time together, the last intimate time I would ever have with him. We spoke mostly of Mother. Her presence was still so powerful that we wanted to hang on to it for as long as we could. It was healing to both of us and remains a memory I treasure.

==

Three years after Mother's death, Father told me of his plans to marry Martha Baird Allen and asked me what I thought. Martha was a widow and almost twenty years younger than Father. She had been married to Arthur Allen, an old friend and college classmate of Father's. The Allens had lived in Providence but summered in Seal Harbor for several years before World War II, and so had kept in close touch with my parents.

Although I had been aware for some time that Father was seeing Martha, when he asked me how I felt, I did not say, "I think that would be wonderful." I knew Mother had not thought highly of Martha, and I said so, expressing my reservations in general to the idea of his remarrying. In retrospect this was unwise and certainly unkind. I should have realized that Father was seeking my blessing on a decision he had already made, not asking for my opinion. I had put Mother's memory before Father's happiness. I knew how lonely he was and that it was natural and right for him to find a companion with whom to share his final years.

My indiscretion caused no outright rupture between us, but it may well have contributed to a gradual distancing on Father's part from his children. There were no scenes, no dramatic episodes or quarrels. Overtly, our relationship remained the same: emotionally muted and perfectly proper and correct. In fact, shortly after he married Martha, Father created a new series of trusts with a combined value of slightly more than $61 million, one for Martha and one for each of the brothers, giving us the option of naming our children income beneficiaries for all or part of the new trusts.

Be that as it may, from that time on he and Martha became increasingly distant and withdrawn. Martha was largely responsible for this. She was always polite but made it clear she preferred to see us as little as possible. Father acquiesced. Martha was by nature reclusive and, when she was not with Father, spent most of her time in the company of her employees. Given Father's temperament, which was certainly not gregarious, he found it easy to comply with her desire to avoid other people, even his children. Other than Martha, he saw only a few members of his office staff. I was saddened by Father's isolation since it meant our children had little opportunity to know their grandfather.

Father's marriage to Martha made the last years of his life happier, but his withdrawal from the family became progressively greater over time. Because they spent much of the spring and fall in Williamsburg, Virginia, and the winter months in Tucson, Arizona, they were rarely in New York, Maine, or Pocantico, where informal contacts with Father normally would have been easier.

As the decade wore on, Father's health declined visibly. Part of this was his age (he turned eighty-five in 1959), but he also experienced difficulty breathing—the result of his chronic bronchitis—and developed a prostate condition as well. He had a serious operation in late 1959 but kept the prognosis secret, and after recuperating he went to Tucson for the winter. Since he refused to divulge the nature of his illness, it was difficult for family members to know what actions to take.

The only link we had was Mary Packard, the widow of Arthur Packard, Father's longtime philanthropic advisor. A trained nurse, Mary had cared for Father after Mother's death. She continued in that role after Father's remarriage and also established a close relationship with Martha. Mary was willing to communicate with Peggy and me, and it was through her that we learned in early 1960 that Father had prostate cancer and had been hospitalized in Tucson. However, we were unable to contact either Father or Martha directly to confirm the diagnosis or even express our concern.

Father's doctor in Tucson refused to give me a satisfactory answer about the severity of his condition, and I became even more concerned. Finally, I sent word to Father through Mary and the doctor that I thought he should have a second opinion on his illness and that I would like to visit him.

A PAINFUL LETTER

A few days later I received the most painful letter of my life. It was signed by Father. The tone was cold, even hostile, and said in part:

> I am now physically able to speak frankly with regard to certain actions on the part of some of you boys in recent months, which have amazed and deeply wounded me. . . . Many weeks ago, I realized that the judgment of both my wife and my trusted friend, Mrs. Packard, was being questioned by some of you. I realized that, in opposition to my own decisions and wishes, pressures and interference were being brought to bear upon the doctors, which led me to ask some straight questions. Reluctant though they also were to answer, I insisted on their telling me the full facts and made very clear to them my resentment at the tactics used and their full implications. . . .
>
> The added burden—not to say shock—that this must have been to one who was devoting her utmost of heart and intelligence to my welfare during a difficult period cannot as yet be estimated. Under doctors' orders, she is at long last having a complete rest, which is felt to be the only means by which she can regain her strength. . . . Acutely conscious as I have been of the burdens she has carried because of my uncertain health in recent years, my heart is even heavier at the thought that my own sons should have added by one iota to these strains.

Father ended the letter by forbidding me or anyone else in the family from intervening any further in the matter.

This was a devastating letter to receive. But as I reread it and discussed it with Peggy, I realized it was totally unlike Father in style and content. Father was always direct and meticulous, but this letter was circuitous and disjointed; even his signature, slightly askew on the page, shaky and barely recognizable, seemed to have been added as an afterthought in order to give it legitimacy. Peggy believed, and I came to agree with her, that Martha had written it and somehow induced Father to sign it. And as we found out later, that was exactly what had happened. Father's doctor later told me the letter was written in its entirety by Martha, and Father had on four occasions refused to sign it. I felt helpless, but Peggy was convinced we could not let the situation lie.

A FINAL GOOD-BYE

An opportunity for me to do something came a few weeks later. I was scheduled to attend a meeting of the Association of Reserve City Bankers in Phoenix in early April 1960. Since I would be close to Tucson, I called Mary to tell her I was coming to see Father. Mary didn't try to dissuade me, and I believe she respected my request not to tell Martha of my proposed visit. I drove to Tucson and stopped first at the Arizona Inn where Martha and Mary were living. I did not see Martha but met briefly with Mary, who told me that Martha was bedridden and had not been to see Father for some weeks.

I was shocked by Father's appearance; he was so feeble, he could hardly raise his head from the pillow. But he recognized me and showed unmistakably that he was touched I had come. I took his hand and told him that I loved him and that all of us in the family were deeply worried about his condition. There was no mention of the letter, but he made a special point of bringing up Martha. "She has been very good to me," he said. "I hope that when I'm gone you boys will look after her."

Father died on May 11, 1960. Peggy and I were in Madrid when we heard of his death, and returned home immediately. Nelson and Laurance had flown to Arizona when they learned that Father's condition had become critical, but did not get there until after his death. They brought his body back to Pocantico, stopping in Little Rock to pick up Win. We followed the Rockefeller tradition of cremation and interred Father's ashes next to Mother's in the family cemetery in Tarrytown. Harry Emerson Fosdick, senior minister at Riverside Church, whom Father greatly admired and respected, presided at the graveside ceremony. Forty members of the family were present on a beautiful spring afternoon, the air sweet with the smell of lilacs and the dogwoods in full bloom.

UNFINISHED BUSINESS

The formality with which Father approached relationships, even with his sons, created a distance that was bridged only on rare occasions. His death finally allowed me to see how much he had given me and how much I owed to him. His hard work and devotion to duty, his unwillingness to let his basic insecurity prevent him from becoming engaged with the affairs of the world, had set me a powerful example. His great wealth made his philanthropy possible, but money was just a lever. The force that enabled him to succeed was a determination rooted in his strong Christian values: that one should love one's neighbor as oneself, that it is better to give than to receive.

Starting life with considerable insecurities myself, I am not sure I would have been able to go out and wrestle with the world had I not grown up with Father's example, had I not learned from my earliest conscious moment that there are things that must be done whether one likes it or not. At times I reacted negatively to Father's strong sense of duty because he made it seem too dreary and burdensome. But as I have learned, duty is liberating. It forces you to transcend your own limitations and makes you do things that may not come naturally but must be done because they are right.

Perhaps, too, having become a father myself and learned of my own inadequacies in that role, I became more sympathetic to Father's idiosyncrasies and limitations. You do the best you can. Father certainly gave me a lot to be thankful for. My visit enabled me to tell him how much I owed him and how deeply I cared for him. I would never have forgiven myself if I had not done so.

═══

My brothers and I wanted to create a memorial to Father and agreed that a stained-glass window at Union Church—symbolically joining him with Mother—would be most appropriate. Given the death of Matisse, we had some difficulty identifying an artist of comparable stature who could do the window. Luckily, the year following Father's death, Peggy saw an exhibition at the Louvre of Marc Chagall's stained-glass windows, destined for the Hadassah Hebrew University Medical Center in Jerusalem. She was greatly impressed and thought Chagall might be the artist we were looking for. She convinced me to see the so-called Jerusalem Windows before leaving Paris, and I came away equally enthusiastic.

After discussing the idea with my siblings and the Union Church congregation, we agreed to approach Chagall. I visited him at his home in St. Paul de Vence, and he agreed immediately to accept the commission. He consulted extensively with the family about Father and produced a beautiful window based on the parable of the Good Samaritan, the biblical story that seemed most fitting.*

DIVIDING THE ASSETS

Father's death removed the man who had established the standards of excellence and provided the moral leadership not only for the family but also for the institutions he and Grandfather had created over the previous half-century. His principal heirs—my brothers and I—had to deal with a number of difficult issues relating to the management of these institutions at the same time that we struggled to find a new balance in our relationships with one another.

A lifetime devoted to philanthropy, the high cost of building and operating Rockefeller Center, and the creation of generous trusts for his wives, children, and grandchildren had substantially diminished Father's fortune from its billion-dollar value in the mid-1920s. His estate was probated at $157 million. Father's will divided these assets just about evenly between Martha and the Rockefeller Brothers Fund. It may seem surprising that Father left nothing to his children or grandchildren, but in fact he had provided for all of us handsomely through the 1934 and 1952 Trusts and a number of direct gifts. By dividing his estate in the way he did, Father sheltered most of his remaining assets from "death duties" and provided my generation with additional philanthropic resources.

Father had given the matter a great deal of thought before choosing the RBF as the recipient of the charitable portion of his estate. By further endowing the RBF, Father made it one of the ten largest foundations in the country and made us stewards of the philanthropies he had done so much to promote. My brothers and I made up the majority of the board, and we would have the predominant voice in developing the RBF's philanthropic program.

---

*At the dedication ceremony in 1963, Chagall told me that apart from Matisse's Rose Window, the eight nave windows were not of very high quality. Could anything be done about that? he asked. I replied that it certainly could—if he would be willing to do the others. Chagall agreed and suggested the Old Testament prophets as his central theme. Chagall designed one window in memory of Michael Rockefeller, Nelson's son who had died in Papua New Guinea in 1961, using the text from John's Gospel, "Seek and ye shall find." After Nelson's death the "Joel" window was dedicated to him. In June 1997 the congregation consecrated the "Ezekiel" window in memory of my wife, Peggy.

THE END OF THE EYRIE

The distribution of Father's real estate and tangible assets, such as works of art and furnishings, proved to be complex. My brothers and I had purchased Father's Maine properties in the early 1950s through Hills Realty with the understanding that Martha could use the Eyrie for as long as she desired after Father's death. Martha had little inclination to return to Maine, however, so when she renounced her rights to the Eyrie, Nelson and I bought all the Maine property from Hills and decided to tear down the Eyrie. Its one hundred rooms made it completely impractical for any of us to use, but the Eyrie had many memories that we didn't want to lose. Even though Martha had spent little time in Maine, she had redecorated the Eyrie extensively. It was understandable that she would not want to live under Mother's shadow, but Martha's taste was not Mother's or mine. The thought occurred to me that before demolishing the house it would be nice to restore the interior to the way it had been when Mother was alive and then photograph it so we could remember it the way it had been.

I accomplished this with the help of a number of people who had worked at the Eyrie during Mother's time. It was surprising how detailed our combined recollections were. When I couldn't remember exactly where something belonged, I would close my eyes and imagine my Mother there, surrounded by the paintings and Oriental objects she adored, and their precise arrangement would come back to me. When my memory failed, somehow the others remembered.

We filled the house with flowers and even lit fires in the living room and dining room just as my parents had done on foggy days when we were children. When everything was ready, Ezra Stoller, the great architectural photographer, went to work and photographed the entire interior.

Once Stoller was finished, all my siblings came to Seal Harbor for the distribution of Mother's belongings, which we accomplished by lottery. Every piece had been appraised and was numbered and catalogued; each of us drew lots to decide the order of choice. Then we picked items in turn until each of us had drawn our proportional monetary share. Several lawyers and secretaries attended the distribution and took meticulous notes on each choice. Peggy and I had done our homework pretty well, and so had Nelson and John, who was already forming a distinguished collection of Asian art. Win probably knew least but showed wonderful taste and made astute selections. It hardly mattered; Mother's collection was so extensive and of such high quality that no one could fail to get many beautiful pieces.

With that final task completed, Nelson and I, who had inherited all of Father's Maine property, gave the order to dismantle the building. All that remains of the Eyrie today is the brick and granite terrace along its southern side, from which one can still enjoy its magnificent view of the island-spotted ocean.

PASSING THE BATON

Some time later I studied a photograph taken of the six of us in the Eyrie living room the day the distribution of furnishings took place. We are grouped around Babs on a large sofa, laughing about something one of us had just said. The photographer captured us in midlife, each of us launched on our careers, with our own families and responsibilities, but all of us tied to one another and to a home that had meant much to each one of us when we were growing up.

Babs married her third husband, Jean Mauze, an affable southerner and a senior vice president of the U.S. Trust Company, in 1953. Although Babs was still shy and reserved, she had overcome many of her earlier problems coping with a strict, strong-willed father. She had become more involved in family affairs and joined the board of the RBF in the early 1950s.

Win left New York in 1954 in the midst of a painful and public divorce from Barbara (Bobo) Sears. Arkansas had more favorable divorce laws, but he also discovered that he liked the slower pace and rural rhythms of the state. He decided to make Arkansas his permanent home, bought a large ranch on Petit Jean Mountain north of Little Rock, and soon became involved in local politics and civic affairs. Although he detested the racism of Governor Orval Faubus, Win accepted the chairmanship of the State Industrial Development Commission and worked hard to attract corporations to the state and ease the regulatory burdens on those already there. His success in this post persuaded Win that he might have a future as a politician. He created the framework for a modern Republican Party in Arkansas, building it from the ground up. Meanwhile, Win married the former Jeannette Edris in 1956 and seemed quite happy with his new life.

John emerged from his struggles with Father in the late 1940s and early 1950s determined to make his own way as a philanthropist. He assumed the chairmanship of the Rockefeller Foundation in late 1952 and helped to channel its immense resources toward the support of scientific research and the application of that knowledge to the solution of a broad range of social problems around the world. Most significant, he championed Norman Borlaug's work in hybrid seed production that would lead to the Green Revolution of the 1960s in Asia and Latin America.

However, it was John's work in the field of population that was even more influential. When the foundation's board proved unwilling to challenge the Catholic Church by adopting a comprehensive program of population measures—including support for birth control—John created the Population Council to do that work. By the mid-1950s, John had also emerged as a strong advocate of improved relations with the countries of East Asia and had created a particularly strong personal link with Japan. In New York, John led the effort to create a performing arts center that would become Lincoln Center, one of the world's great centers of music and dance.

For most of his life Laurance had seemed willing to dwell in Nelson's shadow, content to act as his surrogate and alter ego. This is actually an unfair characterization because Laurance's roles as a venture capitalist and conservationist were highly innovative and even visionary, and owed nothing to Nelson. When Nelson started his political career and had little time for family affairs, Laurance became the principal executive of the organizations central to our family, running the Family Office and chairing both the RBF and Rockefeller Center. By assuming these heavy responsibilities he allowed the rest of us to pursue our independent careers. Laurance had a quiet strength and a sharp intelligence, but because he was so self-effacing, the importance of what he was doing for the family and for society was easily overlooked.

And finally there was Nelson, governor of New York, a potential president of the United States, and self-acclaimed and broadly accepted leader of our generation. I need to say more about Nelson because my relationship with him underwent a profound transformation beginning at this time.

NELSON AND THE POLITICS OF DIVORCE

A family advisor once said the two most expensive things a Rockefeller can do are run for public office and get divorced. Nelson did both. Even at the time he became governor of New York in 1958, Nelson already had his sights on the presidency. In 1959 he told his brothers he planned a publicity campaign to increase his national visibility. It was not a full-fledged campaign, yet he estimated it would cost a million dollars, and that proved to be just the beginning. Over the next decade each of us responded to his

appeal for political contributions, but Laurance was by far the most generous. Brooke Astor, a longtime friend, also gave large sums to his campaigns,
sometimes a million dollars at a time. However, it was Martha, whom
Nelson assiduously cultivated after Father's death, who became his most
generous supporter, providing the largest share of his support, second only
to the funds that Nelson had drawn from his 1934 Trust.

In November 1961, Nelson announced that he and Tod had agreed to a divorce. For the family the announcement came as no surprise, but it was a
painful time for us all. I have always identified it as the beginning of my dis-
illusionment with Nelson, when the scales fell from my eyes and I no longer
saw him as the hero who could do no wrong but as a man who was willing
to sacrifice almost everything in the service of his enormous ambition.
While I would continue to admire his great vision and capabilities and remained devoted to him to the end of his life, I would never again feel the un-
alloyed admiration of my youth.

Perhaps Peggy and I had been naive. It often happens that those who are
closest are the last to find out. When we first heard about Nelson's affair
with Happy, we were shocked. Happy (her full name was Margaretta Fitler
Murphy) and her husband, Robin Murphy, had been among our closest
friends for many years.

Robin was the son of Dr. and Mrs. James Murphy, who had a summer
home in Seal Harbor where they had long been good friends of my parents.
Robin met Happy after the war, and they married in 1948, returning regularly to Seal Harbor in the summers; it was there that Peggy and I became
friends with both of them. Robin crewed for us when we raced our interna-
tional-class sloop in races of the Northeast Harbor Fleet, our local yacht
club, and the four of us often cruised the coast of Maine in the *Jack Tar.*

I helped Robin secure a position as a biomedical researcher at the
Rockefeller Institute, and he and Happy moved into a town house directly
behind ours on 65th Street. We, along with Nelson, encouraged Father to
sell them property owned near the Pocantico estate when they wanted to
build a weekend country home. Father rarely sold Pocantico land to anyone
outside the family, but he was as fond of them as we were. At the time I
thought Nelson was supportive simply because he thought Robin and
Happy would be nice neighbors. Later on I learned that Nelson had played
an important role in encouraging Father to make the sale.

I have no idea how long the affair had been going on, but while Father
was alive, Nelson did not show his hand. After Father's death, Nelson was

liberated from many restraints and free to be himself. He decided before long to follow his strong impulse to divorce Tod and marry Happy.

STRAINED RELATIONS

O f the six siblings only Laurance attended Nelson's second wedding in May 1963. Sensing our feelings, Nelson had not invited any of the rest of us. He had not only torn apart his own family, he had broken up the marriage of two of our close friends. Happy continued to circulate around our lives in Pocantico and in Maine, but for many years Peggy and I could no longer feel the same affection for her. Time is a great healer of wounds, however, and over the years my friendship with Happy has been restored; today she and her sons, Nelson, Jr., and Mark, are active members of the family.

Robin felt badly burned and would have nothing more to do with any of our family. Peggy and I attended his second wedding a few years later in an effort to keep in touch with him, but basically he vanished from our lives.

Tod had been my friend ever since our trip to Egypt in 1929, during which I pretended to propose to her on Nelson's behalf. Peggy and I considered her part of our family and had no intention of cutting her off. But matters were not made any easier for Tod by Nelson's choice of living arrangements. He divided their thirty-two-room duplex apartment on Fifth Avenue in two; Tod lived on one floor, and Nelson and Happy on the other. While they had separate entrances, it was not a comfortable situation for anyone.

=

Soon after the divorce Nelson and I had our first serious confrontation. My brothers and I did not object when Nelson told us he wanted to move into Kykuit once Martha indicated she didn't wish to live there after Father's death. The four of us—Babs and Win were not involved—owned Kykuit jointly, but John, Laurance, and I were comfortably settled in our own homes nearby and not interested in moving. Kykuit's formal decor and stately setting were more suited to Nelson's needs as governor.

The problem arose over the furnishings, which Father and Mother had left jointly to the four of us. Nelson took it for granted that despite the terms of Father's will, John, Laurance, and I would leave all the furnishings and art in place as long as he was living there. I told him that I could readily understand his desire to keep most of the furnishings and I had no thought of taking a great deal, but Peggy and I were particularly fond of several objects and would like to have them for our home. I suggested we follow the same lottery system that we had used in distributing the Eyrie furnishings, but in this case it seemed likely that little would be taken by his three brothers as long as he was living there.

Nelson found my suggestion unacceptable and became absolutely livid, angrier than I had ever seen him. He couldn't believe that I would challenge him. He said that as governor he needed Kykuit to entertain and that he wanted it left unchanged. Nelson claimed that his public service was in the family's best interest, and for that reason it was essential to allow him to keep Kykuit intact. I was in no mood to give in. In the end the law was on my side, and there was nothing he could do but conform to the terms of Father's will. He conceded and said each of us should take what we wanted without a formal selection procedure. Typically, once he had lost the battle, Nelson accepted the decision, and it was never mentioned again. He never carried a grudge.

THE CONSUMMATE CAMPAIGNER

Nelson's political career proceeded apace, as did his need for money to sustain it. In 1962, Nelson defeated Robert Morgenthau, then and now the U.S. Attorney for the Southern District of New York, decisively winning a second term as governor. In 1964 he entered the Republican presidential primary but was swept away by the conservative Barry Goldwater tide. In 1966 he narrowly won a hard-fought campaign for reelection as governor. Nelson made one final try for the presidency in 1968. Although Richard Nixon had a clear lead in the polls and among delegates to the nominating convention, a number of moderate and liberal Republicans, led by Spiro Agnew, urged Nelson to enter the race. In mid-March, after months of vacillating, Nelson seemed to have reached a decision. He had to enter the race immediately if he wanted to demonstrate his popularity in the West Coast primaries.

I had lunch with Nelson at Kykuit at the time and discussed the pros and cons of his entering the race. Nelson knew that right-wing Republicans would violently disrupt his campaign, as they had in 1964. Happy was also deeply disturbed by this possibility, a fact that weighed heavily on his mind. Despite this, and because I knew this would be his last real chance at the presidency, I encouraged him to become a candidate, and by the end of our conversation he told me he was determined to go forward.

He then scheduled a press conference a few days later to make the announcement. But an hour or two before he was to appear, Nelson reached me by telephone in my car as I was making customer calls to tell me that he had changed his mind. His announcement bitterly disappointed and disillusioned his supporters and wrapped up the nomination for Nixon.

I thought Nelson had made a serious miscalculation. The year 1968 was a volatile one, and I think Nelson seriously underestimated his national support, a point underlined when President Lyndon Johnson announced that he would not seek reelection. The disarray in the Democratic Party over the Vietnam War coupled with the surprising strength of George Wallace among conservative voters meant the political center, where national elections are won or lost, was up for grabs. But timing in politics is the most important factor, and when Nelson changed his mind yet again and entered the race at the end of April, it was much too late. Most people saw him as an opportunist and not a politician with a credible set of ideas. His last chance to be elected president effectively came to an end on that day in March when he had failed to rise to the challenge.

==

Between 1958 and 1970, Nelson ran for office every two years—a total of seven campaigns. The financial cost to him was high, almost ruinously so. I was never a major contributor to his campaigns, and he never pressed me for support. That changed as Nelson's financial situation grew more and more precarious in the mid-1960s. In 1967 he asked me to buy his share in our Brazilian ranch, Fazenda Bodoquena, as a means of generating additional campaign funds. Actually, he didn't *ask,* he *demanded.* Nelson insisted I pay him $2 million for his share.

Lindy Lindquist felt Nelson's asking price was substantially more than its market value. When I informed Nelson of this, he again became furious. "I have drawn down from the '34 Trust all that they [the trustees] will let me have," he said. "I don't have any other source of funds." When he was in such a mood, he became very tough and cold. I was ungrateful, he said, given all he had done for me, particularly persuading Father to sell us Rockefeller Center.

I wrote him that I appreciated all he had done for us in the past, but I resented "that on more than one occasion you have chosen to use this as a lever to achieve objectives of your own." While I agreed to the price he wanted, I insisted that he agree in the future "in any negotiations we might have of a financial nature or otherwise to deal on the basis of the facts at hand without reference to past considerations." I advised him to remember that "in other ways, at different times, other members of the family have contributed to the common good, sometimes specifically in assisting you in causes of vital interest to you. This is all natural and as it should be. Perhaps the balance of contributions to the family as a whole is still weighted in your favor. I would not wish to argue to the contrary. But I regret on more than one occasion you have chosen to use this as a lever to achieve objectives of your own."

LARGER THAN LIFE

Even though Nelson's personal behavior could often be very high-handed, I never lost sight of his enormous talents as a public servant. He had a sure touch and a considerable understanding of public needs. He was utterly self-confident and relished the life of a politician—stumping the state, speaking in every Elks Club he could find, and kissing every baby within reach. He was one of the first politicians to make effective use of television, conducting televised "town meetings," much like contemporary politicians, moderating them himself and tussling skillfully with the audience. He could broker a deal behind closed doors, knock heads together, and forge a compromise better than any union boss. He had as much love for the game of politics as any ward politician, and just as much charm—something I was just as susceptible to as the average voter.

I remember in particular one Wall Street rally during the 1970 gubernatorial campaign. It wasn't that common for me to become publicly involved in Nelson's campaigns, but when he came to "my territory," I felt a brotherly obligation to appear with him. After I made a few brief remarks, Nelson strode across the stage, his grin enveloping his face, and lifted my arm in the air, eliciting cheers from the crowd. A photograph perfectly captures Nelson's exuberance and its effect on those around him, including me. I'm not normally inclined to make expansive public gestures, but in the photograph I'm grinning as broadly as he, loving it just as much because I, too, was affected by his charisma.

Nelson taught me invaluable lessons about people and the way the world works. There was a greatness to him that enveloped those around him, and they honestly loved him for it. He loved to give pleasure to others, and he was warmed by their gratitude. He taught me to loosen up, to *enjoy*, to take pleasure in the "great game" of life. And if my brother sometimes played that game with too much abandon, he helped me play it more ardently and with greater zest.

CHAPTER 15

CREATING
A GLOBAL BANK

As the Chase's president and co–chief executive officer, I was responsible for directing the bank's strategic planning, modernizing our management structure, and overseeing our domestic and foreign expansion. I suspect that George Champion hoped I would busy myself with planning exercises, organizational charts, personnel seminars, and filling One Chase Plaza with art he disliked, leaving the management of the bank to him. While I did pay a great deal of attention to improving Chase's corporate structure and the quality and diversity of our personnel, I focused principally on internationalizing the bank, a course that George and others sharply opposed. Their opposition to my efforts to broaden the bank's foreign business undoubtedly would have continued throughout the 1960s had there not been two fundamental changes in the global banking environment that literally forced Chase onto the international stage.

PAYING FOR DEPOSITS

The first change involved the cost and availability of funds—the lifeblood of banking. Beginning in the 1930s the Federal Reserve had strictly regulated the amount of interest commercial banks could pay on time deposits and prohibited the payment of interest on demand deposits, which then became the primary source of funds used for lending. Thus, the vast bulk of our lendable funds cost us very little and increased bank earnings. In the late 1950s, however, this system began to change as the United States entered a period of economic expansion, which was accompanied by a dramatic increase in the demand for credit. Neither Chase nor the other commercial banks could sustain the growth in deposits necessary to keep pace with the surge in demand for loans. As bank credit became less available, corporations turned to non-bank financial sources, such as insurance companies, and began to issue their own commercial paper. Banks reacted to this competitive threat by purchasing additional funds in the market—largely by means of a recently developed financial instrument called the "negotiable certificate of deposit" and by entering the "Eurodollar" market.

Certificates of deposit (CDs) are time deposits on which a bank has agreed to pay a fixed amount of interest for a specific period of time. In 1961, in an effort to make CDs more attractive to corporations, the major New York banks, with City Bank taking the lead, issued these traditional bank instruments in negotiable form. As an added inducement, banks created a secondary market so that investors could sell their CDs for cash. In short, corporations could earn interest on their working capital while retaining full liquidity. Banks gained access to a new source of lendable funds, but only at a substantial new cost.

During this same period American banks also began to enter the market for Eurodollars (U.S. dollars that circulate outside the United States) in search of additional lendable funds. Since Eurodollars were not subject to Federal Reserve regulations on interest rates or reserve requirements, American banks took advantage of this new source of "unregulated" deposits for lending overseas. Banks could borrow more favorably, and depositors could obtain better rates on their money.

While the emergence of CDs and Eurodollars solved the "availability of funds" problem, we now had to pay interest on a much larger portion of our lendable funds. As a consequence CDs had a negative effect on bank profits. Since we could not pass on to our customers the full cost of the higher interest rates we now paid for lendable funds, we were caught in a profit squeeze. This fundamentally transformed the role of commercial banks in the United States—away from their historical role as the prime lenders of funds to corporate America and toward becoming brokers of loans and sellers of fee-based services. Consequently, banks had to look beyond the United States for additional sources of income.

THE EMERGENCE OF MULTINATIONALS

A second fundamental change—the expansion of the world's major corporations beyond their national borders—put even more pressure on banks to expand overseas. Many U.S. corporations were building production and sales facilities in Europe and Latin America, and wanted their U.S. bank to be there with them. At the same time many European and a few Japanese companies extended their operations into the United States and were competing for markets in Asia, Africa, and Latin America. In order to satisfy the needs of both American and foreign multinationals, commercial banks had no alternative but to provide a full range of banking products and services overseas as well as at home.

Competition among U.S. and foreign banks for this new multinational business was intense. If Chase wanted to maintain its leadership position at home, it had to compete overseas for the business of *foreign* corporations even if this alienated our foreign correspondent banks, as the old guard predicted. But gradually the need for fundamental policy changes that allowed us to lend to foreign corporations and implement a strategic program of global expansion became more widely accepted in the bank. This change in attitude strengthened my hand in dealing with George Champion.

MIXING BUSINESS WITH FRIENDSHIP

Establishing contact with key local businessmen and government officials in the countries where we wished to do business was a sine qua non if Chase was to build an effective international presence. And that meant my foreign travels assumed an added importance.

During my thirty-five years at Chase I visited 103 countries; this included forty-one trips to France, thirty-seven to England, twenty-four to West Germany, fifteen to Japan, fourteen each to Egypt and Brazil, and three extensive tours of sub-Saharan Africa. At home I called on bank customers in forty-two of the fifty states. I logged more than 5 million air miles (the equivalent of two hundred round-the-world trips), ate approximately ten thousand business meals (more if you count the ones that I consumed in New York), and participated in thousands of customer calls and client meetings—as many as eight to ten a day when we were on the road. I also met more than two hundred heads of state and government, many of whom I got to know on a personal basis. Though at times the pace was a bit hectic, I found these trips productive and enjoyable, and essential to the globalization of our operations. Fortunately, I was blessed with the Rockefeller traits of energy, stamina, and good health!

Some observers at the time criticized my extensive travel as "irrelevant" or "a waste of stockholders' resources." They completely missed the point. The reason for these trips was to generate business for the bank, and from the start they produced important links with business and political leaders in Europe, Latin America, the Middle East, Asia, and Africa that were critical to the bank's expansion. Further testimony to their value came from the fact that Chase officers, both domestic and foreign, continually requested that I travel with them because their customers were eager to talk with me on a broad range of political and economic subjects in addition to banking relationships. (Even today, many years after my retirement, Chase's management still asks me to travel on behalf of the bank.) I think it is fair to say that my visits to the far corners of the world in the 1950s and 1960s helped lay the groundwork for the expansion and consolidation of Chase's global position in the 1970s.

As an international banker with an equally heavy commitment to a wide range of not-for-profit organizations, I had continual contact with a large number of people. This was not a burden because I have always enjoyed meeting people and learning about their personal concerns, ideas, and activities—finding out what makes them tick. I have been fortunate in the number and quality of the friendships I have made with people from all walks of life. I am always open to and aware of the potential of a new relationship, whether for its intellectual challenge or the emotional pleasure it brings, or because it opens up the prospect of a new business or philanthropic opportunity. I often have immediate feelings of empathy and compatibility with others, but I am equally capable of feeling the reverse.

My interest in others has helped me cut through cultural differences to establish a quick rapport. This direct and uncomplicated approach applies to people I meet every day as well as world leaders. I have never felt that a close personal friendship and a good business relationship need be mutually exclusive. In fact, I firmly believe that the most successful business associations are based on trust, understanding, and loyalty, the same qualities that are essential to a close personal friendship.

ESTABLISHING INSTITUTIONAL ROOTS

In the early 1960s I began the task of putting down roots in the major countries of the world. Since we had a very thin network of branches in Latin America, Europe, and Asia. I knew that creating a comprehensive global branch system de novo would be too costly and time-consuming. A more promising course would be to affiliate with indigenous banks throughout the world, commencing in an area with which I was most familiar: Latin America.

=

For some time I had tried to establish a Chase presence in Brazil, the largest and most promising of Latin America's economies. Our failure to do so had been particularly frustrating because many Brazilian businessmen understood that foreign capital was essential to their economic growth and diversification.

In 1961 an associate of Nelson's informed me that Antonio Larragoitia, the chairman of Sul America, the largest insurance company in South America, wanted to sell a majority interest in its Brazilian banking subsidiary, Banco Hipotecario Lar Brasileiro. Although Banco Lar was small by Brazilian standards, it was well managed and profitable, so I immediately contacted Larragoitia, who confirmed that he was willing to sell 51 percent of the stock of his bank for $3 million. He agreed to give Chase management control, which would allow us to transform Banco Lar into a full-fledged commercial bank. We had an unprecedented unique opportunity to establish an immediate presence within a dynamic economy at a bargain basement price. Furthermore, I viewed the acquisition as a test of both my ideas and my clout as president and co-CEO.

George Champion reflexively opposed the deal. He was put off by Brazil's political instability, chronic fiscal and budgetary problems, and dizzying inflationary spiral. Admittedly, it was a precarious time politically, since Brazil's new president, João (Jango) Goulart, was a populist with strong socialist convictions. One couldn't be sure how things would turn out, and clearly our purchase would involve a risk. But the low price reflected that risk, and in my judgment if we waited until a country was risk-free before moving, we would never go anywhere. When George remained obdurate, I took the matter to the board, where we debated the issue several times. Despite the opposition of George's allies, I persevered, and the board gave its assent to the deal in April 1962.

We gradually added to our equity interest in Banco Lar, and in 1980, as a result of an informal conversation over cocktails at my home in New York with Carlos Langoni, governor of the Brazilian Central Bank, we were able to purchase the balance of the shares. I simply told him that Chase wanted to increase its ownership and asked if the Brazilian Central Bank would allow us to proceed. To my great surprise he agreed, and Chase purchased the rest of the bank.

Over the years Banco Lar proved to be a solid acquisition for Chase. Now known as Banco Chase Manhattan, it is one of the leading foreign banks in Brazil with assets of more than $1.1 billion. Not bad for an initial $3 million investment.

A similar affiliation in Venezuela in 1962 went a lot more smoothly. Chase had maintained a representative office in Caracas for a number of years, and our strong position with the petroleum industry made the advantages of a strategic alliance there acceptable even to George Champion.

Luís Emilio Gómez Ruíz, whom I had met when he was his country's foreign minister, had become president of the Banco Mercantile y Agricola, which was controlled by the Vollmer family. I approached Gómez Ruíz in 1961 about an affiliation with Chase and, after several meetings in New York and Caracas, eventually persuaded him and Gustavo Vollmer to sell us 42 percent of the bank's stock for $14 million. This deal gave us a controlling interest in one of Venezuela's leading banks; it had assets of more than $71 million and fifteen branch offices throughout the country.

We followed up on this promising start with other strategic affiliations in Peru, Colombia, Argentina, and Honduras over the next five years. The process of Latin American expansion was not always smooth and trouble-free. We encountered problems with populist politicians and restrictive regulations wherever we went—not unlike our experience in some areas of the United States. But by the end of 1962, having successfully rebuffed internal opposition, I felt encouraged by the pace of our expansion in Latin America and set out to find similar opportunities in other parts of the world.

MISSED OPPORTUNITY IN CANADA

As important as Latin America was to my strategy of international expansion, I considered Canada even more important. Canada was, and is, our nation's largest trading partner, and U.S. firms controlled more than half of Canadian mining, petroleum, and manufacturing. Many of Chase's most important customers were active there. Even though Canadian law prohibited foreign banks to have branches, I believed it necessary for us to have a direct presence north of the border.

There were a few hopeful signs. I had enjoyed good relations with many of Canada's business and political leaders dating back to Father's friendship with Mackenzie King. Soon after World War II, I had gotten to know Lester (Mike) Pearson personally when he was secretary of state for external relations and represented Canada at the United Nations. In April 1963, Mike became prime minister and called for strengthening political and economic ties with the United States. His positive attitude suggested to me that there might be a more favorable climate in Ottawa toward foreign banks.

The need for Chase to do something became urgent in July 1963 when City Bank bought the Mercantile Bank of Canada, the smallest national bank and the only one already owned by foreign interests. City Bank's purchase created a nationalist uproar, but it fundamentally changed the banking equation in Canada. I felt this was a challenge we could not ignore. Affiliation with one of the principal chartered banks seemed to be our best alternative. Toronto Dominion, Canada's fifth largest, with assets of $2.2 billion and more than six hundred branches, looked especially attractive. Moreover, we received an encouraging letter from Alan Lambert, TD's chairman, indicating that he "would understand if it later developed that you people found it necessary to make some move into this area." I had developed a cordial relationship with Lambert and decided to approach him with an offer to purchase as much as 40 percent of Toronto Dominion's stock. This was my intention when I flew to Canada on November 13, 1963.

Lambert had offered to host a lunch for me and suggested we meet privately in his office for a few minutes beforehand—the perfect opportunity to advance my proposal. To my great surprise Lambert opened our conversation by asking me whether Chase would be interested in buying one-third of TD's stock. I told him the idea had great appeal to me and that I would explore it with George Champion. Lambert's proposal would have required a Chase investment of almost $60 million, more than triple the amount we had invested in *all* our foreign affiliations up to that time. I realized that such a large commitment required careful consideration, but I felt instinctively that we should seize what might be a fleeting and unique opportunity to link two of North America's largest financial institutions.

George Champion did not dismiss the proposal outright but insisted that we first ascertain whether our U.S. corporate customers would find it helpful if we had a stake in a major Canadian bank. From my perspective this was the wrong question. As I saw it, our primary interest in affiliating with TD would be to generate more business directly with leading *Canadian* firms. What our domestic customers thought about the move seemed relatively unimportant.

When George determined that our domestic customers were indifferent to our having a stake in a Canadian bank, he used that as an excuse to postpone making a decision. That was a serious error because our window of opportunity was rapidly closing. Walter Gordon, minister of finance, had introduced legislation that would limit foreign ownership of domestic banks by any one individual or institution to no more than 10 percent.

In a last-ditch effort to save the original terms of the deal, I flew to Ottawa in November 1964 to see Prime Minister Pearson. I tried to convince Mike that restricting Chase's ability to do business in his country, while allowing City Bank a free hand, was unfair to Chase and probably detrimental to the economic development of Canada. Mike said he agreed with my views and promised to review the legislation. But a few months later Lambert told us Gordon had informed him that "he had the complete sympathy and support of the prime minister in his proposed legislation, and that any impressions obtained from Pearson to the contrary are without validity." And that was that.

TD's loss was a terrible setback. The debacle was a glaring consequence of divided authority at the top of Chase and our inability to develop a unified vision for the bank. It was one of the most frustrating experiences of my joint tenure with George Champion.

TURNING POINT IN EUROPE

D espite George's visceral distrust of foreign operations, the irresistible tide of global change forced him to temper his position, and he did not resist the incremental growth of our European and Asian operations. The turning point in George's thinking about Europe resulted, oddly enough, from bad loans we had made in South Africa and managed from our London offices. Initially, George viewed the loan problem as confirmation that little good could come from venturing outside the safe confines of the United States. He dispatched a trusted lieutenant to London to straighten out what he considered the mess made by the International Department.

Soon after he arrived, George's emissary realized just how strongly entrenched City Bank had become, not only in London but in almost every major Western European country. It was doing business directly with European corporations and starting to make strong inroads with Chase's domestic customers with overseas operations—a danger that I had long warned of.

All this was reported to George, who finally agreed that we should strengthen our European management to counter this threat. A subsequent study, conducted by the same Champion loyalist, confirmed that Chase's competitiveness depended on establishing a foothold in virtually every country in Western Europe. This study changed everything. George might discount *my* enthusiasm for expansion, but he could not dismiss the considered views of one of his most trusted men. As a result we initiated plans to acquire affiliates across the continent, a process that took the rest of the decade. During that period Chase completed a number of important acquisitions and affiliations.

In Belgium we bought 49 percent of the Banque du Commerce from its parent, the Banque du Bruxelles. Chase also acquired a 30 percent interest in the Nederlandse Credietbank, which had more than sixty branches throughout Holland. We entered a joint venture with the Bank of Ireland, and we acquired a controlling interest or complete ownership of banks in Austria and Switzerland. And we continued to expand the scope and authority of our flagship branches in London, Paris, and Frankfurt and established new branches in Greece and Italy.

By the end of the decade Chase had a presence in every major European capital.

EXPANDING IN ASIA

Our initial expansion in Asia was much more modest but eventually produced enduring benefits for the bank as well. As late as 1963, Chase's Asian presence was limited to our two branches in Japan along with a representative office in Bombay. Our two Chinese branches had fallen victim to the Communist revolution, and we had unwisely closed the Hong Kong branch a short time later. We clearly needed a radical change in the character of our operations in the vast Asia-Pacific region.

In the late 1950s, Jack McCloy had made an effort to enlarge our pitifully small Asian presence by offering to purchase an equity interest in the Mercantile Bank of India, a small British-based commercial bank with twenty-eight branches scattered across south and southeast Asia. While the management of the Mercantile Bank responded positively to our offer, Lord Cromer, the governor of the Bank of England, demurred granting permission. He suggested instead that we buy the east Asian branches of the Chartered Bank, another large British colonial bank. Cromer then persuaded the much bigger British-owned Hong Kong and Shanghai Bank to buy Mercantile out from under us, thus reinforcing British banking dominance in Asia.

We had much better luck in 1963 when the Dutch-owned Nationale Handelsbank sold us its network of branches in Singapore, Bangkok, Hong Kong, and Japan for $2.5 million. This acquisition got us back into Hong Kong and gave us a new direct presence in two promising countries: Thailand and Singapore. Along with these well-placed branches came more than thirty experienced Dutch managers whose talents and contacts were invaluable in Chase's regional expansion. Later in the decade we opened a new branch in the former Handelsbank building in Jakarta and other branches in Malaysia, South Vietnam, and South Korea. By the decade's end we had positioned ourselves to play a strong role in financing the region's exponential economic growth in the 1970s.

Establishing a foothold in the newly independent African nations south of the Sahara proved a formidable undertaking. Traveling across that continent in 1959 I had seen a number of opportunities but just as many obstacles to the entry of American banks. The former colonial powers had granted independence but also ensured that their banks would continue to dominate. This fact neatly dovetailed with strongly nationalist policies in most African nations and made the task of entering these countries difficult and time-consuming for American banks.

We did establish branches in Johannesburg, South Africa; Lagos, Nigeria; and Monrovia, Liberia, but it was clear that full coverage of this enormously rich continent would depend on Chase's affiliating with one of the major British, French, or Belgian overseas banks already located there. Such an opportunity came unexpectedly in 1965 when Sir Cyril Hawker, the chairman of the Standard Bank, literally walked in the door and offered us a minority participation in his bank's South African subsidiary as a way of protecting it from the threat of nationalization.

Hawker had just merged Standard with the Bank of West Africa, creating an institution with more than eleven hundred branches spread over much of anglophone Africa and the Persian Gulf. We determined that the parent institution would be more suitable to our objectives and proposed to buy 25 percent of the Standard Bank itself. Both Hawker and the Bank of England balked at our taking such a large stake but eventually did agree to our purchasing 14.5 percent of Standard's shares for $21 million, making us their largest shareholder.

An added benefit was that Sir Cyril, a conservative British banker, hit it off famously with George Champion. The two of them began to formulate a "grand design," a powerful global banking unit that covered Africa, Asia, Latin America, and the United States. It would seem that George had become a convert to my views, but he never acknowledged the fact.

Although Standard promised Chase operational influence and the chance to increase our own business in major African markets, it did not work out that way.

From the outset I had insisted that Chase needed to increase its stake in Standard to ensure our real voice in their global operations and to enable us to leverage our activities in Africa. Hawker and Champion discouraged this as antithetical to their grand design. Within a few years it became obvious, as an internal study concluded, that "a gradual erosion of Chase's management participation had taken place." This was hardly the global partnership that had been envisioned.

After George retired in 1969, I decided to remedy the situation. I discussed the issue with the chairman of Britain's National Westminster Bank, which owned a much smaller but still significant percentage of Standard's shares. We agreed that each of us would seek to increase his bank's holdings to 20 percent, which would give us effective control of Standard's operations. Hawker and his board (including George Champion even after his retirement from Chase) adamantly opposed our move, as did the Bank of England, which intervened, probably at Hawker's request, to prevent us from acquiring shares on the open market.

With our strategy revealed, Hawker retaliated quickly. Without consulting either National Westminster or Chase, Hawker carried out a preemptive merger of Standard with the other British colonial giant, the Chartered Bank. Hawker's action diluted Chase's interest in the merged bank to less than 10 percent.

The merger also created an insurmountable obstacle to our continued ownership of Standard-Chartered stock because included in the Chartered Bank's vast worldwide holdings was a small two-branch bank in San Francisco. Even though Chase had only a minuscule indirect interest in the California bank, the Federal Reserve ruled that Chase was in violation of the regulation prohibiting U.S. banks from branching across state lines. We asked Standard-Chartered to sell the California subsidiary, but they refused. As a result, in 1975, after numerous appeals to the Federal Reserve, we had to sell our interest in Standard-Chartered.

Although we realized a $42 million profit on our investment in Standard, the termination of the relationship marked a substantial setback for Chase. Our presence in most African nations was obliterated overnight, and we had to begin anew the task of creating a regional network.

FAILURE WITH GLOBAL INVESTMENT BANKING

While the development of a global branch network was critical to Chase's emergence as a multinational bank, so, too, was our ability to expand into other international financial areas, particularly investment banking. Lacking the needed expertise ourselves, we decided to form a consortium with some of our oldest European and British banking friends to provide international bond underwriting and loan syndication.

We approached three banks in the Rothschild group. Since both Evelyn de Rothschild, chairman of L. M. Rothschild, and Leon Lambert, chairman of Banque Lambert (a Rothschild through his mother), were personal friends, I had positive initial conversations with them.

At the same time we met with Hermann Abs, chairman of the Deutsche Bank in West Germany; Alfred Schaefer, chairman of the Union Bank of Switzerland; and Marcus Wallenberg of Sweden, whose family controlled the Stockholm Enskilda Bank. Of these three, only Wallenberg expressed interest and agreed to proceed. Abs and Schaefer, the two most powerful and influential European bankers of their day, were decidedly negative to the proposal. Despite that, we thought the combination of Chase, the Rothschild-related merchant banks, and the prestigious Enskilda Bank gave us substantial strength and was worth doing. After extensive negotiations with the leaders of the other institutions, I thought we had hammered out a firm deal. A press release was ready for distribution following a luncheon at Chase in the fall of 1966 at which the new bank was to be launched.

Late in the morning of the appointed day, only hours before the announcement, Marcus Wallenberg, Jr., came to see me at my office at Chase Plaza. He was obviously distraught. As he stammered out his story, I learned why. Earlier that morning Marcus had paid a courtesy call on J. P. Morgan and Company, Enskilda's principal U.S. correspondent bank. Senior Morgan executives told him the proposed consortium bank was unacceptable to them and implied they would retaliate if Enskilda proceeded with the venture. Marcus had then called his father in Stockholm and received instructions to withdraw from the consortium. Despite my efforts to change his mind, young Marcus said he was sorry but his father's decision was final.*

When young Wallenberg announced Enskilda's withdrawal at the lugubrious luncheon, the aristocratic Evelyn de Rothschild responded by saying that without the Swedish bank, L. M. Rothschild was not prepared to sign the final papers, either. Although I suggested we delay a decision to see if we could find another European commercial banking partner, it was

---

*The vacillating behavior of the Wallenbergs ended on a tragic note. The elder Wallenberg, one of the world's most prominent and successful businessmen, had given his son increasingly heavy responsibilities, leaving him little time for his wife and young children. That, coupled with the pressure he was under, was apparently too much for young Marcus to handle, and five years later he committed suicide.

painfully clear that our plan for a Chase-led consortium had fallen apart. I heard later that both Abs and Schaefer had put pressure on Wallenberg and the Rothschild group to withdraw from the venture. The Europeans were simply not going to allow a large and aggressive U.S. commercial bank into their territory without a fight. My desire to create an investment banking vehicle for Chase would have to wait.

ENHANCING GLOBAL ACCESS AND INFLUENCE

I had far greater success in strengthening Chase's access to the most important and powerful industrial leaders of the world. To enhance our global visibility worldwide, we decided in the late 1960s to create an International Advisory Committee (IAC). It was to be composed of prominent and respected businessmen, many of whom were my personal friends, in the countries we considered most essential for our operational success. We were not the first to attempt this concept. Other New York banks had already formed similar committees, and I thought the idea had real merit for us also—particularly if we could attract the caliber of person I sought.

John Loudon, the distinguished chairman of Royal Dutch Petroleum, agreed to take on the critical job of IAC chairman. John's executive capabilities and diplomatic and managerial skills had brought him recognition as perhaps the world's most prominent and respected businessman. I had met him at Bilderberg and other international gatherings over the years and had come to like and admire him greatly. As we had hoped, John helped recruit a stellar group of chief executives of nonfinancial firms—ten Americans and eleven foreigners. Among them were the following:

Giovanni Agnelli was chairman of the Fiat Group, Italy's largest and most profitable corporation. One of our first choices, Gianni had a strong interest in domestic Italian politics and was committed to the process of European integration. I thought he would bring exactly the right combination of personal, political, and business skills to the IAC's deliberations. He has now been a member of the committee for over thirty years.

Wilfred Baumgartner, the president of Rhône-Poulenc, served as the IAC's French representative. Wilfred was an *inspecteur des finances* in the Ministry of Finance, a position held only by a few select individuals. He later became governor of the Bank of France and then minister of finance. He spoke French with an elegance matched only by Charles de Gaulle.

Taizo Ishizaka was an octogenarian whose selection enhanced our plans to expand in Japan. His position as honorary chairman of the Keidanren and chairman of two hundred corporations afforded him immense prestige and access to the upper echelons of Japanese business and government.

J.R.D. Tata was the chairman of his family's enormous steel and industrial empire. Far and away India's most prominent and successful businessman and also one of her most public-spirited citizens, he was a man of great modesty, simplicity, and wisdom who contributed greatly to the standing of Chase in South Asia.

Sir Y. K. Pao was one of the world's leading shipping magnates. Another colorful and influential member of the committee, Y.K. had been a banker in Shanghai before World War II. After Mao's revolution he moved to Hong Kong and built a shipping fleet that surpassed the Soviet Union's merchant marine in size. Y.K. had heard about the formation of the IAC and requested a private meeting in my Rockefeller Center offices to tell me of his interest in being included in the group. We were more than happy to comply with his request.

We balanced our distinguished foreign membership with an equally impressive list of American chief executives, including William Blackie of Caterpillar, Carl Gerstacker of Dow Chemical, William Hewitt of John Deere, and David Packard of Hewlett-Packard. Over the years Chase maintained the IAC's reputation by recruiting such prominent individuals as C. Douglas Dillon, Rawleigh Warner, Henry Ford II, Cyrus Vance, Lord Carrington, and Henry Kissinger. At the working sessions senior bank officers review aspects of the bank's operations, prominent individuals frequently address the group on specific economic issues, and individual members comment on economic and political developments in their countries.

Periodically, the IAC convenes in a foreign country where the head of state or government usually receives the group with other prominent government and business leaders. Visits to historic sites and cultural institutions form an integral part of our program as well. And the press often covers the visit. On our first visit to France, for example, we organized a dinner with French leaders and their wives in the Salon de Battailles of the Palace of Versailles. We then moved to the theater of Louis XV and listened to a Mozart program played by the Paris Opera chamber music ensemble.

I became the chairman of the IAC upon my retirement from Chase in 1981. During recent years, as Chase merged first with Chemical Bank and then with J. P. Morgan, the advisory committees of the three banks have also merged. Nonetheless, the IAC remains a valuable vehicle for today's Chase, just as it was when we began it more than three decades ago.

A DECADE OF GROWTH

Despite divided leadership and costly delays, the 1960s was a period of real progress toward Chase Manhattan's becoming a truly international bank. We began the decade with branches in only eleven foreign areas and ended it with direct operations in seventy-three. We had spread our network to six continents: North and South America, Europe, Asia, Africa, and Australia. By 1969 deposits in our overseas branches formed almost one-third of all Chase deposits, and foreign loans constituted one-fourth of our total portfolio. Earnings from the international side were expanding and would soon surpass domestic income.

With George Champion's retirement, my challenge as sole chief executive officer was to ensure that the bank continued to strengthen its leadership role in the United States, even as it expanded its presence and position as a world financial power.

CHAPTER 16

TAKING THE HELM

When I took over as CEO on the morning of March 3, 1969, I had been with the bank for almost twenty-three years. In contrast to Winthrop Aldrich and Jack McCloy at the time they assumed command, I knew the bank intimately from the inside and had been exposed to most aspects of its varied business. But unlike George Champion, I was not an experienced lending officer. I sensed that my lack of credit training and lending experience made some directors and senior officers skeptical about my ability to run the bank effectively and profitably. Leading these men (and all the directors and senior officers of the bank were men) would not be easy, but I was convinced that my vision for the bank was the correct one and that I was uniquely qualified to lead the Chase at a time of great change.

I was proud of Chase's reputation among U.S. banks for integrity, quality, and excellence. The leading corporations of our nation were our clients, and no other bank was more respected for the creativity and professionalism of its lending officers. Furthermore, Chase was an institution that acknowledged its responsibilities as a constructive player in the effort to build a more equitable society. All of that I was determined to preserve.

My principal challenge, then, was not to dismantle the bank but to build on its strengths by expanding our global capacity and by introducing the techniques of modern management that would make Chase a leading global financial institution.*

SIX KEY CORPORATE CONCERNS

As CEO I considered at least half a dozen areas critical if Chase was to continue to compete effectively in the world of global banking.

International Expansion. Even though we now operated in East Asia, Latin America, Europe, and Africa, there were still great gaps in our foreign coverage both in terms of our direct presence in many countries and the diversity of the services we offered. By the late 1960s, U.S. businesses—many of them Chase customers—had become increasingly involved in foreign trade and had located their manufacturing and production facilities abroad. Thus, there was no longer any doubt, at least in my mind, that Chase had to become more of an international bank at the same time that we continued our domestic expansion.

My first priority, then, was to develop a coherent global strategy, a comprehensive program and a specific timetable for expansion and diversification on every continent. For instance, having failed in our earlier effort with the Rothschilds and Wallenbergs, I was determined to set up an international merchant banking consortium to provide Eurocurrency term loans to multinational corporations and governments, and to engage in underwriting and bond placements worldwide. The possibility of direct branching into a number of areas, particularly the oil-rich Middle East, seemed especially promising, and I wanted to explore dawning opportunities in the Soviet bloc countries and China. The key to this process would be finding, training, and deploying personnel capable of managing this ambitious program of expansion. That would require, in turn, a very different attitude toward the recruitment and training of our staff.

Human Resources. Chase desperately needed a more professional approach to human resources. Although we had an excellent credit training program, we had no organized plan for identifying talented employees and developing

---

*I had outlined my ideas on the importance of good management practices in banking and the need for banks to play a greater role in economic development at home and abroad in the McKinsey lectures at Columbia University in 1964. These lectures were later published as *Creative Management in Banking.*

a career path for them. There was no system of performance evaluation and no incentive compensation program. Some progress had been made in hiring and promoting women and minority employees, but we lacked a policy affirming that all employees would have an equal opportunity for advancement based solely on the quality of their individual performance. I extended this policy to include foreign employees who had correctly perceived that there were limited opportunities for them to move up in the bank.

Organization Planning. Chase's gradual transformation from a largely domestic wholesale bank into a full-service international bank required fundamental structural changes, which had been delayed, avoided, or only partially implemented during the years of conflict between George and me in the 1960s.

Our differing positions on reorganizing as a one-bank holding company, a key issue during the last year of our joint tenure, exemplified the situation. The other major New York City banks had adopted this form of organization, but George opposed it, fearing that the bank would lose its identity by becoming a mere subsidiary of the larger corporation. I favored it because the holding company would enable us to enter a number of new and potentially profitable domestic fields such as insurance, mortgage banking, management consulting, and computer-based services—all of them prohibited to commercial banks by Federal Reserve regulations.

I wanted to create a holding company as soon as I became chairman as the preliminary step to other structural changes I hoped to introduce. I also wanted to upgrade our internal planning process, which was far below the standards of topflight industrial corporations such as General Electric, IBM, and Standard Oil of New Jersey.

Marketing. While marketing was in urgent need of improvement, Chase had real strengths in this area that we could capitalize on. Credit officers who traveled the U.S. districts had developed strong ties with their corporate customers and often with their families as well. International officers had begun to establish the same relationships with our overseas clients. The loyalty of our customers was legendary in the banking world and a strong foundation on which we could build. However, we needed a more systematic approach to marketing and a more formal overall strategy for developing, pricing, promoting, and selling the bank's services that would generate an image of Chase as a professional, aggressive, and modern bank.

Technology. At the core of any bank's ability to operate effectively and profitably is its back office—the people and technology executing hundreds of thousands of daily customer transactions accurately, expeditiously, and at a reasonable cost. The application of advanced technology to the banking business had intrigued me almost from the beginning of my career with Chase. In 1954 I had persuaded Jack McCloy to commission the Laboratory for Electronics (LFE), a company I had helped start, to study the bank's operations and custom-design a computer to control our operations. The timing was premature and the effort failed, but the LFE's work gave us the courage to pursue a more comprehensive approach to modernizing our operational procedures and staff. In fact, by the early 1960s virtually all of our operations were computerized.

Unfortunately, at the time I became chairman, we had twenty-seven different computer systems in operation! We first had to rationalize these incompatible systems and then make sure there was better interaction and linkage among our technical operations people, the line officers responsible for account relationships, and the top management of the bank, who were blissfully ignorant of both the potential and the problems of the imminent electronics revolution. I knew this was an area I would have to get involved with personally, but I didn't realize that the back office would become a major problem area for the bank before we finally brought it under control.

Social Responsibility. Finally, there was the bank's public role and responsibilities. The consensus that had unified the country in the postwar period had ended abruptly in the mid-1960s. Strong popular opposition to the Vietnam War and rising unrest in our cities were accompanied by a growing antipathy toward business in general and big banks in particular. While I considered the more extreme of these criticisms irresponsible and ideologically inspired, I believed Chase did have a responsibility to help redress the legitimate social and economic problems that confronted the country.

I had felt this way for some time. Indeed, in the fall of 1968, a few days before the public announcement of my promotion to chairman, I addressed a meeting of the Financial Executives Institute on the subject of the "urban crisis" and told them that what we faced as businessmen was not a single problem: "Rather it is a kind of witches' brew blended from all the major ills of our country—inadequate educational systems, hard-core unemployment, hazardous pollution of natural resources, antiquated transportation, shameful housing, insufficient and ineffective public facilities, lack of equal opportunity for all, and a highly dangerous failure of communication between old and young, black and white. All of these are problems that cry out for immediate action."

I believed then and I believe now that the private sector has an obligation to understand and help solve such societal problems.

Chase had a strong tradition of civic involvement, but I wanted to broaden and deepen the bank's involvement with its community. The manner in which an institution gives expression to its relationship with the community has an important bearing on its public image. I was eager to have Chase perceived as a modern, progressive, and open institution. To forge a new "image," I targeted three areas:

First, I wanted to transform our uncoordinated corporate charitable giving into a broad-based and carefully conceived program that focused on the complex urban issues of the day. I believed that personal participation and leadership by Chase officers should be part of this effort and was as important as the contribution of corporate philanthropic funds.

Second, I planned to use the distinguished modern architecture of One Chase Manhattan Plaza as a model for the design and construction of new branches and facilities around the world.

Third, I believed that our art program, which had started out as a way to make One Chase Plaza less austere, could be expanded into a powerful expression of the bank's enlightened role in the culture of the modern world.

During our joint tenure George had taken little interest in any of these programs; at best he considered them peripheral to the bank's principal activities. But with his departure I would have a freer hand to pursue these and other initiatives more aggressively.

CHARTING A NEW COURSE

At the beginning of my tenure as chairman I was fortunate in finding an extremely able executive assistant, Joseph Verner Reed, Jr., who was recommended to me by Eugene Black, a Chase director and former chairman of the World Bank. Joseph had been Gene's assistant at the World Bank and had stayed with him when he returned to New York. A few weeks before I took over as chairman, Gene told me that my success would depend to a considerable degree on finding a capable personal aide who could supervise the wide-ranging responsibilities of my office. Reed, he said, had all the qualities that were needed, and he urged me to take him on.

Joseph—a man of uncommon spirit and *joie de vivre*—proved to be all Gene Black claimed he would be. During the twelve years I served as chairman, Joseph's friendship, loyalty, and managerial capability were critical in enabling me to handle the broad range of tasks I had to cope with and to survive many difficult moments.

In addition to Joseph I had strong support and wise counsel from Dick Dilworth, who in addition to being a Chase director was also the chief financial advisor to the Rockefeller family and a close personal friend. Dick helped me steer through several perilous moments during my tenure as chairman. Joseph and Dick were especially helpful during the early years when I was struggling to build a senior management team at the bank. As it turned out, I needed all the friends I could find.

A RELUCTANT DEPARTURE

At the outset of my tenure I lacked the full authority and independence that I needed to do my job and accomplish my goals. This situation resulted from George Champion's refusal to let go of the reins of power and my own reluctance to fully assert my authority.

While no longer an officer of the bank, George remained a director and at the monthly board meetings continued to second-guess my decisions, make pronouncements that sounded like orders, and act much as he had when he was chairman. I have no doubt George thought he was acting in the bank's best interest, making a last-ditch effort "to save the bank" from my quixotic schemes, but even his supporters on the board recognized that this situation was intolerable. After two years of his constant sniping, I convinced the board to amend the bylaws and lower the board retirement age to sixty-eight, which was, not coincidentally, George's age at the time. For some years after that I would occasionally run into George, who stayed active in the New York business community, and after a few drinks he would pour out his feelings in scathing terms about how I was ruining the bank.

In one sense I can't blame George for his bitterness. Our shared leadership had been deeply frustrating for him. He had devoted his career to the Chase, an institution I'm sure he loved as deeply as I did, yet he was never allowed to run the bank entirely on his own. He was honestly convinced that my "radical" ideas were dangerous, just as I was convinced they were essential to the bank's survival and growth. Our visions were so diametrically opposed that no real compromise was possible, only accommodation. Certainly, Chase had lost valuable ground, especially to City Bank, that we would never entirely make up. On the other hand, had I simply resigned in 1960—my only real alternative—and left the bank in George's hands, Chase would never have developed into the great international bank that it became.

CHAMPION'S REVENGE

George had also limited my authority through more direct means. In the fall of 1968, six months before he retired, George pushed through a reorganization of the upper level of the bank's management via the creation of the "executive office of the chairman" that would commence operations on the day I took over. He pointed out, in defending his move, that other leading New York banks, including J. P. Morgan, had recently done the same. The executive office would be composed of me as chairman; Herbert Patterson, the new president and chief administrative officer; and John Place and George Roeder, newly appointed as vice chairmen. Efficiency was the ostensible reason for the change. Although I had serious reservations about the reorganization, I defended it at the press conference where I was introduced as the next chairman. I said in response to a reporter's question, "It's obvious that not one or even two people can deal effectively with the complex problems of a bank as large and diverse as Chase."

While there was some truth to my statement, it certainly was not the whole story. The reorganization should have been called "Champion's Revenge," because it effectively prevented me from becoming the chief executive officer. The procedures instituted by George required a unanimous vote of all four of us before any major decision could be made. And since Patterson, Place, and Roeder had all risen through the ranks under George's tutelage and subscribed to most of his views of banking, this was clearly a technical device to keep me under control. It was as if George, embittered by our years as co-CEOs, could not accept the idea of my attaining the position that had been denied to him.

The executive office would guarantee even more delay and stagnation, which the bank could ill afford. I realize now that I should have objected immediately to this rigged system, but I had never been a CEO before and lacked the confidence to move promptly and decisively to rectify it. In truth, the arrangement was so intrinsically unmanageable that it could not last long. In early 1971 I persuaded the board to disband the committee as an operating entity and make it purely advisory to me.

FISTFIGHT AT A UNITY MEETING

Ironically, the biggest problem the bank faced in the first few years of my chairmanship was the result of the one decision both George and I had agreed on: appointing Herb Patterson president and chief operating officer.

Herb was a good credit officer and was well liked in the bank. A graduate of Yale, he had successfully run both the United States Department—where he worked for George Champion—and the International Department, where he had truly grown into the position, developing a keen interest in promoting our foreign activities, something that obviously appealed to me.

The first indication that we might have made a serious error in promoting Herb came at a retreat I had arranged for the bank's senior management in Princeton, New Jersey, in late January 1969, just before I took over as chairman. I had convened the meeting "to build unity" among my most senior managers. The decade-long rift between George and me had created a massive fault line within the bank, and the Princeton retreat was my effort to mend fences and promote a sense of teamwork and camaraderie.

It was no secret that Herb Patterson enjoyed a cocktail, but I was certainly not prepared for his performance that first evening at Princeton. After downing a few too many, Herb started a shouting match with Charlie Agemian, the bank's feisty comptroller. A man of considerable girth, Charlie had a quick temper and was not the easiest person to get along with, but he was also extremely knowledgeable and a very competent officer who would need to be a fully participating member of Herb's and my core management team. The shouting soon turned to shoving, and before we knew it, Herb and Charlie were throwing punches at each other and the rest of us were trying to separate them. At the height of the debacle, as he was being escorted from the room, Herb shouted that Charlie should be fired. My unity meeting had degenerated into a total fiasco.

I was angry and disheartened by this incident. Instead of forging a closer working relationship among my top officers, I had only succeeded in exposing the deep fissures that existed within the bank. The next morning as I rode back in the car to New York, I realized something had to be done; I simply could not afford to tolerate this kind of behavior.

I was in an impossible position, however. Firing Herb a month before he was to take office as president would undermine the fragile consensus in the bank and also create a furor in the financial community that might have a strongly negative impact on Chase's business relationships and operations. My options were severely limited. The following Monday morning I called Herb to my office and told him that another such incident would force me to fire him. Herb was contrite and assured me nothing like that would ever happen again. There were no more fistfights, but personal tensions continued. More important, I began my tenure as chairman of the bank with grave doubts about whether I could rely on the man who would be my chief operating officer.

THE FIRING

Herb and I assumed our new responsibilities on March 3, 1969, and for the first two years Herb's performance was respectable. He had, after all, done an exemplary job managing two of the bank's most important departments. However, in the early 1970s I began to notice that many of the routine managerial and administrative functions I expected Herb to deal with were being neglected or mishandled. As time went on he seemed to freeze under the pressure. He retreated into his office, which was next door to mine, and rarely emerged during the day. From my perspective Herb appeared unwilling or almost incapable of making a decision, but he also refused to allow important issues to be brought to me, even for my advice or comment. "Mr. Rockefeller can't be bothered," he would say, and I would only find out about it later, sometimes when it was much too late. Herb was supposed to run the day-to-day operations of the bank, allowing me to focus on broader issues of policy and planning, but even routine decisions were not being made.

Herb's lifestyle was taking a visible toll on him. His first wife was a lovely woman who had kept him on the straight and narrow path, controlling his drinking and keeping him focused on his work. She had died, and Herb soon married an attractive socialite who enjoyed her status with the New York "jet set." However, it was impossible to run a major commercial bank after staying out all night; the pressure and fatigue only compounded Herb's drinking problem. I learned of several incidents at important banking functions when Herb had become conspicuously drunk and had to be led, staggering, from the room. His associates and friends tried to conceal or rationalize his behavior, but word about these bouts spread rapidly around Wall Street.

I spoke with Herb a number of times, voicing my growing concern about his performance and style. Herb always listened patiently and contritely to my admonitions and complaints, but nothing changed. As a result, morale at the bank suffered, and the upper echelon of management started to grumble.

By early 1971 a number of Chase directors had spoken with me about Herb's work. A few demanded that I take immediate action. Therefore, in order to strengthen the senior level of management and to ease the burden on Herb, I recommended to the board in late 1971 that we appoint two new vice chairmen to become part of the executive office and absorb some of Herb's responsibilities. While the performance of the bank improved modestly, Herb's passivity remained a problem. I grew more and more frustrated, and by the late summer of 1972 I decided that Herb had to go. During the annual meeting of the American Bankers Association in Dallas in early October of that year, I asked him to come to my room. I told him I was disappointed with his performance and that I was planning to replace him. Herb agreed that things were not going well, and he seemed relieved by my decision. There was some press criticism over the apparent abruptness of Herb's departure, but people who understood the circumstances felt I should have fired him much earlier.

FINDING A NEW PRESIDENT

One of the reasons I had given Herb a number of second chances was that there was no obvious replacement for him. Bringing in someone from outside the bank would have been hard on morale, and, indeed, I saw no outside candidates who fitted our needs. There was a limited field within the bank as well.

In the end only one person stood head and shoulders above the rest: Willard Butcher. Bill had served ably as vice chairman for the previous nine months and had an easygoing personality and an exceptional knowledge of modern banking. Ten years my junior, Bill was a Phi Beta Kappa graduate of Brown University and had joined the bank as a management trainee in 1947. He had spent most of his career in the Commercial Banking Department, mainly in the highly competitive New York City branches, and had risen rapidly. I was impressed with Bill's knowledge and personal touch, and in 1969 appointed him head of the International Department, where he was an aggressive exponent of foreign expansion.

Bill Butcher was a pleasure to work with. A hands-on administrator, he went about his job aggressively and enthusiastically. We worked well together, conferring often and talking easily. There were no walls or awkwardness, just a plain, straightforward give-and-take. Bill understood my plans for Chase and ably administered its day-to-day implementation. Almost immediately the bank gathered momentum.

MY OWN TEAM

It had taken me four years to secure full authority as CEO of the Chase Manhattan Bank. Admittedly, I should have moved more quickly to consolidate my power and to end the Champion era. I didn't, and that was a mistake. But once I became comfortable with my role and position as CEO, I moved swiftly and correctly in making the difficult and painful decision to fire my chief operating officer, a man I liked personally but who was not performing acceptably.

These were difficult and frustrating years for me. Despite my many years at the bank, I felt isolated, with few close friends or supporters. As a result I acted with considerable caution, even timidity, insofar as the bank's internal structure and management was concerned, and I regret my hesitation in this area. Fortunately, my timidity was balanced by a boldness in leading the bank in a number of other areas.

I helped lay the groundwork for our future growth and expansion by convincing the board to organize as a one-bank holding corporation and by beginning to improve our management process.

We moved quickly and effectively to establish a direct presence in many parts of the world—in the expanding industrial and financial centers of Europe, the rapidly modernizing countries of Latin America and the Pacific Rim, throughout the critical petroleum-producing countries of the Middle East, and later in the bastions of the Communist world, the Soviet Union and China.

Finally, in the realm of external relations—in our philanthropic support for the local community and the larger society, and our willingness to speak out in defense of the system we represented—Chase was viewed by many as a model company.

I was extremely proud of these accomplishments and took it as my special mandate to strengthen Chase's position as a leader in global banking by continuing to expand our presence in new markets around the world.

CHAPTER 17

ENGAGING THE SOVIETS

To become a global banking leader Chase would have to confront the reality that much of the world was dominated by governments fundamentally opposed to democratic principles and to the operation of the free market. As a practical necessity, then, if Chase was to expand internationally, we would have to learn how to deal with regimes that were autocratic, totalitarian, and anticapitalist in their orientation and policies.

Even though I was totally unsympathetic to these regimes, I believed the bank should work with them. Throughout my Chase career I never hesitated to meet with the leaders of my country's most militant and obdurate ideological adversaries, and with rulers whose despotic and dictatorial style I personally despised, from Houari Boumedienne of Algeria to Mobutu Sese Soko of Zaire, from General Augusto Pinochet of Chile to Saddam Hussein of Iraq. I met them all.

I talked at some length with Marshal Tito of Yugoslavia, President Nicolae Ceaușescu of Romania, General Wojciech Jaruzelski of Poland, and General Alfredo Stroessner of Paraguay. I sat for extended discussions with all the modern leaders of racist South Africa: Henrik Verwoerd, B. J. Vorster, P. W. Botha, and, later, the more enlightened F. W. de Klerk. I persevered through lengthy meetings with Zhou Enlai and other senior members of the Chinese Communist hierarchy while the Cultural Revolution still raged. I debated virtually every leader of the Soviet Union from Nikita Khrushchev through Mikhail Gorbachev, and, even more recently, confronted Fidel Castro during his 1996 visit to New York.

Critics from both the left and the right have vilified me for doing this. Indeed, mine has not been a particularly popular or well-understood position. My critics claim that "David Rockefeller has never met a dictator he didn't like." But at no time in more than four decades of private meetings with foreign leaders have I ever deferred to their point of view when I disagreed with them. On the contrary, I have used these meetings to point out respectfully but firmly the flaws in their systems as I saw them and to defend the virtues of my own. I pursued these opportunities because I believed that even the most entrenched authoritarian systems would succumb eventually to the superior values of our system.

BEGINNING THE DIALOGUE

M y contacts with the Soviets began in 1962 when I was invited to attend an American-Soviet citizens conference. Initiated by Norman Cousins, publisher of the *Saturday Review,* the "Dartmouth Conference," as these meetings came to be called, was one of several Cold War efforts designed to improve understanding between the two superpowers through face-to-face meetings and dialogue. The value of the meetings was proven at the first one I attended in Andover, Massachusetts, in late October 1962.

In the midst of the Cuban Missile Crisis, the participants continued their sessions even as our two nations faced each other in an unprecedented and terrifying nuclear confrontation. Both sides saw that the time had come to step back from the threshold of atomic annihilation and seek other ways to pursue our rivalry. The next Dartmouth Conference took place two summers later in Leningrad, and it was on this trip that my daughter Neva and I met Nikita Khrushchev, the first secretary of the Soviet Communist Party. The idea for the meeting had actually come from U Thant, the secretary-general of the United Nations, who mentioned it to me at a reception I hosted for the U.N.'s senior staff at Pocantico. When I told him I was planning a trip to Leningrad, the Secretary-General said he thought the top Soviet leadership would benefit from exposure to an American banker. A personal meeting with Khrushchev during my trip to Russia might help in a small way to improve relations between the two superpowers.

U Thant agreed to send word to him, but I heard nothing definite about the meeting before leaving for Leningrad in late July. The day after the Dartmouth delegation arrived, however, I received a message from the Kremlin summoning me to a meeting the following day in Moscow. In order to get there in time, Neva and I took the overnight train—watched carefully by a KGB agent who had attended the conference itself.

=

Moscow in those days was a study in contrasts. Khrushchev had claimed that the USSR would surpass the United States in terms of gross domestic product, but he had issued this pronouncement from a city mired in economic stagnation and suffering from decades of neglect. Elegant buildings from the Czarist days stood unpainted and in disrepair; offices and apartment houses built during the more recent Stalinist era looked shabby and uninviting. There were few automobiles, but the center lanes on the broad main boulevards were kept open to accommodate the speeding Russian-built Zil limousines carrying members of the Politburo on official business. People queued on long lines to buy meager quantities of poor-quality food, and in department stores the shelves were virtually empty of goods. On this, my first trip to the heart of the Soviet Empire, I found myself wondering about the economic strength of the country that was the subject of Khrushchev's bluster.

THE EMBODIMENT OF CAPITALISM

To the Soviet propaganda machine the Rockefeller family had always been "capitalist enemy number one." Some years before, *Pravda* had published a book on me and my four brothers entitled *Ever Knee Deep in Blood, Ever Trampling Corpses.* An article at about the same time in the English-language *New Times* magazine explained that "of all the billionaire dynasties reigning in the world, the most powerful is that of the Rockefellers." The thesis was that, having made exorbitant profits on oil during World War II, we then plowed the money into armaments and took control of the manufacture of atomic weapons. The fact that the Rockefeller Foundation had helped rescue Enrico Fermi, Leo Szilard, and Edward Teller from European Fascist regimes in the 1930s was provided as supporting evidence of our family's intent to fuel the Cold War to increase our own profits.

Just a few months before I arrived in Moscow, *Izvestiya* editorialized that as chairman of the Museum of Modern Art I was promoting decadence in order to corrupt the population at large: "Under the Rockefellers' tutelage, abstract art is summoned to play a definite political role, to distract the attention of thinking Americans from real life and to make them stupid."

I met many Russians over the years who were convinced my brothers and

I were a cabal, pulling strings behind the scenes to shape American foreign policy. The Soviets had no conception of how a pluralistic democracy works and believed elected officials, up to and including the president of the United States, were only figureheads acting out the roles dictated to them by the real "powers that be"—in this case, my family. Not infrequently Soviet officials would admonish me to "tell your president to grant most-favored-nation trading status to us," or some other thing on their minds, as if it were just a question of my saying so, and it would be done. I would try to explain that the United States had a different kind of government and that I didn't wield that kind of power, but it was clear they didn't believe me.

UNDER LENIN'S GAZE

In the midafternoon of July 29 a battered Russian-built Fiat collected Neva and me from our hotel and drove us through the high, red, crenelated walls of the Kremlin to a rather simple and sparsely furnished room in a modest building that had been used by Lenin. His successors had maintained offices there, trying, I suppose, to convey the impression that they were making sacrifices on behalf of the proletariat.

The interview had been granted to me alone, but when Khrushchev greeted us in the anteroom, I asked if Neva could remain to act as note taker. I thought it would be important for me to have a record of the conversation and a memorable experience for her. Khrushchev graciously assented.

There were only four of us present: Neva, me, Khrushchev, and his excellent interpreter Victor Syhodrev, who was born in Brooklyn and translated for the Soviet leaders. We sat on hard wooden straight-backed chairs around a large, varnished oak table, Khrushchev on one side, and Neva and I across from him. Syhodrev sat at the end of the table between us. There was little decoration in the room apart from a large portrait of Lenin that dominated the room. Once or twice during the conversation that followed I glanced up to find Lenin staring at me in disapproval.

THE CONVERSATION

While there had been a definite thaw in the Soviet Union's internal repression under Khrushchev—a welcome change from Stalin's incredible brutality—his image was still that of the crude bully who had taken his shoe off in the U.N. to pound his desk, interrupting British Prime Minister Harold Macmillan's condemnation of Soviet actions. There was a question in my mind as to how Khrushchev would behave in our meeting since it would not be without strong symbolic meaning; the "prince of capitalism," as some labeled me, confronting the modern "Czar of all the Russias." I began with a few pleasantries and offered him as a gift two etchings by Grant Wood, thinking them appropriately American and close enough to approved Soviet tastes that he wouldn't take offense. There were no telephone calls or other interruptions during our meeting, which lasted well over two hours.

Almost immediately Khrushchev challenged me. He claimed that Nelson, through the Rockefeller Brothers Fund study *America at Mid-Century*, had called for a massive increase in U.S. defense expenditures to counter the growing Soviet military threat. "I believe," Khrushchev said, "that had your brother Nelson been elected, his policies would differ little if at all from those presently followed by President Johnson."

In an attempt to be diplomatic I spoke of the importance of high-level contacts and said I hoped he and President Johnson would be able to establish close relations, but in a non sequitur, Khrushchev complained bitterly about U.S. interference in Soviet internal affairs. Russians, I found, were surprisingly sensitive to U.S. criticism of their regime.

After that our conversation began in earnest. The interview, as transcribed by Neva, who was scribbling furiously at my side, captures the thinking of Khrushchev at a crucial time in U.S.-Soviet relations and also a crucial moment in his career: Barely two months later, in mid-October 1964, Khrushchev was deposed. What follows is largely verbatim, although I have paraphrased some sections and added personal comments in parentheses.

=

NK: As regards all internal matters [referring to third world countries], we believe that they are and must be resolved from within by the people of that country. We conduct all our relations with any state *as it exists* and with the internal order of that country, which is the sole reasonable basis for peaceful negotiations.

DR: That is one of the areas that gives me cause for concern. In recent cases, particularly in Latin America, we feel that you make use of local Communist parties to bring into power governments that favor the Soviet Union. When this happens, it endangers the existing power structure and is opposed to the interests of the United States. So I am pleased to hear that this is not your policy. [The Secretary appeared to be irritated.]

NK: *Nyet.* A revolution cannot be organized or instigated just at anybody's will. The people of the country must accomplish it themselves. When the revolution occurred in Russia, Lenin wasn't even in the country. The revolution took place because our people accomplished it themselves. Hungry women went out into the streets of Leningrad, and the government fell. This is the case in other countries. It is the people who cause a revolution; it can never be accomplished by another state or party. Examples are South Korea and South Vietnam. In South Vietnam there is terrible strife, while in Korea the situation is relatively calm. Doesn't that show that revolutions are not dependent on anyone's wish or will? They depend on the maturity of conditions. We do believe that revolutions will occur in all countries, even in the United States. *When,* one can't say, but when it *does* occur, it will be accomplished by the people of your country. Meanwhile, we want peace, good relations, and good business contacts with the United States.

When the revolution triumphed in Cuba, Castro wasn't even a member of the Communist Party. Even after victory he didn't recognize this country for one or one and a half years. But the revolution developed further, resulting in the present government in that country. We recognized that the revolution had fulfilled itself. We recognize every people's right to establish a system of its own choice in its own country, without interference in internal affairs. Such interference can only result in chaos.

DR: I would draw different conclusions than you did from the examples of history which you cited. South Vietnam is the cause of chaos today, as I see it, because the Vietcong have received massive support from North Vietnam and, more importantly, from the People's Republic of China. All the United States seeks to accomplish there is to stop the aggressive policies of North Vietnam and the People's Republic whose efforts to take over South Vietnam are inimical to our vital interests. The United States would welcome a chance to get out of Vietnam and to see it neutral. Perhaps this could be done through the United Nations, but as the situation is now, I don't see how neutral independence can be accomplished, other than with our assistance.

[At this point Khrushchev took a paperweight in his hand and began to thump it on the table.]

In Southeast Asia the interests of our two countries are one and the same. I can hardly imagine that it is in the interest of the Soviet Union to see the People's Republic of China sweep over the whole of Asia, but I fear there is a danger of this without your continuing participation with us in the stabilization of Vietnam, and in Laos through the International Control Commission you set up with President Kennedy. There must be cooperation between us so that Southeast Asia is not a threat to the whole world.

NK: [The Secretary continued thumping.] You're mistaken. You're mistaken because you think the Chinese are interfering in Vietnam. The Chinese are no less interested in South Korea, and yet nothing of the kind has happened there, which goes to show that a desire alone is not enough. China is the neighbor of both countries, but the situations in them are different. So you see it is the objective situation and not the subjective one that counts. So don't try to put all the blame on the neighbors.

DR: No, not all—only ninety-five percent! There has been no popular uprising in South Vietnam, but the People's Republic has been successful in sending in a large amount of arms and in stirring up trouble. I'm afraid I can't agree with the Chairman in his interpretation of the case.

NK: [Apparently irritated.] Here we have a basic difference. But if you say that China is the main factor there, surely the United States could send in more arms. But the Vietnamese don't want to take those arms because the guerrillas will take the arms away from them. Arms sent into the country from the outside are certainly *not* a factor.

[Khrushchev's voice had been rising, and the thumping got louder. I felt I should probably change the topic, but then I thought of one more thing I had to say.]

DR: I appreciate the Chairman's views and am glad to hear him speak on this subject. I think our basic differences are such that nothing will be gained from pursuing this particular subject. I would like to say one more word on Cuba. I agree with you that it was the corrupt Batista regime which made possible an internally generated revolution in Cuba. But it was not at first—not until Cuba received massive economic and military assistance from the Soviet Union—that the character of the government was changed. And here the Soviet Union did interfere in internal matters for her government's betterment and to the detriment of our government. This is precisely the sort of situation that creates so much concern and apprehension on the part of the people of the United States.

NK: That is a very profound delusion! As I said, Castro only recognized our country diplomatically about twelve or eighteen months after the revolution, so the revolution was won when we didn't even know the leader of the revolution, and then—well, to think that Cuba could at any time be a bridgehead for an attack on the United States by the Soviet Union is ridiculous. Cuba is separated from the Soviet Union by eleven thousand kilometers, and all these communication lines are completely controlled by the United States. And even assuming we wanted to make war on the United States from Cuba, we have no means. You were in the Army, I know; you will understand this. We haven't the transportation to supply food and ammunition to troops based in Cuba.

Now we do have rockets, we have nuclear weapons, with which we keep the United States covered, but we can do that from our own country. If at one time we placed rockets on Cuba, it was only in order to deter the United States from attacking Cuba. And we then reached an understanding with the President, and we took out our rockets—we had forty-two or forty-four there, I believe. In return, Kennedy gave his word that neither he nor his allies would invade Cuba. Should this agreement at any time be violated, we could support Cuba from our own country. We have rockets and nuclear weapons. For this purpose we don't need Cuba's territory. And then your understanding is completely counter to ours. You believe the Soviet Union wants to subordinate countries, but that is no longer possible.

[I thought it preposterous at the time that Khrushchev could say this with a straight face after the brutal Soviet repression of the 1956 Hungarian Revolution and the continued presence of Soviet military forces from Estonia in the north to Bulgaria in the south.]

NK: The colonial system has toppled; the remnants of it are now falling. I believe each people should be free to have its own setup. *This* is the reason we support Cuba. Cuba has nothing we don't have in our own country—

DR: Except, perhaps, proximity to the United States!

NK: [The Secretary was now quite agitated.] What does that give us? Do you really believe all that rot, that we want to seize the United States? If you think that is possible, tell me how, tell me by what means. We *can* destroy the United States, but why? As for Cuba, it makes much sugar, but so does the Soviet Union.

DR: I suppose, judging from what I've seen, that you use Cuba as a base to activate the Communist movements in other parts of Latin

America. There is no thought of an attack on the United States—serious-thinking Americans don't feel you want to take us over by force. Our fear is that by the kind of activity I have suggested you would cripple the United States, weaken our position. [At this point I thought it might be a good idea to shift the conversation to less controversial ground.]

I don't want to take too much of your time, but I feel this is directly connected with the question of trade, and I would like to speak to you on this matter if you would permit me.

[Khrushchev perked up when I mentioned the subject of trade and began to listen very intently.]

In relation to trade and all other relationships between our countries—rightly or wrongly—we feel our position to be jeopardized by the actions of the Soviet Union. Naturally, we are not eager to take steps which will lead to the facilitation or the hastening of that process. All of the relations between our countries must be based on confidence, and at present that confidence is lacking.

[I went on to congratulate him for the role he had played in the "lessening of tensions"—diplomatic blandishment, pure and simple—and then itemized some of the obstacles we had to surmount.]

NK: As for lend-lease, we paid for that with our blood. Do you know how many soldiers we lost in the war? Twenty million.

DR: We are very mindful of the tremendous human sacrifices that your country made, but our claims in this matter do not have to do with the war or with the war effort; the transactions took place subsequent to hostilities.

NK: [Speaking slowly, with his eyes cast down, occasionally even closed.] We must proceed from the major issues. You are a capitalist and a Rockefeller. I am a Communist. You are a banker. I was a miner. You represent a capitalist nation, while I speak for the Soviet Union. Whatever you say or do, you sympathize with the strengthening of capitalism. Whatever I say or do, I sympathize with the cause of communism, which I believe to be the strength of the future, the up-and-coming philosophy. We believe capitalism has reached its sunset. The time will come when she [here he pointed to Neva] will be allied with me and my ideas. But we believe that while both systems do continue, we must work for peaceful coexistence. You say we threatened you in Cuba, but we feel threatened by you in Turkey, Denmark, Norway, and Italy, and by your allies. It is a fact that your allies are closer to us than Cuba is to you. Some of their territories are contiguous to ours. But we're not afraid of that—we can destroy you within a matter of minutes. It is the possession of nuclear weapons that determines the conditions today and makes peaceful coexistence so necessary. I know that you are aware that we are not afraid of you or your allies, or of the fact that you have arms near our borders. We sympathize with Cuba. We feel that she has taken a significant road of development away from the declining order of capitalism. Capitalism, as Marx understood so profoundly, is not destined to survive. We lay the blame not on Cuba or on any socialist system but on the weakness of capitalism for the new developments in all these countries.

And about trade: If you want to trade, good; if not, you needn't. We can live quite well without trade. Its usefulness lies in its political implications, which we believe will lead to the consolidation of peace in the world.

DR: I agree with you on the necessity for peace in the world. This is the reason I am here. This is the reason I am grateful to you for being generous enough to give me so much of your time. It is true, as you say, that there are irreconcilable differences between our countries. It is true, as you say, that either of us can destroy the other. It is true that we are both strong and independent peoples who are willing to accept death rather than subjugation. The only solution is to find more means of contact through which we may avoid unnecessary and irresponsible conflicts which could lead to disaster.

NK: I agree with you.

DR: Good.

We ended our discussion with mutual pleasantries, Khrushchev saying he appreciated the fact that I, "a man who owns such vast assets," understood the necessity for peace.

It had been an extraordinary meeting—tough, at times combative, even hostile. But despite the difficult nature of the issues we had discussed, I never sensed a personal animosity toward me. On the contrary, I came away feeling a great respect for Khrushchev, and I think the feeling was reciprocated. I also came away from our encounter with a strong sense—call it a banker's instinct—that the top Soviet leadership wanted to expand financial and commercial ties with the United States, and despite Khrushchev's confident assertions about Soviet self-sufficiency, I felt his nation was confronting serious economic problems.

DEBRIEFING LYNDON B. JOHNSON

Soon after my return I sent a copy of Neva's notes to Secretary of State Dean Rusk, who shared them with other senior officials in the Johnson administration. In late August, President Johnson wrote, personally inviting me to come to Washington immediately after the Democratic convention "so that we can discuss your trip."

We met at the White House in mid-September. I already had a good relationship with the President. Johnson was extremely bright and had an intuitive grasp of the politics of any situation with which he dealt. While I disagreed with the cost and invasiveness of his "Great Society" programs, I liked him personally. LBJ was easy to work with as long as he was not crossed on a sensitive subject.*

At our meeting in the Oval Office, Johnson questioned me about Khrushchev's mood and his attitude toward the United States. Few Americans had met personally with Khrushchev up to that time, and the President and his advisors wanted my assessment of him and the potential for change. I told them that beneath Khrushchev's tough and dogmatic language, he was clearly opening the door to further contact with the United States.

The President seemed reassured by my account and agreed that we needed to take concrete steps to expand the opportunities for trade and other commercial ties with the Soviet Union. However, reelection was LBJ's top priority, and he would not do anything openly until after the November elections so that Goldwater could not accuse him of being "soft on Communism."

THE DARTMOUTH CONFERENCES

As the two superpowers circled each other warily during the late 1960s and early 1970s, private citizens and nongovernment groups began to play a greater role in the effort to stabilize and improve relations between the

---

*I remember one occasion on which I was the object of LBJ's irritation. I had made a speech in Chicago critical of his economic policies and a week or so later attended a meeting in the White House along with a number of union leaders. I had to leave early, and as I attempted to depart quietly, Johnson called out, "David, I didn't appreciate what you said about me in Chicago last week."

two countries. The Dartmouth Conferences were particularly important in this process.

For Dartmouth's first decade, Norman Cousins dominated the selection of American participants, and more often than not they were his friends or celebrities of one kind or another: Margaret Mead, Marian Anderson, Bill Benton, James Michener, and Agnes deMille. While there was a smattering of academics and businessmen, few of them could be considered Soviet experts—George Kennan and Marshall Shulman being notable exceptions.

In 1971 the Kettering Foundation assumed principal responsibility for funding the conferences, with additional support from the Rockefeller Foundation and the Lilly Endowment. At a time when American and Soviet diplomats were discussing treaties on defense spending and the control of antiballistic missiles, Dartmouth began to be viewed in official circles in both Moscow and Washington as a serious forum that might contribute to the broader dialogue. Celebrities disappeared from the American roster and were replaced by experts on Soviet affairs such as James Billington, Richard Gardner, and Paul Warnke; scientists such as Paul Doty of Harvard and Harold Agnew of the Los Alamos Laboratory; and businessmen whose companies had an interest in the Soviet Union, such as General James Gavin of Arthur D. Little, G. William Miller of Textron, and William Hewitt of John Deere. A number of U.S. senators, including Frank Church, Mark Hatfield, Hugh Scott, and Charles (Mac) Matthias, also attended.

There was a comparable change on the Soviet side. Minor Russian luminaries and literary figures were supplemented by members of the Supreme Soviet; senior governmental officials; renowned academicians who specialized in the study of Europe, North America, and the Middle East; and retired military officers. Georgi Arbatov, head of the U.S.-Canada Department of the Soviet Academy of Sciences, assumed principal responsibility for the Soviet group in the early 1970s.

═══

During the first half-dozen Dartmouth meetings, the temptation to use them for propaganda and ideological posturing got in the way of substantive discussions. Speaker after Soviet speaker would rise to denounce U.S. policy in the Middle East, Vietnam, and Europe; to denounce the power that Zionists had in the United States; or to reaffirm his belief in various aspects of Marxist-Leninist thought. Anyone familiar with the Soviet manner of discourse knew that these set pieces were arranged in advance and made partly to prove to their comrades that they were being appropriately tough. I noticed, however, that in small group discussions most of the party line rhetoric was dropped, and we actually had useful discussions on practical steps that could be taken on many issues.

During the Kiev meeting in the summer of 1971, I asked Georgi Arbatov to go for a walk with me. I told him that our side found these exaggerated attacks offensive and counterproductive. I suggested we open each conference with a brief gathering that would be followed immediately by meetings of smaller groups, which would discuss specific subjects such as defense spending and trade. Arbatov agreed, and we adopted the new format for all subsequent conferences. Soon after that the Kettering Foundation asked me to take on greater responsibility for organizing the meetings, which I agreed to do.

The new format and the participation of experienced and knowledgeable individuals from both countries resulted in substantive discussions that had a direct influence on Soviet-American commercial negotiations during the first half of the 1970s, the high point of détente. After that date the growing stalemate in negotiations over nuclear arms reduction, defense spending, and trade had a negative impact on the tenor of the Dartmouth meetings. However, even as relations between the superpowers cooled, conference participants continued to deal with one another forthrightly and directly. The level of discussion on all the salient issues remained high, but convincing our respective governments of their merits became much more difficult.

Dartmouth provided me with an opportunity to get to know a number of Russians in an informal setting. I was particularly impressed with Yevgeni Primakov, who later became Russian foreign minister, and with Vladimir Petrovsky, who rose to deputy secretary-general of the United Nations.

While the Dartmouth Conferences did not change the course of history, they did provide an arena where critical issues could be discussed and new ideas proposed. Each of us who participated, whether American or Russian, learned something about the beliefs, motivations, and aspirations of our counterparts, which made it impossible to think only in the rigid ideological categories of the Cold War. Dartmouth broke down barriers and made change possible.

TRADING WITH THE "ENEMY"

Even before the Dartmouth group began to play a role in Soviet-American relations, I had become one of a small group of American businessmen who advocated increasing trade with the Soviet Union and her Eastern

European satellites. From a purely economic viewpoint, the United States did not need Soviet trade. Its usefulness to us lay in its "political implications," as Khrushchev had noted during our meeting.

It is important to remember that from the 1950s until well into the 1980s few people thought Communism would collapse or the Soviet Union itself would disintegrate. During those years people on both sides of the great Cold War divide were seeking practical ways to lessen tensions.

I made my first public statement on the issue of East-West trade in San Francisco in September 1964, shortly after I had met with Khrushchev. In it I made the following observations: If two great and rival systems are somehow to endure side by side on this planet, then each must know more about the other, and that knowledge must extend beyond the narrow confines of pronounced ideology. We must know people, their attitudes, their manner of life, the social organism that they have created and that in turn has given them shape. We need to know their history, their culture, how they think and react, and what aspirations we hold in common that may be irreconcilable but not necessarily intolerable.

Trade could be a vehicle for achieving this objective. Thus I said in the same speech that a greater trade in material goods should be in the forefront of efforts to improve our relationship with the Soviet Union.

=

President Nixon regarded broadening commercial intercourse with the Soviet Union an integral element in his policy of détente. The Soviet leadership, hungry for access to the modern technology and capital resources of the West, were eager to oblige, and the framework for a trade treaty was incorporated in the agreements signed at the 1972 Moscow Summit that inaugurated a "new era in Soviet-American relations." As part of the "new era," a Soviet-American Commission was created to work out the details that would lead to most-favored-nation (MFN) status for the Soviets.

To accomplish these general goals, the State Department set up a working group with the Russian Ministry of Foreign Trade and the Bank for Foreign Trade, and in June 1973 the two nations signed a protocol creating the U.S.-USSR Trade and Economic Council, a private group that would seek to foster normal economic relationships between the two countries.

I was not among those selected to serve. This bothered me because I felt my active involvement with the Soviets over the past decade entitled me to be a member. I never discovered if my omission was the result of a deliberate action by a government official or if others on the council preferred not to have me included for competitive reasons. I am inclined to believe the latter was the case. When I asked Secretary of Commerce Frederick Dent about it, he told me that since I was already serving on the U.S.-China Business Committee, everyone assumed I would not be interested in serving on the one dealing with the Soviet Union. Since the question had never been posed to me, I doubted the truthfulness of this explanation. In any event, Soviet minister of foreign trade Nikolai Patolichev indicated that my omission was "preposterous," and in the end Henry Kissinger intervened to have me added to the group.

The council made significant progress initially, but then our work collided with American domestic politics. The Jackson-Vanik Amendment to the Trade Reform Act of 1974 tied the grant of MFN status to Communist nations to freedom of emigration for their citizens, particularly the right of Soviet Jews to emigrate to Israel. The amendment was aimed directly at the Soviet Union, and its inclusion made Leonid Brezhnev furious. In response to quiet pressure from Henry Kissinger, he had already substantially increased the number of Soviet Jews allowed to emigrate. He felt entitled to a positive response from our side, not punishment. Faced with the amendment and the denial of MFN, Brezhnev refused to sign the trade accord. He also reversed course on Jewish emigration and imposed an even more restrictive policy. In the end the amendment not only killed any possibility of a trade accord between the United States and the USSR, but it also effectively ended Jewish emigration from the Soviet Union.

Many experts date the end of détente to this shortsighted congressional action, and I agree with them.

THE FIRST AMERICAN BANK IN THE SOVIET UNION

My conversation with Khrushchev in 1964 made me keenly aware of the Soviet desire to expand commercial and financial ties with the United States. I was eager to see this happen and to have Chase play a role in the process. Historically, Chase was the leading American correspondent bank for what we called in those days the "socialist markets": the Soviet Union and the "COMECON" nations of Poland, East Germany, Czechoslovakia, Hungary, Bulgaria, and Romania. Chase had long maintained relationships with both the Soviet Central Bank and the Bank for Foreign Trade, and we had also served as the lead American bank for Amtorg, the Soviet agency that purchased supplies for the Red Army during World War II. However, in the intervening years Chase had done little business with the USSR.

Our big breakthrough came when we served as one of the lead American banks in financing the billion-dollar Soviet grain deal of 1971. The following year we began discussions with Soviet authorities about opening direct operations in Moscow. In November 1972, Chase received permission to establish a representative office—the first American bank to receive a license.

We located the office at One Karl Marx Square, officially opening for "business" in May 1973. I put business in quotation marks because our activities there were tightly circumscribed, though I hoped that with time they would be allowed to expand. I had originally proposed to Ambassador Anatoly Dobrynin that we assign James Billington to head the branch. Jim, a Russian expert who spoke the language fluently, was then serving the Chase as full-time advisor on Soviet matters (he subsequently became the Librarian of Congress). Dobrynin told me politely that it wasn't necessary to send anyone who spoke Russian; they had excellent interpreters, whom they would provide. It might be more appropriate, he said, to send someone else. Later on, Dobrynin jokingly told me that we should be less demanding of the interpreters; after all, he said, they not only had to work for Chase all day, they had to stay up all night writing reports for their supervisors in the Ministry of the Interior.

Chase's gala Moscow opening reception at the Metropol Hotel was an enormous success, not least in terms of the size of the crowd. We attracted every Communist functionary in Moscow: they swarmed like locusts, and in a matter of minutes the tables, covered with delicacies imported from abroad, were literally picked clean, and hardly a drop was left in any of the bottles of wine and vodka.

The Soviets gave permission to City Bank and several other American banks to open representative offices in Moscow soon after. While the Soviet market never developed for any of us, the symbolic significance of Chase—the "Rockefeller Bank"—being the first U.S. financial institution in the Soviet Union could not be denied.

CONVERSATIONS WITH KOSYGIN

I visited Moscow almost every year during the 1970s, either for Dartmouth Conference meetings or on bank business. My principal government contact during that time was Alexei Kosygin, one of the USSR's most important political figures. Kosygin had participated in the coup that overthrew Nikita Khrushchev in 1964. A tall, thin, and rather sad-faced man, Kosygin was an able manager who had done wonders administering the unwieldy Soviet economy. By the time I met him, he had lost the power struggle within the Kremlin to Communist Party chief Leonid Brezhnev and had been subordinated to the position of premier—the chief operating officer of the Soviet economy.

While my talk with Khrushchev had become a debate on the relative merits of our respective ideologies and philosophies, my conversations with Kosygin were always pragmatic and business-oriented. In retrospect, the substance of these discussions was illuminating because of what they implied about the potential economic relationship between the United States and the USSR.

=

I first met Kosygin in the summer of 1971 after a Dartmouth meeting in Kiev. It was my first visit to Moscow since my memorable encounter with Khrushchev. I found the Soviet capital had changed markedly in those intervening years.

Kosygin's emphasis on producing goods for the consumer sector had resulted in more cars on the streets and a greater availability of clothing and other items. There were massive road construction projects everywhere, and the Moscow subway system was a marvel—modern, clean, comfortable, and cheap. Moscow itself was relatively clean and litter free, and hippies and long hair were largely absent. Western fashions were making an impact. I observed that "skirts are about four inches above the knees, though what is exposed often leaves something to be desired!"

I was part of the Dartmouth delegation that paid a courtesy call on Kosygin in his Kremlin office. We spent most of our time talking about trade, and Kosygin urged our group to work "to remove the obstacles" in the United States that hindered trade with the USSR. It was clear the Soviets were anxious to expand commercial relations. Our second meeting coincided with the opening of the Chase office in May 1973. Kosygin was pleased with this development and seemed optimistic that the "obstacles" preventing increased U.S.-Soviet trade would now be eliminated. He focused on the large gas field explorations in Siberia, at one point brandishing a pointer and locating strategic deposits on a wall map. "On the economic side," he said, "we are ready to proceed, but we do not know how far the United States will go."

By 1974, Kosygin's concerns had shifted dramatically. This was by far our most technical and economically oriented dialogue. He expressed deep concern about the OPEC oil price increases and the impact they were having on the U.S. dollar, and European and Japanese balance of payments. He was eager to hear my analysis of the consequences of these developments. We discussed the relative merits of alternative energy sources such as coal and atomic power.

Kosygin said he was convinced that Western nations would have trouble reducing their energy consumption and that effective solutions would take years to implement. The Premier suggested that increased atomic power production would ultimately drive down the cost of oil. He then asked if Chase would help finance the construction of nuclear power plants in Russia, to be jointly owned by the United States and the USSR. I was astonished by his revolutionary proposal because it indicated how important both U.S. investment and technology were to the Soviets and how far they were willing to go to secure both. Although he promised to send me a proposal on this unique idea, I never heard from him again on it.

Kosygin concluded our meeting by saying that those "who are endeavoring to block the new relationship between the United States and the USSR would be proven wrong by history," and the "leadership in the Soviet Union had faith in the leadership of the United States, and they were unanimous in their desire to seek new ways of continuing this new relationship between the two countries."

UNCONVERTIBLE CURRENCY

In each of the first three meetings Kosygin had been upbeat and expansive, eager to suggest potential areas of cooperation and ways in which joint ventures could be pursued. Our April 1975 encounter followed a different direction. In the wake of the Jackson-Vanik Amendment and Brezhnev's bitter denunciation of the American failure to grant MFN to the USSR, Kosygin displayed a confrontational style I had not seen before. Using rhetoric eerily reminiscent of Khrushchev's, he extolled the superiority of the Soviet economy and his country's growing influence in world economic affairs.

I challenged him by asking, "If the Soviet Union is truly to become a world economic power, it must be a major factor in world trade. How is that possible if you do not have a convertible currency, one that is accepted everywhere in the world?" In fact, I noted, the ruble was not accepted anywhere outside the Soviet bloc. I said I realized that to make the ruble convertible would create other complications for the USSR "because your ideology requires that you severely restrict the movement of people, goods, and currency. How do you reconcile these two realities?"

He looked at me for a second, rather nonplussed, then gave a confused, not particularly relevant response. He clearly had never given serious thought to the practical implications of a convertible currency.

About a week later I was lunching at a restaurant in Amsterdam when Fritz Leutwiler, governor of the Swiss National Bank, saw me and strode across the room. Leutwiler said he had just come from Moscow. He said that after my visit Kosygin had learned he was in Moscow and summoned him to his office. Kosygin was concerned about what I had said, and they had spent two hours discussing the implications of convertibility for Russia.

For the Soviets there was no satisfactory answer to the question I had posed. It precisely defined their dilemma: They could not become an international economic power without a fully convertible currency, but that was impossible as long as they adhered to Marxist dogma and maintained a repressive authoritarian society.

EPILOGUE

In December 1987, Mikhail Gorbachev, the energetic and able general secretary of the Soviet Communist Party, came to Washington for his third summit meeting with President Ronald Reagan to sign the Intermediate-Range Nuclear Forces Treaty with the United States. While this was an enormously important event in relation to disarmament, most people, including myself, were equally interested in Gorbachev's proposals for reform of the Soviet domestic economy and political order.

Through *perestroika*, which could be loosely translated into English as "restructuring," and *glasnost*, or "openness," Gorbachev proposed to renew and revitalize Soviet society by granting genuine legal and political freedoms. Lost in the American acclaim for Gorbachev and his proposals was the fact that he remained strongly committed to the essentials of a centralized Communist economy. He might be a "Socialist reformer," but he still rejected "bourgeois capitalism" and the market economy.

Peggy and I were invited to several of the official ceremonies connected with his visit, including the formal welcoming of Gorbachev and his wife, Raisa, to the White House and the state dinner that same evening. Gorbachev impressed us with his charm and easy manner, so different from the stiff and distant demeanor of the other Soviet leaders I had met.

Two days later I attended a formal reception at the Soviet embassy. Ambassador Yuri Dubinin had invited a number of American financial and business leaders to meet Gorbachev, who spoke at some length about the changes that he planned to introduce, including freer trade and broader contacts with the capitalist world. He then opened the floor to questions.

Gorbachev pointed to me, and I reprised the question I had asked Kosygin a dozen years earlier. I told him I was pleased to hear that the Soviet economy would be opening up, but I wondered what the implications of this policy would be for the ruble. How could he expect to play a major role in international markets if his currency was not accepted in satisfying commercial transactions outside the USSR? On the other hand, could the ruble become an international currency without removing restrictions on the free movement of people and goods across international borders?

Gorbachev responded quickly. "We are studying this issue and will be making some important decisions before long." And that was the extent of his answer.

Ultimately, while Gorbachev recognized the difficulty of operating a centrally planned economy within the context of a dynamic global market system, he never produced a workable solution to the inherent contradictions the Soviets faced. In the end, despite introducing important political reforms, Gorbachev failed in his effort to shore up a dying economic order. Within four years he fell from power and with him went the last vestiges of the Marxist ideology that had sustained his country's totalitarian system for most of the twentieth century.

CHAPTER 18

PENETRATING
THE BAMBOO CURTAIN

Late in the evening of June 29, 1973, barely a month after the opening of Chase's Moscow office, Peggy and I sat in the Great Hall of the People in Beijing talking with Premier Zhou Enlai, a man second in rank and power only to Mao Zedong.

This was my first trip to China, and it was a historic one, as I was the first American banker to visit the People's Republic of China (PRC). That afternoon I had signed an agreement that made Chase the first U.S. correspondent bank of the Bank of China since the Communist takeover twenty-five years earlier.

In 1973 a trip to China could be viewed as quixotic, given the Communist antipathy to what the Chase and I represented. The Chinese remained implacably hostile to capitalism, and their xenophobia knew no bounds. The country was still in the brutal grip of the Great Proletarian Cultural Revolution, and Mao Zedong's enigmatic leadership style made it impossible to judge whether the radicals headed by Mao's wife, Jiang Qing, or the moderate reformers, who were being quietly sustained by the cautious Zhou, would prevail.

I could only speculate on their motives for agreeing to invite me. One possibility was that in the wake of Nixon's visit Mao and Zhou were seeking ways to broaden the range of contacts with the United States. A remark I had made in 1970 in Singapore, during a tour of Chase's Southeast Asian branches, may also have played a role. At a press conference I was asked about the Nixon administration's decision to relax restrictions on trade with the PRC. I said that it was a "logical and good step toward seeking some sort of contact." In fact, I noted it was unrealistic for the United States "to act as if a country of 800 million people did not exist." While my statement attracted only a modest amount of attention in the United States, I have a feeling that the Chinese leadership took note of it.

Admittedly, when I made those remarks, I imagined it would take years even to begin the process of restoring relations with the PRC, so deep was the enmity between our two nations. Thus, I was surprised and encouraged when Nixon linked the process of détente with the Soviet Union to an equally powerful initiative directed at promoting rapprochement with the PRC. Nixon's visit to Beijing in February 1972, followed a few months later by his Moscow summit with Brezhnev, shattered the Cold War stalemate that had controlled international relations for a generation and transformed the global balance of power.

I saw Nixon's China initiative as a potential business opportunity for Chase, similar to the ones we had pursued and recently secured in the Soviet Union and other Communist bloc countries of Eastern Europe. In addition, I hoped it would provide me with an opportunity to renew my connections with a country in which my family had had an important interest for many years prior to the Communist revolution.

THE ROCKEFELLERS IN CHINA

Grandfather, like many entrepreneurs of his generation, had been eager to tap the potential of the "China market." "Oil for the lamps of China" was one of Standard Oil's first advertising slogans, reflecting the enormous demand for kerosene that developed throughout that vast country during the last years of the nineteenth century. In fact, by the mid-1920s, Socony-Vacuum (one of Standard Oil's successor companies) had established a comprehensive marketing network that stretched from the Great Wall in the north to Hainan Island in the south.

China also had been a focus of my family's charitable giving ever since Grandfather contributed a few pennies from his first paychecks to well-established Baptist missionaries working there. By the second decade of the twentieth century, this early and primarily religious interest had been replaced by larger philanthropic disbursements, from both my father directly as well as Rockefeller-related foundations, to a broad array of projects ranging from comprehensive economic development efforts in the Yangtze Valley to the restoration of the Ming Tombs near Nanjing, public health and medical education, and even an effort to reform the Chinese Customs Service.

In terms of enduring impact, however, the Rockefeller Foundation's support for the Peking Union Medical College (PUMC) was the most notable. Beginning in 1915, the foundation officers created a first-class research institute focusing on parasitology, communicable diseases, and nutritional deficiencies, problems endemic to China at the time. The PUMC also trained a generation of physicians and nurses who played an important role in developing China's public health system between the two world wars.

My parents traveled to Beijing in the summer of 1921—the only time they visited Asia—to participate in the formal opening of the PUMC. More than seventy-five years later I vividly recall having missed them very much during their three-month absence in Japan, Korea, and China. It was a consequential trip for both of them; their interest in Asian art deepened, and they became collectors of ceramics, textiles, prints, paintings, and sculpture from all three of the cultures they encountered. More important, Father was persuaded that while American philanthropy had an important role to play in the modernization of China, traditional American missionary work had become outmoded and irrelevant to the needs of the country. The lessons drawn by each of my parents had not only an enduring impact on them but also on the lives of my brothers and me.

THE NEW CHINA

During the half-century separating my parents' trip and my own journey, China had experienced a long period of internal disorder, a devastating war with Japan, and finally a civil war that drove Chiang Kai-shek's Guomindang government from the mainland to the island fortress of Taiwan. Mao's victory in 1949 began an era when the Communist Party attempted to obliterate all traces of Western influence. The PRC closed Christian missions and forcibly suppressed the practice of all religious faiths, abolished private property, expropriated the assets of foreign corporations and banks, expelled representatives of Western foundations and other charitable organizations, and stripped the educational system of its Western faculty and purged its "corrupt" curriculum. In a small but telling example of this antiforeign fervor, in the mid-1960s PUMC's name was changed to the Anti-Imperialist Medical College.

Mao and his compatriots sought to build a "new China" through Leninist means adapted to Chinese circumstances. Modernization would be achieved through the restoration of national unity and the creation of a powerful centralized government. The power of the state would then be used to communalize agriculture and stimulate rapid industrialization. Mao initially pursued these goals by turning to the Soviet Union for assistance. Thousands of Soviet advisors helped China's new leaders create a Stalinist-style command economy and plunge China into an era of extreme isolation.

From the start the United States refused to accept the new regime in Beijing and continued to recognize Chiang Kai-shek as the legitimate ruler of all of China. With the outbreak of the Korean War in 1950 we interposed the U.S. Navy in the Taiwan Straits, supplied billions of dollars in foreign aid, and supported Chiang's retention of China's seat as a permanent member of the U.N.'s Security Council.

The PRC, for its part, supported revolutionary movements in Asia and Africa that fought for independence from European colonial powers; when combined with their passionate commitment to Marxist-Leninist ideology, this brought our two nations into direct conflict, especially across the western arc of the Pacific Rim from Korea in the north to Indonesia in the south and, most tragically, in Vietnam.

The United States and the PRC viewed each other as eternal enemies. Each government had implemented political, economic, and military strategies designed to weaken and ultimately defeat the other. Of course, by the early 1970s, neither government had achieved this objective, and many people, including me, thought the time had come to try something new. Thus, Nixon's willingness to explore a new strategy with the leadership of the PRC had set the stage for a dramatic new chapter in East Asia.

CHASE'S RETURN TO ASIA

At an earlier point in its history, Chase had been an active participant in China's export trade. During the decade following World War I, the Equitable Trust Company had opened branches in Shanghai, Tientsin, and Hong Kong, all of which specialized in trading silver bullion. After the 1930 merger Chase became known as "Dahtong Yinhang," roughly translated as "the silver bank doing business all over the world." Our branches prospered during the uncertain years of the 1930s and up to the time the Japanese closed them after Pearl Harbor. We reopened the branches in 1945, but with Chiang's defeat, we again terminated our business on the mainland—or, more accurately, it was terminated for us in 1950 when the PRC nationalized our branches and interned our employees.

Chase's fortunes in Hong Kong also took a decided turn for the worse the following year. When the People's Liberation Army intervened in the Korean War by crossing the Yalu River and driving General Douglas MacArthur's forces back down the peninsula, most American government and military officials felt this was the opening of a broader Communist Chinese offensive and that Mao had set his sights on Hong Kong, Taiwan, and the rest of Southeast Asia. Winthrop Aldrich agreed with this view and abruptly closed our Hong Kong operations. His decision was a significant mistake since other foreign banks decided to await developments and did not follow our lead. When the PRC failed to move against the Crown Colony, our Hong Kong clients felt we had abandoned them.

To give Winthrop credit, however, he had shown foresight in persuading the Defense Department in 1947 to allow Chase to open military banking facilities in Occupied Japan. With the growing American military presence in the region after the outbreak of the Korean War and the signing of the United States–Japan Security Treaty, these facilities flourished, and a few years later the Japanese government permitted us to add full commercial branches in Tokyo and Osaka.

Thus, during the 1950s, while other nations in the region struggled with the political and economic consequences of independence, Japan's economy boomed, and Chase emerged as the principal private banking source of dollar funding for the Japanese government. We provided hundreds of millions of dollars for the rebuilding of the Japanese economy when they desperately needed external dollar financing. This was a bonanza for Chase while it lasted.

By the early 1960s, however, this profitable business began to dry up when surging exports enabled the Japanese to accumulate huge dollar surpluses on their own. By then the economic prospects of a few other Asian countries started to look more promising, and a number of our major corporate clients started to expand into Southeast Asia and South Korea. We realized then that we ran the risk of losing their business if we failed to move beyond our Japanese base to accommodate their needs.

All of these factors compelled Chase to purchase the three Far Eastern branches of the Dutch-based Nationale Handelsbank, giving us a position for the first time in both Bangkok and Singapore, and getting us back into Hong Kong. A crucial component of the deal was our ability to retain the services of the able group of Dutch bank managers we inherited from the Handelsbank. They had the language skills and expertise to deal with local businessmen, and also helped us retain the regional business of several important international corporations.

Chase took advantage of the region's evolving economies and during the course of the 1960s opened additional branches in Kuala Lumpur, Seoul, and Jakarta, as well as Saigon to supplement the military banking facilities we had established throughout Vietnam at the request of the Defense Department. Asia, or at least a small part of it, was on the move, and I was delighted that Chase was positioned to participate in it.

======

The one uncertain element in this otherwise positive picture was the attitude of the Chinese leadership in Beijing. China's huge population, massive military establishment, and latent economic strength made its future course of action of great interest to everyone. Would the PRC maintain its domestic isolation while continuing to support revolutionary movements elsewhere in Asia, or would they adopt more moderate economic and political policies that would make them part of an emerging market-oriented system in the region? This was the critical question that preoccupied many thoughtful people as the decade of the 1960s drew to a close. It certainly was on the minds of those of us involved with implementing Chase's strategy of expansion in Asia.

A SUITCASE FULL OF MONEY

Once Nixon's China strategy became clear and relations between the United States and the PRC started to improve, I began to consider the possibility of visiting China myself. The prospect of doing so became more realistic after the PRC replaced Nationalist China in the United Nations in November 1971. This event signaled the end of mainland China's years of isolation and its intention to become a responsible player in world politics.

Shortly after Nixon's return from Beijing in 1972, I asked Henry Kissinger for advice on the best way to get permission to enter China. He told me to contact Ambassador Huang Hua, the PRC's permanent representative to the United Nations and the senior Chinese diplomat stationed in the United States; Huang was well connected with Zhou Enlai's faction of the Politburo. Henry counseled patience since the Chinese continued to be extremely cautious about granting access to foreigners in general and, at least at that time, seemed to prefer carefully stage-managing visits of selected journalists and scholars rather than hosting bankers and businessmen.

Henry was right. It took more than a year to arrange an invitation. Henry's support was certainly crucial, but astute marketing by one of the bank's officers also contributed significantly to my success. When Leo Pierre, the Chase vice president responsible for relationships with the United Nations, learned that Huang and his entourage would arrive in New York, he guessed they might find it difficult to obtain "spending money" to tide them over their first few days. Leo filled a suitcase with $50,000 in cash and spent all day in the lobby of the Roosevelt Hotel waiting for the Chinese delegation to arrive. When they finally turned up, he presented himself to the Ambassador, explained his purpose for being there, and handed over the suitcase, politely refusing even to accept a receipt for the instant loan.

Huang was impressed by Leo's gesture, and soon afterward the Chinese mission opened an account with Chase. With this positive background I asked Leo in January 1973 to deliver a letter from Peggy and me to the Ambassador and his wife, Li Liang, asking them to join us for tea at our home. We received a prompt acceptance. Even though they had been in New York for more than a year, it turned out that this was their first visit to a private home. At first they appeared a bit uncomfortable with the surroundings. We quickly ran through the formalities, and the conversation began to drag. Peggy valiantly tried to keep the ball rolling by apologizing for not being able to offer them a traditional "tea ceremony." When Peggy saw my appalled expression, she realized she had confused a Japanese tradition with the Chinese and beat an embarrassed retreat! Our polished Chinese guests never gave the slightest indication that Peggy had made a gaffe.

Only as they were leaving did I mention my interest in visiting China. The Ambassador was studiously noncommittal. He said only that he was returning to Beijing for a short visit and would enjoy seeing us again when he returned.

Secretary-General Kurt Waldheim had invited us to a farewell dinner that same evening for George Bush, who was retiring as U.S. ambassador to the U.N. There were only sixteen guests, and among them were our afternoon "tea" companions. Ambassador Huang was surprised to see Peggy and me at what he thought was a diplomats-only function. It was a happy coincidence and may have suggested to him that I had interests and contacts beyond banking, which may have strengthened my chances of securing another meeting with him.

A few months later the Ambassador wrote to let me know he had returned to New York. I invited him to visit the Museum of Modern Art, which he had never seen, and to have lunch afterward at our home. As we sipped an aperitif, Huang casually mentioned that Peggy and I were on the invitation list for Pakistani Airline's inaugural flight from Rawalpindi to Beijing. He said it had occurred to him that we might prefer to travel to China di-

Waiting at the Tarrytown railway station for the arrival of Grandfather's casket, May 25, 1937. Left to right: Father, me, Nelson, Winthrop, Laurance, and John. (CORBIS)

Standing with Grandfather and my great-uncle William A. Rockefeller at the Eyrie, our summer home overlooking Seal Harbor on Mount Desert Island in Maine, in the summer of 1920. Grandfather and Uncle William had built Standard Oil into the greatest corporate enterprise of its day. (DR photo collection)

Mother and Father shortly after their marriage in 1901. (Courtesy of the Rockefeller Archive Center)

A panel of the Unicorn Tapestry that hung in Father's special gallery next door to our house on West 54th Street in Manhattan. I would often take visitors on tours and explain the story of the unicorn, an allegory of Christ's death and resurrection. (Courtesy of the Rockefeller Archive Center)

The Eyrie. (Photo by Ezra Stoller Associates; courtesy of the Rockefeller Archive Center)

Roller-skating to school along Central Park
during the 1920s. Father insisted on daily
exercise, and this was my way of doing it.
(DR photo collection)

Learning to sail aboard the
Jack Tar in Maine.
(DR photo collection)

The six of us in Maine in the mid-1930s. Winthrop and I are still in knickers, flanked by Laurance,
Nelson, John, and our sister, Babs, who would marry David Milton the following year.
(DR photo collection)

A stop in the desert near Megiddo on the way to Damascus after our trip down the Nile in the spring of 1929. Dr. James Breasted, the famous archaeologist from the Oriental Institute at the University of Chicago, is third from the right. Father and Mother are to his right. Mary Todhunter Clark, whom Nelson married the following year, is fashionably dressed for the journey in cloche hat, furs, and high heels! I am third from the left. (Courtesy of the University of Chicago)

Rockefeller Center under construction. The Center was Father's great gamble with the fortune Grandfather had entrusted to him. This 1932 photo shows the RCA Building nearing completion, with the graceful spire of the Chrysler Building in the background.
(Courtesy of the Rockefeller Center Archives)

Hitler striding through the streets of Munich in December 1937. I pushed my way to the front of the crowd and snapped the photo just as the dictator passed. (DR photo collection)

Peggy and I on our wedding day, September 7, 1940.
(DR photo collection)

My brothers and I just after
our return from the war.
Nelson has already begun to
assume the leadership of our
generation from John.
(Photo by Philippe Halsman;
courtesy of the Philippe
Halsman estate)

The leadership team at the
new Chase Manhattan Bank in
1956. Jack McCloy is in the
center, with Stewart Baker, the
former chairman of the Bank
of Manhattan Company, on his
left. George Champion is standing. The great rivalry between
George and me, which would
dominate the bank's affairs for
almost fifteen years, began at
this time. (Courtesy of the J.P.
Morgan Chase & Co. Archives)

The construction of Chase's
new headquarters in the early 1960s.
Our building was the first step in the
revival and redevelopment of Wall
Street. (Courtesy of the J.P. Morgan
Chase & Co. Archives)

Father and Martha. Father's remarriage severely strained relations within the family. (UPI; courtesy of the Rockefeller Archive Center)

Nelson and I on Wall Street during his 1970 gubernatorial campaign. Despite our personal differences, Nelson could always bring a smile to my face. (Photo by Arthur Levine; courtesy of the J.P. Morgan Chase & Co. Archives)

The life of a banker: trying out a motor scooter at a customer's production facility near Milan, Italy, 1957. (Publifoto; DR photo collection)

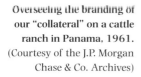

Overseeing the branding of our "collateral" on a cattle ranch in Panama, 1961. (Courtesy of the J.P. Morgan Chase & Co. Archives)

The Twin Towers of the World Trade Center near completion in July 1971. This project marked the culmination of Wall Street's redevelopment, which began when Chase decided to locate its new headquarters downtown. The old elevated West Side Highway runs along the base of the towers, and at the extreme right is the fill from the World Trade Center, upon which the World Financial Center would rise in later **years.** (Photo by the Downtown–Lower Manhattan Association; courtesy of the Rockefeller Archive Center)

I'm looking for a Job.

Retirement. The shirt was only partially facetious, as I would soon discover. (Photo by Arthur Levine; courtesy of the J.P. Morgan Chase & Co. Archives)

My memorable meeting with Nikita Khrushchev in the Kremlin in 1964. The Soviet leader assured me that my daughter Neva would eventually live under a Communist system in the United States. Viktor Sukhodrev, the interpreter, is also pictured. (Courtesy of Wide World Photos)

Introducing Peggy to Zhou Enlai on the steps of the Great Hall of the People in Beijing in 1973. (Courtesy of the J.P. Morgan Chase & Co. Archives)

In November 1969, Henry Kissinger, the National Security Advisor, and I listen to President Richard M. Nixon deliver a speech. A few weeks later, word that I had urged the President to pursue a "more balanced course" with regard to Israel and the Arab states leaked to the press and caused both me and the bank a great deal of trouble. (White House photo; courtesy of the J.P. Morgan Chase & Co. Archives)

A meal with Golda Meir, the Prime Minister of Israel, part of my effort to achieve balance for Chase in the turbulent Middle East. (Courtesy of the J.P. Morgan Chase & Co. Archives)

King Hussein on the steps of the Chase plane in Amman, Jordan. Hussein was an able politician and a quiet force for peace in the Middle East. (Courtesy of the J.P. Morgan Chase & Co. Archives)

With the incomparable Anwar Sadat in Cairo in January 1974. Sadat was mercurial and demanding, and our relationship had its difficult moments. (Courtesy of the J.P. Morgan Chase & Co. Archives)

On my way to the *qat* party in San'a, Yemen, in 1978. (Courtesy of the J.P. Morgan Chase & Co. Archives)

Peggy and I with Joseph Verner Reed, my friend and indispensable executive assistant during my tenure as the chairman and CEO of the bank, at an International Advisory Committee dinner in 1978. (Courtesy of the J.P. Morgan Chase & Co. Archives)

Best Wishes to David Rockefeller   *Jimmy Carter* 4/80

President Carter's geniality quickly disappeared this day in April 1980 when I pressed him to allow the Shah of Iran to enter the United States. (White House photo; courtesy of the J.P. Morgan Chase & Co. Archives)

George Landau (left) and I meet with President George Bush, Secretary of State James Baker (second from right), and National Security Advisor Brent Scowcroft (right) at the State Department in May 1990 to support the North American Free Trade Agreement. (White House photo; DR photo collection)

The end of a marathon session with Fidel Castro in Havana in February 2001. Pete Peterson, chairman of the Council on Foreign Relations, is on Castro's left. My back is to the camera. (Photo by Jeffrey A. Reinke; courtesy of the Council on Foreign Relations)

A group from the Council on Foreign Relations met with Chairman Yasser Arafat in Gaza in 1999, before the most recent outbreak of violence in Israel and the West Bank. (Photo by Jeffrey A. Reinke; courtesy of the Council on Foreign Relations)

Nelson Mandela is the most courageous and compassionate human being I have ever met. Here, I am introducing him to a group of businessmen at a breakfast I hosted in New York in 2000. (Associated Press/Wide World Photos)

During the New York City fiscal crisis, Pat Patterson of J.P. Morgan (second from left), Walter Wriston of Citibank (third from left), and I tried to persuade Secretary of the Treasury William Simon and President Gerald Ford to provide federal loan guarantees to assist our effort to save the City from bankruptcy. (White House photo; DR photo collection)

Tension among the brothers: Laurance, John, Nelson, and I trying to resolve some of the issues that confronted us in the 1970s. The photo was taken before the annual Christmas family dinner at Kykuit in 1976. (DR photo collection)

Kykuit, with the Playhouse in the distance. (Courtesy of the Rockefeller Archive Center)

Rockefeller Center at the time of its sale to Mitsubishi Estate Corporation in 1989. I had resisted the demands of the 1934 Trust Committee to sell this valuable property for almost a decade. (Courtesy of the Rockefeller Archive Center)

My family at the JY Ranch in the Grand Tetons in the summer of 1980. This vacation helped heal the generational wounds of the 1970s. Standing, left to right: Neva, David, Jr., Peggy, Abby, and Eileen. Richard is kneeling. (Photo by Mary Hilliard)

Groundbreaking for the new Museum of Modern Art, May 10, 2001. I am joined by, from left to right, Agnes Gund, Yoshio Taniguchi, Ronald Lauder, Donald Marron, Jerry Speyer, Mayor Rudolph Guiliani, and Glenn Lowry. (Photo by Eric Weis; DR photo collection)

After a century of biomedical research, The Rockefeller University has exceeded the expectations of Grandfather and Father. In June 2002, I sat with four men who epitomize the institution's scientific excellence: from left to right, Alexander G. Bearn, Maclyn McCarty, former president Frederick Seitz, and former president Joshua Lederberg, a Nobel laureate. (Photo by Karen Smith)

The entire Rockefeller family helps Laurance and me celebrate our ninetieth and eighty-fifth birthdays in 2000. It was a wonderful occasion, made even better by the closer relationship that Laurance and I have developed in recent years. (Photo by Matthew Gillis; DR photo collection)

Peggy and I sailing off the coast of Maine. This is my favorite picture of the two of us. I still miss her terribly. (DR photo collection)

rectly and on our own. I was delighted by this rather oblique invitation, which I immediately accepted. At my request he agreed to include in the invitation my executive assistant, Joseph Reed, and his wife, Mimi; Frank Stankard, the head of Chase's Asian operations; and James Pusey, a China scholar and the son of my old friend Nathan Pusey, the former president of Harvard, who acted as our interpreter.

BONING UP ON CHINA

O nce the formal invitation had been extended by the Chinese People's Institute for Foreign Affairs (PIFA), I set out to learn more about China's history and its contemporary political and economic situation. We met with experts from the Council on Foreign Relations, who a few years earlier had recommended the adoption of a two-China policy by the American government, and also with two eminent China scholars, John K. Fairbank of Harvard and Michel Oksenberg of Columbia University.

Mike's three lengthy briefings were invaluable. He stressed that Mao's greatest accomplishments were the unification of China and the imposition of a stable political order in the 1950s after many years of war and upheaval. The Chinese people revered him for this. But there was a darker side as well. Mao had undermined his own achievements by ruthlessly pursuing radical social and economic change. The "Great Leap Forward" of the late 1950s and the "Great Proletarian Cultural Revolution" that had started in 1966 were the equivalent of a civil war, producing enormous social chaos, widespread economic disruption, and terrible famine. Mike believed that China was then in the midst of a period of transition and that it was impossible to predict what the outcome would be. Mao, while old, ill, and paranoid, was still very much in charge, but a major power struggle over the succession was in process. In Mike's view, Zhou Enlai represented the principal voice of moderation within the inner circle of the Chinese leadership, and he urged us to see him if at all possible.

Shortly after my first meeting with Ambassador Huang, Secretary of Commerce Frederick Dent invited me to join the National Council on U.S.-China Trade. The Nixon administration organized the council in early 1973 as part of its strategy to bolster public support for its China policy. It was a mixed public-private group that worked to increase the opportunities for trade with the PRC. I became vice chairman of the council and attended its first conference in Washington in May 1973, only a few weeks before leaving for China.

I also talked with the heads of three organizations in which I had long played a leadership role—Bayless Manning of the Council on Foreign Relations, Joshua Lederberg of The Rockefeller University, and Richard Oldenburg of the Museum of Modern Art—and asked them if it would be helpful for me to explore contacts for them with the PRC. All three responded enthusiastically and in the affirmative. Accordingly, carrying the portfolios of a number of organizations—the Chase, the U.S.-China Council, and the three not-for-profits—we set off for China.

RETURNING TO THE MAINLAND

Physically entering China in those days was not easy.

We flew first to Hong Kong and then set off the following day on a two-hour train ride from Kowloon to Luo Wu, a small village on the border of the New Territories in China's Guangdong Province. We stepped off the train into the humid, tropical air of a south China summer day and carried our own bags across the railroad bridge that spanned a small river, while loudspeakers blared "The East Is Red" and a medley of other Chinese patriotic songs. The eerie voices and martial music were strangely foreboding. But just as we stepped into China proper, we encountered W. Michael Blumenthal, president of the Bendix Corporation and later Secretary of the Treasury, on his way out. Seeing the familiar face of someone actually returning from China gave us heart.

An unenthusiastic official processed our papers, and then we waited at the Shenzhen station for a few hours before boarding another train to Guangzhou. There we transferred to the airport, only to discover our scheduled flight to Beijing had departed without us. We waited among throngs of Chinese while several passengers were unceremoniously dumped from the next flight so that special seating could be arranged for us in the front of the plane. Early in the evening we touched down in the capital, having flown for three hours across China's endless and ancient landscape.

We drove into Beijing along a rough road packed with people on bicycles and wagons drawn by horses and teams of oxen. We saw few motor vehicles either then or during the rest of our time in China. Finally, we arrived at the once elegant Beijing Hotel in the heart of the city, only a few blocks from Tiananmen Square and the Forbidden City. Built early in the century to cater to European travelers (my parents and Aunt Lucy had stayed there in the 1920s), the grand old hotel was now suffering from years of neglect. Nevertheless, these were the best accommodations in town, and the staff was polite and attentive to our needs.

INFORMAL/ACCOMMODATING, RIGID/INFLEXIBLE HOSTS

On virtually every business trip I made for Chase during my thirty-five-year career, I would approve a prearranged schedule of meetings before leaving. This trip was different. We had no idea of our itinerary or whom we would see until after we arrived in Beijing. Soon after we unpacked, our official host from PIFA, a retired Chinese diplomat, called on us to ask where we would like to go and whom we would like to see. We told him that we hoped to spend four or five days in Beijing and were eager to meet with senior government officials—mentioning Zhou Enlai specifically—and to visit the Great Wall, the Ming Tombs, and the Forbidden City. We also asked for permission to travel to Xi'an, Shanghai, and Guangzhou. He said most of this could be arranged, but meetings with senior officials, particularly Zhou, would remain uncertain until toward the end of our stay in Beijing.

We had learned before leaving New York that traveling within China would be difficult, so I had asked Huang if we could use the Chase plane for that purpose. Huang demurred, claiming that facilities to service private aircraft were not available, but the government would put a plane at our disposal. And they did: a four-engine Russian Tupolev with seating for twenty-four and a crew of four, more than adequate for our party of six plus four interpreters. Given the extremely limited airline service in China at the time, such a gesture was a clear indication of the importance the Chinese placed on our visit.

While in Beijing the government assigned us a large, black Chinese-made Hongqi limousine with a driver and an interpreter-guide. Due to our host's rigid concept of protocol, however, only Peggy and I were allowed to ride in it. The other members of our group had to be content with much smaller cars. Joseph and Frank were not very happy with this inequity, but the Chinese refused to yield an inch, to the point of refusing to allow anyone to ride with us even for short distances.

In other respects our hosts were remarkably informal and accommodating. We were told at our initial briefing, for instance, that our spouses were welcome to participate in all meetings, including those with senior officials, and that except at official banquets we should dress in casual clothes, such as slacks and shirts without ties, because of the summer heat.

By chance our visit coincided with the arrival of Ambassador David Bruce, the newly appointed chief of the U.S. Liaison Office, and his wife, Evangeline. I had first met David in Paris in 1945 when he headed the OSS mission attached to General Eisenhower's headquarters. David subsequently served with great distinction as ambassador both to France and Great Britain.

The Bruces invited Peggy and me to have lunch with them in the newly built U.S. residence in the Diplomatic Quarter a few blocks from our hotel. Their furniture had not yet arrived, so we ate on a card table in their bedroom. David touched on the intense power struggle being waged between moderates and hard-liners within the Chinese Communist Party. David's account of turmoil within the leadership stood in stark contrast to the orderly way in which our visit was being orchestrated, but it also confirmed my sense that creating a presence for Chase or any American organization would require patience and hard negotiations.

WITNESS TO THE CULTURAL REVOLUTION

Mao instigated the Great Proletarian Cultural Revolution in the mid-1960s in a brutal bid to solidify his own grip on power. While he succeeded in eliminating or neutralizing his opponents within the Communist Party, Mao lost control of his chosen instrument, the zealous and bloody-minded Red Guards, cadres of young, fanatical Communist Party members who ran rampant until the Red Army finally brought them to heel a few years later. During this time, extremist political factions, egged on by Mao's wife, Jiang Qing, inflicted profound misery on millions of people and ripped apart the fabric of Chinese society. Indeed, we saw constant evidence of the Cultural Revolution's effects and soon came to realize that it had not yet run its course. Three vignettes may serve as illustrations of what we observed.

At Beijing University a distinguished scientist, who still bore the title of vice president, accompanied us to the campus but sat in silence while three members of the Revolutionary Committee in their early twenties presided at the meeting. In response to a question about university entrance requirements, they made it clear that academic preparation was secondary to unquestioning loyalty to Mao's teachings. The disastrous impact this had on the quality of scholarship and teaching for a full generation can well be imagined.

It was the same story at the recently renamed Capital Hospital, formerly the PUMC, where James (Scotty) Reston of *The New York Times* had undergone an emergency appendectomy, anesthetized with acupuncture, two years earlier. Although several doctors trained before the revolution were still on staff, they remained in the background while members of the

Revolutionary Committee led us on a tour. These student leaders boasted of the medical care available to "the masses" because of Mao's leadership, but it was apparent that the facilities were primitive and the hospital lacked the most basic surgical instruments and medicine, even though it was considered the best in China. As chilling proof of this, we looked through the open door of an operating theater just after a leg amputation had been completed; the temperature was above 90 degrees, and flies buzzed around the severed leg, which stood upright in a bucket beside the operating table.

We visited a ceramic factory outside Guangzhou established during the Tang dynasty and famed for the finely wrought pieces it had produced for more than a thousand years. The factory was now mass-producing poor-quality imitations of those earlier masterpieces. We asked if workers were permitted to create original pieces and were told that nothing could be produced for "elite individuals" that was not also available to the masses.

Throughout our visit no one said anything, even when we were alone in the car, that deviated in the slightest degree from strict Maoist doctrine. Had they done so, they would have doubtless been banished to the countryside for "reeducation." In fact, nothing gave us much hope that the Chinese leadership was about to relax its iron grip on the country.

NEGOTIATING WITH THE BANK OF CHINA

Despite these depressing encounters, our meetings in Beijing with Chinese officials went well. The most important was with the chairman of the state-owned Bank of China, which managed the country's external financial and banking relations. The chairman seemed suspicious of even the most rudimentary Western banking practices and dubious about adopting them. He explained that paying interest was inconsistent with Marxist doctrine and then said, "You must realize, Mr. Rockefeller, that we have no experience with either lending or borrowing money." He gave us little reason to think this policy was about to change.

It became clear that even if we established a relationship with the Bank of China, it would be a very limited one. I was quite surprised, therefore, when after more than an hour of pointing out all the reasons that China could not open its doors to foreign trade or investment, the chairman suddenly declared that the Bank of China would be interested in establishing a limited correspondent relationship with Chase. I had to assume he had received instructions from a superior to make the offer, and I lost no time in accepting the proposal.

The implementation of even this modest arrangement was neither easy nor quick. A correspondent relationship normally requires the foreign bank to open an account in New York by making a dollar deposit. In this case such a seemingly innocuous deposit would have triggered calamitous consequences; there was an estimated $250 million in claims against the PRC for assets seized from Americans after the revolution, and the U.S. government had frozen $75 million in Chinese assets in the United States in retaliation. Had the Bank of China deposited money with us before an agreement was reached on these blocked balances, the PRC's funds would have been seized by the U.S. government. As a temporary expedient, therefore, we adopted the unusual course of making a dollar deposit with the Bank of China to enable them to satisfy the modest letter of credit and remittance business they proposed conducting with us. While many criticized Chase for doing business with yet another Communist country, I was persuaded there was great potential in being the first American bank in China—even though it might be some time before the relationship was profitable. I felt our new connection was supportive of broader American interests as well. The diplomatic opening achieved by Nixon and Kissinger had enormous significance, but if the full fruits of rapprochement were to be realized, contact with the PRC at the private as well as at the government level would be necessary. To bring about a fundamental change in China's closed and suspicious society would be a slow and arduous process. This could only be accomplished by personal contact and through a gradual process of building closer relationships. It gave me satisfaction to have played a part in that process.

ZHOU ENLAI

When our last day in Beijing rolled around with no word on whether Zhou Enlai would receive us, we became concerned that it might not happen at all. That afternoon, however, we were told not to leave the hotel for dinner and to wait for instructions. There was no further explanation of what might be in store for us.

Sometime after 9:00 P.M., one of the officials from PIFA walked into my room and told us the Premier would receive us at precisely 10:45 in the Great Hall of the People. It was a hot, muggy night, and after a hectic day and a copious Chinese meal, we had largely given up hope of meeting Zhou and were thinking instead of sleep and our departure the next day. His words quickly revived us.

We left the hotel at 10:30 and drove through dimly lit streets the short distance to Tiananmen Square. The pink walls of the Forbidden City and the huge portrait of Chairman Mao looming over the Gate of Heavenly Peace were barely visible in the darkness. We moved slowly around the square and stopped at an entry on the south side of the Great Hall of the People precisely at the appointed hour.

Zhou Enlai himself stood at the top of the steps to greet us. Winston Lord, one of Henry Kissinger's aides on his historic trip to China and later our ambassador there, subsequently told me this was an unusual gesture for Zhou to make; he had not done this for either Nixon or Kissinger. The Premier looked even smaller and frailer in person than in his pictures. He was dressed in a regulation dark gray "Mao tunic" with the red badge of the Politburo affixed to it. He shook hands with each of us and posed for a photograph in front of a large painting called the *Welcome Guest Pine.* We then moved inside to the "Taiwan" room (the symbolism was not lost on us), a large carpeted room where we were seated in a formal square around Zhou in overstuffed armchairs. Beside each chair stood a white porcelain spittoon, standard equipment at all our formal meetings. I sat on Zhou's right. Nancy Tang, his young Brooklyn-born interpreter, was just behind him.

Zhou had a surprising amount of knowledge about my family. He also asked about T. V. Soong and H. H. Kung, high-ranking Chinese bankers who were also relatives and strong supporters of Chiang Kai-shek, and seemed surprised that I did not know them, not realizing, among other things, that I was a generation younger than they. I heard no rancor in his voice when he talked about them or even when he mentioned his old adversary, Generalissimo Chiang.

In fact, Taiwan came up for discussion only in relation to its remarkable economic growth. Zhou agreed that Taiwan's growth had been impressive. But he dismissively noted that Chiang had set up a free port "like Hong Kong" by importing raw material, manufacturing cheap goods with exploited labor, and then exporting the finished products at a profit. While this was good for Chiang and his coterie, he said, "it was not good for the workers, who didn't benefit at all."

Zhou referred positively to Nixon's visit and the broader contacts with the United States that were now possible. He attributed this result to "the decisiveness" of Chairman Mao. As one of the few senior Party members who had survived Mao's reign of terror during the Cultural Revolution, Zhou was careful in every word and gesture never to raise himself above the Chairman. We talked about Henry Kissinger, and Jamie Pusey later told me that Nancy Tang, when speaking to Zhou, had referred to Henry as "the

Doctor," apparently his nickname among the inner circle of the Chinese leadership.

Zhou seemed most interested in discussing the international economic and monetary situation. He questioned me about the weakness of the U.S. dollar, which had effectively been devalued by 20 percent over the previous two years, the high inflation rate in the United States, and the volatility of international exchange rates. He mentioned the disastrous devaluation that China had experienced right after World War II and the runaway inflation in Germany after World War I, which he remembered from his student days in Paris and Berlin in the early 1920s. He asked if something like that could happen in the United States. Zhou noted that his conversations with both Nixon and Kissinger had convinced him that neither "seemed to be very interested in or to know very much about economics."

The Premier seemed genuinely concerned that our economic problems might have an effect on China and asked me to explain the international monetary system—quite an undertaking for that time of night without any preparation! I said that I would try, but it might take a while. While I am sure my colleagues blanched at the prospect of listening to this midnight lecture, Zhou simply nodded his head for me to proceed.

I began with the Bretton Woods agreement, the Marshall Plan, the dramatic expansion of world trade in the 1950s and 1960s, and on to the emergence of the Eurodollar market. I spoke of the onset of the U.S. inflationary spiral in the mid-1960s that resulted from LBJ's disastrous "guns and butter" fiscal and budgetary policies. Those policies, I said, had produced balance-of-payments deficits, which in turn had led to Nixon's decision to go off the gold standard and impose wage and price controls in 1971. I concluded my *tour d'horizon* almost an hour later by suggesting that it was faulty U.S. economic policies rather than fundamental economic ills that had created the troubles for the dollar. If we followed more prudent economic policies, I felt, the strength of the dollar would return.

Zhou listened attentively to my discourse, unlike some of my colleagues who could barely keep their eyes open. When I finished, he questioned me on some of the points I had made about trade and currencies. Zhou acknowledged that trade could be useful for China's growth and development, but would not concede that changes in his country's managed economy would have to be made in order to facilitate foreign investment and participation.

The potentially destabilizing effect of foreign trade on the yuan, China's currency, seemed to trouble him the most. Like his Soviet counterpart, Alexei Kosygin, Zhou was perplexed by the hard reality of currency inconvertibility and seemed not to understand the tremendous limitations this imposed on China's ability to trade with the rest of the world. If anything, the Chinese were even more unsophisticated than the Russians on these matters. Zhou believed that the yuan's greatest strength was that it was *not* an international currency, and "because of that," he said, "it is very strong, backed by the economic strength of our country."

The meeting ended shortly before 1 A.M., and Zhou courteously accompanied us to the door to bid each of us good-bye.

=

It had been a fascinating meeting. Zhou had been friendly, and I was surprised at the degree of his interest in exploring serious issues. Unlike the Russians, especially Khrushchev in our 1964 meeting, Zhou was uninterested in scoring ideological points. I suspect he thought the severe problems then besetting the United States and the free market economies of Western Europe and Japan were not the result of imprudent policies, as I had suggested, but rather the product of the fundamental "contradictions of capitalism." But if so, he was too polite to correct me.

=

China paid an immense price for Mao's dictatorship. The Cultural Revolution destroyed an entire generation of the country's ablest people engineers, teachers, scientists, factory managers. In 1973 we knew almost nothing about the enormity of Mao's crimes or the complicity of his closest associates, including Zhou Enlai. I found Zhou to be urbane, charming, and erudite. It was a shock to learn later that he had tolerated such crimes against humanity.

OBSERVING CHINA'S TRANSITION

I visited China five more times over the next fifteen years and met with the successors of Mao and Zhou on a number of occasions. These trips gave me the opportunity to observe the evolution of China's position in the world.

My second visit in early January 1977 came less than a year after the deaths of Mao and Zhou, and at a time when the transition from the radicalism of Mao's final years had barely begun. The infamous Gang of Four had been imprisoned in late 1976, and the ineffectual Hua Guofeng had just become chairman of the Communist Party.

PIFA had again invited me, this time in my capacity as chairman of the Council on Foreign Relations, with whom they wanted to establish closer ties. I accepted the invitation with the understanding that I would also be able to discuss banking matters with Chinese officials. Nurturing the relationship between PIFA and the CFR was important to me, but I was more interested in prodding the Chinese to be a bit more imaginative about Chase's operations. Five years had elapsed since Nixon's historic visit, but full diplomatic relations had not been restored between the United States and China. Each country had been distracted by internal political concerns—the death of Mao and the protracted Watergate crisis. As a result Chase's correspondent relationship with the Bank of China had been slow to develop.

With this in mind I visited Washington before leaving for the Far East to determine the attitude of the incoming Carter administration toward normalizing relations with China. I met with Cyrus Vance, who was about to take over as Secretary of State, and Zbigniew Brzezinski, who would serve as national security advisor. I also met briefly with Jimmy Carter. All three of them indicated that resolving the remaining areas of disagreement with the PRC was high on their list of priorities, and they gave me permission to convey this information to the senior officials I was scheduled to see in Beijing.

I raised the issue with both Vice Premier Li Xiannian and Huang Hua, who by then had become minister of foreign affairs. To my dismay they were notably cool in their response. They insisted that the principal obstacle to normalization was our country's continued support for the "criminal regime" on Taiwan. Until we changed our policy there, nothing would be done. I found most of the senior leaders I met almost as suspicious of the United States as they were of the Soviet Union, which they invariably referred to as the Polar Bear. Although courteous to me, my requests to expand Chase's operations met with a firm refusal. All in all it was a very disappointing trip.

THE OPEN DOOR

A little less than two years later, sentiment had changed completely. Deng Xiaoping displaced Hua Guofeng and rapidly consolidated his power over both the Party and the State. The Carter administration was prepared to complete the process begun by the Nixon administration. In December 1978, American and Chinese diplomats finally agreed to a formula that finessed the intractable issue of Taiwan's independence, and with it came the restoration of full diplomatic relations between the United States and the PRC.

Chase benefited immediately from the agreement. With the "blocked assets" issue resolved, we established a full correspondent relationship with the Bank of China, which finally opened a substantial dollar account at our home office in New York. In addition, the Ministry of Finance authorized a Chase representative office in Beijing, and soon after we made our first loan—to the Chinese Ministry of Mining and Metallurgy. The Chase World Information Corporation, our information services subsidiary created in 1972, began to introduce American businessmen to investment opportunities in China.

In many ways Chase served as China's point of entry into the United States. We hosted a business luncheon in New York for their minister of finance in 1979, and in June of the following year organized a China forum attended by senior representatives of more than two hundred American companies. In the fall of that same year I hosted a small private luncheon in Pocantico for Vice Premier Bo Yibo, who was accompanied by Rong Yiren, the chairman of the China International Trust and Investment Corporation (CITIC). This gave me the opportunity to meet the man who would do more to implement his country's opening to the West than any other.

Rong was the scion of an old Shanghai banking and manufacturing family that had extensive investments in China, Hong Kong, and the United States before the revolution. After Mao took power, Rong remained as a favored "national capitalist," continuing to run his family's many enterprises with only nominal supervision from the government. Eventually, however, the Red Guards caught up with Rong, confiscated his property, and submitted him to torture. Only the intervention of his protector, Deng Xiaoping, had saved him from a long term of "reeducation" on a rural commune.

After Deng consolidated his hold on power in the late 1970s, he appointed Rong to head CITIC. Deng knew that China desperately needed foreign capital to finance its development and turned to Rong as one of the few Chinese with the requisite knowledge and contacts in the Western world. Rong was an able and farsighted businessman who quickly became the focal point for all foreign investment in China. Over time, he and I became good friends.

The door to China had swung open, and Chase was waiting on the other side as American companies began to walk through it.

=

I next visited China in May 1981, shortly after I retired from the Chase, and found more evidence of change. Deng Xiaoping's moderate faction of the Politburo had wrested control from the hard-line Maoists and had begun to repair the damage done during the decades of Mao's harsh rule. There was a new openness and a tolerance for foreign ideas that had not existed on my earlier visits.

A measure of this change was the Chinese leadership's willingness to meet with a delegation from the Trilateral Commission. After a plenary session of the Trilateral in Tokyo, a group of us went to Beijing to discuss opportunities for economic cooperation between China and the Trilateral countries with a dozen or so senior Chinese intellectuals. The highlight of the trip was our meeting with the three Chinese vice premiers, including Deng himself.

Deng was a diminutive man with an extraordinarily weathered face. He was seventy-seven years old when I first met him and looked much older. He smoked nonstop during the course of our one-hour meeting. It was apparent he was very much the man in charge. Both of his companions, although his equal in rank within the government, deferred to him constantly.

Deng was quite willing to discuss any and all topics. He was fully engaged throughout the meeting and seemed eager to reassure us of his commitment to continued economic liberalization.

THE CAVES OF DAZU

In April 1986, Peggy and I returned for a vacation trip at the invitation of my old friend Ambassador Winston Lord and his wife, Bette, the author of *Spring Moon*, a widely acclaimed novel about China in the early twentieth century.

Before leaving Beijing I had the chance to meet and talk with Premier Zhao Ziyang, and I liked him immensely. Zhao was considered by many the logical successor to Deng once the aging leader fully retired. Zhao seemed fully committed to the process of change and eager to experiment with new ideas. He was comfortable talking about economic matters and candid about the difficulties that China faced in making its transition to a more market-oriented economy. In talking with him I felt a sense of compatibility I had never experienced with other Chinese leaders. He had Zhou Enlai's urbanity and cosmopolitan interest in the rest of the world.

Rong Yiren gave a splendid banquet for Peggy and me at one of the guest houses adjacent to the Forbidden City, where Nixon and Kissinger had stayed in 1972. It was an indication of Rong's power and influence that he was able to do this in a place normally reserved for heads of state. Rong and his wife also entertained us at their home—the only time I have ever been to

a private home in China. They lived in a beautiful old house built in the tra-
ditional style with several rooms arranged around a large inner courtyard.
We were served a delicious formal Chinese "tea," and Rong told us about his
family's long and interesting history. Later, after we returned to New York,
Rong sent me an unusual reclining wooden chair that I had admired in his
house. These two gestures of friendship were unique to my experience in
China and ones I would have expected from a senior official in the old
Imperial China, but not from the representative of a Communist govern-
ment.

When Rong learned we would be traveling to Chongqing to begin our
journey down the Yangtze, he made a suggestion that turned an exotic vacation into a deeply memorable experience. He told us about Dazu, an eight-
hundred-year-old Buddhist complex and pilgrimage center located fifty
miles west of Chongqing, which he said was one of the great artistic treasures of China. We followed his suggestion even though we had to leave our
hotel in Chongqing at 4 A.M. in order to get back in time for the departure of
our riverboat.

The drive to Dazu gave us our first glimpse of rural China—men and
women planting young rice plants by hand in the flooded paddies, and huge
water buffalo pulling single-bladed plows behind them. Our car was the only
modern piece of equipment in sight. Dazu itself was incredible: Buddhist
monks had hollowed out caves in limestone cliffs where they lived, and during the twelfth and thirteenth centuries they carved more than fifty thousand statues of Buddha and other religious figures on the cave walls and on
the faces of the cliffs. Dazu was comparable in quality to the much older
(first century B.C. to eighth century A.D.) and more famous Ajanta and Ellora
caves in India, which may have been, I learned on a visit many years later,
the inspiration for the caves in Dazu.

In May 1988, I traveled with the Chase IAC to Beijing for a four-day visit. We
met with Zhao Ziyang, who had by then reached the pinnacle of power as
general secretary of the Chinese Communist Party, Premier Li Peng, and
Deng himself, who at the age of eighty-four still exercised the ultimate
power through his position as head of the Red Army. Winston Lord said he
did not recall any other private group being received by the three senior
leaders in one day.

On my previous visits I had met with Chinese officials at the Great Hall of
the People or in their offices. This time our meetings were held in the
Ziguangge, the Hall of Purple Effulgence within Zhongnanhai, the exclusive

enclave next to the Forbidden City, where the highest officials of the Communist Party had lived since coming to power in the late 1940s. The area was exquisite; traditional Chinese homes were set on well-tended grounds surrounding two beautiful lakes.

Deng was even more diminutive and frail, but his mental faculties were as sharp as ever. Deng claimed he was semiretired because he wished to make way for younger leaders. He noted with pleasure the presence of Henry Kissinger, an IAC member with whom he had met on many occasions, and commented favorably on the meeting he had held with my Trilateral group seven years before.

Deng pointed with pride to the progress China had made over the previous decade and stated that both Zhao and Li were committed to the forceful implementation of a program of economic reform. However, Deng also provided a frank appraisal of China's current situation. His country was weak economically, hampered by a low level of technology, and pressed by an ever-increasing population. The solution lay in economic growth and the campaign to limit population growth. But China also needed foreign investment and infusions of modern technology. Deng was optimistic that this would happen and expected that by the end of the century China would have made considerable progress in meeting all these goals.

In a reflective mood, Deng talked about his vision of the world. He saw the twenty-first century as the "Century of Asia," with Latin America gradually becoming a force. He even saw a time when Africa would be a world leader. By implication he saw the stars of Europe and the United States waning, although he knew that China would be dependent on the Western world for technology and capital for some time.

In closing the meeting he said that China had no option but to pursue reform and to improve relations with the developed world. He was pressing his successors to move swiftly. Deng conceded that mistakes would be made but felt that this should not deter the reform effort. "China should not be afraid to make errors," he said, "but it should avoid repeating them." He indicated, ominously as it turned out, that in the event too many errors were made, he would not hesitate to reexert his authority and make changes in his country's leadership.

This was a chilling prophecy. A year later, with the Tiananmen Square demonstrations, Deng sent in the tanks to crush the dissidents. This reprehensible act has tainted Deng's place in history, but it should not obscure his pivotal role in breaking with China's immediate past. It must be remembered that it was Deng who authorized the dismantling of China's inefficient communal farm system, opened the country to foreign trade and investment, and initiated, albeit quietly and slowly, the process of political decentralization and democratization.

At the start of the twenty-first century China has become a far more open and tolerant society than the one I observed almost three decades earlier.

CHAPTER 19

EMISSARY FOR "BALANCE"
IN THE MIDDLE EAST

Nowhere in the world was my family and our close connections to the petroleum industry so complex and so easily misconstrued as in the Middle East. In turn, Chase's involvement in the region stemmed from its close and longtime association with the major U.S. oil companies.

The bank had been one of the earliest financiers of the American petroleum industry, and as new sources of oil were discovered in Latin America, the Far East, and the Middle East, Chase underwrote the shipment of both crude oil and refined products all over the world. By the mid-1930s, oil had become so central to Chase's profitability that Winthrop Aldrich created a separate Petroleum Department, which was soon recognized as the best in the business. In 1947, Winthrop opened a branch in Beirut, the financial center of the region, as part of his international strategy. But we faced difficulties there from the start. The main problem was the regional dominance of the large British and French overseas banks, but we simply did not assign enough resources to the area. A single officer, James Major in the Foreign Department, was expected to cover all the Middle Eastern countries outside Lebanon from New York. He made one trip a year to keep in touch with our correspondents and other customers, hardly sufficient to develop meaningful new business.

In 1953, Jim asked me to accompany him on his annual trip even though I had shifted to the domestic side of the bank by then. The visit was an eye-opener. Both the Saudis and the al-Sabahs, the rulers of Kuwait, retained important aspects of their Bedouin heritage. They were courageous, shrewd, and daring people with little knowledge of Western culture or the modern world. Riyadh, the capital of Saudi Arabia, was encircled by a high crenellated wall, and its tall wooden gates were closed every night against intruders. Women in veils, muezzins calling the faithful to prayer from the tall minarets, and desert warriors in long robes with curved ornamental daggers in their belts presented the Western visitor with a colorful mosaic of a time that seemed long past. As if to keep the modern world at bay, foreign embassies were required to locate in Jidda on the Red Sea, more than five hundred miles distant from the capital.

In 1950, Winthrop Aldrich convinced King Ibn Saud to allow us to open a branch in Jidda. But the follow-up was poor, and Saudi officials declined to approve the request. Although we maintained an important depository relationship with the Saudi Arabian Monetary Agency (SAMA), their central bank, and with a number of Saudi private banks, and also served as the personal bank for some members of the Saudi royal family, we still needed a direct presence in the country.

In contrast, City Bank took a more aggressive approach and succeeded in getting permission to open a branch in 1955. This gave them an enormous advantage when Saudi oil production increased in the ensuing years.

Recognizing the weakness of our position, I made the Middle East an integral part of my plans for international expansion after I became co-CEO of the bank in 1961. I called on political leaders and banking officials in Lebanon, Kuwait, Saudi Arabia, Bahrain, and Iran during the course of a round-the-world trip in February and March 1962, a trip on which Peggy accompanied me.

I saw signs of change everywhere we went in the Middle East. The increasing flow of oil wealth had provided the funds to build new highways, airports, desalinization plants, and vast housing projects, and governments throughout the region were signing contracts with American and European companies to do the work.

I wanted to make Chase's presence more visible and effective, but we were late in arriving and encountered serious obstacles everywhere. Tough legal restrictions prevented direct branching by foreign banks in almost all the oil-producing states of the Persian Gulf. And hard-line Socialist governments in Egypt, Iraq, Syria, and Libya were actively hostile to foreign investment and foreign banks. While it was possible to do business with these governments, it was not easy, and with the exception of Egypt, we soon terminated our relationships with them.

For the region as a whole, however, it was the conflict between Arabs and Israelis that posed the greatest obstacle and the greatest potential danger to

Chase, particularly because of our determination to do business with both sides. Inevitably, I became involved in the complex politics of the region, both as an agent for change and an object of controversy.

CHASE AND ISRAEL

Even at the time of my 1953 trip, Arab-Israeli enmity was an intractable reality. The leaders of the frontline Arab nations—Syria, Lebanon, Jordan, Iraq, and Egypt—refused to recognize Israel and vowed to "drive the Zionists into the sea." While the 1947–48 conflict ensured Israel's survival, it also created a quarter of a million Palestinian Arab refugees, most of whom eked out a marginal existence in camps run by the United Nations Relief and Works Agency for Palestine Refugees (UNRWA) in the Near East in Lebanon, Jordan's West Bank, and Egypt's Gaza Strip. Peggy and I visited two of these camps in southern Lebanon in 1962 and were appalled at the atrocious conditions under which the refugees lived, with little or no prospect that the situation would improve.

On the other hand, the Jewish people, after the horrors of Hitler's Holocaust, now had a nation of their own. The Jews had a powerful moral claim on the conscience of the world, one that had a particularly strong resonance in the United States. The American commitment, which began with President Harry S. Truman's solid support for the creation of the Israeli state in 1948, gradually strengthened and expanded over the years. It is a great tragedy that an equitable division of land between the Palestinians and Israelis was not accomplished at the most opportune moment in 1948. Sadly, because of the failure to resolve this issue, the world has had to live with the consequences ever since.

Initially, Chase's business with Israel was quite limited. We had a correspondent relationship with the Israeli central bank and a small number of private banks, but the flow of business was limited, largely because the Socialists who dominated Israel's government for almost thirty years were not especially welcoming to foreign banks. However, one financial connection was of great significance for both Chase and Israel. In 1951 the Israeli government selected Chase as the American fiscal agent for Israeli bonds. The sale of these bonds produced a huge flow of funds critical to Israel's economic development. Chase handled the interest payments on these bonds and provided other custodial services for a fee, a business that turned out to be quite profitable and also strengthened our relationship with Jewish organizations in the United States.

Chase's business with Israel, many Arab governments, and the major oil companies grew significantly in the 1960s. We attempted to walk a tightrope of commercial neutrality in the region, but from time to time we would hear complaints from the Arab world that we were contributing to the well-being of the Zionist state and should refrain from doing so.

BOYCOTT

In May 1964, Chase received a letter from Anwar Ali, the governor of SAMA. The letter was blunt and to the point.

> The Commissioner General of the Israeli Boycott Office of the Arab League has received information from certain banks that your bank is the headquarters for promoting the sale of Israeli bonds in all the states of the world and that your bank is the financial agent of the Israeli bonds and it performs all the technical services required of the issuance of these bonds. Your bank is also responsible for the appointment of the foreign banks which work as your correspondents for these bonds in foreign countries.
>
> Furthermore, it has been alleged that your bank gave El Al Israeli Airlines Ltd. a loan for the purchase of its requirements for its aircraft and spare parts; thus you are clearly supporting the Israeli economy. The above two actions will subject you to two of the principles of the Israel boycott, any one of which will lead to stoppage of dealings with you.
>
> I am to express the sincere hope that the Chase Manhattan Bank, in view of its important relationship with us and other Arab countries, will extend its maximum cooperation in avoiding any action which may be construed as jeopardizing its existing happy relationships with our group of countries.

A few weeks later the thirteen Arab League countries voted "to ban dealings with the Chase as from the first of January 1965." Anwar Ali informed us that the "ban can be obviated if your bank should cancel its financial agency for the Israeli loan bonds and all relationship with these bonds and undertake not to extend any further loans in future to any person or institution in Israel."

If the Arab states carried out this threat, we would have had to close our Beirut branch, and approximately $250 million in deposits (mostly from

SAMA) would be withdrawn. To make matters worse, ARAMCO, the Arabian American Oil Company, a consortium made up of Standard Oil of New Jersey, Mobil, Chevron, and Texaco, which held the exclusive rights to develop Saudi Arabia's oil reserves, informed us that unless an acceptable solution could be found, they would be forced to stop doing business with us as well. Chase stood to lose tens of millions of dollars in deposits and earnings.

Fortunately, this worst-case scenario never materialized. Both Saudi Arabia and Egypt were responsive to the argument that in serving as a banker for Israel we were simply discharging our responsibilities as an impartial and apolitical international bank. In the end these two influential countries refused to accept the economic consequences a boycott would inflict on them as well. In addition, the U.S. government acted forcefully to defend us, and the threat of a general Arab boycott subsided.

I had learned a valuable lesson from this tense and worrisome time: If Chase was to survive future crises, I needed to develop a better relationship with the leaders of the Arab world.

NASSER

In the 1960s, if one wanted to have influence on politics in the Arab world, Gamal Abdel Nasser was the man to meet. Although many in the United States considered him a dangerous rabble-rouser, in his own region Nasser was a respected and charismatic figure, the prophet of a new Arab nation who refused to compromise with the "Western imperialists." Nasser had stood his ground during the Suez Crisis of 1956, first nationalizing the waterway and then weathering a British-French-Israeli invasion aimed at toppling him from power.

Nasser emerged from the Suez crisis as a hero. He consolidated power in Egypt and then stepped forward as the leader of the radical, modernizing forces within the Arab world. Millions throughout the Arab world listened to Nasser's weekly broadcasts over Radio Cairo, where he exuberantly outlined his colorful, if somewhat vague, vision of a Pan-Arab Socialist utopia, and attacked the traditionalist regimes of the Gulf.

Eugene Black, who had joined the Chase board in the early 1960s, felt the Anglo-American refusal to finance the Aswan High Dam at the time of the Suez Crisis had been a disaster and had driven a reluctant Nasser into the arms of the Soviets. Gene insisted Nasser was much more flexible and less hostile to the West than his public pronouncements suggested. He believed contacts with Western businessmen would help persuade Nasser to adopt a more moderate position, and, in the wake of our brush with the Arab boycott, encouraged me to meet him.

Gene arranged my first meeting with Nasser in December 1965, and we met in his modestly furnished office in a small, nondescript building not far from the Cairo airport. Photos of Nasser with foreign government leaders crammed every available inch of space on his desk and surrounding tables and bookshelves. Included among them were autographed photos of Nikita Khrushchev, Zhou Enlai, Jawaharlal Nehru, and Josip Broz Tito, the latter two leaders with Nasser of the Non-Aligned Movement. Most of the others were from third world or at least Socialist countries. I do not recall any from Western Europe and none from the United States.

Nasser and I candidly discussed the Middle East situation, during which he passionately denounced unconditional U.S. support for Israel. Despite his obvious displeasure with U.S. policy, he said he would welcome my keeping in touch with him through the Egyptian ambassador in Washington. I reported this to the State Department, but the Johnson administration was consumed by the expanding Vietnam War and was either unwilling or unable to consider implementing a more balanced policy in the Middle East. I had the feeling that Washington hoped the Middle East would not boil over while it focused on more urgent matters. That was wishful thinking.

AFTERMATH OF WAR

The situation in the Middle East worsened after the 1967 Six-Day War. Israel's decisive preemptive strike crippled Arab military forces almost before they got out of their barracks. The Israeli army seized the Sinai Peninsula and the Gaza Strip from Egypt, the Golan Heights from Syria, and East Jerusalem and all of the West Bank from Jordan. Arab leaders who had boasted for years that they would destroy the Israelis were humiliated, and their reaction was sharp and immediate. They viewed our military resupply of Israel during the fighting as a hostile act and immediately severed diplomatic relations with the United States.

Soon after the fighting ended, Charles Malik, a former foreign minister of Lebanon and former president of the U.N. General Assembly, called on me at Chase. Malik was a man of impeccable integrity, and I respected him greatly. He told me the Arabs were very angry with the United States because we had acquiesced in Israel's occupation of Arab land and seemed unconcerned about the hundreds of thousands of new Palestinian refugees caused by the war. Malik said Americans claimed to have deep humanitarian sympathies, but most Arabs perceived us as concerned only about Israel.

Malik's visit forced me to think about the war's impact on the people of the Middle East, in particular the refugees. I called James Linen, the publisher of *Time* magazine, and Arthur K. Watson, who ran IBM World Trade Corporation and chaired the International Chamber of Commerce, and told them of Malik's visit. They agreed something needed to be done to show there was concern and sympathy in the United States for the new Palestinian refugees.

Since the U.S. government's hands were tied by the break in diplomatic relations, we had to act on our own. We established Near East Emergency Donations (NEED), and persuaded former President Eisenhower to serve as honorary chairman. We enlisted the support of a number of prominent Jewish leaders, including Edgar Bronfman, the chairman of Seagrams, to demonstrate that our effort was broad-based and nonideological.

We raised almost $8 million in just over four months, most of it from the major American oil companies. I contributed $250,000 to the effort, which the Rockefeller Brothers Fund matched on behalf of the other members of my family. We turned over the funds to UNRWA for distribution.

Early the following year I toured the refugee camps in Jordan to see first-hand what the conditions were. One camp stood forlornly on the bleak, treeless slopes above the Jordan River valley. It was mid-winter when I arrived by helicopter from Amman, and a cold, bitter wind was blowing from the north. The ground was muddy from melting snow. There were no permanent structures, only floorless tents standing in a sea of mud. More than one thousand people lived there without adequate sanitation or running water, and barely enough food to sustain them. I vividly remember a small child sitting in the bright sun wearing a white hooded jacket. She never moved, even when the crowd shoved past her. These people were living in sight of their former villages on the West Bank but had not been allowed to return. There was a sense of hopelessness about them, but also a deep anger.

It was the anger and desperation of the refugees that were the most enduring legacies of the Six-Day War. They fueled the radicalization of the Palestinians and the emergence of Yasser Arafat and his Palestine Liberation Organization (PLO). Before the war, the refugee problem had been manageable; afterward, the PLO emerged as a separate and strident political force with its distinct objectives, particularly the creation of an independent Palestinian state. Arafat and his followers were no longer content to allow Egypt and the other Arab states to carry on the struggle for them or, as they saw it, to sell them out when it was to their advantage to do so. Another element of instability had been introduced into the regional equation that would make a resolution of the Arab-Israeli conflict even more difficult to achieve.

A few days after visiting the refugee camp, we went on to Beirut. A ceremony had been arranged in which I would hand over a check from NEED in the amount of $1 million to Ian Michelmore, commissioner general of UNRWA. Still disturbed by the scenes I had witnessed, I put aside my prepared remarks and said:

> When a group of private American citizens established NEED to provide emergency funds to aid the refugees, we were only partially aware of the character, scale, and intensity of the problem. Now some of us have seen it for ourselves, and we are conscious not only of the humanitarian challenge that it presents, but also of the urgency in finding a solution to the problem. These refugees, some of them in flight for the second time in twenty years, are victims of political conditions over which they have no control. Their plight is a rebuke to a world that is unable to find and implement a just solution to their problem. I am convinced that until this is solved, there will not soon be peace in the Middle East.

While NEED by itself could do little to relieve the enormous distress of the refugees, the effort at least demonstrated that there were American citizens who wanted to help. We also sent a message to both Arab leaders and American politicians of the urgent need to balance all the conflicting interests within the region before the situation deteriorated any further. Sadly, four decades later, such a balanced policy still remains beyond our grasp.

THE SEARCH FOR BALANCE

The new political conditions that emerged after the 1967 war made it imperative for me to maintain regular contact with Arab leaders. Doing that became more difficult, however, since a number of these nations had severed diplomatic relations with the United States, and the level of hostility toward the West had increased dramatically. Since most Arab political leaders could not or would not come to the United States, I began to travel to the Middle East much more, often twice a year.

Gene Black, who served as a financial advisor to the emir of Kuwait, encouraged me to improve my personal relationships with these Arab leaders.

If they respected me and felt confidence in my fair-mindedness, he pointed out, they would be less likely to penalize the Chase for our Israeli business. NEED's contributions to Palestinian refugees was a good case in point; my credibility with King Hussein of Jordan and other leaders had advanced greatly as a result of this effort.

Since I was one of relatively few Americans who had access to the senior leaders in the region, I soon found myself playing the role of a diplomatic go-between. Before each of my trips in the late 1960s and throughout the 1970s I called on U.S. government officials to learn about changes in U.S. Middle Eastern policy. I would meet with the same officials upon my return to inform them of what I had seen and heard.

A MESSAGE FROM NASSER

In the autumn of 1969, shortly before a bank trip to the Middle East, Egypt's ambassador to the U.N. came to see me at Chase. He said Nasser wanted me to know that he had not had any "meaningful contact" with the United States and hoped I would see him while I was in the area.

I recognized Nasser's request as a potentially significant opening. Diplomatic relations between the United States and Egypt had still not been restored, and efforts to bring the Israelis and Arabs to the bargaining table had been fruitless. I decided to fly to Washington and lay the matter before Henry Kissinger, Nixon's national security advisor. I thought it important to have the administration's approval for the meeting before I replied to Nasser.

I was not optimistic about the reception I would receive from the Nixon administration. Nixon was a strong supporter of Israel, and during the 1968 presidential campaign he had insisted that "the balance of power in the Middle East must be tipped in Israel's favor" and pledged to support a "policy that would give Israel a technological military margin to more than offset her hostile neighbors' numerical superiority."

Once in office, however, Nixon proceeded more cautiously. Wrestling with the need to fully revise U.S. foreign policy, Nixon and Kissinger began to formulate the concepts that would be used to reshape the role of America in the world—détente with the Soviet Union, the opening of China, and the "Nixon Doctrine," which called for smaller powers to carry the burden of defense against Communist expansion and subversion in their own regions. Both men were realists and committed to an objective, almost ruthless appraisal of American objectives and the means to achieve them. Thus, at an early point in the administration, as the process of Vietnamization of the

Indo-China War began, a comprehensive review of U.S. foreign policy, including the Middle East, was also initiated. So the timing of my meeting with Henry was fortuitous.

Henry and I talked at some length about Nasser's request. Henry admitted he knew little about the region but agreed that seeing Nasser might be useful. A few days later Henry called to say that both the White House and the State Department "thought it would be a constructive thing for our government" if I were to maintain "some kind of dialogue" with Nasser. He also asked me to brief President Nixon on my return.

With this green light from Henry, I rearranged my schedule to allow for a brief stopover in Cairo. I met with Nasser in his Cairo home. He looked older and tired, barely recovered from a heart attack he had suffered a few months earlier. When I entered the room, I noticed he had a signed photograph of Lyndon Johnson standing amid his collection of Socialist leaders and Marxist revolutionaries.

I told Nasser I would be seeing Nixon after my return and would be pleased to pass on any message he might have. Nasser readily agreed to my taking notes for this purpose.

As in my prior meeting, Nasser insisted the real obstacle to peace in the Middle East was Israel's refusal to abide by U.N. Resolution 242, which required withdrawal behind the borders that existed prior to the 1967 war, before negotiations for a general peace agreement could begin. Nasser had said this before, and I began to wonder if I had traveled to Cairo just to be harangued. Then he switched gears. In a confidential tone he said that while Resolution 242 should provide the general framework for peace, he was willing to support some border rectifications and also the demilitarization of Syria's Golan Heights, which Israel viewed as a grave threat to its security. In return, Israel's right to exist would be accepted by all Arab nations. This constituted a significant change in Nasser's position. His willingness to concede Israel's right to exist and to negotiate on other issues might enable a regional peace accord to be reached.

I wondered what had caused Nasser to change his mind. He said there were a number of reasons. He was worried about the growing radicalism and instability in the region. "The Fedayeen [Palestinians] are growing stronger every day. A year ago King Hussein could control things in his country, but no longer today—the Fedayeen are too strong. The ability of Egypt to exercise any control over them may also prove to be short-lived. Israel holds the view that the longer a peace settlement is deferred, the greater the chances that his [Nasser's] government would fall and that they would be able to deal with a more flexible man."

Nasser believed the opposite would be the case.

"Prolongation of the conflict has weakened the conservative govern-ments. Changes in government in the Sudan and Libya are examples. In Saudi Arabia there was an attempted coup, which with the aid of the CIA was put down, but the last has not yet been heard from it."

Nasser was also worried about his own domestic position. He was frus-trated by Egypt's total dependence on the Soviet Union for military assis-tance and economic aid. He said that the loss of most of Egypt's military capability in the '67 war had made the Russians his only alternative for re-building his army and air force. With a note of regret he added, "We were a free country until 1967, now we no longer are. We have to depend on the Soviets until the war is settled."

The crux of Nasser's argument was that the situation would become worse unless movement toward a lasting peace started immediately. And for that to occur the United States would have to put pressure on the Israelis in order to reassure Arab governments of our goodwill.

I told Nasser that I would report all of this to President Nixon upon my re-turn. It was the last time I saw Nasser. The Egyptian president died of a heart attack the following year.

A WARNING FROM KING FAISAL

I then flew to Riyadh for a meeting with King Faisal.

The Saudi-Egyptian rivalry had long divided the Arab world. The two countries epitomized the divergent political and economic tendencies of the region. Nasser represented the Pan-Arab vision and Socialist ideas of the first generation of Arab reformers. The Saudis, bolstered by their enormous oil wealth, held fast to the structures and beliefs of the more traditional Islamic world. While the Saudis remained staunch American allies, they were under great pressure from the rest of the Arab world to demonstrate their solidarity with the Palestinians and their independence from the United States. As a result the Saudis had taken the lead in the affairs of the Organization of Petroleum Exporting Countries (OPEC), and they had begun to talk openly about using their enormous economic power to resolve the conflict in the Middle East. Faisal was a hereditary monarch who kept the reins of power securely in his own hands. One of more than fifty sons sired by the great desert warrior Ibn Saud, who had created the nation of Saudi Arabia, Faisal became king in 1964 after a palace coup in which he toppled his ineffectual half-brother. A good part of Faisal's power derived from his religious role within Islam. His formal title was Custodian of the Two Holy Mosques, and he was a devout Muslim and strictly observed all the dictates of his religion.

The al-Sauds regarded their country as a family economic enterprise, and Faisal's principal duty was managing the large and fractious royal family. To keep them loyal and satisfied, Faisal distributed the first 20 percent of oil revenues among the six hundred or so members of his family before making the remainder available to the government. There was more than enough to go around. In 1969, with oil selling at $2 a barrel, Faisal had almost a billion dollars a year to distribute among his relatives, an amount that would rise to almost $24 billion by the early 1980s. Even this was not enough to maintain family peace; Faisal was assassinated by a deranged nephew in 1975.

Faisal greeted me warmly when I arrived. We exchanged gifts, and he reminisced about the lunch I had given him at Pocantico in 1966 at the time of his state visit to the United States. I told him I was interested in hearing his views about the current situation in the region and that I would report them directly to President Nixon upon my return to the United States.

Faisal was even more emphatic than Nasser about the disastrous consequences of U.S. Middle Eastern policy. His opinions were inflexible and his language unrestrained, and his dark, piercing eyes seemed to bore right through me. My notes from that meeting read, in part:

> Faisal feels our policy in the Middle East is dictated by U.S. Zionists and is entirely pro-Israel. It is driving more and more of the Arab nations away from us. He is convinced that it is this policy which has given the Soviets a growing foothold in the Middle East. He feels we have actually encouraged radical elements in countries to overthrow more conservative regimes. . . . Faisal is convinced the U.S. is steadily losing friends and influence in the Middle East. Our only friends now are Saudi Arabia, Kuwait, Jordan, Lebanon, Tunisia, and Morocco. If the war with Israel persists, we will soon have none at all.

Faisal's views on Israel were, frankly, bizarre:

> Faisal believes that all the troubles in the Middle East stem from Zionism and Israel. He says most of the Jews in Israel come from Russia, that Communism is a product of Zionism, that the Israelis are a Godless people, that Israel is a socialist state which only pretends friendship with the United States, and that Israel and the Soviets have

a secret understanding whereby all of the Arab world is to fall into Communist hands.

Faisal dismissed my attempt to counter his argument. But Faisal also said he had no desire "to push Israel into the sea." There was now an element of flexibility in the Saudi ruler's position that had been missing previously.

As I left the meeting, I reminded Faisal that I would report the essence of our conversation to President Nixon. The King responded by saying that the former governor of Pennsylvania, William Scranton, had made the same offer to him a year earlier and had publicly supported a more even-handed U.S. Middle Eastern policy. The public outcry, Faisal noted, had all but ended Scranton's political career. He hoped I would not suffer the same fate.

INFORMING THE PRESIDENT

I returned to New York deeply concerned about what I had learned. Both Nasser and Faisal had been clear and unambiguous. They perceived U.S. policy as actively hostile in tone and substance toward the Arabs. They saw Soviet penetration of the area as the direct consequence of this policy and believed its continuation might have an adverse effect on the global flow of oil. On the other hand, both men seemed willing to compromise and negotiate if the United States would modify its unwavering support of Israel. It was this message I felt obligated to convey to President Nixon.

A few days after my return from the Middle East, I saw Henry Kissinger in Washington and informed him of the substance of my conversations. Henry told me the administration was well along in the process of reassessing its Middle East policy and would announce a more balanced position in the near future in an effort to bring the Israelis to the bargaining table. He thought it might be valuable for President Nixon to hear my assessment firsthand.

A month later I was invited to the White House, but I was surprised to discover that the Oval Office meeting would also include Jack McCloy, Standard Oil chairman Kenneth Jamieson, Mobil chairman Rawleigh Warner, Amoco chairman John Swearingen, and Robert Anderson, a former Secretary of the Treasury, who had developed extensive and somewhat controversial business interests in the Middle East. I had hoped for a private meeting to candidly report what I had learned from Faisal and Nasser, but found myself part of a larger group concerned primarily with oil, which gave the meeting a very different cast from the one I would have chosen.

Each of us shared his concerns about the situation in the Middle East and his hopes for a more balanced U.S. policy at the meeting on December 9. Jack McCloy and the others expressed alarm about the pressure the radical regimes in Libya, Algeria, and Iraq were putting on the oil companies and about the possibility that the Soviet Union might increase its influence in the area and limit American access to the region's resources. While I shared my colleagues' views, I was more interested in pointing out that both Nasser and Faisal were offering us a legitimate way to resolve the crisis and that it was important for the United States to respond positively.

Nixon said he agreed with our concerns, and he showed us the speech that Secretary of State William Rogers would deliver that evening which would spell out U.S. proposals for a Middle East settlement. After months of behind-the-scenes negotiations with the Russians, Secretary Rogers would urge the "withdrawal of Israeli armed forces from territories occupied in the 1967 war," in return for a binding peace agreement from the Arabs. The Secretary included a statement about the importance of a just settlement of the Palestinian refugee problem, and also proposed that Jerusalem become a "unified" city, open to people of all faiths. Although it did not appear that either the Nixon administration or the Soviets had discussed any of these issues with either the Israelis or the frontline Arab states, all of us agreed that the Rogers speech was a constructive step. I left the Oval Office believing that positive changes might be imminent.

Rogers's speech met with a mixed reception. While *The New York Times* endorsed it, other papers denounced the change in policy. The Israeli government rejected it out of hand. Prime Minister Golda Meir accused Rogers of "moralizing," and to show their independence, the Israelis immediately announced that all of heavily Arab East Jerusalem would be opened to Jewish settlement.

This provocative act should have been met with a stern response from the Nixon administration, especially if it wanted to show Nasser, Faisal, and the other Arab leaders a new U.S. commitment to a policy of balance. Instead, the administration did nothing.

A LEAK TO THE *TIMES*

And there matters might have remained—except that someone in the White House leaked the fact of our meeting with Nixon. Tad Szulc reported it on the front page of *The New York Times* two weeks later. He reported the facts accurately but implied that economic self-interest had led us to urge the President to adopt not just a balanced policy but a "pro-Arab" position. Szulc wrote:

> According to officials familiar with the discussion, the consensus in the group was that the U.S. must act immediately to improve its relations with oil producing and other Arab states. The group was said to feel this was necessary to deflect what the group feared to be an imminent loss of U.S. standing in the Middle East that might be reflected politically as well as in terms of American petroleum interests in the area.
>
> The group was said to feel that United States weapons deliveries to Israel, including the recent shipment of supersonic Phantom jets, and Washington's alleged support of Israeli policies in the Middle East conflict were turning moderate and conservative Arab leaders as well radical Arabs against the United States.

Szulc failed to report, or perhaps the "leaker" had not informed him, that we had not counseled abandoning Israel to the tender mercies of the Arabs. However, the affiliations of those involved in the meeting—the heads of three major American oil companies, a Wall Street lawyer with close connections to the petroleum industry and to Chase, and my own historic ties to Standard Oil—made Szulc's inference that we had acted out of self-interest seem plausible.

In retrospect, all of this may well have been a setup. Instead of meeting Nixon alone to discuss my conversations with Nasser and Faisal, I had been drawn into the controversial politics of Arab oil and Israeli security. But perhaps this was the point all along. The composition of the group seemed a deliberate attempt to serve up scapegoats to explain the reason for Nixon's change in policy if public opinion turned negative.

In any event, a tidal wave of criticism broke over me and the Chase. The resulting controversy effectively killed any chance for the introduction of a more balanced policy toward the Middle East.

CONFRONTATION WITH KOCH

Democratic congressman Edward Koch fired the first salvo. He wrote a letter to me demanding to know if the "thrust" of the story was correct and accusing me of acting as a shill for the oil industry. Before I even received the letter, Koch had distributed it to newspapers and TV stations in the City and done a number of live interviews. And that was just the beginning. *Newsweek* covered the story with a photo of me that carried the caption "Rockefeller: Blinded by Oil?" Even my brother Nelson, facing a difficult reelection campaign in 1970, quickly distanced himself from me and demanded an "explanation" from the Nixon administration about their policy on Israel. I began to wonder if King Faisal's warning about the fate of Bill Scranton might be coming true.

Chase was swamped with letters and phone calls protesting my alleged anti-Israeli bias. Prominent rabbis, some of whom I had known for years, came to my office to complain; several Jewish businessmen organized a boycott; and a number of important accounts were withdrawn from the bank.

In order to clarify my position I issued a public statement in early January 1970 describing my meeting with President Nixon. It read in part:

> A recent trip to the Middle East reinforced my conviction that the continuing hostilities there could easily escalate into full-scale war. . . . My observations during my trip convinced me that thoughtful Arabs are beginning to question whether the current turmoil in the area really furthers their own interests. More and more of them appear disposed to explore reasonable compromises.
>
> In expressing my views at the recent White House meeting, it was my intention merely to suggest that the United States encourage these more positive and conciliatory sentiments.
>
> I believe, as I always have, that the United States must do everything it can to safeguard the security and sovereign existence of Israel. My sole interest is in seeing that hostilities are ended and peace is achieved.

The controversy ignited by the *Times* story obscured the real issue: the need to move toward reconciling the increasingly entrenched and inflexible positions of the Israelis and Arabs. By January 1970, Nixon himself backed away from the Rogers initiative, and the level of violence in the region—terrorist acts against Israel, Israeli counterattacks into Jordan and Lebanon, and pitched battles between the PLO and forces loyal to King Hussein in the streets of Amman—mounted steadily. The PLO also launched a campaign of bombings in Western Europe and hijacked a number of commercial airplanes. The dangers Nasser and Faisal had warned about, and which I had passed on to Nixon, were coming to pass. "Balance" was as elusive as ever in the Middle East.

VISITING THE OTHER SIDE

There was one positive outcome of the Koch controversy. Although I had met Prime Minister Golda Meir, Foreign Minister Abba Eban, and Ambassador Yitzhak Rabin in New York on a number of occasions, I had never actually set foot in the State of Israel. This was due in great part to the complications of reaching Israel from other countries in the Middle East. All Arab states prohibited direct flights to Israel, requiring a stop in either Cyprus or Athens before flying on to Tel Aviv, which made a visit there tied in with a trip to Arab nations difficult to arrange. In addition, Israel's heavily regulated private sector and the inconvertibility of the shekel made the country unattractive from a banking perspective. However, Koch's reckless accusations made me realize that never having visited Israel could add to the spurious notion that I was anti-Israeli. I thought it wise to visit Israel as soon as possible.

The atmosphere surrounding my first visit in March 1971 was understandably tense. Golda Meir and the other leaders I met were personally pleasant, although they remained inflexible on the issue of withdrawing from any of the occupied territories.

Politics aside, one of the real joys of this trip was meeting Mayor Teddy Kollek of Jerusalem. Teddy took me on the first of many tours to view the restoration work he had initiated throughout the Old City to restore the glory of the past and honor the three religions that consider Jerusalem the Holy City. We need more broadly tolerant people like Teddy if the problems of the Middle East are ever going to be resolved.

=

By 1973 I had been involved in Middle Eastern affairs for the better part of two decades, and I was one of a very few Americans with access to the Arab leaders of the region. I would find my knowledge and relationships severely tested as the Middle East entered a new and extremely dangerous period in the early 1970s.

CHAPTER 20

SURVIVING OPEC

On September 22, 1973, Joseph Reed and I arrived in Cairo for an appointment with President Anwar Sadat. He wasn't there. We were told he was at his summer retreat on the Mediterranean, and an Egyptian air force plane would fly us to Alexandria. I had requested the meeting before leaving New York in order to deliver a message from Secretary of State Henry Kissinger, who wanted Sadat to know unofficially that he was eager to explore ways to lessen the tensions between the United States and Egypt.

From Alexandria we were driven west along the old coastal highway to Sadat's residence near the village of Burg-el-Arab, where he ostensibly had fled the heat of Cairo for the cool breezes of the Mediterranean coast. We were escorted to a small anteroom by an official who told us Sadat was meeting with the Soviet ambassador. Nearly an hour later the ambassador emerged from Sadat's office, nodded curtly to us, and hurriedly left the building.

During our only previous meeting two years earlier, Sadat had been distant toward me and unable to repress his hostility toward Israel, his disdain for the United States, and his contempt for Henry Kissinger. I braced for more of the same. But he greeted me warmly and seemed calm, relaxed, and very much at peace with himself. Nevertheless, he seemed distracted as I delivered Kissinger's message. Without any preliminaries he asked, "Mr. Rockefeller, would you be interested in establishing an office of your bank in Egypt?" I was taken totally by surprise. Fifteen years earlier Sadat's predecessor, Gamal Abdel Nasser, had nationalized not only foreign banks but all

Egyptian banks as well. But here was his successor inviting Chase to be-come—just as we had in Russia and China—the first American financial in-stitution allowed back into the country.

I responded cautiously. I said Chase would be interested in exploring the possibility but that a final decision would have to be based on a careful busi-ness analysis. I also reminded Sadat of Chase's long-standing relationship with Israeli banks and our position as an agent for State of Israel bonds. "Mr. President," I said, "how would you feel if we opened a branch in Tel Aviv at the same time we open one in Cairo? Would this be acceptable to you?" I readied myself for an angry outburst, but instead Sadat responded with an enigmatic smile and said, "Mr. Rockefeller, it is all a matter of timing."

Two weeks later I understood what Sadat meant.

We were on our way home from an extensive tour of Africa when the pilot informed us that Egypt had launched a massive air-land assault across the Suez Canal into the Sinai Desert. I thought immediately of our meeting with Sadat and his cryptic remark. I said as much to Joseph, who suggested that perhaps we should have been forewarned by the many warplanes on the tarmac at the Alexandria air base. Obviously, even as he spoke to us that afternoon in Burg-el-Arab, Sadat had been preparing the attack.

AN EARLY WARNING SIGN

A great deal was changing in the United States during the second half of the 1960s: the musical tastes of the young, hairstyles for men, and the length of women's dresses. Everything but the price of gasoline. Cheap en-ergy, especially gas at about thirty cents a gallon, had become an "entitle-ment" to most Americans. These halcyon days came to an end in December 1973 when OPEC raised the posted price for Saudi Arabian light crude to $11.65 a barrel.

This fourfold increase in oil prices within a year had little to do with the law of supply and demand. It was the direct result of the unresolved Arab-Israeli dispute and the protracted contest between the oil-producing states of the developing world and the great American and European oil compa-nies as to who would benefit most from the "rents" resulting from the ex-traction, refining, and marketing of petroleum. Whatever its causes, the increase in the price of petroleum would have a profound economic and psychological impact on the entire world. It would also greatly enhance the role of American commercial banks like Chase that served as depositories for the enormous volume of "petrodollars" generated by these price increases and also became financial intermediaries between the OPEC countries and the oil-importing nations facing an unprecedented "liquidity crisis."

My first intimation that oil prices were in for a dramatic jump came in Algeria in September 1973. I had stopped in Algiers at the request of President Houari Boumedienne prior to my meeting with Sadat; he wanted to discuss the financing of his country's enormous petroleum reserves and natural gas fields in the wake of his nationalization of France's interests in 1971.

Boumedienne was a quixotic character. He had fought for more than a decade in his country's bloody war of independence and was intensely anti-French, but it was clear that Napoleon was his hero. A very short man, he wore a flowing black cape and was given to lavish gestures that emphasized his sense of grandeur and self-importance. Boumedienne was playing a leading role in the efforts of the nonaligned countries of the third world to forge a "new international economic order" and consistently demanded increases in the price of crude oil. Despite his reputation we spoke pleasantly in French for more than an hour, about the role Chase might play in his country's economic development.

After meeting with Boumedienne I attended an extravagant luncheon at Chez Madelaine, a superb French restaurant overlooking the sparkling Bay of Algiers. An otherwise pleasant meal with succulent seafood and surprisingly good Algerian wines was marred by the truculent minister of finance, who recited a litany of complaints about the policies of Western corporations and banks, and then proclaimed that those days were over. He promised the price of crude oil would be up to $10 a barrel—a more than 300 percent increase—by the end of the year. Already offended by his manner, I was outraged by the absurdity of his prophesy. Unfortunately, the ominous forecast by this arrogant character turned out to be correct.

OPEC AND THE ARAB OIL EMBARGO

From Algiers I proceeded to my meeting with Anwar Sadat. My conversations in Algeria and Egypt alerted me that something was about to break in the Middle East, but I had no idea what.

When Sadat ordered his army across the Suez Canal on October 5, 1973, he probably knew he would not be able to defeat the Israeli army. While he lost the war, his bold gamble paid off in other ways. First, he created the conditions that allowed him to negotiate with Israel as an equal. Henry

Kissinger, recognizing that the balance of power in the region had shifted, began his campaign of "shuttle diplomacy" that would eventually produce cease-fire agreements with Egypt and Syria, and then establish the basis for more comprehensive negotiations between Israel and the other frontline Arab states. And while the landmark peace treaty between Egypt and Israel was not signed until the Carter administration, it was based on the foundation of trust that Henry had so arduously constructed from late 1973 to early 1977.

Sadat's decision to roll the dice had a second, even more profound consequence: the Arab oil embargo. Following Egypt's initial military success in the Sinai, the United States had resupplied the beleaguered Israeli forces. This action further inflamed Arab opinion against the United States and led the Arab oil-producing countries to agree to the proposal by the Saudi oil minister, Sheik Ahmed Zaki Yamani, to cut oil production by 5 percent each month until their political objectives—Israeli withdrawal to the borders existing prior to the 1967 war—were accepted.

When President Nixon proposed on October 20 a $2.2 billion military aid package for Israel, the Saudis, soon joined by the other Arab producers, announced a total embargo on oil shipments to the United States. By the end of the year the Algerian finance minister's prediction had become a reality. A new oil weapon—or, in Henry Kissinger's words, "a weapon of political blackmail"—had been forged that strengthened the hand of the Arabs in their political struggle against Israel and in their economic contest with the West.

The massive increase in the cost of energy roiled financial markets in Western Europe and throughout the Western Hemisphere, disrupted international patterns of trade, and threw the industrial world into a deep and prolonged recession. In the United States unemployment soared, and the inflationary spiral that had emerged in the late 1960s intensified. By mid-decade "stagflation," rampant inflation combined with sluggish economic growth, had sapped economic growth and eroded income for everyone. Anyone who lived through those days remembers the long lines of cars waiting at service stations and the feeling of almost desperate helplessness that afflicted policy makers.

While it was difficult for us, it was disastrous for nations in the developing world whose fragile economies teetered on the brink of collapse. In many nations, ill-considered "import-substitution" policies made the process of adjustment to higher energy prices almost impossible to accomplish.

The most immediate effect of the oil shock was the surge in the flow of dollars from oil-importing nations into OPEC's coffers. Between 1973 and

1977 the earnings of the oil-exporting nations expanded 600 percent, to $140 billion. The capital that had fueled economic growth across the globe was now diverted to a few oil-producing states.

Ultimately the adjustment process would require conservation, improved technology to increase energy efficiency, and exploration to find new sources of oil. But all this would take time—in the best of circumstances several years. The crisis confronting the world monetary system was immediate. It was imperative that some way be found to pump that capital back into the oil-consuming nations to "recycle" the petrodollars, or recession and stagnation might turn into a full-blown worldwide depression.

RECYCLING PETRODOLLARS

The task of recycling dollars and maintaining the system of global trade and finance fell to the major international commercial banks, including Chase. The OPEC nations, too, faced a serious problem: how to invest the huge sums they were generating. In the case of the major Middle Eastern countries, their central banks and finance ministries were more than willing to cooperate in the recycling process. Each nation, however, pursued a different course of action.

Saudi Arabia, the world's largest exporter, placed most of its enormous new revenues with U.S. banks as CDs or in U.S. Treasury bonds. Their cautious policy enabled us to efficiently recycle funds to oil-consuming nations.

The Kuwaitis, less conservative, invested most of their revenues in the U.S. and European money and stock markets, and saw their financial reserves grow proportionately even faster than those of Saudi Arabia. The Shah of Iran dedicated a large portion of his new oil wealth to a visionary plan of internal investment, including economic diversification, defense spending on an enormous scale, the building of a new hydroelectric grid, and the expansion of his nation's educational system.

Chase's long-standing relationships with the Saudi Arabian Monetary Agency and the Bank Markazi, Iran's central bank, gave us ready access to the region's funds. Our strong position in the Eurocurrency markets, through which much of the surplus was recycled, enabled us to place funds outside of the regulatory restrictions imposed by the Federal Reserve, and was essential in preventing the long-term disruption of capital markets.

We recycled most of the petrodollars as loans to foreign businesses and industries, although in Latin America, Africa, and parts of East Asia most went to state-owned enterprises that dominated those economies. On occasion we lent directly to governments to finance balance-of-payment deficits. One memorable incident occurred in early 1974. Italy faced a multibillion-dollar account deficit and was having trouble financing the purchase of petroleum. In the middle of lunch at the Bank of Italy, Guido Carli, the bank's governor, asked me for an emergency $250 million loan. I must say I wasn't in the habit of granting loans of that size over cups of espresso, nor did we encourage loans to governments unless they were tied directly to productive investments. But in this case, because of the urgency of Italy's situation and Chase's long-standing relationship with the Bank of Italy, I agreed on the spot to the loan. Chase's prompt action was hailed in Italy, and, most important, the loan was repaid on schedule.

Chase and the other international banks were able to forestall the breakdown of the global financial system that so many feared. The banks could only manage the process for a time; coordinated action by governments was needed to deal with the fundamental problem. But these failed to materialize, and broader global economic problems ensued.

THE DEBT CRISIS

While most of Chase's foreign loans had been extended to the industrialized world and the OPEC nations, about one-third went to the developing countries of Latin America. By 1982 the lingering effects of the recession and the impact of the 1979 oil shock initiated a massive withdrawal of liquid capital from many of these countries. First Mexico, then Brazil and many others announced a moratorium on interest payments on their debt, thereby precipitating a banking crisis and a second, even more serious threat to the world monetary order.

One consequence was that Chase and the other recycling banks suffered huge losses during the 1980s. As this process unfolded, bankers received a great deal of criticism for lending to state enterprises rather than to private companies. Since large, privately owned companies were a rarity in Latin America and the developing nations of Asia and Africa, we had no alternative if petrodollars were to be recycled. Most critics conveniently ignored this point in their efforts to prove that commercial bankers were, at best, irresponsible.

The debt crisis of the 1980s was the longer-run consequence of the oil crisis of 1973 and the abrupt restructuring of the world economy that followed. The fact was that both governments and the private sector had more than enough time during the intervening years to make the difficult budgetary cuts and regulatory reforms necessary to minimize the impact of large-scale borrowing on future productivity. Instead, the major industrial nations of the world and the governments of the emerging nations chose the easier and less confrontational course. Despite the intermediating role the major American and European commercial banks performed during these years—a role I would call heroic—it was not enough to stave off the day of reckoning.

EXPANDING IN THE MIDDLE EAST

While the Arab-Israeli dispute and the OPEC oil increases imposed tremendous burdens on Chase, they also presented us with unusual opportunities. In response we developed a strategy of aggressive growth in the Middle East and North Africa. The basic objective was to develop a presence everywhere we were permitted, provided that economic conditions justified the effort and expenditure. In 1970 our regional network consisted of a single branch in Lebanon, a representative office in Bahrain, and a joint venture bank in Dubai. By mid-decade we had opened another representative office in Tunis and a new branch in Amman, Jordan, and created joint venture banks in Iran, Egypt, Saudi Arabia, Kuwait, Qatar, and Abu Dhabi.

By traveling frequently in the region I got to know the rulers and senior political officials who allowed Chase to establish banking operations. In Egypt, for example, within four months of the time Sadat had asked us to open a branch, I returned to give him an affirmative answer.

A COMPLICATED PERSONAL RELATIONSHIP

Sadat was in an expansive mood when I saw him in Cairo in January 1974. By then he had met Kissinger, and his opinion of American diplomacy had undergone a marked change since my first conversation with him in 1971, when he had angrily denounced Kissinger's preoccupation with "power politics" and Nixon's refusal to deal evenhandedly with Egypt. "I liked Henry," he said. "We did much together. He is the first American politician I have met that I have respected."

Sadat was eager to discuss his plans for Egypt, which included a duty-free zone along the Suez Canal, an oil pipeline from the Red Sea to Alexandria, and what he called "something big enough for a Rockefeller," the building of a new Suez canal. Suddenly he leaned forward, interrupting me in the middle of a sentence, smiled, and said, "You know, David, if I had slipped that day we talked in Burg el-Arab and told you about my plans, I would have had to keep you here. I could not have allowed you to leave and tell everyone of my intentions."

We returned to banking matters, and I told him Chase thought it best to create a joint venture with the National Bank of Egypt instead of opening a wholly owned branch with a more limited scope of operations. Sadat said, "I think your business activities here may cause trouble for you at home. The Israelis will raise hell for you in the States." I indicated that so far the opposite was proving to be the case; in fact, "the Israelis were very positive about our economic relations with Egypt. In effect, the Israelis have given us their blessing."

In January 1975 we signed the joint venture agreement with Sadat creating the Chase National Bank of Egypt (with Chase owning 49 percent), and over the next few years we opened branches in Cairo, Alexandria, and Port Said.

A COMPLICATED BANKING RELATIONSHIP

My own and Chase's relationship with Israel continued to be complicated and tortuous. During a visit to Jerusalem in January 1975, Finance Minister Yehoshua Rabinowitz asked me to consider opening a Chase branch in Israel. This put me in a difficult position as I was about to close the Chase National Bank of Egypt deal with Sadat. Nonetheless, I told the Finance Minister we would consider the proposal.

Again I decided to check first with Sadat. Two days later in Cairo I asked him what the reaction would be if Chase opened a branch in Israel. He said Libya, Syria, and Iraq would cause trouble but that he would not oppose it and would resist efforts to put Chase on the Arab boycott list. Sadat counseled, however, that it would be useful to advise the Saudis and King Hussein of Jordan of our plans. He said I could tell them that Sadat approved our proposal.

Both King Hussein and Prince Fahd readily agreed. In fact, Fahd noted, "It is delicate and sensitive, but since Anwar Sadat knows and approves, I will go along with him."

In the end our internal analysis concluded that we would not be able to generate enough local business in Israel to justify opening a branch there. All the major U.S. banks had reached the same conclusion. While we based our decision solely on economic criteria, the Israelis were very unhappy and told us so.

Once our decision became known, there was a flurry of criticism of me in both Israel and New York's Jewish community. The Anti-Defamation League accused Chase, five other companies, and two government agencies of "knuckling under to the Arab boycott." CBS Radio ran a three-part editorial denouncing American companies, specifically naming Chase, for "bowing to the most degrading kind of extortion. They are trading law and principle for profit." Although we never stopped doing business with Israel and none of the major American banks had a direct presence there, Chase was singled out for criticism.

A SURPRISE JOB OFFER

My increasingly cordial personal relationship with Sadat took an unusual turn in 1976. I had touched base with him first in Cairo in February, and then I set off to visit other countries in the region. My final stop was to be Israel. However, a week later, as I left a meeting with the Shah of Iran, I received a call from the Egyptian ambassador saying Sadat wanted to see me in Egypt before my return to New York. Since I could not cancel my meetings in Israel, I sent word to Sadat that I would be able to see him only if I could fly directly from Tel Aviv to Cairo, without the usual stop in Cyprus required by the Arab League boycott restrictions. In order to accommodate me, Sadat agreed to a compromise: We would file a flight plan in Tel Aviv for Cyprus, but once outside Israeli airspace, we would be permitted to alter our course for Cairo.

Sadat sent his personal helicopter to fly me from Cairo to his home at the Barrage in the Nile Delta. As we flew above the narrow green ribbon of the Nile valley, I was puzzled as to why I had received such an urgent summons. A few weeks earlier Sadat said he was also about to set off on a tour of the Gulf states, and I wondered if he might want to compare impressions.

But Sadat had another surprise to spring on me. As soon as I entered his office, Sadat asked me to become his economic advisor. It soon became clear he was thinking of more than occasional informal advice from a friend; he actually wanted me to serve as an official financial advisor on Egypt's economic development program. I was flattered by his offer but pointed out that as chairman and CEO of Chase, it would be difficult for me to perform the role he had in mind. I said, however, that I wanted to help in any way I could and would get back to him after giving the matter further thought.

On our flight to New York I discussed Sadat's proposal with my Chase colleagues. We agreed it was not feasible for me to accept. On the other hand, turning him down without suggesting a suitable alternative could easily cause offense. By the end of the flight I had come up with another candidate. Richard Debs, chief operating officer of the New York Federal Reserve Bank, had recently announced his retirement. Dick was thoroughly familiar with the economic situation in the Middle East and specifically with Egypt's critical financial problems. Dick was the perfect candidate for the job, and I spoke with him as soon as I returned to New York. Within a few days he flew to Cairo to meet Sadat and agreed to take on the assignment on a pro bono basis.

ANGER AND RECONCILIATION

The warm relationship Sadat and I had enjoyed for nearly a decade ended abruptly in the summer of 1980, the product of sloppy staff work on my part. During a tour of major European countries Bill Butcher and I took just prior to my retirement from Chase, I received a message from Mohammad Abushadi, a prominent Egyptian banker, to the effect that a group of American, European, and Arab investors were organizing a bank that would operate in the Middle East. He invited Chase to take a 5 percent interest in it. The message stated that Sadat knew of the project and had even suggested Chase's participation. Since we were in the midst of a whirlwind tour, I asked our Paris office to analyze the proposal and give me its recommendation as quickly as possible. The Paris office concluded that Chase's role would be too small to be financially meaningful and that we would have little or no control over the new bank's management, and advised a declination. Bill Butcher and I concurred with this analysis and asked Ridgway Knight, our political advisor in Europe and a former U.S. ambassador to Syria, to call on Abushadi to inform him of our decision.

Even though the message from Abushadi had cited Sadat's interest, I had not heard directly from him or from Ambassador Ashraf Ghorbal, Sadat's customary emissary for important matters. In retrospect I should have checked with Ghorbal to determine the level of Sadat's interest before reaching a decision. I later discovered Sadat had indeed suggested that Chase be included and was offended we had turned down the proposal without calling him. Six months later I learned the full extent of Sadat's displeasure.

In April 1981, Bill Butcher and I were in Cairo as part of my final tour of the Middle East. When we tried to set up an appointment, Sadat inexplicably refused to see us. I was embarrassed that my old friend would not see me on my farewell visit to his country, and I called on both Ghorbal and Vice President Hosni Mubarak, who told me the rebuff was the direct consequence of Chase's decision not to invest in Abushadi's project. In an effort to make amends I sent Sadat a handwritten letter of apology while we were still in Cairo. I received no response.

In August of that same year, however, Sadat came to the United States on an official visit. Ambassador Ghorbal invited me to a special dinner in Washington for Sadat, which I took as a hopeful sign even though he and I did not have a chance to do more than shake hands. The following day Sadat spoke at the Council on Foreign Relations in New York, and I introduced him. Afterward he invited me to ride back in his car to the Egyptian mission. We had a quiet talk there about the Abushadi incident, and all was forgiven.

Some years later I related this story to U.N. Secretary-General Boutros Boutros-Ghali, who had served as Sadat's foreign minister for a number of years. I was relieved to discover that I was not the only one who had fallen into Sadat's bad graces. Sadat, Boutros said, often took offense at relatively minor slights and would not speak to his closest associates for several weeks at a time. In fact, he said, it had happened to him.

My reconciliation with Sadat came just in time. On October 6, 1981, just two months after our talk in New York and exactly eight years after he launched the Yom Kippur War, Sadat was assassinated by a group of fundamentalist Egyptian army officers. With the rest of the world I mourned the loss of a man I truly considered a hero and a friend.

JORDAN'S KING HUSSEIN AND CROWN PRINCE HASSAN

Another Middle Eastern leader with whom I developed a close relationship and whose courage I admired was King Hussein of Jordan. Few leaders in the world have been tested more. He survived numerous assassination attempts, personally fighting off assailants on more than a few occasions, and weathered the many turbulent political storms of the region. A descendant of the Hashemite Sherifs of Mecca who fought with the fabled Lawrence of Arabia against the Ottoman Turks during World War I, Hussein ascended the Jordanian throne in 1952 at the age of sixteen, after the murder of his grandfather Abdallah by Arab extremists and the deposition of his father, Talal. Throughout his reign Hussein showed a deep commitment to his people and a willingness to compromise for the sake of a comprehensive Arab-Israeli settlement. He was a remarkable leader and a good friend of the United States.

In March 1971, during a round-the-world tour for Chase accompanied by both my wife and my daughter Peggy, I stopped briefly in Jordan to see the

King. Amman was still an armed camp, and the King had moved his head-quarters out into the country. Both Peggys remained on the Chase plane while my Chase colleagues and I drove out to see Hussein. When I told him they had remained at the airport, he apologized for not inviting them to lunch. To make amends Hussein personally flew us back to Amman in his helicopter. He boarded the plane to say hello and concluded his visit by giving my daughter his card and private telephone numbers!

At about the same time I also became good friends with Crown Prince Hassan, to whom the King had delegated responsibility for economic development and for encouraging foreign investment. Hassan took me on a number of tours by car and helicopter of projects he was sponsoring. We also had a memorable visit to the mysterious Nabataen and Greco-Roman ruins at Petra.

Hassan believed Jordan's future depended on granting greater access to foreign companies and banks, something that government bureaucrats were less willing to acknowledge. When Chase's efforts to open a branch in Amman were rebuffed by the governor of the Bank of Jordan, Hassan intervened to have the decision reversed. In 1976, after visiting Prince Hassan's home, I made arrangements with the Israelis to quietly cross over the Allenby Bridge from Jordan, thereby avoiding the always irritating excursion to Cyprus. Hassan insisted on flying me there himself. He landed his helicopter behind the brow of a hill, and I then carried my bag across the bridge where my Israeli hosts met me. Hassan preferred that the Israelis not learn the identity of my "driver," although he had no problem with the fact that Israel was my destination.

I stayed in close touch with King Hussein until his death in 2000 and have maintained my friendship with Prince Hassan. Both men played quiet but critical roles in the changes that have occurred in the region over the past four decades and have ensured that Jordan, despite its size, will continue to be an important player in Middle Eastern affairs.

SHEIKS, SULTANS, AND SADDAM

My friendship with President Sadat and King Hussein, and my extensive contacts with the Saudi royal family, had taken a long time to establish, but they exemplified the kind of high-level relationships Chase needed in order to build its business in the region. The OPEC price increases revealed the financial power of the region's oil-rich nations, both large and small. Decisions taken by a relative handful of men in Saudi Arabia, Iraq, Iran,

Algeria, and even in the smaller sheikdoms scattered along the Persian Gulf's southern littoral could have profound consequences for the world's economy.

These vast energy reserves magnified the strategic significance of the region, particularly the nine nations bordering the Persian Gulf. The British decision to withdraw militarily from "east of Suez" at the end of 1971 terminated their century-long role as political mentor and military protector of the smaller Arab sheikdoms and sultanates along the Persian Gulf's Trucial coast and created an economic and security vacuum that American policy only partially filled. The so-called Nixon Doctrine, with its reliance on regional powers such as Iran, Saudi Arabia, and later Egypt to bear the burden of local peacekeeping, ignored the importance of the smaller powers.

KUWAIT'S SHEIK JABBER

One of the world's largest producers and exporters of petroleum and a leading member of OPEC, Kuwait had been ruled by the al-Sabah family for more than two hundred years. My primary Kuwaiti contact was Sheik Jabber, whom I had first met in the early 1960s soon after Kuwait gained its independence from Great Britain. As Kuwait's finance minister he attended one of the luncheons I gave at Pocantico for the world's finance ministers and central bank governors following the annual Washington meetings of the World Bank and IMF. Subsequently, Jabber visited Hudson Pines with his son, who was studying in the United States, and the young man rode El Assad, our full-blooded Arabian stallion.

Jabber became prime minister in the mid-1960s and then emir in 1977, and I saw him frequently on my Middle Eastern journeys. On one visit I presented him with a small painting by Fritz Glarner, an American abstract painter. It was a rather unusual gift for a traditional Arab ruler; however, I was aware that works of art depicting natural forms—animal, plant, or human—were violations of Islamic law. Jabber seemed genuinely delighted with the painting, and I noted with satisfaction on a subsequent trip that he had hung it prominently in his home.*

---

*On another occasion I attempted to bring a copy of my brother Nelson's art catalogue to a friend in Saudi Arabia. A customs official confiscated the book because it included the image of a female nude by Henri Matisse. I had to ask the Saudi finance minister to intercede in order to get the book released.

Jabber was a reserved man who understood that profound changes would accompany his country's sudden accumulation of wealth, and he guided its social and political transition quite deftly. Apparently he also managed his more traditional obligations with comparable ability. The Sheik was entitled to spend the night with young, unmarried Kuwaiti women from traditional villages, with whom he would frequently produce children. The women he selected were said to consider this a great honor.

Over the years my friendship with Sheik Jabber helped Chase navigate through the complexities of the Kuwaiti bureaucracy, including the approval in 1973 of an agreement allowing us to manage the Commercial Bank of Kuwait in return for a percentage of its earnings. Once we succeeded in turning the bank around and made it profitable, however, the Kuwaitis canceled the contract, not wanting us to share in the bank's burgeoning profits. This was a disappointing outcome. We had hoped that a strong performance by Chase managers would persuade the authorities to allow us to broaden our operations. That never happened, and while we maintained our strong depository relationship with their central bank and a number of wealthy individuals, we failed to persuade the Kuwaitis to use us as their investment advisors or as providers of other financial services.

The Kuwaitis were shrewd negotiators and well known in the Gulf for being prickly and inflexible in their relationships. Accordingly, our business seemed to depend on how individual finance ministers or members of the Sabah family were feeling about us on a given day. Our relationship with Abdul Rachman al-Atiqi, a longtime Kuwaiti finance minister, was typical. Respected for his integrity and candor, he was nonetheless suspicious of Western bankers and could be abrupt and arbitrary over minor matters. I arrived one day at the Kuwaiti finance ministry for what I knew would be another exasperating meeting over some minor issue and got stuck in the tiny, rickety elevator leading to his office. When we finally emerged, I said, "Mr. Minister, I see you even trap us in the elevator to express your irritation." Although Atiqi laughed, he knew I was only half-joking.

BAHRAIN AND BEIRUT

In contrast to the Kuwaitis, the Bahrainis are accommodating and eager to do business with the outside world. An archipelago of small, barren islands just off the Arabian mainland, Bahrain was the location of the first oil discovery on the Arabian Peninsula in 1932, and revenues from petroleum have provided the government with the lion's share of its income ever since.

Sheik Isa al-Khalifa's family has ruled Bahrain since the mid-1700s. After gaining full independence from Great Britain in the early 1970s, Sheik Isa prudently employed his limited but steady petroleum revenue to diversify his country's economy. He also encouraged the development of "offshore" banking, insurance, and other financial services, which enabled Bahrain to supplant Beirut as the financial center of the Middle East when Lebanon fell victim to the prolonged civil war and the widening Palestinian crisis of the 1970s.

===

Beirut had been the focal point of Chase's Middle Eastern operations for years. The city flourished from the early 1950s through the mid-1970s, and our branch prospered, although it never generated the broader regional business that we had expected. We gradually learned that wealthy Saudi and Kuwaiti businessmen viewed Beirut as a resort where they could escape the strictures of Koranic law, and only secondarily as a financial center. Nonetheless, it was an immensely attractive and cosmopolitan city with a stable political system and an internationally oriented business sector.

In the early 1970s, however, the political compact between the Maronite Christians and Sunni Muslims began to fray, and the Syrians, led by the aggressive Hafez el-Assad, intervened more directly in Lebanon's internal politics. In addition, the PLO, driven from its sanctuaries in Jordan, began to operate from refugee camps in southern Lebanon, which invited Israeli retaliation. Lebanon rapidly degenerated into a state of anarchy.

My last visit to Beirut was in March 1977 when a brief lull in the fighting allowed us to reopen our branch. I wanted to reassure the staff that I was aware of the risks and concerned for their well-being. At the Beirut airport the bank's plane was forced to taxi to a location far from the terminal. A squad of fully armed soldiers in armored cars met us and escorted us into town. Fighting among the different factions and artillery shelling from the surrounding hills had turned the city into a shambles. The King George Hotel, where I had always stayed, was completely gutted. When I entered the Chase branch, the soldiers formed a phalanx around me. After I greeted the staff, the branch manager presented me with an artillery shell, carrying Russian markings, that had exploded just outside the building. The "Paris of the Mediterranean" had taken on the appearance of the Germany I had seen at the end of World War II. The seemingly calculated destruction of Beirut by unyielding religious and political zealots ranks as one of the great man-made tragedies of the post–World War II era.

=

Bahrain, where we had opened a branch in 1971, was well positioned to take advantage of the opportunity presented by Beirut's agony.

I first met Sheik Isa in the early 1960s, soon after he became emir. He was barely five feet tall but large in friendliness and generosity, and renowned for the liberality of his gift-giving. He once presented me with a beautiful Damascene sword that had a scabbard studded with pearls; it is now part of the Chase collection. On my last visit to Bahrain in 1997 the Sheik adjourned a cabinet meeting in order to introduce me to his prime minister and the rest of his ministers, many of them his relatives, and on that occasion he gave me a handsome Rolex watch. His astute leadership allowed his small country to play a significant role among its powerful neighbors.

THE UNITED ARAB EMIRATES

The United Arab Emirates, seven small oil-rich sheikdoms scattered along the barren coast of the Persian Gulf between Saudi Arabia and Oman, joined together as a confederation in 1971 at the time of the British withdrawal from the Gulf. The two largest, Abu Dhabi and Dubai, have dominated the affairs of the UAE from the start.

The first time I set eyes on the town of Abu Dhabi in 1974, I was not impressed. Small adobe houses sprawled haphazardly along the coastal lowlands and swamps, and a sharp wind off the Gulf filled the air with dust and sand. Sheep and goats wandered everywhere along the unpaved streets. A large fort, constructed by the British a century earlier, dominated this uninspiring scene. In the absence of a more suitable structure, the fort served as the seat of Abu Dhabi's essentially nomadic government.

The ruler, Sheik bin Sultan al-Nahayan Zayed, was away, and his brother received us in a room furnished in traditional Bedouin fashion. We sat on cushions placed along the walls and drank small cups of strong Arab coffee poured from brass coffeepots with long curved spouts. Our host, who wore fine Arab robes, had a large dagger in his belt and was surrounded by others in similar garb. He was courteous, speaking through an interpreter, but gave the impression that he would be more comfortable on horseback in the desert than discussing finance with Wall Street bankers.

On my next visit two years later, oil revenues had already begun the transformation of Abu Dhabi. International-style skyscrapers were under construction, and an elaborate road system had replaced the dirt roads. Abu Dhabi had become a modern city, and the old fort seemed a relic of the distant past. As in Saudi Arabia, all of the oil revenue, by this time several billion dollars a year, flowed directly into Sheik Zayed's treasury.

The Sheik was an impressive man with a strong, sharply chiseled face and piercing eyes. He spoke no English but was always in full command of the conversation. I was impressed that his home was quite modestly decorated and bore a striking resemblance to a Bedouin tent—not at all like the pretentious palaces so common by then in Saudi Arabia. It was Sheik Zayed's custom to receive visitors late at night, after the heat of the day had dissipated. In addition to obligatory cups of coffee, he served us hot spiced camel's milk in small glasses. I found it very sweet and rather pleasant, but not everyone who accompanied me agreed.

Like many Arab rulers, Zayed loved hunting. During one of my visits he told me he had just returned from Pakistan where his prized falcons—costing up to $100,000 each—had bagged a number of bustards. Bustards are a bit smaller than our wild turkeys and, like them, are crafty and difficult to hunt, so Zayed was quite pleased with his triumph. He asked if I had ever tasted bustard, and when I answered in the negative, he insisted I take a few with me. I explained we were in the middle of a long business trip and had no means of storing the bustards. He asked whom we would be seeing after we left Abu Dhabi, and when I told him Sheik Isa in Bahrain, he was delighted. Sheik Isa's chef, he told me, was particularly proficient at preparing bustard.

So we carried the bustards with us to Bahrain, where Sheik Isa immediately dispatched them to his chef. Since Isa had arranged a dinner for us that evening and we were leaving early the next day for Yemen, we would not be able to eat the bustards in Bahrain. Instead, the next morning a picnic basket—actually a large hamper carried by two people—was delivered to the Chase plane. We loaded it on board and took off for Yemen. After landing there, we drove over the mountains and stopped for our picnic lunch of bustard and the other delectables Sheik Isa had stuffed in the hamper. Unfortunately, by then the bustards were cold and rather tough. Nevertheless, we enjoyed the experience of eating Central Asian bustards snared by Sheik Zayed's falcons in Pakistan, cooked in Bahrain, and finally consumed by a carload of hungry Chase bankers on a hillside in Yemen!

Sheik Zayed may have preferred the desert and falcon hunting, but he was a good businessman who, for the most part, prudently managed his nation's immense oil earnings. He did, however, become involved in the Bank of Credit and Commerce International (BCCI) scandal in the early 1990s. He provided more than $1 billion to shore up this institution during the 1980s, and a court settlement required the Sheik and a number of his close associates to provide another $1.8 billion to reimburse BCCI shareholders.

Before that unfortunate incident, Chase had worked closely with him through our new investment banking operation based in Bahrain and headed by Nemir Kirdar, an officer of Iraqi origins. Nemir was an excellent credit officer, and his knowledge of the area did much to promote our business throughout the Gulf. Prior to one meeting with the Sheik, Nemir suggested that I raise the issue of Chase involvement with the Abu Dhabi Investment Authority. At our meeting I asked the Sheik to "allow us the opportunity to serve you as an advisor to the Investment Authority." Shortly thereafter, Nemir received the go-ahead for Chase to manage $200 million of the Authority's assets.

Chase's presence in the Persian Gulf grew dramatically during the 1970s, and we eventually had a staff of two hundred. One indication of the bank's growing clout was a $350 million Chase-led financing for four industrial projects in Qatar, which was named the "1977 Deal of the Year" by *Institutional Investor* magazine.

SULTAN QABUS OF OMAN

Oman, standing astride the Straits of Hormuz at the mouth of the Persian Gulf, through which a good part of the world's supply of crude oil must pass, is the oldest and, in many ways, the most sophisticated nation on the Arabian peninsula. The Albusaid family gained control of Muscat and much of the hinterland in the mid–eighteenth century and extended their maritime empire as far south as Zanzibar, off the coast of East Africa. In the nineteenth century the British protected the ruling family from both the Ottoman Turks and marauding Bedouin tribes from the interior, and built a strong political and financial relationship with the Sultan.

The British withdrawal in the early 1970s had created an opportunity for the United States in Oman. However, when I arrived in Muscat for the first time in January 1974, I discovered the United States had no permanent diplomatic staff based there. The State Department seemed not to have grasped the growing economic and political importance of the region. I reported these facts to Henry Kissinger after my return. I told him that despite continuing British economic influence, the rulers were looking for a closer relationship with the United States. Henry was fully absorbed by the effort to work out a cease-fire between the Israelis and Egyptians at the time, but within a few months he appointed an ambassador to Oman and another to the UAE.

At the time of my arrival Sultan Qabus was actively involved in suppressing an insurrection in the western province of Dhofar, supported by the Soviet-sponsored government of South Yemen. The Shah of Iran, with American financial and military assistance, had provided the Sultan with three thousand soldiers to help in the campaign. We flew to Salalah, the capital of Dhofar, to meet the Sultan. Sharpshooters and antiaircraft were stationed in the hills overlooking the city, and we had to make a long, low approach over the water in order to avoid their fire. The Sultan was impressed that we had made such a dangerous journey in order to see him, and the meeting came off rather well.

Sultan Qabus had only recently taken power when I met him. With British help he had staged a successful coup in 1970 against his father, a rather disagreeable man who had kept his son under a form of house arrest for six years. Qabus had been educated at Sandhurst and was only thirty-four at the time I met him. He was a strikingly handsome man with an erect bearing, a full black beard, and dark piercing eyes, and he always wore an elegant turban. Over the ensuing years he and I developed a good relationship. While I was visiting the Sultan in January 1979, I received word that my brother Nelson had died of a heart attack. The Sultan offered to send me home in his plane, but since I had the Chase plane, I declined his gracious offer.

YEMEN AND A *QAT* PARTY

By the late 1970s one of the few areas in the Middle East I had not visited was Yemen, site of the biblical kingdom of Sheba and the place where the fabled "Frankincense Road" had its beginning. At the time of my 1977 visit the country was in the midst of a savage civil war pitting the traditional tribal groups of the north against the radical Marxist forces that dominated the southern portion of the country. North Yemen (the Yemen Arab Republic) was closely allied with Saudi Arabia, while the People's Democratic Republic of Yemen was a Soviet client state. In fact, the republic had granted the Soviet navy access to the former British naval base at Aden, providing them with a strategic base that controlled access to both the Red Sea and the Horn of Africa.

North Yemen had little oil but considerable economic potential because hundreds of thousands of Yemenis worked in the Persian Gulf fields and sent home millions of dollars in remittances each month. The main reason for my visit was to ask Prime Minister Abdalaziz Abdal Ghani if Chase might establish a broader relationship with his government. On our arrival we learned that Abdal Ghani was with some friends at his home some twenty or so miles outside San'a. He left word that we were all invited to his home.

When we arrived, we found only men were in attendance. They were sitting on the floor on cushions and rugs listening to Arab music. Occasionally two men would get up and dance with each other. There were no chairs, tables, or other furniture. The Prime Minister didn't interrupt the party but warmly incorporated us in it. The most unusual aspect of the party, however, was the refreshment provided. Alcohol is prohibited in most Islamic countries. In Yemen the stimulant of choice, so to speak, is *qat*, a rather mild narcotic said to produce hallucinogenic effects. The leaves of the plant are chewed and then formed into a little ball that is placed under the lower lip. If one chews enough of it over a long enough period of time, it will produce an enjoyable experience. We had joined a *qat* party. All the guests were chewing *qat*, and I was given a few leaves to chew as well, which I did. The leaves had little taste, and I experienced no hallucinations. Years of drinking martinis straight up had probably immunized me sufficiently! However, to my surprise, the Prime Minister did ask me to dance, a rather unusual way to get to know a potential client. It was a rather memorable afternoon!

Unfortunately, the Prime Minister came to a gruesome end only a few weeks after our meeting. A "special emissary" from South Yemen called on him with a gift from the president of South Yemen. The gift was actually a bomb, which the emissary triggered once he was inside the Prime Minister's office. Both men were killed instantaneously.

IRAQ AND SADDAM HUSSEIN

Saddam Hussein emerged in the late twentieth century as one of the world's most ruthless dictators, willing to subject his people to constant warfare and incredible privations in order to maintain his grip on power. I met him only once.

Hussein was a product of the Ba'ath Party, an extreme political faction organized in the 1940s by Syrian and Iraqi intellectuals who propounded a mixture of Socialism, anticolonialism, and Arab nationalism. Ba'athist rhetoric was both enormously popular with the mass of the Iraqi people and riddled with political and economic contradictions. The party seized power in 1958, killing King Faisal II by dragging him through the streets of

Baghdad behind a car. That was the way they behaved then and, it would seem, are still behaving today.

Iraq's new rulers immediately adopted a pro-Soviet foreign policy, nationalized the assets of foreign companies, and established a police state. Iraq became a radical voice within OPEC, arguing consistently for higher prices and strict limits on the shipment of oil to Western industrial nations. In many ways Iraq also emerged as Israel's most implacable enemy in the Middle East. Saddam Hussein and his predecessors not only participated in all the Arab wars against Israel but also provided funding for Arafat's PLO, sponsored terrorist groups around the world, and persecuted their own indigenous Jewish population.

While Chase did little direct business with Iraq, we maintained a modest correspondent relationship with their central bank, the Bank Rafidian, for many years. When the Iraqis severed diplomatic relations with the United States after the 1967 war, this connection provided one of the few links between the two countries. Henry Kissinger, searching for the means to include the Iraqis in a comprehensive Middle Eastern peace process, asked if I would try to establish contact with the Iraqi leadership during one of my trips to the region.

I agreed to do this and through the president of the Bank Rafidian I obtained a visa allowing me to enter Baghdad to discuss banking matters. I was also able to secure an appointment with Foreign Minister Sadoom Hammadi. Hammadi was a graduate of the University of Wisconsin and spoke fluent English, but his manner was hostile from the moment I entered his office. It became even more pronounced when I told him I had come at Henry Kissinger's request to deliver a message to Saddam Hussein, who was widely regarded as the strongman of Iraqi politics.

Hammadi said, "Totally impossible. He couldn't possibly receive you." I replied, "I will be in Baghdad for twenty-four hours, and I am available to meet with him at any time of the day or night." Hammadi was insistent. "A meeting is impossible, so give me the message." "I'm sorry, Mr. Minister," I said, "but my message is for the ears of Saddam Hussein alone, and I am not authorized to give it to anyone else." When Hammadi insisted a meeting would not occur, I said, "I am going to be here until midday tomorrow and would appreciate your advising Saddam Hussein that I have a message from the Secretary of State and that I would be happy to see him if he wishes to receive me."

That evening as I was about to leave for a dinner hosted by the Bank Rafidian, I received a message that Hussein would receive me at nine o'clock that evening in his office. I was instructed to come alone.

I was taken by car to the National Council building on the banks of the Tigris River. The building radiated an aura of foreboding, which was not dispelled by a long walk down an endless series of darkened corridors past armed sentries. When I finally arrived at his office, a small, bare, windowless room deep in the bowels of the building, Hussein greeted me courteously. He was a man of average height with a sturdy build. His face was stern and unsmiling, and even then he wore his trademark mustache.

We spoke for more than an hour through an interpreter. Although there were only the three of us present in the room, a few days later an almost verbatim account of the conversation appeared in the Beirut newspaper *an Nahar*. For whatever reason, Saddam wanted the substance of our conversation made public.

I explained that Henry Kissinger felt it was contrary to the best interests of both Iraq and the United States that no means of communication existed and that the Secretary wanted to find a way to establish a dialogue. I asked how to accomplish this.

Pointing his finger at the door by which I had entered the room, Saddam said, "The door might be opened a crack if two conditions are met." First, the United States had to stop supplying arms to Israel that might be used against Iraq and begin to play a "decisive role in securing the rights of the Palestinian people." Second, the United States must stop selling arms to Iran or at least make the sales conditional on Iran's promise not to use those arms against "Iraq or any other Arab nation." Saddam insisted that as long as the Shah continued to arm the rebelling Iraqi Kurds, he would not be interested in resuming diplomatic relations with the United States.

I reported this to Henry Kissinger upon my return to the United States. Saddam's first condition regarding Israel was, of course, one that the United States was never going to meet. However, within a few months a rapprochement between the Iraqis and Iranians did lead to the end of military assistance to the Kurds and, within a few years, a dramatic improvement in U.S.-Iraqi relations.

Saddam seemed an essentially humorless man who was adamant but not hostile to me in the presentation of his views. Sitting opposite him that night I had no reason to believe that within a relatively few years he would become known to all as the "Butcher of Baghdad," as ruthless and contemptible a leader as the world had ever known.

=

The historical continuity of the Saudis and the Kuwaitis, the discipline and financial acumen of the emirate shciks, the sinister intelligence of Saddam

Hussein, the tragedy of Lebanon and the Palestinian people, the strength and courage of the Israelis, the honor and heroism of King Hussein and Anwar Sadat—all these images come to mind when I consider my experiences in this confounding and unpredictable region of the world. How "unpredictable" I would learn as I became embroiled in the effort to find a refuge for the exiled Shah of Iran.

CHAPTER 21

BUSINESS TURBULENCE

In October 1972, with Bill Butcher in place as Chase's chief operating officer, I felt confident for the first time since becoming CEO three years earlier that my effort to transform the bank into a stronger, more innovative
and competitive institution would now be pursued purposefully and aggressively. The top leadership was now in place to sustain Chase's drive toward
global success.

Neither Bill nor I anticipated the significant bumps in the road we would
encounter. As the decade wore on, well before our reforms and strategies
could be fully implemented, Chase and I were subjected to a series of
harsh—and occasionally savage—public attacks. Our management competence, investment policy, and strategic direction were all openly questioned.
Throughout those painful days I never lost confidence in my vision for
Chase as a great international financial institution or in the quality of the
corps of capable officers we were assembling. I was committed to seeing the
bank through the rough patches that it—and I—would inevitably encounter.

PROBLEMS FOR THE BANK AND ITS CHAIRMAN

A quality that has served the Rockefeller family well over the generations
has been a thick skin. While on the one hand we are mindful that we
have been blessed with great wealth and abundant opportunity, on the

other we recognize that the privileges we have been accorded often cause others to look upon us with suspicion and resentment. The actions of a Rockefeller—particularly a "public" Rockefeller—like those of a movie star or sports hero, are analyzed microscopically, and when we fail, critics duly note it. Thus, ever since the 1880s, when the muckraking journalists attacked Grandfather and Standard Oil, Rockefellers, especially "public" Rockefellers, have had to develop thick protective skins. And so it was that when I opened the *New York Times* business section on the morning of Sunday, February 1, 1976, I was fully prepared to absorb yet another attack. But my heart sank as I read the page-one headline: "The Chase and David Rockefeller: Problems at the Bank and for Its Chairman." I only needed to scan the first paragraph to understand the article's main thrust: "The Chase Manhattan Bank has emerged in the public spotlight as a symbol of the nation's troubled banking system at one of its most difficult moments. In the process, the job security of David Rockefeller, its well-known chairman and chief executive officer, has come under question."

The most respected newspaper in the land in its most widely read edition of the week had indicated that I might soon be fired. I have to concede that the *Times* story was neither unexpected nor entirely unfair. The mid-1970s had been a difficult period for Chase. A series of problems adversely impacted the bank's performance and profitability, which raised questions about my effectiveness as chief executive officer.

The first problem was an almost total collapse in our operations management systems—the document-processing and record-keeping function that lay at the heart of the bank—producing an alarming deterioration in service, a commensurate increase in customer complaints, and a steep decline in earnings. This was followed by a forced restatement of our balance sheet as a result of an overvaluation in our bond trading account that cost us $33 million.

Soon after that we had a disastrous run of losses in our real estate portfolio that culminated in the eventual bankruptcy of Chase Manhattan Mortgage and Realty Trust (CMART), the real estate investment trust that, regrettably, carried the bank's name.

During the same time we were overtaken by our archrival, Citibank, in terms of total assets and earnings.

The final indignity was the flaunting of our problems in a front-page *Washington Post* story, picked up by other national media, that hinted at a potential Chase insolvency.

The confluence of these events placed the bank and my management under a microscope where every decision was dissected and every misstep recorded. Few companies, then or since, have been held to such a level of public scrutiny.

During the first half of 1976, *Business Week* called Chase a "floundering giant." *Institutional Investor* asked on its cover, "Can David Rockefeller Ever Get His Act Together?" And in perhaps the most ignominious of all, *Financial World* ran a seventy-two-point, all-cap headline on its cover: "WHY DAVID ROCKEFELLER SHOULD FIRE HIMSELF."

Even as these difficult problems were aired by the press, Bill and I had already taken a number of concrete steps to correct the problems for which we were being pilloried and which had long characterized Chase's "culture." Through it all I continually reaffirmed my confidence that the bank would regain its position of leadership in terms of both profitability and respect *and* that I would remain as CEO to see it reach these goals.

But sitting in my living room that cold winter morning and reading the *Times* story that picked apart my management style and business acumen, I realized most people would not give me much of a chance of achieving my goals or even of serving out my full term as CEO.

HERSTATT HARBINGER

The first years of the 1970s were characterized by worldwide inflation and recession, disruption in the balance of payments between nations, and the gradual breakdown of the international monetary system. The huge increase in energy costs occasioned by the OPEC price increases provided the coup de grâce to the steady economic growth and relative stability that had characterized most of the post–World War II era, ushering in a period of great risk and uncertainty. In the early summer of 1974 we found out just how risky and uncertain the world had become.

=

On June 26, Bankhaus I. D. Herstatt, a small family-owned bank in West Germany, went belly up. The cause of Herstatt's collapse was a $100 million loss they had taken speculating in the increasingly volatile foreign exchange market. Chase was Herstatt's principal correspondent and dollar-clearing bank; all claims against their account came through us.

Under normal circumstances the monies paid into each correspondent bank's account would cover the debits to that account by the end of each business day. However, during the course of any given day, claims against an individual customer would often exceed its balance with us so that for a few hours we would be extending, in effect, a loan to that bank. Prior to the 1970s these amounts were quite modest, but as the speculative fever in the foreign exchange markets mounted, "intraday" loans in the millions of dollars suddenly became the rule rather than the exception. The income from the balances in these accounts made it a profitable business for us, but we also faced much greater risks.

In Herstatt's case we were lucky. The foreign exchange trader at our Frankfurt branch learned of the failure at 4 P.M., European time. He called New York, where it was 11 A.M., and we immediately froze the $156 million we had on deposit. By the end of the day the claims against Herstatt considerably exceeded the $156 million. By acting quickly Chase avoided any losses. Other banks holding unpaid claims had to wait months for the American courts to allocate limited funds among the many claimants.

We had dodged the bullet, but the broader lessons of Herstatt's failure could not be ignored. International financial markets had evolved to the point where the old regulatory mechanisms could no longer manage them properly. The collapse of a small bank in Germany, which most people had never heard of, had disrupted markets for a significant period of time. The insolvency of a major bank could have produced a world economic crisis. While the central bankers of the world struggled to replace the existing system of fixed exchange rates with something more flexible, the private sector also needed to adjust.

Chase had been struggling for some time with the inadequacies of our operational systems and internal controls. Indeed, by the mid-1970s problems with the bank's back office had become as critical as any that faced the institution.

THE BACK OFFICE

Chase had been among the first of the major banks to automate its operations beginning in the late 1950s. Banks had enormous record-keeping requirements—an avalanche of paper. Accordingly, the new technology was introduced to all of the bank's operational areas: check processing, demand deposit accounting, stock transfer services, payroll, installment credit, and the like. The computer also allowed us to centralize our back office operations in a new building especially constructed for that purpose and to begin to apply rigorous cost analysis methods so that management had the tools to measure quickly and by sector the profitability of our products and the effectiveness of our organizational units.

That was the good news.

The bad news was that the new electronic technology changed frequently and was quite expensive to install and operate. In addition, automation required a host of new employees, programmers, systems analysts, and operations research technicians. Integrating these new employees with those handling the more traditional tasks of banking, and ensuring that the technical personnel communicated effectively with the credit officers, proved to be a daunting task, especially when most of us at the senior level of the bank had only a superficial understanding of computers and their capabilities.

In the summer of 1972, I invited Frank Cary, the chairman of IBM, which was an important Chase customer, to have lunch with me. Frank took advantage of the occasion to warn me that Chase was not doing a good job in managing its back office operations. He said we would never correct the situation until the top management of the bank understood the basics of computer technology and how to integrate it into our daily operations. He invited me to make use of IBM's special weekend course on computers for senior corporate executives. Although I was intrigued by the idea, I did not follow up on it until two years later.

At that time about twenty of Chase's top executives, including Bill Butcher and me, traveled to IBM's training center in Poughkeepsie. It was an eye-opener for all of us. By that time, however, we had experienced several painful and well-publicized operational glitches. The most embarrassing of them occurred in February 1974. Shortly before we were scheduled to exchange our obsolete UNIVAC for a new IBM mainframe, disaster struck. An overzealous janitor mistook the spare parts of the UNIVAC for junk and threw them out. The UNIVAC soon gave out completely, and we were forced to rely on a manual record-keeping operation for a number of months before the new IBM system was ready. Even after the new IBM began operating in July, there were many glitches and delays. We had, as our operations vice president put it, "garbage in, garbage out, and a backlog of garbage."

In the midst of this debacle the bank examiners from the Comptroller of the Currency arrived for their annual visit. Not unexpectedly, they found deficient operating systems in a number of our departments and issued a report to the Chase directors that termed our operations "horrendous." Bill and I devoted a good deal of our time over the course of 1974 and 1975 to solving this problem and assuaging the complaints of customers. It was an embarrassing period, and our operational problems contributed significantly to a number of our difficulties during those years. By mid-1975 we had largely overcome these problems and returned our operations to a high level of efficiency. But the damage, in terms of customer relations and public perception, had been done.

SCANDAL IN THE BOND DEPARTMENT

Technology was not our only problem. Chase was also bruised by a scandal that was even more damaging to our reputation.

The scandal involved the bank's bond department, which, in addition to trading bonds for others, held U.S. government, state, and municipal bonds for our own account. Securities law required banks to issue quarterly reports on their holdings, but establishing a fair market value for state and municipal securities, which at that time were usually long in term and thinly traded, was not an easy proposition. Most banks, including Chase, solved this problem by using a formula that estimated their current market value. Federal regulations also required that whenever bonds dipped below their book value, the shortfall had to be reported in a bank's quarterly income statement.

What got us into trouble in October 1974 was that the senior vice president in charge of the bond department guessed wrong on interest rates. Anticipating that rates would fall and prices would rise, he loaded up on government bonds—adding about $1 billion to our portfolio by the middle of 1974. Unfortunately, interest rates did not perform according to his prediction. He held on as interest rates moved up, gambling that the market would correct itself and his position would be covered. Unfortunately, he failed to report the accounting loss, thus violating the law.

Unaware of this omission, Chase issued an inaccurate third-quarter statement at the end of September 1974. After a routine internal audit revealed the truth, the bond department head admitted he had purposely concealed the losses in the hope that values would recover.

Bill Butcher and I were in Washington for the World Bank/IMF meetings and were hosting Chase's annual dinner when we received the news. Without finishing dessert we left our guests and flew back to New York. We arrived at my house on 65th Street at about 11 P.M. Chase director Dick Dilworth, our outside counsel, and several senior officers were assembled. They had been working at a frenzied pace all day, and none of them had taken time for dinner. Peggy cooked hamburgers and prepared hot chocolate while they briefed Bill and me on the situation.

The next day, after informing all the bank's officers, we released a statement admitting that serious errors of judgment had been made and that the senior vice president in charge of bond trading had been asked to resign. We estimated that the bond trading account had been overvalued by some $34 million and that this would lower Chase's published after-tax earnings for the preceding nine months by $15 million. It was front-page news in both the *Times* and *The Wall Street Journal* the following day. Ironically, within a few months interest rates did decline, and the $15 million unrealized loss was erased.

It made little difference. The debacle brought into question the effectiveness of Chase's supervision and reporting, damaged the bank's hard-earned reputation for integrity, and raised questions about the competence of its chief executive officer.

MEDIA ONSLAUGHT

Recessions are rarely kind to business and frequently disastrous for banks. The steep 1974–75 recession was particularly damaging to large commercial banks in the United States. And as our problems at Chase accumulated and our earnings plunged by more than 42 percent, from $182 million in 1974 to $105 million in 1976, the media singled out Chase and me for special attention.

Part of the problem was the impressive performance of Citibank. Capitalizing on its aggressive expansion overseas in the 1950s and 1960s— when I was arguing vainly that Chase pursue a similar course—Citi had moved decisively ahead of Chase by the mid-1970s. In 1970 the two banks were in a dead heat in terms of earnings; by 1975, Citi's earnings had moved well ahead of ours, thanks largely to its enormous international advantage. As Citi swept past Chase, the critics let us have it. Chase management, they reported, had gotten flabby. They pointed to the failure of Herb Patterson's presidency, the bond trading fiasco, a $97 million loan to bankrupt retailer W. T. Grant, Chase's large holdings in suspect New York City obligations, and finally and most particularly, the bank's mounting problems with real estate loans.

The pressure on the bank and me was unrelenting. *Time* magazine reported "rumors that Rockefeller's job is at stake." *Newsweek* indicated that Chase directors were "sounding out at least one prospect to succeed the sixty-year-old Rockefeller as chairman." A *Newsweek* reporter asked Treasury Secretary William Simon if he would be my replacement. Simon responded, "I could turn that situation around in six months to a year."*

All in all, it was not a happy time to be chairman of Chase.

THE CHASE REAL ESTATE INVESTMENT TRUST

The primary cause of my many woes at the bank was the collapse of the national real estate market. With the onset of the recession in late 1973 the real estate market, which for several years had been exceptionally strong, began to weaken. Chase had been a major and successful real estate lender, but when the recession hit, we discovered we had taken greater risks in our real estate lending than we had realized.

Our principal problem was Chase Manhattan Mortgage and Realty Trust (CMART), the real estate investment trust (REIT) we had created in April 1970 to take advantage of the surging property market. REITs became fashionable as a result of changes in the tax code designed to encourage broader private investment in commercial real estate. Before then, commercial real estate development had been financed almost exclusively by commercial banks and insurance companies. To make stock ownership of REITs more accessible and attractive to individual investors, Congress decreed that they would be taxed at a lower rate than other corporations as long as they paid out 90 percent of their revenue annually to their shareholders. REITs quickly became popular investments. On the other hand, the stockholder payout requirement also added a substantial element of risk by preventing the accumulation of reserves that might be needed in an emergency. When the recession deepened in early 1974, this element would lead to disaster for REITs in general and CMART in particular.

Chase had been in the real estate business for a long time and had developed substantial expertise and extensive connections throughout the country. Ray O'Keefe, the executive vice president who ran the department, was considered the dean of the industry. That is why when Ray extolled the benefits of a REIT as a potential generator of profits, I listened. General Lucius Clay, a senior partner at Lehman Brothers, whom I had first met in 1947

---

*Simon's comment sounded like revenge for President Nixon's having asked me to serve as Secretary of the Treasury after George Shultz's resignation in 1973. As Treasury undersecretary, Simon thought he should have been the first choice. Reportedly, he was deeply offended that he got the job only after I had declined.

when he was one of the Allied military governors in Berlin, was also a persuasive proponent of the REIT, as were most of my senior bank associates. Despite some misgivings about the risks, I was finally persuaded by their arguments and gave my approval.

In 1970, Lehman Brothers and Lazard Frères underwrote the successful offering of CMART stock. Although the REIT was a legal entity totally independent of Chase and with its own board of directors, it carried the bank's name. This proved a significant mistake. As we would learn, when investors purchased CMART securities, they looked to us to take care of them if things went wrong.

For its first three years CMART prospered, generating large fee income for the bank and impressive dividends for its shareholders. However, the initial success experienced by CMART and many other REITs played a large role in their eventual downfall. New capital flooded into the REIT marketplace, and the pressure increased to find new projects. In response, REITs and their sponsors lowered their lending standards. Chase's Real Estate Department was no exception.

CMART was highly leveraged, drawing its funds from capital markets, bank loans, and commercial paper. The commercial paper it used was in turn backstopped by bank lines of credit. This meant that if CMART could not pay off its debt when it came due, the bank was committed to lend it the money necessary to make good on the REIT obligations. This leverage would turn out to be Chase's undoing.

By the spring of 1975, CMART had loans to developers approaching $1 billion and bank credit of over $750 million, including $141 million from Chase. At the same time, 46 percent of its assets were no longer producing income, and CMART was operating at a loss. In July 1975, CMART announced a $166 million six-month loss. This resulted in a negative net worth of $50 million. CMART was technically bankrupt.

In retrospect, agreeing to the creation of CMART, allowing it and the Chase Real Estate Department to fall victim to overly aggressive and poorly supervised lending policies, and christening it with the Chase name clearly constituted the worst decisions I made during my tenure as chairman.

A DISASTROUS BOARD MEETING

The problems we experienced with CMART and our own real estate lending were not unique to us. Most banks were overextended and had bad loans, but because Chase was bigger, the consequences of our mistakes were bigger, too. In the three years between 1971 and the end of 1974, Chase and its subsidiaries had increased their real estate lending from $2 billion to $5 billion. The full dimensions of the disaster we faced crystallized in a single event: the Chase board meeting on July 16, 1975. That board meeting is engraved on my memory because it almost cost me my job.

Once a month the Chase board gathered in the executive dining room on the top floor of One Chase Plaza for lunch and informal discussions. On one wall of the dining room hung a large mural by the Italian artist Campigli, originally commissioned for the *Andrea Doria,* the ocean liner that had gone down in a spectacular ocean disaster. It was an alarming portent.

After lunch the directors assembled in the wood-paneled boardroom forty-three floors below. Reviewing the antiseptic formal minutes today, it is hard to believe the afternoon was such a nightmare. Only two sentences referred to the REIT: "A review was made of a proposed workout plan for Chase Manhattan Mortgage and Realty Trust and related resolutions. After discussion, it was decided to defer action to a special meeting of the Board of Directors which would be called by the Chairman."

The reality had been much more dramatic.

After taking care of routine business I called for an update on Chase's obligations to CMART. A competent lending officer with little real estate experience, who had been assigned to head the Real Estate Department when Ray O'Keefe left to run CMART in 1973, stepped to the podium. It soon became apparent that the disaster he inherited had become too much for him. His presentation was inarticulate and confused. When board members pressed him to clarify certain points, he was almost incoherent, and the board became even more confused and agitated. Recognizing the magnitude of the disaster that was unfolding before me, I interrupted the disjointed and dispiriting presentation and proposed that the discussion be postponed until a more thorough analysis of CMART could be prepared for a special board meeting I would convene the following week.

I had no illusions about where I stood with the directors. The presentation had unnerved them because of what it intimated about the bank's position and my management. They knew CMART was in deep trouble, but they expected top management to have a plan for dealing with the deteriorating situation. The scene they had just witnessed was far from reassuring.

I scheduled the special board meeting for the following Thursday, July 24.

The next day Dick Dilworth flew up with me in the Chase helicopter to Hudson Pines for dinner. This was the first opportunity I had to discuss with him the prior day's meeting. Dick told me that he had been sounding out other board members during the day. As we flew past the Cloisters and out over the Hudson, he told me that he had found considerable concern about my leadership of the bank. He said a few directors were quite outspoken in their criticism of me—John Swearingen, chairman of Amoco, and Fred Lazarus, chairman of Federated Department Stores, prominent among them. Neither of them had been supportive of me, so I was not surprised by their reactions. I was more concerned that Richard Shinn, chairman of Metropolitan Life, whom I considered a friend and supporter, had also been critical.

Dick phrased his words as constructively as he could, but there was no doubt what he was telling me. Though one of my principal backers on the board, he never lost sight of his own responsibilities as a director. By the time we reached the Tappan Zee Bridge, Dick had warned me that the special board meeting was a make-or-break occasion for me as chairman.

I had less than a week, literally, "to get my act together."

PREPARING FOR ARMAGEDDON

If I was going to convince the directors that I was on top of the situation, I had to *be* on top of the situation. That meant preparing a detailed, objective analysis of the full extent of our liabilities—no rosy scenarios. There had been far too much wishful thinking. We had to assume the worst and demonstrate exactly what we would do to control the damage.

As a first step I immediately restructured the line of command in the Real Estate Department and put together a small working group to crunch the numbers and propose alternatives. John Haley, the executive vice president whose responsibilities included real estate, headed the group with able assistance from Richard J. Boyle, a senior vice president who was barely thirty years old. Dick had come to my attention a few years earlier through his work at Detroit's Bank of the Commonwealth, with which we had huge outstanding loans. When that venerable institution reached the verge of bankruptcy in 1970, we seconded John Hooper, one of our executive vice presidents, to serve as chairman and CEO to straighten out their problems. Hooper had included Boyle on his team, and I had been impressed by his excellent analytical skills and capacity for hard work.

After working around the clock for days, the CMART task force determined that Chase had about four times the value of its equity capital exposed in real estate. We had $827 million in loans to REITs, of which $141 million represented loans to CMART. The analysis also showed that CMART's failure would lead its creditors to demand that Chase's loan be subordinated to theirs, meaning that our loan would be wiped out completely. Our CMART liabilities alone represented one-tenth of Chase's equity.

The costs of lawsuits and claims by creditors against the bank and the REIT could cause an overall loss of confidence in the bank and lead to a sharp decline in the value of our stock. Thus, the worst case was that Chase might go under or be so badly crippled that it would never be a viable institution again. That wasn't a likely scenario, but it was a possibility—a very anxiety-provoking one for the board and a deadly serious one for me as Chase's CEO and as its largest shareholder.

Their dismal analysis confirmed my worst fears, but I decided to present the complete picture in all its painful detail to the board and accept the consequences, whatever they might be.

DAY OF RECKONING

It was a very somber group that filed into the meeting room at 410 Park Avenue, Chase's midtown Manhattan headquarters, on the afternoon of July 24. Almost every board member—many from distant parts of the country and most of them CEOs of major corporations—was in attendance. Concern was etched into their faces, and I noticed that some of them were quite guarded, as if they had already decided my fate and now wanted to distance themselves from me. Their attitude of skeptical watchfulness added to my own discomfort and sense of foreboding.

Up to that point the day had not gone well. An early-morning meeting at Gracie Mansion with Mayor Abraham Beame had been disastrous. Beame still refused to accept the severity of the City's deepening fiscal crisis or to take any significant steps to resolve it. When I reached Chase, there was more discouraging news. Bill Butcher told me that our auditors, Peat, Marwick and Mitchell, had just informed him that the valuation procedures we wanted to use would have to be scrapped. As a result, for the most important meeting of my life, we would have to discard our carefully crafted presentation, complete with booklets filled with multicolored pie charts and fancy overhead visuals, and improvise. I kept thinking about the *Andrea Doria*!

John Halcy started the meeting by summarizing the bank's real estate lending history, including our loans to REITs, and outlining Chase's current position. Dick Boyle then described in stark terms precisely what our current position was. Forty-six percent of CMART's assets were nonperforming, and we were in the midst of negotiations with CMART's forty other creditor banks, the trustees of CMART, and numerous outside lawyers. The creditor banks and the trustees of CMART wanted Chase to subordinate its CMART notes and agree to several other onerous conditions that were totally unacceptable, but those were the demands we faced.

Boyle then presented our workout strategy. Standing at a blackboard with chalk in hand, Dick took the board through the process. We would purchase $210 million worth of loans from CMART, extend $34 million in new credit for buildings not yet completed, and, along with the other creditors, reduce the interest we were charging CMART to well below market rates. Chase would not be permitted to select only the good loans—many of those we would acquire would not be of high quality—but at least we would reduce our exposure to manageable proportions. Boyle estimated that losses in the first two years could amount to $100 million.

Dick cautioned that CMART was still in a precarious position and that our workout plan was no guarantee of its future viability. If the market got worse, Chase might be required to provide even greater financial assistance to CMART. But without the workout, CMART would have to file immediately for bankruptcy, and Chase would be involved in expensive and protracted litigation from everyone involved. The bankruptcy of CMART could lead to the bankruptcies of other REITs, leading to still greater losses in Chase's own portfolio. The adverse impact of a bankruptcy on Chase's reputation and its ability to attract funds was incalculable and had to be avoided categorically.

After Boyle's presentation, board members asked a number of questions, but there was a great sense of relief in the room, not because the proposal he presented was optimistic—even the best case meant real pain for the bank—but because the directors finally understood the true parameters of the problem. More important, they now believed that management had the situation under control, at least the part of it we could control.

After the meeting Dick Dilworth told me the mood of the directors had changed. "The sense I get," he said to me, "is that they are considerably happier than they were last week; but they're waiting to see. I'd say you have about a year to turn things around." That was a relief, but we still faced a big challenge.

Despite our best efforts, CMART did default on its obligations and filed for bankruptcy in 1979. From 1975 to 1979 the bank charged off $600 million in real estate loans, and the total cost, including the loss of income from nonperforming assets, was almost $1 billion. While CMART had been a bitter lesson, we had managed the bailout process in an orderly manner and mitigated the impact of its final failure. Fortunately, the income that we generated from other sources, especially from our international loans and operations during this same period, enabled us to cover the heavy losses we had sustained, and Chase never suffered an operating loss during that period. It had been a difficult, painful, and expensive experience for Chase.

ONE FINAL INDIGNITY

The only time I ever threw a reporter—or anyone else for that matter—out of my office was in January 1976, shortly after I had sat down for an interview with a reporter from *The Washington Post*.

The reporter, Ron Kessler, had asked to see me, ostensibly to review world banking trends. Shortly after we began, however, Kessler pulled from his briefcase a confidential report from the Comptroller of the Currency. The report was the same one we had received eighteen months earlier that detailed our many operational deficiencies in 1974. I was shocked that the *Post* had obtained this privileged information, and even more dismayed when Kessler displayed a confidential Federal Reserve memorandum that listed Chase as one of a number of big banks on the Comptroller's "Problem Bank List." I told him that I refused to discuss confidential government documents and asked him to leave.

On Monday, January 12, the front page of *The Washington Post* carried an eight-column headline: "Citibank, Chase Manhattan on U.S. 'Problem' List." The story cited our abbreviated interview, quoting me as refusing to "discuss the examiners' findings, saying their reports are 'privileged.' " It added that while the examiners rated Citibank's future prospects "excellent," Chase's prospects were listed as only "fair."

It is true that the Comptroller's report had characterized operating conditions at Chase as "horrendous" and that it had specifically noted "a large volume of clerical errors in certain accounts," poor internal controls and audit procedures, and insufficient staff and inexperienced personnel in vital positions. However, when we received this report in August 1974, we immediately addressed the issues that it raised, and by the time of the *Post*'s revelations, we had largely corrected them. In fact, the Comptroller's 1975 report had readily acknowledged this fact, as would their 1976 annual audit. So the breathless *Post* article on January 12, 1976, was largely based on very old news.

Because the *Post* story sent shock waves through the financial community, Comptroller of the Currency James E. Smith immediately issued a statement that both Citibank and Chase "continue to be among the soundest banking institutions in the world." I issued my own statement that Chase was "sound, vital, and profitable" and that the article was based on information which was more than eighteen months old.

Even then Kessler and the *Post* refused to back off. In fact, this was only the first in a weeklong series of articles, including one in which Kessler cited for the first time a Federal Reserve Board memorandum that criticized Chase's operations. Kessler's use of this confidential document was particularly outrageous because its author had simply quoted from the Comptroller's earlier report, although Kessler made it appear that these were entirely new criticisms of Chase.

As soon as I read the article, I called Arthur Burns, the chairman of the Federal Reserve Board, urging him to consider making a public statement in light of the damage the *Post*'s misleading stories were having on Chase and the American banking system. Burns agreed, and the following day *The New York Times* carried his statement that read in part: "In the year and a half since July 1974, the Chase Manhattan Bank has taken numerous steps to improve all aspects of the Bank's operations that were criticized. As a result of these efforts, significant improvements in the Bank's operations have been realized. . . . It is my judgment that the Chase Manhattan Bank is a responsibly managed and financially sound institution."

Nevertheless, the damage had been done. Frankly, there was little we could say to challenge the story. Virtually every national newspaper and magazine picked up the *Post* "exclusive" and discussed the "nation's banking crisis," with Chase as the centerpiece.

At the height of this furor I received a vote of confidence from one of the directors. At the January 1976 Chase board meeting, the bank's outside directors requested that all the "inside" directors leave the room except me. I thought initially of Dick Dilworth's warning to me six months earlier. My anxiety quickly dissipated when John Connor, chairman of Allied Chemical Corporation, read the following statement and asked for it to be incorporated in the minutes: "In my opinion, the Bank and Corporation have a very strong top management team with David Rockefeller as Chairman and Bill Butcher as President. . . . As for the media criticisms, we all know that the problems described are about two years old. Starting at that time, the outside Directors expressed concern to the Chairman. . . . Management proved to be very responsive to the suggestions made, and as a result the Chairman and President carried out a new program that has resulted in a greatly strengthened organizational situation and sound loan programs and operating procedures."

As to the public's perception of Chase, the only way we could dispel the negative publicity and silence the critics was to perform, and that Bill and I were determined to do.

THREE-YEAR DEADLINE

By the middle of 1977 we had gone a long way in correcting our operational problems, integrating our new computer systems, and working out our real estate mess. Bill Butcher and I had righted the ship, but valuable time had been lost, especially in comparison with our major competitors, who had substantially increased their earnings between 1974 and 1976. During that same period, Chase's net income had fallen by more than 40 percent. We had to improve our profitability and performance for our shareholders.

I had three years left before reaching the mandatory retirement age of sixty-five, and I wanted to go out a winner. Not only was I committed to turning the bank around but I was confident we could do it. For one thing the disasters of the mid-1970s gave Bill Butcher and me the opportunity to transform the Chase culture that had contributed substantially to our many difficulties. We reorganized the bank along more efficient, functional lines and also recruited seasoned outside specialists to head the critical areas of human resources, planning, corporate communications, and systems.

Two former General Electric executives played an instrumental role in this process of change and modernization. Alan Lafley, an experienced human resources executive, overhauled our recruitment, training, and compensation policies, and helped strengthen our internal communications at all levels. Alan also helped identify individuals to handle the other key non-credit-related areas of the bank. Gerald Weiss, a brilliant strategist, retooled a planning process that had been inept and ineffective. Their combined impact was just what I had hoped, and it went a long way toward making Chase the kind of professionally managed organization I had always felt it should be.

===

As a sign of our confidence in what we were doing, in 1977, we allowed *Fortune* magazine to write a story about the bank based on interviews with all of our top managers. Carol Loomis, one of the country's most respected financial journalists, wrote the story. Her article, while not complimentary, was a fair and evenhanded appraisal of Chase's situation. She wrote, "In one sense, Rockefeller has succeeded splendidly; he is a world-renowned figure, clearly this nation's leading business statesman. Yet in another sense, Rockefeller must be judged at this point to have flunked."

She recounted the problems that had afflicted the bank in the 1970s under my chairmanship and the task that I still confronted: "Rockefeller is

62 years of age and must retire as chairman in three years. If it is David Rockefeller who gets the bank where it should be, the job is going to have to be accomplished in pretty short order. . . . Some people have questioned whether running a bank is David Rockefeller's cup of tea. He has his own 'final days' to settle that matter once and for all."

Carol Loomis had identified the challenge that lay before me, and I was comfortable with her words. I knew we were building a stronger and better bank, and I invited her to return in three years to see with her own eyes the Chase turnaround.

FAMILY TURMOIL

In March 1976, *The Rockefellers: An American Dynasty* was published and soon became a best-seller.

Written by Peter Collier and David Horowitz, erstwhile editors of the radical magazine *Ramparts*, the book was a disparaging account of my family as seen through the lens of Marxist theory and counterculture politics.*

A blend of fact and fiction (mostly the latter) that depicted us as the incarnation of capitalist greed and the cause of much that was wrong with contemporary American and global society, the book was carelessly researched, based on questionable sources of information, and contained little about the first three generations of the family that had not already been dealt with by earlier muckrakers of the left and the right. However, it was the section on the "cousins"—my children, nieces, and nephews—that was quite sensational, and particularly troubling to me.

The authors, posing as sympathetic friends, met with a number of cousins. They encouraged them to speak freely about their disenchantment with the Rockefeller family and its institutions, and their estrangement from

---

*One of the minor ironies of contemporary politics is that Collier and Horowitz, having made their names and a good deal of money writing as left-wing Marxist critics of American capitalism and the American establishment in books on the Rockefellers, Kennedys, and Fords, have now become the darlings of the right wing of the Republican Party. Horowitz is the director of the Center for the Study of Popular Culture in Los Angeles, which receives significant funding from Richard Mellon Scaife and other conservative activists. Politics does indeed make strange bedfellows.

their parents, in some cases promising confidentiality. Those interviews formed the core of the book, focusing on the personal lives and struggles of the younger generation of my family, including five of my own children. The portrait drawn by Collier and Horowitz showed an unhappy, conflicted group of people, many of them attracted to radical social causes and revolutionary ideas, who were eager to distance themselves from their reactionary and unsympathetic parents. After the book was published, my children told Peggy and me that the authors had misled them about their real intentions, claiming they were writing a book on philanthropy and promising that nothing they said would be printed without their permission. They said their words had been purposely misconstrued to fit the ideological framework of the writers, not the facts of their own lives. Nonetheless, there had to be some truth in what they said, which made the book very painful reading for Peggy and me.

Ironically, by the time the book appeared in 1976, all of our children had graduated from college, and even those who had been active in radical politics during their undergraduate days had long since moved on with their lives. Thus, while the immediacy of these rancorous issues, related to the Vietnam War and the struggle for social justice, had dissipated, all of us— each of our children as well as Peggy and me—had to face, as we never had before, the existence of several basic differences and strong tensions that had never been resolved.

As we began to deal with these issues more calmly in the mid-1970s, we all realized that despite our very real differences we shared a number of common desires: to create a more just world that was free of racial intolerance and bigotry, to eliminate poverty, to improve education, and to figure out how the human race could survive without destroying the environment.

It took some time for that realization to sink in, but when it did, the possibility of a different and more respectful relationship among all of us became stronger. Prior to that time, however, we had gone through a decade where confrontation rather than comity characterized our parent-child relationships.

PROBLEMS OF PARENTHOOD

Peggy and I found it curious that two of our children, Abby and Peggy, were deeply attracted to the revolutionary ideas and causes of the 1960s while the other four were much less involved with the turbulent politics of those years. We had raised all of them according to the same moral principles, based essentially on Christian precepts, that Peggy and I had been brought up to believe in. I am still amazed at how differently each of them responded to their upbringing and to the events of the 1960s.

I have no doubt that my lengthy absences during their early and most formative years had a detrimental effect. Dave, Abby, and Neva, born just before or during my World War II service, spent a good portion of their first years without me. Peggy, a young mother, did her best to give them love and guidance, and they absorbed her passion for nature and music as well as her enthusiastic embrace of life in all its diversity. Peggy, Richard, and Eileen were all born after the war, but even as a junior officer at Chase I traveled a great deal and was often away from home. Thus, with the younger children as well, I was unable to give them the time and attention they needed and deserved.

Peggy found the burdens of motherhood difficult to bear. Although she was a devoted mother and much of the time had an exceptional capacity to communicate with the children, for the first twenty years of our married life she also suffered sporadic periods of acute depression. The children learned to stay away from her while she was in the depths of these black moods. Although Peggy worked assiduously with an excellent psychiatrist and eventually succeeded in largely overcoming her problems, it seems likely that her depression, combined with my heavy work schedule and frequent absences, created insecurities and anxieties for at least some of the children.

Peggy and I were dedicated to being responsible parents and to providing our children with a safe home and a good education. When the children were young, they attended well-known day schools in New York City—the girls went to the Chapin and Brearley and the boys to Buckley—which gave them a solid educational grounding even though they lacked cultural diversity.

We spent most weekends at Hudson Pines in Tarrytown where the children rode horseback, played outdoors, and on rainy or cold days enjoyed the Playhouse, often with friends they had invited. We also took them on trips around the United States and to other parts of the world, as my parents had done with me. Our house was always filled with guests from around the world so that from an early age the children were exposed to a variety of interesting and accomplished people—such as Pablo Casals, the great cellist; Pedro Beltrán, the prime minister of Peru; Nate Pusey, the president of Harvard; and General George Marshall. The children responded well to these visitors, and it was an educational and enjoyable experience for them. Our many contacts with the outside world developed in them a variety of interests—languages, art, the natural world—that they have pursued with great enthusiasm.

In 1952, Father had made provision for my children's future financial needs by creating a series of irrevocable trusts. In doing this Father followed the same model he had used in creating the 1934 Trust which provided my siblings and me with most of our income. Prior to creating the 1952 Trust, Father asked me how I wanted them structured.

Peggy and I decided that each of our children should receive a modest annual income—beginning at $5,000 at age twenty-one—that would increase every year until they turned thirty. At that time each of them would receive all the income earned by their trust. We also stipulated that, with the approval of the trustees, each could withdraw as much as 50 percent of the principal of the trust once they reached twenty-one. We felt these provisions and Father's generosity would allow our children to lead independent lives as adults and be able to determine for themselves how best to allocate their own resources.

STRAINED RELATIONSHIPS

Once the children began to leave home for boarding schools in the mid-1950s, our relationships with them began to change. Part of this was the natural consequence of their growing up, an understandable desire to make their own decisions, to find their own way in the world, to establish an identity of their own. However, another part of it involved their discomfort with the Rockefeller name and the traditions, associations, and obligations that membership in the family seemed to imply. Two of our daughters adopted other surnames from Peggy's side of the family. Today, however, they have reconciled themselves to being part of the Rockefeller family, even to recognizing that the name may have a few advantages!

DAVID, JR.

Our oldest child, David, was the first to leave home when he prepared for college at Phillips Exeter Academy in New Hampshire. Dave had never openly rebelled, but neither had he been particularly close or open with either of his parents. Exeter and Harvard seemed to widen the communications gap. His form of rebellion was aloofness, not outright antagonism.

I have often wondered whether I simply did not have much talent as a father, because my efforts to establish a connection with my children often misfired. In 1965, for instance, I gave Dave a share of my equity in L'Enfant Plaza, a Washington real estate development. It seemed probable the stock would appreciate significantly in value as the buildings were completed and the debt was paid off. I thought the gift would be a good way to pass along significant financial resources to my oldest son, but, more important, I hoped the details of the project itself would interest him and serve as a vehicle for bringing us together in a natural way. Although my gift benefited Dave financially, he showed little interest in learning about L'Enfant or even discussing it with me. Some years later Dave said he regretted that we didn't have a closer relationship. When I mentioned L'Enfant, he was surprised that bringing us closer had been an important reason for the gift. I realize now that my thinking was somewhat unrealistic given Dave's attitude toward me at the time, but my intentions were sincere and hopeful.

Dave graduated from Harvard Law School in 1965, then studied economics at Cambridge University before returning to the United States and marrying in 1968. He decided to remain in the Boston area and to follow his interests in music and arts education rather than return to New York for a career in business or the law. He worked for the Boston Symphony Orchestra for a number of years, served on the boards of the National Endowment for the Arts and National Public Radio, and chaired an important arts education panel that was partially supported by the Rockefeller Brothers Fund.

Dave, like most members of his generation, rejected the family's traditional Republicanism. He preferred a politics that placed more emphasis on protecting the environment, ensuring civil rights for all citizens, and ending the war in Vietnam. In the late 1960s he helped finance a "vigorously anti-establishment" Boston weekly, *The Real Paper,* along with a number of his contemporaries who had similar views, including William Weld, a future governor of Massachusetts, and Mortimer Zuckerman, who became a successful publisher and real estate developer. (Ironically, years later I would become a business partner of Mort's in Boston Properties, his very successful real estate investment trust.) While personal relations with Dave were always pleasant, he remained distant until later in life when, I am happy to say, our relationship has blossomed, and we have become very close.

ABBY

Abby was the most rebellious and strong-willed of all our children. From her earliest childhood Abby had forceful and even passionate reactions to most things she encountered. When Peggy started to wean her from breast-feeding, Abby decided to switch immediately to the bottle, giving her mother considerable discomfort. But she always shared her parents' love of nature. As a teenager she became an ardent bird watcher and could imitate their songs so convincingly that birds would actually respond to her call.

Abby and her mother were very close when Abby was a child. Each admired the other's independence and willingness to defy convention. But both of them had strong personalities, so while they adored each other, they engaged in fierce verbal battles. Abby disliked the formality of school but loved music and played the cello with great feeling. In 1963 she enrolled in the New England Conservatory of Music to develop her talent. She also met a number of teachers who encouraged her growing disenchantment with "the inequities of American life." She was drawn to Marxism, became an ardent admirer of Fidel Castro, and joined the Socialist Workers Party for a brief time. As the United States strengthened its military commitment to Vietnam, Abby became a financial backer of antiwar organizations, including *Ramparts* magazine, and worked as a draft resistance counselor in Boston.

Abby's deepest commitment came to be feminism. In 1967 she vowed never again to wear a dress as a protest against women's second-class status in society. *New York* magazine featured her in a story on "Cell 16," the Women's Liberation Group to which she belonged in Cambridge. Abby was described as a "sexual segregationist" and quoted as saying that "love between a man and a woman is debilitating and counterrevolutionary." (Abby denies ever having said this.) Whenever she came home during those years, she would engage us in heated arguments about the capitalist system and our family's continuing complicity in its sins. Our dinners together often ended with angry words.

In the early 1970s, Abby's interests began to shift toward environmental and ecological issues. Most surprising, given her disdain for the private enterprise system, she set up a company to manufacture and market a Swedish-designed composting toilet, the clivus multrum, which was in limited production by early 1974. Peggy and I were more than a bit amazed by Abby's commercial interest but not surprised by the passionate way in which she pursued it.

Despite the vehemence of Abby's rebellion and her angry rejection of most things her family and I stood for, I believe that in her heart of hearts she never forgot the close relationship she had with her mother as a child or the times she and I had spent looking for Caddis fly larvae and whirligig beetles in our pond at Pocantico. For most of the 1960s and well into the 1970s, however, our relations with Abby were, to say the least, tempestuous.

Even when her behavior was most exasperating, her mother would say to me, "Never forget, if anything happens to either of us, Abby will always be there." Sure enough, at the most critical moments in my life, Abby has always provided me with her full measure of love and support.

NEVA

Neva was just thirteen months younger than Abby. As children they shared a room and were inseparable, although their personalities were very different. Abby was the dominant, forceful leader. Neva played a more passive role but was extremely intelligent and an avid reader. Often she would outsmart her older sister, who envied Neva's ability to read fast and do well at school.

It was unfortunate that Neva's maternal grandmother, for whom Neva was named, never concealed the fact that she had hoped Neva would be a boy. Both she and Peggy's older sister, Eileen, made it clear that they adored Abby, who for them could do no wrong, while ignoring and disparaging Neva. This was very hurtful and unfair to Neva.

As a teenager Neva was never openly rebellious but preferred to keep her distance from Peggy and me. She graduated from Concord Academy in 1962 and went on to Radcliffe. Although Abby was living close by in Cambridge, the two of them had had a falling out and rarely saw each other. Thus, while Neva shared Abby's concern for the environment, civil rights, and other social causes, she never became personally involved with radical groups. Neva graduated in 1966, just before the most intense period of student activism broke over the nation's campuses. She married a Harvard professor later that same year and within a few years became the mother of our first grandson and granddaughter.

Neva, ever the intellectual, was drawn to the ideas of R. Buckminster Fuller, the inventor of the geodesic dome, whom she first met at the Dartmouth Conference meeting in Leningrad in the summer of 1964, on the same trip that we met Khrushchev in the Kremlin. Neva was particularly intrigued by "Bucky" Fuller's compelling system of technologies that would maximize the social uses of the world's energy resources and remained in contact with him for a number of years. Subsequently, Neva followed in my footsteps by taking a doctorate in economics, and then she specialized in the connections between poverty and environmental degradation. Neva also joined me as a trustee of The Rockefeller University in the late 1970s. In Seal Harbor, where she and her family spent the summer, she developed a great interest in gardening and eventually succeeded her mother as the manager of the Abby Aldrich Rockefeller Garden.

PEGGY

P eggy entered Radcliffe in the fall of 1965, and her undergraduate years coincided with the most intense period of student protest and the rise of the counterculture. While she quickly fell under Abby's spell and became an active supporter of a number of antiwar organizations, Peggy's own powerful sense of social justice drove her to question the fairness of a system that provided her with enormous wealth and opportunity while consigning millions of others to the worst kind of poverty.

Abby's fiery exhortations influenced Peggy's thinking on many subjects, but she discovered the nature of poverty by herself while working in Brazil in the mid-1960s. Our friends Israel and Lina Klabin invited Peggy to visit them in Rio de Janeiro the summer before she entered college. Peggy accepted their invitation but only on the condition that she could "do something worthwhile" during her stay. Shortly after her arrival, Peggy joined an anthropological team that was studying the *favelas*, or shanty towns, of Rio de Janeiro. Finding the work compelling, she returned the two following summers. She became fluent in Portuguese and moved in with a favela family for her final summer in Brazil. I happened to pass through Rio on a Chase business trip that summer, and Peggy invited me to share a meal with her and "her family" in the favela. Peggy had developed a warm relationship with her host family, who treated her as one of their own daughters.

Peggy was devastated by the poverty she saw and enraged by the political and economic obstacles that prevented meaningful change from occurring. She believed the capitalist system that I represented was a significant part of the problem. After she graduated from Radcliffe in 1969, she enrolled in Harvard's Graduate School of Education and earned a master's and then a doctorate. For most of that time she also worked as the co-director of the STEP Program for disadvantaged and at-risk youth at Arlington High School in Massachusetts.

Peggy was passionate in her efforts to reform the world and seemed unable to disassociate her family and me from what she felt was wrong. For several years she distanced herself, and her trips home to see us became more infrequent. Happily, with the passage of time, Peggy and I reestablished a good relationship. We have worked together on many projects in New York City and have traveled widely together around the world.

RICHARD

The war in Vietnam was still raging when our two youngest children, Richard and Eileen, entered college—Richard at Harvard and Eileen at Middlebury—and the tide of student protest was still running high. However, neither of them became involved with any of the radical movements that in varying degrees had attracted their older sisters.

Richard was troubled by Vietnam, but he remained relatively aloof from the issue during his undergraduate days. Because Dick was more dispassionate than either Abby or Peggy, the two of us could talk about it more calmly. By then, as a result of my experience with the other children and my more general exposure to college students, I was able to deal with him less emotionally.

But it was not easy to answer Dick's probing questions or to justify my strong support for a war that might eventually claim him as a victim. In reality there was no simple solution to the dilemma our country faced, although there were many on both sides who insisted there was. Vietnam involved complex and contradictory geopolitical and moral issues that were a challenge to both the nation as a whole and to every family, including mine.

Dick and I discussed issues like Vietnam at great length. I was grateful he was willing to listen to my arguments even though he was clearly more sympathetic to the radical views of his siblings. I also learned a great deal from Dick about the deep feelings of betrayal and mistrust that many members of the younger generation had developed because of our government's actions in relation to the Vietnam War.

Dick graduated from Harvard in 1971 and spent the next few years "deciding what to do with his life." He worked for a missionary group that served the isolated indigenous populations of northern Quebec and Labrador. Through his work Dick fell in love with flying and qualified for his pilot's license as soon as he could. He also took courses at Harvard's School of Education before deciding on a career in medicine. He graduated from Harvard Medical School in the late 1970s and then built a successful family-oriented medical practice in Portland, Maine.

Dick set himself an orderly and purposeful course in life, centered around his family and his profession. Recently he has been active in helping to lead the effort to permanently protect important wildlands and forests in the northeastern United States. He also is using computer technology to build partnerships between patients and their doctors and to encourage people to become more active participants in their own medical care. Richard is a bright, compassionate, and dedicated man, and a steadying influence in our family.

EILEEN

Our youngest child, Eileen, seemed unaffected by most of the issues that had so deeply entangled her siblings. Instead, resolving the emotional struggle within our family became her preoccupation. She had always been close to her mother, and when her sisters were quite hostile in their attitudes toward Peggy and me, Eileen tried to act as a conciliator, passing information back and forth in an effort to keep the lines of communication open.

In the end Eileen did go through a rebellious phase, but it played itself out on a personal rather than a political or ideological level. She resented that Peggy and I did not appear to take her views on important issues seriously. Her feelings were easily hurt, and this, too, led to tensions. There was a period of estrangement following her lengthy trip to Africa in the mid-1970s when she decided to live apart from us after her return.

Eileen's early efforts to mediate within the family became a central focus of her life after she met Norman Cousins, the editor of the *Saturday Review*, at a Dartmouth Conference meeting in Williamsburg, Virginia, in 1979. Norman had just published *Anatomy of an Illness*, which detailed his successful battle to overcome cancer through the healing ability of the human mind. Eileen was impressed with Norman's philosophy, and for a time he became her mentor. Subsequently, she set up a foundation, the Institute for the Advancement of Health, to encourage scientific study of mind-body relationships in health and disease. This led her to found the Collaborative for the Advancement of Social and Emotional Learning to promote social and emotional intelligence throughout the country.

THE TRAGEDY OF VIETNAM

For more than forty years after the end of World War II I believed that "containing" the threat posed by the Soviet Union and counteracting its consistent and unrelenting support of "wars of national liberation" around the world was the most important task the United States faced as a superpower. The defense of South Vietnam fit into the broader global strategy of containment. If Ho Chi Minh's Communists, with the backing of China and the Soviet Union, conquered all of Vietnam, then it would be only a matter of time before the other "dominos"—including Indonesia, India, and the Philippines—would fall one after the other. It was an article of faith for me and for most of the people I knew and respected that only the United States had the power to prevent this from happening.

A trip to South Vietnam in September 1966 only confirmed my belief that we had to do everything we could to prevent the triumph of the Vietcong and the North Vietnamese. I had gone to Saigon to open a Chase branch that would serve the growing number of American troops stationed there. General William C. Westmoreland, the commander of American forces, briefed us on the progress of the war and his strategy to defeat the enemy. Westmoreland believed the United States had the capability to win the war if we were prepared to commit enough combat troops and "to stay the course."

Westmoreland's greatest concern was that growing antiwar sentiment at home would prevent us from fighting the war to the finish. He was particularly upset by the editorial stance of *The New York Times*, which he felt undermined what we were doing and how we were going about it. I had also been concerned by these editorials, written by John Oakes, head of the *Times* editorial board, whom I had known when we were stationed at Camp Ritchie during World War II. I contacted John when I returned to New York and suggested that he go to Vietnam and meet with Westmoreland. John did go to Saigon, but he was so convinced we should negotiate a settlement with Ho Chi Minh as quickly as we could and get out that nothing Westmoreland said could disabuse him of his strongly held views.

I had a very different perspective. I was disturbed by the numbers of young Americans, including my own children, who had lost their sense of patriotism and pride in their country, and I was saddened by the cynicism and mistrust that so many felt about our government and its actions.

After the Tet offensive in early 1968, however, it became clear that Westmoreland's strategy of massive military intervention had not worked and that disenchantment with the war had reached a fever pitch at home. I realized then that we had no choice but to negotiate our withdrawal on the most acceptable terms possible. There had already been too much damage done to our national fabric and cohesiveness for the conflict to be sustained any longer. I look back on Vietnam, as others do, as a terrible tragedy for our country.

Nonetheless, our intervention in Vietnam did secure time for the rest of the region to stabilize and begin the transition toward democratic market-oriented economies. A conversation in late 1998 with Lee Kuan Yew, the former prime minister of Singapore, confirmed this view. He told me, "America lost the Vietnam War in the United States, not in Vietnam." Lee was convinced that had we not intervened in South Vietnam, all of Southeast Asia would have fallen under Chinese Communist domination. I doubt whether many Americans would look upon this result as much of a consolation for the damage done to our country.

CONFRONTATION AT HARVARD

I also encountered the rebelliousness of the sixties in many places outside my home, especially on college campuses, where my appearances frequently generated protests. On one occasion I canceled a speech at Columbia University's Business School when the central administration refused to provide more than token security, even though there were indications that my appearance might be physically resisted.

The protestors I encountered accused me of responsibility for all the world's ills—from the Vietnam War to institutional racism to fluoride in the water supply. I regret to say that some of the experiences that I found most offensive occurred at Harvard, my alma mater. Surprisingly, one had to do with a gift my family and I made to the Harvard Divinity School.

In 1962 I had been elected to a second six-year term on the board of overseers at Harvard, and in 1966 I was asked to be president of the board for my last two years of service. Throughout those years I worked closely with Harvard's president, my good friend Nathan M. Pusey.

The Divinity School affair began quite innocently in the spring of 1967 when a fellow overseer and chair of the Divinity School Visiting Committee asked me for a contribution to the school. Harvard was in the midst of a $200 million capital campaign, of which the Divinity School was trying to raise $7 million to construct a new dormitory and dining facility, and to endow scholarships and fellowships. I was asked if my family and I would provide $2.5 million for a new building, which would be named in honor of my father.

Since Father had been an active supporter of Nate Pusey's efforts to restore the Divinity School to its former position as a major center for Protestant ministerial training, I agreed to try to encourage the family to join me in providing the necessary funds. My stepmother, Martha, and I each gave $750,000, and the remainder was put up by my brothers and two family foundations.

Nate Pusey and the dean of the Divinity School were overjoyed by our gift. Edward Larrabee Barnes was selected as the architect, and we all looked forward to a ground breaking in the fall of 1969 and a completed building in the latter part of 1970.

In April 1969, President Pusey was forced to call in the Cambridge police to clear University Hall of militant student protesters. His action led to a student strike that effectively closed down the campus. Although classes resumed soon thereafter, campus disruption continued. Plans for Rockefeller Hall became hostage to more general student demands that the university cease its expansion into surrounding neighborhoods, restructure the governance of the university, renounce all defense contracts, eliminate ROTC from campus, and purge its investment portfolio of stock in corporations that continued to operate in South Africa.

A small group of students at the Divinity School demanded that the money contributed by the Rockefeller family either be rejected or used for other purposes, such as buildings for low-income housing in the Cambridge area. They sneered that Rockefeller money was "tainted" and that the family was trying to buy respectability with the gift. While their demands were rejected by a majority of the Divinity School faculty and students, the radicals enjoyed enough power to insist that a delegation be appointed to visit me in New York to explain their position on Rockefeller Hall.

With considerable reluctance I agreed to meet with them at Chase on the morning of June 10, 1969, the day before commencement weekend at Harvard. Some of the group were honestly concerned about the future direction of the Divinity School and wondered if the funds designated for the building might be spent in a more socially responsible way. Two of them took the position, however, that accepting money from the Rockefellers for any purpose would compromise Harvard morally. One of them, a graduate student in religion, reeking with self-righteousness, asserted that Father was a hypocrite, "no real Christian at all," who had given money away only to purge his conscience.

It made me so mad, I could hardly speak. I can't think of a moment in Father's life when his actions were not motivated and shaped by his deep religious beliefs and concern for his fellowman. This was unfair to him and my family, and a most disagreeable encounter for me.

=

I left that night for Cambridge to attend our daughter Peggy's graduation ceremonics at Radcliffe and to receive an honorary degree at the Harvard commencement—along with New York's mayor John Lindsay, Interior Secretary Stewart Udall, and labor leaders Marianne and Walter Reuther.

I learned that Students for a Democratic Society had threatened to disrupt the graduation exercises unless they were allowed to speak. Nate felt it necessary to accede to their demands. Thus, when I was called to receive my degree, a young SDS representative stood on his chair with a loudspeaker and harangued the audience: "David Rockefeller needs ROTC to protect his empire, including racist South Africa, which his money maintains. . . . Harvard is used by the very rich to attack the very poor. . . . Every minute of this commencement Harvard continues to attack people, including us as students. In the context of Harvard's training of officers, of Harvard's racism, of Harvard's expansion, this commencement is an atrocity. . . . Our interests as students do not lie in this tea party with these criminals, these Puseys and Bennetts and Rockefellers."

Of course there was no chance to respond to his invective. I stood there grimly as a small scattering of those attending cheered and applauded. Although the incident was personally unpleasant for me, I felt the real victim was Harvard. A strident ideological minority who cared little for civility, free speech, or democratic principles had tarnished a solemn event at a great university.

Eventually the protests dissipated, and Rockefeller Hall now stands proudly on Harvard's campus. Nevertheless, the 1960s were years embittered by angry protests and saddened by periods of family estrangement and conflict.

HAPPY ENDINGS

As memories of the war in Vietnam began to fade, so did much of the rebellious mood it had generated. As our children matured and started to have families of their own, frictions and misunderstandings between them and their parents rapidly diminished.

An important breakthrough came in 1980, the year that Peggy and I celebrated our fortieth wedding anniversary. To our surprise and delight, several weeks before the date of our anniversary, the children came to us as a group and invited us to spend a week with all of them, including spouses and children, anyplace in the world we would select, at their expense.

We chose the JY Ranch in Jackson Hole, Wyoming, where Peggy and I spent our honeymoon. It was a total success; neither a harsh nor an unkind word was spoken. We enjoyed the beauties of the Grand Tetons and being together as a family. After our week together the dark clouds lifted. In the years since, we have strengthened our bonds as a family. We still disagree on many important issues, but we have learned to count on one another for love and support in both good times and bad.

BROTHERLY CONFLICTS

By the mid-1970s the circle of family conflict had broadened considerably beyond my own children.

Winthrop died of cancer in February 1973, and Babs succumbed to the same disease in May 1976. With their passing, my three brothers and I found ourselves at loggerheads over the future of the Rockefeller Brothers Fund, the Family Office, and the Pocantico estate. Our debates and disagreements over these family institutions were affected by the attitudes and actions of the "cousins" during this time—so much so that a divisive intergenerational struggle briefly threatened the cohesion and continuity of the family itself.

Each of the brothers had experienced some degree of friction within his own immediate family during the course of the 1960s and early 1970s, but the sharp conflict between Nelson, who, ironically, had been the great advocate and architect of family unity, and John, our generation's foremost philanthropist, now became the focus of family tensions.

AN EMBITTERED LEADER

In late January 1977, Nelson returned to the Family Office from Washington, crowned with the laurels of an exemplary public career spanning four decades, a career that had brought him within a heartbeat of achieving his lifelong quest for the presidency of the United States. But despite his significant achievements, Nelson became deeply embittered by the events of the two preceding years.

In the wake of Watergate and Richard Nixon's ignominious resignation, President Gerald Ford selected Nelson as his vice president. Nelson properly viewed his selection as a great honor that would allow him to serve his country in high office at a time of crisis. He handled the arduous and intrusive congressional confirmation process with characteristic equanimity, and the Senate approved his nomination in December 1974.

The vice presidency was frustrating for someone who was accustomed to running his own show, but this was balanced by Ford's willingness to utilize Nelson's enormous expertise in domestic policy and foreign affairs. In addition, if Ford chose not to run for reelection, as had been rumored, Nelson would have the inside track for the Republican nomination in 1976.

None of this played out the way Nelson had anticipated. In November 1975, Ford informed Nelson that he had decided to seek a second term but that Nelson would not be his running mate. The President's decision reflected the thinking of his inner circle of advisors, especially his chief of staff, Donald Rumsfeld. They were convinced that Nelson's liberal Republicanism would be a liability in the primaries against Ronald Reagan, the darling of the increasingly dominant conservative wing of the party. There was no doubt—in Nelson's mind, at least—that Rumsfeld's own presidential ambitions had played a significant role in the decision-making process. Ford proceeded to select Senator Bob Dole as his running mate and defeat Ronald Reagan in the hotly contested struggle for the Republican nomination; but then he lost the November election in a squeaker to Jimmy Carter.*

Ford's decision devastated Nelson. The stark reality was that his hopes of becoming president were now permanently dashed. Nevertheless, to his great credit, Nelson never voiced any public criticism of Gerald Ford. He even campaigned vigorously on behalf of the Republican ticket.

After 1976, however, Nelson never again campaigned for another candidate. He lost all interest in politics, letting his network of political friends and allies languish. Thwarted when the greatest political prize seemed within his grasp, he had become an angry and deeply bitter man.

Nelson also found himself in a difficult situation financially. Years of operating at the highest level of state and national politics—including four gubernatorial campaigns and three runs for the presidency—had been

---

*Years later at a public dinner I attended in New York, Ford acknowledged that dropping Nelson from the ticket was one of the biggest mistakes of his political career and that in his opinion Nelson's presence would have made the difference in his winning the 1976 election.

costly to him personally. Apparently the combined income from his 1934 Trust and his personal investments had been insufficient to sustain both his political career and his expansive lifestyle, which included the creation of an extensive and magnificent art collection. To make ends meet he had invaded his trust on a number of occasions to a point where the 1934 Trust Committee decided they would no longer allow him to draw down any more principal. Nelson, while still a wealthy man, faced the need to economize for the first time in his life.

Despite political disappointments and financial problems, Nelson retained his boundless physical energy. Denied the public stage, that energy would now be expended within the family.

Nelson had always considered himself the de facto leader of our generation and the guiding force behind all family organizations. He assumed he would simply reclaim these positions now that he had left government for good. Nelson's assumption that he would automatically pick up the mantle of leadership seemed, at least to me, more than a bit presumptuous. He made his intentions clear even before he returned to New York by announcing, without consulting anyone in the family, that he would undertake a detailed study of the Family Office and the RBF.

As soon as he reoccupied his old office on the fifty-sixth floor of 30 Rockefeller Plaza, Nelson made it clear that he would brook no opposition to his plans. He seemed to have lost his political skills, or perhaps he felt he didn't need to apply them in dealing with his own family. In pursuing his objective of control he quickly succeeded in offending both the cousins and his siblings, most particularly our oldest brother, John.

A STUBBORN IDEALIST

John's strenuous and vocal opposition to Nelson could not have been anticipated. John had always been a shy and reserved man, who had allowed the more ebullient and aggressive Nelson to shoulder him aside and to assume the role of leader for our generation—in the purchase of Rockefeller Center, the ownership of the Pocantico estate, and the always intricate task of dealing with Father. But this would not be the case with philanthropy. John viewed himself as the legitimate "heir" of the Rockefeller tradition of philanthropy, which he also considered the core value of the Rockefeller family and the only activity that could over time hold family members together.

While Nelson rose to national prominence as a political figure, John had quietly developed a reputation for strong leadership and significant accomplishment in the field of American philanthropy. He had served as an innovative chairman of the Rockefeller Foundation for twenty years; he had been the driving force behind the creation of New York City's Lincoln Center, the nation's preeminent performing arts center; he had tackled the controversial issue of global overpopulation through the Population Council, which he had founded in the early 1950s and largely financed himself for many years; and he had developed a network of relationships in the Far East, most impressive in Japan, through his personal support and advocacy of economic development projects and cultural exchange programs. Along the way John also rejuvenated the Japan Society and brought the Asia Society into being. For most of the 1950s and 1960s, John's charitable contributions had averaged about $5 million a year—more than 60 percent of his annual income.

Philanthropy was John's field, and he resented Nelson's assertions that it was he, rather than his older brother, who should guide the future of the family's primary philanthropies, particularly RBF.

John's stiffening opposition to Nelson resulted, at least in part, from a strong shift in his political views. John, like many of us, had been deeply concerned about the social upheaval of the time, but instead of denouncing the younger generation for their perplexing attitudes and rebellious behavior, he set out to understand the causes of their discontent. John and his associates spent hundreds of hours with young people—from Black Panthers to Ivy League undergraduates—listening as they related their complaints, political beliefs, and hopes for the future, and he found himself sympathetic to much that he learned. It was a transforming experience for John, and he wrote a book, *The Second American Revolution,* that distilled his experience.

The book was very much a reflection of the times, particularly in its suggestion that all wisdom reposed in the young and that the older generation, which had made such a mess of the world, should look to their children for guidance. The book caused quite a stir; senior members of the establishment do not often make common cause with society's malcontents or even youthful critics. But for those of us who knew him well, John's ideas and conclusions were not that surprising. He had increasingly come to be what we used to call a "parlor pink," and the years he spent dealing firsthand with serious and intractable social problems had strengthened his instinctive sympathies for the underdog and the underclass. His political views, as a consequence, had drifted ever more to the liberal side of the spectrum.

In retrospect this was one of the principal sources of conflict between Nelson and John. As governor of New York, Nelson moved consistently to the right on most social issues—the "Rockefeller" drug laws, his suppression of the Attica prison riot, and his last-ditch defense of American intervention in Vietnam were all examples of his more conservative political posture. Nelson was scornful of John's liberalism and his embrace of many individuals and organizations that had been vitriolic in their attacks on him. He was also outraged by the behavior and beliefs of the cousins and determined that they not gain control of important family institutions. Thus, the stage was set for a contentious struggle, beginning with the future of the RBF.

ROCKEFELLER BROTHERS FUND: THE FIRST BATTLEGROUND

By 1973 the RBF had become the country's twelfth largest foundation, with an endowment of $225 million. The fund's program had changed greatly from its inception in 1940 when we five brothers created it in order to manage our annual support for organizations such as the Girl Scouts, the YMCA, and more than ninety other community agencies in New York City and Westchester County. Father's gift of almost $60 million in Rockefeller Center notes in 1951 provided the RBF with an endowment for the first time (up until then the RBF had depended on annual contributions from each of the brothers) and allowed us to broaden the fund's scope beyond our "citizenship" giving to provide significant support for organizations that had been initiated and led by individual brothers. Among the principal recipients were John's Population Council, Nelson's American International Association for Economic and Social Development, and Laurance's Jackson Hole Preserve, Inc.

In 1961 the RBF received an additional $72 million for its endowment from Father's estate. This sizable increase in resources enabled us to broaden the fund's program even further. The RBF continued to handle our "citizenship" giving and to fund the work of a number of family-led organizations, but we now began to reach out to a broader array of groups and institutions. As a result the RBF began to evolve into a more traditional kind of foundation. My brothers and I were comfortable with this process, because we had every reason to believe our children would wish to assume responsibility for the RBF and, through it, pursue their own philanthropic interests.

That change was already well under way by the mid-1960s and was strongly reflected in the RBF's support for groups working in the area of civil rights and equal opportunity, which were very much in harmony with the interests of many of the cousins. But while my brothers and I strongly supported the RBF's broader program, we felt a continuing responsibility to "our" family-led organizations that had received significant financial support from the RBF over the years. As we contemplated our own imminent retirement from leadership roles in these organizations, we concluded that simply cutting them adrift without providing adequately for their future would be irresponsible. We envisioned devoting as much as $100 million, or roughly half, of the endowment for this purpose, with the thought that once the grants were made, the RBF "would be relieved of any further continuing responsibility to these organizations." The RBF board approved our proposal and immediately launched a review process, supervised by RBF president Dana Creel.

Within a year it became apparent that each brother had different expectations and objectives for what we called the "Creel Committee process." John's primary goal was to preserve as much of the RBF's endowment as possible, so he favored sharply limiting the number and amount of the "terminal" grants. Laurance and I did not disagree with John; we also wanted to ensure that our organizations were strengthened for the future. Two institutions in particular—the Memorial Sloan-Kettering Cancer Institute in Laurance's case and The Rockefeller University in mine—required substantial financial assistance if they were to survive as centers of excellence. Therefore, Laurance and I strongly endorsed significant capital grants to each. John strongly opposed the amounts we proposed, calling them "inappropriate and self-serving."

While Nelson took little interest in the early stages of the Creel Committee process, he would be heard from soon enough.

"GIVING AWAY" THE RBF

The Tax Reform Act of 1969, designed in part to regulate philanthropic foundations, had added another layer of complications to our discussions. The act included strong prohibitions on self-dealing by trustees of foundations, most of which were reasonable. However, John, who had played an important role in the Tax Reform Act while it was wending its way through Congress, insisted that there was strong support in Congress for additional legislation that would do away with foundations *altogether.* Consequently, John argued that since the law implied that donors should begin to relinquish control over their foundations, we should set an example at the RBF by voluntarily reducing family control of the RBF.

To accomplish this John wanted to add more outside directors so that family members would be a minority on the board. In my view, John's position challenged the basic premise upon which the RBF had been established. It was only because of our common interest in the social, economic, and political issues of the day that the RBF had emerged as one of the country's most respected foundations. Reducing the role of the brothers in order to placate a temporary political majority in Washington I felt would be a great mistake. But my arguments failed to convince John.

John's patronizing manner and the implicit assumption that he was arguing from a superior moral position made matters more contentious. While his ideas and manner annoyed Laurance and me, Nelson, who rejoined the RBF board in early 1977 after an absence of almost twenty years, was positively infuriated by them. Nelson accused John of trying to "give away" the RBF in the same way that he earlier had allowed the family's influence to be diminished and then extinguished at the Rockefeller Foundation.

While I was willing to make some concessions to John's position in the interest of peace and harmony, Nelson was in no such mood. No doubt Nelson's condescending approach to John had always rankled, but until then their differences had never erupted into open hostilities. In the past John usually had given in to Nelson, whose innate political instincts had always stopped him before he pushed his older brother too far. But not this time.

John's sympathy for the cousins and the views they had expressed to Collier and Horowitz in their book drove the wedge in even further. Nelson was livid over what he considered the cousins' act of disloyalty. Why bother to save the fund if we would simply be turning it over to a younger generation who had publicly spurned the family and who were committed to causes Nelson saw as profoundly objectionable. Nelson's solution was to distribute the entire RBF endowment to that small group of institutions that had been of the greatest importance to the brothers. Failing that, Nelson wanted to reassert the brothers' earlier dominance over the RBF's program and management.

CIVIL WAR

Beginning in early 1977, discussions at RBF meetings became increasingly acrimonious. Angry exchanges between Nelson and John increased, and Laurance occasionally abandoned his role as chairman in order to join the fray. This would have been distressing enough if these family squabbles had taken place in private, but the outside trustees—including Gerald Edelman, a Nobel laureate from Rockefeller University; William McChesney Martin, former chairman of the Federal Reserve; and John

Gardner, a former Secretary of Health, Education and Welfare—were forced to witness these intemperate scenes.

The hostilities commenced within days of Nelson's return to Room 5600 when he declared to the family that he wanted to become chairman of the RBF. Nelson had served briefly as head of the fund in 1956 and 1957, succeeding John, who had held the position for fifteen years. Now, with Nelson back, Laurance insisted he was happy to stand aside since, as he put it, he had only been "filling in for Nelson for the previous twenty years." John promptly objected, suggesting it was *my* turn to become chairman. I declined, citing the heavy obligations of my final years at Chase. Laurance reluctantly agreed to remain as chairman until I retired from the bank four years later.

Undaunted, Nelson continued to push his plan to secure control of the RBF. At a nominating committee meeting in March 1977, Nelson proposed Nancy Hanks, former director of the National Endowment for the Arts, and Henry Kissinger for membership on the board. A number of trustees, including brother John, were concerned about their independence as trustees because of their long affiliation with Nelson. On the other hand it was difficult to deny their outstanding ability, and both were elected.

Nelson also proposed that the RBF resume its original role as a vehicle for supporting the personal philanthropy of the brothers and that all the other trustees, both cousins and nonfamily, should serve only as advisors. Nelson's outrageous idea was a "nonstarter," but John Gardner was especially offended by the proposal.

Gardner asked for a private meeting with Laurance and me, and we met in my office at Room 5600. Gardner fairly bristled with indignation at Nelson's proposal, pointing out that under the laws of New York State every trustee of a publicly incorporated foundation has equal legal and fiduciary responsibilities; the vote of an outsider could never carry less weight than the vote of a brother. I fully agreed with Gardner and told him so. But much to my surprise Laurance vigorously defended Nelson's position and lashed out at Gardner, impugning both his motives and his personal integrity. Visibly angered by Laurance's tirade, Gardner stalked from the room.

Within days Gardner resigned from the RBF board, and shortly thereafter a *New York Times* article reported the RBF controversy in depth. I am convinced that Gardner played a role in leaking the story and casting the issue in terms of ethical impropriety on Nelson's part. Gardner's strong reaction to Nelson's machinations and Laurance's tirade was certainly understandable, but Nelson's proposal had no chance of being accepted. That's why I was extremely disappointed that John Gardner allowed the story to become public. The adverse publicity sullied the RBF's reputation for some time thereafter.

But Nelson, ever the hard charger, refused to be bridled. He exploded another bombshell at the June 1977 board meeting, proposing that the RBF provide a $3 million grant to help underwrite the construction of a new college of osteopathy at the New York Institute of Technology on Long Island, a proposal inspired by Dr. Kenneth Riland.

For many years Nelson had been under the care of Dr. Riland, who became a trusted friend and permanent fixture in Nelson's entourage, traveling with my brother wherever he went and carrying along his portable table to administer treatments. It was not unusual when visiting Nelson at Kykuit to find him on Dr. Riland's osteopathy table, having his joints cracked and his limbs twisted and pulled in all sorts of seemingly uncomfortable ways. On Nelson's recommendation Babs and Laurance also made use of Dr. Riland's expertise, and they, too, swore by it.

Nelson's proposal produced a strong negative reaction from the other trustees, who felt he was trying to tap into the RBF's resources to support a project of dubious merit sponsored by a close friend. But Nelson refused to back off, and as a compromise the board allocated $100,000 to study the financial feasibility of the college.

The duel between John and Nelson flared up again over a grant proposal for the Metropolitan Museum of Art in the spring of 1978. Nelson asked that the Met be placed on the Creel Committee list for a project that would honor his son, Michael, who had been lost on an anthropological expedition to Papua New Guinea in 1961. Nelson had donated his important collection of primitive art, including a number of artifacts collected by Michael, to the Met. The museum created a new wing to house the collection and named it in Michael's memory. It was a wonderful solution: Nelson's collection had a permanent home, it was a splendid tribute to Michael, and a conspicuous gap had been filled in the Met's own collection.

The family responded generously to Nelson's initiative. Martha Baird provided most of the funds for construction of the new wing. The RBF contributed almost $1.5 million for the installation and permanent maintenance of the collection, and a number of other family members, including Laurance and me, also supported the project. However, there had been cost overruns that Nelson could not meet, and he asked the RBF to consider a supplemental capital grant of $150,000. Most board members had no problem with this additional grant, but John objected. He argued that the Met had already received its full capital grant from the RBF and was not entitled to any further support. It was another case where John's "holier than thou" attitude antagonized the rest of us. In the end the board approved the additional grant, with John petulantly abstaining from the vote.

And there matters rested in mid-1978, with John and Nelson each eyeing and jibing at each other across the boardroom table and making RBF meetings an uncomfortable experience for the rest of us.

SKIRMISH AT THE FAMILY OFFICE

In the spring of 1977, Nelson completed his unsolicited study of the Family Office and submitted his recommendations to his three brothers. Up until then the Family Office, which Grandfather had established in the mid-1880s, had functioned on an informal basis. First Grandfather and then Father had hired a small number of professionals to help manage the family's business and philanthropic interests. But after World War II, as my generation became more active, it became necessary to create departments to handle the family's growing legal, real estate, accounting, investment, and philanthropic interests.

Father generously continued to pay for most of these services, which amounted to millions of dollars annually, until his death in 1960. Thereafter his widow, Martha, who had inherited half of his estate, agreed to pay for half the office costs, with my generation picking up the rest of the tab. Martha died in 1971, after which the brothers, with assistance from Babs, shouldered the full burden of office expenses. From that point on, spiraling inflation and the increased demand for services by the cousins and their children drove costs to a higher level each year.

Nelson's study contained several constructive and valuable recommendations. He suggested a total reorganization of the office through the creation of a family-owned corporation that would charge clients for services rendered. Nelson took as his model the Bessemer Trust Company that the Phipps family had organized a number of years earlier, and proposed marketing its services to outside clients as well. This "Rockefeller Trust Company" would be governed by a board of directors and run by a chairman and chief executive officer. Nelson's plan promised huge cuts in our costs by rationalizing office operations. It dealt with the difficult issue of family continuity and the transfer of power between the brothers and the cousins. In many respects Nelson's proposal offered a plausible solution to the problems the family faced.

But Nelson, inexplicably, misjudged the politics of selling his idea to the rest of the family. His troubles began when he brazenly proposed that he become chairman and CEO of the new corporation. That meant replacing Laurance, who had been the nonexecutive chairman of the office for almost twenty years, and J. Richardson Dilworth, who had been the able manager and, in effect, the CEO of the office during that same period. Nelson also proposed restricting membership on the new corporation's board of directors to individuals with "proven capacity in the outside world." According to Nelson's criteria, only he, Laurance, and I, and John's son, Jay, then governor of West Virginia, passed the test from within the family. Nelson insultingly dismissed John and all the other cousins, including his own children, as "unqualified."

This aspect of Nelson's plan had all the characteristics of a power grab, and most family members reacted very negatively to it. The issue came to a head at the "cousins weekend" in June 1977 in Tarrytown, the annual gathering when many of the family return to Pocantico for fun, relaxation, and meetings on a variety of family-related issues.

On Friday night Nelson attended a dinner at his son Rodman's house along with a number of cousins and their spouses. This was the first time that Nelson had seen many of them since the Collier and Horowitz book had appeared the year before. Nelson first made clear his distaste for the book and his low opinion of the cousins who had cooperated with the authors. He then proceeded to explain his plan for the office with himself as chairman and CEO. The cousins were outraged. They attacked Nelson for the imperious manner in which he was trying to seize control of the office. Nelson responded in kind. It was a tense and unpleasant evening for everyone present.

The following morning the four brothers gathered in the Card Room of the Playhouse while the cousins convened outside by the swimming pool to discuss formally Nelson's proposal. Because office management had never been determined by voting, Nelson assumed his plan would go into effect once his brothers approved it. He was dumbfounded when we were sent word that the cousins had voted unanimously to turn it down. They insisted Laurance should remain as head of the office while other aspects of the plan were considered. Nelson was as angry as I have ever seen him, and he demanded that his three brothers support the implementation of his entire plan immediately.

I must say I favored Nelson's becoming head of the office, but not with the absolute authority he demanded. I also felt empathy for him because of his genuinely hurt feelings and the hostility he had encountered. But he seemed oblivious to how much he had provoked the cousins. Despite his demands for personal support, I thought the time had come for diplomacy in order to end the confrontation. For the next hour or so I acted as a conciliator, first with Nelson and then with the cousins. After Nelson calmed down a bit, I left my brothers and walked down to the pool. I urged the cousins not to reject Nelson's proposal out of hand. It took a good deal of persuasion, but eventually they softened their position, but not by much. They continued to insist that Nelson's reorganization plan be shelved. They did agree to his becoming chairman but not the CEO, and only on the condition that the office would be run along more democratic lines, with their needs receiving greater recognition. When I returned to the Card Room, John, Laurance, and I prevailed upon Nelson to agree to this compromise, but his anger at the family continued to simmer for months.

Two decades later, as I think back on that sunny Saturday at Pocantico, I realize that family dynamics began to change irrevocably on that day. Nelson, the architect and advocate of family unity who for so long had been accepted as the family's undisputed leader, had suffered a devastating defeat. His rejection forced him to draw back from the family and its principal institutions. At the same time, and quite unexpectedly, as a result of my stepping up to help craft a compromise between the cousins and the brothers, my role as a family leader began to become more prominent.

SHOWDOWN OVER POCANTICO

At the same time that we battled over the RBF and the Family Office, my brothers and I also faced difficult decisions about Pocantico, the family estate in Westchester County. This issue generated yet another bitter quarrel between John and Nelson.

By the early 1950s we came to realize not only that the estate was a very valuable economic asset, but also that it had genuine historical and aesthetic attributes. We began to explore our options—a process that was not fully resolved until the late 1970s with the deaths of John and Nelson. Our early deliberations were made more difficult by the intricate ownership structure of the property.

Pocantico, like the Gaul of Caesar's *Commentaries,* was divided into three parts. First, there was the Kykuit mansion and the area immediately surrounding it, which we referred to as "the Park" or the "historic area"; it consisted of about 250 acres. From the mid-1950s on, John, Nelson, Laurance, and I owned this portion of Pocantico as tenants in common. Second was the "open space," almost 2,000 acres in extent, owned by all five brothers through Hills Realty. There were our individually owned properties: John's

Fieldwood Farm; Nelson's Hunting Lodge; my Hudson Pines Farm; and Laurance's five distinct parcels, including Rockwood Hall, on the Hudson River.

Beginning in the early 1960s we began to develop plans for the future disposition of these properties, especially the open space. None of these plans met our needs, so in 1972 we asked the noted landscape architect Hideo Sasaki to address all of the concerns that had emerged over a decade's worth of discussions and prepare a plan that would yield the "highest and best use" for the entire Pocantico estate.

A MONUMENT TO NELSON

Nelson had never been particularly concerned about what happened to our jointly owned property "outside the fence." When it came to planning for the future of the estate, Nelson tended to think primarily, if not exclusively, about Kykuit. He viewed the mansion as the family's ancestral home and the symbolic center of the Rockefeller universe. He considered it of great importance that he was its occupant in lineal succession to Grandfather and Father. So great was Nelson's sense of ownership that few of his guests were aware that he was not the actual owner of Kykuit but rather a joint tenant of the property along with three of his brothers. It was Nelson who pushed for its designation as a National Historic Landmark, a distinction bestowed by President Ford in an impressive ceremony in December 1976.

Here again John differed strongly with Nelson. The historic preservation of Kykuit, which in his view would simply be creating a "monument to Nelson," was not high on his list of priorities. His prime concern was to ensure that the open spaces in the other reaches of the estate ultimately would be devoted to public purposes.

In this instance Laurance agreed with John, but his loyalty to Nelson made it difficult for him to resist his brother's plans. Laurance's deepest personal commitment was to conservation, and he was averse to applying his personal financial resources to other aspects of planning for the future of the Pocantico estate. He was strongly drawn to the idea of creating a public park out of the open space as a legacy to both his own life's work and to Father's. I would later discover that as far as Kykuit was concerned, Laurance would not even have been sorry to see it torn down.

My own view was that we should try to safeguard the open space *and* preserve Kykuit because I believed there were compelling arguments for both.

The plan that Sasaki submitted in 1974 skillfully balanced our different preferences and provided the framework for resolving our competing objectives. Sasaki told us that the "highest and best use" for the property was to keep Pocantico exactly "as it is." He argued that Kykuit and the park area should be preserved for its historical, architectural, and aesthetic significance, and that most of the open space should be preserved for "park purposes" for the benefit of the general public. The plan was diplomatically presented, and the family's reaction was positive, even enthusiastic.

There remained two overarching questions: To what private entities would the property be given, and how would it be financed? Even if we donated most of the open space to a governmental entity as parkland, the cost could be considerable, especially if the agency selected required an endowment to maintain Father's original carriage roads as well as the fields and forests. Preserving Kykuit would be an even more expensive proposition; indeed, the estimate of the endowment needed just for the historic area was $35 million.

Although some of this amount could be raised by selling marginal areas of the open space, most of the endowment would have to come from our own resources. Nelson proposed that the RBF supplement the funds that each of the brothers would commit. Once again John strenuously resisted, arguing that a grant from the RBF would be "inherently self-serving." This particular issue would become the final battleground between John and Nelson.

AN OUT-OF-CHARACTER LETTER

Shortly after the cousins' revolt at the Playhouse in June 1977, John wrote Nelson a letter, which he had hand-delivered from his office in the northwest corner of the fifty-sixth floor to Nelson's office in the northeast corner. It read in part: "You have always indicated to me that there were two things you wanted to accomplish in your lifetime. The first was to become President of the United States, and the second was to become the leader of the family and be sure it lived up to the great traditions bequeathed to us by Father and Grandfather. Obviously, you have failed in the first of these objectives, and you are in danger of failing in the second, unless you modify your behavior."

Nelson wrote back immediately, demanding that John's letter be "withdrawn." It was a private letter, of course; no one else had seen it. But Nelson was adamant. He said that unless John withdrew the letter immediately, he would break off negotiations on Pocantico and pursue plans to build a hotel and conference center on his own portion of the property. Eventually John did take the letter back, and negotiations resumed.

Once again I found myself in the middle of a John-Nelson contretemps. They both had legitimate points but had lost sight of the common good. After much bargaining we reached a compromise: Nelson agreed to the donation of a large portion of the open space as parkland, on condition that each of us insert language in his will committing $5 million for the endowment of the historic area and that our $20 million be supplemented by a $15 million grant from the RBF, thereby ensuring an adequate endowment to fund the historic preservation aspects of the Pocantico plan. John went along with the agreement, and the prospects for a permanent—and amicable—solution seemed bright.

But matters were not quite settled. After years of battling with Nelson, John decided he could be just as contrary and irascible as Nelson in trying to get what *he* wanted. Before changing his will, John insisted that Laurance include Rockwood Hall—the beautiful property along the Hudson River—in the park. While the future disposition of any part of our separately owned property had never been part of the negotiations, John arbitrarily decided that Rockwood Hall had to be included, or he would call off the deal.

Laurance resented John's unilateral reopening of the negotiations with new conditions. He found this end run intolerable and refused to consider the proposal. John persisted, but the more he lectured Laurance about his "duty," the madder Laurance got. Finally, John came to me and suggested that he and I approach Laurance and offer to buy Rockwood Hall ourselves as a means of including it in the proposed park. It was with great reluctance that I agreed to join him, and we got the reaction I feared. Laurance was furious, wouldn't discuss the matter, and essentially pushed us out the door.

After that incident John finally accepted the fact that Laurance wasn't going to budge, and he agreed to modify his will, as the others of us already had, to include $5 million for the Kykuit endowment. Being a stickler for detail, however, he methodically reviewed draft after draft, suggesting minor changes and raising marginal issues for reconsideration by his lawyer. We all assumed that John's revisions were completed and that the Pocantico issue had finally been put to rest. No doubt this would have been the case if tragedy had not intervened.

THE DEATH OF JOHN

I last saw John on July 9, 1978. He and Blanchette came to Hudson Pines for Sunday lunch with Peggy and me. We had a relaxed meal on the dining terrace in the shade of a big elm tree. Peggy told John of her new interest in raising purebred Simmenthal cattle. As with everything else she undertook, Peggy had become passionately involved with farming, and after lunch she persuaded John to go for a carriage drive to see some of her prize animals. I stayed back at the house with Blanchette to discuss Museum of Modern Art matters.

John was impressed by what he saw, and the following afternoon, after spending the day working on his will with his secretary, he took her to see the cattle on his way to the railway station to catch a train back to New York. His secretary was driving because John was still recovering from ankle replacement surgery.

As they proceeded along Bedford Road, a Volkswagen driven by a young man, who had just left his house upset over an argument with his parents, was approaching from the other direction. Rounding a bend in the road, he lost control of the car, careened off a tree, and slammed directly into John's approaching vehicle. John's secretary was severely injured; her recovery would be long and painful. The young boy died at the scene of the accident. John was killed instantly.

When I learned the news, I thought not of our annoying disputes but of all the little kindnesses he'd shown me when we were younger, things that he had probably forgotten but that had meant so much to me. Even though John was almost ten years my senior, he had made the greatest effort of all my brothers to reach out to me. We were not really close, but his comforting support when I needed it led me to ask him to be the best man at my wedding.

As with Father, life had been difficult for John, but he left behind a legacy of accomplishment in the field of philanthropy of which even a Rockefeller could be proud. Like all of us, John had imperfections, but he was a decent, honorable, and compassionate man who cared deeply about the world, hated injustice, and devoted his time, talent, and resources unstintingly to those causes that held the greatest promise for producing real and lasting change. His courageous campaign to reduce the alarming rate of world population growth, his generous support of the arts, and his visionary efforts to link the peoples and nations of the Far East more closely to the United States have had a lasting impact. I regret that the full measure of John's accomplishments have never been adequately understood or recognized.

NELSON'S REVENGE

D eath does not always soothe passions or put an end to hostilities. Ironically, John's death actually reignited them. Nelson learned that John's will did not include the $5 million provision for Pocantico; he was beside himself. As the pertinent provisions were read to us, I could see Nelson's eyes harden with anger. It made no difference to Nelson that John had finally included the $5 million in his will; all that counted was his failure to have signed it. As far as Nelson was concerned, Johnnie had double-crossed him, and he wasn't going to put up with it.

Nelson promptly summoned his lawyers and rewrote his will, removing the $5 million for the Pocantico endowment, leaving his share of the open spaces to Happy, and bequeathing his portion of the historic area specifically to the National Trust for Historic Preservation. He provided his executors with no flexibility to modify these provisions in the event of his death.

Nelson did not inform either Laurance or me about these changes until almost six months later, in December 1978. At that time he called us to his office and informed us that if we wanted to proceed with the Pocantico plan as originally negotiated, we would have to buy his portion of the open spaces from Happy after his death. I was outraged and told Nelson so. Nelson retreated a bit when he saw how angry I was. He said his will was not final, and he hoped we would be able to get things back on track. But it wouldn't turn out that way.

When I asked him why he had made these changes, Nelson explained that Carl Humelsine, the head of the National Trust for Historic Preservation, had assured him the trust, by congressional action, would be the recipient of millions of dollars from the sale of offshore oil leases and would easily be able to develop and maintain Kykuit for historic preservation and public visitation; therefore, none of us would have to put up any of our own money for the endowment.

I shook my head in disbelief. Nelson knew enough about the promises of politicians (he had made a number of them himself) to know that such things are subject to change—as, sure enough, they were. The legislation appropriating these funds did not pass Congress. Nevertheless, motivated by a desire to strike back at John and show who was in command, Nelson did not change this provision in his will and provided his executors with no discretion in the matter. His will automatically transferred his interest in the historic area to the National Trust. Nelson's final gesture would cost me, and to a lesser degree Laurance, many millions of dollars and even more headaches over the next fifteen years.

NELSON'S FINAL MONTHS

As Nelson's drive to take over the Family Office and the RBF was thwarted, he drew back from family affairs. He devoted his time instead to two colorful new enterprises.

The first was a company that made reproductions of objects in his personal art collection and sold them to the public. In some ways this was quite appropriate since Nelson's greatest hobby and form of relaxation was collecting art. Nelson had come across an amazingly accurate process for reproducing art and speculated that there might be a fairly large market for high-quality reproductions—especially if his name was linked to them. To that end he reproduced many of his finest works and sold them from a shop that he leased on 57th Street in Manhattan and through Neiman-Marcus stores. Although the company soon began to show a modest profit, most of us in the family, with the exception of my wife Peggy, looked on the idea with considerable skepticism.

The second project was even more ambitious. Together with George Woods, a former president of the World Bank, Nelson formed the Saudi Arabian–American Corporation (Sarabam). In partnership with a few prominent Saudi businessmen, Woods and Nelson planned to use Saudi oil revenues and American managerial expertise to carry out social and economic development projects in the Middle East. They hoped to persuade the Saudi government and a few other Arab producers to invest a billion dollars of their surplus funds and then give the partners 50 percent of the profits for managing it. While directing Arab oil money into more productive uses than bank CDs and government bonds certainly made sense, it was naive to think that Arab governments would put up all the money and then share evenly in the profits with Nelson and his partners. It was a grandiose scheme, characteristic of Nelson, but I wasn't surprised when the Saudis backed out.

Nelson always wanted to make money, and he greatly respected those who were successful in business. It was largely for that reason that he and Peggy had a rapprochement. One Sunday at lunch Peggy told him she had sold one of her prize Simmenthal bulls for a million dollars. One could see

Nelson's expression change at the news; he looked at Peggy with a new-found respect and was exceedingly interested in all the details of her business. It was curious that after all the years of a respectful but formal relationship, Peggy became the person in the family with whom Nelson felt most comfortable.

In the final months of his life Nelson struck me as a very unhappy man. He was fatalistic about many things and seemed to have lost the will to live. He had heart problems, but he never told Happy and refused to see a heart specialist. He consulted only Dr. Riland, who would put him on his table to manipulate his back and limbs three times a week. In mid-January 1979 I left on a Chase trip to the Middle East. Before departing I called Nelson, and I remember thinking at the time that he was warmer and more solicitous than he was wont to be when I was just going on a trip, which, after all, was a frequent occurrence for both of us. I remember wondering if I would ever see him again. It was, in fact, the last time we ever spoke.

THE DEATH OF NELSON

I was in the Sultan of Oman's anteroom in Muscat when I learned Nelson had died. I was shocked, but I felt it only courteous to see Sultan Qabus briefly. He expressed his sympathy in the warmest terms and even offered to have me flown back to New York in his own 747. Although grateful for his offer, I returned on the Chase plane. When we touched down at the White Plains airport, Peggy was waiting on the tarmac. She took me aside to tell me the circumstances surrounding Nelson's death, all of which would soon appear in the papers. It was a sad ending for a man whose career had been so distinguished. But with the passage of time, memory of this unfortunate episode has faded, and Nelson's extraordinary accomplishments have been properly recognized and understood.

=

From the time he was a teenager Nelson seemed to know what he wanted to do in life and how to get there. While he greatly admired both of our grandfathers, politics—Grandfather Aldrich's calling—intrigued him the most. And once embarked on that course, Nelson set his sights even more firmly on the ultimate position of power: the presidency of the United States. He understood that leadership within the family would be critical to his plans. After graduating from Dartmouth he played active roles with Mother at the Museum of Modern Art, and with Father in building Rockefeller Center.

Nelson was also the driving force in organizing his brothers into a cohesive unit.

From the time of his service as President Roosevelt's Coordinator of the Office of Inter-American Affairs, Nelson demonstrated the qualities that would become legendary: hard work, great ingenuity, and personal magnetism. He learned to speak Spanish fluently and could even hold his own in Portuguese. Nelson became an expert on the politics and security needs of the region, and earned the lasting friendship and admiration of many Latin American leaders. Indeed, in many countries he was looked upon as a hero.

After the war Nelson worked briefly for President Truman, served as the first deputy secretary of the Department of Health, Education and Welfare, and finally as a special assistant to President Eisenhower. Through it all Nelson proved himself to be an able administrator and an innovative policy maker on both domestic and international issues.

His greatest public contributions, however, were made during his four terms as governor of New York. He believed, as did I, that government had an essential role to play in creating a more humane and progressive society. Although a Republican, Nelson established close and enduring ties with organized labor and minority groups. Never one to let tradition stand in his way, Nelson transformed the nature and function of New York State's government by reforming its structure and infusing it with a spirit of change and innovation. Among his many accomplishments was the development of the state's system of higher education, a dramatic expansion of its parks, and a thorough revision of its system of taxation. Under Nelson, New York became a model of progressive state government.

Nelson hoped to translate his successes in New York into enduring national power. But in this he failed. He was never quite at home in the National Republican Party. He was also considered too liberal on social issues for the emerging conservative wing of the party. To this day "Rockefeller Republicans" are anathema to staunch right-wingers. Finally, Nelson's divorce from Tod and marriage to Happy set him back both in the party and in the polls, and he never recovered.

Nelson was a strong, creative leader and one of the most effective American politicians and administrators of the twentieth century. He was also one of the few visionary international statesmen that our country has produced. He would have been a magnificent president.

CHAPTER 24

THE SHAH

It is ironic that of all the people I have known during my life, the only non-family member to whom I feel compelled to devote a chapter in these memoirs is the Shah of Iran. While I admired the Shah, he and I were little more than acquaintances. We had a cordial but formal relationship; he addressed me as "Mr. Rockefeller," and I addressed him as "Your Imperial Majesty." The primary topic in all our meetings was business. I felt my having contact with the Shah would enhance Chase's stature with the government of Iran; the Shah saw Chase as a financial resource that was useful in his efforts to quicken his country's economic growth and improve its social well-being. In fact, my relationship with the Shah was similar to those I had with most national leaders in countries where Chase operated.

My association with the Shah became the subject of intense public scrutiny only after the seizure of the American embassy in Tehran in November 1979. As the "hostage crisis" unfolded, the search for scapegoats to blame for the debacle began. Media reports about my alleged role in "forcing" President Jimmy Carter to allow the Shah to enter the United States for medical treatment in October 1979 provided the American public with an inaccurate picture of my relationship with the Shah and his regime.

The media, learning that Henry Kissinger and I, along with a few others, had helped the Shah find sanctuary, first in the Bahamas and then in Mexico, concluded we had "pressured" the President to allow him into the United States. "For eight months," Bernard Gwertzman would write on the front page of the November 18, 1979, *New York Times,* "Mr. Carter and Mr.

Vance had resisted intense lobbying from American friends of the Shah, such as David Rockefeller, the Shah's banker, and former Secretary of State Henry Kissinger, to stop treating the deposed ruler like, in Henry Kissinger's words, 'a flying "Dutchman" unable to find a safe haven.' " Others would claim my motive was greed—the desire to retain the "Shah's billions of dollars" for the Chase.

Actually, I had no contact with the Shah until two and a half months after he was forced to leave Iran, and then only because the Carter administration had seemingly turned its back on him. Several months later when I learned the Shah had cancer, I informed the Carter administration of this fact, but my communications with the U.S. government were brief and formal.

Until now I have never provided the full story of my involvement in this controversial episode.

MOHAMMAD REZA PAHLAVI

Mohammad Reza Pahlavi owed his seat on the Peacock Throne to foreign intervention during World War II, and for the next four turbulent decades Iran's enormous oil reserves and proximity to the Soviet Union ensured that it would be in the interest of the Western powers to keep him there. For the first three decades of the Shah's reign, Great Britain exercised predominant political and economic influence in Iran, as it had for more than a century throughout the Persian Gulf. This changed in 1968 when Prime Minister Harold Wilson announced his country would withdraw its military forces from east of Suez by early 1971. The task of containing the Soviet Union and protecting the vital oil reserves of the region now devolved on the United States.

The Nixon Doctrine, which called for smaller regional powers supported and supplied by the United States to carry the burden of defense against Communist expansion around the world, became the controlling policy, and in the Persian Gulf the "twin pillars" would be Saudi Arabia and Iran.

The Shah took action to bolster his own position. He systematically eliminated political opposition and centralized control of Iran's economic affairs in his own hands. The Shah sought to transform his traditionalist Islamic society by introducing a public health system, establishing public schools throughout the country and making education compulsory for women as well as men, and instituting universal suffrage, giving women the right to vote for the first time.

The Shah's modernizing reforms met strong opposition from Muslim clerics and the bazaar merchants. They inveighed constantly against what they saw as the degradation of Iran's Islamic culture through the effects of westernization and prosperity: the short skirts, jeans, movies, and discotheques.

In the early 1970s when huge amounts of oil revenue flooded into Iran, the Shah poured money into infrastructure: roads, ports, airfields, electrification, hospitals, and schools. And he emphasized the diversification of industry, producing an enviable economic growth rate that was unparalleled in any other country at that time, at least for a few years.

While the Shah did much to transform Iran into a modern state, there was a dark side to his regime. SAVAK, the secret police, repressed those who opposed the regime or simply demanded a more democratic political order. Over time he became more and more isolated from the realities of life in his own country, and his regime became increasingly inflexible and repressive. Therein lay the seeds of his demise.

MEETING ON THE SLOPES

Prior to the 1970s my contacts with the Shah were confined to two brief meetings: an audience in Tehran in 1965 and a dinner in 1968 when Harvard awarded him an honorary degree. Chase, on the other hand, had long maintained strong correspondent relationships with the Bank Markazi, Iran's central bank; the Bank Melli, the largest commercial bank; and a dozen other commercial banks. More important, by the mid-1970s we had become the lead bank for the National Iranian Oil Company (NIOC), the state-owned corporation that dominated the country's economy. We had even been able to briefly penetrate Iran's highly protected domestic banking system by setting up a development bank there in partnership with Lazard Frères in 1957. However, the Iranian government subsequently restricted both our ownership percentage and the operations of the institution, snuffing out a promising opportunity.

For the next decade I looked for a way to establish a direct commercial banking presence in Iran, but with no success. A realistic opportunity finally emerged in the early 1970s, for which we needed the permission of the Shah to proceed.

＝

In January 1974, only a few months after the first "oil shock," I stopped off to see the Shah in Saint-Moritz with some Chase associates and my son

Richard. We were on our way to the Middle East and had learned the Shah was skiing in Switzerland. Richard took notes of the meeting, which lasted nearly two hours and covered many subjects.

The Shah believed the price of oil should be determined by the cost of extracting oil from shale, a price even higher than the one artificially imposed by the OPEC cartel. He pointed out that petroleum was a nonrenewable resource that would be depleted within a finite number of years; therefore, a high price would be good because it would force the world to develop new sources of energy. Oil's most valuable use, he said, was for petrochemicals, and we should use other energy sources for fuel. He insisted that high oil prices were a favor, not a disservice, to the industrial world.

The Shah envisioned a golden future for his country as a result of higher oil prices. Iran, he assured us, would become an industrial power and, within twenty-five years, one of the top five economies in the world, alongside the United States, Russia, China, and Brazil. He claimed incorrectly, but I did not challenge him, that Tehran had already replaced Beirut as the financial center of the Middle East and that before long it would rival both London and New York.

Our two-hour conversation—the longest I would ever have with him—touched on many topics, from Soviet designs on Iran to President Nixon and his Watergate troubles. Henry Kissinger had told me the Shah was an exceptionally able man with a strong grasp of international affairs. I certainly found this to be the case, but there was also an arrogance that underlay his pronouncements on many of these issues; they lacked plausibility and betrayed an alarming isolation from political and economic reality.

The Shah seemed to think that because he believed something, it was automatically a fact. The term *hubris* occurred to me as I sat listening to him outline his startling vision of an imperial Iran reclaiming the ancient domain of the Medes and the Persians. He seemed unconcerned about the havoc the oil price increases had already caused in the global economy, let alone what his extravagant proposals would generate.

A few days later in Tehran, I discussed the meeting with Ambassador Richard Helms. Dick, who had only recently taken up his post after serving as the director of the CIA, felt the Iranians were really "feeling their oats." Oil wealth and their predominant military position in the Gulf, largely the result of assistance from the United States, had transformed Iran's strategic and economic position. But Helms also noted that "their biggest problem is that they have the money, the materials, but not the trained manpower necessary to handle them. What is perhaps even more serious, the ministers are not sophisticated or experienced enough to cope with the added governmental complications which their sudden enormous wealth is bringing them."

"SOMETHING REALLY BIG"

I had not stopped in Saint-Moritz to tap the Shah's geopolitical expertise but rather to discuss Chase's effort to purchase an interest in an Iranian commercial bank. Six months earlier I had raised this issue at a brief meeting at Blair House during one of his visits to Washington. The Shah, who was in the process of negotiating an economic and arms agreement with the United States, gave me authorization to explore the possibility of purchasing an Iranian bank. However, the two banks we had been allowed to approach were, to put it mildly, lemons—badly managed and with negative cash values.

When I told the Shah in Saint-Moritz this was not the opportunity Chase had been looking for, he agreed and said, "It might be best to permit the establishment of an entirely new bank. I have recently permitted three or four new merchant banks, so why not one more?" He said he would wire Tehran that night giving the necessary instructions. He urged me not to become involved with small commercial loans but to "do something really big."

The Shah was as good as his word, and over the next year and a half we put together a joint venture with the state-owned Industrial Credit Bank to form the International Bank of Iran (IBI) to finance economic development projects as well as help with the formation of an Iranian capital market. Chase invested $12.6 million and owned 35 percent of the new bank. The Shah's help had been essential, but it was the only time he ever intervened on Chase's behalf.

After Chase established a physical presence in Tehran, it was the bank's deposit gathering and trade finance activities from which we benefited most substantially. As Iran earned more from the sale of oil after 1973, Iranian deposits maintained with Chase increased dramatically. In addition, our trade finance business boomed because we continued to finance a significant portion of Iran's oil exports. By the mid-1970s as much as $50 to $60 million a day passed through Chase, and Iranian deposits at one point in late 1978 exceeded $1 billion. When Iran entered the international capital markets in the mid-1970s to finance its large public sector projects, Chase took the lead in floating eight syndicated loans. By 1979 we had served as agent for syndications totaling $1.7 billion, of which our portion was about $330 million. These were significant but by no means extraordinary amounts, given that Chase's total foreign lending at the end of 1979 was more than $22 billion and our total deposits exceeded $48 billion.

Moreover, none of these financial links depended on my having a "special relationship" with the Shah; they were the result of Chase's leading role in world financial markets. Ironically, we were never successful in attracting the Shah himself as a customer; he preferred to keep most of his money in Switzerland.

A PESSIMISTIC PICTURE

The promise of the Shah's regime depended largely on how the Iranian monarch used his newfound oil wealth to reform his country's political and economic structure. There was certainly enough money to do this, but money by itself was not the answer. This was one of the messages that I delivered to him in Saint-Moritz.

In 1975, when diplomatic and political relations between the United States and Iran grew closer as a result of the Nixon-Kissinger initiatives, I was asked to join the board of the newly formed Iran-U.S. Business Council, the private sector counterpart of the U.S.-Iran Joint Committee. The latter had been formed by Henry Kissinger and Hushang Ansary, the minister of finance and economy, to explore ways in which the two nations might improve their economic ties. In late 1975 the Joint Committee asked the Business Council to organize a conference in Tehran to advise the Iranian government on the steps they needed to take in order to play a larger role in global financial markets.

Hushang Ansary told me that the Shah understood the need for reform and urged that the meeting be convened as soon as possible. I asked our Chase economists to put together background papers for the conference, which I would chair. We scheduled the meeting for March 1976 in Tehran and assembled a distinguished group of Americans that included Paul Volcker, then president of the New York Federal Reserve Bank; Donald Regan, chairman of Merrill Lynch & Co.; Peter G. Peterson, chairman of Lehman Brothers; and the heads of several major U.S. commercial banks. The Iranians fielded a delegation of senior cabinet ministers, bankers, and businessmen.

The Chase economists painted a pessimistic picture of Iran that was difficult to reconcile with the Shah's own vision of financial and economic hegemony. Iran had large quantities of oil money and every expectation that this source of income would continue to grow. But almost nothing else was in place to ensure this windfall would be turned to productive use. Iran lacked both an organized money market and a stock exchange; its currency was weak, and its foreign exchange was in disarray. Even more important, the Iranian legal and governmental system lacked transparency, accountability, and credibility, all necessary for attracting foreign investment. The government owned everything of any economic consequence and managed everything from the top down and from the center out, which produced tremendous waste, inefficiency, and corruption. To get anything done required paying bribes, knowing someone in power, or both. The Shah's family and members of his inner circle benefited from this system and did not wish to see it changed. Until these basic conditions were changed, there was little likelihood that the Shah would realize his vision of Tehran as an international financial center or of Iran as an important global economic force.

The Iranians were not pleased with our findings. At the dinner that concluded the conference Prime Minister Amir Abbas Hoveyda subjected us to an impassioned harangue for exporting "a lack of morality" to Iran. He denounced American companies for bribing Iranian officials and then accepting kickbacks for multimillion-dollar military procurement deals. Hoveyda's remarks were a self-serving, gratuitous attempt to blame the West for problems that seemed to be deeply embedded in the Iranian system.

When we called on the Shah to report the conference's conclusions, he promised to study them, but I think he already sensed that Iran's sudden increase in wealth had intensified but had not solved his country's problems. The Shah had inaugurated a process of social and political change, but it remained to be seen whether he would control it or if it would control him.

But for the moment the Shah's domestic position remained strong and his relations with the United States firm. In late 1977, President and Mrs. Carter paid an official visit to the Shah in Tehran. At a state banquet on New Year's Eve, President Carter in televised remarks spoke of the importance of U.S.-Iranian relations. He said in part: "Iran, because of the great leadership of the Shah, is an island of stability in one of the more troubled areas of the world. . . . We have no other nation with whom we have closer consultation on regional problems that concern us both. And there is no leader with whom I have a deeper sense of personal gratitude and personal friendship."

THE END OF THE DYNASTY

On my final visit to Iran in March 1978, everything appeared calm, but I sensed an increasing discontent with the Shah's rule among those with whom we talked. When I called on the Shah at the Niavaran Palace, he was polite and interested in what I had to say, but we learned from others that he had become more and more isolated, impatient of criticism, and indecisive. The dramatic growth of the Iranian economy had leveled off after 1975 and had been replaced by recession, a severe retrenchment in government expenditures, and growing unemployment. We saw evidence in the streets of Tehran of the religiously driven civil unrest that within a few months would become a full-scale revolution against the Shah's regime.

Nine months later the Shah took the controls of a Boeing 707 and flew out of Tehran for the last time. His odyssey had begun.

THE SHAH IN EXILE

When the Shah departed Tehran in mid-January 1979, I assumed he would come directly to the United States where President Carter had offered him political asylum. Instead, he and his entourage flew to Egypt at Anwar Sadat's invitation. I did not give much thought to his movements because I was more concerned about the Iranian revolution's impact on Chase. As it turned out, the new Iranian government, headed by Mehdi Bazargan, a moderate nationalist who wanted to both democratize and modernize his country, soon permitted foreign businesses to resume operations, and Chase's financial relations with Iran returned to normal. Thus, while I personally regretted the circumstances of the Shah's departure, I had no reason to think I would have anything further to do with him.

=====

A few days after the Shah left Tehran, I embarked on a trip to the Middle East. My first stop was Egypt, where I was to meet with Anwar Sadat in Aswan on January 22, 1979. Sadat was late and apologized, explaining he had been at the airport bidding farewell to the Shah, who was bound for Morocco at the invitation of King Hassan. Sadat said he had urged the Shah to remain in Egypt so that he could return quickly to Iran if conditions changed. The Shah had shrugged off his advice, claiming the Americans "had forced him out" and would never allow him to return.*

---

*Chase officer Archibald Roosevelt, cousin of Kermit Roosevelt, the CIA officer who had engineered the 1953 coup that restored the Shah to the throne, was with me on the trip. Archie, who had also worked for the CIA, had an astonishing political and historical knowledge of central Asia and the Persian Gulf region. Archie said he thought the "game was up" for the Shah in Iran.

The Ayatollah Ruhollah Khomeini's triumphant return to Iran in early February eliminated any possibility that the Shah might be restored to his throne. Adoring crowds chanting "Death to the Shah" greeted the elderly cleric, and the interim government installed by the Shah as well as the Iranian army and air force quickly capitulated. Even though Khomeini initially backed Bazargan's government, they disagreed profoundly on many issues, and the question of who would rule Iran remained in doubt for a number of months. While Bazargan worked assiduously to rebuild external relations, the Ayatollah's hatred of the United States became a potent force in Iranian politics. In mid-February, Iranian radicals seized the American embassy and briefly held Ambassador William Sullivan and his staff hostage until Bazargan intervened to have them released.

Despite this incident, the United States officially recognized the Bazargan government in late February. The Carter administration had decided to work with the moderates in the hopes of strengthening their position against the two extremes that had emerged in the Iranian political landscape: the Marxist left and the fundamentalist right. As a result, the Carter administration quietly changed its position on granting the Shah political asylum.

=

Before the Shah left Iran, Ambassador Sullivan had given assurances that he and his family would be welcomed in the United States. The President himself publicly reinforced this invitation when he noted at a press conference on January 17, "The Shah's now in Egypt and he will later come to our own country." Soon after the Shah's arrival in Morocco, Ambassador Richard Parker assured him that President Carter's offer of asylum in the United States remained open, but suggested that he might want to expedite his departure in case circumstances changed. The Shah ignored the Ambassador's advice and remained in Marrakesh for several more weeks.

King Hassan of Morocco was a gracious host, but he had his own problems with Islamic fundamentalism. In addition, in early April, Hassan would host a meeting of the Islamic Conference, which included Arab leaders who had been hostile to the Shah. Consequently, the King asked the Shah to leave and to do so not later than March 30. The Shah then informed Ambassador Parker that he was ready to accept President Carter's offer of asylum. But, as I would soon learn, it was already too late.

By early March the Carter administration had determined that supporting the Bazargan government had to take precedence over granting the Shah asylum. The National Security Council, with National Security

Advisor Zbig Brzezinski vigorously dissenting, concluded that the Shah should not be allowed to enter the United States. President Carter concurred and asked Secretary of State Cyrus Vance to, in Carter's words, "scout around to help find him a place to stay."

TURNING DOWN THE PRESIDENT

I first became aware of the change in policy on March 14, 1979, when David Newsom, Under Secretary of State for Political Affairs, telephoned me in New York. Newsom said he was calling on President Carter's behalf. The President had reviewed the situation in Iran, including the threat that Americans might be seized as hostages if the Shah came to the United States, and had decided it was no longer prudent to allow him to enter the country, at least at that time. Newsom asked if I would fly to Morocco and inform the Shah of the decision.

Newsom's request surprised me, not least because my relationship with the Shah had never been that close. Taken aback, I immediately refused. One does not lightly turn down a request from the President of the United States, but I told Newsom I found it incomprehensible that the President would ignore American tradition by denying political asylum to a man who had been a great friend of our country. I refused to become complicit in the decision.

Henry Kissinger said later that Newsom had called him first, and he had rejected the request just as firmly as I. Henry called the decision "a national dishonor." In the end, Ambassador Parker delivered the message and also told the Shah that the State Department, after extensive inquiries, had found only two countries, South Africa and Paraguay, willing to receive him. The Shah was unwilling to go to either country.

A SISTER'S PLEA

A little more than a week after my conversation with David Newsom, I received word from Princess Ashraf, the Shah's twin sister, that she wanted to speak with me. I had met Ashraf casually on a few occasions when she was Iran's representative on the U.N.'s Women's Rights Commission. Joseph Reed and I called on her at her Beekman Place town house in New York late on Friday afternoon, March 23.

Ashraf, a tiny woman, was fiercely devoted to her family and very tough-minded. In obvious distress she described her brother's dire situation and begged me to intervene with President Carter to reverse his decision or at least help to find the Shah a haven somewhere else. Ashraf informed us that King Hassan had set a deadline of seven days hence for her brother's departure from Morocco. "My brother has nowhere to go," she said, "and no one else to turn to."

I was in an awkward position. There was nothing in my previous relationship with the Shah that made me feel a strong obligation to him. He had never been a friend to whom I owed a personal debt, and neither was his relationship with the bank one that would justify my taking personal risks on his behalf. Indeed, there might be severe repercussions for Chase if the Iranian authorities determined that I was being too helpful to the Shah and his family. Therefore, I listened to the Princess with interest and concern without making a commitment to take any action.

That same evening I had dinner with Henry Kissinger and Happy Rockefeller, Nelson's widow, at her home in Pocantico. Henry and I discussed our telephone calls from David Newsom and the Shah's plight. Happy told me of Nelson's close friendship with the Shah and about the weekend they had spent with him and Farah Diba, the Shah's wife, in Tehran in 1977. Happy reminded me that when the Shah realized he would have to leave Iran, Nelson offered to find a suitable property for him in the United States.

We also talked about the precedent that President Carter had established by refusing to admit the Shah into the United States. Both of us believed our allies, particularly those in the Middle East such as Sadat and King Hussein, who had taken great risks on our behalf, were likely to entertain second thoughts about the dependability of the United States in light of this action. In view of these concerns and Nelson's offer, Henry and I agreed to do what we could to help the Shah while the Carter administration continued to mull over whether and under what circumstances he might be admitted to the United States. Jack McCloy, one of the "wise men" of American foreign policy who had counseled the President on a number of matters during his first years in office, soon joined our effort.

FINDING A SAFE HAVEN

We had learned that no European or Middle Eastern country other than Egypt was willing to risk the wrath of the new satraps of Persia by granting the Shah asylum, so we concentrated our efforts on the Western

Hemisphere. The response was not good, but in the nick of time Henry persuaded the foreign minister of the Bahamas to grant the Shah a temporary visa to enter his country. The Shah and his party arrived there on March 30.

The Shah was met in Nassau by Robert Armao; this young public relations man had served on Nelson's gubernatorial and vice presidential staffs, and had continued to work for him after he retired from public life. Princess Ashraf had retained Armao to improve her brother's public image in the United States in late 1978, and it was Armao who negotiated the initial arrangements for the Shah's stay in the Bahamas. Armao faced a difficult task because of the unwillingness of American officials to provide assistance, so I asked Joseph Reed to help him in any way he could. For the next few months Joseph and Armao found themselves, quite unexpectedly, in the position of having to manage most aspects of the Shah's life in exile—from hiring security guards to finding schools for the Shah's children. In addition, Joseph served as liaison with the U.S. government, reporting regularly to David Newsom at the State Department on the Shah's situation and occasionally passing information back to him.

In early April 1979 none of us could anticipate either the length or the nature of the Shah's exile, or, indeed, where he would eventually find a permanent refuge. Henry and I assumed, based on what administration officials told us, that, after a relatively short sojourn in the Bahamas, the President would allow the Shah to enter the United States.

That, alas, did not happen. It soon became apparent that the Bahamas' prime minister, Linden Pindling, and his associates were much more interested in making money from the Shah than in providing him with privacy and security. Pindling insisted, for instance, that the Shah's party stay on Paradise Island, the tourist area just outside Nassau in which Pindling had a personal interest. Both Armao and Joseph reported that the Shah was worried about rumors of "roving hit squads" sent by the Ayatollah; and he was incensed that Pindling and his cronies seemed to be bleeding him for every dime he had. The Shah's treatment in the Bahamas was so disgraceful that after a few weeks we began looking for alternatives.

AN ICY WHITE HOUSE MEETING

Just after the Shah arrived in Nassau, I made my one and only direct effort to persuade President Carter to admit him into the United States. The Shah, Joseph reported to me, was "deeply wounded by the personal disloyalty of Carter." A month or so earlier I had scheduled a meeting with the President for April 9 to discuss the Westway project in New York City. I decided to use the opportunity to inform the President about the concerns that a number of foreign leaders had recently expressed to me about our treatment of the Shah. I prepared a one-page brief, which I handed to the President at the end of our Oval Office meeting. My paper noted in part:

> During the past several months, I have had an opportunity to visit more than twenty countries in Asia, Africa, Europe and the Middle East. Many of the countries I visited are relatively small and not of primary significance to United States objectives, but nevertheless, tend to consider themselves friends of the United States.
>
> With virtually no exceptions, the heads of state and other government leaders I saw expressed concern about United States foreign policy which they perceive to be vacillating and lacking in an understandable global approach. In this regard, the uneven application of laudable human rights objectives were frequently alluded to. As a result of events in China and Taiwan, and the implications they perceive for Taiwan and the Shah, they have questions about the dependability of the United States as a friend.

I suggested it would be useful for the President to invite the leaders of these countries to Washington in order to reassure them that they could continue to count on our support. Carter reacted coolly, indicating only that he would discuss the matter with his advisors.

Before leaving I also urged the President to permit the Shah to enter the country. I told him that if there were threats to our Tehran embassy, we should take the necessary precautions, but it seemed to me that a great power should not submit to blackmail. The President was clearly irritated, and after I finished, he stiffly brought our meeting to an end.

＝

With conditions worsening in the Bahamas and the American option firmly closed, at least temporarily, both Henry and I looked elsewhere for a country that would accept the Shah and to which he would willingly go. There were not many names on the list, but one possibility was Austria. In late April at a meeting of the Bilderberg group in Vienna, I spoke with Chancellor Bruno Kreisky, who seemed sympathetic to the Shah's plight. "As a Jew," he told me, "I know what it is to be a refugee." I left Vienna believing Kreisky would admit the Shah. We maintained contact with him, but a formal invitation was never issued.

Henry Kissinger had more luck. The two of us had met with Mexico's president, José Lopez Portillo, a number of times in the late 1970s and had established a good relationship with him. Henry persuaded Lopez Portillo to override the objections of his foreign minister, who felt it wasn't Mexico's role to bail out the United States, and issue visas to the Shah and his family, who arrived in Cuernavaca on June 10, 1979. The Mexican government was considerate, and the Shah found his new surroundings quite pleasant.

TURNING DOWN THE PRESIDENT AGAIN

With the Shah safely settled in Mexico, I had hopes that the need for my direct involvement on his behalf had ended. Therefore, while Henry continued to publicly criticize the Carter administration for its overall management of the Iranian crisis and other aspects of its foreign policy, and Jack McCloy bombarded Cyrus Vance with letters demanding the Shah's admission to the United States, I did nothing else, publicly or privately, to influence the administration's thinking on this matter.

Despite President Carter's irritation with me for trying to persuade him to allow the Shah's entry into the United States, he seemingly did not hold that against me. My relations with him and other senior members of his administration remained good—so good, in fact, that on July 19 the President called me out of a Chase board meeting to ask me to replace Mike Blumenthal as Secretary of the Treasury. I went to Washington the following day to discuss the matter with him, but we quickly realized our views on managing the nation's financial affairs were too far apart to bridge easily. The President appointed William Miller, then chairman of the Federal Reserve Board, to the Treasury post.

To my surprise, a few days later Miller called on the President's behalf to ask if I would consider replacing him as chairman of the Fed! It was an offer I considered seriously, but in the end I declined it as well. I would have been responsible for implementing a set of draconian policies to wring inflation from the economy and stabilize the dollar. As a wealthy Republican with a well-known name, and a banker to boot, it would have been extremely difficult for me to make the case for tight monetary policy and sell it to a skeptical Congress and an angry public. I spoke with my friend Andre Meyer, and he agreed that the obstacles were too daunting to overcome. I reported my decision to Bill Miller and strongly recommended Paul Volcker, then the president of the New York Federal Reserve Bank, for the job.

"ADMITTED FOR HUMANITARIAN REASONS"

President Carter's Iranian policy began to unravel during the summer of 1979. The Bazargan government hung on to power, but just barely. His efforts to get Iran's economy up and running again had shown some success; oil began to flow once again to the tankers waiting patiently to take on their cargoes at Kharg Island. American and European companies, including the Chase, resumed operations in the spring as soon as the disorders produced by the Shah's departure and the return of the Ayatollah died down. However, the balance of political forces was precarious, and any unexpected event, even a minor one, might undermine the still fragile situation and produce another crisis.

Such an event began to unfold in Cuernavaca during the summer of 1979 when the Shah became ill. Joseph Reed saw him in early August and noticed his watchband was extremely loose, but passed it off as some sort of royal affectation. A month later Joseph found the Shah had lost more weight and was clearly suffering from jaundice; Joseph was told the Shah might have malaria.

Late in September, Bob Armao told Joseph that the Shah's condition had deteriorated and asked him to contact Dr. Benjamin Kean of New York Hospital, a tropical medicine specialist. Kean flew to Cuernavaca, examined the Shah, and concluded he had obstructive jaundice caused by either gallbladder disease or pancreatic cancer. He wanted to do further tests, but the Shah refused. Joseph informed David Newsom of this development, saying it might be necessary for the Shah to come to the United States for medical treatment. Newsom replied that a "substantial medical case" would have to be made before he would be allowed to enter the country.

The Shah's condition worsened, and three weeks later, on October 18, Dr. Kean was again summoned to Mexico. At that time the Shah told Kean he had lymphoma and that a team of French doctors had been treating him secretly for a number of years. Only a few people close to the Shah, his wife among them, knew this. Amazingly, no one in the United States in or out of government had any inkling of the Shah's illness. Kean immediately informed the State Department's medical officer that the Shah was suffering from a malignant lymphoma complicated by a possible internal blockage that had produced the jaundice. In terms of treatment, Kean said that, given time, a medical team could be assembled to treat the Shah in Mexico, but it would be better for him to go to New York. Kean also called Joseph in New York, and I then instructed Joseph to telephone Newsom and inform him that the severity of the Shah's medical problems argued in favor of his immediate admission to the United States and that I would be willing to make the arrangements at a hospital in New York.

President Carter and his advisors considered these facts at a meeting on October 20. As Cyrus Vance noted in his memoirs, *Hard Choices,* "We were faced squarely with a decision in which common decency and humanity had to be weighed against possible harm to our embassy personnel in Tehran." After careful consideration, President Carter announced that the Shah would be allowed to come to New York for "diagnostics and evaluation on humanitarian grounds."

Prime Minister Bazargan was personally notified of the Shah's condition by the U.S. Chargé d'Affaires. While the Iranian leaders warned there would be hostile demonstrations, they felt the American embassy would be safe. The administration also received assurances from President Lopez Portillo that the Shah would be allowed to return to Mexico following his medical treatment in the United States.

The Shah was then informed on October 22 that he could proceed to the United States. However, the U.S. government still took no "official" responsibility for the Shah. When his chartered plane landed in New York early in the morning of October 23, it was met by Bob Armao, who accompanied him to New York Hospital, where Joseph Reed had arranged to have him admitted under the pseudonym "David Newsome," which the real Newsom didn't think very amusing when he found out.

THE HOSTAGE CRISIS

The reaction to the Shah's arrival in New York was muted. A few hundred protestors took up station outside New York Hospital and denounced the Shah, but they were largely ignored. In Iran the reaction was very different. Within days, massive demonstrations erupted all across the country, culminating in the attack on the U.S. embassy and the seizure of more than seventy Americans on November 4. Ominously, the "students" holding the embassy, who claimed they were "following the Imam's line" on behalf of the Ayatollah Khomeini, demanded the Shah's extradition to Iran to stand trial for his crimes as the price for the release of the hostages.

The Ayatollah had an "event," and the more radical phase of the Iranian revolution was about to begin.

Bazargan's efforts to free the hostages were unavailing, and within two days his government dissolved, replaced by one more in tune with Khomeini's anti-American and fundamentalist views. Abolhassan Bani-

Sadr, the new foreign minister, demanded the Shah's extradition, the return of all his wealth, and the end of American "meddling" in Iranian affairs, in return for the hostages. The Carter administration rejected these demands and then began ratcheting up the economic pressure on Iran in an effort to force the release of the hostages.

On November 14, Bani-Sadr threatened to withdraw all of Iran's reserves in American banks, about $9 billion, unless the Shah was immediately extradited to Iran. Within hours of Bani-Sadr's announcement President Carter froze official Iranian assets and deposits both in the United States and those held in the overseas branches of American banks. At that point Chase had outstanding loans and other claims against the Iranian government of $366 million, but we also held deposits of just over $509 million. We immediately complied with the presidential order; the following day we declared the Iranian government in default of its obligations and offset our loans against their deposits, and paid off all our claims against Iran.

On November 15 I called President Carter and told him the situation had reached the point where private citizens could no longer deal with it. I said the Shah, then undergoing radiation treatment for cancer, recognized the problems he had caused by coming to New York and felt he would be well enough to travel in a few days. I asked the President to send a senior representative to New York to handle the situation. The President refused on the grounds that he did not want to be seen as having forced the Shah to leave the United States because it might be interpreted as yielding to Iranian pressure. Thus, despite the intensifying crisis, the President was still unwilling to take official responsibility for the Shah.

Two weeks later, on November 30, the story took yet another bizarre turn. I was about to deliver a speech in Minneapolis when I received a telephone call from one of Lopez Portillo's senior assistants informing me that he had decided to withdraw permission for the Shah to remain in Mexico after his visa expired on December 10 because his presence was a threat to his country's national interests. When I asked why I had been called, he said Lopez Portillo had become exasperated with the Carter administration's handling of the Iranian crisis and preferred to send the message through me rather than the State Department. I pointed out how awkward this abrupt reversal in Mexico's position was since the Shah had planned to return to Cuernavaca and had nowhere else to go. He told me the decision was irrevocable and asked me to pass the message along to President Carter, which I did through the White House staff.

Lopez Portillo's refusal to honor his promise forced President Carter to assume responsibility for the Shah and his movements. Soon after my call to the White House, the President sent his counselor, Lloyd Cutler, to New York. With Cutler's arrival, I could at long last bow out completely.

=

The subsequent story of the Shah—his hospitalization in Texas, his mistreatment in Panama, and his return to Egypt where he died in June 1980—is a sad one. Robert Armao remained with him until the very end, but all further arrangements were handled by the Carter White House as part of the effort to free the American hostages.

My last meeting with the Shah was on October 23, 1979, the day he arrived in New York. I entered New York Hospital secretly through a back entrance to avoid the protestors and the press. Farah Diba and Hushang Ansary, his former finance minister, were with him. The Shah and I exchanged only a few words; he was clearly exhausted and looked thin and pale. He was in great pain. He shook my hand and thanked me for the help I had given him over the previous months. I wished him well—there was little else for me to say—and then I left.

THE SHAH IN RETROSPECT

In preparing these memoirs I have reviewed the writings of those in the Carter administration—including both Jimmy Carter and Cy Vance—who made the critical decisions concerning the Shah. Their books cover the course of American foreign policy during those years, often in minute detail, and include their own unceasing efforts to establish a modus vivendi with the new Iranian government, to which they assigned a high priority.

They are less forthcoming, however, about how they dealt with the Shah during his exile. Neither President Carter nor Secretary Vance mention that, having decided to bar his entry, they asked private citizens to deliver the "official" message. They also leave unanswered why, over the course of the next seven months, they refused to provide any official assistance to the Shah or to have any official communication with him, while they indirectly sent word to him on a number of occasions that they hoped to admit him to the United States in the not-too-distant future. The fact is that the Carter administration, for admittedly pragmatic reasons, washed its hands of the Shah while he was still in Morocco but never quite mustered the courage to say so publicly. Instead, they cast him adrift on a hostile sea and relied on a few private citizens to sustain him.

The Shah's strange odyssey coincided with the suffering of the U.S. hostages in Iran. Their agony would continue for many months and was made even more complicated by the freeze of Iranian assets held by Chase and other American banks. The 444 days of their captivity was a horrible ordeal, as was the ordeal of our nation as we impotently watched our fellow citizens being harassed and humiliated.

But even in hindsight I believe our government should never have submitted to blackmail in the first place. It showed weakness. Not only our hostages but our nation paid a severe price for our cavalier treatment of the Shah. When it comes to principle, nations must stand for something; they must keep their word. We failed to do this with the Shah, who, despite his imperfections as a ruler, deserved more honorable treatment from the most powerful nation on earth. Undoubtedly the new Iranian government would have reacted severely if the Shah had come to the United States in February or March 1979. However, coping with that kind of crisis would have been far less damaging to American prestige and credibility than the abandonment of a friend when he most needed us.

As to his tenure as Iran's ruler, the Shah was a patriotic nationalist who sincerely wanted to improve the lives of his people. Given the militantly fundamentalist and viciously anti-American regime that followed—a regime with a human rights record far worse than the Shah's—the interests of the United States would have been better served had the Carter administration acted to keep the Shah in power while working to strengthen the more democratic elements that were beginning to emerge in Iran.

=

As for my own role in these events, as a banker I had developed ties with Iran that were important to Chase, and after the Shah's exile I worked diligently to protect our position with the new government. Chase's relationship with Iran remained stable for most of 1979, literally until the day the embassy was seized in early November. The government did reduce the balances they maintained with us during the second half of 1979, but in reality they had simply returned to their historic level of about $500 million. Carter's "freeze" of official Iranian assets protected our position, but no one at Chase played a role in convincing the administration to institute it. In early 1981, as part of the comprehensive deal freeing the hostages, Chase (along with all the other American banks involved) received all the monies that were due and suffered no losses.

On the personal level, despite the insistence of journalists and revisionist historians, there was never a "Rockefeller-Kissinger behind-the-scenes campaign" that placed "relentless pressure" on the Carter administration to have the Shah admitted to the United States regardless of the consequences. In fact, it would be more accurate to say that for many months we were the unwilling surrogates for a government that had failed to accept its full responsibilities.

The Iranian crisis had little impact on Chase, but it would take years for my personal association with the Shah to be placed in proper perspective.

=

One of the more dubious rewards of being a public figure is that *The New York Times* periodically sends a reporter to update your—as they benignly put it—"biography." Literal translation: "obituary." In 1981, shortly before I retired as chairman of the bank, a reporter came by for one such biographical update. We talked for a full hour, and 90 percent of his questions involved the Shah. As far as the *Times* was concerned, my experience with him was the most important, perhaps the only important, issue in my life. In 1986 another *Times* reporter stopped by, and this time only about half the questions were about the Shah. In 1996 yet another reporter conducted yet another update, and this time only 20 percent or so of the questions were Shah related. If I live another couple of decades, I may be able to outlast my bad press.

CHAPTER 25

REDEMPTION

The public furor over my involvement with the Shah of Iran did not divert me from my primary task: presiding over the recovery of the Chase Manhattan Bank.

Two decades later I hope it is not immodest to conclude that "we did it." I say "we" because Chase's turnaround and recovery was the result of a team of people pulling together to reach a common goal.

"It's a Stronger Bank That David Rockefeller Is Passing to His Successor" was the way *Fortune* magazine headlined Carol Loomis's follow-up account of the Chase comeback. Few articles have made me prouder.

CREATING A MANAGEMENT PARTNERSHIP

Sailors know that it takes time before you can bring a ship onto a new course; the larger the ship, the longer it takes. After the difficult meetings with the Chase board over our burgeoning real estate problems in the summer of 1975, I took my vacation in Maine and spent some delightful days sailing the waters off the coast of Mount Desert Island with Peggy and other members of my family. I remember thinking about the difficult task we faced at the bank, not unlike threading my way through the narrow passages and treacherous shoals between islands, constantly correcting course for the wind and tide. We had shown the board how we planned to manage our severe real estate exposure, but we needed a comprehensive approach to deal with the full range of our challenges—from back office operations problems to front office management development.

That was what I set out to achieve in early September 1975. By my side as chief operating officer was Bill Butcher. Together we would confront and ultimately conquer our considerable challenges. Bill and I had quickly established an excellent working relationship. We understood each other's roles and responsibilities. I was the CEO, the final arbiter of policy and strategy; Bill was the COO, responsible for seeing that all the bank's day-to-day operations were consistent with our strategies and our profitability objectives.

Unlike George Champion and me, who butted heads constantly when we were co-CEOs, Bill and I never got in each other's way. He had grown up in the bank, knew our business intimately, and handled the day-to-day business flawlessly.

Our offices adjoined on the seventeenth floor of One Chase Manhattan Plaza, and the two of us talked daily during 1975 and 1976 about policy and personnel issues. It was this latter area that we both felt needed bolstering, particularly the critical nonbanking functions of marketing, planning, systems, and human resources, which in the Chase tradition had usually been headed by credit officers who were untrained for these specialized jobs.

BUILDING THE TEAM

I often think one of the best decisions we ever made at the bank was bringing in Alan Lafley to run our human resources department; Alan was key to helping change the bank's culture. Bill and I first met Alan in 1974, on the same inauspicious day we had announced news of the bond trading account scandal. Alan had been in charge of human resources for a large segment of General Electric and came to work for us in 1975. He developed a strategic organization plan and helped us determine what our staffing needs would be in the next several years. This, in turn, led to an in-depth analysis of the qualifications of our senior staff and to a system of rotating talented officers through different departments in order to broaden their experience and test their skills. Some moved up and some moved to different positions within the bank; others who did not measure up were encouraged to move out of the bank altogether.

At the same time we drastically altered the system of executive evaluation and compensation, becoming much more attentive to performance in relation to clearly defined jobs. For the first time in the bank's history we tied an individual's compensation directly to results, offering bonuses and more rapid pay increases to those producing the most outstanding results. Most important, we instituted annual executive reviews throughout the bank to identify the most talented people and to decide how they could be used to best advantage. Today, of course, such management systems are routine. But in the "comfortable" Chase culture of those days, the steps we instituted were considered positively radical.

The board's compensation committee periodically reviewed with management the performance of our most senior officers. Several directors headed industrial corporations noted for excellent management policies, and they were particularly helpful in honing our program.

By the late 1970s, for the first time in Chase history, we considered an orderly management succession plan, identifying a handful of candidates best qualified to assume top leadership positions. One of these was Thomas Labrecque, who had worked as secretary of the executive office and had played a key role in dealing with the New York City fiscal crisis in the mid-1970s. Tom later became president and then succeeded Bill Butcher as chairman and CEO. Beyond identifying these new senior leaders we also stocked the bank with a cadre of high achievers, and we began to provide the training they would need to lead Chase in the future.

TRANSFORMING THE CULTURE

We also took actions to reorganize the bank on a more efficient basis and to create a culture built on the cornerstones of competence, character, and accountability.

The Chase "culture" had often been criticized for allowing semiautonomous fiefdoms ruled by powerful department heads who concentrated on guarding their turf rather than creating synergy with other parts of the institution. Early in my tenure as chairman, we had sought to address this problem of internecine warfare by restructuring into three new line units: corporate banking, institutional banking, and personal banking. This change went a long way toward integrating the bank but did not completely solve the problem. Restructuring to streamline our organization became commonplace. But creating a new culture based on cooperation and shared responsibility involved much more than a simple structural reorganization.

One program that played a central role in our cultural evolution was the Corporate Social Responsibility Program. Few companies in the 1970s made charitable contributions, and still fewer had programs whereby a planned percentage of annual earnings were contributed to charity. Even these formal giving programs tended to be an extension of the chairman's office, with the CEO arbitrarily directing funds to his favorite nonprofit organizations or acting in response to customer requests. This was not acceptable to me.

Instead, we established clear guidelines and objectives—contributing 2 percent of our annual net income before taxes to a diverse array of carefully identified nonprofit organizations. The program was managed by a Corporate Responsibility Committee, which met quarterly and included the entire executive management team. Subcommittees proposed grants in such areas as the arts, social service, community development, public policy, and a host of others. The twenty-five-member committee convened to consider the merits of each organization proposed by the subcommittees. We debated the level of support we would provide to civic organizations such as hospitals, symphony orchestras, and universities, as well as to more controversial groups such as Planned Parenthood and Covenant House. These discussions were among the most worthwhile we had within the bank. We learned from one another and about one another, and we began to understand how Chase fitted into the broader society around us.

My rationale for an active corporate responsibility program was simple: Businesses could not afford to become isolated from the larger society of which they were an integral part. I said as much at a meeting of the American Bar Association in October 1972: "Any business that does not respond creatively to this world and its growing insistence on an improved quality of life is cutting off its future nourishment. For, however you interpret its role, the corporation depends on the health of its society. Just as society's perception of us molds the laws that govern us, society's health determines whether we will have a vigorous or slack marketplace."

The broadening of executive sensitivity to the important underlying societal issues of our time became one of the most powerful components of the evolving Chase culture and helped our institution become qualitatively different from the vast majority of major American companies.

FRAMING THE STRATEGY

By early 1976, Bill Butcher and I had brought our real estate and back office problems under control and began to focus on developing longer-term growth strategies. We worked intensively on a three-year strategic plan to establish earnings targets for each year. We presented it to the board at an all-day session at my family estate in Pocantico in November 1976.

Our plan positioned Chase to cope with the profound changes that had overtaken the financial services industry worldwide. In essence, we radically redefined the bank and the products on which we would place our principal emphasis. We had to do this because the domestic and international marketplaces within which we operated had now altered irrevocably.

=

Through most of its existence Chase had been a major supplier of credit, first to the largest U.S. corporations and later to companies around the world. Chase also played a leading role both domestically and internationally in providing services to other banks. Thanks to the 1955 merger with the Bank of Manhattan, we had become strong in retail branch banking in New York City as well.

By the early 1970s, however, it had become apparent that the profitability of our most important product, lending to major corporations, was eroding. This resulted from the growing competition we faced from European and Japanese banks and, even more important, from the appearance of new financial instruments, particularly the growing use of commercial paper issued by corporations themselves.

Moreover, the proliferation of investment and merchant banks introduced another area of bank competition in the international capital markets, even in the provision of short-term banking needs.

Faced with increased competition in our traditional core businesses, Chase had to diversify; we had to identify other profitable fee-generating products and markets to meet our earning targets. We told the board that we wanted to accelerate our movement in three areas in particular:

- The first was our declining corporate lending business. We sought to expand our capital markets and investment banking business. After two attempts to form consortium banks in Europe in the late 1960s, we now proposed to develop a capital markets capability of our own, first in London with what became Chase Manhattan, Ltd., and then in Asia through the purchase of the charter (for the bargain basement price of $6!) of a Hong Kong merchant bank that had not yet begun operations. From this modest beginning grew Chase Manhattan Asia, Ltd., which by 1979 was co-managing syndicated loans of $10 billion a year and was playing a leading role in the Eurocurrency markets that had spread to Asia.
- The second was the marketing of retail products, such as credit cards and home mortgages, on a nationwide basis. Even though Federal Reserve

regulations prevented us from directly accepting deposits outside New York, it was permissible to have out-of-state offices that marketed other products. A retail expansion of the kind we proposed represented a major departure for Chase, and some of our directors resisted it at first. However, over the years this business became a reliable and rapidly growing source of revenue for the bank.

- The third was a renewed concentration on private banking, which provided trust and custody services and investment advice to wealthy individuals, along with the creation and development of other institutional investment services. Our earlier efforts to enter the private banking business had failed. By the mid-1970s, having learned from these earlier false starts, we formed the Chase Investors Management Corporation and brought in experienced people from outside the bank to manage it. CIMC attracted upscale investment clients from all over the world. Today the businesses of private banking, investment management, and custody have become great global strengths for Chase.

BEATING THE DEADLINE

At a special board meeting in November 1976, Bill and I projected a three-year plan of earnings of approximately $310 million by the end of calendar year 1979—nearly triple the expected earnings in 1976. It was an ambitious goal, and many of the directors may have thought it wishful thinking. But Bill and I were confident that we were on the right track and that the programs we had launched were taking hold and would produce the results we projected.

By the end of 1979 we posted earnings of $311 million—even better than our ambitious forecasts. *Fortune*, which had earlier given me "three years to turn the bank around," summarized our progress this way: "Chase made it back, and Rockefeller beat his deadline." For a change the story was rather pleasant reading. I was gratified—actually, considerably relieved—that our plan had worked and the bank had made it all the way back.

When I stepped aside as CEO on January 1, 1980, I felt a great sense of accomplishment that our efforts to reassert Chase's leadership in the world had succeeded.

Between 1969 and 1980 we opened sixty-three new foreign branches and seventeen new representative offices. By the early 1980s we operated in more than seventy countries, and our foreign activities accounted for the majority of the bank's income. Income from international operations grew from just over $29 million in 1970 to $247 million in 1981. Our aggregate earnings during my decade of Chase leadership had nearly tripled, from $133 million in 1970 to almost $365 million in 1980.

Most important, the "culture" of the bank, which had seemed so intractable through much of my career, had clearly changed. Chase had become a modern corporation. Equally important, the bank's idea of social responsibility—once a revolutionary concept—had become an integral part of the Chase philosophy. Our commitment to social responsibility extended beyond our annual charitable contributions to include programs of minority hiring, "lending" executives to schools and not-for-profits, making loans and extending credits in low-income areas, and many other social initiatives. It was indeed a "stronger" bank that I was passing on to my successor.

REDEMPTION AND RETIREMENT

On June 12, 1980, I reached the ripe old age of sixty-five, and in accordance with Chase bylaws, it was my time to retire. The same board that six years earlier had seriously contemplated asking for my *early* retirement now requested that I stay on for an extra nine months as chairman, until the next annual meeting in 1981.

I was proud that my thirty-five years in the service of The Chase Manhattan Bank ended on a high note. I was even more delighted that our plans and strategies resulted in a bank that was vindicated on all counts. The Chase was back. The team had triumphed.

Looking back, there is no other career I would have preferred. Banking gave me a chance to meet the leaders of the world in government, finance, and business—and to keep in touch with many of them over four decades in a way no other job I can think of in any field would have made possible.

But when I completed my tenure on April 20, 1981, by presiding over my final board of directors and stockholders meetings, I felt no pang of regret at leaving. Bill Butcher provided me with an office and secretary at the bank, and I would continue to serve as chairman of the International Advisory Committee and a member of the Art Committee. Bill also asked me to continue to travel abroad with senior bank officers, and I am pleased that subsequent Chase CEOs have continued to request my support from time to time. While my management responsibilities had ended, my links to the Chase would remain strong.

CHAPTER 26

NEW YORK, NEW YORK

Although my retirement from Chase in 1981 brought to an end a distinct phase of my life, there would be important continuities with the past. One of these was my involvement with the affairs of my hometown, New York City.

I began to learn about New York as a schoolboy. Father was my principal mentor. Soon after he was graduated from Brown University in 1897 and entered Grandfather's office, he immersed himself in many of the Progressive reform movements of the time: education, health, housing, regional planning, and parks. All had a strong urban focus, and my brothers and I were motivated by his example.

Attending school in the City also had a powerful influence on me. In the late 1920s, as part of a Lincoln School project, I delivered Thanksgiving food baskets to poor families living in "old law" tenements in Harlem, which lacked running water and adequate ventilation and lighting. As I climbed the stairs, it became darker and darker. The halls reeked of garlic, cabbage, and urine from the common bathrooms at the end of each floor. No doubt the residents were surprised when they opened the door to find a teenager accompanied by a liveried chauffeur in full uniform who helped me hand over a basket filled with a turkey, fresh fruit, and canned goods. This was a very memorable experience because I was faced for the first time with the reality that many people in the City were living in dire poverty and would not have had a Thanksgiving meal had we not brought it.

On our weekend drives to Pocantico we often stopped to inspect one of the many construction projects that Father was sponsoring, such as Riverside Church on the Upper West Side of Manhattan or the Cloisters in Fort Tryon Park in northern Manhattan. Father also had a keen interest in providing decent and affordable housing without government subsidies. He financed the construction of both the Paul Lawrence Dunbar Apartments in Central Harlem and the Thomas Garden Apartments on the Grand Concourse in the Bronx, demonstrating that there were innovative ways for the private sector to help solve this chronic urban problem. The projects he sponsored were undertaken before the New Deal housing program was initiated in the mid-1930s.

My stint with Mayor Fiorello La Guardia during the early 1940s broadened my knowledge of the City. La Guardia's charismatic personality and enormous popularity allowed him to tackle difficult problems that others preferred to avoid. The "Little Flower" enthusiastically deployed the powers of government to tackle the problems caused by the Depression. He secured funds from the federal government that put the unemployed to work building highways, schools, bridges, sewer systems, hospitals, airports, and public housing. As his aide, I often accompanied him in his oversized seven-passenger Chrysler on "flying tours" around town to open new housing projects or dedicate new public schools. My year and a half in City Hall gave me invaluable exposure to how effective a competent government could be in addressing important public issues.

I also believed then, as now, that the private sector had much to contribute. A case in point was Father's construction of Rockefeller Center during the Depression, despite formidable financial risks. His decision generated seventy-five thousand jobs at a time when there was virtually no other private construction in the City.

Both Father and Mayor La Guardia showed me in their different ways that the most effective response to urban problems would result from intelligent public-private cooperation.

LEADING AN UPTOWN TRANSITION

My first opportunity to put these principles to work came in a neighborhood with which I was intimately familiar: Morningside Heights on the Upper West Side of Manhattan. In the early twentieth century the

Heights had become home to many of the City's most prestigious educational and religious organizations—Columbia University, Barnard College, Union Theological Seminary, Jewish Theological Seminary, the Cathedral of St. John the Divine, Riverside Church, and International House, among them—and to a residential community of graceful town houses and elegant apartment buildings.

By 1945 the so-called Acropolis of America faced an uncertain future. Harlem, located just to the east and north, had gone through a dramatic transformation during the 1920s and 1930s, changing from a predominantly middle-class Irish and Jewish community to a Black ghetto of more than three hundred thousand people. The quality of life had begun to deteriorate markedly during the early 1930s because of the lawlessness associated with Prohibition. During World War II, areas of Morningside Heights were even ruled off-limits to servicemen because of the high incidence of prostitution and crime.

The leaders of the Morningside Heights institutions feared that they would have difficulty attracting and retaining faculty, students, and staff if conditions didn't improve.

=

Soon after I returned to New York, I was elected chairman of the Executive Committee of International House (I House), the residence for foreign students that Father had built in the mid 1920s at Riverside Drive and 124th Street. My first initiative was to hire Will Munnecke, a distinguished sociologist from the University of Chicago, to conduct a survey of the area. Munnecke had done a similar study for Chicago, which also confronted the challenge of adjusting to its changing Hyde Park neighborhood. As a university trustee I had been impressed with his work.

Munnecke's Morningside report identified the high crime rate and the scarcity of decent affordable housing as two preeminent issues that I House should confront. The board followed Munnecke's recommendation, and in early 1947 the fourteen major institutions in the area created Morningside Heights, Inc. (MHI) and elected me chairman. In accepting the position I told my colleagues that personal participation by the head of each institution was essential if we were to deal effectively with the problems we faced. I promised that they would be required to attend meetings only when important decisions were being made, and I encouraged them to appoint representatives to handle routine matters. All of MHI's constituents, including General Dwight D. Eisenhower, the president of Columbia, made this commitment and agreed to this approach, which worked well in practice.

We soon realized that unless middle-income housing was developed, there would be little chance to stabilize the area. But land costs were high, and none of the institutions had funds to devote to residential construction. Moreover, private builders were unwilling to accept the risk of construction in such a transitional neighborhood. The situation was exacerbated by New York City's invidious rent control laws, which persist to this day, long after any realistic economic rationale can be made for them. Builders feared they would not be able to recover their costs, and landlords lost any incentive to upgrade or even maintain their properties.

As a result, by the end of the 1940s, New York had become the nation's principal "housing laboratory," experimenting with a series of publicly financed housing schemes.

MHI took advantage of one such measure, the National Housing Act of 1949, which encouraged slum clearance or urban renewal by providing federal money to help defray the cost to private sponsors of land purchase and demolition to finance new housing. To take advantage of this new law we needed the approval of Robert Moses, the fabled "power broker" who headed Mayor William O'Dwyer's Commission for Slum Clearance, for approval to replace ten acres of densely packed "old law" tenements with a cooperatively owned apartment complex on the northern edge of the Heights.

Moses liked the idea. He had been looking for a reliable not-for-profit group to manage the City's first urban renewal site and expeditiously ushered our proposal through the maze of federal and city bureaucracies. After the MHI institutions subscribed $500,000, the Bowery Savings Bank agreed to supply a $12.5 million construction mortgage, thanks largely to Earl Schwulst, its imaginative chairman, who was active on the board of MHI. This meant private funds would account for 80 percent of the project's cost.

In October 1951 we announced the plans for Morningside Gardens, a six-building cooperative apartment complex that would house almost a thousand middle-income families from all ethnic backgrounds. At the same time the New York City Housing Authority—also headed by Bob Moses—agreed to complement our project by building a two-thousand-apartment public housing project, the U.S. Grant Houses, just to the north of Morningside Gardens. The two worked well together in catering to different income levels in the community.

Despite the obvious benefits of Morningside Gardens to the community, there was opposition. The most bothersome bunch, "Save Our Homes," who claimed that MHI was purposely dislodging low-income people, even recruited Republican congressman Jacob Javits to their cause. We had some sharp exchanges on the subject, but Javits realized he had been misled and recognized the benefits the project would provide the community.

Morningside Gardens taught me some important lessons: the necessity of sound organization and planning, the indispensability of public-private cooperation, and the crucial role of delegation of responsibility to staff. In regard to the latter, I knew I could be effective in such a complex project only if I had a trusted aide to whom I could delegate responsibility. I convinced Warren T. (Lindy) Lindquist, my friend from the military attaché's office in Paris, to come to work for me. Lindy's first job was to assume day-to-day responsibility for Morningside Gardens.

Lindy developed good relations with Robert Lebwohl, Moses's chief of staff. Lebwohl would tell Lindy if the imperious Moses was upset about some real or imagined slight, giving me time to intervene in order to placate him. This division of labor saved me time, avoided possible blowups, and kept our uptown project on schedule. It also enabled me to play a leadership role by leveraging my time to the maximum.

SPEARHEADING A DOWNTOWN REVIVAL

Soon after we began Morningside Gardens, I approached Moses with a request critical to Chase's future. In order to build our new headquarters in lower Manhattan we needed the City's permission to "demap" or close a one-block stretch of Cedar Street, a narrow but heavily traveled thoroughfare. If the City refused, the modern skyscraper we envisioned would be a nonstarter.

Permanently closing a city street was not a routine request, but ours was the kind of daring and visionary project Moses liked. He acceded to our request, but he also cautioned me: "You'll be wasting your money unless others follow suit." He pointed out that many Wall Street businesses had already moved uptown or were about to leave the City altogether. If any more left, Chase's decision to remain would be viewed as a colossal blunder.

Moses's point was well taken. There had been almost no new construction in the Wall Street area since the 1920s. The Financial District was cramped, dirty, congested, and a ghost town after 5 P.M. It was easy to understand why so many banks, insurance companies, and other corporations had left the area.

The construction of a new Chase headquarters could make a difference but by itself would not be enough. If the physical infrastructure and public services in lower Manhattan were not radically upgraded, the exodus from

Wall Street would continue. Moses suggested that I put together an organization that could speak on behalf of the downtown financial community and offer a cohesive plan for the physical redevelopment of Wall Street to persuade the politicians to allocate the necessary resources.

With this objective in mind I took the lead in organizing what became the Downtown–Lower Manhattan Association (D-LMA). To ensure a high-powered and influential board I personally recruited such influential downtown business leaders as Cleo Craig, chairman of AT&T; Henry Alexander, chairman of J. P. Morgan; Howard Shepherd, chairman of National City Bank; John Butt, chairman of the Seamen's Bank for Savings; Ralph Reed, treasurer of U.S. Steel; Keith Funston, president of the New York Stock Exchange; Harry Morgan, senior partner of Morgan Stanley; and others of similar stature. Importantly, all of them accepted and took an active interest in the affairs and activities of D-LMA.

I served as chairman, and Lindy became chief operating officer. We recruited experienced city planners to suggest practical ways to redevelop the entire area below Canal Street. Our first report proposed the comprehensive rezoning of the entire area, followed by a series of public sector projects to stimulate and encourage private redevelopment within the 564-acre zone from Canal Street to the Battery.

Among other proposals we recommended rehabilitating the rim of lower Manhattan by removing rotting piers and bulkheads and replacing them with parks, a heliport, and a boat basin; reducing traffic congestion through street widenings and closings, improvements in mass transit, and building the Lower Manhattan Expressway, an elevated highway that would link the Manhattan Bridge with the West Side Highway; relocating the old Washington Square Wholesale Fruit and Vegetable Market that extended for a dozen blocks along the waterfront on the West Side, and clearing the long-abandoned warehouse and tenement district on the East Side, to create an expanded financial services industry; and promoting Wall Street as an "around-the-clock" community (while four hundred thousand people worked there, only about four thousand lived in the area) by building affordable housing in Coenties Slip and in the run-down blocks south of the Brooklyn Bridge.

Mayor Robert Wagner loved our plan, as did *The New York Times*, which called me the "billion dollar planner" in a page-one article. Our infrastructure proposals would require the investment of more than half a billion dollars of public funds, but they were essential for the future of Wall Street. While it took substantial arm twisting with City budget and planning officials, eventually expenditures were approved, and the process of revitalizing Wall Street began.

CREATING THE WORLD'S TALLEST BUILDING

Two years after our first report, D-LMA proposed the construction of a World Trade Center that would firmly establish lower Manhattan as the world's trade and financial capital. In those days moving beyond the core of Wall Street meant entering a veritable commercial "slum."

On the west side, squat, low-rise buildings and warehouses built in the late nineteenth century were now occupied by hundreds of stores whose dirty windows featured hand-lettered signs for cheap electronic gadgets. The east side was even worse. A defunct elevated railway, slowly rusting away and home to thousands of pigeons, loomed over a neighborhood of abandoned piers and warehouses. Just north, the Fulton Fish Market added a unique redolence to the area, especially on hot summer days.

We concentrated first on revitalizing the east side, which offered the greatest opportunities. It was Lindy who suggested that we capitalize on lower Manhattan's historic strengths as a hub of international commerce by creating a trade-oriented center along Water Street. D-LMA commissioned Skidmore, Owings and Merrill to develop a plan for a 13.5-acre site that included a seventy-story hotel and office building, an international trade mart and exhibition hall, and a central securities exchange building where we hoped the New York Stock Exchange would relocate.

It would be a costly undertaking. The Port Authority of New York and New Jersey—an independent agency chartered by both states to manage New York's maritime shipping, the area's three airports, and regional transportation—seemed to be the only entity capable of financing such a massive project. Lindy and I discussed the matter at considerable length with Austin Tobin, executive director of the Port Authority, who enthusiastically agreed with our proposal and the Port Authority's role.

With the Port on board, we presented the proposal to those government officials whose endorsement was required. Mayor Wagner was supportive. So, too, was the governor of New York—my brother Nelson. But Governor Robert Meyner of New Jersey, who liked the idea in principle, balked at locating it on Water Street. He argued that New Jersey commuters arrived through the "tubes" on the west side of Manhattan and would be inconvenienced if they had to walk across town to work. Meyner's objection could have torpedoed the project, so as a compromise Tobin suggested moving the trade center to the west side and building it above the existing train terminal for New Jersey commuters. This gave the project a closer link to New Jersey and quieted complaints from that side of the river. With that issue resolved, I was optimistic that the project would move ahead immediately.

Alas, we hadn't considered the "special interests" who would be adversely impacted by the trade center. Midtown real estate developers saw the downtown trade center as a threat to their rents and property values. Organized by Larry Wien, who owned the Empire State Building, this group posed as "valiant defenders" of the small downtown merchants threatened with relocation. They backed a series of legal challenges to the trade center, which held up the project for several years.

=

The trade center plans called for 10 million square feet of office space, mostly in two 110-story buildings (taller than the Empire State Building, which may explain Larry Wein's opposition) situated on a large plaza that would also include a number of smaller structures. Critics insisted the space would never be fully rented and demanded the project be scaled back. Nelson immediately rode to the rescue by announcing that New York State, which wanted to consolidate its operations in the City, would lease 1 million square feet of office space, becoming the largest tenant. In 1965, after excavation for the "twin towers" (dubbed Nelson and David by the New York tabloids!) had begun, Nelson decided to take an additional million square feet of space. Nelson's announcement elicited another chorus of jibes—some claiming I had interceded with Nelson to ensure sufficient tenants. In point of fact, neither I nor the D-LMA had anything to do with the construction or rental of the trade center once the Port Authority assumed responsibility for the project.

Years of litigation and delays added dramatically to the trade center's final price tag of $1.5 billion, an amount five times the original estimate. The buildings were completed and fully occupied in stages between 1970 and 1977. The towers, at least for a time, would be the world's tallest buildings and provide office space for more than fifty thousand people. They used as much electricity as a city of four hundred thousand, and their forty thousand tons of air-conditioning were enough to cool refrigerators for a city of one million.

The World Trade Center soon became one of the City's greatest assets. Like Chase Manhattan Plaza before it, the trade center helped anchor the financial community more solidly in lower Manhattan. It provided new homes for Wall Street's commodity exchanges and office space for all manner of large and small businesses. It was an essential public investment that brought immense benefits.

D-LMA's second report, issued in 1963, advocated a new round of public improvements for the area. The most gratifying aspect of our work downtown was the response of the private sector. Over the next several years more than forty new office buildings were constructed below Canal Street, and an additional 100 million square feet of office space was built and occupied. There is no question that Chase's decision to build a new headquarters, the formation of the D-LMA with its roster of influential and involved CEOs, and the building of the World Trade Center were all pivotal in the revitalization of lower Manhattan. By almost any measure—employment, new construction, quality of life, property values, level of economic activity—our efforts to breathe life into a moribund downtown community had succeeded beyond our wildest expectations.

NELSON'S LANDFILL

The excavation for the trade center land resulted in yet another opportunity to quicken the transformation of lower Manhattan. Landfill from the project was dumped in the Hudson River, where it joined fill from dozens of other building projects to form a ninety-acre addition to the Island of Manhattan. This meant that for the first time in decades there was now land in Wall Street's congested precinct on which to build. This possibility generated a great deal of excitement and also involved me in an interesting contretemps with Nelson.

The D-LMA's 1963 Report endorsed the City's proposal to build affordable housing and a hotel/office building on this parcel, although no plans had been drawn up. That is, not until one morning in May 1966 when an obviously agitated Lindy rushed into my office at Chase waving a copy of *The New York Times*. Had I seen what Nelson had done? he asked. I hadn't. The article reported that at a press conference Nelson had announced plans for Battery Park City, a megadevelopment that would combine four high-rise office buildings, a hotel, and seventy-five hundred units of middle- and low-income housing on the landfill site. The article provided detailed plans and a photograph of the model that was prepared by Wallace K. Harrison and Nelson himself.

I must say I was annoyed. Clearly Nelson and Wally had been working on these plans for months without having the courtesy to mention them to me. I was, after all, chairman of the Downtown–Lower Manhattan Association and, not incidentally, Wally's friend and Nelson's brother! I guess this was a measure of how strained my relationship had become with Nelson as a result of his recent divorce and remarriage, and how rarely we saw each other.

When I called Nelson in Albany, he feigned surprise. "Surely you've heard about it," he said. "Only just this moment while reading the *Times*," I replied sharply. He admitted that it was a "rather extraordinary oversight." Perhaps Nelson envied the favorable publicity I had received as a result of the trade center and resented that his own role had been downplayed; he wanted to make sure there was no doubt that the landfill project was his.

As it turned out, Nelson would have been bitterly disappointed had he lived to see the fruition of his project. When the initial phases of Battery Park City were completed in the early 1990s, they bore little resemblance to the plan he and Wally had secretly developed thirty years earlier. Nelson's original scheme became a casualty of his political rivalry with Mayor John Lindsay and of the financial earthquake that jolted New York City in the early 1970s.

THE FISCAL CRISIS

The roots of New York's fiscal crisis of 1975 can be traced to John Lindsay's election as mayor in 1965. John was a complex individual. I first met him when he was a Republican congressman representing Manhattan's "Silk Stocking District"; in fact, he was my congressman, and I had contributed to his campaigns. He was a "Rockefeller Republican," and I thought his unique combination of charisma and moderation would make him a great mayor. But when John was inaugurated on January 1, 1966, he suddenly became a "populist." He proclaimed that the power brokers would no longer be welcome at City Hall. Presumably, that included me, since he refused to return my phone calls.

Unfortunately, John was not as assertive with New York's powerful municipal labor unions. Within hours of taking office the Transport Workers Union, led by the uncompromising Michael J. Quill, went out on strike and closed down the City's mass transit system for two weeks. Lindsay finally caved in and agreed to every one of Quill's demands. (Quill said at the time that he did not expect the Mayor to capitulate so totally, but what could he do—give it back?) Lindsay's surrender to the transit workers opened the floodgates to large across-the-board salary increases for *all* municipal workers. Over the next few years this would have a staggering impact on the City's budget.

By the end of the decade, as opposition mounted to the escalating tax burden and the local economy entered a period of recession, municipal officials began to rely increasingly on the sale of short-term debt to fund the City's operating budget. When that debt came due, they simply rolled it over and resorted to a variety of accounting gimmicks to disguise the City's true financial plight. The operating deficits grew larger and larger until they became so big that they couldn't be hidden any longer. By early 1975 the City had a structural deficit of $3 billion in its operating budget of $12 billion and needed to raise an additional $7 billion to pay off the short-term debt that would be coming due that year alone.

—

Some have suggested that the big commercial banks were culpable for allowing this deception to continue for as long as it did. In fact, it was the banks that finally forced the parlous state of the City's finances out into the open, with the City fighting us every inch of the way. In October 1974 a record $475 million bond offering sold poorly, and two subsequent issues required an interest cost of 9.5 percent, the highest in the City's history, before buyers could be found. Chase, as one of the City's principal bankers, warned the City's comptroller, Harrison Goldin, that the market was saturated with city securities and that steps had to be taken immediately to bring expenses in line with revenues.

Our private warnings had little impact on him or on the new mayor, Abraham Beame. Mayor Beame called a "summit meeting" at Gracie Mansion in January 1975. It brought together the CEOs of the six principal underwriting banks and leaders of the municipal unions with the Mayor and his principal aides. To my amazement Mayor Beame began the meeting by accusing the banks of "disloyalty to the City." He insisted that it was our duty to go out and "sell the City to the rest of the country." If we did so, he assured us, the problem would go away. I was stunned by the Mayor's refusal to accept the gravity of the City's financial situation.

I told the Mayor that the bond market was extremely skeptical of the City's financial management and that he had to cut spending and balance the budget if he wanted to regain investor confidence in New York City debt. I suggested that rather than calling each other names, the Mayor should ask the banks to work with the City in fashioning a solution, and I recommended that Ellmore (Pat) Patterson, chairman of Morgan Guaranty, head such a working group. The Mayor acquiesced, and a few days later the Financial Community Liaison Group (FCLG), chaired by Patterson, began its last-ditch attempt to enable the City to regain control of its own finances.

FCLG made some progress, but it soon became clear that the City would not change of its own accord. The banks informed the Mayor they would no longer underwrite or purchase any more debt until there was credible evidence that fundamental budgetary and fiscal reforms had been undertaken. Beame immediately accused the banks of blackmail, and City Council president Paul O'Dwyer attacked us for holding the "power of life and death over municipal institutions" and demanded an investigation of the banks.

BIG MAC AND THE FINANCIAL CONTROL BOARD

By early June 1975 the City was in a desperate position; it had nearly run out of funds to pay for its daily operations and had no way of refinancing almost $800 million in short-term debt. City officials and the leaders of municipal unions still insisted that it was someone else's problem and matters would improve in time. The Mayor even asked the banks for a bridge loan to keep the government functioning until the economy recovered—a request we promptly denied.

It was time to seek outside intervention. I had several talks with Governor Hugh Carey about my concerns, and on June 10, the day before New York City would have defaulted, a new state agency was created, the Municipal Assistance Corporation (MAC), to assist the city in overcoming its financial problems. While MAC couldn't force the City to balance its budget, it could audit the City's expenses and issue its own long-term bonds—backed by sales tax revenues—to replace the City's short-term debt. Once MAC was in place, Mayor Beame blithely declared, "The fiscal crisis is over."

It wasn't. By mid-July 1975 investors refused to purchase any more of the $3 billion in notes that MAC was selling, and the City again approached default. It became apparent that the market would respond only if the City was persuaded to surrender "all control" of its financial affairs to a more credible body.

That duty fell to me.

On the morning of July 22, I held a press conference at Chase and released a letter that had been sent to the head of MAC. In effect the letter stated that the bankers would not purchase any more MAC securities unless measures mandating "spartan control on the expenses of the City" were adopted.

Within a week Mayor Beame relented, agreeing to an immediate freeze on wages, the elimination of twenty-seven thousand city jobs, an increase in the subway fare, and the state takeover of certain city responsibilities. In return the banks agreed to a further purchase of almost a billion dollars of

MAC securities. But even this was not enough to attract general investors back into the market for New York City debt. Thus, with another half-billion dollars in debt coming due beginning in October 1975, the situation once again reached a critical point.

Despite everyone's best efforts, it appeared that the City would finally be forced to default on its debt, a potentially catastrophic action.

Working behind the scenes, Carey and his capable budget director, Peter Goldmark, proposed the creation of yet another state agency, the Emergency Financial Control Board (EFCB), that would assume full control of the City's budgetary powers, in much the same way as a trustee in a corporate bankruptcy. The state legislature immediately passed legislation stripping City officials of their remaining financial power. Mayor Beame and the City's other elected officials would now become mere spectators as the crisis moved through its final difficult phase.

DROP DEAD!

There remained one final obstacle.

The markets still remained skeptical about the City's capacity to generate enough revenue to amortize the debt that MAC had assumed. MAC bonds were selling at huge discounts, and the City's financial institutions were awash in MAC securities that we couldn't sell. All of us in New York—the commercial banks and the state government in particular—had done as much as we could. We needed an insurance policy, a guarantee, that would reassure investors beyond a shadow of a doubt that the crisis had passed.

We turned for help to the federal government. But winning Middle America's support for New York City was not an easy sell in Washington. I went to Washington a number of times with Walter Wriston and Pat Patterson to present the case for federal backing of the City's obligations. President Gerald Ford, who had just announced his decision to seek reelection and was facing a difficult challenge from Ronald Reagan, did not look benignly on our request. Evidently, opening the federal purse to the profligates of New York and eastern bankers wouldn't play well in Peoria. At least that was the impression we gained at a frustrating session in mid-October in the Oval Office with President Ford, Treasury Secretary William Simon, Federal Reserve chairman Arthur Burns, and my brother Nelson, then the vice president.

Nelson, although sympathetic, kept his own counsel, perhaps because he still hoped that Ford would retain him as his running mate in 1976. The others were entirely unsympathetic, especially, and most surprisingly, Bill Simon. Even though Bill had been an investment banker in New York and had served as an advisor to Mayor Beame, he urged the President to let the City declare bankruptcy. Burns, though less adamant, leaned in that direction as well. We left the meeting quite discouraged.

A few weeks later President Ford delivered his definitive response in a speech at the National Press Club. The President used the occasion to itemize the City's litany of fiscally irresponsible acts and promised to veto any "bailout" bill. The *Daily News* summarized the speech in a famous page-one headline: "FORD TO CITY: DROP DEAD."

The backlash from that headline, especially the prospect that Ford would resoundingly lose New York State in the next election, had a mitigating impact on the administration's hardline position. With yet another city-state financial plan in place, Congress authorized $3.6 billion in loans over a three-year period, which required the City to repay the amount borrowed with interest at the end of each fiscal year. This, then, was the "insurance policy" that the City needed to reassure investors. President Ford announced this compromise at a Thanksgiving Eve press conference, and with his statement the fiscal crisis came to an end.

═

I look back on the City's financial travails with a deep sense of sadness. Abe Beame was a good and honest man who found himself adrift in a sea of red ink brought on by decades of unsound fiscal policies. He and his municipal government colleagues were either unwilling or unable to face up to the City's serious problems. Nor was the situation helped by the cavalier and irresponsible attitude of our national political leaders.

The end of the fiscal crisis also marked the end of an era in the history of New York City. The terms of the financial rescue put the City in a budgetary straitjacket that made it impossible to sustain the high level of social activism and income redistribution that had characterized the Lindsay and Beame mayoral years. Even before the money ran out, however, it had become clear to many, including me, that the intellectual underpinnings of liberal reform of the day had become bankrupt as well. Decades of high taxes, intrusive regulations, and special interest politics had not resulted in a more prosperous and civil society but just the opposite: a decaying infrastructure, a declining population, an eroding employment base, an increasing crime rate, and a failing school system.

Perhaps the only positive outgrowth of the fiscal crisis was that it forced bankers and union leaders, two species not normally known to associate, to begin to work together in search of common solutions. During the course of our difficult negotiations, business and labor developed mutual respect for one another. This would prove to be an important foundation as we cast about for ways to restore a once-great city's prominence in the aftermath of a destructive financial crisis.

UNITING BUSINESS AND LABOR

With the fiscal crisis behind us, I spoke with Harry Van Arsdale, president of the New York City Central Labor Council of the AFL-CIO, about strengthening the relationship between business and organized labor. He agreed that it would be useful to continue our association. We persuaded other businessmen and labor leaders to join us in forming the Business Labor Working Group (BLWG), which included Peter Brennan of the New York City Building and Construction Trades Council, Sol Chaikin and Murray Finley of the Textile Workers Union, Edgar Bronfman of Seagrams, Richard Shinn of Met Life, Preston Robert Tisch of the Loews Corporation, W. H. James, publisher of the *Daily News*, and Howard Clark of American Express.

Not wanting to duplicate the efforts of other organizations, we decided that BLWG should disband after it completed a comprehensive analysis of the City's problems and potential. We recruited more than 150 people to work on the study and reported our findings in late 1976. Our report emphasized job creation by the private sector and suggested the elimination of many obstacles to economic growth: excessive regulation, an uncompetitive tax structure, and bureaucratic red tape.

The fact that both businessmen and labor leaders collaborated on the report gave it a special significance. For that reason many of our specific recommendations were acted on immediately; others became part of the new policy debate that began in New York City during the late 1970s about the City's direction. Even more important, the BLWG offered the promise that business and elements of organized labor could work together to realize common civic goals.

WESTWAY: OF BASS AND MEN

The BLWG report strongly endorsed two major public projects to jumpstart the City's anemic economy.

The first was a modern convention center, which the City desperately needed. The plans for what would become the Jacob K. Javits Convention

Center were approved in early 1978, and it opened in 1986. It has been a great success and annually accounts for about 2 percent of the City's economy.

The second was Westway, an innovative but controversial highway project along the Hudson River shoreline of Manhattan that was designed to be constructed from landfill. Building Westway, we said, would, among other things, create jobs, alleviate air pollution, expedite traffic flow, revitalize a badly deteriorated section of the West Side, support development of the downtown business community, and help many smaller industries such as printing, retail, and garment.

Most New Yorkers overwhelmingly supported Westway. In the past, projects such as Westway, backed by top business and labor leaders, endorsed by the leading newspapers, and promoted by most politicians, would have been quickly approved and expeditiously completed. But none of us realized that a new political force—environmental activism—would be able, in the end, to frustrate the implementation of a plan that would benefit all New Yorkers.

=

By the 1960s the elevated highway along Manhattan's Hudson shoreline was in such poor condition that it was under constant repair. In late 1973 a dump truck carrying asphalt to repair the highway broke through the rotting roadbed and plunged to the ground below.

Even before the West Side Highway collapsed, the City Planning Commission and the Urban Development Corporation had developed an ambitious plan, which became known as Westway when it was formally announced in 1974. It called for four miles of new highway to be built on landfill between what is now Battery Park City and 42nd Street. The landfill would create more than 150 acres of parkland as well as residential and commercial development. Although it was finally estimated that Westway would cost slightly more than $2 billion, 90 percent of the money would come from the Federal Highway Trust Fund and New York State would supply the remaining 10 percent. The City would not have to spend a penny.

I was among the plan's strongest advocates. I intervened with four successive secretaries of transportation in Washington to keep the project alive. I helped convince Governor Hugh Carey, though he had originally opposed the development, to become a supporter. I also helped convince Ed Koch, after his election as mayor in 1977, to abandon his strident opposition.

Westway's opponents included advocates of mass transit who wanted to "trade in" the highway money for funds to improve the subways, community activists concerned about the impact of construction on their neighborhoods' quality of life, and environmentalists. These opponents waged a protracted battle to prevent Westway's construction, delaying the approval of the air-quality permit for more than three years and forcing federal officials to conduct exhaustive reviews.

Finally, in the summer of 1981, the Army Corps of Engineers issued the final, essential approval: the dredging and landfill permit. President Ronald Reagan came to New York on Labor Day and presented Mayor Koch with an $85 million check to purchase the rights of way for the highway. The President declared, "The Westway project begins today." If only that had been the case.

Shortly after Mario Cuomo became governor in 1983, he told me he had learned as a lawyer that it was possible to stop anything if you persisted and knew the right techniques. In Westway's case, Cuomo was prophetic.

Almost as soon as Reagan delivered the check, the opponents of Westway were back in court. Activist Marcy Bienstock and her New York Clean Air Campaign petitioned Federal Court Judge Thomas Griesa to block the permit, alleging errors in the environmental studies conducted by the Corps. Judge Griesa agreed and ordered the Corps to assess more fully the impact of Westway on the Hudson's striped bass population, which seemed to favor the rotting piers along the waterfront for procreative pursuits.

The Corps announced in 1983 that it would conduct a two-year survey of the landfill's impact on the bass. In February 1985, the Corps found that Westway would have only a minor impact on the striped bass and issued a new dredge and fill permit. More than eight years after the initial federal approval and almost twelve years after the old West Side Highway had collapsed, it appeared that the construction of Westway would finally begin. I joined Governor Cuomo and Mayor Koch for a triumphant posting of the permit on Pier 59 in Chelsea.

Our triumph was short-lived. That same day Bienstock and her allies paraded into court and sued to have the permit set aside. Incredibly, the judge concurred with the environmentalists. Griesa held new hearings on the way in which the Corps of Engineers had conducted its environmental studies, found them lacking, and on August 6, 1985, issued a permanent injunction on the spending of federal funds for the construction of Westway. When the United States Court of Appeals for the Second Circuit affirmed Griesa's decision a month later, Westway was dead.

Although New York received about $1 billion in mass transit money and about $500 million for the construction of a Westway replacement, much more than money was lost in the exchange. The dogged opposition of a small group of ideological extremists had defeated a project that was in the best interest of all New York's citizens. What was lost is immeasurable: a magnificent new waterfront along most of Manhattan's West Side, with skillfully landscaped parks and walkways overlooking the river, and concomitant new jobs and revenues for the City.

=

Ed Koch tells a story about Westway that in my more forgiving moments I find funny. One day an anti-Westway activist went to City Hall to object to Koch's support for the project. She told the Mayor he had to stop the project because it was "killing people." When he said he wouldn't, she threw herself on the floor, clutching her throat, and screamed that she was dying because of lack of oxygen. The sad part is that this woman and her allies won. New York—along with reason and common sense—lost. I fought for Westway for ten years; I chaired countless meetings, wrote op-eds, gave speeches, and lobbied in Washington and Albany—all for naught. In the end, sadly, the striped bass trumped the public interest.

CREATING A LASTING PARTNERSHIP

The failure of a sound and sensible project like Westway was illustrative of a city in decline and disarray, lacking, in particular, strong leadership.

If the City was ever to recover, it would require a collaborative approach between government and the private sector. Complicating this was the fact that New York's private sector was itself disorganized and fragmented. This was precisely the concern of three gentlemen—Walter Wriston, Richard Shinn, and William Ellinghaus—who asked me to breakfast one morning in late 1978. As a result of our meeting I agreed to join forces with them to charter a study by J. Henry Smith, the retired chairman of Equitable Life, to see what could be done. Smith concluded that consolidating all business groups within one organization was the only way to ensure that the private sector could have an "effective and unified voice to support the economic growth of the city."

Smith also observed that the chief executive of the new organization would have to be "decisive, articulate, diplomatic, and imaginative—much like an effective chief executive of a large corporation." After a number of meetings it was concluded that, for a variety of reasons, the logical individual was me. And so in October 1979 I assumed the chairmanship of what would come to be called the New York City Partnership, deriving its name from the partnership we sought between government and the private sector.

Because the Partnership was a tax-exempt organization, we decided to retain the New York City Chamber of Commerce as a subsidiary in order to legally lobby in New York, Albany, and Washington. And to symbolize our new citywide vision, we moved our headquarters from the chamber's old building in lower Manhattan to a new office in Midtown.

=

One of our principal goals was to persuade organized labor—particularly the heads of the municipal unions—to participate. We were unsuccessful. These labor leaders adamantly opposed working with the Chamber of Commerce; they said it would be like mixing oil and water.

We were a great deal more successful in expanding our membership beyond the Manhattan-dominated big business community of male corporate leaders. We actively recruited smaller businesses in all the boroughs, many of them headed by women, Blacks, and Hispanics, and secured the active participation of the leaders of many of the City's leading not-for-profit organizations as well. The result was the most inclusive, focused, and, I believe, effective private-sector organization in New York City's history.

From the beginning we focused on enhancing economic growth—creating jobs, improving the business climate, and reducing the cost of government. That was the Partnership's strategic vision in 1980, and it remains so to this day.

=

During the years of my chairmanship, the Partnership made demonstrable progress in several key areas. The first job we tackled in June 1980 was providing summer jobs. At the urgent request of Mayor Koch, a number of our member corporations, especially AT&T and Brooklyn Union Gas Company, provided almost three thousand jobs that first year. In subsequent years, with more time to organize, the Partnership provided summer employment for tens of thousands of young New Yorkers, most of them from minority groups. As a result Mayor Koch, who had been skeptical and even somewhat dismissive of the Partnership, became a strong supporter.

Improving the quality of education in the City's public schools presented a more daunting challenge. Our long-term goal was to address the growing imbalances between the needs of business and the lagging abilities of graduates of the system. My daughter, Peggy Dulany, a former teacher, served for several years as a Partnership vice president in this critical area.

Through the Adopt a School program, companies provided administrative support to specific schools. Recently, through its Breakthrough for Learning program, the Partnership committed $25 million to turn around underperforming school districts.

Economic development has always been a strong focus of the Partnership. We have worked collaboratively with the City and State on a number of important economic development issues. One notable initiative has been to persuade corporations to shift their back office operations to less costly space in the outer boroughs. Thousands of jobs are involved—information storage, data processing, and the like—that don't require prime real estate in Manhattan. Retaining such jobs in the City has been of the utmost importance. The development of Metrotech in Brooklyn to house Brooklyn Union Gas and Chase's back office operations has been among the most conspicuous successes.

The Partnership has had its greatest impact in the area of housing, which, as noted, has been an interest of mine from the days of Morningside Gardens. In the mid-1970s I helped organize the Community Preservation Corporation (CPC) as a nonprofit affiliate of the New York Clearing House to finance the rehabilitation of existing housing stock in deteriorating areas of the City. CPC used the financial resources and acumen of its membership of commercial and savings banks to provide millions of dollars in low-cost loans to enable owners to upgrade their property—and their neighborhoods.

While CPC filled an important niche, there was also an enormous need for new housing construction as well. This seemed like a prime opportunity for the Partnership to do something. At a Partnership-sponsored luncheon, at which President Ronald Reagan spoke, in January 1982, I announced our plan to provide thirty thousand units of housing over a period of five years.

After considering an array of possibilities we concentrated on the construction of new two- and three-family homes. Since 1984 the Housing Partnership has produced more than thirteen thousand moderately priced homes in fifty neighborhoods—almost 50 percent of the affordable housing built in the City during that time. In this way the Partnership has spurred the reemergence of housing markets in the most distressed areas of the City.

Most recently the Partnership has expanded its economic development efforts through the creation of the New York Partnership Investment Fund, co-chaired by Henry Kravis and Jerry I. Speyer, to provide venture capital for high-technology businesses that promise to diversify New York's economic base and generate employment.

===

During the course of the mayoralties of Ed Koch, David Dinkins, and especially Rudolph Giuliani, the Partnership has become a highly visible fixture in New York City affairs. As the *New York Daily News* recently observed, it has "served as a model public-private organization" showing what can be accomplished when petty differences are set aside for the improvement of the entire community.

CHAPTER 27

PROUD

INTERNATIONALIST

M y lifetime pursuits as an internationalist might best be summarized by one rather extraordinary day in 1995.

October 23 was a busy day at the Council on Foreign Relations. The fiftieth anniversary of the United Nations had drawn almost two hundred heads of government to New York, and many had asked to speak at the Council. But even then the day was unusual for the diversity of the speakers: Jiang Zemin, president of the People's Republic of China and heir apparent to Deng Xiaoping; Václav Havel of the Czech Republic, the former political prisoner who had eloquently guided his country through its "Velvet Revolution"; Yasser Arafat, leader of the Palestine Liberation Organization, considered by many a terrorist and by others as the key to an enduring Middle East peace settlement; and, finally, Fidel Castro, charismatic leader of the Cuban revolution and implacable opponent of the United States for almost forty years.

The ironies abounded. With the exception of Havel, these men had vowed to fight to the death against imperialist America. Now, with the end of the Cold War, they flocked to the center of world capitalism, eager to meet and close deals with American bankers and corporate executives, or at least to be seen with them—even Castro. *El Presidente* wanted especially to meet me, but a convenient time had not yet been found. Failing this, at the formal reception hosted by Secretary-General Boutros-Ghali at the U.N., Castro spotted me, charged across the delegates lounge, and grabbed my hand, shaking it warmly. I was chagrined, sensing the photo frenzy about to erupt. But I smiled as the paparazzi snapped away. Predictably, the photo of "the Capitalist and the Communist" appeared on the front page of newspapers from Ankara to Zanzibar; and just as predictably I was criticized for appearing with a man considered one of our nation's bitterest enemies.*

POPULIST PARANOIA

For more than a century ideological extremists at either end of the political spectrum have seized upon well-publicized incidents such as my encounter with Castro to attack the Rockefeller family for the inordinate influence they claim we wield over American political and economic institutions. Some even believe we are part of a secret cabal working against the best interests of the United States, characterizing my family and me as "internationalists" and of conspiring with others around the world to build a more integrated global political and economic structure—one world, if you will. If that's the charge, I stand guilty, and I am proud of it.

The anti-Rockefeller focus of these otherwise incompatible political positions owes much to Populism. "Populists" believe in conspiracies, and one of the most enduring is that a secret group of international bankers and capitalists, and their minions, control the world's economy. Because of my name and prominence as the head of the Chase for many years, I have earned the distinction of "conspirator in chief" from some of these people.

Populists and isolationists ignore the tangible benefits that have resulted from our active international role during the past half-century. Not only was the very real threat posed by Soviet Communism overcome, but there have been fundamental improvements in societies around the world, particularly in the United States, as a result of global trade, improved communications, and the heightened interaction of people from different cultures. Populists rarely mention these positive consequences, nor can they cogently explain how they would have sustained American economic growth and the expansion of our political power without them.

---

*My daughter Peggy has visited Cuba a number of times since 1985 and developed a good rapport with President Castro. This may partially explain Castro's exuberant behavior. I did meet privately with Castro the following day at the Council on Foreign Relations building on Park Avenue.

Instead, they want to wall off the United States by rejecting participation in such constructive international activities as the World Trade Organization and the North American Free Trade Agreement, eviscerating the World Bank and the International Monetary Fund, and assaulting the United Nations. In staking out these positions the new Populists misunderstand history, misconstrue the effectiveness of the international effort that the United States organized and led after World War II, and misjudge the importance of constructive global engagement to our nation's future. Global interdependence is not a poetic fantasy but a concrete reality that this century's revolutions in technology, communications, and geopolitics have made irreversible. The free flow of investment capital, goods, and people across borders will remain the fundamental factor in world economic growth and in the strengthening of democratic institutions everywhere. The United States cannot escape from its global responsibilities. Today's world cries out for leadership, and our nation must provide it. In the twenty-first century there can be no place for isolationists; we must all be internationalists.

THE COUNCIL ON FOREIGN RELATIONS

It was my parents who first impressed on me the importance of the world beyond the United States. Father was a staunch supporter of the League of Nations, an active participant in the worldwide Protestant ecumenical movement, and, through the Rockefeller Foundation and other family foundations, one of the principal funders of health, education, and cultural endeavors around the world. Mother, of course, was deeply engaged by art from all parts of the world.

Like many in my generation I returned from World War II believing a new international architecture had to be erected and that the United States had a moral obligation to provide leadership to the effort. I was determined to play a role in that process, and I found the Council on Foreign Relations in New York the best place to pursue my interest in global affairs.

=

The Council was formed in 1921 in the aftermath of World War I and the U.S. Senate's rejection of the Treaty of Versailles. Despite the timing, the Council was not established to promote American membership in the League of Nations but "to afford a continuous conference on international questions affecting the United States." The distinction is an important one because from the outset the Council has eschewed taking a position on any issue that it discusses save one: that American citizens need to be informed about foreign affairs because events in other parts of the world will have a direct influence on their lives.

For example, in the 1930s the foreign policy debate centered on America's response to the rise of dictators in Europe and the Far East and the outbreak of war. Many Council members, John Foster Dulles among them, favored a strict American neutrality, while others, including my uncle Winthrop Aldrich, urged an active intervention short of war on the side of Britain and France in their struggle against Nazi Germany. The Council provided both sides with a forum.

After World War II the Council played an important role in alerting Americans to the new threat posed by the Soviet Union and in crafting a bipartisan consensus on how to deal with the worldwide expansion of Communism. In 1947, *Foreign Affairs,* the Council's distinguished journal, published the famous "X" article, "The Sources of Soviet Conduct" (written anonymously because George Kennan was serving in the State Department at the time). It outlined the doctrine of containment. George wanted to alert the foreign policy establishment to the dangers of Soviet imperialism and knew that the most effective way to do this was through the pages of *Foreign Affairs.* His article became the defining document of U.S. Cold War policy.

A decade later Henry Kissinger, then a professor of political science at Harvard, chaired a Council study group, of which I was a member, to examine the impact of nuclear weapons on international relations. Henry's seminal work, published by the Council in 1957, unexpectedly became a best-seller and required reading in both Washington and Moscow. The deployment and control of nuclear weaponry would become the critical negotiating point between the United States and the Soviet Union for the next four decades.

From the early 1950s on, then, the Council's program of speakers, study groups, and publications has provided a forum where critical issues are examined and discussed. Vietnam, the opening of China, détente with the Soviet Union, balancing world population with food resources, the Arab-Israeli conflict in the Middle East, economic development in the Third World, the expansion of NATO—these and many other issues have found their place on the Council's agenda through the years. But the essential point is that the Council never takes a position—official or unofficial—on any foreign policy issue even though its members are free to do so.

What, then, gives the Council its strength and reputation?

There are several interrelated factors, beginning with the quality and diversity of its membership. New York City's businessmen, bankers, and lawyers once dominated the proceedings, but during the past thirty years the membership has been broadened to include men and *women* from the communications industry, colleges and universities, and the not-for-profit world. In 1971 the Council had seventeen female members; there are now more than seven hundred, and 20 percent of the directors are women. Now more than thirty-six hundred strong, one-third of our members live outside New York and Washington. Increasing geographical, ethnic, professional, and gender diversity has been accompanied by a considerable broadening of the political, economic, and even cultural viewpoints represented within the Council's membership, ranging from William F. Buckley, Jr., Condoleezza Rice, and Newt Gingrich to Mario Cuomo, Madeleine Albright, and Bill Clinton.

In short, the quality of its membership, its central location, the excellent staff and facilities, and the tradition of rigorous debate and nonpartisanship—rather than a secret pipeline into the White House and the State Department—are the reasons that the Council on Foreign Relations continues to influence the formulation of American foreign policy.

=

I was elected to the Council's board of directors in 1949. At thirty-four I was its youngest member and retained that distinction for the next fifteen years. In 1970 I succeeded Jack McCloy as chairman and immediately became embroiled in a controversy that rocked the usually civil halls of the Council.

The board had selected William P. Bundy to replace Hamilton Fish Armstrong, who was retiring after more than forty years as editor of *Foreign Affairs.* Bill was a man of quality and culture, the younger brother of McGeorge Bundy who served both John F. Kennedy and Lyndon B. Johnson as national security advisor during the tumultuous 1960s. Bill was assistant secretary of defense in the mid-1960s as the Vietnam War escalated and then moved to the State Department as assistant secretary for Far Eastern affairs, where he helped design our Indo-China policy.

Bill Bundy's selection, which I strongly supported, angered many Council members who believed American involvement in Vietnam was not only a mistake but an immoral act perpetrated by corrupt and power-hungry men. They considered Bill a war criminal and went public in their efforts to deny him the position. I thought their charges were intemperate, but Vietnam had so poisoned the atmosphere that, quite frankly, it would have been impossible to choose anyone involved in the conduct of American foreign policy during those years without stirring passions. With time, Bill's ability as a writer and his proficiency as an evenhanded editor came to be widely appreciated, even by his strongest critics. But the affair clouded my early years as chairman.

The dissension over Vietnam was only one problem facing the Council and my chairmanship in the early 1970s. If the Council wished to remain relevant, we needed to make significant reforms. In terms of structure we decided to recruit a full-time chief executive officer and selected Bayless Manning, the dean of the Stanford University Law School, to fill the post of president. Bayless and his successor, Winston Lord, who would later serve as American ambassador to China, made my fifteen-year tenure as chairman a great deal easier and more productive.

In terms of program, the Council faced much stiffer competition than it ever had from research institutions, university faculties, and think tanks. And, of course, television had expanded the global awareness of most Americans. If the Council was to remain relevant, we had to be forward looking and responsive. To meet the challenge Manning launched the "1980s Project," a comprehensive effort to identify the issues that would dominate international affairs in the future, and over the next decade we expanded the Council's purview beyond its traditional concerns with regional conflicts, arms control, and military balance to include human rights, environmental degradation, and the knotty issues of development economics and international trade.

=

When I retired as chairman in 1985, I had served as a Council board member for thirty-six years. I was succeeded by Peter G. Peterson, a former Secretary of Commerce and now chairman of the Blackstone Group. Pete has introduced a number of innovations that have strengthened the Council. One of his initiatives, in which I participate, are periodic Council trips overseas. These visits are designed to probe beneath the smooth surface of diplomacy by allowing us to assess the situation in strategic regions of the world. Our visits to Israel in 1999 and Cuba in 2001 were typical.

We drove from Jerusalem to the Gaza Strip for a luncheon meeting with Yasser Arafat. Although the Israelis had given us permission to cross the border into Gaza, we were detained for more than an hour while heavily armed Israeli soldiers carefully scrutinized our papers. The schedule became a shambles, but Arafat—a small, canny, and charming man obviously suffering from Parkinson's disease—met briefly with us anyway. He insisted that Israel must withdraw from the West Bank and allow its incorporation into a fully sovereign Palestinian state.

Gaza was one of the most forlorn places I have ever visited. It is a ghetto, physically isolated, crammed with substandard housing, and teeming with people, most of whom have to travel long distances every day through heavily guarded border checkpoints to their jobs in Israel.

Returning to Jerusalem we met Prime Minister Ehud Barak, a self-confident, assertive man who explained why Israel would never agree to

Arafat's demands to return to the 1967 borders. Thus, despite the apparent gains of the Oslo Agreement and the Wye Accords, I came away with the impression that there is still a great distance to travel before real peace comes to the Middle East. Unfortunately, the surprising election of hardliner Ariel Sharon as Israeli prime minister and the renewed outbreak of violence in the aftermath of the attacks on the World Trade Center and the Pentagon now threaten an even wider war.

More recently, in the winter of 2001, a group of Council members visited Cuba at the invitation of the Cuban government and with the approval of the U.S. State Department. We spent four days in Havana, a magnificent city that has escaped the worst ravages of modern urban development and maintained the quiet charm I remembered from my last visit there in the late 1950s.

Havana's unusual calm—few cars, many pedestrians, clean streets, virtually no new construction—is not the product of planning but the direct result of Fidel Castro's rigid dictatorship. The combination of the U.S. embargo, the collapse of the Soviet Union, which ended the financial subsidies that kept the country afloat for decades, and Castro's Marxist economics has turned Cuba into a basket case. In my view the country is worse off now than it was in the 1950s; it is completely dependent on sugarcane production, tourism, and the generosity of Castro confreres like Hugo Chávez of Venezuela to make ends meet. Despite the impressive accomplishments of the regime in the areas of education and health care, Cuba faces a hard and uncertain economic future.

Our visit culminated with a six-hour dinner meeting with Castro that began at 11 P.M. Dressed in his familiar military fatigues but without his trademark cigar, Castro harangued us continuously throughout the night. When I intervened to ask him if there were areas where he had not achieved his goals, he paused briefly but had trouble thinking of any.

Cuba remains largely isolated from the rest of the world, and its people are ensnared in an anachronistic economic and political trap. Unfortunately, I think there is little possibility for change while Castro remains in power, although he does seem willing to negotiate on many important issues.

BILDERBERG

If the Council on Foreign Relations raises the hackles of conspiracy theorists, the Bilderberg meetings must induce apocalyptic visions of omnipotent international bankers plotting with unscrupulous government officials to impose cunning schemes on an ignorant and unsuspecting world. At the risk of disappointing these conspiracy mongers, the truth is that Bilderberg is really an intensely interesting annual discussion group that debates issues of significance to both Europeans and North Americans—without reaching consensus.

Prince Bernhard of the Netherlands convened the first conference in May 1954 at the urging of Joseph Retinger, a Pole of aristocratic origins who had served with British intelligence during World War II. Retinger, a dynamic and energetic man who spoke with a heavy accent and walked with a pronounced limp, was concerned about the tense relations within the Atlantic community. He persuaded Bernhard to convene a group of prominent individuals to discuss these matters.

I was one of eleven Americans invited, and we joined fifty delegates from eleven Western European countries—a lively mosaic of politicians, businessmen, journalists, and trade unionists. I was surprised to have been invited in the first place and even more taken aback when Retinger asked me to prepare a background paper on prospects for the world economy from the American perspective. Retinger indicated that Hugh Gaitskell, a former Labour Chancellor of the Exchequer, had agreed to address the same topic from the European point of view. I was a bit intimidated by the prospect of going up against such a formidable opponent.

Gaitskell foresaw a dreary and dismal future. By contrast, my paper predicted steady economic growth in the United States and a strong recovery in the volume of world trade. Within the year my confident forecasts had been borne out. The paper undoubtedly helped establish my credibility with a sophisticated group of senior politicians and business leaders.

The conference had served a useful purpose, and the consensus was that we should meet again the following year under the continuing chairmanship of Prince Bernhard. We also decided to call the gathering "Bilderberg" after the hotel in Oosterbeek where we had first assembled.

=====

For the first twenty years Bilderberg meetings were marked by the sharp clash of opposing views. Once Europe recovered its economic strength, many of the old national rivalries and suspicions began to resurface, along with a strong distrust of American intentions and even accusations of an American drive for hegemony in Europe. These attitudes grew in strength during the 1960s and came to a head in the 1970s as a result of the economic disarray of those years and the steady improvement in U.S.-Soviet relations resulting from détente.

If these fissures had not been addressed, the consequences for the Atlantic Alliance might have been disastrous. While it is not Bilderberg's role to resolve disputes among sovereign states, individual participants are free to report on what they have heard to those who do wield official power in their respective countries.

=

In 1976, Bilderberg faced a scandal that almost resulted in its collapse. Early that year in testimony before the Senate Foreign Relations Committee, it was alleged that Prince Bernhard had approached the Lockheed Corporation with an offer to use his official position to influence Dutch defense procurement policies in return for a significant financial consideration. As the year wore on, the evidence against Bernhard accumulated, including indications that he had met with intermediaries during Bilderberg events. The 1976 conference was canceled, and it appeared for a time that Bilderberg was finished.

Although there were several indignant resignations and a few others who thought the meetings had outlived their usefulness, many more believed we should try to find a way to keep them going. A specially appointed committee recommended that Bilderberg be continued but that meetings be modified to involve younger participants who would help diversify the political viewpoints represented.

Lord Alec Home, the respected former British prime minister, accepted the chairmanship, and the 1977 meeting in Torquay, England, was an outstanding success. Lord Home was the first in a line of distinguished chairmen: Walter Scheel, the former president of the Federal Republic of Germany; Lord Roll of Ipsden, chairman of SBC Warburg; Lord Carrington, a former British foreign secretary; and, most recently, Etienne Davignon, the chairman of the Société Générale de Belgique. I am pleased to report that as the new millennium begins, a reinvigorated Bilderberg continues to thrive.

"CONSORTING WITH REACTIONARIES"

Bilderberg overlapped for a time with my membership in a relatively obscure but potentially even more controversial body known as the Pesenti Group. I had first learned about it in October 1967 when Carlo Pesenti, the owner of a number of important Italian corporations, took me aside at a Chase investment forum in Paris and invited me to join his group, which discussed contemporary trends in European and world politics. It was a select group, he told me, mostly Europeans. Since Pesenti was an important Chase customer and he assured me the other members were interesting and congenial, I accepted his invitation.

Jean Monnet, Robert Schuman, and Konrad Adenauer were founding members of the group, but by the time I joined, they had been replaced by an equally prominent roster that included Antoine Pinay, a former French president; Giulio Andreotti, several times prime minister of Italy; and Franz-Josef Strauss, the head of the Christian Social Union in Bavaria and a perennial contender for the chancellorship of the Federal Republic of Germany. The discussions were conducted in French, and usually I was the sole American present, although on a few occasions when the group assembled in Washington, Henry Kissinger, at the time President Nixon's national security advisor, joined us for dinner.

Members of the Pesenti Group were all committed to European political and economic integration, but a few—Archduke Otto of Austria, the head of the house of Hapsburg and claimant to all the lands of the Austro-Hungarian empire; Monsignor Alberto Giovanetti of the Vatican and a prominent member of Opus Dei, the conservative Catholic organization; and Jean-Paul Léon Violet, a conservative French *intellectuel*—were preoccupied by the Soviet threat and the inexorable rise to power of the Communist parties of France and Italy.

Pesenti set the agenda for our thrice-yearly meetings, and *Maître* Violet, who had close connections with the Deuxième Bureau of the Service des Renseignements (the French CIA), provided lengthy background briefings. Using an overhead projector, Violet displayed transparency after transparency filled with data documenting Soviet infiltration of governments around the world and supporting his belief that the threat of global Communist victory was quite real. While all of us knew the Soviets were behind the "wars of national liberation" in Asia, Africa, and Latin America, I was not personally convinced the Red Menace was quite as menacing as *Maître* Violet portrayed it to be, but my view was a minority one in that group. Even though I found the discussions fascinating, the ultraconservative politics of some participants were more than a bit unnerving. My Chase associates, who feared my membership could be construed as "consorting with reactionaries," eventually prevailed upon me to withdraw.

FURTHERING INTERNATIONAL COOPERATION

I also had a personal hand in the formation of a number of other organizations with an international orientation. I am particularly proud of two: the International Executive Service Corps (IESC), a partnership between the federal government and American corporations that provides technical assistance to the private sector in the developing world; and the Emergency Committee on American Trade (ECAT), which seeks to preserve and expand American involvement in foreign trade.

=

By the early 1960s the problem of poverty in many developing nations had become acute, as had the Communist challenge, which invariably accompanied the process of European decolonization in Asia and Africa. Although the U.S. government had responded forcefully to this challenge, IESC grew out of my conviction that the U.S. private sector could share their knowledge and expertise directly with businessmen in other countries. My own experience had convinced me there was a critical need for them to acquire modern management skills, which were even more urgently needed than capital.

With this in mind, when I spoke at the thirteenth International Management Congress in 1963, I called for the establishment of a Business Executive Corps that would be analogous to the Peace Corps created by President Kennedy a few years earlier. The audience responded positively, and I received several hundred letters about it afterward. With the active involvement of Sol M. Linowitz, the CEO of Xerox, and others, we created the IESC to provide technical advice and managerial assistance in developing countries around the world. President Lyndon Johnson formally launched IESC at a ceremony in the White House Rose Garden in June 1965.

Over the past thirty-five years IESC has sent more than fifty thousand retired executives abroad. They have completed almost thirty thousand projects ranging from the reorganization of a chicken-processing factory in the Philippines to advising the governments of Poland, Hungary, and the Czech Republic on the transition to a free-market economy. IESC is a true partnership, with much of the funding provided by the Agency for International Development and the brains and muscle supplied by American executives. In addition to aiding in the emergence of a more modern private sector in countries throughout Asia, Africa, Latin America, and now Eastern Europe, IESC has also played a significant role in stimulating demand for U.S. products.

FIGHTING PROTECTIONISM

Just after the Kennedy Round of GATT (General Agreement on Tariffs and Trade) negotiations were concluded in late 1967, W. Michael Blumenthal, then a deputy special representative for trade negotiations, spoke to the

Chase International Advisory Committee in New York. Mike warned us that the forces of protectionism were once again stirring in the United States. Twenty years of diminishing tariffs and a dramatic surge in low-cost imports from abroad had placed American textile and steel manufacturers under great competitive pressure, and they wanted quota or tariff relief. According to Mike, Congress was poised to accommodate them. To make matters worse, he said, the American corporate and banking community had done nothing to counter the protectionist arguments. He urged us to take action quickly, or the system of international trade that had produced the dramatic economic expansion of the post–World War II years might begin to crumble.

After the meeting, Eugene Black, William Hewitt, the CEO of Deere & Company, and I went to see Arthur K. Watson of IBM World Trade and persuaded him to take the lead in forming ECAT, a group composed of CEOs from about fifty major American corporations doing business overseas. We hired Bob McNeil, who had been one of the Kennedy Round negotiators, as executive director, and we were able to fend off the immediate threat.

We thought ECAT would be disbanded once protectionist pressures had subsided. They never have, and ECAT has remained in existence and continues to be one of the strongest voices for free trade in an increasingly protectionist Washington.

THE TRILATERAL COMMISSION

No organization with which I have played a founding role has attracted as much public scrutiny and attention as the Trilateral Commission. Pat Robertson has insisted that Trilateral is trying to create a world government and claims that it springs "from the depth of something evil." My son Richard, when he was a student at Harvard in the 1970s, told me his friends assumed that Trilateral was part of a "nefarious conspiracy."

On the lighter side, Garry Trudeau, author of the popular "Doonesbury" comic strip, delights in lampooning Trilateral. In one classic example a slightly paunchy businessman announces to a bartender that he is in the mood to celebrate because he has "just been accepted for membership in the Trilateral Commission." The bartender has never heard of the group, so the businessman explains "it is a powerful coterie of statesmen and international financiers which periodically meets in secret to shape the destiny of the western world." His job, the businessman relates, is to set "world zinc prices."

Trilateral, like Bilderberg, is a much more benign organization than the conspiracy theorists have depicted. It is a broadly based effort to bridge national differences and, in this case, invite the Japanese into the international community.

=

The idea for an organization including representatives from North America, Europe, and Japan—the three centers of democratic capitalism—resulted from my realization in the early 1970s that power relationships in the world had fundamentally changed. The United States, although still dominant, had declined relatively in terms of its economic power as both Western Europe and Japan recovered from the devastation of World War II and entered a period of dramatic economic growth and expansion. As a result the comity that characterized relationships among these regions for more than two decades had deteriorated alarmingly, and I believed something needed to be done.

I spoke about this in March 1972 before Chase investment forums in Montreal, London, Brussels, and Paris, calling for an "international commission for peace and prosperity" composed of private citizens drawn from the NATO countries and Japan to examine "such vital fields as international trade and investment; environmental problems; control of crime and drugs; population control; and assistance to developing nations."

I thought it essential to include the Japanese for a number of reasons. First of all, Japan had become a global economic power, and its high-quality products, especially automobiles and electronics, had made inroads into markets everywhere. Japanese export success, however, had produced a hostile reaction in the United States and Europe, and there was a strong perception that Japan was a "free rider" on the international trading system, aggressively exploiting opportunities abroad while only grudgingly opening their domestic market. Japan's economic prowess combined with its curious reluctance to engage seriously in international dialogue made it imperative to include them in the process I had in mind.

Zbigniew Brzezinski, then teaching at Columbia University, was a Bilderberg guest that year, and we spoke about my idea on the flight to Belgium for the meeting. I had been urging the Steering Committee to invite Japanese participants for several years, and at our session that April, I was again politely but firmly told no. Zbig considered this rebuff further proof that my idea was well founded and urged me to pursue it. I arranged a follow-up meeting with Zbig, Robert Bowie of the Center for International Studies at Harvard, Henry Owen of the Brookings Institution, and McGeorge Bundy of the Ford Foundation, who all heartily endorsed my proposal to form a trilateral organization.

I then convened a larger group, including five Europeans and four Japanese, for a meeting at my country home in the summer of 1972. Among the Japanese were Saburo Okita, who later became minister of foreign affairs, and Kiichi Miyazawa, who would serve as minister of foreign affairs, minister of finance, and prime minister. After a lengthy discussion we determined to set up the new organization. Zbig agreed to serve as director, and Benjy Franklin, my college roommate and colleague at the Council on Foreign Relations, agreed to help with organizational matters.

Trilateral was established on a trial basis; at the end of three years we would review its activities and accomplishments and decide whether it should be continued. Each region had its own executive committee and secretariat. At our first executive committee meeting in Tokyo in October 1973, two task forces reported on political and monetary relations among the three regions, and we published their findings in an effort to influence the behavior of our respective governments. For the second executive committee meeting in Brussels in June 1974—just after the first OPEC "oil shock" and calls for a "new international economic order"—we concentrated on the energy crisis and relations with developing countries.

We cast our nets widely in terms of membership and recruited labor union leaders, corporate CEOs, prominent Democrats and Republicans, as well as distinguished academics, university presidents, and the heads of not-for-profits involved overseas. We assembled what we believed were the best minds in America. The Europeans and Japanese assembled delegations of comparable distinction.

The inclusion among that first group of an obscure Democratic governor of Georgia—James Earl Carter—had an unintended consequence. A week after Trilateral's first executive committee meeting in Washington in December 1975, Governor Carter announced that he would seek the Democratic nomination for president of the United States. I have to confess that at the time I thought he had little chance of success. Much to my amazement, however, he not only won the Democratic nomination but defeated President Gerald Ford in the November election.

Carter's campaign was subtly anti-Washington and antiestablishment, and he pledged to bring both new faces and new ideas into government. There was a good deal of surprise, then, when he chose fifteen members of Trilateral, many of whom had served in previous administrations, for his team, including Vice President Walter Mondale, Secretary of State Cyrus Vance, Secretary of Defense Harold Brown, Secretary of the Treasury Michael Blumenthal, and Zbigniew Brzezinski as national security advisor. In his 1975 autobiography, *Why Not the Best?*, Carter wrote that "membership on this commission has provided me with a splendid learning opportunity, and many of the other members have helped me in the study of foreign affairs." Predictably, I was accused of trying to take control of Carter's foreign policy.

=

As economic conditions worsened in the late 1970s and the United States suffered a series of foreign policy reverses culminating in the Iranian hostage crisis and the Soviet invasion of Afghanistan, Trilateral attracted a great deal of unfavorable attention. In the 1980 presidential primary campaign, for instance, one of Ronald Reagan's supporters ran an advertisement that stated, "The people who brought you Jimmy Carter now want you to vote for George Bush," and highlighted the membership of both in Trilateral. I am not sure how many votes were changed by this ad, but such is the nature of politics in a democratic society. I should note, however, that President Reagan ultimately came to understand Trilateral's value and invited the entire membership to a reception at the White House in April 1984.

=

In December 1999, on the trip back from the ceremonies marking the official return of the Panama Canal, President Carter and I, who were both members of the U.S. delegation, spoke about Trilateral. He again generously credited the commission with broadening his understanding of international issues and their impact on the United States. And that, I would argue, is really the point. Trilateral has never been a sinister force; rather, it has provided an invaluable forum for dialogue among the leadership of three pivotal regions of the world. I am pleased that Trilateral remains a vigorous and effective collaborator on the world scene.

"CONSTRUCTIVE ENGAGEMENT"

These organizations reflect my belief in the principle of "constructive engagement." As an intelligence officer during World War II, I learned that my effectiveness depended on my ability to develop a network of people with reliable information and influence.

Some may feel this technique is cynical and manipulative. I disagree. Such an approach enabled me to meet people who were useful in achieving goals and gave me opportunities to form lasting friendships that have greatly enriched my life.

I have kept a record of most people I have met since the 1940s. Their names are stored in an electronically operated Rolodex that contains upward of one hundred thousand entries. Each card records my first contact and all subsequent meetings, and I can quickly review the nature of my past associations before seeing someone again. In a surprising number of countries—Mexico and Brazil, for instance—I have met every head of state since World War II, several of them many times. The continuity of these relationships has stood me in good stead on many occasions.

The world has now become so inextricably intertwined that the United States can no longer go it alone, as some prominent politicians have urged that we should. We are the world's sole superpower and its dominant nation economically. One of our principal duties is to provide judicious and consistent leadership that is firmly embedded in our national values and ideals. To do otherwise is to guarantee a return to the conflict that characterized the blood-drenched twentieth century. It is that fear, and that hope, that make me a proud internationalist.

SOUTH OF THE BORDER

My retirement from Chase in 1981 also gave me the opportunity to devote more time to my enduring interest in Latin American affairs, which had begun soon after World War II. In fact, I trace the origin of my personal involvement with Latin America to a romantic second honeymoon that Peggy and I spent in Mexico in early 1946. Nelson had given Peggy and me letters of introduction to friends of his in Mexico's vibrant artistic community as well as to businessmen with whom he had worked during the war, so we met a number of people who would become lifelong friends.

After visiting Mexico City, Peggy and I rented a car and driver and traveled north to San Miguel de Allende, Guanajuato, and Manzanillo, and then south to Puebla, Orizaba, and Oaxaca. The tour opened our eyes to a new world: the picturesque villages filled with people dressed in bright colors crowding the *mercados* where everything from tacos to beautifully made handicrafts were sold; and the charming old Spanish city of Puebla on the rim of the Valley of Mexico, which produced such beautiful pottery that we could not resist purchasing a number of pieces. We also learned more about the ancient civilizations of that land. Remains of the ancient Olmecs and Mayans, as well as the more recent Aztecs, were everywhere.

ENCOUNTERS IN BRAZIL

By 1948 I had begun to travel extensively for the Chase in Latin America, beginning with the Caribbean, Panama, and Mexico. I gradually acquired an imperfect but working knowledge of Spanish and quickly became enchanted by the warmth of Latin hospitality.

An added incentive for my first Chase trip to Brazil in 1948 was the chance to travel with Nelson to a country he knew intimately and believed had limitless economic potential. We began our tour in the great industrial city of São Paulo, where I was introduced to many of his friends, including our host, Walther Moreira Salles, a banker, agriculturist, politician, and former Brazilian ambassador to the United States. Walther accompanied us on a tour through the states of Parana, São Paulo, and Mato Grosso. This was the beginning of a friendship I would treasure for half a century.

Coffee was Brazil's principal export, and Walther was one of Brazil's largest coffee growers. Matao, his plantation, had more than a million coffee trees—a most impressive sight. Walther was a cultured gentleman with a broad interest in the arts. His gracious, self-effacing manner belied the fact that he was chairman and principal shareholder of Brazil's third largest bank and had vast holdings in industries throughout the country.

One stop on our weeklong tour was at a huge cattle ranch, Fazenda Bodoquena, in the state of Mato Grosso do Sul on Brazil's wild and untamed border with Paraguay. The ranch was in the geographical center of South America and abounded with wildlife—monkeys, parrots, jaguars, and alligators. Its English owners were offering it for sale because their manager had been murdered by local Indians. Walther had formed a syndicate to buy it and had invited Nelson to join. Intrigued by its romantic remoteness as well as its economic potential, I asked to take a small share as well, and over the next twenty years I visited it several times.

In 1967, Nelson, needing cash to finance his next presidential campaign, asked me to buy his share of Bodoquena. With some hesitation I agreed, realizing that I would have to become more involved in its management, which I had neither the time nor the expertise to do. After talking with Walther we decided to buy out the other members of the syndicate and invite Robert O. Anderson, whom I had known since my days at the University of Chicago, to become our partner. In addition to being CEO of Atlantic Refining, Bob owned one of the largest cattle ranches in the United States. He assumed responsibility for Bodoquena's operation and over the next decade built up the herd to more than ninety thousand. In 1980 we sold it for a substantial profit.

AN ERA OF OLIGARCHS AND ECONOMISTS

Doing business in Latin America was a very different proposition from banking in New York or London. In each country a small group of powerful oligarchs ran the economy, largely to suit themselves. While North American–style democratic institutions existed in a few nations, the majority were controlled by authoritarian regimes: Juan Perón in Argentina, the Somozas in Nicaragua, Fulgencio Batista in Cuba, the Trujillos in the Dominican Republic, François (Papa Doc) Duvalier in Haiti, Perez Jiménez in Venezuela, Manual Odria in Peru, Alfredo Stroessner in Paraguay, and Getulio Vargas in Brazil. These *caudillos* condoned oppression, extravagance, and corruption. Given these conditions it is not surprising that most Latin American countries seethed with social discontent and seemed always on the verge of revolution.

With a few notable exceptions most Latin leaders were ardent nationalists, wary of the United States. By the early 1950s most had established statist regimes and had either maintained or reinstituted protectionist policies similar to those advocated by Argentine economist Raul Prebisch, the first secretary-general of the United Nations Economic Commission for Latin America (ECLA). Prebisch and his colleagues had concluded that Latin American economic growth would be short-lived because of slackening world demand for its primary exports and its failure to develop a strong manufacturing sector capable of producing competitive goods for export.

ECLA's solution was to shift Latin America's capital and labor resources away from the production and export of primary products such as coffee, sugar, and minerals to the creation of manufacturing industries that would permit import substitution, and to encourage greater economic cooperation and integration within Latin America. Prebisch argued that a temporary period of protectionism would allow entrepreneurs to strengthen and diversify their economies while shielding them from destructive foreign competition. This prescription was broadly adopted throughout the hemisphere.

Unfortunately, protectionism and the augmented government powers needed to sustain it became a *permanent*—not a temporary—policy in the larger Latin American countries. As a result foreign investment and trade began to decline in the mid-1950s and accelerated in the 1960s. ECLA's pernicious doctrine not only failed to stimulate the growth of competitive indigenous manufacturing, but it also ushered in a high rate of inflation that depressed economic growth and worsened already abysmal social conditions. The consequences were devastating and enduring. For four decades after 1945, Latin American economies lagged behind other regions of the world. Argentina, historically the most affluent of the major Latin American countries, had a gross domestic product before World War II that was double Italy's. By 1960, Argentina had squandered its advantage and found its GDP lagging behind Italy's and surpassed by those of the newly industrializing countries of East Asia. This poor performance was replicated in every Latin American country.

NELSON AND THE GOOD NEIGHBOR POLICY

Latin America had traditionally been of secondary importance to U.S. relations with Europe, the Far East, and even the Middle East. Indeed, in the years since President James Monroe promulgated his doctrine in 1824, U.S. policy toward Latin America was characterized by long eras of neglect punctuated by periods of political and military intervention in countries such as Cuba, Mexico, Panama, and Nicaragua.

Even President Franklin Roosevelt's Good Neighbor Policy was more a promise to refrain from direct intervention in the affairs of our sister republics than a program of assistance and cooperation. By the end of the decade, however, the United States adopted a more progressive policy, and to implement a portion of it, FDR appointed Nelson to the newly created post of Coordinator of the Office of Inter-American Affairs in 1940. Nelson defined his task as showing Latin Americans that the United States was truly a "good neighbor."

Nelson assembled an exceptionally able staff, and his group crafted programs that addressed Latin America's fundamental problems in public health, education, and economic development. Nelson also inaugurated a policy of "cultural diplomacy"—sponsoring radio broadcasts in Spanish and Portuguese; hiring Walt Disney and Orson Welles to produce movies with a Latin flavor; and dispatching ballet corps, glee clubs, musicians, and academics on tours and welcoming their Latin American counterparts to the United States. He cultivated the leaders in every country, and his charisma and skills in dealing with people created friends for our country throughout the hemisphere.

Nelson laid the foundation for a new "Inter-American" system, a true economic and political partnership within the hemisphere rather than just a security alliance. Perhaps his greatest moment came at the Chapultepec Conference in Mexico City in February 1945. It was there that he, by then Assistant Secretary of State for American Republic Affairs, forged a hemispheric consensus on the structure of postwar international organizations. Against great odds Nelson held this bloc of votes together behind the United States position at the U.N. Organizing Conference that spring in San Francisco.

Nelson's successes came at a price for him at home. His tendency to act independently alienated the career diplomats in the State Department, who felt that they, not he, should control policy. With the death of his mentor, Franklin Roosevelt, Nelson quickly found his activities circumscribed and his advice ignored. He resigned in late 1945 and returned to New York.

Without Nelson's strong advocacy, U.S. relations with Latin America quickly withered. During the war Latin Americans were led to believe that the United States would provide massive economic aid and technical assistance once the crisis had passed. In fact, little of it materialized; instead, the United States poured billions of dollars into the reconstruction of Western Europe and Japan through the Marshall Plan. Latin America received little more than paternalistic advice and sermons.

With government aid on the decline, Nelson shifted his Latin American focus to the private sector. In early 1947 he formed the International Basic Economy Corporation (IBEC) as a vehicle to invest in productive enterprises in Latin America. Nelson was the principal shareholder, but Father and my brothers and I also took shares. My investment of $1 million required an invasion of my trust, but I wanted to show my strong support for Nelson's effort. IBEC invested in supermarkets and a fish cannery in Venezuela and, in Brazil, grain elevators, a farm machinery company, and the first mutual fund established outside the United States.

Nelson's first initiative, even before IBEC, had been the American International Association for Economic and Social Development (AIA), a not-for-profit that provided technical assistance throughout the region. Somewhat later Nelson formed the IBEC Research Institute in Brazil to conduct basic scientific research on hybrid corn, grass seeds, soybeans, and coffee plants. I served on the AIA board and later chaired the institute's board, whose work in improving crop yields has been an essential element in Brazil's economic growth.

Nelson's wartime involvement in Latin America and the subsequent impact he made through the private sector earned him enormous respect and sincere gratitude throughout the region. I believe there was no other American as popular as he was at that time. Nelson derived great satisfaction from his accomplishments and the many friendships he formed there. It is my impression that he looked upon his Latin American years as the happiest and most rewarding of his life.

THE ALLIANCE FOR PROGRESS

The decade of the 1950s was marked by increasing tension in U.S.-Latin American relations. This was the product of many factors: growing nationalism and anti-Americanism, disappointing economic growth, and the perception, after the CIA-sponsored Guatemalan coup in 1954, that the United States preferred dictators over democracy. This resentment came to a head during Vice President Nixon's trip through South America in 1958 when he was greeted by howling mobs and huge anti-American demonstrations in Peru and Venezuela. That experience and Castro's triumph in Cuba a few months later forced the Eisenhower and then the Kennedy administrations to reassess U.S. policy toward the region.

President Kennedy's announcement of the Alliance for Progress in early 1961 met with an enthusiastic response throughout the hemisphere. The basic purpose of the Alliance—"to enlist the full energies of the peoples and governments of the American republics in a great cooperative effort to accelerate the economic and social development of the participating countries of Latin America"—was timely and necessary. Its goal of achieving an economic growth rate of 2.5 percent throughout the hemisphere and of implementing an array of social and political reforms had broad support in the United States and Latin America. How these goals would be accomplished was the question.

I strongly supported the President's initiative, not least because it meant there would be an energetic response to the threat presented by Castro's Marxist regime in Cuba and Communist subversion in other parts of the hemisphere. However, I felt the Alliance had to be a public-private partnership if it was to be successful, while its U.S. architects had a decided preference for state-directed economic development. They assumed the nations of Latin America had to reach the "takeoff" stage of economic growth before anything else could happen, and the quickest way to get results was to put the government in charge.

The vast majority of Latin American political leaders were sympathetic to this approach. The presidents and prime ministers who attended the Alliance for Progress organizational meeting in Punta del Este, Uruguay, in August 1961 eagerly embraced Kennedy's proposal and the promise of significant American aid. The lone exception was my old friend from the London School of Economics, Premier Pedro Beltrán of Peru. Pedro pressed—with diplomatic restraint, to be sure—for a stronger private sector role and for eliminating the restrictions on foreign trade and investment imposed by Latin American governments. Unfortunately, Pedro's plea was largely ignored as the nations of the hemisphere, urged on by the "New Frontiersmen" in Washington, rushed to implement the Latin American Marshall Plan.

ORGANIZING THE AMERICAN PRIVATE SECTOR

The Kennedy administration, in an effort to mobilize the business community in support of the Alliance and to forestall private sector criticism, created the Commerce Committee for the Alliance for Progress (COMAP) under the leadership of Secretary of Commerce Luther Hodges. R. Peter Grace, CEO of W. R. Grace and Company and a longtime booster of Latin America, was named chairman, and I was one of about two dozen businessmen appointed to its board.

Despite a huge public relations effort, enthusiasm for the Alliance soon faded, and by early 1962, President Kennedy's request for a $1 billion congressional appropriation to fund Alliance programs had been cut in half. In an effort to rally support, Peter Grace wrote a fiery 140-page report on behalf of COMAP, denouncing Congress and arguing for $2.5 billion in aid.

While I agreed with Peter that the United States had to remain engaged in Latin America, to my mind throwing good money after bad was not the way to solve the problems. I felt Peter was so obsessed by the "Communist menace" that he was willing to sacrifice everything, including good economic sense. I talked with Walter Wriston, then president of City Bank, and Emilio (Pete) Collado, a director of Standard Oil of New Jersey, COMAP members who shared my views, and we issued a statement dissenting from Peter's position and urging a reappraisal of the Alliance.

We suggested a basic reorientation of the Alliance's focus, emphasizing the role of "private enterprise and investment" and placing "primary stress on improvement in the general business climate as a prerequisite for social development and reform." We urged governments throughout the hemisphere to remove foreign exchange controls, tame inflation and budgetary deficits, and "remove the network of other controls which restrict enterprise and sustain local, high-cost monopolies."

In conclusion we argued that free enterprise had to become the basis of real economic growth in Latin America, and that "the United States must change its role from one that emphasizes short-run economic palliatives combined with recommendations for sweeping social and economic reforms to one that places the greatest emphasis on the longer-run goals of creating an environment in which freedom of the marketplace is recognized for what it is: a major pillar of free and prosperous societies."

Our direct challenge to official U.S. policy was roundly denounced in Latin America as an affront to national sovereignty and a cover for U.S. economic penetration of the region.

=

Convincing the U.S. government to reverse course needed far more than words; it also required a concerted effort by the private sector. Therefore, in the summer of 1963 I began contacting members of COMAP and leaders of other U.S. business groups with a Latin American focus, urging them to meet to discuss forming a new organization. The response was overwhelmingly positive, and at a meeting on October 15, 1963, we formed the Business Group for Latin America (BGLA).*

Meanwhile, I lobbied the Kennedy administration to give the private sector a stronger voice in the formulation of Latin American policy. I met with National Security Advisor McGeorge Bundy twice to press the issue. Mac must have convinced the President that the criticisms of the Alliance had merit because the President wrote me that our group could "provide an exceptional opportunity for improved consultations with the United States Government and the business community on certain aspects of U.S.–Latin American affairs" and asking us to consult with federal agencies on a regular basis for this purpose. A meeting was arranged for this purpose on November 19, 1963, at the "F" Street Club with senior State Department officials to discuss our concerns. It was clear the Kennedy administration was ready to contemplate real changes in its Latin American policy. Tragically, President Kennedy was assassinated three days later.

SIDE-BY-SIDE WITH JFK

I first met Jack Kennedy in London in 1938 at his sister Kathleen's coming-out party at the American embassy. Although we were contemporaries at Harvard, we moved in very different circles. It was almost twenty years be-

---

*BGLA became the Council for Latin America in February 1965 when we formally merged with the Latin American Information Committee and the United States Inter-American Council. In 1970, we changed the name to the Council of the Americas.

fore we met again. By then Jack was a U.S. senator and a leading Democratic candidate for the presidency. I called on him in Washington a few times on bank-related matters, and he once visited Peggy and me at our New York home.

Jack was gracious, polished, and extraordinarily well informed on many subjects. While we differed on a number of domestic political issues, he and I were in broad agreement on American foreign policy—particularly the military and ideological threat posed by the Soviet Union and the need for the United States to play a leading role internationally in countering it.

In 1958, Jack was elected to the board of overseers of Harvard, on which I was already serving. Jack considered this a great honor, as did I. It was one of the few private organizations on which he continued to serve after he was elected president. While he never attended another overseers meeting in Cambridge, he invited us to hold a meeting in Washington and hosted a dinner for us at the White House, at which he did me the honor of placing me next to him.

In May 1962, Peggy and I attended a White House dinner for André Malraux, the well-known French writer and minister of cultural affairs. During the reception the President took me aside for a brief conversation on the state of the U.S. economy. As we parted, he asked me to set down my ideas in writing, which I proceeded to do. The President then responded with a letter to me. Although there were obvious points of disagreement, both of us agreed a tax cut would help get the sluggish economy moving again. Henry Luce asked to see the letters and found them so intriguing that he published them side by side in *Life* magazine in July 1962.

Jack's tenure was so brief that he did not leave behind much of a legislative legacy. But his immense popularity, a result of his personal charm, intelligence, and great courage, coupled with the tragic circumstances of his death, has turned him into a mythic figure.

=

Kennedy's death cut short the promise of the Alliance for Progress. Although I believe the original emphasis of the Alliance had been misplaced, I think that on this, as on many other issues, Kennedy had learned from his mistakes and the mistakes of his advisors. Had he lived, the private sector would have played a stronger role in economic development within the hemisphere. In fact, the Kennedy administration had already shifted its emphasis by late 1963 and was urging Latin American countries to modify their protectionist policies.

In the aftermath of the assassination, however, the new administration did not fully grasp this opportunity. Despite the best efforts of Thomas

Mann, the able assistant secretary for Latin America, the Johnson White House, preoccupied with its own War on Poverty in the United States and the real war in Vietnam, lost interest in Latin America. The Alliance for Progress gradually faded into insignificance. It would be another twenty years before another opportunity to affect the course of Latin American policy would arise.

THE COUNCIL AND THE CENTER

W ith Latin America relegated to the back burner in Washington, it was left to the private sector to pick up the slack. In 1965 I assumed the chairmanship of both the Council of the Americas and its new cultural adjunct, the Center for Inter-American Relations (CIAR). The council would focus on strengthening the involvement of the U.S. private sector in Latin America and would attempt to broaden public awareness in the United States of Latin America's rich cultural heritage.

From the beginning the council's membership included many of the country's largest and most important corporations, representing about 90 percent of U.S. investment in Latin America. Because of this the council quickly emerged as a key player in the ongoing debate over U.S. policy toward Latin America.

The CIAR, for its part, introduced New Yorkers and other Americans to the diversity, beauty, and sophistication of Latin American artists, musicians, and writers. Among other activities the CIAR held the first one-man show in New York for Fernando Botero, the great Colombian painter; sponsored the first New York auction of Latin American art at Sotheby's, which inspired both Sotheby's and Christie's to begin their own auctions of Latin American art; subsidized the translation into English of great Latin American writers, including Gabriel García Márquez's powerful *One Hundred Years of Solitude;* and published *Review* magazine, a literary quarterly that for twenty-five years has brought outstanding but lesser-known Latin writers to the attention of the American public.

ANGEL IN THE FAMILY

I n 1965 the council and the CIAR acquired a permanent home on the Upper East Side of New York through a stroke of good fortune. Our benefactor was Margaret de Cuevas, the daughter of my aunt Bessie Rockefeller. Bessie died in 1906 when Margaret was only eight, and she was raised in

Europe by governesses with little oversight from her father or other family members. Grandfather was inordinately fond of his eldest granddaughter. Bessie was his favorite child, and her death was a great tragedy for him. He often invited Margaret to Tarrytown and Ormond Beach, Florida, and it was in Florida in the mid-1920s during one of my stays with Grandfather that I first met Margaret. Although she was almost twenty years older than me, we became good friends.

Because Grandfather felt that adequate financial provision for Margaret had not been made, as it had for his other grandchildren, she inherited his residual estate of $25 million, which was held in trust for her. After the war Margaret and her husband, George, Marquis de Cuevas, lived in France where George ran the Ballet de Monaco, a money-losing activity that Margaret kept afloat. Margaret did maintain a home in New York on East 68th Street next to the Council on Foreign Relations, but she visited it infrequently.

As we looked for a headquarters for the CIAR and the council, I learned that Margaret had just bought the handsome mansion across 68th Street from her home in order to prevent it from being demolished and replaced by a multistory apartment house that would have cut off her light. I felt sure she had no need for an additional home, so asked her if she would be willing to give the property to the CIAR. Since George, who had died in 1962, was a Chilean by birth, I hoped she might look favorably upon giving it to an organization dedicated to improving relations with Latin America. After some hesitation she agreed to do so. This proved to be the answer to our prayers.

We raised $1.5 million—one-third contributed by me—to renovate the building and incorporate a small gallery on the ground floor where both historical and contemporary works of Latin art could be shown for the first time in New York.

Then in 1970, with my responsibilities as Chase's CEO becoming more demanding, I stepped down as chairman of both organizations, although I remained active on their boards.

The 1970s were not kind to the Center for Inter-American Relations. While the Council of the Americas flourished with the support of its two hundred member corporations, the CIAR, dependent on donations from a relatively few individuals and foundation grants, had a hard time making ends meet. I contributed substantial funds each year to cover operating deficits, but there seemed to be no end in sight. In 1976, somewhat out of desperation, we launched a $3 million endowment campaign. I persuaded the Rockefeller Brothers Fund to contribute $1 million, half of it as a challenge grant. I added half a million dollars, but even then the endowment campaign sputtered. It was hard to find New Yorkers interested in support-ing Latin American cultural programs. When all looked bleakest, once again Margaret de Cuevas came to our rescue.

By the late 1970s, Margaret had become involved with another man, who persuaded her to leave New York permanently. This led me to approach her about her two 68th Street town houses. But this time I found myself in a dilemma. Margaret's houses abutted the Council on Foreign Relations, which needed more space. The CIAR didn't need more space but desperately needed a larger endowment. The situation was further complicated by the fact that I was chairman of the CFR as well as a founder and past chairman of the CIAR. Which hat should I wear when I asked Margaret to make a gift of the houses?

I thought the CFR's need was more compelling and approached Margaret on their behalf. It turned out that the Council had done something to annoy Margaret a few years earlier, so she refused to consider it as a recipient. She felt differently about the CIAR. She agreed to give her houses to it, with the understanding that we did not need the space and would undoubtedly sell them. A year later the CFR bought the property from the CIAR for $1.6 mil-lion. So both organizations got what they needed most—all because of the generosity of Cousin Margaret.

DISMAL DECADES

Beginning in the mid-1960s a powerful tide of intense nationalism, stri-dent anti-Americanism, and revolutionary populism swept across Latin America. In country after country, civilian governments were unable to manage the extreme social tensions that had emerged during the process of modernization. Most were toppled, sometimes violently, and replaced by au-thoritarian military regimes.

By the end of the 1960s the hope for hemispheric cooperation raised by the Alliance for Progress was shattered and replaced by a miasma of con-frontation and suspicion. Latin American nations, with a few exceptions, closed their borders ever more tightly to foreign, especially American, com-panies and capital. The Andean Pact, for instance, formed in 1970 by Chile, Bolivia, Peru, Ecuador, and Colombia, and joined later by Venezuela, se-verely restricted the operations of foreign corporations, and there were a number of outright expropriations.

I was so concerned about the situation that I met with Secretary of State William P. Rogers and National Security Advisor Henry Kissinger to discuss what might be done. Among other things I suggested that President Nixon, as an indication of the importance he placed on improved relations with Latin America, ask my brother Nelson to tour the region as his special emissary. Both Bill and Henry liked the idea and persuaded Nixon to ask Nelson to tour South America on a fact-finding mission. Unfortunately, by this time relations were so bad that even Nelson met animosity almost everywhere, including a massive anti-American demonstration in Venezuela. I was concerned by the depth of hostility Nelson encountered. Clearly it would take more than a presidential emissary, no matter who he was, to repair hemispheric relations.

=

Most emblematic of these dismal years in Latin America was Chile during Salvador Allende's presidency in the early 1970s. The story has become well known and quite controversial. Allende, an avowed Marxist and leader of the Chilean Socialist Party, campaigned in 1970 on a platform of radical land reform, the expropriation of all foreign corporations, the nationalization of banks, and other measures that would have put his country firmly on the road to Socialism.

In March 1970, well before the election, my friend Augustin (Doonie) Edwards, publisher of *El Mercurio*, Chile's leading newspaper, told me that Allende was a Soviet dupe who would destroy Chile's fragile economy and extend Communist influence in the region. If Allende won, Doonie warned, Chile would become another Cuba, a satellite of the Soviet Union. He insisted the United States must prevent Allende's election.

Doonie's concerns were so intense that I put him in touch with Henry Kissinger. I later learned that Doonie's reports confirmed the intelligence already received from official intelligence sources, which led the Nixon administration to increase its clandestine financial subsidies to groups opposing Allende.

Despite this intervention, Allende still narrowly won the election. The Chilean congress confirmed his choice a few months later even though the CIA continued its efforts to prevent Allende's accession to power. Once in office the new president, true to his election promises, expropriated American holdings and stepped up the pace of land seizure from the elite and its redistribution to the peasantry. Most of Doonie Edwards's property was taken, and he and his family fled to the United States where Donald Kendall, CEO of Pepsico, hired Doonie as a vice president, and Peggy and I helped get them established.

Allende's radical program swiftly alienated the Chilean middle class. By September 1973 economic conditions had worsened and political violence had increased. The Chilean military, led by General Augusto Pinochet

Ugarte, revolted. Army units stormed the Moneda presidential palace, and Allende committed suicide. What followed can only be described as a reign of terror as old scores were settled and Allende loyalists, trade union leaders, and others were tortured, killed, or driven into exile.

Despite my own abhorrence of the excesses committed during the Pinochet years, the economic side of the story is a more constructive one. Faced with high inflation and huge budget deficits, and cut off from the international capital markets, Pinochet sought the advice of a group of young economists, many of them trained at the University of Chicago. They counseled the general to free Chile's economy from the restraints and distortions it had labored under for many years. Their daring economic experiment became the basis of Chile's strong recovery after 1985 and the model for other hemispheric nations.

THE DEBT CRISIS

During the 1970s many Latin American countries suffered the same fate as Chile—brutal urban guerrilla warfare, military dictatorships, repression of democratic institutions, and faltering economies. In fact, by the early 1980s Latin America was in the midst of an economic cataclysm. Decades of protectionism and state control had substantially lowered economic growth. Worse, most countries had borrowed heavily abroad after the huge oil price increases of the 1970s to support their overvalued currencies, fund their growing public sector budget deficits, and finance large public infrastructure projects. The severe recession that followed in the early 1980s knocked the bottom out of world commodity prices and drove world interest rates to almost unprecedented levels. The result was economic chaos in Latin America. By the mid-1980s annual inflation rates averaged 150 percent in the region and had reached the astonishing level of 217 percent in Brazil and 1130 percent in Argentina; unemployment rose to 15 percent; and capital flight attained epidemic proportions. The net transfer of assets *out* of Latin America rose to $30 billion a year, and external debt soared to an astounding $400 billion.

In my long experience in banking and finance, I had never seen a comparable situation. I must acknowledge, however, that banks like Chase must bear a large share of the responsibility. They should have seen what was happening and turned off the loan spigot to Latin American governments and businesses sooner than we did.

In August 1982, Mexico, owing more than $80 billion abroad, unilaterally suspended service on its debt, and many feared the other large debtors—Brazil, Argentina, and Peru—would follow suit. The International Monetary Fund and the U.S. Treasury cobbled together emergency loan packages to forestall threatened defaults, which enabled Mexico and the other countries to continue making interest payments on the debt they owed to foreign banks. Many people criticized this "bailout," but I spoke out in favor of it. Without prompt stabilization the world's financial system could have been at risk. Even though it took years and two debt reschedulings to completely stanch the hemorrhaging, the economic crisis had one salutary effect: It set the stage for basic change in Latin America.

By 1985 there was a growing realization throughout the region that sustainable economic growth would require fundamental political and economic reform. I believed the Americas Society and the Council of the Americas could make a real contribution to this process.

REJUVENATING THE INITIATIVE

In 1981, soon after retiring from the bank, I reassumed chairmanship of both the Council of the Americas and the CIAR. Even though the council had played a constructive role in the national debate over the Panama Canal during the late 1970s and the CIAR had firmly established itself as New York City's primary Latin American cultural organization, there was a general feeling that both needed to be reenergized and placed on a more solid financial footing.

As a first step we formed the Americas Society to absorb the assets of the CIAR and enable the council to continue to lobby the federal government. That was the easy part. The hard part was infusing both organizations not only with a new program, but also with a renewed sense of purpose. For that we needed to gain the support and active participation of prominent Latin Americans.

I discovered during three trips to South America in 1982 and 1983 that our organizations, which had been in existence for almost twenty years, were virtually unknown. While we were cordially received everywhere, it was largely because of my previous role with the Chase. The Americas Society and the Council had little visibility and no constituency in Latin America. If it was to be effective, that had to change.

To begin the process I wrote many of my friends in Latin America and invited them to a meeting in New York in late 1983. I told the gathering we wanted to create a Chairman's Latin American Advisory Council for the Americas Society and asked for their reactions. Their response was universally positive. In short order the Chairman's Council was formed with representation from every Latin American nation.

At one of our first meetings it became clear that there were many issues we could fruitfully explore. Foremost among them was the devastating impact the debt crisis had had on most Latin American economies. As a result I approached former Assistant Treasury Secretary Fred Bergsten of the Institute for International Economics, where I was a board member, about examining Latin America's economic problems to see how they could be overcome. Fred agreed to sponsor the project.

The research led to the publication in 1986 of *Toward Renewed Economic Growth in Latin America,* a landmark work that went a long way toward replacing the prevailing economic orthodoxy with a new set of assumptions that would eventually become known as neoliberalism or the Washington consensus. Superbly written and based on exhaustive research, the book outlined the steps by which Latin American nations could reignite economic growth—by lowering trade barriers, opening investment to foreigners, privatizing state-run and -controlled enterprises, and stimulating entrepreneurial activity; in other words, by ending the symbiotic relationship between government and the oligarchs over the economies of the region.

The study had a strong impact. Three of its four authors were distinguished Latin American economists whose prestige gave added heft and substance to the study's recommendations. The book was published in Spanish and Portuguese as well as English, making it more accessible to those we wanted to reach, and members of the Chairman's Council were behind the project from the start. Not only did our Latin American members insist on providing half the financing for the research to demonstrate that it was not just a "Yankee plot," but many of them reviewed the text before publication and made thoughtful changes. Some hosted public meetings in their own countries and made a concerted effort to bring the document to the attention of the media, government officials, academics, and labor leaders. Partially as a result of the study, by the late 1980s there was a discernible movement away from statist solutions and toward more reliance on market mechanisms to stimulate economic growth in many Latin American countries.

TOWARD HEMISPHERIC FREE TRADE

The pressure of the debt crisis forced Latin countries to act. Miguel de la Madrid, the young Harvard-educated president of Mexico, led the way. De la Madrid's courageous initiatives were expanded and consolidated by his successor, Carlos Salinas de Gortari. The Council of the Americas played a supportive role in this difficult and delicate process.

In the early 1980s my nephew Rodman Rockefeller, Nelson's oldest son, became chairman of the Mexico-U.S. Business Committee, an organization affiliated with the Council of the Americas. Rod and the American members of the committee convinced their Mexican business and banking counterparts to abandon their traditional support for high tariffs and other protectionist policies—not an easy feat to achieve. The Mexican members then informed President de la Madrid that a reversal of Mexico's traditional protectionist policy would have their full support. With important elements of the business establishment behind him, de la Madrid, in 1986, took the initial steps. These included unilaterally reducing tariffs, selling off some state-owned companies, and announcing that Mexico would join the General Agreement on Tariffs and Trade—steps that fundamentally altered Mexico's relationship with the rest of the world and set its course for the future.

If the economic reforms being implemented by Chile and Mexico were to be sustained and emulated by others, however, they had to be reinforced by positive changes in the rules that governed trade within the hemisphere. As one country after another adopted the export-driven model of economic growth, they needed a destination for their goods, particularly the U.S. market. Indeed, the authors of the *Growth* study had strongly recommended that the major industrial nations not only initiate a new GATT round of tariff reductions, but also avoid adopting any new import restrictions. It is ironic that just when Latin Americans began to accept the criticality of export markets to their own economic and social well-being, the United States began to seek tariff protection for our own threatened industries.

An exceptionally strong dollar ballooned the U.S. trade deficit to a record $160 billion in 1987, wreaking havoc in many domestic industrial sectors (particularly automobiles, steel, and textiles) and sparking demands for quotas, domestic content legislation, retaliation, and outright increases in tariffs. It was against this backdrop that those of us interested in maintaining the liberal trading regime had to do battle against labor unions, the protectionist right wing of the Republican Party, and environmentalists.

=

I vigorously opposed this protectionist reaction and encouraged the movement toward freer and more open trade. In a speech in Caracas in 1989 I called for intensified efforts toward economic cooperation for the mutual benefit of the U.S. and Latin America. Three years later, at the Council-sponsored Forum of the Americas in Washington, keynoted by President George Bush, I proposed creating a "Western Hemisphere free trade area" no later than the year 2000.

Indeed, in the wake of the passage of the North American Free Trade Agreement (NAFTA) in 1993, the idea of hemispheric free trade gained more general acceptance. President Clinton called for a "Summit of the Americas" in Miami in December 1994 that would consider the entire spectrum of issues that confronted our part of the world: drug trafficking, environmental degradation, and population growth as well as economic relationships.

In the months before the meeting, several of us at the Council of the Americas met often with members of the White House staff, State Department officials, and representatives from Latin countries to press the point that the summit would be an opportune moment to hammer out the framework for the "Free Trade Area of the Americas." A key player in getting the President to move ahead was Thomas F. (Mack) McLarty, Clinton's chief of staff, who became our liaison in the White House.

The Miami summit was an exhilarating moment for those who had fought for closer hemispheric relations. When the heads of state of all thirty-one American republics (all except Cuba) signed the protocol establishing the framework for the Free Trade Area of the Americas, there was a tangible sense that we could and would solve our many problems together. It appeared Chile would soon join NAFTA and that it would be only a matter of time before other Latin American nations would be added as well. Alas, that did not happen.

President Clinton had come to Miami politically wounded by the Republican triumph in the 1994 midterm elections. Partisan political considerations soon took center stage in Washington as the duel between President Clinton and House Speaker Newt Gingrich intensified. In addition, soon after the summit ended, the Mexican peso crisis unfolded and the so-called Tequila Effect placed pressure on these new and fragile reforms throughout the region. Trade issues swiftly slipped into the background.

It was not until the inauguration of George W. Bush as president in 2001 that this situation began to change. In the final years of the Clinton administration a strongly protectionist Democratic Party, insistent upon unrealistic and unworkable labor and environmental standards, joined with the isolationist wing of the Republican Party in the House of Representatives to thwart most trade initiatives—especially granting the president authority to negotiate trade agreements on a "fast track" basis, which Congress could then accept by a simple majority vote, rather than the two-thirds majority required by the Constitution. During a period of unprecedented economic growth and global trade expansion this was not a particularly acute problem, but in early 2000, as worrying signs of recession began to appear, U.S. failure to pry open new markets overseas began to hurt.

Fortunately, President Bush came out aggressively in favor of free trade and made "fast track" (which he referred to as trade promotion authority or TPA) an integral part of his campaign platform. At the annual Council of the Americas meeting in Washington in May 2001, the President spoke eloquently about the power of free markets and the critical importance of free trade. The President, Secretary of State Colin Powell, and U.S. Trade Representative Robert Zoellick, among other senior members of the Bush administration, all laid out cogent arguments for the United States to again assume leadership in the effort to facilitate both regional and global trade agreements.

The Council of the Americas played an integral role in the ultimately successful effort to secure TPA. Along with the Business Roundtable, the National Association of Manufacturers, the Farm Bureau, and other business groups, the Council lobbied hard for the legislation. Although the vote in the House was extremely close (215 ayes to 214 nays), the Senate passed TPA more easily. There is still a long way to go, but the Free Trade Area of the Americas and with it the promise of igniting economic growth within the stagnant economies of Latin America are once again within reach.

FORTIFYING THE AMERICAS SOCIETY

To secure the Americas Society's future, we needed to find a solution to its persistent financial problems. Annual deficits and a small endowment inhibited its effectiveness. I wanted to solve these problems as quickly as possible, so in 1987 we retained a consulting firm to help design a capital campaign.

Their report was not encouraging. No money, they claimed, would be forthcoming from Latin America, and the most we could expect to raise in the United States would be $5 million. We needed at least double that, so we fired the consultants and developed our own plan. We set a goal of $10 million and decided to ask the Latin American members of the Chairman's Council for a considerable portion of that. That in itself would be a real challenge. Wealthy Latin Americans had only just begun to support civil society institutions other than the Catholic Church, and convincing them to give substantial sums of money to a U.S.-based institution would be a difficult task, but I was determined to try.

Successful charitable fund-raising has much in common with managing a business: It requires leadership, persistence, and creativity. Accordingly, in the Americas Society campaign I got the ball rolling with a $1 million contribution to demonstrate my own commitment and set a level of giving for others. Then, because I knew it would be important early on to get at least one substantial commitment from a prominent Latin American, I approached Amalia de Fortabat, owner of the largest cement company in Argentina. I told her of my gift, explained my reasoning, and asked her to match it. Amalia quickly understood the logic of my approach and complied with my request. Our gifts stimulated other contributions; in fact, we raised $11.5 million, more than double what the "expert" consultants had predicted, with fully one-third of it from Latin Americans, who also became more involved in the affairs of the Society.

The rejuvenation of the Americas Society and the Council of the Americas in the 1980s was due in no small part to the strong leadership provided by George Landau. I had known George over the years as he moved from diplomatic post to diplomatic post in Latin America. He was an unusual foreign service officer—forceful, energetic, iconoclastic, and a firm believer in the importance of backing the U.S. private sector with all resources at his disposal. In my experience few career diplomats took such an active role in promoting American business internationally.

George served as president of both the Society and the Council for my final eight years as chairman. Our personal rapport and mutual respect resulted in an unusually effective partnership. They were banner years for both organizations.

=

The society's home on Park Avenue has become an important forum for Latin American governmental and business leaders seeking to connect directly with the New York business and financial community. The society also makes it possible for Latin and U.S. politicians and business leaders to meet informally and privately to discuss specific problems, ranging from tariffs to intellectual property rights to direct investment, and to move them toward resolution. I am proud to say that the Council of the Americas and the Americas Society, bolstered by the Chairman's Council, are among the most influential private sector voices in the United States promoting constructive relations with Latin America.

THE DAVID ROCKEFELLER CENTER

When Neil Rudenstine became president of Harvard University in 1991, I was delighted to learn at a get-acquainted lunch that Latin America was one of his highest priorities. We agreed that the vast majority of Americans knew little about their closest neighbors, and relatively few American universities provided their students with much more than a superficial introduction to Latin American history and culture. Even Harvard was derelict in this regard. Although some of Harvard's faculties offered courses on Latin America, there was no overall coordination, few majors, and almost no visibility.

Neil wanted to upgrade Harvard's teaching capacity in this critical area, and he sought my help. Since I had been looking for just that kind of opportunity, Neil and I had a happy meeting of minds. After our discussion he consulted with the deans of Harvard's several schools and secured their support for the creation of a university-wide Center for Latin American Studies that would focus all of Harvard's considerable faculty talent in one place. The center would be housed in its own building and have its own budget and director. Neil decided to name the new facility the David Rockefeller Center for Latin American Studies.

The cost of the center was estimated at $30 million. To get the project off the ground, Neil asked me to give $1 million, matching a like amount from Harvard. I agreed to this and also to give another $10 million over time, with the understanding that Harvard would raise the remaining $20 million in outside gifts. We both agreed it would be highly desirable to ask Latin Americans to play an important role in the center as well as to contribute financially to its success. This goal was achieved in a remarkably short time.

The center got off to a flying start. John Coatsworth, a distinguished Latin American historian, became director of the center. Harvard Latin Americanists—from historians to public health specialists to zoologists, a core group of fifty scholars—now work closely through the center. As a result, the importance of Latin America within Harvard's curriculum has grown, and the number of Latin American students enrolled there has more than doubled. Harvard has become a focal point in the United States for academic gatherings of all kinds relating to Latin America.

=

At the beginning of the twenty-first century I have become increasingly concerned about the political and economic stability of Latin America. The powerful surge of economic growth that followed the structural reforms of the late 1980s and early 1990s, and which dramatically raised living standards south of the Rio Grande, has now stalled. The two bright spots in the region are Mexico, now under the leadership of President Vicente Fox, and Chile. Both nations have stuck with the free market policies and democratic reforms instituted by their predecessors and have reaped their benefits, although not without a certain amount of pain and dislocation. But the promise of these two nations is, at least in my mind, counterbalanced by the poor economic performance of most other countries and the deepening social crisis that can be clearly observed in a number of others—Argentina, Ecuador, Colombia, and Venezuela in particular. In some ways the situation is very similar to the late 1950s prior to the creation of the Alliance for Progress, or the early 1980s just before the full impact of the debt crisis was felt.

There are, however, two major differences between these earlier crises and the one we now confront. The first is the comprehensive and resilient framework of institutions that has been created to deal with international economic and financial problems. These institutions—from the IMF to the WTO to the U.S. Treasury to the incipient Free Trade Area of the Americas—have been severely tested by the peso crisis and the so-called Asian flu of 1998, and acquitted themselves well, although not without severe criticism from both the left and the right. The second factor is the growing awareness of Latin America within the United States. Economic development, environmental protection, human rights, and narco-terrorism are not just national issues but are hemispheric and can only be resolved through common action. Fortunately, the institutions with which I have been associated during my fifty-year involvement with Latin America—the Council of the Americas, the Americas Society, and the Center for Latin American Studies at Harvard—are now part of a much larger and more intricate fabric. The combination of these two factors will assure, I am confident, an immediate and effective response to whatever problems the future might bring.

A PASSION FOR
MODERN ART

I have been immersed in the world of art since I was a small boy. Among my first memories—aside from being left disconsolate on the dock in Seal Harbor while everyone else went off to see the stranded whale—are of Mother amid the Asian art in her incense-misted Buddha room or studying a Toulouse-Lautrec print in her gallery in our home on 54th Street. Father's art—especially the wonderful Unicorn Tapestry—has also left an indelible imprint, but his formidable collection of fragile Chinese porcelains, old masters, and austere religious works, beautiful as they were, did not invite intimate contact. It was clear as well that Father believed we should admire their perfection and absorb their timeless beauty from a distance. Mother was different. Although she had an expert's understanding, Mother also approached art emotionally, and she wanted her children to revel in the full beauty of a painting, print, or piece of porcelain. Above all she taught me and my siblings to be open to all art—to allow its colors, texture, composition, and content to speak to us; to understand what the artist was trying to do and how the work might provide a challenging or reassuring glimpse of the world around us. It was often a deeply enthralling experience. I owe much to Mother, but her patient transmission of her love of art is a treasure beyond calculation. Her death in April 1948 left a deep hole in my life.

I had not fully realized the extent of my devotion to her and the influence she had and would continue to have on my values, artistic tastes, and appreciation for the intrinsic quality of all people. Apart from her devotion to Father and her children, the Museum of Modern Art (MoMA) was Mother's consuming passion. From the early 1920s everyone in the family knew of Mother's growing enthusiasm for almost all forms of contemporary art, although many of us, particularly Father, were mystified by it. MoMA was a logical extension of this passion, and the nurturing of the museum became her strongest priority.

My involvement with MoMA—indeed, my interest in modern art—took much longer to develop. In fact, it was not until I was asked to replace Mother on its board that I took any real interest in the museum.

It is true I had had a front-row seat during the museum's creation in the late 1920s. Many of the planning sessions were held at our home on West 54th Street, and it was there I first met Lillie Bliss and Mary Quinn Sullivan, who shared my mother's determination to create a museum where the work of younger, more innovative artists could be shown to a larger public. A few prominent businessmen and important collectors, intrigued by the ideas of the three ladies, also attended these meetings, which were often long and drawn out. I remember Father waiting impatiently for them to end.

Once Mother and her associates decided to create a new museum, a director had to be found. Professor Paul Sachs, head of the Fogg Museum at Harvard, recommended Alfred Barr, a young art historian who was then teaching at Wellesley, where he had initiated the first college course on modern art. Barr was a risky but inspired choice. Barely thirty at the time, he was a scholar and an aesthete with a broad acquaintance among European and American artists, among them Pablo Picasso and Henri Matisse, two of the greatest artists of the twentieth century. Over the course of the next forty years Alfred built MoMA's collection of unparalleled modern masterworks and helped shape the taste and sensibilities of the art world and the general public.

NELSON TAKES COMMAND

Within a year of graduating from Dartmouth in 1930, Nelson had immersed himself in MoMA's activities. Together with several bright, energetic friends he joined the Junior Advisory Committee, which had been established to attract younger people to the museum. Nelson and his contemporaries were brash enthusiasts who insisted that artists working in more abstract styles should have a prominent place in the museum's exhibitions and programs. This brought them into conflict with older, less venturesome trustees who were comfortable with more conventional exhibitions. They stirred a debate that still rages today over the appropriate boundaries of "modern" art in terms of ever more radicalized art forms. In the 1930s this debate raged around the relationship between the classical work of Degas and Monet, on the one hand, and the more controversial offerings of Ernst, Mondrian, de Chirico, and Klee on the other. Today the tension centers on the connection between these older artists and the sometimes shockingly graphic, sometimes bewilderingly nonrepresentational practitioners of contemporary art. The traditional belief that art should be beautiful seems irrelevant to many younger artists today.

Even in the early 1930s everyone knew Nelson wanted to be president of MoMA (not to mention the United States), but he was reluctant to seek the office too aggressively as long as Mother was still active. It turned out that he had an unlikely ally in Father, who frankly disliked modern art and resented the leading role that Mother was playing at "her" museum. Mother served as treasurer and first vice president during the museum's early years, but Father pressured her to decline the presidency when it was offered to her. Finally, in 1936, he used Mother's worsening heart problems to persuade her to resign altogether from her official posts. Nelson had his opportunity. He replaced Mother as first vice president and treasurer, and in 1939, just as MoMA's building was completed, was elected president.

Nelson was an enthusiastic collector of modern and contemporary art. He was quick to find merit in controversial art forms, which comprised the bulk of his purchases. His favorite pastime for most of his life was to pore over auction catalogues, carefully marking the objects on which he would bid. Nelson's enthusiasm and willingness to take risks enabled him to help MoMA become the kind of cutting-edge institution that Mother had intended it to be.

Nelson's partner in this endeavor, really his alter ego, was René d'Harnoncourt, who became MoMA's director in 1949. René was a great bear of a man, standing more than six and a half feet tall. A chemist by training, he became an expert in pre-Columbian art after emigrating to Mexico in the 1920s. René was charming and well educated, and he bubbled over with ideas. Nelson and René assembled a stunning collection of primitive art from Africa, Oceania, and Central and South America, and exhibited it at the Museum of Primitive Art, which Nelson created in 1954; it was located just to the west of MoMA. It was this collection that Nelson donated to the Metropolitan Museum in memory of his son Michael.

Nelson and René's partnership transformed MoMA, making it more accessible to the general public and taking it down new and ever more daring paths.

After Mother's death in 1948, I was honored to be asked to fill her seat on the board. I was somewhat intimidated by the responsibility and my lack of preparation for it. After I left home for Harvard in 1932, I had few direct contacts with the museum other than attending an occasional exhibition. In addition, I was very conscious of joining a board on which my older brother was the dynamic president and realized it would be best to "learn the ropes" before I attempted to take a more active role in MoMA's affairs.

The one area in which I did take an interest was the unfinished garden along 54th Street, site of my childhood home, which Father had demolished in the late 1930s after he and Mother moved to their Park Avenue apartment. In 1949 I donated the funds for the design and construction of the Sculpture Garden. At my request Philip Johnson, whose architectural talents were already widely recognized, agreed to take on the commission, and it quickly became a favorite feature of MoMA. That was a happy way for me to begin my active participation in the museum's affairs.

SURROUNDED BY MEN IN RED COATS

Part of learning the ropes at MoMA was enhancing my own knowledge and appreciation of art. Peggy and I were fortunate to find a wonderful mentor in Alfred Barr.

I had come to know Alfred through Mother. His passion for ornithology and mine for entomology gave us a common link through the world of natural history. After I joined MoMA's board, he became a good friend of Peggy's and mine, and served as a bridge between us and Mother's museum. While there were many others over the years who helped us in the selection of paintings for our collection, Alfred had the greatest impact.

When we were first married, my income was strictly limited, and so was our ability to purchase art. We used what little money we had to purchase a few paintings, which served as wall decorations. Almost all the works we hung in our first homes were gifts from Mother, including several watercolor landscapes of France and Italy by Arthur B. Davies, whom Mother had discovered early in his career. Mother also gave us a large, handsome George Inness landscape, which we prized. But most of our walls were filled with prints: an entire folio of prints of the Hudson River; a number by John James Audubon, though none of his important ones; and some not particularly good examples of Currier & Ives, which we placed in less conspicuous places. After Mother's death we received from her estate a number of prints by the Japanese master Ando Hiroshige and a set of black-and-white prints by Honoré Daumier.

The first painting of any consequence we bought was a portrait of a handsome young gentleman, attributed (falsely, as it turned out) to Thomas Sully. We paid $10,000 for it in 1946, which was a great deal of money for us at the time. We liked it very much, and for many years it hung over the living room mantel in New York. At about the same time, because they were reasonably priced, we bought other minor eighteenth-century English portraits, two featuring men in bright red coats and one of a girl, vaguely—and inaccurately—ascribed to Thomas Gainsborough. They at least filled blank spaces on our walls, and we found them agreeable.

Shortly after I joined the museum board, we invited Alfred and his wife, Marga, to see our new house on Manhattan's East Side. While we were having tea, Marga looked around the living room, clearly dismayed at what she considered an extremely banal collection of paintings. "How can you stand to be surrounded by so many little men in red coats?" she asked. Peggy and I were taken aback by her bluntness and more than a little annoyed but, upon reflection, had to admit the art on our walls wasn't of great caliber. We decided then and there to place more emphasis on quality in our purchases even if we could not afford anything approaching a masterwork. In this endeavor we frequently sought Alfred's advice.

Over a decade or more, Alfred brought to our attention works of high quality. Peggy and I were drawn to the French Impressionists and Postimpressionists, and the first significant painting we bought under Alfred's tutelage was a beautiful Pierre Bonnard flower painting. This was followed by a Matisse still life and, in 1951, Renoir's stunning nude *Gabrielle at the Mirror*, for $50,000. It was our first important Impressionist painting and by far the most expensive. We hung it proudly in our living room in the City, although some of Peggy's conservative relatives were scandalized at the sight of a nude woman so prominently displayed!

Alfred introduced us to several dealers from whom we bought Impressionists, including Sam Salz, Justin Thannhauser, and Dalzell Hatfield of Los Angeles. We also became active clients at the Wildenstein and Knoedler galleries.

In 1955, Alfred learned that the French dealer Paul Rosenburg had acquired a substantial part of Mrs. A. Chester Beatty's collection of Impressionist paintings, reputed to be one of the finest in England. Among its treasures was Paul Cézanne's *Boy with a Red Vest*. Alfred considered it one of Cézanne's masterpieces and was anxious to acquire it for MoMA. Since the museum did not have the funds to purchase it, Alfred made us a proposal: If we would buy it and agree to leave it to the museum, he would ask Rosenburg to give us the first opportunity to see the entire collection. We accepted his proposal and ended up buying not only the Cézanne but also Georges-Pierre Seurat's *The Roadstead at Grandcamp* and Edouard Manet's magnificent still life *La Brioche*. We were so impressed by the quality of the paintings in the Beatty collection that had we been able to afford it, we would gladly have purchased them all. Nonetheless, the three we did buy are without doubt among the finest paintings in our collection.*

EMERGING AS SERIOUS COLLECTORS

The following year we acquired two of Claude Monet's *Water Lilies.* Monet's later works were considered inferior at the time, but Alfred Barr strongly encouraged us to buy them.

The large mural-sized landscapes Monet painted during his later years depicting sedges, reeds, and water lilies floating on the surface of the pond that he created near his home at Giverny on a tributary of the Seine were initially regarded by critics as inferior to his earlier, more representational studies of railway stations, haystacks, and other familiar scenes. In his mid-seventies and nearly blind when he began his final Giverny *Water Lilies* cycle, Monet painted with his brushes fastened to the end of long sticks. The massive canvases—some of them twenty or more feet in length—were almost abstract in design. When they were exhibited in 1925, the reaction was strongly negative. Only the intervention of Monet's friend Premier Georges Clemenceau, the "Tiger of France," prevented the artist from destroying them. For years these canvases were locked away in a barn at Giverny, all but forgotten.

In the early 1950s, Michel Monet sold thirty of his father's Giverny paintings to Madame Katia Granoff, a Paris dealer. Alfred Barr saw them and recognized what most art historians had missed: Monet's anticipation of abstraction in modern art. The connection between Monet's later works and the overpowering canvases of the New York School of Abstract Expressionism—exemplified by Jackson Pollock, Mark Rothko and Willem de Kooning—seemed startlingly suggestive to Alfred. In 1955, with funds pro-

---

*Our *Boy with a Red Vest* is one of four Cézanne painted. The others hang in the National Gallery in Washington, D.C., the Barnes Collection in Philadelphia, and the Musée d'Orsay in Paris.

vided by Mrs. Simon Guggenheim, Alfred purchased a large *Water Lilies* canvas and had it displayed prominently at MoMA. Critics soon recast Monet's last Giverny paintings as an extraordinary advance in the history of art.

Peggy and I saw and admired the painting at MoMA, and before we left for Paris in June 1956, Alfred informed us that Katia Granoff still had several *Water Lilies* canvases and encouraged us to visit her gallery. As we entered, one painting—white lilies floating on the indigo surface of Monet's luminous pond—immediately caught our attention. We bought it and one other on the spot. In 1961 we purchased a third canvas from the Wildenstein Gallery in New York. Although too large for most of our walls, we finally found an excellent place to hang all three in the stairwell at Hudson Pines.

Peggy and I were now fully launched into the exciting world of collecting, and for the next three decades we continued to expand the scope and deepen the quality of our collection.

In late 1959 we were guests of Stavros and Eugenie Niarchos for a week's sail through the Aegean aboard their three-masted schooner, *The Creole.* Owner of one of the world's great shipping fleets, Stavros along with a few other Greek magnates—Aristotle Onassis, future husband of Jacqueline Kennedy, was another—dominated the global maritime industry. Widely considered one of the world's wealthiest men, Stavros had homes scattered across the globe, a stable of thoroughbreds in England, and a superb collection of modern art. I had met Stavros six years earlier when he came to Chase's headquarters for a business meeting. I found him to be an extremely shrewd and talented businessman who had already begun to expand his corporate empire. Peggy thought him witty and entertaining, although she was put off by his racy lifestyle. Even though Stavros and I had little in common, we developed a good personal relationship and became business partners in many real estate deals in the United States, including the purchase of Rockefeller Center.

Our friends Jack and Drue Heinz of Pittsburgh were also on that 1959 voyage, as were Hans (Heini) Heinrich and Fiona Thyssen-Bornemisza, whom we met for the first time. Heini was the grandson of the famous August Thyssen, the "Rockefeller of the Ruhr," founder of Germany's Vereinigte Stahlwerke, for many years the world's largest mining and steel cartel. Our cruise brought out the fact that we were all interested in art.

The following May, Peggy and I dined with Stavros and Eugenie Niarchos at their home on the Rive Gauche, built originally by Napoleon for his mistress Madame Tallien. We then all flew to Lugano to spend the weekend with the Thyssens. Heini's father, Heinrich, had devoted himself to art rather than the family business and had assembled one of the world's greatest collections of Renaissance art. We had heard much about it but had never seen it. When we arrived at Heini's home, the Villa Favorita, we were awestruck. Heini had greatly expanded his father's collection by adding both old masters and fine examples of twentieth-century artists. It was the most comprehensive and beautiful private collection we have ever seen.*

While in Lugano, Heini told us there was to be an auction of twentieth-century art in Stuttgart. Stavros convinced the group to fly there on his plane to take a look at the objects being offered. Peggy and I went along largely to have a good time with our more daring friends. When we arrived, we saw a number of items that appealed to us and were emboldened to place bids on several of them. After returning to New York we learned to our pleasant surprise we had acquired a Paul Klee painting; watercolors by George Grosz, Lyonel Fenninger, Emil Nolde, Maurice de Vlaminck, and Wasily Kandinsky; and a sculpture by Käthe Kollwitz, none of whom were represented in our collection.

BECOMING ENGAGED AT MoMA

In 1958, after a decade of relatively inactive board membership, I suddenly found myself thrust to the center of MoMA's affairs when Nelson resigned from the chairmanship to run for governor of New York. My sister-in-law Blanchette was the logical choice to replace him because of the vital role she was already playing as a trustee, but my brother John, who felt much the same way about modern art as Father had, was opposed to her doing so. Therefore, I agreed, with some reluctance, to serve as chairman on an interim basis. Fortunately, Blanchette overcame John's opposition and was duly elected to relieve me as chair of the board after about six months.

In 1962 I was elected to a full term as MoMA's chairman. Despite my heavy responsibilities at Chase, I felt able to accept because the chairmanship is largely honorific, and the president is the senior trustee position. I also knew the museum's operations were in René d'Harnoncourt's capable hands. But René retired in 1968, and Eliza Parkinson, the president, indicated that she, too, wanted to relinquish her post. Quite unexpectedly, MoMA needed a new top management team, and as chairman I had to lead the effort to find their replacements.

---

*The Thyssen-Bornemisza Collection is now housed in the Villa Hermosa in Madrid.

I was convinced that MoMA needed a president with business experience as well as recognized competence in the arts. William Paley was the best candidate. A trustee since the 1930s, Bill had an outstanding collection of modern art and, as the founder and chairman of CBS, had been an innovator in the communications industry. Bill was an extremely busy man, however, and it was not clear he would accept. After considerable persuasion by Blanchette and me, he agreed to take on the job. This was a godsend for MoMA, if not for Bill, as the next four years proved to be the most turbulent in the museum's history.

In the late 1960s, after forty years of operations, MoMA had become the citadel, sanctuary, and principal testing ground for modern art in the United States. Attendance had grown dramatically from year to year, as had membership. Our broadly diversified collections of paintings, prints, drawings, sculpture, film, and the other artifacts of modern art—including a helicopter dangling from the rafters of the fourth floor—had also grown exponentially. MoMA's staff developed and dispatched exhibitions across the nation and around the world. And we had just completed the first expansion of the museum since the late 1930s with the completion of the East Wing and the incorporation of the old Whitney Museum into our new West Wing in 1964. This was all positive and heartening.

Below the surface, however, two critical business problems threatened the institution: money and management. The recurring operating deficit approached $1 million a year and was worsening. Our thirtieth anniversary endowment campaign had raised $25.6 million, but the annual deficits quickly eroded this reserve. In addition, the finance committee had invested in a portfolio of then fashionable high-technology "go-go" stocks that turned out to be a disaster, wiping out one-third of our all too meager endowment.

Our financial woes were exacerbated by a poor management structure, a result of a decentralized system in which each department enjoyed considerable autonomy in terms of exhibitions, acquisitions, and program. Furthermore, influential trustees often aligned themselves with the curators of departments in which they had a special interest and for which they became strong advocates and financial backers. Since no one wanted to antagonize important trustees, exhibitions and acquisitions were often approved without regard for overall policy guidelines or the museum's fragile financial condition. There was no museum-wide budget process, and curators and exhibition planners rarely allowed cost to figure adequately into their calculations; they assumed the trustees would find ways to cover the bill.

This unbusinesslike process was symptomatic of a deeper problem: the lack of consensus about the composition of MoMA's permanent collection and the direction our collecting should take in the future. Some trustees strongly advocated continuing to collect the work of emerging contemporary artists while carefully culling the collection of its less outstanding holdings to finance new acquisitions. Many others preferred that the collection be limited to the "golden age" of modernism: from the 1880s, when the Postimpressionists first emerged, to the 1950s with the advent of the New York School. I was in the camp favoring a "pioneering spirit" in our acquisitions, as originally defined by Mother and her collaborators, that would not restrict the collection to a specific period but instead would continue to identify, purchase, and exhibit works of the avant-garde. Bill Paley and I agreed this course required strengthening our fund-raising capacity and correcting our financial and administrative problems. This was MoMA's principal challenge as we headed into the last quarter of the twentieth century.

MANAGEMENT TURBULENCE

Our first task was to find a suitable replacement for René d'Harnoncourt. For almost twenty years, René had been a tower of strength and a skillful diplomat who harmonized the talented but temperamental curators working under him. He also found a way to utilize Alfred Barr's genius in developing the museum's permanent collection, while relieving him of management responsibility, at which he was not proficient. René was also extremely adept at dealing with the trustees and integrating their varied abilities and interests for the benefit of the museum. In retrospect, however, René had created a management structure that depended far too much on his own personal abilities. Because he had not delegated sufficient authority, that structure began to fall apart soon after his retirement.

Bates Lowry, our choice as René's successor, was a well-respected art historian. He seemed the ideal choice, but his honeymoon was short-lived. Shortly after he became director, Bates announced he would also become curator of the Department of Painting and Sculpture, MoMA's most important curatorial position and a full-time job in itself. The other curators saw this as a power grab and believed their departments would get short shrift in the future. Bates also alienated the trustees by insisting we provide him with "suitable" housing so that he could entertain on behalf of the museum. But after we did what he asked, he refused to entertain because, he said, it was his home! He renovated his office suite at the museum without getting board approval for the expense. When Bill Paley saw the bill, he was furious and fired Bates on the spot, after only ten months on the job. Bill's unilateral action upset a lot of people, but I thought it was necessary under the circumstances even though we were left without a director.

It was not until a year later that our search committee proposed John Hightower as director. As executive director of the New York State Council on the Arts, John had generated strong financial support for the arts throughout New York State and was considered a man who understood the importance of the bottom line. More important, John was not an art historian, so, unlike Bates Lowry, he posed no threat to the museum's curatorial staff. John came to the museum full of enthusiasm, and initially we were optimistic about his appointment.

John soon ran into trouble. He believed museums had an obligation to help society resolve its problems. Since Vietnam was one of the principal societal problems of the day, John thought MoMA should participate in the national debate. Before long the museum's lobby resembled an antiwar protest headquarters. He allowed the bookshop to sell a poster of the infamous My Lai massacre, with the caption "And babies too . . ." and "The Museum of Modern Art" emblazoned in bold letters along the bottom. When President Nixon's invasion of Cambodia provoked widespread unrest on the nation's college campuses, Hightower dropped the museum's admission fee, ran continuous showings of antiwar films, and permitted MoMA staff members to stand outside distributing antiwar pamphlets.

This was followed by the infamous "information" exhibition in the summer of 1970. John had a black flag flown outside the museum. Inside, museum-goers were asked to vote on the question: "Would the fact that Governor Rockefeller has not denounced President Nixon's Indochina policy be a reason for you not to vote for him in November?" They were also invited to "dial a revolutionary" and hear recorded messages from Black Panther Bobby Seale and Yippie Jerry Rubin that exhorted them to action. To accommodate the "sexual revolution" there were burlap-draped cubicles within which couples could romp about. It was all quite outrageous.

John was entitled to voice his opinions, but he had no right to turn the museum into a forum for antiwar activism and sexual liberation. In response to questions about the artistic validity of the show, John responded by saying, "There are a lot of things individually and collectively that affect my existence: the war, J. Edgar Hoover, the Establishment, the Rockefellers, the Defense Department." He continued, "Artists are bound and determined to bite the hand that feeds them, especially when the integrity of art is revered in the evening and dismissed during the day." I found his statement personally insulting, and so did other trustees.

When MoMA's professional and curatorial staff went on strike in 1971, John immediately yielded to their demands to form a union. With the staff in disarray, contributions drying up, and the trustees in open revolt, Bill Paley, with my full support, fired Hightower in early 1972.

Having failed twice with external candidates, we looked within MOMA for a replacement. The strongest candidate was Richard Oldenburg, brother of the artist, Claes. Dick had run the Publications Department with great ability and had even broken precedent by turning in a modest profit for a few years! Broadly knowledgeable about the arts, Dick was a calm and gracious man, and appeared to be the right person to steer the museum onto a new course. He was appointed director in 1972 and ran MoMA with considerable success for the next twenty-two years.

BUYING THE STEIN COLLECTION

In 1968 the sudden availability of a portion of the fabled Gertrude Stein collection attracted the attention of much of the art world.

Gertrude Stein, an avant-garde American writer, had lived in Paris for many years, presiding over a salon attended by many writers and artists, including Pablo Picasso, Henri Matisse, and Georges Braque. Gertrude and her brother Leo were among the first collectors of Cubist and other radical art forms during the early decades of the twentieth century. They started collecting when most of these artists were unknown, unappreciated, and often indigent. By the 1930s they had assembled an outstanding collection that was displayed in Miss Stein's Paris apartment. When she died in 1946, she bequeathed part of her collection—consisting of forty-seven paintings, thirty-eight by Picasso and nine by Juan Gris—to her three great-nieces and nephews, subject to a life interest for her longtime companion, Alice B. Toklas.

After Miss Toklas's death in 1967 the Stein heirs decided to sell the collection. William Lieberman, then director of MoMA's Department of Prints and Drawings, learned they would be pleased to have the collection go to the museum *if* we made a competitive offer; otherwise, it would be sold to the highest bidder. The problem was that MoMA, facing a deficit and chronically short of acquisition funds, had no funds available for this purpose.

I felt this was too good an opportunity for us to miss, so I formed a syndicate to buy the collection; it included my brother Nelson; William A. M. Burden; André Meyer, the senior partner in Lazard Frères; Bill Paley; and John Hay (Jock) Whitney, publisher of the *New York Herald Tribune.** The six of us agreed to subscribe equal dollar amounts. When Bill Burden dropped out, I voluntarily assumed his share as well.

MoMA's curators were not interested in the entire Stein collection, but they did want six Picassos to fill gaps in the collection. Syndicate members agreed in advance that these six would go to the museum either outright or in the form of a testamentary bequest by whoever acquired them.

To determine the price that we would offer the Stein heirs, we asked Eugene Thaw, the respected art dealer, to appraise the entire collection. Gene estimated its value at $6.8 million, a price the Steins accepted. We also asked Gene to place a valuation on each work so that we could divide them equitably among us. Gene assigned prices ranging from about $750,000 for the most important Picasso to barely $2,000 for one of the smaller Gris.

The syndicate members gathered in a large room in the Whitney wing of MoMA on the afternoon of December 14, 1968, for the final selection. The paintings had been placed along the walls and made a colorful and impressive sight. Drawing on my experience with the distribution of Aunt Lucy's estate years before, I suggested a procedure to which the others agreed: We put six numbers in an old felt hat and passed it around. I drew last, and as luck would have it, numbers one and three were left. Each of us then selected a painting in sequence until we reached our dollar quota of $1.1 million (double that for me) or had chosen as many as we wanted.

Peggy and I selected Picasso's *Girl with a Basket of Flowers*—the first choice, we later learned, of everyone except Nelson.† Bill Paley then chose a similar Picasso pink nude of the same period, enabling us to draw our second choice, Picasso's *The Reservoir, Horta de Ebro* (one of his first Analytic Cubist paintings and therefore of considerable historical importance). I could see the consternation on Nelson's face as soon as I announced our choice. Peggy and I ended up with eight Picassos and two Gris, at a total cost of $2.1 million. Nelson, inordinately fond of Picasso's work, selected twelve

---

*A few years earlier I had organized a similar syndicate to purchase the Edward G. Robinson Collection, only to have Stavros Niarchos snatch it away from us with a higher bid.

†Leo Stein purchased Picasso's *Girl* in 1905 for a few dollars from an art dealer; we paid just under a million in 1968, and it was recently reappraised at $25 million.

by the great Spanish master, a few masterpieces but several of them smaller and of lesser importance. Jock and André chose well but sparingly, and Bill Paley selected only two, both major Picassos. Five Grises and seven Picassos were not selected; they were subsequently sold, enabling us to recoup a portion of our original investment.*

———

The paintings we acquired during the 1950s and 1960s established standards of quality and beauty that I have tried to maintain in my collecting ever since. Some of our earliest purchases would now command prices a hundred times more than what we paid for them, a reflection of their high quality and the boom in the art market that began in the 1980s and continues today. While we never bought paintings as an investment, our art collection has become one of my most valuable assets and represents a significant part of my personal wealth.

THE EXPANSION OF MoMA

The major problem since the museum's opening in 1939 has been accommodating the rapid growth of its permanent collection. As a result, the major expansions since 1939 have been complex, costly, and contentious. I have been involved in all of them.

By 1960 the museum had completely outgrown its five-story Art Deco building. Attendance had skyrocketed, and the number of objects in the collection had grown from just under three thousand to more than eighteen thousand, most of which had to be stored in rented space because there was no room on 53rd Street. The museum's staff worked out of cramped quarters and had to fight each other tenaciously for gallery space to mount exhibitions. As a consequence we launched a campaign to raise $25 million, half of which would be used to add a new wing to the existing building.

Rockefellers were major contributors to the campaign. I gave $1.6 million and along with Nelson persuaded the RBF to make a $6 million grant to assure the campaign's success. Most important, my aunt Alta Prentice, Father's sole surviving sibling who had lived in the two brownstones on

---

*Three of my Picasso selections—the *Reservoir,* a Cubist landscape of 1908, and *Woman with a Guitar*—were among the six identified by MoMA in advance. We gave the landscape and *Woman with a Guitar* to MoMA in the mid-1970s but still retain *Reservoir,* which will go to the museum upon my death.

53rd Street just to the east of MoMA for most of her life, made the expansion possible by agreeing, at my request, to give her houses to the museum. Philip Johnson, then the head of MoMA's architecture department, designed the new East Wing, which opened in the spring of 1964.

At the same time that we broke ground for the East Wing, we expanded to the north by acquiring the Whitney Museum building, which was in the process of moving to new quarters on the Upper East Side. As chairman, I presided over the board's decision to buy the property and contributed another $700,000 to help defray the cost of incorporating it into the larger complex. These were rather simple and straightforward projects. Future expansions would be infinitely more complex and expensive.

THE MUSEUM TOWER

By the mid-1970s the space we had added was fully utilized through the rapid growth of the collection and the development of our educational programming. While another expansion was needed, there was no reasonably priced contiguous land available, and our finances were in abysmal condition. A new addition would be problematic at best.

For a banker, reading the MoMA balance sheet was a painful experience. The operating deficit in 1974 was $1.5 million, our ninth deficit in a row. The money raised in previous capital campaigns was being frittered away in paying for the deficit, and our endowment had dropped to $15 million from a high of almost $24 million only five years earlier. My own contributions during those years had to be used primarily to help cover the annual shortfall.

The fund-raising outlook was dismal. Consultants advised us that major foundations and corporations, our strongest supporters in the past, had already shifted their resources away from the arts to focus on the pressing "urban crisis." The consultants were equally dubious of our ability to raise new money from trustees and close friends of the museum. Under the circumstances most trustees believed the best course would be "to learn to live within our means." That would require, at the least, dramatically limiting acquisitions of contemporary art. While I agreed that we needed to get our financial house in order, failing to refresh the permanent collection would compound rather than solve our problems. I believed then, as I do now, that without continued growth in its collection MoMA would lose its public appeal, stagnate, and eventually wither. At best we would become a twentieth-century Frick Museum: a perfectly beautiful place, but a testament only to a brief moment in time.

In light of the consultants' pessimistic forecast about our fund-raising capacity, it was clear that we had to explore other ways to solve our financial and space problems. We found it with the innovative "tower" project. Richard Weinstein, an architect who had worked with me on projects in lower Manhattan, came up with the idea of packaging properties owned by MoMA along 53rd Street and selling them and the "air rights" above the museum itself to a developer, who would build his own residential or commercial building. Selling air rights (the unused portion of a building's zoned height) to allow the construction of a taller building nearby has been common practice in New York ever since the enactment of the Zoning Law of 1915. However, few not-for-profits had ever been in a position to take advantage of the provision.

We had to proceed carefully, however, because we had to maximize our financial returns without jeopardizing our tax-exempt status or compromising our ability to expand in the future. Selling the air and development rights would provide a much needed infusion to the endowment but by itself would not cover the cost of the building expansion. Our lawyers came up with an ingenious plan: the creation of "The Trust for Cultural Resources of the City of New York," an agency of New York State that could hold property, borrow money, collect taxes, and apply the taxes collected to the maintenance of private cultural institutions. The trust's ability to issue tax-exempt bonds to finance building construction was key because it provided us with direct access to low-cost financing for the project. The trust would collect the equivalent of property taxes from the owners of the new building to amortize the bonds and, after deducting expenses and other costs, pay over the remaining funds to the museum each year.

After the trustees endorsed the project, we approached Mayor Ed Koch, who, in the midst of the City's fiscal crisis, happily supported the idea. Assemblyman Roy Goodman introduced the bill for us in the New York State legislature, where it took two days of intense lobbying by me and other trustees before the Assembly finally approved it. Warren Anderson, majority leader of the New York State Senate, was especially helpful in ushering the bill through his chamber, and Governor Hugh Carey signed the law creating the trust.

In 1979 the museum conveyed its property and development rights to the trust for a total of $17 million, and the trust sold the property and rights to The Museum Tower Corporation, a private company created for that purpose, for the same amount of money. Over a period of years the trust will reimburse the museum for the cost of the new addition, and the museum, in turn, has leased the building from the trust for $1 a year for ninety-nine years.

Cesar Pelli, dean of Yale's School of Architecture, designed the building, which opened in 1984. The tower's crisp modern style fits the neighborhood well. The project more than doubled our exhibition areas, providing for the first time large interior spaces where large contemporary works could be displayed. The lower six floors, which are also used for workshops, classrooms, and offices, sit snugly below the graceful forty-four-story residential tower. Inside the museum one is totally unaware of the large tower rising over it.

The Museum Tower was a creative solution that brought together government, the private sector, and philanthropy in an effective partnership that was beneficial to the museum and the public at large.

CHANGES IN LEADERSHIP

For most of the 1970s and into the 1980s, Blanchette, Bill Paley, and Dick Oldenburg guided MoMA's physical expansion, refined its program, and added to its already lustrous collection. Bill, unfortunately, became ill and had to step down as chairman in early 1985, and Blanchette took over as board chair. Sadly, Blanchette's own battle with Alzheimer's disease forced her premature retirement only a few years later. With no obvious replacement for Blanchette, the board asked me in 1987 to serve for the third time as chairman. I agreed to do so even though I was already deeply involved with Rockefeller Center, the Americas Society, and the New York City Partnership.

There was much to be done. A 1986 outside study concluded that we needed to resolve three critical issues: board composition, our chaotic management system, and our persistent need for new space.

The problem with the board was clear: We were too old. MoMA had no mandatory retirement age for trustees, and in 1991 nine trustees out of forty, including me, were seventy-five or older, and a number of others were not far behind. While many of us had been generous and effective members, we had to make room for the next generation. Our solution was the creation of a new category, a "life trustee," who would be eligible to chair committees, attend board meetings, and participate in discussions but would not have a vote. While the logic of the proposal was undeniable, its implementation had to be handled skillfully so as not to offend loyal museum supporters. I agreed to take the job of selling the idea to the others. I called on each one, and all of them accepted my proposition with grace and understanding, if not happiness. There were no adverse consequences, as some had feared. Among those added to the board in subsequent years were Mrs. Akio Morita, the wife of the Sony Corporation's chairman; Patricia Phelps de Cisneros, an art patroness from Venezuela; and Michael Ovitz, the powerful Los Angeles–based media and entertainment executive.

We also made substantial progress on restructuring management. Dick Oldenburg had done an admirable job as director, but the position had increased in scope and complexity. It was unrealistic to expect Dick to handle all these responsibilities unassisted.

Initially, we created a new post—a paid president—to share administrative responsibilities with the director. After searching aggressively for more than a year it became clear that individuals of the quality we were looking for were not prepared to share authority with a director who had been in place for more than twenty years. In the fall of 1993, just before I was scheduled to step down as chairman, Dick announced his intention to retire the following June. His decision allowed us to search for a single individual who would be the sole CEO of MoMA.

Within a relatively short period of time we found the perfect candidate. Glenn Lowry was forty years old and a graduate of Williams College with a Ph.D. in Islamic Art from Harvard. He had worked at the Smithsonian and as director of the Art Gallery of Ontario in Toronto, Canada. Because he specialized in a very different field of art history, Glenn was not a threat to any of MoMA's curators. Glenn is brilliant, tactful, full of energy, and a natural leader.

The final issue—determining where and how to expand as well as how to finance such an expansion—would take much longer to resolve. Within a few years of the opening of the Museum Tower in 1984, MoMA had once again run out of space. Our permanent collection, including almost thirteen thousand films, dozens of classic cars, and numerous oversized modern sculptural works, in addition to our vast holding of paintings, prints, drawings, and other items chronicling life in the twentieth century, now totaled more than a million objects. More than one million people a year poured through MoMA's doors, and complaints about long lines and crowded galleries had become common. Clearly we needed to expand, but our immediate neighbor on 53rd Street, Saint Thomas Episcopal Church, would not consider selling, and the owners of the Dorset Hotel to the west on 54th Street wanted a price we could not afford.

Our other options—moving the museum to a new location, acquiring a satellite facility, and burrowing into Manhattan bedrock to create more storage and exhibition space—were all rejected for one reason or another.

When I stepped down as chairman in 1993, we still had not resolved the issue. But my successors did.

Agnes Gund, president of MoMA and one of the nation's premier collectors of contemporary art, and Ronald S. Lauder, the chairman of the Estée Lauder cosmetics firm, led the way. In 1996, after three years of negotiations, we finally persuaded the Goldman family, owners of the Dorset Hotel, to sell us their property. The Dorset site was unquestionably the best solution to MoMA's space problem. Even though the $50 million price tag was very high, MoMA's board quickly concluded that we could not afford to reject it. That may well have been the most important decision the board has ever made.

"THE FINEST MUSEUM OF MODERN ART IN THE WORLD"

In early 1996, with Glenn Lowry in charge and the Dorset property acquired, we turned to the arduous task of developing plans for the new museum and raising the funds necessary to build it. Although I was chairman emeritus by this time, Aggie Gund and Ron Lauder urged me to play an active role in the monumental task of fund-raising.

We estimated land acquisition and construction costs would be $450 million and assumed another $200 million should be added to the endowment to carry new programs and operations. It was a very ambitious goal. The success of the campaign would depend in large part on our ability to raise large sums of money right at the start, and most of it would have to come from our own board. I agreed to put up $15 million and persuaded Ron Lauder, Sid Bass, and Aggie Gund to provide leadership gifts. So we began the drive with $55 million in hand.

To sustain this early momentum I suggested we create a new donor category: Founder of the Museum of Modern Art of the 21st Century. To join this group required a contribution of at least $5 million. It was a daring strategy, but within two years of the campaign's inauguration in early 1998, thirty-three individuals and corporations had pledged or contributed at least that amount.

Those of us at the heart of the campaign knew that without substantial public support, a "new" Modern would take much longer to build. Because of MoMA's positive impact on New York City's economy—we now attracted almost 2 million visitors a year, many of whom stayed in the City's hotels and dined in its restaurants—we approached Mayor Rudolph Giuliani with a request for a $65 million capital contribution from the City. The Mayor responded enthusiastically, and after a short, sharp struggle with the City Council, the funds were included in the City's capital budget.

After that exceptional beginning on the fund-raising front, we initiated an international design competition, which attracted more than one hundred submissions and resulted in the selection of the distinguished Japanese architect Yoshio Taniguchi. His design will almost double MoMA's exhibition space and provide larger and more flexible galleries for the display of contemporary art as well as temporary exhibitions. In addition the museum will now include an extensive educational and research center, a new administrative complex, another movie theater, and a dramatic lobby gallery that will overlook our beloved Abby Aldrich Rockefeller Sculpture Garden. All in all the museum will expand by more than 250,000 square feet, and its configuration will be dramatically altered into an innovative campus complex. In my opinion this design captures the exciting future of MoMA while remaining faithful to our storied and essential past.

In the fall of 2000, with more than $460 million in hand, the Dorset was demolished in preparation for the construction of "the finest museum of modern art in the world."

=

The building of a new MoMA has not settled the argument between the advocates of modern versus contemporary art. That discussion still rages within the walls of MoMA and without. While I have supported those who insist the museum must be continuously open to evolving forms of artistic expression, I am often startled and even angered and repulsed by the strange directions and provocative content of the new forms that seem to pop up every few months. For instance, on my first visit to the P.S. I Contemporary Art Center, MoMA's contemporary art center, I found many of the exhibits baffling. Strange videos, distorted and grotesque paintings, graffiti, and perverse photography lined the halls and crowded the walls. They made the "fenders" sculpture, which had caused such a controversy at Chase in the 1960s, seem tame and charmingly naive.

I was relieved when the tour ended and I returned to the comforting confines of my home and its Cézannes, Signacs, and Derains glowing peaceably before me. As I looked at them, however, I remembered that these men had once been members of a revolutionary artistic vanguard themselves, and quite often their revolutionary zeal was not limited to their palette. They had banished perspective, grappled with the disturbing currents coursing through their societies, and insisted that their vision and methods were as valid as those that had gone before. They had also been roundly denounced by the establishment of the day and their work ridiculed as pointless, grotesque, and without beauty. They had "invented" modern art and changed the way in which the world was perceived. Perhaps, like the Neo-Impressionists and Fauves, this latest generation of "modern" artists had more to offer than I was giving them credit for.

I know that would have been my mother's reaction.

CHAPTER 30

ROCKEFELLER CENTER

REDUX

No physical structure is more associated with my family than
Rockefeller Center, majestically situated in the heart of midtown
Manhattan.

Father's courageous decision to move forward with the Center, in the
depths of the Depression, is his crowning legacy and an enduring symbol of
hope and optimism of which all his descendants are proud. Indeed, since
1934, Rockefeller Center has served as the family's "nerve center" for its diverse business operations.

As solid as the Center's standing in the City has been over seven decades,
its financial history has been surprisingly turbulent—from Father's scram-
bling to keep the property afloat at its conception to my own intercession
sixty years later to help rescue the center from an ignominious bankruptcy.

It has been a curious and memorable evolution.

THE TRUSTS

My generation's ownership of Rockefeller Center stemmed from the creation of the 1934 Trusts, which Father established for his six children
during the Depression. These trusts, in particular, have been the primary
source of the preservation, enhancement, and transfer of the family's
wealth from generation to generation.

At the time Father set up the trusts, all of us were relatively young; I was
only nineteen. As I have noted, Father had a number of compelling reasons

for creating the trusts even though he worried whether we could handle the responsibilities of great wealth at such a young age.

Father resolved the dilemma by setting up sizable trusts for each of us but limiting the income we could receive from them before the age of thirty and prohibiting us from drawing down on the trust principal before then. To ensure his wishes were carried out, he appointed a five-member Trust Committee from among his closest advisors—all experienced men he could count on to provide us with prudent counsel. However, while the trustees were given important powers to dispense or withhold income, he gave the Chase National Bank's Trust Department sole responsibility for investing the principal.

Father recognized that our need for financial guidance would diminish as we grew older. For that reason he included provisions in our trust indentures that allowed each of us, once we turned thirty, to withdraw portions of the principal if the Trust Committee concurred with the request. Indeed, Father also gave each of us the right to withdraw the entire principal and dissolve our trust altogether if we wished.

Father realized, however, that continuing the trusts might be in our best interest and those of our descendants. For that reason he directed that the principal of each trust be passed automatically to our children.

THE BROTHERS, THE CENTER, AND THE TRUST COMMITTEE

For nearly fifty years the relationship of my brothers and me with the Trust Committee was routine and eminently satisfactory. Over the course of that time, in fact, there was only one financial transaction between the brothers and our trusts that turned out to have unexpected and complicating repercussions: the transfer of ownership of Rockefeller Center.

From time to time we asked for permission to invade our trusts for some special purpose, and the committee was always sympathetic and responsive, as Father had intended it should be. Once a year at Christmas time the trustees invited the beneficiaries to lunch with them. On those pleasant occasions the Chase officer responsible for investing the funds would report on the trust's financial performance, and we would discuss the financial markets and any changes there might be in investment policies. The market value of the trusts grew substantially over time, as did the income from them.

In 1955 our lawyers advised my brothers and me that our joint ownership of Rockefeller Center placed us in a precarious position if one of us were to die unexpectedly. Such an event, they said, might trigger the liquidation of our ownership in order to pay estate taxes. To guard against that eventuality they urged us to transfer all Rockefeller Center stock out of our personal portfolios as quickly as possible.

That was much easier said than done because the lease agreement with Columbia University prohibited us from selling or otherwise disposing of our shares without the university's consent. When Columbia's lawyers understood our dilemma, they agreed to allow us to sell our shares, but only to the 1934 Trusts, thereby ensuring the family's continued involvement in the Center. The Trust Committee agreed to buy our stock and gave us shares of the former Standard Oil companies in return. The deal netted each of us slightly more than $12 million.

While the sale took care of our individual estate problems, it did not resolve two other important issues: Rockefeller Center's divided ownership—the trusts now owned the buildings and Columbia University owned the land—and the continuing illiquidity of the asset itself. The resolution of those issues had to be deferred to the future. Over time an even more troublesome development arose: the increase in power of the Trust Committee rather than the Rockefeller family over the operations and destiny of Rockefeller Center. Initially no one was concerned by what seemed like a technical change in ownership, but thirty years later this exchange led to a controversial and infuriating confrontation.

NEW CHAIRMAN, NEW COURSE

In March 1982, a year after retiring from Chase, I became chairman of Rockefeller Center, Inc. (RCI), which by then owned not only the original Rockefeller Center but also a number of other properties as well. The restrictions imposed by the Columbia lease limited our ability to manage and expand the company. I had long believed that if RCI were able to acquire the land under the Center, it could become an asset of far greater value for my family. Indeed, I felt it could become the financial engine for future generations of the Rockefeller family, just as Standard Oil had been for the first three. That was my vision. I would soon discover that neither the Trust Committee nor several members of my family shared my view.

==

Nelson had been directly involved in the Center's management from the early 1930s through the mid-1950s. In fact, it was he who had taken the lead in persuading Father to sell us the property in 1948 for $2.2 million.

When Nelson entered politics in 1958, Laurance succeeded him as chairman of RCI, and under his leadership and that of his successor, Dick Dilworth, the head of the Family Office, the modernization of the Center was successfully completed. Laurance and Dick also led the Center's physical expansion across Sixth Avenue through the construction of the Exxon, Time-Life, McGraw Hill, and Celanese buildings.

The real estate and stock market booms of the 1960s were followed by the prolonged economic malaise of the 1970s. Dick Dilworth was forced to act and, along with Alton G. Marshall, RCI's president and CEO, began to diversify the company in order to free it from its overwhelming dependence on a single property in a city that was experiencing a strong "shakeout" in real estate values. Starting in 1975, RCI purchased Cushman & Wakefield, one of the country's largest commercial real estate brokers; Trinity Paper & Plastics Corporation, the nation's largest paper grocery bag producer; Wessely Energy, a petroleum exploration and production company; and the Tishman Realty and Construction Company. They also launched Rockefeller Center Television (RCTV), a cable television company, and expanded the Center's involvement in property development outside New York City. These actions soon had the desired effect: The losses of the mid-1970s were replaced by record operating profits, $19.9 million in 1979 and almost $21 million in 1980.

=

Despite several valiant attempts, Dick Dilworth was never successful in convincing Columbia to sell us their land. He did, however, negotiate important modifications in the lease, the most important of which eliminated the $12 million escrow account that required RCI to hold three years of rental payments at all times. In return for this important concession and other technical adjustments, RCI increased its rental payments to the university from $4 million to $9 million a year.

Dick Dilworth and RCI's management substantially improved RCI's financial position, but many changes still needed to be made. More than 70 percent of the company's assets were still concentrated in real estate, primarily in midtown Manhattan. And while earnings had improved, they were still a minuscule percentage of the company's estimated market value of more than $400 million.

=

RCI's record of modest earnings and erratic performance, and its uncertain prospects, soon became a point of contention within the family.

After the deaths of Winthrop, Babs, John, and Nelson, their children replaced them as direct income beneficiaries of the 1934 Trusts. This meant that in the case of three trusts—those of Babs, John, and Nelson—income would have to be divided among more individuals. Many of the new beneficiaries were disappointed when they learned how limited their income would be. In their eyes the main culprit was RCI, which had never paid dividends on its common stock. While RCI began to pay a nominal dividend of $1 on a class of preferred stock in 1976, the only trusts to benefit were mine and those of Babs, John, and Laurance. In view of this fact, Nelson's children were the most vocal in insisting that RCI should distribute dividend income to all shareholders in an amount commensurate with its net worth. I opposed that option because to do so would entail paying income in excess of earnings and because it might require selling assets without due regard for their longer-run potential. I suggested instead that we move aggressively to improve RCI's profitability by hiring a new management team and adopting a new business plan. Mine was a distinctly minority view within the family in the late 1970s and early 1980s. Laurance had an even more radical view: He thought it was time to sell RCI. Most of the family seemed to agree with him.

REVITALIZING THE CENTER

Soon after I retired from the Chase in April 1981, Dick Dilworth and I began a series of discussions with the RCI board and members of the family about the challenges facing Rockefeller Center. It had become painfully apparent that RCI needed to be restructured from the ground up if it was to become a profitable company capable of meeting the ambitious demands of its family shareholders.

As a first step I agreed to replace Dick as RCI chairman when he stepped down in March 1982. Next, we desperately needed a new business plan and a strong CEO to implement it. Heidrick & Struggles, the search firm we hired, identified Richard A. Voell, the president and chief operating officer of Penn Central, as a prime candidate. After a successful career at Beatrice Foods, Voell had managed Penn Central for a three-year period, diversifying the company and increasing its revenues. Although Voell was reluctant to leave Penn Central, he was intrigued with our situation and agreed to review our portfolio of investments and advise us on how to proceed. Voell concluded that many of the companies we had acquired during the previous seven years had now reached their apex in terms of market value and should be sold. He advised us to continue diversifying out of real estate and suggested focusing on investments in the communications industry, which he considered the most promising alternative for us. It was a radical proposal whereby RCI would first divest itself of all corporate properties other than Rockefeller Center and then transform itself over five to seven years into a real estate, communications, and financial services conglomerate. Once the transformation was accomplished, Voell said, we should sell RCI to the public.

Dick Dilworth and I were so impressed by Voell's creative recommendations that we eventually persuaded him to become RCI's president and CEO in order to implement his plans. He took over on March 19, 1982, the same day I was elected chairman. He and I quickly established a close and effective partnership.

=

Dick Voell and his planning team, led by Lorian Marlantes, who holds a Ph.D. in economics from the Stanford Business School and had worked on Penn Central's diversification, spent the next year developing a strategic plan for RCI. It was an exhaustive effort that examined every aspect of RCI's current operations and studied dozens of industry sectors for profitable investment opportunities. The result was a three-pronged strategy that would beautify, diversify, and unify Rockefeller Center.

Beautification involved a multimillion-dollar program of capital improvements designed to make the Center a more attractive location for our tenants. It focused on modernizing the Center and involved everything from cleaning and relighting murals and other artwork to rewiring the entire complex to meet the power requirements of high-speed computers. The lower concourse and restaurants surrounding the skating rink were completely refurbished, and *Prometheus,* the Paul Manship statue that hovers over the rink, was given a new coating of gold leaf. The Rainbow Room was brought back to its original Art Deco glory, and the other restaurants on the sixty-fifth floor were also renovated and brought under new management. The sixty-fourth floor was entirely done over to include dining, meeting, and conference rooms, each a masterpiece of period decoration.

The second step was diversification. In order to move RCI decisively out of the real estate business, we sold most of the assets purchased during the 1970s, including Wessely Energy, Trinity Paper Bag, and a number of our real estate joint ventures in other parts of the country, most at the top of the market. We also sold RCTV, which was losing about a million dollars a month, to a joint venture owned by Hearst and ABC, which eventually transformed the operation into the Arts and Entertainment Network.

We then purchased Outlet Communications, which owned a group of radio and TV stations in a number of strong markets across the country, for $330 million. In 1983, the company's name was changed to the Rockefeller Group, Inc. (RGI), to reflect our broadened base of holdings.

Our final strategic step was unification—persuading Columbia University to sell us the twelve acres of land it owned under the old Center so that RGI could unite the Center as a single unit. I had always considered this the key to unlocking the value of Rockefeller Center and to our long-run success. How in the end we achieved that objective was little short of miraculous.

In late January 1985 I asked Dick Voell to be my guest at the annual dinner of political and corporate luminaries at the Alfalfa Club in Washington. Dick had been negotiating with Columbia to purchase the land under the Center for most of 1984 and thought he was close to a final deal. We were more than a bit disturbed to learn from a reliable source just before we left for the capital that General Electric was about to close a deal with Columbia for $400 million.

When we took our assigned seats at the Washington Hilton that evening, I was pleasantly surprised to find Jack Welch, the chairman and CEO of General Electric, sitting directly across from me. During dinner I leaned across the table and asked Jack point-blank if the rumor that GE was on the verge of buying the Columbia land was true. He said it was. I explained to him why we were anxious to buy it and asked if he would object if we talked to Columbia before GE completed the deal. Graciously, he said he had no objection.

The Alfalfa dinner was on Saturday night, January 26. Early Monday morning I called Michael I. Sovern, the president of Columbia. I told him of my conversation with Jack Welch and asked him if he would be willing to resume negotiations with RGI. I explained how vital it was for Rockefeller Center to own the land and pointed out how important our lease payments had been to Columbia over the years. I suggested that given our historic relationship they might even owe us a favor! To my delight he agreed to sell the land to us.

The following Sunday we closed the deal for $400 million, the same amount that GE had offered. At $32 million an acre, it was the highest per-acre price ever paid for a parcel of urban real estate. But for the future of the Rockefeller family, I was convinced it was a price well worth paying.

=====

With the Center buildings and the Columbia land finally united, Dick Voell and I were overjoyed that we had accomplished the objectives established only three years earlier. We had transformed RGI into a more aggressive company and dramatically enhanced its potential. It was now time to initiate the second part of our plan: the refinancing of the Center.

It was our thought to generate cash by mortgaging Rockefeller Center to the public through the sale of a Real Estate Investment Trust (REIT). The bulk of the proceeds from the public sale of the REIT, which we expected to produce $1.3 billion, would be used to finance other acquisitions to further enhance the value of RGI. Given enough time for our investments to mature, we would generate the additional income my family was demanding. The plan made great sense and only needed to be implemented.

DISASTER IN PARADISE

Standing in the way of carrying out our plan was the Trust Committee, the custodian of the vast majority of RGI's shares.* It was a distinguished group chaired by R. Manning Brown, chairman of the executive committee of New York Life, and its other members were William G. Bowen, president of Princeton University; Hannah Gray, president of the University of Chicago; George Putnam of Putnam Funds; and John Whitehead, a former senior partner and co-chairman of Goldman Sachs.

The acquisition of Columbia's land, the upgrading of the Center's buildings, and our strategic diversification had enhanced RGI's appraised value from $600 million to almost $740 million in three short years. RGI stock had come to represent more than half the net asset value of the 1934 Trusts. The difficulty was that its dividend yield was far lower than that of many of the other assets in the trusts. The RGI board, under pressure from the family and the Trust Committee, had instituted a small common stock dividend in 1981, which had been quickly increased to $17 a share in 1984, but apparently this was not enough. Several family members even insisted that it was time to sell Rockefeller Center.

To come to grips with these differences, Dick and I thought it prudent to brief the RGI board and the Trust Committee in detail about our plans for the REIT and how they would affect future income, stock appreciation, and dividends. We knew our ideas faced strong opposition, but we believed our

---

*Beginning in 1982 the Trust Committee sold about 14 percent of RGI stock to a company owned by Gianni Agnelli of Italy, to the family of William Hewitt of California, and to B. K. Johnson of Texas, in order to provide certain Rockefeller family trusts with greater liquidity and additional income for the beneficiaries.

plans were sound and that we could persuade the doubters of their merit. Accordingly, we scheduled a special RGI board meeting to which we invited the Trust Committee for the weekend of March 28–31, 1985, at Caneel Bay, my brother Laurance's Rockresort on Saint John in the U.S. Virgin Islands.

We chartered the Chase corporate jet and flew the Trust Committee, the RGI board, several of RGI's senior officers, and some guests, including Michel David-Weill, senior partner of Lazard Frères and RGI's investment banker, to the Caribbean. On the way down, the plane stopped in Princeton to pick up Bill Bowen, the Trust Committee's ranking member in the absence of Chairman Manning Brown, who was terminally ill with cancer.

Although Bill had been a member of the Trust Committee for a number of years, I did not know him very well. He was an economist by training and as president had done a superb job of rebuilding Princeton's endowment and strengthening its faculty and curriculum. Bowen had been close to my brothers John, who had left the university a substantial bequest, and Laurance, who had also been very generous to his alma mater. The flight lasted a couple of hours, during which Bowen and I chatted amiably. Although the Trust Committee already knew about the REIT proposal, Bowen gave me no indication that he had any concerns or even strong opinions about the plan.

=

The meeting in Caneel was a disaster.

Dick and I knew we did not have the support of at least two of the other five members of the RGI Board. George O'Neill, husband of my niece Abby, and William Pounds, the executive head of the Family Office, thought the plan "too risky." They were concerned about the continued illiquidity of RGI's stock and also believed the REIT would further delay the payment of larger dividends to the family.

Their dissent was no surprise. What we had not anticipated was that the Trust Committee would be unanimous and categorical in its opposition. Bowen, Hannah Gray, John Whitehead, and George Putnam (who also sat on the RGI Board) listened to our presentation. Then Bowen dropped the bomb. He said the business plan was "too aggressive" and did not meet the needs of the shareholders. While the committee authorized us to proceed with the REIT, they directed Dick Voell and me to disburse the $1.3 billion we expected to generate in a totally different way:

- $400 million would be used to pay off the debt incurred by purchasing the land from Columbia.

- $250 million would be invested in an escrow account to support dividend and interest payments to the REIT shareholders.
- $250 million would be applied to the purchase of RGI's shares from the 1934 Trusts, thereby enabling the Trust Committee to achieve its objective of reducing RGI's total value in the trusts. These funds were passed directly to the income beneficiaries in the Rockefeller family, including me.
- An additional $100 million would be reserved for dividend payments to the family shareholders through the trusts over the following five years.
- $200 million was reserved to complete capital improvements in and the modernization of Rockefeller Center.
- RGI would be allowed to retain only $100 million, less than 8 percent of the total proceeds, for the aggressive acquisitions program we had contemplated, essentially eliminating this as a viable strategy.

The decision took me completely by surprise. I was outraged by what I considered an imprudent policy, and I said so with some vehemence. By ordering the withdrawal of capital to buy back shares and to pay dividends in excess of income, the Trust Committee had decreed the partial liquidation of RGI. In effect they were mandating that RGI remain a real estate company, and one that would be even more dependent on Rockefeller Center as its key asset than it had been before. They had vetoed the aggressive program of diversification that Dick Voell and I had begun to implement in the early 1980s. Michel David-Weill, one of the world's most astute financial strategists, agreed. He likened RGI to a goose that could lay golden eggs and believed the Trust Committee's action "would be slitting the goose's throat."

In order to ensure that their policies were implemented, they commissioned Samuel Butler, a senior partner at Cravath, Swaine and Moore, to convey their wishes directly to management, effectively bypassing the RGI board altogether. Frustrated and angry, I retained Judge Simon Rivkind, a respected senior member of the New York State Bar, to advise me on the legality of the Trust Committee's actions. Judge Rivkind concluded, much to my regret, that the powers given to the trustees under the original trust indenture were so extensive that, short of illegal actions, they could dictate whatever course they felt was best for the beneficiaries—including the dismantling of RGI if they so wished.

For the next four years Bowen, who became chairman of the Trust Committee after the death of Manning Brown in late 1985, regularly interceded with both management and board prerogatives—an unprecedented role for the Trust Committee and one that I doubt Father had in mind when he created it.

THE REIT

The REIT, formally named Rockefeller Center Properties, Inc. (RCPI), was duly created and went public in September 1985. I served as chairman, and the other board members included my old friend Pete Peterson of the Blackstone Group; Benjamin Holloway, the head of Equitable Life's real estate unit; Paul Reichmann, one of the principals in Olympia & York; and Dick Voell. Goldman Sachs and Shearson Lehman underwrote what would prove to be the largest REIT offering in history, issuing 37.5 million shares of stock at $20 a share that raised $750 million in the United States and marketing $335 million of bonds in Europe and $215 million of notes in Japan.

The REIT lent RGI the $1.3 billion it had raised, receiving a mortgage on the buildings and land of the original Rockefeller Center in return.* The proceeds were disbursed as the Trust Committee had directed. RGI would make regular payments to the REIT from Rockefeller Center rents, and the REIT, in turn, would pay dividends to its shareholders of 95 percent of its annual taxable income as required by REIT regulations.

Under the terms of the REIT, as specified in its prospectus, dividends would increase from $1.75 in 1986 to $6.63 in 2000 when the shareholders would have the option of either converting the mortgage into a 71.5 percent ownership of Rockefeller Center or awaiting the return of their principal in 2007. The REIT prospectus clearly stated that for the first nine years of operation rental income would be insufficient to service the mortgage but that RGI would cover the estimated $250 million shortfall by drawing down on its own reserves.

We were satisfied that our projections for the REIT were realistic and achievable since 40 percent of the Center's leases, more than 2.3 million square feet of space, would roll over in 1994. We believed, and most experts concurred, that New York City's real estate market would continue its strong recovery from the recession of the early 1980s. We estimated, therefore, that by 1994 we would be able to raise rents to an average of $75 a square foot, a 100 percent increase. We also believed that the remaining leases coming up for renewal between 1995 and 2000 would command between $80 and $100 a square foot. Thus, early losses would be replaced by handsome profits, and if the REIT shareholders exercised their ownership

---

*The funds were actually lent to two partnerships owned by RGI, Rockefeller Center Properties and RCP Associates, in order to insulate the parent company from a long list of legal and financial contingencies.

option in 2000, we would hand over to them, as promised, a successful property.

Our forecasts proved to be right on target for the first five years. The REIT began to repurchase its bonds and notes (almost $480 million of the $550 million outstanding), paid dividends on time and in the amount promised, and even began to return capital to its shareholders, a total of $1.58 a share by the end of 1988. The strong stock market of those years bolstered the escrow fund and limited the contributions RGI had to make out of its own cash flow. In addition, new leases appreciated in line with our expectations. The REIT was in excellent shape.

The same was true of RGI. At the Trust Committee's insistence we had sold Outlet Communications, the centerpiece of our earlier diversification strategy for a tidy $236 million pre-tax profit. Likewise, RGI's other holdings—especially Cushman & Wakefield and the totally revamped Radio City Music Hall, the nation's leading concert venue with annual profits approaching $9 million a year—were showing positive growth. Thus, despite the cash withdrawal of $250 million by the trust for the benefit of my family, RGI's balance sheet remained strong. In fact, by year-end 1988, its net worth had surged an additional $350 million, to $1.1 billion, a double-digit growth rate in only three years.

Ironically, this healthy appreciation in value proved to be a double-edged sword. Once again the value of RGI had grown to more than 50 percent of the total value of the 1934 Trusts, thereby causing consternation among the members of the Trust Committee.

SELLING A LANDMARK

Toward the end of 1988, Dick Voell and I began meeting regularly with the Trust Committee to discuss the future of RGI. Bowen told us that he and his fellow trustees considered it "unsound" for RGI to represent such a large portion of the trusts' assets. They were particularly concerned about RGI's vulnerability to a decline in New York City real estate values. Paul Volcker, who joined the Trust Committee in 1987 after he retired as chairman of the Federal Reserve, agreed with Bowen, as he was particularly wary of real estate in New York City. Dick Voell reported that Paul Volcker told him that he felt "real estate was not a suitable trust investment; he was not comfortable with the debt necessitated by real estate investment, and, even more important, he had little faith in New York City politicians."

The Trust Committee concluded that to protect the interests of the beneficiaries, the value of RGI stock as a percentage of the value of the trusts would have to be reduced from 50 percent to something closer to 15 percent. In order to accomplish that goal they wanted to reduce the trusts' ownership of RGI stock from 86 percent to about 25 percent as quickly as possible. Once RGI management had accomplished that goal, Bowen assured us, the Trust Committee would no longer intervene in the policies and operations of RGI but would treat the company as just another substantial investment.

In essence, then, it was the Trust Committee rather than the Rockefeller family or the board of RGI who ultimately decided that owning Rockefeller Center was no longer "in the Rockefeller family's best interest."

To comply with the Trust Committee's *diktat*, Voell and I recommended selling a controlling interest in RGI. The Trust Committee gave us the green light to proceed with a sale in September 1989. However, they imposed two conditions that made our job more difficult: an impossibly high minimum price of $1,000 a share and completion of the sale by the end of the year— or they would consider other options.

Dick Voell and his team identified twenty companies in the United States, Europe, and Japan who might be interested in RGI. The Mitsubishi Estate Corporation, flush with cash from the boom in the Japanese real estate market, offered a staggering $1,350 a share, a preemptive bid that essentially ended the auction. In late October 1989 the RGI board accepted their proffer.*

The 1934 Trusts sold Mitsubishi 80 percent of the outstanding shares of RGI over a period of fifteen months in 1990 and 1991 at a total price of $1.373 billion. The trusts paid almost $533 million in taxes on this total and another $40 million in expenses, leaving about $800 million to be divided proportionally among the fifteen 1934 Trusts. The trust of which I am an income beneficiary netted $171.3 million from the Mitsubishi sale, not a bad return considering that I bought my original 20 percent interest in Rockefeller Center from Father in 1948 for $442,000! Despite the enormous taxes that had to be paid, the deal was clearly a good one for the family financially, and the Mitsubishi Estate Corporation was a wholly appropriate buyer.

The sale of Rockefeller Center to the Japanese, however, ignited a firestorm of criticism in the United States—hysteria, I would call it. "Japan,

---

*We later learned informally that Mitsui Fudosan would have offered about $1 billion for the property. However, that price may have gone higher if the two Japanese companies had entered into a bidding war.

Inc." was described as a monolithic giant taking advantage of naive Americans in the subtle warfare of trade and then buying up America's patrimony. What more telling symbol was there than New York's greatest landmark, Rockefeller Center? Some said the verdict of World War II had been reversed. In the overwrought mood of the moment, a crucial point was overlooked: The Rockefellers through the 1934 Trusts would still own a 20 percent stake in RGI and Rockefeller Center.

AN "UNTHINKABLE" BANKRUPTCY

Dick Voell and I were optimistic about RGI's partnership with the Japanese, particularly since they showed confidence in our management by asking me to remain as chairman and Dick Voell to continue as president and CEO. Mitsubishi Estates was a well-run company with more than $26 billion in assets and extensive interests around the world. We even had reason to hope that Mitsubishi's management might pursue some of our ideas regarding the expansion of RGI as a holding company, which the Trust Committee had firmly rejected.

Alas, in the end the purchase of RGI proved to be a nightmare for the Japanese. They had bought control toward the end of the 1980s real estate boom. No one at RGI or Mitsubishi could have predicted the depth or duration of the worldwide real estate recession that began less than a year later or its particular severity in New York City.

The recession's impact on RGI was almost immediate. Instead of rolling over leases at $75 a square foot, by mid-1990 demand had flattened and it was difficult to retain tenants at $35. The Center's rental income soon fell even further below its interest obligations to the REIT; its appraised value declined from $1.4 billion to $1.1 billion in 1993; and annual operating deficits climbed from $40 million in 1990 to $61 million in 1993. Mitsubishi and the 1934 Trusts were obliged to step in to cover the shortfall. Mitsubishi's investment swiftly became a financial drain with the potential of turning into a financial disaster unless remedial action was taken promptly.

To make matters worse the REIT itself was rapidly running out of reserves. It had borrowed almost $400 million in the short-term commercial paper market to finance the repurchase of bonds and notes to lessen costs down the road when interest rates on both classes of debt would increase automatically. By mid-1992 the REIT faced a credit crisis and turned to RGI for emergency financing.

As chairman of both RGI and the REIT, I was acutely aware that I had a conflict of interest. To avoid any appearance of impropriety I resigned as chairman and director of the REIT in December 1992. Claude Ballard, a limited partner of Goldman Sachs, replaced me.

===

By 1993 it was mandatory for RGI to act decisively if continued financial deterioration was to be averted. While the recession had ended, there was still no prospect that the Center would be able to renew leases at the higher levels we had anticipated. With lower rents RGI would not be able to handle its obligations to the REIT, and Mitsubishi and the 1934 Trusts would be forced to cover deficits amounting to hundreds of millions of dollars after 1994. I advised Mitsubishi that its only viable options would be to restructure the debt or buy out the REIT. Because the REIT shares had fallen to below $10 a share, I thought the latter was the more tenable alternative.

In early 1994, with REIT shares then trading at $6, Mitsubishi tendered $4.35 a share to the REIT. The REIT board promptly rejected the bid but, still facing a severe credit crunch, secured financing from Goldman Sachs's Whitehall Realty in the form of $225 million in debentures carrying an interest rate of 14 percent. As a result Whitehall, headed by Daniel Neidich, would become a dominant player in the REIT's affairs, and relations would become adversarial between the REIT and RGI.

As Rockefeller Center's losses continued to mount—reaching a cumulative total of $575 million in 1994—Mitsubishi made one final effort to buy out the REIT. In cooperation with the 1934 Trusts, Mitsubishi offered $7 a share, or $270 million in total, with Mitsubishi providing $216 million and the 1934 Trusts $54 million. The REIT countered with a demand for $310 million.

The Japanese balked and insisted that any additional funds would have to come from the 1934 Trusts. Mitsubishi had already invested almost $2 billion in the property and would go no further. In response Bill Bowen insisted that any increased investment from the 1934 Trusts would make business sense only if Mitsubishi offered concessionary terms, including a preferred five-year equity investment with a 12 percent dividend rate. He also demanded control of RGI if Mitsubishi missed four dividend payments. The Japanese were infuriated by Bowen's terms and immediately backed away from the deal, indicating they would not make any more payments to the REIT. The prospect of the unthinkable—a Rockefeller Center bankruptcy—had become a real possibility.

AN ILL-FATED TRIP TO TOKYO

E ven though my role in all of this had largely been reduced to that of an observer, I felt strongly that bankruptcy should be avoided at all costs. I thought a personal appeal to Mitsubishi's senior management might bring them back to the bargaining table, so Dick Voell and I flew to Tokyo to press their top executives to reconsider their decision. As I was entering Mitsubishi's headquarters on the morning of our meeting with Takeo Fukuzawa and his senior colleagues, I slipped, fell, and broke my leg. It took thirty uncomfortable minutes for a wheelchair to arrive. By the time it did, my adrenaline had taken over, and the pain had momentarily subsided. I insisted that we proceed with the meeting before I was taken to the hospital.

Mr. Fukuzawa and his associates were aghast when I was wheeled into the boardroom. They listened respectfully while I spoke about the dangers and stigma of bankruptcy, and beseeched them to reopen negotiations with the REIT. I remained at the meeting for nearly an hour, but ultimately neither my broken leg nor my arguments persuaded them.

The purchase of the Rockefeller Group had been Mitsubishi's largest overseas investment, although the more conservative members of their board had opposed it from the start. With the Japanese economy in the process of a meltdown and Rockefeller Center in serious trouble, this faction now held the upper hand. While negotiations continued for the next few months and at one point it looked as though Mitsubishi and the 1934 Trusts were close to working out a deal, it was to no avail. On May 11, 1995, the Mitsubishi board in Tokyo voted to walk away from the property.

On that same day members of the RGI board assembled in the ornate boardroom on the fifth floor of the Simon & Schuster Building on Sixth Avenue and 49th Street. It was a somber meeting. There was only one item on the agenda: a resolution to withhold the $20 million payment to the REIT and thereby precipitate a default. I made one last attempt to prevent the bankruptcy, noting the damaging consequences of a default to Mitsubishi, the Rockefeller family, and the Center itself. Drew Lewis, George Scharffenberger, Dick Dilworth, Dick Voell, and I voted against the resolution. We were outvoted by Mitsubishi's directors and George Putnam, the 1934 Trusts' representative on the board. Two days later RCP Associates and Rockefeller Center Properties—the two partnerships that had borrowed the money from the REIT a decade earlier—filed for bankruptcy protection. Dick Voell, finding himself in an increasingly untenable position, resigned as RGI president within six weeks.

Mitsubishi's unfortunate decision had a painful financial consequence for them. Under the terms of the original deal, the 1934 Trusts had the right to "put" to Mitsubishi the 20 percent of RGI shares they continued to own at a price of $1,495 a share. The trusts exercised their right and received an additional $160 million from the Japanese in 1997. Thus, while Mitsubishi gained full ownership of RGI, the full burden of the loss fell on them.

RECLAIMING A JEWEL

Soon after the embarrassing and well-reported bankruptcy, Prudence Abraham, the judge overseeing the case, invited bidders to present plans to deal with the Center's mortgage, which was now controlled by the REIT. Rockefeller Center was again "in play."

Much to everyone's surprise, the REIT had been able to stave off bankruptcy, but its financial condition was, to say the least, fragile, and a number of large real estate companies were clearly interested in picking up the property at a bargain price. I was concerned about the Center's future and let it be known that I would be willing to join a new ownership group. The members of my family whom I approached were not interested in a continuing role in the Center, so I had to look elsewhere for partners.

During the course of the summer I kept in touch with events through my associate, Richard E. Salomon, and my lawyer, Peter Herman of Milbank, Tweed. Gianni Agnelli told me he would be helpful if there was a need for his investment. A few weeks later he called from Europe and told me that he had spoken with Stavros Niarchos, who was also intrigued with the idea of investing in the Center.

Gianni and Stavros each agreed to put up $61 million. Jerry Speyer, one of the principals in Tishman Speyer, also became involved in the discussions and expressed an interest in managing the Center. In the end Jerry and I each committed $15 million, or about 5 percent each of the funds required. With those commitments in hand we struck a deal with Goldman's Whitehall Realty for a 50 percent ownership in a joint venture to purchase the REIT. In November 1995 the REIT board accepted our offer of $8 a share plus our assumption of the $845 million debt the REIT owed to its shareholders, and the REIT shareholders ratified the decision in March of the following year. Rockefeller Center was ours.

Despite claims from some quarters—notably *Barron's*—that "mom and pop" investors had suffered huge losses in buying shares of the REIT, the fact was that original investors recovered their initial investment and actually made a modest profit. Between 1985 and 1995 the REIT paid $10.13 in dividends and returned $4.87 in capital for each share. Shareholders also received $8 per share when we assumed control of the property, producing a total return of $23 per share on a $20 investment—by no means a spectacular return, but at least not a loss.

Since one reason for my participation was to prevent the Center from being summarily dismembered, Whitehall agreed, at my insistence, to maintain ownership of the property for five years before considering a sale. And to underscore their good faith I was elected the nonexecutive chairman of the company RCPI Trust.

The irony of a Rockefeller once again "owning" Rockefeller Center, albeit a very small percentage, was not lost on the media. I said at the time that Rockefeller Center represented a "crown jewel, not only for New York but for the nation." I was confident that our group would not only maintain the Center's cachet, but also add to it.

ROCKEFELLER CENTER RENAISSANCE

We began our tenure as the new owners of the Center by asking Jerry Speyer to design a business strategy that would enhance its value and realize its full potential at a time when New York had finally shaken off the last vestiges of the recession of the early 1990s. Jerry responded by crafting a comprehensive plan for a "new" Rockefeller Center: a redesign of the plaza, the redevelopment of the underground concourses, and a retail strategy to attract upscale stores and tenants. The result has been a brighter, more colorful, and more dynamic Center epitomized by NBC's *Today Show* broadcast from the plaza that attracts thousands of visitors every morning.

In addition we reduced the Center's enormous debt load by selling to NBC's parent company, General Electric, a condominium interest in 30 Rockefeller Plaza and other portions of the complex for $440 million in mid-1996. This seemed a fitting conclusion to my initial conversation with GE chairman Jack Welch about Rockefeller Center at the Alfalfa dinner a decade earlier.

＝

My confidence in the inevitable renaissance of Rockefeller Center has been rewarded. The resurgence of the American economy in the latter half of the 1990s truly lifted all boats, including the large ocean liner named Rockefeller Center. By the year 2000, with refurbished facilities, space-age elevators, prominent new tenants such as Christie's auction house, and an array of upscale retail outlets, the Center had reclaimed its position as one of the most sought-after treasures of American real estate.

A TOUCH OF SADNESS

Rockefeller Center had recovered much more rapidly than any of us could have anticipated. In view of this fact I agreed with Dan Neidich in the spring of 2000 when he proposed selling the property. We hoped to obtain in excess of $2 billion for the Center, but the offers from the four final bidders fell well below that level. In late December 2000, during an early morning conference call, we learned that the highest bid was still $50 million short of our $1.8 billion minimum price. We discussed the possibility of refinancing the property but came to no definite decision. However, at the very end of the call, Jerry Speyer said that he would be willing to pay $1.85 billion and asked that we accept or reject his offer by noon of that same day.

I discussed Jerry's bid with Gianni Agnelli, the executors of Stavros Niarchos's estate, and my own advisors. Goldman clearly wanted to sell, and the others seemed interested in accepting Jerry's offer. I was convinced that Jerry and his associates, the Crown family of Chicago, would maintain the Center's integrity and quality, and exhibit the same sense of public obligation that had characterized my family's ownership of more than seventy years. So in the end I agreed to sell as well.

This "final" sale of Rockefeller Center netted me about $45 million after taxes and expenses, a threefold gain in my investment in barely four years. While I was pleased with this happy outcome, of course, I must admit to a touch of sadness as well. Barring some extraordinary development—and the history of Rockefeller Center has been full of unusual events—this will mark the end of my family's long involvement with the Center that dates back to Father's daring decision to build an innovative urban showcase in the middle of Manhattan during the depths of the Depression.

CHAPTER 31

PARTNERSHIPS

M y wife, Peggy, meant more to me than anyone else.
We were married for fifty-six years, and her death in 1996 left an ir-
replaceable gap in my life. Her affection, wisdom, and wit were a source of
strength throughout our life together. Her love enabled me to become more
self-confident in facing the many responsibilities I had inherited or assumed,
but she also saved me from the error of self-satisfaction when I was blessed
with success. Peggy and I shared a deep pleasure in many things: sailing,
collecting art, listening to fine music, carriage driving, and travel, especially
when we could get away by ourselves. Yet while we enjoyed being together,
we also had different interests, which we pursued independently. This was
the key to our long and very happy marriage.

PEGGY

P eggy loved working with her hands—planting flowers, driving tractors,
even making furniture for our bedroom in Maine. She embraced new
projects with an intensity that was wondrous to behold, and became expert
on subjects as esoteric and diverse as the artificial insemination of cattle and
the identification of antique porcelain. Peggy was not a dilettante; rather,
she was serious about anything she undertook. Never satisfied to just sit on
the board of any organization, she was a font of creative ideas and always
willing to do her share to implement them. Two organizations in particular,

the Maine Coast Heritage Trust and the American Farmland Trust, occupied much of her time and energy during the last two decades of her life and reveal the passion and commitment she brought to everything she did.

Sailing in Maine became an absorbing pastime for both of us soon after World War II. We spent many happy days of our annual summer vacations cruising among the islands of Maine's rugged coast in a thirty-six-foot wooden-hulled sloop without an engine or a "head" in the company of family and friends. Later we graduated to a forty-two-foot Hinckley Sou'wester but continued to handle the sailing ourselves.

Peggy's concern for the future of our beloved cruising ground led her to join forces with our fellow sailor and friend Thomas Cabot to form the Maine Coast Heritage Trust (MCHT) to help protect the islands from inappropriate development. Largely through Tom's and Peggy's leadership, MCHT became an effective preservation force by encouraging landowners to place conservation easements on their property. This innovative legal tool has enabled MCHT to protect 115 privately owned islands and more than twenty-five thousand acres of Maine's magnificent coast.

In the 1970s, Peggy became interested in raising beef cattle and pursued this new interest with her characteristic enthusiasm and energy. She surveyed the American beef cattle industry and discovered that Simmenthals, a recently introduced European breed with a larger frame than the more familiar Black Angus, was gaining in popularity. Peggy believed she would have a greater chance of success with Simmenthals, rather than with older, more established varieties. Although making a profit in the cattle business was by no means assured—production costs were high and demand uncertain—Peggy was determined to go ahead.

She began with a small herd of polled, or hornless, animals (a characteristic also coming into vogue, in part, because of the ease in handling them) at Hudson Pines. Her first real success was an impressive bull whom she named "Keep It Clean" because all his progeny, even when he was bred to horned cows, would be polled.* Peggy's purebreds quickly gained favor, and her auctions at the handsome Stone Barns, which Father had built in the 1930s at Pocantico, attracted buyers from around the world.

Peggy soon expanded operations from Tarrytown to Maine and began to look for land in upstate New York. She finally settled on Livingston in Columbia County, about seventy-five miles up the Hudson from Pocantico, and eventually purchased almost three thousand acres there, much of it in

---

*The technical term is heterozygous, which means the polled bull's gene for hornlessness is dominant and overrides the genes of the horned cow.

pasture where several hundred Simmenthals could graze. Later she converted most of the acreage to the commercial production of corn, soybeans, and wheat.

Columbia County's beauty enchanted us. Nestled along the Hudson River with the Catskill Mountains to the west and the Berkshires to the east, the area had been settled for hundreds of years. After buying the land we discovered the area had been home to my Rockefeller ancestors when they emigrated from the German Rhineland early in the eighteenth century. As Peggy became more absorbed with the Livingston farm, she commissioned the architect Edward Larrabee Barnes to design a residence for us, which we named Four Winds. In the years before she died, Peggy spent a day or two a week there. Since her death I have kept the farm going, though I am only able to get there several times a year.

Peggy's burgeoning involvement with raising cattle and farming in Columbia County deepened her awareness of modern agriculture's new economic realities. Increasing costs and the arrival of the global marketplace had made good management and adequate financial resources essential if one was to remain in business. At the same time the inexorable growth of urban areas spawned a surge of development into rural areas that was gobbling up much of the nation's best farmland without regard for the quality of the land or the consequences to future generations. Small family farms had once abounded in Columbia County and other parts of the northeastern United States, but many of their owners had succumbed to the pressure and sold their land to real estate developers at high prices. Large subdivisions of suburban tract homes were appearing in erstwhile farming communities.

In an effort to stem the tide, Peggy helped to organize the American Farmland Trust (AFT) in 1980. The AFT did not want to prevent all development; it wanted to impose order on the helter-skelter process while championing the cause of farmland preservation. A key tool was the conservation easement, which allowed landowners to place legally binding restrictions on the future use of their property, limiting it, for instance, to agricultural purposes or keeping it "forever wild." The AFT also lobbies state governments to appropriate and set aside permanent financial reserves to acquire these easements and thereby provide small farmers with the necessary liquidity to stay in business.

While development pressure in farming communities has continued to intensify, the AFT has made a significant difference in protecting vulnerable areas across the nation. Nineteen states now have easement purchase programs, and hundreds of localities have imposed agricultural conservation zoning ordinances or created land trusts and other creative programs to enable farmers to remain on the land.

=

By the early 1980s, Peggy and I had developed different interests, all time-consuming and with little overlap among them. This might have caused the two of us to gradually drift apart—leading separate lives and seeing less and less of each other. We had both seen it happen to close friends and family members, but we did not let it happen to us. We made a conscious effort to understand each other and support each other's interests and activities. Since we also had many interests in common, there was a fortunate balance in our lives. I was happy to provide financial support for her organizations, and she was helpful to me with the ones of my special interest. Our partnership was enduring and endearing, and Peggy was the perfect partner.

GOVERNMENT

I suspect my relationship with Peggy would have been threatened had I pursued any of the opportunities I had to enter politics. As it was, my career at Chase required extensive travel, attendance at many public functions, and enormous amounts of entertaining. Peggy was often at my side for these events, but it was not something she enjoyed. The even more onerous obligations of a political career might well have been more than she could accept. I am glad I did not put the issue to a test, but I did pass up some fascinating opportunities.

The most unusual was Nelson's offer to appoint me to Robert F. Kennedy's United States Senate seat after Kennedy's assassination in June 1968. To this day I have no idea whether Nelson was serious, since he also asked a number of other people, including my brother John and my nephew Jay Rockefeller. While I was certainly tempted, I recalled how President Kennedy had been criticized for choosing Bobby Kennedy as attorney general in 1960, and was not eager to be subjected to charges of nepotism, so I declined Nelson's offer.

I also had to decline the cabinet-level appointments that were offered to me during the 1960s and 1970s. Richard Nixon made two of them. The first was in November 1968 as the president-elect assembled his cabinet. Nelson told me that Nixon wanted me as his Secretary of the Treasury. I told Nelson I preferred not to be considered because I had just been elected chairman of the Chase and could not in good conscience step aside at that critical moment. Nelson passed along my decision to Nixon and his advisors.

A few days later I made a courtesy call on the new president at the Pierre Hotel in New York. John Mitchell, the attorney general–designate, whom I had known for many years, and Bryce Harlow, Nixon's chief political advisor, were also present. Although we spoke for almost two hours and the conversation ranged across many topics, including relations with the Soviet Union and measures to control inflation domestically, I found it surprising that Nixon never mentioned or even obliquely referred to the Treasury position. He disliked being turned down, and I suspect this was his way of showing his displeasure.

Five years later Nixon more formally offered me the Treasury post. In late January 1974, in the midst of the first Arab oil embargo and as the Watergate scandal entered its penultimate phase, I was on a bank trip in the Middle East. I had just arrived in Kuwait and was about to leave for an audience with the emir when I received a phone call from General Alexander Haig, then an assistant to President Nixon. Haig informed me that George Shultz was stepping down as Secretary of the Treasury, and Nixon wanted me to be his successor. The General asked me to return immediately to Washington to meet with the president. I told him that I was only at the midpoint of my trip and still had scheduled engagements with senior government leaders in Saudi Arabia, the Persian Gulf states, and Israel, as well as a critical meeting in Cairo with Anwar Sadat. In light of this, I explained, it would be awkward to cut short my trip. Haig was insistent, emphasizing that Nixon himself had made the request. I assured him I would come to Washington immediately after returning to the United States.

The morning after I returned from Cairo in early February, I flew to Washington to discuss the appointment with Haig. It was clear from our conversation that if I accepted, I would be expected to carry out the President's commands and that my own input on the development of policy would be limited. A few years earlier, in a futile effort to wring inflation out of the economy, Nixon had imposed wage and price controls, and I sensed there would be more of that kind of thing in the offing. Since my own inclination was to allow the markets to have freer rein, I wondered what role I could honestly play as a member of Nixon's cabinet.

With all the serious economic problems looming on the horizon—worsening inflation, flagging productivity growth, a widening current account deficit in our foreign trade, and the oil crisis itself—tough measures would be required. I felt it would be awkward, at best, for a Rockefeller to impose these measures on a reluctant public and that I might well end up a scapegoat for unpopular policies. Furthermore, since the Chase was itself confronting a number of challenges, I questioned whether it would be right to leave at that critical time. All things considered, I respectfully declined the President's offer. A few days later William Simon, formerly Treasury undersecretary, who was serving as the "Energy Czar," was appointed Shultz's successor.

While political considerations had a great deal to do with my declining these offers (as was also the case when President Carter talked to me about both Treasury and the chairmanship of the Federal Reserve in the summer of 1979), so did my commitment to the bank. It wasn't just a convenient excuse. I felt an intense loyalty to Chase and a sense of obligation to those I worked with and for. Furthermore, I thoroughly enjoyed my job and believed I would be able to accomplish much that would benefit the United States as an "ambassador without portfolio."

During my years at the bank I regularly met senior political leaders in the countries I visited on behalf of the bank. Perhaps for that reason the State Department and occasionally the President asked me to perform official or semiofficial missions on their behalf. For example, I helped maintain a back channel to the Wojciech Jaruszelki government after the suppression of Lech Walesa's Solidarity Movement in Poland; and in early 1981, at the request of President Ronald Reagan, I rallied the American business community to support the newly elected conservative government of Edward Seaga in Jamaica.

During my years at Chase there were many who claimed these activities were inappropriate and interfered with my bank responsibilities. I couldn't disagree more. My activities resulted in establishing better relations with foreign governments as well as forging strong public-private partnerships within the United States. Moreover, my so-called outside activities were of considerable benefit to the bank both financially and in terms of its prestige around the world.

I have never been particularly dogmatic in my political or economic beliefs. Rather, I have supported effective people and backed practical policies. It is clear to me that both government and the private sector have important roles to play in fostering economic growth and providing a more secure and prosperous society both in the United States and around the world. Relying on either government or the market alone to solve all problems and cure all ills has always seemed to me to be more doctrinaire than realistic. Government should set and enforce the rules, but implementation should be left to the private sector. The best results occur when there is close cooperation between the two.

PHILANTHROPY

O ne of Father's favorite New Testament stories was the parable of the
Good Samaritan. Most people are familiar with the story of the man
who is attacked on a lonely road, beaten, robbed, and left for dead. Other
travelers pass him by until a Samaritan—a member of a group considered,
during biblical times, to be untrustworthy and dangerous—stops to help
and saves his life. Who is your neighbor? What are your obligations to him?
That is the point of the story. To Father the moral was clear: Everyone is your
neighbor. He would emphasize that point over and over again at our prayer
sessions before breakfast each morning when we were children: You must
love your neighbor as yourself. The story of the Good Samaritan—it was the
theme that Marc Chagall chose for the window memorializing Father at
Union Church in Pocantico Hills—epitomized Father's life and inspired his
philanthropy. For him philanthropy was about being a good neighbor.

Father, drawing on Grandfather's earlier actions, established a powerful
example for all members of the Rockefeller family, including me. In addition
to donating most of his personal fortune to charity, he also demonstrated
that philanthropy—the "third sector"—could play a seminal role in helping
society find solutions to its most pervasive and persistent problems and
serve as a valuable bridge between the private and public sectors. In my
opinion, that is his most important legacy.

I have tried to emulate Father by contributing to a variety of not-for-
profit organizations throughout my life. I have also been closely associated
with The Rockefeller University for more than sixty years, an involvement
that has given me intense satisfaction.

The university's mission—"to benefit humankind throughout the
world"—was an ambitious goal, reflecting the depth of Grandfather's and
Father's concerns that their wealth be used wisely. They recognized that
progress in public health was critically dependent on scientific advances in
the understanding of the human body and the nature of disease. And to accomplish this, Father and his associates assembled the most outstanding scientists working in the fields of physiology, anatomy, biology, and medicine,
and provided them with the best facilities and equipment, insisting they be
totally free from outside pressures or influence in their work.

The university has been in the vanguard of the scientific revolutions that
have swept through the life sciences during the course of the twentieth century. The discipline of cell biology was born in Its laboratories; it was here

that Peyton Rous first demonstrated that viruses cause cancer; and it was where some of the mysteries of the structure of DNA's double helix began to be unraveled. Today the university's eighty laboratories, each headed by a senior scientist, have come a long way from the half-dozen that were operating there a century ago. Molecular geneticists, theoretical physicists, neuroscientists, immunologists, molecular biochemists, biophysicists, and many other scientists use the most advanced technologies—the latest generation of magnetic resonant imagers and high-speed computers among them—to constantly push back the frontiers of human knowledge. They have contributed to our increased knowledge of cellular functions, helped map the human genome, and charted the underlying chemistry of human life—work that holds promise for not only the defeat of mankind's most ancient enemies but the extension of life itself.

The Rockefeller University continues to rank as one of the half-dozen leading medical research institutions in the world, and twenty-one Nobel Prize winners have served on its faculty over the years. My family's support for the university over more than a century illustrates how individuals with substantial financial resources can promote and enhance the general welfare and advancement of society through regular and generous philanthropy.

CAPITALISM

Contrary to the views of many, the ability to make profits is a critical element in society's progress. The lure of profits generates employment, creates wealth, and empowers people in ways that no other social or economic system has been able to. That is why no one should feel guilty about making money.

Nor should anyone feel guilty about taking prudent risks. This is a fundamental truth that I learned from Joseph Schumpeter, who believed that without entrepreneurs willing to bring new products and ideas to the market and investors ready to finance them, it would be impossible to achieve real economic growth. The alternative, as we have learned to our sorrow in the twentieth century, is government control of the factors of production with results that can be seen in the devastated landscapes and abandoned factories of Russia and Eastern Europe, and the scarred lives of billions of human beings throughout Asia, South America, and Africa.

My long-standing investment in Rockefeller Center, throughout its various stages of uncertainty and crisis, is an example of my willingness to take risks commensurate with the prospect for gain. Perhaps even more so has been my experience with what some have called "Rockefeller Center West"—Embarcadero Center in San Francisco.

The Embarcadero project grew out of San Francisco's effort to revitalize its decaying central business district along the waterfront through the federal urban renewal process, which provided for a substantial write-down in the cost of the land in order to attract qualified developers. By the mid-1960s much of the downtown area east of Montgomery Street was filled with dilapidated slums, produce markets, and flophouses. The San Francisco Redevelopment Agency (SFRD), under the capable leadership of Justin Herman, was formed to revive this historic area. Justin had a vision that was strikingly similar to Father's hopes to revitalize Midtown Manhattan through the construction of Rockefeller Center.

In 1969 I joined a partnership that included Texas developer Trammell Crow, Atlanta architect John Portman, and my brother Winthrop to bid on a portion of the land that the SFRD was offering. We proposed building a hotel and four office towers linked by plazas and walkways that would include substantial retail space for restaurants and shops. It was a creative design, and SFRD quickly approved the proposal. Our contract called for taking down each piece of land separately and sequentially, and erecting the five buildings over a ten-year period. We persuaded the Prudential Insurance Company to become a 50 percent partner and to supply the construction financing.

We began construction in 1971 and over the following three years completed the first two office buildings and the Hyatt Regency Hotel, with a signature Portman atrium at its center. Unfortunately, by the time we completed construction, the recession had crippled San Francisco's real estate market.

With the second Embarcadero office tower half empty and not a single tenant signed up for the third 700,000-square-foot tower (EC3), Prudential declined to take an equity position in EC3, although it was still obligated to provide the mortgage financing if we proceeded with the building. So in 1976, with both Crow and Portman out of Embarcadero because of financial problems elsewhere and the executors of Winthrop's estate unwilling to put up more money, I faced a dilemma. I could either drop out of the project or go it alone. If I dropped out, the agreement with the SFRD would prohibit me from participating in the construction of EC4. However, financing it myself would require me to provide the full $60 million—the equivalent of my personal net worth outside of the trust—and an additional $1 million a month until things turned around. Thus, if I went ahead with the project and the recession persisted, I ran the risk of personal bankruptcy.

Even though Dick Dilworth and my other advisors counseled me not to take on this additional risk, I decided to take it. I was convinced that once the recession lifted, space at Embarcadero Center would be in great demand. Nonetheless, the risk in continuing alone was awesome.

The first three months of my sole ownership were not promising. The building remained empty long after its completion in the summer of 1976. We kept the lights on at night so the tower wasn't dark, but it was little comfort to peer out the windows at the Hyatt Regency and realize that, except for the night watchman, there wasn't a living soul inside to pay rent.

Thankfully, sooner rather than later the San Francisco market turned around, and tenants began taking space in EC3. By mid-1977 rents had reached a level that put the building on a profitable basis. The Prudential agreed to provide the mortgage financing for EC4 and begged me to allow them to take their proportional share in the equity financing as well. I agreed, but only if they bought back their 50 percent share in EC3 at its new and higher valuation. This resulted in my recapturing my investment not only in EC3 but in the entire Embarcadero Center project. The risk I had taken in staying the course had proved exceedingly rewarding.

Some years later we expanded by building Embarcadero West (EC West), only to discover that the new investment was jeopardized by a real estate recession and the Bay Area earthquake of 1989. By the early 1990s, with a huge bank loan to repay, EC West teetered on the precipice of bankruptcy. But I continued to believe in San Francisco's long-term prospects, and despite my advisors' hesitance, I was determined to persevere.

By mid-decade the real estate market had recovered, aided by the citizens of San Francisco, who were alarmed by the city's rapid growth and voted to drastically restrict new commercial construction. In 1998, Boston Properties, the real estate firm controlled by Mort Zuckerman, purchased all of the Embarcadero Center office buildings for $1.8 billion. Since I received payment in the form of obligations from Boston Properties, I retained an indirect stake in Embarcadero but in the process diversified my investment to include prime properties in key areas around the country.

My thirty-year association with Embarcadero Center has been profitable for me and has helped spark the renaissance of San Francisco's historic downtown and waterfront. As with the development of Rockefeller Center, Embarcadero illustrates the benefits that can flow to the community when thoughtful government leaders join with risk-taking capitalists to improve the urban environment.

TODAY AND TOMORROW

My life today, at the age of eighty-seven, remains busy and fulfilling. I continue to travel extensively for business as well as enjoyment and have recently completed fascinating journeys to northern Thailand, Laos, Burma, Western China, and Tibet, as well as a wonderful sailing tour of the Hebrides Islands of Scotland and a boat trip up the Rio Negro in the Amazon. In recent years I have often traveled with members of my family, all of whom have sought ways since the death of Peggy to bring me comfort. Although only a few of them live in New York, they visit me often and make my Manhattan home their base of operations whenever they are in town.

As my children have grown older, each of them has discovered fields of special interest in which they have excelled and through which they have made contributions to the society in which we live. In many ways I think my proudest accomplishment—and one that I attribute in large part to my wife, Peggy—is these six vigorous, intelligent, and committed individuals. Although we have disagreed about many things in the past and continue to view the world in quite different ways, I now realize they have embraced their heritage as strongly as I did and have used their resources to improve the world or at least try to change it. I am immensely proud of each one of them.

THE ELEMENTS OF SUCCESS AND HAPPINESS

In thinking back over my life I realize how fortunate I have been. Thanks to Grandfather and Father, I inherited substantial means that enabled me to make what I wanted of my life without being concerned about where financial support was coming from. I realize, too, that inherited wealth unaccompanied by the guidance of wise parents can be a curse rather than a benefit. Over the decades there have been conspicuous and regrettable examples of just that. Fortunately, my parents set exceptional examples of social responsibility in addition to treating me with love and respect. With that backing I was able to work my way through the normal perils of adolescence, which was complicated by the floodlights of a society fascinated by, but always inclined to look for flaws in, the scions of great wealth.

In addition, I have been blessed with more than an average amount of energy and good health. In fact, I still exercise at the gym several mornings a week. This has enabled me to pursue a broad range of interests with a minimum of stress. For the most part what I am able to do in a day is limited only by the number of working hours.

My life has been further enriched through learning from the world around me, especially by savoring the observations arising from a busy life of work, recreation, and travel. I find intense pleasure in many of the episodes of life, large and small, consequential and inconsequential.

My satisfaction derives from the simple fact that I enjoy meeting people from all walks of life, from different races and nationalities, and with divergent views. That is not to say that I am enthralled with everyone I meet. Some people bore me unbearably, and others I take an immediate dislike to. But being with people energizes me and makes life worth living. My family and close friends have given me the sense of confidence I lacked in my youth. Without that underpinning, many of my daily encounters would have seemed threatening, and life would have been unnerving rather than the exciting and pleasurable challenge it has been.

Despite my share of disappointments, setbacks, and periods of unhappiness, I have found great satisfaction and enjoyment in life. That has been due primarily to the principles established by my parents and to the nourishing support of my wife, children, and many friends.

It has been a wonderful life.

EPILOGUE

September 11, 2001, was a day—to borrow a phrase from President Franklin D. Roosevelt—that "will live in infamy."

I watched from the window of my office on the fifty-sixth floor of the General Electric Building in Rockefeller Center that morning as two plumes of smoke billowed blackly upward from the World Trade Center towers and then drifted out to sea across Brooklyn and through the Verazzano Narrows. Shortly before 10 A.M. the South Tower collapsed and a cloud of dust enveloped the southern portion of Manhattan. Beneath it lay the Wall Street area, where I had spent most of my career.

I knew immediately that the physical destruction would be immense and the loss of life catastrophic. Moreover, the hopes and dreams of thousands of victims and millions of survivors were buried in that rubble. For the first time since December 7, 1941, when I heard the news of the attack on Pearl Harbor, I experienced a physical sense of dread about the future.

In the immediate aftermath of the attacks, like all New Yorkers and Americans, I struggled with the incredible dimensions of the disaster and tried to comprehend its causes. It was only with time that I began to understand the connection between the terrorist attacks on the World Trade Center and the Pentagon and the failure over a period of almost fifty years to resolve the dilemma of the Middle East. President Nasser's 1969 warning to me about the "growing instability and radicalism" throughout the region resonated strongly. Despite efforts by people of good faith on all sides, this dangerous cancer has never been excised, and it now threatens the stability and prosperity of the entire world.

In the months following those horrible attacks, the leadership of President Bush, Mayor Giuliani, and Governor Pataki heartened me, and the courage and compassion of New Yorkers, in particular, made me proud.

We New Yorkers are resolute people, and we Americans are optimists by nature. I have no doubt, therefore, that a new, even more vibrant lower Manhattan will rise from the ashes of devastation and personal loss. The process, in fact, is already well under way. And when lower Manhattan is ultimately "reborn" yet again, I have every hope and expectation that I will be right here to witness it.

ACKNOWLEDGMENTS

Writing these memoirs has been a labor of love that took more than ten years to complete. Fortunately, I did not have to do it alone. I had many companions who made it an interesting and enjoyable experience. I gratefully acknowledge them for the assistance they all provided.

Randolph Bergstrom and David Robarge collected, organized, and analyzed much of the historical material upon which the manuscript was based. These fine young historians were followed by a number of other capable researchers who developed additional information on more specific topics when the need arose. Among this latter group, Rees Doughty, Amy Houston, Emily Landsman, Melissa Manning, and Simon Middleton stand out for the quality of the work they performed.

Dr. Darwin Stapleton, director of the Rockefeller Archive Center in Sleepy Hollow, New York, and his fine staff, including Dr. Kenneth Rose, the Center's assistant director, the incomparable Thomas Rosenbaum, and Michele Hiltzik, the photo archivist, answered complicated questions on many institutions and events with courtesy and alacrity, and made their superb collection of photographs available for use. Jean Elliott, vice president and archivist at J.P. Morgan Chase & Co., where my business papers are deposited, found the essential documents related to Chase's international expansion and many other matters, and was always available for expert advice and consultation. Shelly Diamond and Nancy Palley, consulting archivists at Chase, located many of the photographs that are found in this book. Bjorg Lema and Michael Stern of the Rockefeller Family Office patiently and cheerfully filled my incessant requests for organizational files and personal letters. Jim Reed of the Rockefeller Center Archives was most helpful in locating photographs of Rockefeller Center.

Many of my friends and close associates made themselves available for lengthy interviews, and a number of them read portions of the manuscript (a few of them many times). All of them provided useful criticism, and often saved me from grievous error. I am particularly beholden to Richard Voell, Lori Marlantes, Jonathan Greene, Vince Silvestri, Richard A. Salomon, Ambassador Joseph Verner Reed, Bill Butcher, Frank Stankard, Charles Fiero, Richard Fenn, Richard J. Boyle, the late Tom Labrecque, Christopher Kennan, Warren T. Lindquist, the late J. Richardson Dilworth, Donal C. O'Brien, Jr., Peter Herman, Colin Campbell, Bill Dietel, Bayless Manning, Winston Lord, Betty Bao Lord, Bill Pounds, Jim Phelan, Wright Elliott, Mike Esposito, the late Ridgway Knight, the late Archie Roosevelt, Schuyler Chapin, Richard Debs, Steve Reifenberg, John Coatsworth, Fred Bergsten, George Landau, Ambassador Richard Helms, Robert Armao, Charles Heck, Zbig Brzezinski, Henry Kissinger, the late William Jackson, Dick Oldenburg, Rona Roob, and Glenn Lowry.

The members of my immediate staff were enormously helpful in the process of research, writing, and revision. At one time or another, everyone who has worked for me over the past decade was drawn into the process. I am therefore indebted to my associates Marnie Pillsbury, Patricia Smalley, and the late Jack Davies, as well as Dorothy Kenner, Clare Eastman, Laura Hepler, Christine Olson Hunt, Chrissy Bonanno, Linnea Bozynski, Teri Recca, Dorothy Smith, Joan Ferris, Marion Mooney, Laura Opdenaker, and Betsy Gude. Richie Cataldo helpfully explained complex financial transactions and located important files dealing with my art holdings. James Ford and Bob Donnelly accompanied me on many of the trips described herein. Alice Gavitt deserves special mention for the many hours she spent typing and editing drafts of the manuscript. Bertha Saunders, my art curator, supplied critical information on art collecting. My associate Alice Victor and Barb Harju, my personal secretary for many years, made my life much easier by deftly balancing my busy schedule with the demands of writing.

I am also grateful to Joe and David Nolan for the work they did at an early point in the evolution of this book, and to Josh Gilder for completing a partial first draft.

My friend and associate Peter J. Johnson has supervised this project from its inception, playing many roles and wearing many hats. Without his persistence, patience, and stamina, this book might never have been completed. Peter combined profound historical learning—including a compendious knowledge of the Rockefeller family and our many institutions—with a keen literary sense that was essential to the book's creation. Among his most important contributions was his suggestion, at a critical point, that we add a third member to the "memoirs team." Fraser P. Seitel was an inspired choice. I had worked with Fraser for many years at the Chase, and his understanding of the bank's culture sharpened my understanding. More important, Fraser's quick wit and sense of humor enlivened the process and improved the book's quality.

Andrew Wylie, my literary agent, has been a strong supporter and wise counselor throughout. Robert Loomis at Random House demonstrated time and again why he is considered the best editor in the business. His suggestions dramatically improved the book. Dominique Troiano, his assistant, cheerfully kept the process flowing and ensured that I paid attention to all the details.

Finally, my children—David, Abby, Neva, Peggy, Richard, and Eileen—and my grandchildren—David, Miranda, Michael, Clay, Christopher, Rebecca, Ariana, Camilla, Danny, and Adam—were lovingly supportive during the long years that it took to complete this memoir. I appreciate them more than they will ever know.

While I could not have written this book without the assistance of all these fine people, I absolve them from any errors that may remain. That responsibility is mine alone.

DAVID ROCKEFELLER
Pocantico Hills, New York
July 2002

INDEX

ABOUT THE AUTHOR

DAVID ROCKEFELLER was chairman of the board and chief executive officer of the Chase bank for many years. He has since retired and currently sits on many project and charity boards. He lives in New York City.

ABOUT THE TYPE

This book was set in Photina, a typeface designed by José Mendoza in 1971. It is a very elegant design with high legibility, and its close character fit has made it a popular choice for use in quality magazines and art gallery publications.